Poverty in America: A Book of Readings

Poverty

Edited by
Louis A. Ferman
Joyce L. Kornbluh
and Alan Haber
Introduction by Michael Harrington

in America

A Book of Readings

Revised edition

Ann Arbor
The University of Michigan Press

Second printing 1969
Copyright © by The University of Michigan 1965, 1968
All rights reserved
Library of Congress Catalog Card No. 68-29261
Published in the United States of America by
The University of Michigan Press and simultaneously
in Don Mills, Canada, by Longmans Canada Limited
Manufactured in the United States of America

*To Norman Thomas in his eighty-fourth year
in tribute to a lifetime of crusading
against the causes of poverty.*

Such poverty as we have today in all our great cities degrades
the poor, and infects with its degradation the whole neighborhood
in which they live. And whatever can degrade a neighborhood can
degrade a country and a continent and finally the whole civilized world,
which is only a large neighborhood. . . . The old notion that
people can "keep themselves to themselves" and not be touched
by what is happening to their neighbors, or even to the people who live
a hundred miles off, is a most dangerous mistake. The saying that
we are members one of another is not a mere pious formula
to be repeated in church without any meaning: it is a literal truth;
for though the rich end of the town can avoid living with the poor end,
it cannot avoid dying with it when the plague comes.
People will be able to keep themselves to themselves as much as
they please when they have made an end of poverty; but until
then they will not be able to shut out the sights and sounds
and smells of poverty from their daily walks, nor feel sure
from day to day that its most violent and fatal evils will not reach
them through their strongest police guards.

—From *The Intelligent Woman's Guide to Socialism and
Capitalism* (New York, 1928), by George Bernard Shaw

Introduction

Michael Harrington

THE ISSUES RAISED by this book of readings, *Poverty in America,* are not simply those of the problems of poverty, but the problem of poverty in its larger context and how, in a sense, that problem meets the issue of the Great Society. For, when we declare a war against poverty, we are reaching out to touch a problem which has first come to the poor but which, if not solved in terms of the poor, will threaten to engulf the entire society.

Individual articles in this comprehensive anthology focus on definitions and prevalence of poverty, the structure of poverty, the relationship of poverty to the economy, the values and life styles of poor people, and various programs and proposals that have been suggested to meet the problems of social, economic, and cultural deprivation.

The point is made in this book that in contrast to the old poverty of immigrants who came with high hopes to a new land and an expanding economy and found unskilled or semi-skilled factory jobs, the new poor are internal aliens in this affluent country. They are the rejects of the past. They are the people who have been driven off farmlands, workers displaced by technological advancement, old folks who face poverty in their declining years, women left alone to raise their children, unemployed teenagers and youths who have dropped out of school but can't find jobs. This is a new kind of poverty in a new kind of society. This is the first poverty of automation, the first poverty of the minority poor, and a poverty that under present conditions could become hereditary, transmitted from generation to generation unless the typical cycles of poverty are broken. Let me share some observations about the growing edge of poverty in this society.

Between 1962 and 1963, this economy increased the number of manufacturing jobs by 152,000 and the number of service industry jobs by 283,000. The production worker earned an average of $99.63 a week and the typical service worker received a weekly pay of $47.58. Between 1962 and 1963, this economy created almost three times as many jobs for people in the field of education as it did for factory hands. All this means is that this economy is going through a fundamental change in the way it produces goods and services. At some point we must face up to the social consequences of technology and what it is doing to the skill levels of our society.

America's automating technology has already created a tremendous number of social problems in addition to persistent and chronic rates of high unemployment during this decade: the devastation of regions such as Appalachia; a setback to the economic progress of the Negro; and a tremendously bleak future for the one-third of the young generation lacking a high school education in a time of increasing demands for skilled workers within the economy.

These are only a few instances of deepgoing problems which cannot be wished away, and an indication of possibly greater difficulties in the future. One need not predict a Thirties-type crash to say that America has not solved all of its contradictions. And, more importantly, the solutions to problems such as automation-induced unemployment, the plight of uneducated youth, the tenacious fact of the slums, all point toward the need for some fairly basic—and controversial—changes in the social and economic institutions of the United States.

By 1980, the government tells us, America will have to have over one hundred and one million jobs, and even that incredible figure is projected on the assumption that unemployment will remain well above three percent. This figure, and many others that have come out of Washington in recent months, defines one of the most fundamental problems in the United States. It raises two basic questions: Will the economy generate this many new employments? And if so, what will the work be—poverty jobs, or Great Society jobs?

In 1965 President Johnson's manpower message and the Manpower Report predicted that the decline in the number of blue-collar workers would continue into the indefinite future. It was in 1956 that the white-collar work force became more numerous than the blue, and there is nothing in the present technology that would make one expect a reversal of this trend. This, of course, means that the United States confronts a critical challenge: With millions of young people coming into the labor force in the next fifteen years, a third of them with less than a high-school diploma, where will they go? The jobs which are on the ascendant are either highly skilled, requiring an education well beyond that possessed by the typical poor, working-class youth, or else they are miserably paid, unorganized jobs in the service sector of the economy, menial tasks in hospitals, schools, hotels, and restaurants.

These considerations make it fairly clear that the nation is going to have to go well beyond its present commitments to deal with the problems of poverty and unemployment. And this raises a basic question. It was assumed by the New Dealers in the Thirties that the government's function was to prime the pump—and the private economy would do the rest. This policy was fixed at the time of the "second" New Deal when Roosevelt abandoned the corporate-dominated, planned economy perspective of the NRA. And it was reasserted by John F. Kennedy when social change was once more put on the agenda in 1961.

Full employment will require much more massive outlays for expanding the public, social sector of our economy. And although business has learned the profitable common sense of a tax cut, and even of pump priming in its patriotic noncompetitive form of defense spending, it has been something else again to speak of the government's helping to redesign the cities and rural areas of this country and plan some changes in our institutions that would lead to a qualitatively better life for its citizens—the Great Society that President Lyndon Johnson has so eloquently suggested.

American liberalism is now in favor of government social investments, i.e., in direct federal participation in the building of housing, schools, transportation systems and the like. This point of view is represented by the A.F.L.–C.I.O., the Americans for Democratic Action and thinkers like John Kenneth Galbraith and Leon Keyserling. On the other hand, the more conservative Keynesians—and that camp now includes the sophisticated, tax-cutting corporation presidents—do not want direct government investments but indirect stimulation of the economy.

The new debate of the coming period will not be over whether the government should intervene in the economy, but how the intervention will take place, for Keynes has finally conquered the entire political spectrum. However, the manner of federal intervention is, to put it mildly, a most crucial question. A conservative intervention which limits itself to stimulating the economy through fiscal and monetary means will have the most reactionary consequences. It may well achieve business "prosperity" but there is no evidence that it will generate sufficient new employments, or the right kinds of new jobs to give youths their economic opportunity.

The labor-liberal view avoids these pitfalls. As the Clark Senate Subcommittee demonstrated in the spring of 1964, had the Administration then pledged itself to annual increments of five billion dollars in social spending, unemployment would have been reduced to three percent by 1968. Secondly, the direct federal outlay approach—the technique of making investments—consciously allocates the funds to make up the enormous deficiencies in our social consumption.

In addition, this debate raises the question of fundamental economic power in the society. In the face of these tremendous transformations of the work force and technology, what is being timidly posed is that most basic of all issues: the necessity of subjecting economic power to the democratic will of the people. Or, in classic terms, this is a first and tiny installment in the ideological struggle to make human need, rather than private profit, the criterion for economic decisions.

By now, America has had its first glimpse of the war on poverty and it is now possible to take its resulting proposals with the seriousness that they deserve. The ideas of massive social investment in low-cost housing, schools, hospitals, and transportation systems have now become politically relevant. The various pre-school education proposals and demonstration projects indicate the beginning of an awareness that the slum child is frequently educationally retarded before he even sees the inside of a school. Finally, all these programs are profoundly related to the most dynamic component of the social change movement in the United States: the Negro freedom struggle. As even the FBI understood, the causes of the riots in the summer of 1964 were not to be found in the Communists, the Nationalists, or any other organized group, but rather in the unspeakable conditions under which Negroes live, North and South.

Beyond the immediate proposals of the war on poverty, there lies the extraordinary fact that the President of the United States is talking in the historic vocabulary of utopianism: "Ahead now is a summit where freedom from the wants of the body can help fulfill the needs of the spirit."

But there are some problems with the war on poverty which I raise within the context of an enthusiasm that we have a government program at all. In this society we need to create jobs for the people. It is good under the program of the Economic Opportunity Act of 1964 to train people for jobs, but in addition, jobs must be created for which people can be trained. I would suggest as a strategy in the war against poverty the following simplified slogan: Let us abolish poverty by hiring the poor to abolish poverty. Let us make a massive social investment in the destruction of the slums. Just think of that for a moment.

In 1949, Senator Robert Taft said that we needed to build 810,000 new units of low cost housing in four years. In 1968, if the present housing program goes through, we will have just about reached Senator Taft's 1953 goal. How can we have a really profound and serious war against poverty that does not have a pledge to tear down every slum in the United States; could we not, by tearing down these slums, create employment for the people who need work? By building schools, hospitals, and transportation systems, could we not hire the poor to help us build the Great Society?

I think it is clear that we are going to have national economic planning in the United States. The United States is a curious exception in the world, because the typical American reaction to the word "planning" is that it equals red revolution, and bringing Brezhnev to the White House, and having some bureaucrats determine the brand of toothpaste which the citizens use. We are the only people who think this way. In France, a conservative general and a banker Premier plan. In Britain's last election, the Tory Party ran against the Labor Party on the antisocialist program that businessmen can plan better than trade unionists. In Italy, the Vatican knows about planning. And in the United States we are going to have to understand that a modern, integrated economy needs national economic planning.

In this context, the Majority Report of the Senate Subcommittee on Manpower and Employment published under the direction of Senator Joseph S. Clark of Pennsylvania is one of the most significant public documents of recent times. This report poses concretely the need for national planning in this country based on the premise stated in Senator Clark's foreword that there is a "manpower revolution" taking place in American society. The Clark Subcommittee proposes that a goal be set: the reduction of unemployment to three percent by 1968. The President should, in his economic report, estimate the size of the gross national product required to attain this objective, and the Council of Economic Advisors should engage in even longer range projections. If the rate of unemployment is greater than three percent, the President is legally obliged to submit governmental programs which would increase the gross national product to such a level that will reduce unemployment below three percent. Americans must understand, as Europeans have for some time, that if a country's gross national product is unsuitable, that country goes out and makes one that is. And it makes one based on social standards. In other words, the poor are hired not only to abolish poverty but to help to begin to build a Great Society.

What are some other relationships between the war on poverty and the Great Society? It is excellent that we are at least talking about a Great Society and that Americans have their eyes lifted up beyond this year or next, or even this decade and the next, to the idea of a new society with qualitative social changes.

Far from being rhetoric, Lyndon Johnson's concept of a Great Society is a very serious intellectual proposition, behind which is an implied political science and sociology. The Great Society will be, presumably, the creation of business, labor, the consumer, the religious believers, the atheists. It will be, it is implied, brought about through the consensus of all these groups. In a sense, the President is participating in the mood which first appeared among intellectuals around the phrase, "the end of ideology," popularized in this country by Daniel Bell. The President is saying that we are going to have a revolution without the painful inconvenience of changing basic institutions and the reason we can do so is that now we live in a society which is so abundant that it need no longer have class conflict in order to make economic decisions, because all reasonable claims can now be satisfied and politics will now proceed by way of consensus rather than by way of conflict.

It seems to me that this view of reality fails because if we are going to eliminate poverty and create a qualitatively new society, we are in for some radical changes. There are going to be more than a few conflicts when we throw so much of the conventional and outlived wisdom overboard and start acting a new way.

For example, we now have to begin to redefine work in this country. First of all, we have to redefine what we mean by public work. The concept of public work grew up in the United States in the 1930's and was based on the theory that the private economy had temporarily broken down in providing employment for willing workers and that the government would temporarily provide public work until the private economy could be put back together again. As a result, the concept of public work had a temporary and pejorative aspect to it; many people regarded it as a form of relief. But, faced with the new economic and social conditions in our society, confronted with the problems raised by automation in the private sector of our economy and the greater social consumption needs of the public sector, our concept of public work has to change.

There has already been a tremendous growth of one type of public work: in the field of education more new jobs have been opened in the last several years than in any other sector of the economy. If we can do that for school teachers with college degrees, why can't we do it for other people, too?

Secondly, the concept of education must be brought more and more under the heading of productive work. I would argue that we should have a GI bill in the war against poverty and pay people to go to school, pay for their tuition, their books, and give them an additional living allowance if they have a family. The GI bill was one of the most successful social experiments this society has ever had. Why does it require a shooting war for us to be so smart? Why can't we in the war on poverty say that the most productive thing a young person between ages 16 and 21 can do is go to school, and that this is an investment in the Great Society?

In addition, I think we need to go out and invent new kinds of work, a new concept of work, creative work, the kind of work that a computer can't do. This year, the star of the antipoverty program is the concept of the indigenous worker. People have discovered, for example, that you can have a social worker with less than an eighth grade education, and that a bright, talented, and sympathetic slum dweller has some abilities that a person with a master's degree in social work may not have. If we look, we can find all kinds of new jobs to create for people if we are willing to make these investments.

We are now making a change in our whole social philosophy. We are breaking with the theory of custodial care for the poor, the supportive care for the poor. We are now taking on a much greater obligation as a nation—to lift people out of poverty and change the quality of their lives. And I think in order to do so, we must change some of the ways we think, establish new definitions of work, pay people for things we once called leisure-time activities, and invent new kinds of jobs. The government has made a start in this direction in the war on poverty through such programs as the Economic Opportunity Act, Medicare, the Appalachian Development Act, but only a start, which thus far has fallen short of what needs to be done to liberate people from poverty by involving them in planning and working to abolish poverty and to start creating a Great Society.

I believe that many of the most well-intentioned and committed Americans are deceiving themselves and the public when they speak of abolishing the slums. The slums can be abolished, but not in the way they suggest. A number of programs have been proposed to end the scandal of the rat-infested, deteriorating, inhuman housing of the poor. Yet every one of these suggestions—and that they are honestly and even passionately made only makes the fact more tragic—fails to face up to what is needed. There must be a massive investment of billions of dollars of federal funds and the creation of new institutions of democratic planning, or else the outrage of the slums will persist and even worsen.

Although my analysis is radical, it can be documented in the official statements of the United States government.

The Council of the White House Conference on Civil Rights (a body composed of businessmen as well as of Negro leaders, trade unionists, and others) said that the United States must build 2 million housing units a year, with at least 500,000 especially designed for the poor, if it is going to live up to its responsibilities.

President Johnson in 1967 proposed building 165,000 units of low cost housing, or 335,000 less than the White House Conference minimum. If past experience is any guide, the actual number constructed will come to a bit over 30,000 or a deficit of 470,000 units.

Moreover, none of the proposals now being discussed comes near to the required number. For example, Senator Robert Kennedy's

approach was clearly motivated by great compassion, yet it would only
have provided 400,000 units over seven years through a $1.5 billion tax
subsidy to private enterprise.

And there can be no creative federalist panacea, enlisting
business in a social crusade, which will deal with this problem. The
corporate sector, as Mr. David Rockefeller testified with great candor
before the Ribicoff Subcommittee, is concerned with making money.
Banks and other business institutions can only invest funds if they are
going to get a return.

Yet the slums are, in business terms, a bad risk. Until August
1967 the FHA itself excluded blighted areas from its mortgage insurance programs on the grounds that such undertakings were "economically unsound." I assume that the bloodshed in Detroit motivated the
revision of this policy in August 1967. A governmental agency can
thus decide, in the name of public social priorities, to make an
"uneconomic" investment of money. A private enterprise will not and
cannot.

This problem cannot be dealt with by providing public subsidies to private builders. All such proposals now before the country—
from Senators Percy and Robert Kennedy among others—are designed to operate on a publicly supported profit principle. Yet even
with this federal support in terms of tax incentives or artificial interest
rates, every one of these suggestions ends up providing housing for
families with incomes well over $4000 a year.

There is certainly a need to give governmental support to the
housing needs of people with incomes between $4000 and $8000. It is
one of the great postwar scandals that lavish, but discrete, subsidies
have been provided for the homes of the middle class and the rich in
the form of cheap, federally guaranteed credit, income tax deductions, and other genteel doles while effectively excluding everyone
with incomes of less than $8000 from the benefits.

But the fact remains that the Kennedy and Percy proposals, if
the published reports of their rent levels are correct, would not
provide any housing for the poor and the almost poor. The rents
would be too high for, among others, the majority of Negroes in the
United States.

And even if some way were found to bring the private sector
into the slums, it could not and should not play the leading role. It is
precisely the commercial calculus of land value which has exacerbated our crisis, and it can hardly solve it. As Mayor Lindsay's task
force on urban design reported to him; beauty, charm, and history

cannot compete with office buildings, and even a venerable structure like the Plaza Hotel will be torn down if present trends continue. Within the framework of such an "economic" approach, one builds most cheaply and most profitably, and social and aesthetic considerations are secondary.

The issue raised here is simple: Who is going to design the "second America" which President Johnson tells us we must build between now and the year 2000? We must construct more housing units than now exist. How? I submit that businessmen, whatever other qualifications they have, are not competent to design a new civilization and, in any case, have no democratic right to do so. The fundamental decisions on what America shall look like and what life in it will be like should be made by the people. And this is particularly important in the case of the slum poor who have been excluded from the making of every important decision in the nation.

In arguing thus, I do not want to suggest that there is no role for the private sector. It is just that the social and aesthetic choices—those "uneconomic" options—must be democratically planned and, because of the logic of money making, publicly financed. Then, and only then, the companies and corporations can contract to carry out the public will, but not to determine it.

The necessity of such innovation cannot be evaded by magic schemes for "rehabilitation" either. The worst of our urban slums are criminally overcrowded. To rehabilitate them successfully would mean removing half to three-quarters of the people now living there to new housing. Moreover, the rehabilitation formulas often take the reality of segregation as a given factor.

I believe that our present crisis allows this country a marvelous opportunity to promote racial integration.

In fact if not in theory, our postwar housing has financed segregated, white suburbs. Now that the government has officially recognized that we must more than double the present supply of housing in the next third of a century, there is the possibility of reversing this ugly policy. There should not be one federal cent for "new towns," either outside of the present metropolitan areas or within them, which are not designed to promote racial integration.

But this points up the need for new public institutions of democratic planning. Our postwar housing deficit is not measured in simple terms of our scandalous discrimination in favor of the rich and against the poor; it is a matter of the failure of the democratic imagination as well. Without thought of social or aesthetic consequences, we have proliferated superhighways and suburbs and made slums more miserable, employment more distant for the poor, age more lonely for those left behind in the central city, and so on.

There is obviously no simple solution to such a complex crisis. But we should start immediately by adopting Senator Ribicoff's proposal of January 1968 and by spending approximately a billion dollars on finding out what we want to do. This would be a wiser investment, as the Senator suggested, than the present Model Cities program. (The monies which Ribicoff spoke of were the $287 million budgeted for three years of the Demonstration City Program.) We cannot go on forever "demonstrating" techniques and leaving the main problem areas untouched.

And in the process of such a massive planning expenditure, every level of American society should be involved in the debate. I do not say this simply out of democratic conviction or populist sentimentality. For I am convinced that where decisions on public subsidy are made at high levels of expertise, there the priorities of money, rather than those of society prevail. There is only one way of establishing the social and aesthetic values which will guide the "uneconomic" expenditure of money. That is through democracy.

The urban crisis also requires pioneering and imaginative efforts by the federal government. The government should immediately begin to build a model city to provide good housing, jobs and income, and public facilities for 250,000 persons. This planned city should be fully integrated economically and racially and provide the optimum cultural and social environment for the strengthening of democratic values. It should be both a pilot project and a yardstick for furthering such developments.

Business firms, including General Motors and Gulf Oil, have built New Towns to meet some of the industrial problems. The federal government can do no less to solve the myriad human and social problems created by the deterioration of the nation's urban areas.

In summary, we know that we have to build 500,000 units of housing for the poor every year.

In market terms, business cannot be expected to go into the job of slum eradication because it is a bad risk.

Even if the market terms are modified by federal subsidy, as in various proposals now before the nation, all the poor and the majority of Negroes would be effectively excluded from the benefits.

There must, therefore, be an "uneconomic" investment of public funds motivated by considerations of social and aesthetic value rather than by a calculus of private profit. In this process the private sector must play a subordinate role as the contractor for the popular will. For the basic decisions involved are not susceptible to business priorities and are even hostile to them. These are issues in the public sector of American life.

Rehabilitation will not evade these problems for, even if such a program be undertaken, it would be necessary to create new housing for millions. Moreover, the urban crisis *allows* the country a chance to use federal funds to promote, rather than, as has been the case until now, to thwart racial integration.

Finally, the enormous undertaking which I outline here clearly requires new public institutions for democratic planning. There is no other way to design a new civilization.

In his *Politics* Aristotle indirectly referred to the subject of automation with a simile which is relevant today. In the course of defending slavery Aristotle said that slavery was inherent and necessary to a society. There was, however, one circumstance under which masters would not need slaves, and managers would not need subordinates. He said that a slaveless society could come about if the statues of Daedelus were to come to life—if inanimate objects could, by intelligent anticipation, do things.

I suggest that we are living through that period of mankind when the statues of Daedelus, that cunning craftsman of Greek legend, have come from myth and are becoming reality, that automation and cybernation are the statues of Daedelus and that we are coming into a period when inanimate objects will, by intelligent anticipation, do the things which the slaves and underlings of former societies were set to do. If we want to look into the future, maybe we are talking about the creation of a new Athens. In the old Athens there were human slaves at the bottom of the society. But the Greek citizen knew that the proper work of man was the work of the intellect, the work of the body in sports, the work of the arts. Perhaps we are entering a period when it will be possible for advanced technology to abolish progressively the menial, routine, and bitter work and to liberate society for the things that are truly human: the sports, the thought, or the arts.

Thus, when we look at the question of poverty and the issues that are raised in the war on poverty and discussed in the articles in this collection, we are not just looking at the poor people whom we are going to help. We are looking from a particular vantage point at the problem of the twentieth century, and more so, of the twenty-first. For I suggest that in abolishing poverty in the United States, we shall have begun to construct a Great Society for us all.

In *Poverty In America,* the causes of, and cures for, the types of poverty in our country are described by government and labor leaders, economists, social workers, psychologists, and other specialists. The result is a balanced, comprehensive book which presents an up-to-date and accurate picture of this nation-wide problem. It is a collection which should prove useful in raising issues for continued discussion and research.

Preface to the Revised Edition

ALTHOUGH IT IS A FACT OF LIFE that the poor are always with us, it is nevertheless true that every generation in America *rediscovers* poverty. Poverty was no less a fact in 1890 when Jacob Riis wrote *How the Other Half Lives* than in our present-day affluent society. The poverty remains, but its structure and the social context within which it occurs has changed. The poor immigrants of the early 1900's have been replaced by large numbers of native-born Americans who find themselves outside the mainstream of economic life—the urban ghetto dweller, the rural, marginal farm worker, the immigrant to the city from the rural area, the welfare recipient and the ADC mother, the technologically displaced, both young and old workers who do not have the educational and skill credentials for the modern labor market, the resident in depressed Appalachia, the minority group members who are discriminated against in employment, education, and housing. In the first quarter of this century the bulk of poverty was represented by new immigrants and Negro farm workers in the South. Poverty today is represented by many different faces, a condition generated by social, technological, and economic currents both in the city and on the farm.

Nor is this the whole story. For many, especially the minority group member with disadvantages in education and skill, poverty is qualitatively different than it was 50 years ago for the immigrant. Poverty is not viewed by these people as a transitory state but as a human condition of life. The opportunity structure is perceived as restrictive and not easily susceptible to change. The immigrant in 1900 could hope for the American Dream to touch his children, but the ghetto Negro today can only see his child caught up in the same cycle of disadvantages that he has experienced.

Poverty in this generation was rediscovered in a social and political context that has given a public awareness and scrutiny of the problem relatively unique in our history. Although numerically more whites than Negroes are poor, the poverty problem has become closely identified in the public mind with current civil rights unrest. As civil rights tensions mount, more and more thought is given to measures to reduce and eliminate poverty. It should also be noted that the elimination of poverty has become the stated national goal of a presidential administration. Not since the administration of Franklin D. Roosevelt has such prominence been attached to the elimination of poverty, nor have funds been specially allocated for this purpose. Both national political parties now seem firmly committed to a war on poverty as a national goal, although there are substantial differences on the means of eliminating poverty. Finally, the rediscovery of poverty paralleled an increasing national commitment of resources in the Vietnam War—a commitment that severely restricted resource allocation for any domestic war on poverty. The result has been a wide debate and conflict on national priorities, goals, and patterns of resource allocation that will undoubtedly have far-reaching consequences for American life.

The current public concern with the issue of poverty required the development of a book that could serve as a resource for a broad-based audience on the nature of poverty, its causes, the social conditions that sustain it, and the range of proposed policies to deal with the problem. When the first edition of *Poverty in America* was prepared, it was the intention of the editors to develop a *basic primer* on poverty that would be useful in a wide variety of educational situations. That is still our goal. Although the temptation was great in this second edition to evaluate the "federal war on poverty" or to discuss new and current issues of American poverty, the decision was made to solicit and include new materials that would be relevant to the plan developed in the first edition. We sought to include articles that would give a more complete introduction to the poverty problem in our industrial society. We refrained, therefore, from including considerable material that has been written on the federal war on poverty. An evaluation of the latter would undoubtedly be worthwhile, but it was clearly beyond the scope of this book.

In organizing the material for this second edition, we have been cognizant of some of the shortcomings of the first edition. The latter was heavily weighted toward poverty in urban centers and among Negroes. We have tried to provide a better balance in the present edition, including more material on rural poverty and an article on the poverty profile of Spanish-Americans. The discussion on policies to combat poverty has also been expanded. We feel that these changes greatly improve and strengthen the anthology and make it more useful to a broad audience.

Understanding Poverty

What are the irreducible assumptions and perspectives that must be grasped if the problem of poverty is to be understood? This is the central question to which we have addressed ourselves in the following seven chapters. We believe that there are seven intellectual reference points to which the reader of this book should orient himself if he is to achieve maximum intellectual gain from the material.

1. Any poverty-line definition of the poor is relative to time and place and is more a reflection of political and cultural assumptions about poverty than of any absolute economic reality. The poverty line is a pragmatic device to separate affluence from poverty and may not have any psychological meaning for the poor themselves.

2. Identification of the many varieties of poverty is important but explains little about the causes of poverty. Far more important in a causal analysis is the need to analyze institutional processes in our society that may intentionally or unintentionally cause and sustain poverty.

3. There is a political economy of poverty where community and national patterns of resource allocation are determined by the special interests and needs of a select number of groups. The tendency is to rigidify patterns of resource allocations that discriminate against the poor and deny them the means to break the poverty pattern. This has the consequence of producing and sustaining certain poverty roles in the society.

4. The causal argument in poverty should proceed from social structure to personal characteristics, rather than vice versa. The popular tendency is to attribute the causes of poverty to personal inadequacies rather than to inadequacies of opportunity. Thus, the unemployed poor are frequently explained by low motivation or personal apathy rather than by impediments (for example, exaggerated skill requirements and race discrimination) that are posed by a restrictive opportunity structure.

5. The reduction of poverty is made more difficult by a series of stereotypes about the life of the poor that dominate the attitudes of the American middle class. Behavior, norms, and values of the poor are evaluated by criteria based on middle-class experiences and socialization. Skills, competencies, and social patterns of the poor may either be invisible or condemned because they cannot be understood within the framework of middle-class life.

6. Much of the behavior that is viewed as a product of "the culture of poverty" is actually class-based and comes from sharing common economic life chance situations. The variation of such situations among the poor is extensive, and a prototype of *the* poverty family is just not grounded in fact.

7. Policy schema to eliminate poverty must be viewed along a number of dimensions. What assumptions are made about the poor

and their problems? Is the policy aimed at damping out a brushfire or does it have a long run emphasis and strategy? Is the policy broad based or does it touch only a small number of the poor? Does the policy assume social change in the wider society, and, if so, what provisions are made to develop these changes? Finally, does the policy contain provisions for implementation?

Our book is built around these seven intellectual perspectives. In a broader sense this book recognizes the basic value conflict that has been built into our society: the desire for increased economic efficiency and an increasing level of national productivity versus the desire for increased social sufficiency and distributive justice for the poor. Our society has assumed that the achievement of one of these goals must necessitate curtailment of the other, since resources in any society are not infinite. Any understanding of the poverty problem in our society must recognize this fundamental conflict and appreciate its significance.

Acknowledgements

This revised edition was developed after intensive discussion with teachers and researchers in the poverty field. We would like especially to thank Professors Sydney Bernard and Philip Booth of The University of Michigan School of Social Work, who spent many hours with the editors making suggestions and reporting conclusions reached after using the text in classes. Dr. Sar A. Levitan of the George Washington University also made himself available constantly and contributed a number of valuable suggestions. Finally, we are appreciative of the continuing support given to us in our work by the codirectors of the Institute of Labor and Industrial Relations of The University of Michigan and Wayne State University—Ronald W. Haughton and Charles M. Rehmus.

Editors' Preface

SERIOUS PUBLIC CONCERN with the problem of poverty is not a new phenomenon on the American scene, although the present excitement about poverty and its consequences may have created such an impression. Henry George in his *Progress and Poverty* referred to the United States of 1869 as a land where "amid the greatest accumulation of wealth, men die of starvation and puny infants suckle dry breasts." In 1890, Jacob Riis wrote *How the Other Half Lives,* a reporter's observations and anecdotes on life in the New York slums, which created a sensation at the time. In his State of the Union Message in 1933, Franklin D. Roosevelt referred to "one third of the nation that is ill-clothed, ill-housed, and ill-nourished." There has always been a "lowest third" or a "lowest fifth" in the sense that some groups of people in the nation have always been *relatively* disadvantaged in their access to opportunities and adequate financial resources. However, the composition of these groups, the nature and prevalence of poverty, attitudes toward the poor, and government involvement in the solution to the problem have varied over time.

The Changing Structure of Poverty

The great majority of the Negroes in America have always been among the poor—first as slaves in the plantation system, then as indentured sharecroppers in the rural areas of the country, and finally as the residents of the black ghettoes of the large cities. Until recent years, the remainder of the poor were largely immigrants from other lands—the bondservants of colonial times, followed by the immigrant masses from western and eastern Europe. With the recession of immigration, the poverty-stricken have included farm workers displaced by the advent of the large mechanized farm; white and Negro migrants from the rural areas to eroded urban city centers; unskilled workers in unprotected and underpaid industries; displaced workers, victimized by technological change, who cannot find new roles in the labor market; and finally those individuals who because of age, physical or emotional disability, undereducation or lack of skill do not participate in the labor market, or if they do, only in marginal roles.

Changes in the Nature of Poverty

The nature of poverty changed with these shifting groups. The immigrant saw poverty as a *temporary state* and looked forward to the day when he or his children could gain a greater access to opportunity and financial resources. The poor of today are more inclined to regard poverty as a *permanent way of life* with little hope for themselves or their children. This change in the outlook of the poor can be explained by changes in the opportunity structure. Unlike earlier times, the labor market of today does not have a place for the undereducated, the underskilled or the old. Increasing technological sophistication makes the future prospects of these groups even bleaker than they are at the present time. Disadvantage breeds disadvantage, and the offspring of today's poor, even though more educated than their parents, will find serious limitations in opportunities for employment and social participation. The general affluence of the society means very little to this underclass of individuals and families.

Changes in Attitudes Toward the Poor

Early attitudes toward the poor in America were compounded by feelings of contempt, repugnance and fatalism. For the most part, the affluent ignored the plight of the poor. Poor people were "the damned" or they were "the losers" who could never be righted to a decent life but were committed to a lifetime of inequality. In a society dedicated to success and achievement, the poor could only be viewed as an abnormality. Although this view was softened with time, it was still popular to assume that the roots of poverty were in *individual* laziness, thriftlessness, and immorality.

The post-Civil War period posed the problem of new poverty in the wake of industrialization, immigration, and urban growth. The new poor lived in the filth and squalor of the urban ghettoes, which were only too visible. These ghettoes posed a twofold problem for the affluent in the cities. First, it became recognized that the substandard living conditions of the poor were breeding grounds for the dread epidemics of the period—typhoid, cholera, and smallpox. Second, the slum environment was viewed as the incubator of the undesirable and lawless groups that posed a direct threat to the institutions of the society. Thus, the city dweller found himself forced to recognize the existence of poor people and their problems. The proximity and interdependence of city life brought a new attention to poverty, its causes, and its cures.

The post-Civil War period also marked the beginnings of the new philanthropy. The conscience of liberal reformers was awakened to the problems of poverty and a subtle shift of attitudes toward the poor occurred. Attention was focused on systemic and structural causes of poverty rather than on properties of the individual. *The individual was viewed as a victim and not as a causal agent of poverty.* It became popular to discuss faulty resource allocation and structural impediments to opportunity. The classic analysis by Henry George was typical of this shift of emphasis which reached its culmination in the 1930's in the policies of the New Deal.

Public attitudes toward the poor today are a mosaic. The poor are viewed with some compassion but are also frequently seen as immoral, unmotivated, and childlike in their behavior. There is still a public lack of appreciation of the debilitating effects of poverty and the stresses that result from a lack of adequate resources. Hostility and racial prejudice may be directed toward some of the poor. In some cases, these attitudes permeate the leadership elites of communities, making the task of poverty reduction more difficult. In truth, history has widened the social distance between the poor and the affluent since life in suburbia makes it possible for the affluent to carry on day-to-day activities with little intimate awareness of the poor or their problems in the crowded urban ghettoes.

Federal Involvement in Antipoverty Programs

Although humanitarian reformists of the nineteenth century pressed for aid and relief to the poor, the main response came from private charity groups. These efforts were uncoordinated and "brushfire" in emphasis. It was not until the Depression of the 1930's that the full resources of the federal government were mobilized to deal with the problem. In his first campaign for the presidency, Franklin Roosevelt pledged participation by the federal government in an antipoverty drive and a good share of New Deal legislation was aimed at improving the minimum purchasing power of every family regardless of their personal circumstances. The Social Security retirement system was set up to maintain income for persons too old to work; unemployment compensation aimed to sustain younger families while the breadwinner looked for work; public assistance was to provide for those unable to work or ineligible for other benefits. These measures undoubtedly made a substantial contribution to the relief of the impoverished during the Depression, but they did not eliminate poverty. Although some of these measures were subsequently broadened, at least one-half of the people now classed as poor were not eligible for these transfer payments. These were the people with low paying jobs, unstable work histories and disabilities that prevented their qualifying for these benefits. The people who needed transfer payments most, received them least.

The 1960's have seen a turning point in federal involvement with antipoverty programs and the greatest outpouring of poverty reducing legislation since the New Deal. Under President Kennedy, the

contract compliance machinery of the federal government was strengthened to provide equal employment opportunities for disadvantaged
minority groups, a measure extended under President Johnson. The
Area Redevelopment Act of 1961 and the Manpower Development Act
of 1962 were developed to revitalize economically distressed communities and to provide more vocational training for the underskilled. The
Vocational Education Act of 1963 emphasized training for the disadvantaged, especially youth. In 1964, the Economic Opportunity Act
provided funds for a direct attack on the problems of poverty, and the
Appalachia Regional Development Act of 1965 developed a program
of poverty reduction for a single area in the United States. Of equal
importance is the recognition in the 1960's that the problems of the
poor will not be solved by magic market forces or the resources of
the poor themselves, but only by a comprehensive program touching all
segments of their lives.

The New Awakening to Poverty

Why has poverty gained a new prominence in the current arena of public
issues? Certainly, the issue of poverty has always existed, although it
was undoubtedly dulled by the economic prosperity of World War II
and the post-war years. We can identify six social currents that have
given a sudden urgency to the reduction of poverty. These are: (1) the
technological revolution of the fifties and sixties with consequent erosion and dislocation of manpower resources; (2) the internal challenge
to our economy posed by the Cold War; (3) the Civil Rights movement
of the 1960's; (4) the increased financial costs of social welfare programs; (5) the increase in crime and juvenile delinquency; and (6) the
youth and school crisis.

Automation and Mechanization

Although technological change has become deeply imbedded in the
American industrial process, the *rate of change* has shown a remarkable increase in the post-war period and will continue to increase in
the predictable future. The immediate effect of these changes is to
eliminate low-skilled jobs or to create a demand for skills that require
extensive preparation. The shrinking of this job base has posed a threat
to the employment opportunities of the undertrained and underskilled,
and has resulted in a concern for improving vocational opportunities for
these groups.

Cold War Pressures

The advent of the Cold War has also created pressures to examine our
current patterns of resource allocation. The best answer to external
criticisms of our political economy would be a viable economic system

with an adequate allocation and distribution of resources to individuals. It could be argued that a country that cannot solve this problem is ill-prepared to exert international leadership and provide a useful model for developing nations to follow.

The Civil Rights Movement

The rise of the Civil Rights movement has also contributed a new sense of urgency to the question of poverty reduction. The core issue in the Civil Rights movement is a maldistribution of economic resources and opportunities to Negroes. Even though the majority of the poverty-stricken are not Negro, the majority of Negroes are poverty-stricken. If one could point to a single current impetus for poverty reduction, it would be the pressures generated by the Civil Rights movement: the demands for better housing, better jobs and better education.

Increased Costs of Welfare Programs

As the number and quality of welfare programs have changed, there has been increasing attention given to the *costs* of these programs. This pressure has been felt at the local and state levels where welfare program financing must compete with other social priorities (e.g. industrial development, service improvement, education, and road construction). Welfare costs have expanded considerably and account for a large proportion of local expenditures. As pressures mount for tax reduction and better services, more and more attention has been given to the financial costs of poverty.

The Increase in Crime and Juvenile Delinquency

The increased rates of social deviancy have focused attention on "the breeding grounds" of such social ills—the slum and the ghetto. The attention has been twofold: (1) what specific conditions of poverty generate these forms of social deviancy and (2) what specific programs can be used as preventive. Basic to this new concern is a desire to treat the cause rather than the symptom.

The Youth and School Crisis

Finally, the recognition of the growing armies of youth who are inadequately prepared for military and occupational service has strengthened the concern with poverty reduction. In an age where better educational preparation is demanded, there has been considerable searching and questioning about possible revisions of the educational system to meet the needs of disadvantaged youngsters.

These are some of the pressures, then, that have generated current interest in poverty, its causes, and its cures. This interest has been articulated in a number of articles and books that, in turn, helped to influence public opinion. Undoubtedly two of the most important were Michael Harrington's *The Other America* (New York: The Macmillan Co., 1962) and Dwight Macdonald's article "Our Invisible Poor" in *The New Yorker* magazine. Both works came to the attention of Presidents Kennedy and Johnson and other public officials and admittedly helped shape action proposals for the current "war on poverty." We are witnessing an intellectual reawakening to the issue of poverty in the United States and an outpouring of popular and technical articles and books on many phases of the subject.

The Purpose and Scope of the Book

In preparing this book, it was our intention to present a selection of articles that reflected both variety and diversity in describing and analyzing the many-faceted problems of poverty in order to contribute to a better understanding of the issue. The book presents an overview of the poverty problem and it is an analytic tool, synthesizing some of the best thinking on the subject. This collection of articles may be as noteworthy for what is *not* included as for what is included. Very little current analyses exist, for example, on the health of the poor, their employment experiences, and their politics. We reached the conclusion in preparing the book that poverty as a subject of inquiry has many unresearched areas and it is hoped, therefore, that this book may prove to be a stimulant for needed research and analyses in these fields.

Acknowledgments

Many individuals contributed to this report. We especially thank the following people. First, we would like to express our gratitude to the Institute of Labor and Industrial Relations, the University of Michigan–Wayne State University, and especially to its co-directors, Ronald W. Haughton and Charles M. Rehmus, who saw the value of the project and made available technical and financial assistance. We were also encouraged and supported in this work by Dean William Haber of the College of Literature, Science and the Arts of The University of Michigan.

A number of people proved to be valuable resources in the development of this book. Space limitations permit us to name only a few: Eugene Feingold, Sydney Bernard, and Benjamin Darsky of The University of Michigan; S. M. Miller of Syracuse University; Hylan Lewis of Howard University; Hyman Rodman of the Merrill Palmer Institute; Robert Lampman of the University of Wisconsin; Sar Levitan of the Upjohn Institute for Employment Research; Irving Jacobs of the Social Security Administration; and Nat Goldfinger of the A.F.L.–C.I.O. Research Department.

Our work was also facilitated by the yeomanlike services of William Murphy, Mrs. Alfreda Wilson, and Mrs. Vicki Wittlich who helped in assembling and typing the materials for this book. We are also indeed grateful for the support and encouragement given to us by Patricia Ferman, Hy Kornbluh, and Barbara Haber.

Contents

Chapter 1

Definitions and Prevalence of Poverty

To all too many people, poverty means merely the absence of money. This is a definition influenced, perhaps, by the belief in American society that if money is lacking, work and determination will provide it, and that in our affluent society no one need starve. Admittedly, nobody starves today and apples will probably never again be sold on the street corners. But it must also be remembered that poverty is not merely a question of food, or of money, or of determination. For poverty deprives the individual not only of material comfort but also of human dignity and fulfillment. Its causes are much more complex, and its cure requires more than merely a relief check or the creation of one or two programs of training and retraining. It must be realized that, because of the growing complexity of modern society, the disadvantaged, in particular, more and more lose the very ability to make choices, to be responsible, to know what must be done, and to take action. In short, poverty has today become a complex interlocking set of circumstances, caused by and in turn reinforcing each other, that combine to keep the individual without money, without help, without work. It can truly be said that today those people are poor who can least afford it.

—From Hearings before the Select Committee on Poverty of the Committee on Labor and Public Welfare, United States Senate, 88th Congress, Second Session on S.2642.

How is poverty defined in the United States and how many people are impoverished? The definition of poverty has implications both for statements about its magnitude and about programs for its reduction. There are four different criteria that could be used to analyze the nature and extent of poverty in this country: (1) the limitation of income resources of a single person or a family; (2) the deficiency of community resources and income substitutes; (3) the combination of negative characteristics for labor force participation; and (4) the presence of a "culture of poverty."

1. *The income criteria:* The most common definition of poverty stresses the lack or inadequacy of income as the distinguishing characteristic of poor individuals or families. Below a defined "poverty-line" individuals are said to have insufficient income to meet the minimum daily needs of life, and above which, it is held, people are able to meet these needs. The "poverty-line" varies depending on assumptions as to what constitutes "the daily needs of life" and the cost of these items.

Current poverty-line definitions vary. In a 1964 report on poverty, the President's Council of Economic Advisors used a cash income of less than $3,000 in 1962 as a poverty-line for families of two or more persons, and an income of less than $1,500 for unattached individuals living alone or with nonrelatives. In all, the Council estimated that between thirty-three million and thirty-five million Americans were "living at or below the boundaries of poverty in 1962—nearly one fifth of our nation."

A variation of the poverty-line definition is urged by liberal economist Leon H. Keyserling who has classified families with an income of less than $4,000 (in 1960 dollars), and unattached individuals with an income of less than $2,000 as poverty-stricken. By this standard, there were ten and a half million families and four million unattached individuals in poverty in 1960. But, in addition to his poverty classification, Keyserling adds a category of *deprivation.* This includes unattached individuals whose income ranges from $2,000–$3,999, and multi-person families with incomes of $4,000 to $5,999, a sum which leaves them in a constant climate of economic insecurity, unable to meet adequate living standards and vulnerable to a marginal social existence. Keyserling estimates that the number of persons in both the poverty and deprivation categories equals about seventy-seven million Americans (forty-three percent of the population) who have less than an acceptable standard of living. This estimate is almost double that made by the President's Council of Economic Advisors.

Until recently, a "poverty-line" definition has failed to distinguish the different minimum needs of families of different sizes, different stages in the life cycle, and different geographic location. Thus, the $3,000 standard would give lead to the impression that a very large, female-headed Harlem family which receives $4,300 in welfare payments was more affluent and less poverty-stricken than a small farm family which earns $2,500. The Social Security Administration has developed a standard which accounts for these differences, but the invariant $3,000 is still widely used.

A second difficulty in using a "poverty-line" is that the line is relative to time. No attempt has been made to use the same methodology to calculate equivalent poverty lines for a number of time periods. For example, the $2,000 guide used in 1949 by the Joint Economic Committee of Congress to define poverty for a four-person urban family has little meaning in current definitions. It was probably too low even in 1949. This fact casts serious doubts on any statements comparing the magnitude of poverty today with that of the 1949 standard.

In calculating the reduction of poverty over time, there is controversy over the relative advantages of a "fixed poverty-line" definition (based on the amount of money in current dollars needed for an unchanging list of goods and services), or a "shifting poverty-line" (where the goods and services considered as the necessary minimum are not fixed but increase with the general increase in the American living standards). As Herman Miller has said in a recent paper, "Changes in the Number and Composition of the Poor,"

> The essential fallacy of a fixed poverty line is that it fails to recognize the relative nature of 'needs.' The poor will not be satisfied with a given level of living year after year when the levels of those around them are going up at the rate of about 2½ per cent per year. Old-timers may harken back to the 'good old days' when people were happy without electricity, flush toilets, automobiles, and television sets; but, they must also realize that once it becomes possible for all to have these 'luxuries,' they will be demanded and will quickly assume the status of 'needs.' For these reasons, it is unrealistic in an expanding economy to think in terms of a fixed poverty line.

Regardless of where the "poverty-line" is set, it is considerably below what is needed to lead a full and fruitful life in American society, a point that will be explored later in this chapter.

2. *Community resource criteria:* Frequently, we hear about pockets of poverty or "communities of poverty." These are communities in which the occupational base has eroded, or employment opportunities are limited to low paid and unskilled jobs. This limited opportunity fosters the outmigration of the young, the skilled, and the energetic, leaving the community with an underskilled, nondiversified labor force, a situation that makes future economic redevelopment of the community even more difficult.

The key to this type of definition is the use of community attributes (e.g., skill composition, unemployment rate, wage levels) as a guideline to the welfare of its inhabitants. In recent years, the Area Redevelopment Administration has used this approach in designating areas in need of federal redevelopment aid. This agency uses as its guide the unemployment rate of the community in relation to the national rate to define a deficiency of community resources. If the unemployment rate is fifty percent or more above the national rate for three consecutive years then the community is designated a redevelopment area in need of program aid.

The area designation approach to poverty has advantages and disadvantages. It is an advantage that special emphasis is placed on areas of substantial and enduring economic problems. Programs can be designed for the particular needs of the distressed community. However, this area designation also has certain disadvantages. It overlooks the large number of economically impoverished individuals and families that live in affluent communities and would not be served by such a community designation system. Also, such an approach rests largely on the willingness and cooperation of community power leaders in accepting a "distressed area" definition of their community and developing a grass roots program coordinated with federal aid. The experience of the ARA program indicates that such federal programs may frequently meet with resistance from local power groups.

There are other ways of looking at community resources as criteria for a definition of poverty. A community may provide public services which serve as *income supplements:* medical care, job training, relocation assistance, surplus foods, retirement pensions, income maintenance during unemployment or disability, and child care centers. The elimination of poverty in Scandinavian countries, for example, relies heavily on such community income supplements. A community may also provide other resources which serve as *adjustment or coping aids.* These provide an individual or family with needed services or emergency assistance, such as psychiatric and other counseling, consumer education, or legal aid. And, a community may provide a *wide opportunity field* for individual development and involvement: cultural activities, good schools, adult and remedial education, voluntary organizations, recreation areas, quality housing, adequate public transportation, and an open political structure where people can play meaningful roles in making community decisions.

Some communities, when viewed in terms of available resources, are poverty-sustaining; others are poverty-reducing. There is a need to develop a "Community Resource Scale" as a component of any adequate measure of poverty. Community resource deficiency handicaps the poverty-reducing potential of personal income; resource richness decreases the income needed for adequate quality of life.

3. *Negative risk criteria:* Frequently we speak of individuals who are undereducated, underskilled, and old as having a *combination of*

risk characteristics which make it difficult to take part in the labor force in anything more than a marginal role. This definition emphasizes finding and holding a satisfactory role in the labor market, since access to economic resources and the rewards of society is largely dependent on adequate income from a steady job.

Education, skill level, and age are not the only characteristics that may combine to affect a person's chances in the labor market. Work experience, previous training, race, seniority record, occupation and industrial attachment are other factors which can combine to limit effectively the labor market opportunities of the individual. This type of definition has a certain utility in isolating the people who are most likely to be economically deprived and providing guidelines for the content of rehabilitation programs. The definition has weaknesses, however, in implying that the cause of poverty lies within the individual and that the treatment of poverty must be oriented toward the individual. This view may bring about a neglect of factors outside of the individual (e.g., the opportunity structure) in the development of an anti-poverty program.

4. *Behavior or attitudinal criteria:* A group of individuals or families may be said to be in poverty when they *share* a distinctive set of values, behavior traits, and belief complexes that markedly set them off from the affluent groups in the society. This set is a *derivative* of prolonged economic deprivation, lack of adequate financial resources, and socialization in an environment of economic uncertainty. This "culture of poverty" is characterized by an intergenerational persistence and transmission to the children of the poor.

There is both agreement and disagreement among scholars and critics as to what themes run through a "culture of poverty." Anthropologist Thomas Gladwin noted in a recent speech before the National Conference of Social Workers that the life of the poor is dominated by two themes: a sense of powerlessness about the events in everyday life (i.e., a sense of failure in the control of the social environment) and a sense of pessimism about the future. Michael Harrington in *The Other America* points to "a personality of poverty, a type of human being produced by the grinding, wearing life of the slums."

The definition of poverty by reference to a culture complex offers certain objections of which the anthropologist is only too aware. The investigators are looking at *different* groups of the poverty-stricken in *different* geographical locations and in *different* opportunity structures. It may well be that we should refer to "*cultures of poverty*" rather than a single "*culture of poverty.*"

One general point should be noted about all of these definitions:

they are criteria for classifying individuals and families as poverty-stricken. But this classification system is developed and applied from the viewpoint of the outside observer. To what extent do these individuals and groups *see themselves* as impoverished? Do they accept this judgment of their life situation by outside observers? There is evidence to indicate that some of them do not. When the Area Redevelopment Administration first began labeling areas as "distressed," some of the very individuals who were the object of this program denied that they were "impoverished" or that their areas were "distressed." The officials of anti-poverty programs are beginning to realize that some individuals and families resent receiving anti-poverty aid because to accept such help is to admit personal failure by the standards of American society. A low-paid worker who earns $3,000 may feel the pinch of inadequate economic resources, but he is not likely to think of himself as a failure, which indeed he is not.

Definitions of poverty are classification systems, designed to suit particular policy or program purposes. They do not reflect the psychological reality of the poor, nor any value judgments as to the quality of life or the actual and potential social contributions of people in America who lack an adequate income.

In this chapter, Dwight Macdonald critically discusses various definitions of poverty and the measure of its prevalence. Oscar Ornati analyzes some of the risk characteristics associated with poverty. In Alvin Schorr's article the point is made that income deficiencies are greater at certain points in the family life cycle and these situations exert considerable pressure for the creation of poverty roles. Herman P. Miller questions whether income inequalities are being reduced in the United States, and his answer is a resounding no. Mollie Orshansky discusses some of the problems of counting the poor and in an author's note discusses the distribution of poverty in 1966. Finally, Martin Rein reviews some of the definitions of poverty and offers a number of criticisms of current fashions in the measurement of poverty.

Our Invisible Poor

Dwight Macdonald

The New Yorker

[This reprint was adapted by the Sidney Hillman Foundation from an article which originally appeared in The New Yorker, *January 19, 1963, and is included by permission of the author and the Sidney Hillman Foundation.]*

IN HIS SIGNIFICANTLY TITLED "The Affluent Society" (1958) Professor J. K. Galbraith states that poverty in this country is no longer "a massive affliction [but] more nearly an afterthought." Dr. Galbraith is a humane critic of the American capitalist system, and he is generously indignant about the continued existence of even this nonmassive and afterthoughtish poverty. But the interesting thing about his pronouncement, aside from the fact that it is inaccurate, is that it was generally accepted as obvious. For a long time now, almost everybody has assumed that, because of the New Deal's social legislation and—more important—the prosperity we have enjoyed since 1940, mass poverty no longer exists in this country.

Dr. Galbraith states that our poor have dwindled to two hardcore categories. One is the "insular poverty" of those who live in the rural South or in depressed areas like West Virginia. The other category is "case poverty," which he says is "commonly and properly related to [such] characteristics of the individuals so afflicted [as] mental deficiency, bad health, inability to adapt to the discipline of modern economic life, excessive procreation, alcohol, insufficient education." He reasons that such poverty must be due to individual defects, since "nearly everyone else has mastered his environment; this proves that it is not intractable." Without pressing the similarity of this concept to the "Social Darwinism" whose fallacies Dr. Galbraith easily disposes of elsewhere in his book, one may observe that most of these characteristics are as much the result of poverty as its cause.

Dr. Galbraith's error is understandable, and common. Last April the newspapers reported some exhilarating statistics in a Department of Commerce study: the average family income increased from $2,340 in 1929 to $7,020 in 1961. (These figures are calculated in current dollars, as are all the others I shall cite.) But the papers did not report the fine type, so to speak, which showed that almost all the recent gain was made by families with incomes of over $7,500, and that the rate at which poverty is being eliminated has slowed down alarmingly since 1953. Only the specialists and the statisticians read the fine type, which is why illusions continue to exist about American poverty.

Now Michael Harrington, an alumnus of the *Catholic Worker* and the Fund for the Republic who is at present a contributing editor of *Dissent* and the chief editor of the Socialist Party biweekly, *New America,* has written "The Other America: Poverty in the United States" (Macmillan). In the admirably short space of under two hundred pages, he outlines the problem, describes in imaginative detail what it means to be poor in this country today, summarizes the findings of recent studies by economists and sociologists, and analyzes the reasons for the persistence of mass poverty in the midst of general prosperity.

In the last year we seem to have suddenly awakened, rubbing our eyes like Rip van Winkle, to the fact that mass poverty persists, and that it is one of our two gravest social problems. (The other is related: While only eleven per cent of our population is non-white, twenty-five per cent of our poor are.) What is "poverty"? It is a historically relative concept, first of all. "There are new definitions [in America] of what man can achieve, of what a human standard of life should be," Mr. Harrington writes. "Those who suffer levels of life well below those that are possible, even though they live better than medieval knights or Asian peasants, are poor. . . . Poverty should be defined in terms of those who are denied the minimal levels of health, housing, food, and education that our present stage of scientific knowledge specifies for life as it is now lived in the United States." His dividing line follows that proposed in recent studies by the United States Bureau of Labor Statistics: $4,000 a year for a family of four and $2,000 for an individual living alone. (All kinds of income are included, such as food grown and consumed on farms.) This is the cutoff line generally drawn today.

Mr. Harrington estimates that between forty and fifty million Americans, or about a fourth of the population, are now living in poverty. Not just below the level of comfortable living, but real poverty, in the old-fashioned sense of the word—that they are hard put to it to get the mere necessities, beginning with enough to eat. This is difficult to believe in the United States of 1963, but one has to make the effort, and it is now being made. The extent of our poverty has suddenly become visible. The same thing has happened in England, where working-class gains as a result of the Labour Party's post-1945 welfare state blinded almost everybody to the continued existence of mass poverty. It was not until Professor Richard M. Titmuss, of the London School of Economics, published a series of articles in the *New Statesman* last fall, based on his new book, "Income Distribution and Social Change" (Allen & Unwin), that even the liberal public in England became aware that the problem still persists on a scale that is "statistically significant," as the economists put it.

The Limits of Statistics

Statistics on poverty are even trickier than most. For example, age and geography make a difference. There is a distinction, which cannot be rendered arithmetically, between poverty and low income. A childless young couple with $3,000 a year is not poor in the way an elderly couple might be with the same income. The young couple's statistical poverty may be temporary inconvenience; if the husband is a graduate student or a skilled worker, there are prospects of later affluence or at least comfort. But the old couple can look forward only to diminishing earnings and increasing medical expenses. So also geographically: A family of four in a small town with $4,000 a year may be better off than a like family in a city—lower rent, no bus fares to get to work, fewer occasions (or temptations) to spend money. Even more so with a rural family. Although allowance is made for the value of the vegetables they may raise to feed themselves, it is impossible to calculate how much money they *don't* spend on clothes, say, or furniture, because they don't have to keep up with the Joneses. Lurking in the crevices of a city, like piranha fish in a Brazilian stream, are numerous tempting opportunities for expenditure, small but voracious, which can strip a budget to its bones in a surprisingly short time.

How Many Poor?

It is not, therefore, surprising to find that there is some disagreement about just how many millions of Americans are poor. The point is that all recent studies* agree that American poverty is still a mass phenomenon.

Thus the Commerce Department's April report estimates there are 17,500,000 families *and* "unattached individuals" with incomes of less than $4,000. How many of the latter are there? "Poverty and Deprivation" (see note below) puts the number of single persons with under $2,000 at 4,000,000. Let us say that in the 17,500,000 under $4,000 there are 6,500,000 single persons—the proportion of unattached individuals tends to go down as income rises. This homemade estimate gives us 11,000,000 families with incomes of under $4,000. Figuring the average American family at three and a half persons—which it is—this makes 38,500,000 individuals in families, or a grand total, if we add in the 4,000,000 "unattached individuals" with under $2,000 a year, of 42,500,000 Americans now living in poverty, which is close to a fourth of the total population.

---

*The studies, all of which are referred to by the author, include, Dr. Gabriel Kolko, *Wealth & Poverty in America* (Praeger); Dr. James N. Morgan, et al, *Income and Welfare in the United States* (McGraw-Hill); "Poverty and Deprivation" (pamphlet), Conference on Economic Progress, Leon H. Keyserling and others.

The reason Dr. Galbraith was able to see poverty as no longer "a massive affliction" is that he used a cutoff of $1,000, which even in 1949, when it was adopted in a Congressional study, was probably too low (the c.i.o. argued for $2,000) and in 1958, when "The Affluent Society" appeared, was simply fantastic.

The model postwar budgets drawn up in 1951 by the Bureau of Labor Statistics to "maintain a level of adequate living" give a concrete idea of what poverty means in this country—or would mean if poor families lived within their income and spent it wisely, which they don't. Dr. Kolko summarizes the kind of living these budgets provide:

> Three members of the family see a movie once every three weeks, and one member sees a movie once every two weeks. There is no telephone in the house, but the family makes three pay calls a week. They buy one book a year and write one letter a week.
>
> The father buys one heavy wool suit every two years and a light wool suit every three years; the wife, one suit every ten years or one skirt every five years. Every three or four years, depending on the distance and time involved, the family takes a vacation outside their own city. In 1950, the family spent a total of $80 to $90 on all types of home furnishings, electrical appliances, and laundry equipment. . . . The family eats cheaper cuts of meat several times a week, but has more expensive cuts on holidays. The entire family consumes a total of two five-cent ice cream cones, one five-cent candy bar, two bottles of soda, and one bottle of beer a week. The family owes no money, but has no savings except for a small insurance policy.

One other item is included in the b.l.s. "maintenance" budget: a new car every twelve to eighteen years.

This is an ideal picture, drawn up by social workers, of how a poor family *should* spend its money. But the poor are much less provident—installment debts take up a lot of their cash, and only a statistician could expect an actual live woman, however poor, to buy new clothes at intervals of five or ten years. Also, one suspects that a lot more movies are seen and ice-cream cones and bottles of beer are consumed than in the Spartan ideal. But these necessary luxuries are had only at the cost of displacing other items—necessary, so to speak—in the b.l.s. budget.

The Conference on Economic Progress's "Poverty and Deprivation" deals not only with the poor but also with another large section of the "underprivileged," which is an American euphemism almost as good as "senior citizen"; namely, the 37,000,000 persons whose family income is between $4,000 and $5,999 and the 2,000,000 singles who have from $2,000 to $2,999. The authors define "deprivation" as "above poverty but short of minimum requirements for a modestly comfortable level of living." They claim that 77,000,000 Americans, or *almost half the population,* live in poverty or deprivation. One recalls the furor Roosevelt aroused with his "one-third of a nation—ill-housed, ill-clad, ill-nourished." But the political climate was different then.

The distinction between a family income of $3,500 ("poverty") and $4,500 ("deprivation") is not vivid to those who run things—the 31 percent whose incomes are between $7,500 and $14,999 and the 7 percent of the top-most top dogs, who get $15,000 or more. These two minorities, sizable enough to feel they *are* the nation, have been as unaware of the continued existence of mass poverty as this reviewer was until he read Mr. Harrington's book. They are businessmen, congressmen, judges, government officials, politicians, lawyers, doctors, engineers, scientists, editors, journalists, and administrators in colleges, churches, and foundations. Since their education, income, and social status are superior, they, if anybody, might be expected to accept responsibility for what the Constitution calls "the general welfare." They have not done so in the case of the poor. And they have a good excuse. It is becoming harder and harder simply to *see* the one-fourth of our fellow-citizens who live below the poverty line.

> The poor are increasingly slipping out of the very experience and consciousness of the nation [Mr. Harrington writes]. If the middle class never did like ugliness and poverty, it was at least aware of them. "Across the tracks" was not a very long way to go. . . . Now the American city has been transformed. The poor still inhabit the miserable housing in the central area, but they are increasingly isolated from contact with, or sight of, anybody else. . . . Living out in the suburbs, it is easy to assume that ours is, indeed, an affluent society. . . .
>
> Clothes make the poor invisible too: America has the best-dressed poverty the world has ever known. . . . It is much easier in the United States to be decently dressed than it is to be decently housed, fed, or doctored. . . .
>
> Many of the poor are the wrong age to be seen. A good number of them are sixty-five years of age or better; an even larger number are under eighteen. . . .
>
> And finally, the poor are politically invisible. . . . They are without lobbies of their own; they put forward no legislative program. As a group, they are atomized. They have no face; they have no voice. . . . Only the social agencies have a really direct involvement with the other America, and they are without any great political power. . . .
>
> Forty to fifty million people are becoming increasingly invisible.

These invisible people fall mostly into the following categories, some of them overlapping: poor farmers, who operate 40 percent of the farms and get 7 percent of the farm cash income; migratory farm workers; unskilled, unorganized workers in offices, hotels, restaurants, hospitals, laundries, and other service jobs; inhabitants of areas where poverty is either endemic ("peculiar to a people or district"), as in the rural South, or epidemic ("prevalent among a community at a special time and produced by some special causes"), as in West Virginia, where the special cause was the closing of coal mines and steel plants; Negroes and Puerto Ricans, who are a fourth of the total poor; the alcoholic derelicts in the big-city skid rows; the hillbillies from Kentucky, Tennessee, and Oklahoma who have migrated to Midwestern cities in search of better jobs. And, finally, almost half our "senior citizens."

The Wrong Color

The most obvious citizens of the Other America are those whose skins are the wrong color. The folk slogans are realistic: "Last to be hired, first to be fired" and "If you're black, stay back." There has been some progress. In 1939, the non-white worker's wage averaged 41.4 percent of the white worker's; by 1958 it had climbed to 58 percent. A famous victory, but the non-whites still average only slightly more than half as much as the whites. Even this modest gain was due not to any Rooseveltian or Trumanian social reform but merely to the fact that for some years there was a war on and workers were in demand, whether black, white, or violet. By 1947, the non-whites had achieved most of their advance—to 54 percent of white earnings, which means they have gained, in the last fifteen years, just 4 percent.

The least obvious poverty affects our "senior citizens"—those over sixty-five. Mr. Harrington estimates that half of them—8,000,000—live in poverty, and he thinks they are even more atomized and politically helpless than the rest of the Other America. He estimates that one-fourth of the "unrelated individuals" among them, or a million persons, have less than $580 a year, which is about what is allotted *for food alone* in the Department of Agriculture's minimum-subsistence budget. (The average American family now spends only 20 percent of its income for food—an indication of the remarkable prosperity we are all enjoying, except for one-quarter of us.) One can imagine, or perhaps one can't, what it would be like to live on $580 a year, or $11 a week. It is only fair to note that most of our senior citizens do better: The average per capita income of those over sixty-five is now estimated to be slightly over $20 a week. That is, $1,000 a year.

The aged poor have two sources of income besides their earnings or savings. One is contributions by relatives. A 1961 White House Conference Report put this at 10 percent of income, which works out to $8 a week for an income of $4,000—and the 8,000,000 aged poor all have less than that. The other is Social Security, whose benefits in 1959 averaged $18 a week. Even this modest sum is more than any of the under-$4,000 got, since payments are proportionate to earnings and the poor, of course, earned less than the rest. A quarter of them, and those in general the neediest, are not covered by Social Security. The last resort is relief, and Mr. Harrington describes most vividly the humiliations the poor often have to put up with to get that.

The whole problem of poverty and the aged is especially serious today because Americans are living longer. In the first half of this century, life expectancy increased 17.6 years for men and 20.3 years for women. And between 1950 and 1960 the over-sixty-five group increased twice as fast as the population as a whole.

The worst part of being old and poor in this country is the loneliness. Mr. Harrington notes that we have not only racial ghettos but geriatric ones, in the cheap rooming-house districts of large cities. He gives one peculiarly disturbing statistic: "One-third of the aged in the United States, some 5,000,000 or more human beings, have no phone in their place of residence. They are literally cut off from the rest of America."

Ernest Hemingway's celebrated deflation of Scott Fitzgerald's romantic notion that the rich are "different" somehow—"Yes, they have money"—doesn't apply to the poor. They are different in more important ways than their lack of money, as Mr. Harrington demonstrates:

> Emotional upset is one of the main forms of the vicious circle of impoverishment. The structure of the society is hostile to these people. The poor tend to become pessimistic and depressed; they seek immediate gratification instead of saving; they act out.
>
> Once this mood, this unarticulated philosophy becomes a fact, society can change, the recession can end, and yet there is no motive for movement. The depression has become internalized. The middle class looks upon this process and sees "lazy" people who "just don't want to get ahead." People who are much too sensitive to demand of cripples that they run races ask of the poor that they get up and act just like everyone else in the society.
>
> The poor are not like everyone else. . . . They think and feel differently; they look upon a different America than the middle class looks upon.

The poor are also different in a physical sense: they are much less healthy. According to "Poverty and Deprivation," the proportion of those "disabled or limited in their major activity by chronic ill health" rises sharply as income sinks. In reasonably well-off families ($7,000 and up), 4.3 percent are so disabled; in reasonably poor families ($2,000 to $3,999), the proportion doubles, to 8 percent; and in unreasonably poor families (under $2,000), it doubles again, to 16.5 percent. An obvious cause, among others, for the very poor being four times as much disabled by "chronic ill health" as the well-to-do is that they have much less money to spend for medical care—in fact, almost nothing. This weighs with special heaviness on the aged poor. During the fifties, Mr. Harrington notes, "all costs on the Consumer Price Index went up by 12 percent. But medical costs, that terrible staple of the aged, went up by 36 percent, hospitalization rose by 65 percent, and group hospitalization costs (Blue Cross premiums) were up by 83 percent."

The Defeat of Medicare

This last figure is particularly interesting, since Blue Cross and such plans are the A.M.A.'s alternative to socialized medicine, or, rather, to the timid fumblings toward it that even our most liberal politicians have dared to propose. Such figures throw an unpleasant light on the Senate's rejection of Medicare. The defeat was all the more bitter because, in the usual effort to appease the conservatives (with the usual lack of success—only five Republicans and only four Southern Democrats voted pro), the bill was watered down in advance. Not until he had spent $90 of his own money—which is 10 percent of the annual income of some 3,000,000 aged poor—would a patient have been eligible. And the original program included only people already covered by Social Security or Railroad Retirement pensions and excluded the neediest of all—the 2,500,000 aged poor who are left out of both these systems.

Mental as well as physical illness is much greater among the poor, even though our complacent cliché is that nervous breakdowns are a prerogative of the rich because the poor "can't afford them." (They can't, but they have them anyway.) This bit of middle-class folklore should be laid to rest by a study made in New Haven: "Social Class and Mental Illness," by August B. Hollingshead and Frederick C. Redlich (Wiley). They found that the rate of "treated psychiatric illness" is about the same from the rich down through decently paid workers—an average of 573 per 100,000. But in the bottom fifth it shoots up to 1,659 per 100,000. There is an even more striking difference in the *kind* of mental illness. Of those in the four top income groups who had undergone psychiatric treatment, 65 percent had been treated for neurotic problems and 35 percent for psychotic disturbances. In the bottom fifth, the treated illnesses were almost all psychotic (90 percent). This shows there is something to the notion that the poor "can't afford" nervous breakdowns—the milder kind, that is—since the reason the proportion of *treated* neuroses among the poor is only 10 percent is that a neurotic can keep going, after a fashion. But the argument cuts deeper the other way. The poor go to a psychiatrist (or, more commonly, are committed to a mental institution) only when they are completely unable to function because of psychotic symptoms. Therefore, even that nearly threefold increase in mental disorders among the poor is probably an underestimate.

The main reason the American poor have become invisible is that since 1936 their numbers have been reduced by two-thirds. Astounding as it may seem, the fact is that President Roosevelt's "one-third of a nation" was a considerable understatement; over two-thirds of us then lived below the poverty line, as is shown by the tables that follow. But today the poor are a minority, and minorities can be ignored if they are so heterogeneous that they cannot be organized. When the poor were a majority, they simply could not be overlooked. Poverty is also hard to see today because the middle class ($6,000 to $14,999) has vastly increased—from 13 percent of all families in 1936 to a near-majority (47 percent) today. That mass poverty can persist despite this rise to affluence is hard to believe, or see, especially if one is among those who have risen.

Two tables in "Poverty and Deprivation" summarize what has been happening in the last thirty years. They cover only multiple-person families; all figures are converted to 1960 dollars; and the income is before taxes. I have omitted, for clarity, all fractions.

The first table is the percentage of families with a given income:

	1935–6	*1947*	*1953*	*1960*
Under $ 4,000	68%	37%	28%	23%
$4,000 to $ 5,999	17	29	28	23
$6,000 to $ 7,499	6	12	17	16
$7,500 to $14,999	7	17	23	31
Over $15,000	2	4	5	7

The second table is the share each group had in the family income of the nation:

	1935–6	*1947*	*1953*	*1960*
Under $ 4,000	35%	16%	11%	7%
$4,000 to $ 5,999	21	24	21	15
$6,000 to $ 7,499	10	14	17	14
$7,500 to $14,999	16	28	33	40
Over $15,000	18	18	19	24

Several interesting conclusions can be drawn from these tables:

(1) The New Deal didn't do anything about poverty: The under-$4,000 families in 1936 were 68 percent of the total population, which was slightly *more* than the 1929 figure of 65 percent.

(2) The war economy (hot and cold) did do something about

poverty: Between 1936 and 1960 the proportion of all families who were poor was reduced from 68 percent to 23 percent.

(3) If the percentage of under-$4,000 families decreased by two-thirds between 1936 and 1960, their share of the national income dropped a great deal more—from 35 percent to 7 percent.

(4) The well-to-do ($7,500 to $14,999) have enormously increased, from 7 percent of all families in 1936 to 31 percent today. The rich ($15,000 and over) have also multiplied—from 2 to 7 percent. But it should be noted that the very rich, according to another new study, "The Share of Top Wealth-Holders in National Wealth, 1822–1956," by Robert J. Lampman (Princeton), have experienced a decline. He finds that the top 1 percent of wealth-holders owned 38 percent of the national wealth in 1929 and own only 28 percent today.

(5) The reduction of poverty has slowed down. In the six years 1947–53, the number of poor families declined 9 percent, but in the following seven years only 5 percent. The economic stasis that set in with Eisenhower and that still persists under Kennedy was responsible. (This stagnation, however, did not affect the over-$7,500 families, who increased from 28 percent to 38 percent between 1953 and 1960.) In the New York *Times Magazine* for last November 11th, Herman P. Miller, of the Bureau of the Census, wrote, "During the forties, the lower-paid occupations made the greatest relative gains in average income. Laborers and service workers . . . had increases of about 180% . . . and professional and managerial workers, the highest paid workers of all, had the lowest relative gains—96%." But in the last decade the trend has been reversed; laborers and service workers have gained 39% while professional-managerial workers have gained 68%. This is because in the wartime forties the unskilled were in great demand, while now they are being replaced by machines. Automation is today the same kind of menace to the unskilled—that is, the poor—that the enclosure movement was to the British agricultural population centuries ago. "The facts show that our 'social revolution' ended nearly twenty years ago," Mr. Miller concludes, "yet important segments of the American public, many of them highly placed Government officials and prominent educators, think and act as though it were a continuing process."

The post-1940 decrease in poverty was not due to the policies or actions of those who are not poor, those in positions of power and responsibility. The war economy needed workers, wages went up, and the poor became less poor. When economic stasis set in, the rate of decrease in poverty slowed down proportionately, and it is still slow. Kennedy's efforts to "get the country moving again" have been unsuccessful, possibly because he has, despite the suggestions of many of his economic advisers, not yet advocated the one big step that might push the economy off dead center: a massive increase in government spending. This would be politically courageous, perhaps even dangerous, because of the superstitious fear of "deficit spending" and an "unbalanced" federal budget. American folklore insists that a government's budget must be arranged like a private family's. Walter Lippmann wrote, after the collapse of the stock market last spring:

> There is mounting evidence that those economists were right who told the Administration last winter that it was making the mistake of trying to balance the budget too soon. It will be said that the budget is not balanced: it shows a deficit in fiscal 1962 of $7 billion. . . . But . . . the budget that matters is the Department of Commerce's income and product accounts budget. Nobody looks at it except the economists [but] while the Administrative budget is necessary for administration and is like a man's checkbook, the income budget tells the real story. . . .
>
> [It] shows that at the end of 1962 the outgo and ingo accounts will be virtually in balance, with a deficit of only about half a billion dollars. Thus, in reality, the Kennedy administration is no longer stimulating the economy, and the economy is stagnating for lack of stimulation. We have one of the lowest rates of growth among the advanced industrial nations of the world.

One shouldn't be hard on the President. Franklin Roosevelt, a more daring and experimental politician, at least in his domestic policy, listened to the American disciples of J. M. Keynes in the early New Deal years and unbalanced his budgets, with splendid results. But by 1936 he had lost his nerve. He cut back government spending and there ensued the 1937 recession, from which the economy recovered only when war orders began to make up for the deficiency in domestic buying power. "Poverty and Deprivation" estimates that between 1953 and 1961 the annual growth rate of our economy was "only 2.5 percent per annum contrasted with an estimated 4.2 percent required to maintain utilization of manpower and other productive resources." The poor, who always experience the worst the first, understand quite personally the meaning of that dry statistic, as they understand Kipling's "The toad beneath the harrow knows / Exactly where each tooth-point goes." They are also most intimately acquainted with another set of statistics: the steady postwar rise in the unemployment rate, from 3.1 percent in 1949 to 4.3 percent in 1954 to 5.1 percent in 1958 to over 7 percent in 1961. (The Tory Government is worried because British unemployment is now at its highest point for the last three years. This point is 2.1 percent, which is less than our lowest rate in the last fifteen years.)

It's not that Public Opinion doesn't become Aroused every now and then. But the arousement never leads to much. It was aroused twenty-four years ago when John Steinbeck published "The Grapes of Wrath," but Mr. Harrington reports that things in the Imperial Valley are still much the same: low wages, bad housing, no effective union. Public Opinion is too public—that is, too general; of its very nature, it can have no sustained interest in California agriculture. The only groups with such a continuing interest are the workers and the farmers who hire them. Once Public Opinion ceased to be Aroused, the battle was again between the two antagonists with a real, personal stake in the outcome, and there was no question about which was stronger. So with the rural poor in general. In the late fifties, the average annual wage for white male American farm workers was slightly over $1,000; women, children, Negroes, and Mexicans got less. One recalls Edward R. Murrow's celebrated television program about these people, "Harvest of Shame." Once more everybody was shocked, but the harvest is still shameful. One also recalls that Mr. Murrow, after President Kennedy had appointed him head of the United States Information Agency, tried to persuade the b.b.c. not to show "Harvest of Shame." His argument was that it would give an undesirable "image" of America to foreign audiences.

There is a monotony about the injustices suffered by the poor that perhaps accounts for the lack of interest the rest of society shows in them. Everything seems to go wrong with them. They never win. It's just boring.

"Address Unknown"

Public housing turns out not to be for them. The 1949 Housing Act authorized 810,000 new units of low-cost housing in the following four years. Twelve years later, in 1961, the a.f.l.-c.i.o. proposed 400,000 units to complete the lagging 1949 program. The Kennedy administration ventured to recommend 100,000 to Congress. Thus, instead of 810,000 low-cost units by 1953, the poor will get, if they are lucky, 500,000 by 1963. And they are more likely to be injured than helped by slum clearance, since the new projects usually have higher rents than the displaced slum-dwellers can afford. (There has been no dearth of government-financed *middle*-income housing since 1949.) These refugees from the bulldozers for the most part simply emigrate to other slums. They also become invisible; Mr. Harrington notes that half of them are recorded as "address unknown." Several years ago, Charles Abrams, who was New York State Rent Administrator under Harriman and who is now president of the National Committee Against Discrimination in

Housing, summed up what he had learned in two decades in public housing: "Once social reforms have won tonal appeal in the public mind, their slogans and goal-symbols may degenerate into tools of the dominant class for beleaguering the minority and often for defeating the very aims which the original sponsors had intended for their reforms."

And this is not the end of tribulation. The poor, who can least afford to lose pay because of ill health, lose the most. A National Health Survey, made a few years ago, found that workers earning under $2,000 a year had twice as many "restricted-activity days" as those earning over $4,000.

Although they are the most in need of hospital insurance, the poor have the least, since they can't afford the premiums; only 40 percent of poor families have it, as against 63 percent of all families. (It should be noted, however, that the poor who are war veterans can get free treatment, at government expense, in Veterans Administration Hospitals.)

The poor actually pay more taxes, in proportion to their income, than the rich. A recent study by the Tax Foundation estimates that 28 percent of incomes under $2,000 goes for taxes, as against 24 percent of the incomes of families earning five to seven times as much. Sales and other excise taxes are largely responsible for this curious statistic. It is true that such taxes fall impartially on all, like the blessed rain from heaven, but it is a form of egalitarianism that perhaps only Senator Goldwater can fully appreciate.

The final irony is that the Welfare State, which Roosevelt erected and which Eisenhower, no matter how strongly he felt about it, didn't attempt to pull down, is not for the poor, either. Agricultural workers are not covered by Social Security, nor are many of the desperately poor among the aged, such as "unrelated individuals" with incomes of less than $1,000, of whom only 37 percent are covered, which is just half the percentage of coverage among the aged in general. Of the Welfare State, Mr. Harrington says, "Its creation had been stimulated by mass impoverishment and misery, yet it helped the poor least of all. Laws like unemployment compensation, the Wagner Act, the various farm programs, all these were designed for the middle third in the cities, for the organized workers, and for the . . . big market farmers. . . . [It] benefits those least who need help most." The industrial workers, led by John L. Lewis, mobilized enough political force to put through Section 7(a) of the National Industrial Recovery Act, which, with the Wagner Act, made the c.i.o. possible. The big farmers put enough pressure on Henry Wallace, Roosevelt's first Secretary of Agriculture— who talked a good fight for liberal principles but was a Hamlet when it came to action—to establish the two basic propositions of Welfare State agriculture: subsidies that now cost $3 billion a year and that chiefly benefit the big farmers; and the exclusion of sharecroppers, tenant farmers, and migratory workers from the protection of minimum-wage and Social Security laws.

No doubt the Kennedy administration would like to do more for the poor than it has, but it is hampered by the cabal of Republicans and Southern Democrats in Congress. The 1961 revision of the Fair Labor Standards Act, which raised the national minimum wage to the not exorbitant figure of $1.15 an hour, was a slight improvement over the previous act. For instance, it increased coverage of retail-trade workers from 3 percent to 33 percent. (But one-fourth of the retail workers still excluded earn less than $1 an hour.) There was also a considerable amount of shadow-boxing involved: Of the 3,600,000 workers newly covered, only 663,000 were making less than $1 an hour. And there was the exclusion of a particularly ill-paid group of workers. Nobody had anything against the laundry workers *personally*. It was just that they were weak, unorganized, and politically expendable. To appease the conservatives in Congress, whose votes were needed to get the revision through, they were therefore expended. The result is that of the 500,000 workers in the laundry, dry-cleaning, and dyeing industries, just 17,000 are now protected by the Fair Labor Standards Act.

Perpetuating Poverty

It seems likely that mass poverty will continue in this country for a long time. The more it is reduced, the harder it is to keep on reducing it. The poor, having dwindled from two-thirds of the population in 1936 to one-quarter today, no longer are a significant political force, as is shown by the Senate's rejection of Medicare and by the Democrats' dropping it as an issue in the elections last year. Also, as poverty decreases, those left behind tend more and more to be the ones who have for so long accepted poverty as their destiny that they need outside help to climb out of it. This new minority mass poverty, so much more isolated and hopeless than the old majority poverty, shows signs of becoming chronic. "The permanence of low incomes is inferred from a variety of findings," write the authors of the Morgan survey. "In many poor families the head has never earned enough to cover the family's present needs."

> For most families, however, the problem of chronic poverty is serious. One such family is headed by a thirty-two-year-old man who is employed as a dishwasher. Though he works steadily and more than full time, he earned over $2,000 in 1959. His wife earned $300 more,

but their combined incomes are not enough to support themselves and their three children. Although the head of the family is only thirty-two, he feels that he has no chance of advancement partly because he finished only seven grades of school. . . . The possibility of such families leaving the ranks of the poor is not high.

Children born into poor families today have less chance of "improving themselves" than the children of the pre-1940 poor. Rags to riches is now more likely to be rags to rags. "Indeed," the Morgan book concludes, "it appears that a number of the heads of poor families have moved into less skilled jobs than their fathers had." Over a third of the children of the poor, according to the survey, don't go beyond the eighth grade and "will probably perpetuate the poverty of their parents." There are a great many of these children. In an important study of poverty, made for a Congressional committee in 1959, Dr. Robert J. Lampman estimated that eleven million of the poor were under eighteen. "A considerable number of younger persons are starting life in a condition of 'inherited poverty,'" he observed. To which Mr. Harrington adds, "The character of poverty has changed, and it has become more deadly for the young. It is no longer associated with immigrant groups with high aspirations; it is now identified with those whose social existence makes it more and more difficult to break out into the larger society." Even when children from poor families show intellectual promise, there is nothing in the values of their friends or families to encourage them to make use of it. Of the top 16 percent of high-school students—those scoring 120 and over in I.Q. tests—only half go on to college. The explanation for this amazing—and alarming—situation is as much cultural as economic. The children of the poor now tend to lack what the sociologists call "motivation." At least one foundation is working on the problem of why so many bright children from poor families don't ever try to go beyond high school.

Mr. Raymond M. Hilliard, at present director of the Cook County (i.e., Chicago) Department of Public Aid and formerly Commissioner of Welfare for New York City, recently directed a "representative-sample" investigation, which showed that more than half of the 225,000 able-bodied Cook County residents who were on relief were "functionally illiterate." One reason Cook County has to spend $16,500,000 a month on relief is "the lack of basic educational skills of relief recipients which are essential to compete in our modern society." An interesting footnote, apropos of recent happenings at "Ole Miss," is that the illiteracy rate of the relief recipients who were educated in Chicago is 33 percent, while among those who were educated in Mississippi and later moved to Chicago it is 77 percent.

Slums and Schools

The problem of educating the poor has changed since 1900. Then it was the language and cultural difficulties of immigrants from foreign countries; now it is the subtler but more intractable problems of internal migration from backward regions, mostly in the South. The old immigrants wanted to Better Themselves and to Get Ahead. The new migrants are less ambitious, and they come into a less ambitious atmosphere. "When they arrive in the city," wrote Christopher Jencks in an excellent two-part survey, "Slums and Schools," in the *New Republic* last fall, "they join others equally unprepared for urban life in the slums—a milieu which is in many ways utterly dissociated from the rest of America. Often this milieu is self-perpetuating. I have been unable to find any statistics on how many of these migrants' children and grandchildren have become middle-class, but it is probably not too inaccurate to estimate that about 30,000,000 people live in urban slums, and that about half are second-generation residents." The immigrants of 1890–1910 also arrived in a milieu that was "in many ways utterly dissociated from the rest of America," yet they had a vision— a rather materialistic one, but still a vision—of what life in America could be if they worked hard enough; and they did work, and they did aspire to something more than they had; and they did get out of the slums. The disturbing thing about the poor today is that so many of them seem to lack any such vision. Mr. Jencks remarks:

> While the economy is changing in a way which makes the eventual liquidation of the slums at least conceivable, young people are not seizing the opportunities this change presents. Too many are dropping out of school before graduation (more than half in many slums); too few are going to college. . . . As a result there are serious shortages of teachers, nurses, doctors, technicians, and scientifically trained executives, but 4,500,000 unemployables.

The federal government is the only purposeful force—I assume wars are not purposeful—that can reduce the numbers of the poor and make their lives more bearable. The effect of government policy on poverty has two quite distinct aspects. One is the indirect effect of the stimulation of the economy by federal spending. Such stimulation— though by war-time demands rather than government policy—has in the past produced a prosperity that did cut down American poverty by almost two-thirds. But I am inclined to agree with Dr. Galbraith that it would not have a comparable effect on present-day poverty:

> It is assumed that with increasing output poverty must disappear [he writes]. Increased output eliminated the general poverty of all who

worked. Accordingly it must, sooner or later, eliminate the special poverty that still remains. . . . Yet just as the arithmetic of modern politics makes it tempting to overlook the very poor, so the supposition that increasing output will remedy their case has made it easy to do so too.

He underestimates the massiveness of American poverty, but he is right when he says there is now a hard core of the specially disadvantaged—because of age, race, environment, physical or mental defects, etc.—that would not be significantly reduced by general prosperity. (Although I think the majority of our present poor *would* benefit, if only by a reduction in the present high rate of unemployment.)

To do something about this hard core, a second line of government policy would be required; namely, direct intervention to help the poor. We have had this since the New Deal, but it has always been grudging and miserly, and we have never accepted the principle that every citizen should be provided, at state expense, with a reasonable minimum standard of living regardless of any other considerations. It should not depend on earnings, as does Social Security, which continues the inequalities and inequities and so tends to keep the poor forever poor. Nor should it exclude millions of our poorest citizens because they lack the political pressure to force their way into the Welfare State. The governmental obligation to provide, out of taxes, such a minimum living standard for all who need it should be taken as much for granted as free public schools have always been in our history.

"Nobody Starves"

It may be objected that the economy cannot bear the cost, and certainly costs must be calculated. But the point is not the calculation but the principle. Statistics—and especially statistical forecasts—can be pushed one way or the other. Who can determine in advance to what extent the extra expense of giving our 40,000,000 poor enough income to rise above the poverty line would be offset by the lift to the economy from their increased purchasing power? We really don't know. Nor did we know what the budgetary effects would be when we established the principle of free public education. The rationale then was that all citizens should have an equal chance of competing for a better status. The rationale now is different: that every citizen has a right to become or remain part of our society because if this right is denied, as it is in the case of at least one-fourth of our citizens, it impoverishes us all. Since 1932, "the government"—local, state, and federal—has recognized a responsibility to provide its citizens with a subsistence living. Apples will never again be sold on the street by jobless accountants, it seems safe to predict, nor will any serious political leader ever again suggest that share-the-work and local charity can solve the problem of unemployment. "Nobody starves" in this country any more, but, like every social statistic, this is a tricky business. Nobody starves, but who can measure the starvation, not to be calculated by daily intake of proteins and calories, that reduces life for many of our poor to a long vestibule to death? Nobody starves, but every fourth citizen rubs along on a standard of living that is below what Mr. Harrington defines as "the minimal levels of health, housing, food, and education that our present stage of scientific knowledge specifies as necessary for life as it is now lived in the United States." Nobody starves, but a fourth of us are excluded from the common social existence. Not to be able to afford a movie or a glass of beer is a kind of starvation—if everybody else can.

The problem is obvious: the persistence of mass poverty in a prosperous country. The solution is also obvious: to provide, out of taxes, the kind of subsidies that have always been given to the public schools (not to mention the police and fire departments and the post office)—subsidies that would raise incomes above the poverty level, so that every citizen could feel he is indeed such. "*Civis Romanus sum!*" cried St. Paul when he was threatened with flogging—and he was not flogged. Until our poor can be proud to say "*Civis Americanus sum!*," until the act of justice that would make this possible has been performed by the three-quarters of Americans who are not poor—until then the shame of the Other America will continue.

Poverty in America

Oscar Ornati

The New School for Social Research

[Reprinted by permission of the National Policy Committee on Pockets of Poverty, Washington, D. C.]

How Many Americans Are Poor?

TRADITIONALLY, A "LINE OF POVERTY" is drawn to separate the poor from the non-poor. The line is drawn at a specific dollar-income level reflecting a judgment as to the minimum needs below which an individual cannot "subsist" or does not live "adequately," or lives in "deprivation." The line is drawn at different levels by different people and reflects differing concepts of justice, of needs, of values and of the influence of geography and occupation.

A survey of the contemporary practice of private and public agencies concerned with the problems of the poor reveals a great variety of definitions. In spite of these differences clusters appear at three levels. The three levels of poverty most generally used are:

1. Minimum subsistence ($2500 per year for a family of four)
2. Minimum adequacy   ($3500 per year for a family of four)
3. Minimum comfort   ($5500 per year for a family of four).

By these standards there are 20, 46, or 70 million "poor" in the United States today.

By whatever standard poverty is measured there are today a very large number of poor Americans. To act against poverty no precise calculation is required. While differences in the use of available statistics explain how various recent studies have arrived at different counts of the poor, once agreement on the standards of poverty is reached no significant difference in the estimate of the number of the poor flows from the use of different statistics, or different imputations of "non-money income" and the like.

Is the Situation Improving?

Various statisticians and government agencies are in disagreement as to whether there are now more or less poor today than in the past. Here different judgments as to how the comparisons are to be made explain the differences. Should the standards of the past be taken as a guide and, having corrected for changes in the value of the dollar, applied to the present? Or, should the opposite be done and current standards be deflated and the extent of poverty of the past so measured?

By taking past standards that go back far enough we are bound to find that there are *no* poor today, which is a patent absurdity.

The President's Economic Report in its statement that "since 1947, prosperity and progress have reduced the incidence of substandard incomes from one-third to one-fifth" suffers from this bias. It is based on the substandard income level used in 1947—17 years ago.

Conversely, by taking present standards and projecting them backwards we would find that Franklin D. Roosevelt's "one-third of a nation" would have been one-half of the nation.

Either exercise tells us more about changing standards than about the number of the poor. If comparisons are to be made, they should be made in terms of contemporary standards. What should be compared is the number who lived "below adequacy" in 1947 by 1947 standards of adequacy with those who lived "below adequacy" in 1960 by 1960 standards. When this is done, we find that the numbers of abject poor, the numbers of those living "below adequacy" and below minimum comfort levels have not changed very much. In 1947, by 1947 standards, 27 percent of all people lived below levels of minimum adequacy and in 1960, by 1960 standards, they amounted to 26 percent. The 1947 proportion living below minimum comfort was 39 percent while in 1960 it was 40 percent.

The story is different when abject poverty is considered. Here, when the number of poor, living at or below subsistence levels in 1947 and 1960 are compared, the proportion decreased from 15 percent to 11 percent although their actual number only decreased from 21 to 20 million.

To do away with poverty the line of poverty approach is *not* useful because:

1. Consensus on the meaning of poverty is hard to obtain and searching for it will delay policy action to do away with poverty; and

2. Viewing poverty as the condition of large but ill-defined populations does not give policy guidance on which action should be taken or on which individuals would be the beneficiaries of which programs.

Far more important than a count of the poor is the identification of the groups that are poor and of the relative risk of poverty that individuals incur because of conditions which are beyond their control.

The Risk of Poverty

For most of the economic history of the United States low income and poverty characterized a considerable part of the population. The old and the young, man and woman, farmer and city dweller, black and white, North and South, almost all shared in the national insufficiency; if one were black or a female family head or Southern, the risk of poverty was greater but not much greater. Many without these attributes shared their fate. The few that escaped from poverty did so by chance, by stubbornness or by personal qualities much more than because they belonged to a particular group.

Since World War II, it has been quite another story. Poverty has become increasingly a burden carried by "special" groups and individuals.

In the United States of the 1960's poverty is more properly and more effectively approached in terms of the programs necessary to improve conditions in which certain groups live, and of the characteristics which they possess.

The contemporary poor are the non-whites, families with no earners, families whose heads are females and men aged 14 to 25 or over 65. The contemporary poor are also those with less than eight years of education, inhabitants of rural farm areas, members of families in which there are more than six children under 18, and residents of the South. These characteristics are, for brevity, called poverty-linked.

Table A shows the proportion of people with poverty-linked characteristics according to the 1960 census that are found at three low income groups.

TABLE A
Poverty-Linked Populations vs. Total Population
1960
Per Cent Distribution

Poverty-Linked Characteristics	Income Class				
	$0–500		$0–2,000		$0–4,500
	Families	Individuals	Families	Individuals	Families
Percent of Total					
Population	2.5	14.6	13.0	54.1	36.7
Non-white	5.7	19.7	31.7	66.7	65.8
Female	8.0	17.1	34.0	60.9	68.0
Age:					
65 and over	3.2	13.7	31.4	79.4	68.0
14 to 24	3.2	25.9	18.3	54.9	58.0
Residence:					
Rural Farm	9.3	32.0	35.8	79.9	70.3
Southern[a]					
All	N.A.	N.A.	21.3	66.3	50.3
Non-white	N.A.	N.A.	44.0	78.7	80.8
Non-earner	12.1	27.7	57.9	88.7	93.4
Work Experience:					
None	7.2	21.0	40.3	86.3	76.8
All Part Time	6.2	20.6	39.6	80.4	71.0
0-26 weeks	8.0	26.3	49.3	86.5	81.9
27-49 weeks	4.2	12.0	32.3	82.4	64.0
Six plus children					
Under eighteen	6.2	—	22.0	—	54.2
Education:					
Less than 8 years[b]	6.2	22.6	33.2	80.3	69.7

Sources: Data for all characteristics except education and southern residence from *Current Population Reports*, Bureau of the Census, 1960, Series P60-37. Education data from *Current Population Reports*, Bureau of the Census, 1956, Series P60-27. Southern residence material from special tabulation Census Bureau (unpublished data).

[a] Total population for southern residence: $0-500, not available for both families and unrelated individuals. For families, $0-2,000, 13.1; $0-4,500, 30.9. For unrelated individuals, $0-2,000, 58.5. Data from *Census Supplementary Report*, PC(S1)—18.

[b] Total population for 1956: (Used because educational income data not available for 1960, see source). For families, $0-500, 3.2; $0-2,000, 15.4; $0-4,500, 16.1. For unrelated individuals, $0-500, 17.7; $0-2,000, 61.1.

Data in Table A involve characteristics and not people. They therefore cannot be added. Indeed the characteristics are overlapping as the individuals involved may have—and, in most cases, do have—more than one such characteristic.

For example, the category "family headed by a female" contains also families with more than six children and such families are often non-white, rural farm, etc. Later, this problem of overlap is dealt with; here we simply examine the extent to which the low income population consists of people with such characteristics.

The major finding highlighted in Table A is that the characteristics studied show a clear, significant and strong association with poverty. Indeed, compared to all families, a much greater proportion of those with poverty-linked characteristics had less than $500 income. Of course, not all the traits are equally tied to low income. But for nine of the fourteen poverty-linked characteristics, possession doubled the risk of abject poverty. For a few traits the risk was even higher. Only very youthful and aged families did not deviate much from the percentage of all families with less than $500 income. Old Age Assistance, Social Security, pensions and savings have insured that only three aged families out of 100 need try to live on an income of less than $500 per year.

At the $2000 income level the situation changes. Here possession of any one of eleven poverty-linked characteristics means a family has twice the normal possibility of living in poverty. At this level, Social Security and Old Age Assistance no longer provide a floor under which income cannot fall. The gap between aged families and families in general has widened; only 13 percent of all American families have incomes under $2,000 as compared with 31 percent for aged families. The same widening of the risk holds for many other categories (non-white, rural farm, etc.).

At the $4,500 income level *all* of the characteristics studied are firmly related to poverty. Indeed, more than half of the families with any one of fourteen traits have less than $4,500 in income, while less than 37 percent of all families are in this situation. The most extreme group is families with no earners, where over 93 percent had incomes of less than $4,500 in 1960.

Unattached individuals with the same characteristics run similarly high risks of being poor. One special feature is added. As the table makes clear, being an unrelated individual is in itself a poverty-linked attribute.

It should be noted that the relative portion of those with poverty-linked characteristics is here understated since comparisons are made with the *total* population, which includes the poverty-linked groups. Had the poverty-linked population been compared with the non-poverty-linked population the contrast would be even more striking. The importance of poverty-linked characteristics as the most effective approach to poverty analysis depends upon our knowledge as to the changing makeup of the total population.

The numerical changes in poverty-linked groups between 1947 and 1960, as well as a tentative forecast for the year 1980, are shown in Table B.

Families and individuals with poverty-linked characteristics are now a larger part of the total population than they were in 1947. If our population forecasts are valid, this trend will continue. By 1980 non-whites will account for more than 11 percent of all families whereas in 1947 they were only 8.4 percent. The growth of the aged in the United States is the best publicized of any poverty-linked group. Again,

TABLE B

Poverty-Linked Characteristics, 1947, 1960 and 1980 (Projected)
Per Cent and Per Cent Change

Families

	Per Cent			Per Cent Change		
Characteristics	1947	1960	1980ᵃ	1947-60	1960-80ᵃ	1947-80ᵃ
Non-white	8.4%	9.5%	11.2%	13.1%	17.9%	33.3%
Female	10.1	10.1	9.7	No Change	−4.0	−4.0
Rural-farmᵇ	14.7	11.3	5.6	−23.1	−50.6	−73.7
Age 65 and Over	11.7	13.7	14.0	17.1	2.2	19.7
Age 14-24	4.9	5.1	8.2	4.1	60.8	67.3
No Earners	6.0	7.3	9.8	22.0	32.1	63.3
Six or More Children Under 18	1.8	2.5	4.2	39.0	68.0	133.0

Unrelated Individuals

	Per Cent			Per Cent Change		
Characteristics	1947	1960	1980ᵃ	1947-60	1960-80ᵃ	1947-80ᵃ
Non-white	11.9%	13.7%	15.9%	15.1%	16.1%	33.6%
Female	53.8	61.5	61.5	14.0	No Change	14.0
Rural-farmᵇ	6.4	5.7	—	−10.9	—	—
Age 65 and Over	28.6	33.5	44.0	17.1	31.3	53.8
Age 14-24	10.3	10.0	10.5	−3.0	5.0	1.9
Non-Earners	33.5	37.0	42.9	10.4	15.9	28.1

Source: Data for 1947 from *Current Population Reports,* Bureau of the Census, Series P60-5; data for 1960 from *Current Population Reports,* Bureau of the Census, Series P60-37.

ᵃ For method of projection see forthcoming *Poverty in an Affluent Society.*

ᵇ For consistency of definition data for 1949, 1958 and 1960 were used instead of 1947 and 1960. Other periods in this line conform to these dates, i.e., 1960-1980 is 1958-60 and 1947-1960 is 1949-1958.

if population forecasts to 1980 are correct, there will be only a small proportional increase in the characteristic "aged family heads," but there will be a proportionately very large increase in the characteristic "unattached individuals over 65." The number of unattached females grew in the fourteen-year span analyzed, but the proportion of families headed by females remained unchanged. In the future this group might diminish in their relative importance. The proportion of families headed by persons 14 to 24 years old increased while the proportion of unattached individuals of the same age group declined. In the future young families can be expected to increase sharply, while young individuals will, by 1980, record only a modest increase. One poverty-linked family group, those with six or more children under 18, increased sharply between 1947 and 1960. This group is expected to increase even more sharply but, in evaluating this change, the smallness in absolute numbers of this group should be kept in mind.

Rural farm residence, a very important poverty-linked characteristic, has declined sharply. Between 1949 and 1958, the number of those residing in rural farm areas declined sharply. It is difficult to forecast rural farm residence for the year 1980. The variables are many and difficult to assess with precision. Our forecast, however, points to a continuing decline in the number of people engaged in agriculture.

The unique behavior of rurality as a poverty-linked characteristic undoubtedly reflects the fact that aside from the non-earner characteristic this is one characteristic from which the individual can theoretically escape by moving. This does not mean that a former rural farm resident is automatically not poor when he reaches the city. All it says is that the moment he reaches the city, he joins a population group whose risk of being poor is lower. One might argue also that education provides another escape. This holds true for the younger person, but less so for the adult currently living on a farm. Historically, Americans escape poverty by pulling up stakes. This is still the case. It has been noted how unattached individuals for the most part fare worse than families. But this is not the case with the locational traits: rural farm and southern residence. For southern residence no reliable forecast could be developed and therefore this characteristic was not included in Table B. Again mobility is the key and unattached individuals behaved as expected: they moved.

An exception which throws light on the interplay of the impact of poverty-linked traits and economic conditions is the curse of the non-white southern individual. The poverty percent of southern individuals is lower than that for southern families. For southern non-whites, as the same table shows, this is not the case. This is not an unreasonable or illogical development. Although as individuals they have greater potential mobility than families, as non-whites poverty already has a hold on them. It prevents them from taking full advantage of their potential mobility. As non-whites they may have discounted the possible benefits of moving which, by itself, does not help them shed the more pervasive poverty-linked trait: color.

In summary, it is clear that population characteristics associated with low income have all increased in importance over the past fourteen years. An exception, and possibly an important offset, to this pattern has been in the declining numerical importance of rural farm dwellers. It is impossible, however, to gauge the total impact of the changes described above by using an additive technique since many of the characteristics are not mutually exclusive. For example, an increase in families with no earners in part reflects the higher proportion of older families. This qualification tempers, rather than contradicts, the initial generalization.

Changes in the Risk of Being Poor

Using data about the risk of poverty of various groups to formulate anti-poverty policies is useful also as it permits comparison over time. What is important is to be able to measure how the risk of being poor for persons with a given characteristic has changed over time correcting the data for the change in the number of people with these characteristics. Such comparisons have been done, where the data were available for 1948 through 1960 on the basis of contemporary standards.

A check on the validity of this whole approach and on the particular findings reported for 1960 is provided by repeating the analysis of the characteristics for a population with *non-poverty-linked characteristics*. This was done for families with the characteristics: white, male head aged 25–34, with two children under 18. The data showed that in 1960 this constellation of attributes was much less frequent in the low income brackets and much heavier in the higher income brackets. Thus individuals with these characteristics appear *not to have a high risk of poverty* which can for 1960 be interpreted as meaning that such individuals are not poor. In 1948 the risk of this type of individual being poor was almost twice as great even by 1948 standards.

The comparison with 1948 strikingly shows that people with low income in 1960 had more frequently those demographic characteristics that have been found to be linked with poverty than did persons with comparable income in 1948.

The fact that in 1960, at income equivalents to those of 1948, poverty-linked demographic characteristics were more frequent is not due to increases in the number of persons at the low end of the income scale. In fact a modest decline in the total number of people in these groups has occurred. *The greater concentration of the population with poverty-linked characteristics at the low income levels of 1960 appears due rather to the fact that persons that moved out of low levels of income since 1948 were predominantly those without those social and demographic characteristics* which have been found to be associated with a high risk of poverty. Obviously the data do not suggest that in 1948 and 1960 the same persons were necessarily involved—some died, new ones were born, some managed to earn more, others less and so on. The data indicate only that populations with poverty-linked characteristics, irrespective of who the particular persons with such characteristics may be, have a greater risk of finding themselves in the low income groups.

The changes in the risk of being poor that have taken place for each of the major groups involved tell a complicated story that is only briefly summarized here:

Non-earners

Despite unemployment benefits, welfare payments, insurance and aid from relatives, living with a non-earner exposes the family to a high risk of being poor. The risk of being poor is *unaffected by changes in business conditions* and *has increased* over the last decade.

Non-earners who do not live in families have a high risk of poverty. The risk of poverty for the unattached individual is not as high as for other poverty-linked characteristics nor has it increased with time.

Non-white

Being non-white makes for a very high risk of poverty. Since 1954 the risk of poverty has increased for all non-whites. The general improvement in business conditions which took place after 1954 and after 1957 was not felt by the non-white families living below subsistence and below adequacy. Following the 1958 recession, improvement was not apparent until 1960. Non-white families living below minimum comfort on the other hand, had a smaller risk of being poor with business expansion and a greater risk of poverty with business contractions. The pattern for non-white individuals was like that of families.

Age 65 and Over

In the last decade the aged seem to have "detached" themselves from abject poverty more than any other group. There is much evidence that, from 1947 to 1960—probably mostly because of Social Security—families with heads 65 and over have moved up, if not out of, abject poverty.

At the level of adequacy and comfort an aged head still exposes the family to a considerable risk of being poor and this risk has increased. The reason the upward movement was limited may reflect the problem older workers have in finding employment to supplement Social Security payments.

The unattached individuals over 65 are worse off than families and, if anything, less sensitive to the cycle. At the lower levels their status has improved somewhat in recent years.

The effect of Social Security is less manifest among the unattached. One possible explanation is that there is a disproportionate number of women among older single individuals and many of them may not have qualified for OASI benefits, since their labor force participation rate in covered employment is, and has been, considerably below the male rate.

Rural Farm

This poverty-linked family group is numerically less important today than in 1948. *The association of the now smaller population with low income, however, has become stronger. Their risk of being poor is much greater.* An additional finding—not unexpected—is that the association appears closely related to the economy's cyclical path. In the 1948 and 1949 recession period, for example, the association became much stronger at all levels of low income and particularly at the $4,500 level. The association weakened somewhat following the recession. A significant tightening of the relationship paralleled the second postwar recession. *Since 1954 the risk of poverty at the abject poverty ($2,500) and minimum adequacy ($3,500) income levels have been less sensitive to the movements of the general economy.*

Although there is some indication that the risk of poverty has increased for rural farm individuals, the trend lacks the strength found for families.

Females

The risk of poverty for a family headed by a female is high, and growing.

Changes in attachment to poverty for such families conflict sharply with changing business conditions. The increase in the risk of poverty for female heads of families was often apparent when the rest of the population was relatively prosperous. The worsening condition of these families appeared to be arrested in years when the rest of the population suffered serious economic setbacks.

The wedding between poverty and single females is not as serious as that in which a family is involved. Their condition is not comparable with that of the female head of household, nor has their risk of being poor increased.

This is not unexpected. Single females suffer from only one economic disadvantage, their sex, while female heads of families face a complex of problems which impinge on their ability to be viable in our economy. There is also no clear relationship between changes in the value of the coefficients· measuring attachment to poverty and the postwar business fluctuations. A factor which blurs whatever relationship there might be is the age composition of this group. It contains a large group of elderly women who were never or are no longer in the labor force, women who are living on their own or their husband's pension, or on welfare or gifts, all of which are sources of income less sensitive to changes in business conditions.

The Large and Young Families

Since 1947 the number of large families has increased. The average increase in the size of the American family does not seem to have affected the poor population very significantly (indeed, different sized families are scattered fairly evenly among consumer units of all incomes). Among low income families, the number with four, five and six persons, has fallen drastically.

Very young families—with the family head between 14 and 24— *comprised a slightly smaller segment of the total population in 1960 than in 1947 but their incidence in the low income population has increased.* Thus, in spite of the lack of any relationship to business conditions, the honor of being called "family head" bestowed too soon brings with it a greater likelihood of poverty, particularly since 1957. For part of this group, poverty may be only a temporary condition. For most, low income is no momentary detour, but the foreshadowing of a life of poverty.

The Convergence of Poverty-Linked Characteristics

The demographic characteristics discussed so far obviously overlap; being non-white may also mean being a farmer, or being aged, or being a female head of family. The poor do not usually have only one problem and many poor families are classified as "multi-problem" families. Available data point clearly to low education and shrinking occupational mobility as one of the major causes of poverty. Here the increased requirements in education for employment are one of the major causes of poverty. In addition, bad physical and mental health contribute to poverty to an undetermined but clearly significant degree.

Our rough estimate is that of the 20 million abject poor more than two-thirds, or somewhere between 12 and 14 million, are deficient in either health, mental or physical, or education, and a very large number of individuals are affected by more than one disadvantage. The proportions do not change significantly at the $3,500 or $4,500 level.

If we are to move against poverty, we must understand the dynamics of the process. Then we can move from the broad discussions of complex causality which determines an individual's risk of being poor to the isolation of characteristics which, in the aggregate, appear to contribute more, and of those that contribute less, to poverty.

Analysis of the 1960 census data allows, at least for that year, a precise count, at different levels of income, of population units which had one or more of four key poverty-linked characteristics. It also provides a set of major preliminary clues as to how to move against poverty along the lines suggested above. Fifteen different poverty-linked family populations were constructed, ranging from units possessing one characteristic to those with all four. Here the problem of overlapping characteristics is eliminated. A non-white family is only non-white. There is no aged family head, no female family head, and no rural-farm resident. The same for the other characteristics. The cumulative total of all families with one characteristic holds no duplication—each family is counted only once. Nor is there duplication when families with two or more characteristics are examined.

As expected, by correcting for overlap, we note that: (1) there are more families with only one poverty characteristic than with two, with three or four; (2) the risk of poverty increases with the number of characteristics. The data in Table C indicate that while the relationship is not perfect, the possession of two characteristics means a greater chance of very low income than the possession of one, three a greater chance than two, etc. The degree of poverty, measured by the proportion of families below the three budget levels varies considerably.

Families that have only one characteristic find between 30 and 40 percent of their membership at or below subsistence, between 55 and 60 percent below the minimum adequacy level and roughly 70 percent below minimum comfort.

Possessing two characteristics condemns a considerably larger portion of the population to subsistence living. For all but one of the six sub-populations with two attributes the proportion below $2,600 is

TABLE C

The Percentage of Each Poverty-Linked Population Below
Three Low Income Levels
(1960)

Characteristic(s) of Family Head	# of Units	%	Per Cent Below 2,500	4,500	5,500
One Characteristic					
Aged	4,276,016	100%	39.6%	60.2%	70.5%
Female	2,387,443	100	38.0	60.4	73.3
Rural-farm	2,434,041	100	34.5	57.5	71.0
Non-white	2,786,211	100	28.6	54.7	70.9
Two Characteristics					
Non-white, Female	743,115	100	64.6	82.2	88.4
Aged, Female	787,975	100	37.2	56.1	68.4
Aged, Rural-farm	489,732	100	54.9	74.7	83.2
Aged, Non-white	331,316	100	62.6	80.1	87.5
Non-white, Rural-farm	208,047	100	78.3	90.8	94.8
Rural-farm, Female	73,842	100	54.8	73.9	83.1
Three Characteristics					
Non-white, Aged, Female	115,444	100	67.5	83.5	89.8
Non-white, Rural-farm, Aged	40,901	100	81.1	91.9	95.4
Rural-farm, Aged, Female	55,444	100	52.5	70.8	80.3
Rural-farm, Non-white, Female	22,784	100	86.6	94.9	97.8
Four Characteristics					
Non-white, Rural-farm, Aged, Female	7,698	100	84.0	93.9	97.0

better than half. For non-white families with the added characteristic of rural farm residence, the probability of abject poverty is three out of four. The chance of living at or below the minimum adequacy level is 75 percent or better for all but one of these twice-cursed families. Ninety percent of all non-white farm families, 80 percent of all the non-white aged and 82 percent of all the non-white families with female heads lived under this level. For all but one of these combinations the chance of escaping from the poverty band is less than 2 in 10. Conversely, families with two poverty-linked attributes rarely have incomes placing them above the poverty level. Extreme poverty is the fate of families with 3 or 4 poverty attributes. For three groups the figure is 8 in 10, for one, 7 in 10, and for one 5 in 10.

The Policy Implications of Convergence

The policy implications of the data and the analysis presented so far should be clear. On the one hand, families with one poverty characteristic make up the largest part of the low income population; on the other hand, families with more than one attribute, although less numerous, suffer the heavier burdens. Noting that they are less numerous in no way means they are insignificant. Families with two characteristics involve roughly ten million men, women and children.

Half of these live below the contemporary subsistence level. Another quarter of a million families are marked by the even more extreme poverty associated with three or four characteristics. They contribute another million human exceptions to American affluence.

Examination of the differential impact of particular characteristics sharpens the focus of policy. Not only does this provide guidelines for the future, it also gives insight into the effect of past policies.

Table D *measures the income effect of removing one poverty-linked characteristic from the population of families with three such characteristics.* The table shows how, in every case, the removal of the *characteristic non-white reduces the percentage of families below sub-sistence to a greater degree than removing the characteristic rural-farm.* The effect is least marked in terms of removing any third characteristic from families with rural-farm as one of their three poverty-linked characteristics.

TABLE D

The Effect of Removing a Poverty-Linked Characteristic
From a Family Possessing Three Characteristics
(Changes in Percentages of Families Below the Subsistence Level)

Characteristic	%	Characteristic	%
Non-white, Rural-farm, Female	86.6%	Non-white, Rural-farm, Aged	81.1%
Minus:		Minus:	
Non-white =	54.8	Non-white =	54.9
Rural-farm =	64.6	Rural-farm =	62.6
Female =	78.3	Aged =	78.3
Non-white, Aged, Female	67.5	Aged, Rural-farm, Female	52.5
Minus:		Minus:	
Non-white =	37.2	Rural-farm =	37.2
Aged =	64.6	Aged =	54.8
Female =	62.6	Female =	54.9

Table E shows—in a manner similar to Table D—the effect of *removing one poverty-linked characteristic from families with two.* The pattern that emerges throws some light on the success of a past policy, Social Security. In the first set of percentages and the fifth set we find that subtracting the aged has a modifying rather than a depressing effect on the percentage of extremely low income units. Rural-farm families headed by aged females were slightly better off than rural-farm families headed by non-aged females. Age is the one area where, adequate or not, there does exist a national policy and program of insurance. Removing the non-white characteristic helps here, too, but less so.

Defining poverty through poverty-linked characteristics leads to the following major conclusions: First, the poverty population in

TABLE E

The Effect of Removing a Poverty-Linked Characteristic
From a Family Possessing Two Characteristics
(Changes in Percentages of Families Below the Subsistence Level)

Characteristic	%	Characteristic	%
Non-white, Rural-farm	78.3%	Non-white, Female	64.6%
Minus:		Minus:	
Rural-farm = 28.6		Female = 28.6	
Non-white = 34.5		Non-white = 38.0	
Non-white, Aged	62.6	Rural-farm, Aged	54.9
Minus:		Minus:	
Aged = 28.6		Aged = 34.5	
Non-white = 39.6		Rural-farm = 39.6	
Rural-farm, Female	54.8	Aged, Female	37.2
Minus:		Minus:	
Female = 34.5		Aged = 38.0	
Rural-farm = 38.0		Female = 39.6	

1960 is characterized by identifying specific socio-demographic attributes. Families that are aged, rural-farm, non-white, headed by females, or combinations of these, account for 70 percent of the abject poor. Second, in absolute terms, the largest groups are those families possessing only one characteristic. Third, the most severe poverty exists among families with more than one attribute and, fourth, among the multi-characteristic families, non-whiteness is most damaging.

In the strictest sense of the word, the poor of today are less endowed. "Underprivileged" has long been a fashionable word. It seemed less offensive than "poor." On the whole, until recent years, it was an inappropriate euphemism. Now it fits. It means those who are less endowed and less able to participate in the Affluent Society. It means those who are out of the mainstream of American life.

The underprivileged are not of, even though they are in, the market society. Their poverty is a poverty of structure. They sit outside as marginal sellers and weak buyers. They are economic as well as physical invalids and are discriminated against socially and economically. *Their poverty is the result of special circumstances*, rather than of the rate of economic activity. They do not directly reflect an inadequate growth rate as they are not part of the economic structure. Our economy takes care of those who are within its embrace, but it does not take care of the underprivileged.

The policy implications are clear. The redefinition presented here casts poverty in a context in which action is possible. Poverty is a structural problem and thus policies to deal with it must be structurally-oriented. This presents many problems. Many policy-makers and economists contend that poverty will be done away with by poli-

cies aimed at bringing about full employment. Such policies are necessary prerequisites and have a social and economic value and priority
of their own. But, the elimination or drastic reduction of poverty in
America demands additional measures pinpointed to those structural
characteristics of the affluent society that have permitted a large pool of
underprivileged in the midst of a relatively efficient economy.

The Family Cycle and Income Development

Alvin L. Schorr

U. S. Department of Health, Education, and Welfare

[From Social Security Bulletin, *February, 1966.]*

IT IS, ON THE WHOLE, a fact that most people who die poor were born
poor. It is also a fact, though partial, that poor people show typical
attitudes and behavior and transmit them to their children. Human
manipulation has made from these observations a non-fact or artifact:
The poor move about in a self-contained aura of attitudes that are
more or less independent of their life experience; the attitudes themselves produce their poverty. It would be hard to imagine a more
comfortable mystique for those who are not poor. It is less flattering
and more taxing to the mind to grasp the play back-and-forth between facts of life and attitudes towards life, between what seems
practical and what one aspires to. Yet this is the task facing those who
want to understand at all how an income-maintenance program may
influence its beneficiaries.

   Some light might be shed on the mystique of the "culture of
poverty" by a simple examination of the effect of poor food or poor
housing on behavior. Ample evidence testifies to the capacity of such
deficiencies to produce the type of attitudes associated with poor
people.[1] However, it will serve the purpose better to take another
approach, attempting to relate the stages through which a family
passes over time to the development of family income. It is the

---

[1]Alvin L. Schorr, *Slums and Social Insecurity,* Social Security Adminis-
tration, Division of Research and Statistics (Research Report No. 1), 1963. Alvin
L. Schorr, "The Non-culture of Poverty," *American Journal of Orthopsychiatry,*
October 1964. I. T. Stone, D. C. Leighton, A. H. Leighton, "Poverty and the
Individual," paper presented at the University of West Virginia Conference on
Poverty Amidst Affluence, May 3-7, 1965.

progress of a child, over time, from poverty to adequacy that is sought. It is a family of some sort that will receive income from any program devised.

Available studies and statistics are poorly suited to outlining the family-income cycle. The problem may be simplified by talking only of poor families, but even so, no one knows whether there are one, two, or several typical modes of development. It is clear only that not every family now poor necessarily started poor or will end poor. In order to attempt to discern a pattern, overlapping and partially sequential stages in family life will be identified. The stages are selected because they represent crises on two planes at once—family development and income development. If the wrong choice, in terms of future income, is made at the first stage, the right choice becomes progressively harder to make at each subsequent stage. The four stages are these: (1) timing and circumstances of first marriage or child-bearing; (2) timing and direction of occupational choice; (3) family cycle squeeze—the conflict of aspiration and need; and (4) family breakdown.

Initial Marriage and Child-Bearing

Women who married for the first time in 1960 were, on the average, about 20 years old. By 27 or 28, the median wife will have had her last child.[2] Within a general trend to young marriage and child-bearing, it appears that the very youngest will have lower incomes and less stable families. The evidence comes from studies that are variously focused and of varying vintage. Arguing 40 years ago that society was moving towards a norm in which 18 would be the youngest age at which girls would marry, Mary Richmond and Fred Hall observed: "The daughter who in the Old Country would have been married at the first chance, must now, for a few years at least, delay marriage—often will wish to do so—in order to help in putting her own and her family's fortunes on a firmer foundation."[3] More recently: "... youthful marriages are less satisfactory to the participants and less stable than marriages contracted by persons who are out of their teens."[4] The incidence of poverty among families with heads 14 to

[2]Paul C. Glick, David M. Heer, and John C. Beresford, "Family Formation and Family Composition: Trends and Prospects," in *Sourcebook in Marriage and the Family*, edited by Marvin B. Sussman, Houghton Mifflin Company, 1963.

[3]Mary E. Richmond and Fred S. Hall, *Child Marriages*, Russell Sage Foundation, 1925.

[4]Lee G. Burchinal, "Research on Young Marriage: Implications for Family Life Education," in *Sourcebook in Marriage and the Family*, cited above.

24 years old, already high by the end of World War II, had increased by 1960. "The honor of being called family head, bestowed too soon," observes Oscar Ornati, "brings with it a greater likelihood of poverty."[5] This observation shows only the relationship of early marriage to income shortly after marriage.

That the relationship of early marriage to low income persists over time can be seen in table 1. Education and occupation are both significant indicators of income. The husbands of wives first married under the age of 17 are far more likely than other husbands, some 20 years or more later, to have the poorest education and work. Their chances of turning up with some college education or a professional or technical job are very small indeed. The age of women at marriage

TABLE 1

Education and Occupation of Husband By Age When Wife Was First Married, For Families in Which the Wife Was 35 Years Old Or Over in 1960

Age of wife at first marriage	Percent of total number of families	*Education of husband (percent)*		*Occupation of husband[1] (percent)*	
		11 years of school or less	*13 years of school or more*	*Operative, service worker, or laborer*	*Professional or technical worker, or manager, official, or proprietor*
14-16	8	83	4	44	12
17 and 18	15	76	6	38	16
19 and 20	19	67	13	32	20
21 and 22	17	60	21	29	26

[1]For husbands with work experience since 1950.
Source: Derived from *U.S. Census of Population: 1960 - Families*, Final Report, PC (2)4A, 1963, tables 52 and 55.

must be permitted to tell the story for their husbands, as the 1960 Census distinguished between men who had married younger or older than 22, without distinguishing below that age. Even dealing with that comparatively advanced age, the data suggest the same conclusion. The men who married between 22 and 27 eventually held better jobs than those who married before 22.[6] It is not surprising to find,

---

[5]Oscar Ornati, "Poverty in America," National Policy Committee on Pockets of Poverty, Washington, D.C., 1964, p. 12.
[6]*U. S. Census of Population: 1960—Families*, Final Report, PC(2)4A, table 48.

too, evidence suggesting that, ". . . early arrival of children is associated with less accumulation of capital by the family, even when adjustments are made for differences in age, education, inheritances, and unemployment experiences."[7] Putting together the two cross-sections, one shortly after marriage and the other a decade or two later, one may conclude that low income is likely to be a continuing experience for those who marry before 18.

The table understates the risk in young marriages. It deals with intact marriages and omits the women whose marriages did not last and who were not, in 1960, remarried. The omission is consequential, for the evidence is also clear that earlier marriages tend to be less stable. If they married before 17, for example, 3 out of 10 women between 25 and 34 are remarried or their husbands are remarried. Only a fraction more than 1 out of 10 who first married at 20 show the same result.[8] Paul Glick has observed that, after a lapse of 30 years, only half of the women married by 17 are still living with their first husband.[9]

These statistics are clear about the risks to income and stability in young marriages, but they do not begin to explain them. To understand the statistics, it is necessary to begin before the marriage takes place. It appears that a substantial number of children (perhaps 20 percent of all legitimate first children) are conceived before marriage.[10] Although the conclusion might once have been that 1 out of 5 marriages has been forced, it now appears that many young people who are planning to be married simply anticipate the ceremony. The situation is rather different among those who marry at 16 or 17. The girl and quite possibly the boy have not finished school. Even if they contemplated marriage, all sorts of practical difficulties would deter them. In fact, the percentage of premarital conceptions among youths is much higher than 20 percent. Studies in a variety of localities show premarital pregnancy rates that range upward from one-third of all school-age marriages to 87 percent where both parties were high

---

[7]James N. Morgan, *et al., Income and Welfare in the United States,* McGraw-Hill Book Company, 1962, p. 91.

[8]*U. S. Census of Population, op. cit.,* table 51.

[9]Paul C. Glick, "Stability of Marriage in Relation to Age at Marriage," in Robert F. Winch, Robert McGinnis, and Herbert R. Barringer, *Selected Studies in Marriage and the Family,* Holt, Rinehart, and Winston, 1963.

[10]Harold T. Christensen and Hanna H. Meissner, "Premarital Pregnancy as a Factor in Divorce," in Robert F. Winch, Robert McGinnis, and Herbert R. Barringer, *op. cit.*

school students.[11] The conclusion is that young marriages are, indeed, forced marriages.

Whether forced or not, young marriages face a number of practical problems. The table above shows that young marriage is associated with less education for the husband. In the climate of postwar attitudes, a young couple readily complete the husband's education while the wife works. If they are very young, however, and already have a baby, this is rather harder to bring off. Forty percent of girls dropping out of high school are willing to tell an interviewer that marriage or pregnancy is the reason.[12] Education and training are increasingly competitive requirements in a period when many youths are unemployed. At any given moment, 1 of 5 youths without a high school diploma is unemployed.[13] At least as many drop-outs are probably not even seeking work.[14] Thus, the young marriage is likely to start with unemployment compounded, when work turns up, by comparatively low wages.

The discussion has proceeded, thus far, as if all families begin with marriage and, of course, they do not. The prevalence of poverty among families headed by women is well documented; obviously, mothers who start out without a husband are no better off. Nor is it to be supposed that pregnancy before marriage or at a young age is the first cause and poverty follows from it, an automatic punishment for transgression. Sometimes, indeed, causality moves in this direction. For example, a pioneer study raised doubt about simple formulations of the relation between fertility and social class.[15] Yet it seemed clear that those couples whose incomes actually declined seemed to have been "selected for initial lack of fertility control."[16]

---

[11]Lee G. Burchinal, *op. cit.*

[12]Vera C. Perrella and Forest A. Bogan, "Out-of-School Youth, February 1963," Part I, *Monthly Labor Review,* November 1964.

[13]Thomas E. Swanstrom, "Out-of-School Youth, February 1963," Part II, *Monthly Labor Review,* December 1964.

[14]Mollie Orshansky, "Who's Who Among the Poor: A Demographic View of Poverty," *Social Security Bulletin,* July 1965.

[15]The theory of social capillarity, stated in 1890, appears regularly in other metamorphoses. Arsene Dumont's theory is stated as follows: "Just as a column of liquid has to be thin in order to rise under the force of capillarity, so a family must be small in order to rise in the social scale." *Dépopulation et Civilization,* Paris, 1890, quoted in Charles F. Westoff, "The Changing Focus of Differential Fertility Research: The Social Mobility Hypothesis," *The Milbank Memorial Fund Quarterly,* January 1953, p. 30.

[16]Ruth Riemer and Clyde V. Kiser, "Social and Psychological Factors Affecting Fertility," *Milbank Memorial Fund Quarterly,* April 1951.

At the same time, it is known that those who are already uninterested in education may more usually engage in premarital relations or wish to get married at a young age. People's ambitions and efforts to achieve them flow together day by day. Whether lack of interest in school leads to marriage or vice versa must be knowledge to which only each youngster is privy, if indeed he knows himself.

When a couple start out together early, they are not only likely to have their first child earlier than usual; they are likely to have more children. White mothers who were married by the age of 18 have an average of 3.7 children by the time their families are completed, and Negro mothers 4.3 children.[17] By contrast, mothers married at 20 or 21 have 2.8 and 4.0 children, respectively. (The first pair of figures is worth bearing in mind, for it will be suggested shortly that four children are qualitatively different from three.) The difference is not simply that the younger couples get a head start. Rather, those who marry young and are fated to be poor tend to have children early and late. The others concentrate their children in a few years and have fewer all told.[18]

Is it that poor people want to have more children? It seems not. All the evidence is that American families, whatever their income, want to have about the same number of children. Those who are poor do not manage to succeed in limiting the number.[19] A study on Growth of American Families puts the matter so:

> Lower status couples don't have more children . . . simply because they want more. They have more children because some of them do not use contraception regularly and effectively. If the wife has a grade school education and if the husband has an income of less than $3,000 a year, then 39 percent have excess fertility . . . The judgment that their fertility is too high is their own opinion.[20]

Describing the handicap to income that more children represent would take the discussion into another stage of the family-income

---

[17]*U. S. Census of Population: 1960—Women by Number of Children Ever Born*, Final Report, PC(2)3A, 1964, tables 18 and 19.

[18]*Ibid.*, table 37.

[19]Ruth Riemer and Clyde V. Kiser, *op. cit.*, Ronald Freedman, Pascal K. Whelpton, and Arthur A. Campbell, *Family Planning, Sterility, and Population Growth*, McGraw-Hill Book Company, 1959. Ronald Freedman and L. Coombs, "Working Paper on Family Income and Family Growth," Appendix B to Social Security Administration Grant Progress Report, June 1963, and "Working Paper on Changes in the Family Situation," Appendix C.

[20]Frederick S. Jaffe, "Family Planning and Poverty," *Journal of Marriage and the Family*, November 1964.

cycle. For the moment, it is sufficient to observe that early marriage sets the stage for a large family. By the rigors of arithmetic alone, more income will be required to escape poverty.

Referring a quarter of a century ago to countless surveys already conducted, Richard and Kathleen Titmuss observed that "children . . . introduce insecurity into the home."[21] Young couples are likely to face the problem of providing for a child quite early. They are likely to face the problem of providing for more than the average number of children. They are likely to face these problems with insufficient training and education. They are more than ordinarily likely to suffer separation or divorce. For a few families, fortunate in money or otherwise, these are no problems at all. The others are not barred, with early marriage, from developing decent income, but the rules of the game are changed for them.

Occupational Choice

By the time a wage earner reaches his mid-twenties, the limits of his lifetime income have in very large measure been established. He will have continued in school or not. The issue is not whether he drops out of school and returns, but whether he has left for several years and is unable to return. In the decade before retirement age a man who has completed college earns two-thirds more, on the average, than a man who has only completed high school and over twice as much as a man who has only completed grade school.[22] The diploma or degree (or qualities attached to getting it) counts for more than the prorated years of schooling it represents. The college graduate referred to earns over $10,000, but the man of the same age with one to three years of college earns $7,000.

Quite apart from education, the young adult will have taken his first job and established a pattern of job movement. White-collar and professional workers (and readers) may be given to thinking of jobs in terms of choice. Studies of manual laborers, blue-collar workers, the lower class, or the working class, make it clear that their entry into the job market is compounded of accident and immediate necessity. A study of youths doing manual work in 1951 summarized their situation as follows:

---

[21]Richard and Kathleen Titmuss, *Parents Revolt*, Secker and Warburg, London, 1942.
[22]Bureau of the Census, *Current Population Reports;* "Consumer Income," Series P-20, No. 43, September 29, 1964, table 22.

Most youngsters (and their parents) approached the choice of a first job with no clear conception of where they were going; the great majority of first jobs were found in a very informal way, preponderantly through relatives and friends; the great majority of youngsters took the *first job* they found and did not make comparisons with any other job; their knowledge of the job before they took it was in most cases extremely meager; and in most cases the job turned out to be a blind alley . . . ."[23] [Italics added.]

In 1964 other researchers were still trying to counter "the myth of occupational choice." S. M. Miller wrote that, on the contrary, working-class jobs are "a recurring and frequently unpredictable series of events in which 'choice' is frequently the obverse of necessity."[24] Despite its chance beginning, the first job is an excellent indication of what the last job will be. The first 10 years of work—with exceptions, to be sure—foreshadow the rest.[25]

The choices that are made by people who are going to be poor may seem haphazard to the observer. The components of this approach to work have been well documented. However, their combined effect is as accidental as the path a trolley car takes. The youth enters upon work unready. He may have left school because he wanted to—whatever that says about his life situation. He may have left school because of sheer financial need. For example, a national study showed that withdrawing public assistance from families who needed it ended the schooling of some of the children.[26] The youth's bargaining power is not good and it is a doubtful favor to tell him otherwise. He knows astonishingly little about the consequences of his choice of job. In terms of immediate payoff, the difference between one job and another may not be great. Their long-range payoff is lost to him in scholarly studies and school administrators' offices. In one sense, help from parents is nonexistent and in another sense, all too available. Although parents tend to want much for their children, they know little about how to prepare for occupations other than their own. The links they can provide are to the work they have known. If

---

23Lloyd G. Reynolds, *Wages and Labor Mobility in Theory and Practise,* Harper and Brothers, 1951, pp. 127-128.

24S. M. Miller, "The Outlook of Working-Class Youth," in Arthur B. Shostak and William Gomberg, *Blue Collar World,* Prentice-Hall, 1964.

25Seymour Martin Lipset and Reinhard Bendix, *Social Mobility in Industrial Society,* University of California Press, 1959. Lloyd G. Reynolds, *op. cit.*

26M. Elaine Burgess and Daniel O. Price, *An American Dependency Challenge,* American Public Welfare Association, Chicago, 1963.

one accepts the interesting, though speculative, concept that careers develop according to a timetable that is learned from others, parents are also passing on not only advice and personal contacts that are limiting but a handicapping sense of the timetable that should normally be followed.[27]

Some youths stay in school only because of the high unemployment rate in their age group.[28] In the circumstances, those who are out of school believe they do well to seize the first job that is offered. Thinking individually and realistically, who is to gainsay this? Over a third of marriages involve boys who are 21 or under. Other boys have responsibilities to parents or brothers and sisters. They are not in a position to refuse even dead-end jobs. As for the rest, any beginning salary may look large compared with what they have had. One should not overlook that a youth may be immature. The penalties of the choice he is making may be hidden, but its benefits—cash in the pocket, independence, adult status—call to his deepest needs. Here is one of the homeliest advantages of higher education. Vocationally speaking, the late teens and early twenties tend to be a "floundering period."[29] The youngster without advanced education enters upon his career uncertain and immature. The youngster who has spent this period in college evaluates work from the vantage point of four more years.

By their middle twenties, youths have made other interlocking decisions that bind them. Women have decided whether or not to work; in their schooling and in their first jobs they too have bounded the sort of work they may do later. Obviously, these decisions influence the family's income, but—equally significant in the long run—women who work will have fewer children.[30] Having a very small family is not typical of ambitious families starting out with decent income. Having one child or none is typical, however, of families starting out with great disadvantage and determined to make their way at all costs.[31] For example, the higher their husband's income, the fewer

---

27See Julius A. Roth, *Timetables,* Bobbs-Merrill Company, 1963.

28W. G. Bowen and T. A. Finegan, "Labor Force Participation and Unemployment," Princeton Industrial Relations Section (undated).

29P. E. Davidson and H. D. Anderson, *Occupational Mobility in an American Community,* Stanford University Press, 1937; Seymour Martin Lipset and Reinhard Bendix, *op. cit.*

30Ronald Freedman, "The Sociology of Human Fertility: A Trend Report and Bibliography," *Current Sociology,* V. X-XI, No. 2, 1961-62, Oxford, England.

31Ruth Riemer and Clyde V. Kiser, *op. cit.*

white women reach menopause without having a child. But among nonwhite women, the largest percentage who are childless are in the $3,000 to $7,000 bracket.[32] Presumably, the struggle by nonwhites to attain a modest income is somehow connected with having no children at all. In nonwhite families with income above $7,000, childlessness is not as common as in the moderate-income group; one senses that a balance point has been attained at which a child does not block the family's aspirations.

Young men, young women, and couples may also have faced a choice about moving where jobs are more readily available. Those who do move are less likely to be unemployed.[33] An English study observes that, in a depressed area, the ages from 20 to 30 are crucial for skilled workers. "Now is taken the vital decision to move or to stay." But for the unskilled, "before they are out of their teens some . . . are almost completely precluded from exercising any free choice in their careers."[34] The evidence in the United States is consistent with this. The highest mobility rate is in the years from 20 to 30; those who are better educated are more likely to have moved.[35] So, too, larger families are less likely to move.[36]

It was noted that young marriages run a high risk of dissolution. By the time the couples are in their mid-twenties, the determination of stability or separation is likely to have been made. Separation creates an obvious income problem for the mother and her children. The father has a problem too, unless he can escape it. He is probably liable for support payments which, if they look small to those who complain of growing irresponsibility, loom large to the father with limited income. Whatever the reason, the jobs of men who have been married only once show steady improvement in the first decade of marriage. In contrast, the status of men who remarry improves rather little.[37] Finally, not only is each job decision important; the se-

---

[32]U. S. Census of Population: 1960—Women by Number of Children Ever Born, Final Report, PC(2)3A, 1964, table 37.

[33]Thomas E. Swanstrom, op. cit.

[34]Adrian Sinfield, "Unemployed in Tyneside," May 1964 (mimeographed).

[35]John B. Lansing, Eva Mueller, William Ladd, Nancy Barth, The Geographic Mobility of Labor: A First Report, Survey Research Center, Ann Arbor, Michigan, April 1963.

[36]Ronald Freedman and L. Coombs, "Working Paper on Changes in the Family Situation," Appendix C to Social Security Administration Grant Progress Report, June 1963.

[37]Jessie Bernard, Remarriage, A Study of Marriage, The Dryden Press, 1956.

quence of jobs is also important. Harold Wilensky has carefully elaborated the consequences of an orderly work history in which "one job normally leads to another, related in function and higher in status."[38] The man with an orderly career shows strong attachment to his work and continues to make progress. The man who shifts about without apparent reason or benefit is likely to be dissatisfied and blocked.

The permutations of even key decisions are numerous, but perhaps several useful *and plausible* generalizations may be extracted from these disorderly patterns. First, occupational and family decisions may be subject matter for different professional disciplines but, as families live, they are a unity. The decision to marry and begin work, for example, is more likely to be one decision than two. Second, one can readily discern extreme family types, even at this early point. On one hand are the heroic families—overcoming their antecedents, husband and wife sticking together (with pleasure or without), studying and working and foregoing children. It is not to be assumed that all of these families achieve reasonable objectives, but obviously some do. Then there are the families defeated from the beginning—pregnant early, married early, dropped out of school, soon separated, and unlikely to have enough income at any time. In between are most poor families, undoubtedly encompassing two or three or several types. Third, the common problem that youths face about school, family, and work, lies in being forced to make decisions prematurely and unprepared. In the situation in which poor youths find themselves, the alternative to one choice for which they are unprepared (completing school) is another choice for which they are also unprepared (early marriage or work). Perhaps what is required are devices to postpone the necessity for any of these choices at 17 or 18 or 20.

Although this conclusion is arrived at by a narrow consideration of occupational development, a parallel psychological argument may be made for providing a "psychological moratorium—a period of delay in the assumption of adult commitment.[39] Because of change and shifting values, today especially youths require a period of relaxed expectation, of experimenting with various kinds of work, or even of

---

[38]Harold L. Wilensky, "Orderly Careers and Social Participation: The Impact of Work History on Social Integration in the Middle Class," *American Sociological Review*, August 1961, p. 522.

[39]Erik Erikson, "Youth and the Life Cycle," *Children*, March-April, 1960, p. 48

introspection to locate their sense of adult identity.[40] The two lines of argument—occupational and psychological—link in the recognition that, in our society, the major source of social identity for men is work. Lee Rainwater has explored this point to argue that if a sense of identity is blocked by the route of work, it may be sought instead through expressive behavior—personal expression in speech, song, behavior, or idiosyncratic ideas. Rainwater observes that the expressive solution is only temporarily satisfying to low-income youths.[41] Given time and opportunity, they may shift to a sense of identity through work. By this line of argument too, one comes to the need for providing time before a youth is finally committed to the work he will do.

In any event, the stage 1 decision, if it begins a family, clearly governs stage 2 decisions: when to begin work and at what. Those who do not marry early retain more flexibility. At the close of stage 2 (say, between 25 and 30), those families who will be poor can be readily recognized. Early marriage and child-bearing, incomplete education, a poor first job, a chaotic work history—any two of these qualities mean a family at high risk of being poor most of the time. Members of such a family are unlikely to change matters very much through their own efforts. A recent study in California, seeking to distinguish between people who receive public assistance and those who do not, confirms this conclusion:

> The main factor involved in the unemployment, underemployment and dependency of the welfare group is not deviant attitude, or deviant personality, but the high-risk objective circumstances of being relatively under-skilled, under-educated, and over-sized. . . .
>
> These high-risk circumstances are shared by a substantial segment of the population which is not currently on welfare . . . but is likely to be at any given time in the future.[42]

---

[40]Erik Erikson, *Young Man Luther,* Norton, 1958, and *Childhood and Society,* Norton, 1950. David Riesman, "The Search for Challenge," *Kenyon Alumni Bulletin,* January—March, 1959.

[41]Lee Rainwater, "Work and Identity in the Lower Class," Washington University Conference on Planning for the Quality of Urban Life, November 25, 1964.

[42]Curtis C. Aller, "Toward the Prevention of Dependency: A Report on AFDC-U Recipients," Preliminary Report, pp. 16, 18. State of California. Department of Social Welfare, *First Annual Report,* January 1965.

Family-Cycle Squeeze—The Conflict of Aspiration and Need

In a study of men who carry more than one job—moonlighters—Harold Wilensky found them to be not necessarily poor, or rich, or in between. Rather, the moonlighter was, typically, a man of any income, squeezed between not unreasonable ambitions and family needs he could never quite satisfy. The key, which Wilensky calls "life-cycle squeeze," is not the man's age but the stage of his family development and, especially, the number of his children:

> The American man most likely to moonlight would be a young, educated Negro with many children, a job such as ward attendant, and a chaotic work history. His mother, a sales clerk whose husband deserted years ago, has fired him with old-fashioned ambition; his wife, a part-time cleaning woman, wants to escape from the ghetto. He is a clerk in his spare time.[43]

In the end, the moonlighter does not realize his ambitions. The needs of his family move more rapidly than he; he has neither surplus money nor energy. Typically, he is blocked and feels deprived.

For a special group, perhaps 6 percent of workingmen, Wilensky has established a dynamic relationship between aspiration and need. (Because family structure determines the changing content of need, this relationship is here called family-cycle squeeze.) Almost all poor families must feel the squeeze and, obviously, most respond otherwise than by moonlighting. Some men, though they would take similar steps, work too many hours or too irregularly.[44] Some poor families send the mother to work, even when the children are relatively young. Some families take the opposite course; instead of expanding their income, they adjust need to their income. They may space their children so their needs can be absorbed. Those who are to be poor appear to have their second child three or four months closer to the birth of the first child than others do.[45] Families may restrict the number of their children, thus limiting need. That families take these steps has been demonstrated over and over again. Studies suggest that at least a number of these families manage to move up a

---

[43]Harold L. Wilensky, "The Moonlighter: A Product of Relative Deprivation," *Industrial Relations*, October 1963, p. 119.

[44]*Ibid.*

[45]Lolagene C. Coombs, "Child Spacing and Family Economic Position," memorandum of May 31, 1965 (unpublished).

step or two.[46] The variety of ways of meeting need illustrate what is, anyway, plausible. The more members in a family, the more income is needed. The necessity to devote all income and more to current needs is associated with inability to make progress.

Beyond this point, discussion frequently mires down in inability to demonstrate either, on one hand, that people have children for the same reasons that they are poor (a tendency to live in the present, etc.) or, on the other hand, that the facts of poverty make it difficult to control the number of births. Poor people have not had the required attitudes, skills, or access to medical resources for effective birth control.[47] But these facts lend themselves to either interpretation. Indeed, the opposing interpretations are probably selective, somewhat biased summaries of the same facts. For, seen day by day, the family that cannot control its course does not seek to control its course, and the reverse is also true. The point here, however, is that the squeeze is felt every day. Whatever its origin, above some threshold the imbalance becomes a hindrance rather than a stimulus to self-improvement.

There is a sprinkling of evidence that the fourth or fifth child represents a point of no return for poor families. The California study cited above concluded that families with four or more children face a substantial risk of poverty.[48] A study of families during periods of unemployment concluded that families with four or more children "found it considerably more difficult to manage financially." The more drastic means of managing—"borrowing money, piling up bills, moving to cheaper quarters, and going on relief—all show sharp increases

---

[46]Seymour Martin Lipset and Reinhard Bendix, *op. cit.* For other citations of studies relating status and fertility, see Ronald Freedman, "The Sociology of Human Fertility . . . ," cited above. Studies have produced inconclusive or negative results if their samples were small or special, if they did not discriminate between families that could afford children and families that could not, or if the hypothesis was formulated too grandly. For example, in the Indianapolis study the "economic tension" hypothesis was stated as follows: "The greater the difference between the actual level of living and the standard of living desired, the higher the proportion of couples practising contraception effectively and the smaller the planned families." (Ruth Riemer and Clyde V. Kiser, *op. cit.*) Large families, quite unrealistic about their aspirations, and small, quite realistic families would blur the findings when the hypothesis is so stated.

[47]Lee Rainwater and Karol Kane Weinstein, *And the Poor Get Children,* Quadrangle Books, Chicago, 1960.

[48]State of California, *op. cit.,* table 20.

with size of family."[49] A third study notes that separations and desertions tend to occur at the time the wife is pregnant. "A major point of pressure for the low-income male," observe the authors, "appears to be an increase in family size with no comparable increase in family income or earning capacity."[50] If four- or five-children families face a special problem, one would expect the children to reflect it. About 7 of every 10 youths rejected for Selective Service come from families with four children or more.[51]

Table 2 sums up the risk of poverty in terms of family size.

TABLE 2
Percent of Families Who Were Poor in 1963, By Number of Children

Number of related children under 18 years of age	Percent of families who were poor
None, 1, or 2	12
Three	17
Four	23
Five	36
Six or more	49

Source: Derived from Mollie Orshansky, "Counting the Poor: Another Look at the Poverty Profile," *Social Security Bulletin*, January 1963, table 8.

Adding a third or fourth child raises the incidence of poverty by 7 percentage points, but the next children raise the incidence by 13 percentage points. "For many families," writes the researcher who developed these figures, "a critical point in financial status may be the arrival of the fourth or fifth child."[52]

Although these figures make the point about risk, they are averages and inevitably crude. It is possible to get somewhat closer to various family types by examining the occupations of the men whose wives have had the most children. These figures (still averages, to be sure) hint at a more common-sense, though complex, relation of birth

---

[49]Wilbur J. Cohen, William Haber, and Eva Mueller, *The Impact of Unemployment in the 1958 Recession*, U. S. Senate, Special Committee on Unemployment Problems, June 1960.

[50]Hylan Lewis and Camille Jeffers, "Poverty and the Behavior of Low-Income Families," paper presented to the American Orthopsychiatric Association, Chicago, May 19, 1964.

[51]The President's Task Force on Manpower Conservation, *One-Third of a Nation*, January 1, 1964.

[52]Mollie Orshansky, "Counting the Poor: Another Look at the Poverty Profile," *Social Security Bulletin*, January 1965, p. 25.

rate and income. The white men who have the most children work, in descending order, as farm laborers and foremen, miners, plasterers, carpenters, truck drivers, and physicians. These are the lowest- and highest-paid occupations listed by the Census for which number of children can be determined. Their incomes fell, more or less, under $5,000 or, for physicians, over $19,000. By contrast, families averaging about three children or fewer per mother are bunched in the occupational range between $4,000 and $9,000, with a scattering up to $15,000.[53] (The pattern for Negro families does not show any high-fertility, high-income occupational groups. This is consistent with the observation made earlier that disadvantaged families moving up are more likely to restrict their family size severely.)

Obviously, several children are not necessarily a bar to decent income. Either income is high enough to support several children, however, or income is destined to be very low indeed. For families of four or five children or more, there is no in-between. Other evidence supports this point: the more children in a family under the Aid to Families with Dependent Children Program, the more the mother owes.[54] In general, the more children in a poor family, the larger is the proportion of needed income that the family lacks.[55]

Children are the most significant element of the family-cycle squeeze, but they are not the only element. An explanation can be assembled for the special difficulty of large families. In finding housing, they experience great hardship; public housing, for example, is less likely to provide a resource. A mother with five children cannot as readily go to work as a mother with two. Yet the problem of a large family is only a midstream example of imbalance between need and resources. In the same sense, the 18-year-old couple with one child faces an imbalance. The problem of the mother without a husband may also be read as a type of family-cycle squeeze. She has very nearly the same need for income but much less in the way of resources than a mother with a husband. In the past decade the median income of such families has increased only about half as fast as that of all families.[56] Entirely apart from children, the relatives of those who

---

[53]U. S. Census of Population: 1960—Occupation by Earnings and Education, Final Report, PC(2)7B, 1963, table 1. U. S. Census of Population: 1960—Women by Number of Children Ever Born, Final Report, PC(2)3A, 1964, table 33.

[54]Greenleigh Associates, Facts, Fallacies, and Future, New York, 1960.

[55]Mollie Orshansky, op. cit., (January 1965).

[56]John Beresford and Alice Rivlin, "Characteristics of 'Other' Families," paper read at the Population Association of America, Philadelphia, April 19, 1963.

are poor are also likely to be poor. As a mother or father approaches 40, *his* parents enter their sixties and may present serious need for financial or other kinds of care.[57] For example, a study of families receiving public assistance shows that the majority of recipients with relatives were giving rather than receiving help.[58]

For all these reasons, need may exceed resources by too wide a margin, forcing choices that are likely to defeat the family. The sorts of choices that are forced have already been named: limited education, limited mobility, dead-end jobs, and family breakdown. Moreover, the couple in their thirties have children growing into adolescence. The quality of their nurture, education, and family life has, no doubt, been affected right along. By adolescence, they begin to make the same categorical choices—more school or less, expect to begin a family early or not. The strains that are implicit in the life cycle of any family have been recognized for some time. But for poor families, whose need is likely continually to outpace resources, disadvantage goes around in a tight descending spiral. In the end, statistics reflect the spiral. The same people have many children, poor education, unemployment, broken families, and so forth. What else is new?

It may be useful at this point to illustrate the type of program question that can be raised on the basis of the family-income cycle. On the whole, public assistance tends to deal with families late in the game. Essentially the same families, with fewer children, are rejected for Aid to Families with Dependent Children (AFDC) who will be granted assistance later, when they have more children.[59] If accepted for assistance, smaller families receive it for a shorter period of time.[60] With stipulated exceptions in a number of States, a surplus of income over minimum requirements becomes the occasion for discontinuing assistance. Standards for minimum requirements are themselves low; in 1963 the standards were below the Social Security Administration definition of poverty in all but six States. In the majority of States, assistance will not be provided if a husband or other man is at home. In short, while the program may relieve desperate need, it deliberately avoids any surplus that will provide

---

[57]Alvin L. Schorr, *Filial Responsibility in the Modern American Family,* Social Security Administration, 1961.

[58]Jane C. Kronick, "Attitudes Toward Dependency: A Study of 119 ADC Mothers," a report to the Social Security Administration, May 15, 1963 (unpublished).

[59]State Charities Aid Association, "Striving for Balance in Community Health and Welfare," Annual Report, New York, 1963.

[60]M. Elaine Burgess and Daniel O. Price, *op. cit.*

room for maneuver. Thus, AFDC is a recognizable element of the poor family's world, relieving need but not providing the flexibility that will tend to alter the direction in which the family is moving. These policies reflect the necessity of distributing insufficient resources equitably, as well as the necessity of discouraging malingering. But from the point of view of objectives, such policies exhibit a curious ambivalence. In a wide variety of ways in the past few years, the program has been bent towards helping to prevent dependency. Yet, AFDC tends to operate too parsimoniously and too late to turn the tide of family-cycle squeeze.

Family Breakdown

With the material reviewed so far, it cannot come as news that many poor families in time become unable to maintain an intact family or a steady income. Some will have reached this stage by the age of 20, having already achieved two or three children and a chaotic family and work history. Others will have struggled doggedly, perhaps experiencing moments of hope, but yielding in the end. Some of the evidence of this outcome has already been seen; it requires now to be brought together.

It has been noted that early marriages tend to break up; only half the women married at 17 or earlier will still be living with the same husband 30 years later. It has also been noted that half of the women married at 17 will have (about) four children or more. Finally, large families create unbearable pressure for low-income men. These are not independent facts. Taken together, they suggest that mothers in broken families are likely to have more children than those in stable families. Although on the face of it, this may seem odd, it is indeed a fact. "Among those females who were mothers by 1960, wives had an average of 2.9 children ever born, and female heads [of families] had an average of 3.7 children ever born." (That the two groups were somewhat different in age and race accounted for only a third of the difference.)[61]

The pattern that these figures represent is not difficult to induce. The early, low-income marriage may begin poorly or it may begin well and earnestly. The problem is not necessarily in beginning but rather in providing the "means for the young adult to meet the demands of marriage and not become a marriage dropout."[62] Howev-

---

[61] John Beresford and Alice Rivlin, *op. cit.*
[62] Hylan Lewis and Camille Jeffers, *op. cit.*, p. 11.

er, with inadequate education and training, money becomes a grave problem. With a second or third child, the marriage may well show strain. When a middle-class marriage shows strain, the wife may settle for being supported comfortably, even if she is unhappy. The wife whose husband is poor does not have that particular alternative.[63] The situation would vary according to the actual economic position of the husband; it has been observed that even unmarried mothers will reject marriage if the man is viewed as an economic liability.[64] From the wife's point of view as well as from the husband's, strain may lead to separation or divorce.

Following separation, there may be reconciliation or the wife may make an arrangement with another man. Contrary to the general impression that only separation is more common among poor families, divorce is also more common.[65] In general, two-thirds of divorced women remarry,[66] and the younger the women are, the more likely they are to remarry. That is, whether a family is broken by separation or divorce, the chances are high that a new family will be formed. The pressures continue, however.

The likelihood that reasonable support will be forthcoming for children is very small and the parents are more heavily burdened than in the initial marriage. Some of these second attempts work out, but more do not.[67] The path that opens before a family is a sequence of marriages or liaisons, with the notion of a stable, intact marriage, if it was present at the beginning, becoming fainter. One study of economically dependent families observes:

> Many of the women who were currently divorced, separated or deserted had been in such situations previously and expected to have similar experiences in future . . . This repetition in behavior was hard for the women we interviewed to explain.[68]

---

[63]*Ibid.*

[64]Charles E. Bowerman, Donald P. Irish, and Hallowell Pope, *Unwed Motherhood: Personal and Social Consequences,* University of North Carolina, 1963. Helen Icken Safa, "The Unwed Mother: A Case Study," in *Fatherless Families: Working Papers,* Youth Development Center, Syracuse University, 1965. G. B. Shaw, not quite the same sort of researcher, had his character say in *Heartbreak House:* "If I can't have love, there's no reason why I should have poverty."

[65]Hugh Carter and Alexander Plateris, "Trends in Divorce and Family Disruption," *Health, Education, and Welfare Indicators,* September 1963.

[66]Paul Glick, *American Families,* John Wiley and Sons, 1957.

[67]Jessie Bernard, *op. cit.*

[68]Paul R. Kimmel, Report on Welfare Administration Project No. 199, 1965 (unpublished).

How, indeed, *explain* a response to circumstances that seems natural and even inevitable. The sound of this pattern is grim. The saving grace for the individuals involved may be that people who reflect such a pattern are sufficiently plentiful and walled off by neighborhood and communication patterns that many regard it as a common, fated way of life.[69]

Thus far, the pattern has been traced with families who were married young; although the overall chances are smaller, some who married later would follow the same course. It must be clear that progressive breakdown in family relations may be accompanied by breakdown in ability to secure a stable income. Without a husband, mothers are, of course, at a disadvantage. They may work, but their earnings are relatively low and they have special costs. If the man feels he must move, he may make a damaging job change. The process of divorce or separation itself involves costs (legal, dislocation) that are large to poor families. Confused legal relationships or casual work patterns may interfere with entitlement to survivors insurance, unemployment compensation, and so forth. Children may be pulled out of school, making for later difficulty. All these costs would be significant for any family; for poor families, they add to the squeeze that is already intolerable.

The discussion, in this stage as in others, has only hinted at extensive research into the feelings associated with deprivation.[70] Such material would reinforce the argument about the critical nature of each of the stages, but might tend to distract attention from the simple relationships of money and family development. As income is the point, this vital aspect had been foregone. Simply to bear in mind that feeling must accompany things and their absence, here is an excerpt from a researcher's interview with a woman who is supporting four children on $27.50 a week, in the stage described as family-breakdown:

---

[69]August B. Hollingshead and Fredrick C. Redlich, *Social Class and Mental Illness,* John Wiley & Sons, 1958. Walter B. Miller, "Implications of Urban Lower-Class Culture for Social Work," *Social Service Review,* September 1959.

[70]See John H. Rohrer, *et al., The Eighth Generation,* Harper and Brothers, 1960; Mirra Komarovsky and Jane H. Philips, *Blue Collar Marriage,* Random House, 1964; Lee Rainwater and Karol Kane Weinstein, *op. cit.;* Frank Riessman, *The Culturally Deprived Child,* Harper and Brothers, 1962; Oscar Lewis, *The Children of Sanchez,* Random House, 1961; Hylan Lewis and Camille Jeffers, *op. cit.,* and other articles by Hylan Lewis; Walter B. Miller, *op. cit.,* and other articles.

If a man has anything and offers to help you out, you don't say to him: "But you'll have to marry me first," she said. You take what he offers right off and offer what you have in return. Of course, you hope that some day he will want to make it legal. But beggars can't be choosers . . . I don't drink whisky but once in a while I'll get myself a half pint of gin . . . But that's about all I spend on myself. I ain't had a new dress for about three years . . . I don't go nowhere to need a new dress . . .

If there's one thing I want it's a back yard, fenced in, so my children don't have to play out in the street . . . I sure hope and pray that some day I can do better. But what can I do now?[71]

By definition, parents who reach their forties poor have not managed to achieve a decent income. A substantial percentage are no longer married and some of the rest have a troubled marriage. The two problems are interconnected. The income problem is a source of reinfection for each new marriage, and each marital failure is likely to add to the income problem.

Stage 5

Only four stages of family-income development have been set forth here; stage five is actually stage one for the next generation. In each of the stages, children have been growing older. In the third and fourth stages for their parents, children are entering the first and second stages. Even if their parents have managed to avoid family breakdown and certainly if they have moved into stage four, the children would tend to begin families early and make a poor career choice. They would make the same mistakes as their parents for the same reasons: little help and example, not enough money to support longer-term alternatives, little hope of doing better, little practical access to ways of doing better. We spoke of the rules of the game changing at the end of stage one. For these children, growing through their parents' third and fourth stages, the rule reads: Go back to stage one and retrace the moves your parents made.

Conclusion

It is a platitude of occupational research that the father's occupation determines the son's. As one discerns the complex and powerful forces that shape choices related to income, one can make a more exact

---

[71]Roscoe Lewis, unpublished report prepared for the Child-Rearing Study, Health and Welfare Council of the National Capitol Area, quoted in *The Washington Post,* January 12, 1964, p. E-5.

statement: The father's circumstances determine the son's and the circumstances that surround them both determine occupational choice.

This article has attempted to distinguish four critical stages in the family and income development of poor people. They may assist in visualizing the stream of life in poor families rather than seeing them always as fractions of a population or at a given point in time. The method of visualizing flow used here is easily as imperfect as an early kinescope. One projects a series of snatches of life and trusts the imagination to provide the intervals. Research that will provide a sharper, truer image is badly needed.

Apart from the detail that is offered here there are some general conclusions to be taken into consideration:

1. Money, as it is paid out, may be regarded as going to individuals. As money is received and spent in a poor family, however, every individual's income and arrangements affect pooled spending.

2. Minimum income for decent living may represent public policy that is responsible and even charitable. It does not necessarily represent a policy that is functional in terms of moving people out of poverty. For such a policy, there are times when surplus (money and time) is required; capital is required. The situation of families taking off from poverty is analogous to that of nations. Take-off awaits "the build-up *of social overhead capital*," together with the necessary skills and a drive for improvement.[72]

3. The stages of family-income development suggest that leverage may more readily be provided at some points than at others. As has been seen, each stage prejudices the next. Therefore, the two stages most open to influence from outside are, in rather different senses, the earliest. First is the period when the family sets out, when it may be induced to postpone childbirths and to make the wisest (and usually most expensive) choices about training and work. Second is the period after the family has 13- or 14-year-old children who may be led to postpone beginning a family of their own, at least until the girl is 18 or 19 and a boy somewhat older. These are not matters of regulating or simply advising against marriage but of making possible a total pattern in which early marriage and early and dead-end employment do not become attractive or necessary.

_____

[72]W. W. Rostow, *The Stages of Economic Growth*, Cambridge University Press, 1960 [italics added].

4. It is not simply availability of money at any given moment that influences the course poor families take, but their expectation that money will be available for certain purposes. Therefore, a *functional* program, in terms of setting them on a course out of poverty, will be predictable and, where necessary, continuous. Families will not only receive money but understand the comparatively simple conditions that determine whether they receive it. And income will not be subject to discontinuance because new policies are devised from year to year or the funds of a demonstration program run out.

5. The description of the family-income cycle may lead to increased understanding of poor people, but it is offered mainly for a narrower and more utilitarian pupose. It is intended to assist in judging the effectiveness and desirability of current and proposed income-maintenance programs. Management efficiency and cost may be appraised fairly readily. Methods are needed for appraising the effectiveness of programs in relation to the Nation's qualitative objectives for the people who are served.

"Is the Income Gap Closed?" "No!"

Herman P. Miller
Bureau of the Census

[From New York Times Magazine, *November 11, 1962.* © *1962 by The New York Times Company. Reprinted by permission.]*

A MYTH HAS BEEN CREATED in the United States that incomes are becoming more evenly distributed. This view is held by prominent economists of both major political parties. It is also shared by the editors of the influential mass media.

Arthur F. Burns, chief economist for the Eisenhower Administration, said in 1951 that "the transformation in the distribution of our national income . . . may already be counted as one of the great social revolutions in history." Paul Samuelson, one of President Kennedy's leading economic advisers, said only last year that "the American income pyramid is becoming less unequal." Several major stories on this subject have appeared in The New York Times, and the editors of Fortune magazine announced not long ago that "though not a head has been raised aloft on a pikestaff, nor a railway station seized, the U.S. has been for some time now in a revolution."

What are the facts about trends in income distribution in the United States? Nobody questions that real incomes have risen for most of the population and that even those who have been left behind enjoy a far higher level of living than most people in other parts of the world. Since the level is so high and conditions are still improving, why consider the gap between the rich and the poor? Isn't it enough that the amount of income received by the poor has gone up substantially? Why be concerned about their share?

The reason is that "needs" stem not so much from what we lack as from what our neighbors have. Except for those rare souls who have hitched their wagons to thoughts rather than things, there is no end to "needs." So long as there are some people who have more, others will "need" more. If this is indeed the basis for consumer behavior then we obviously cannot ignore the gap between the rich and the poor, however high minimum levels of living may be raised.

Has there been any narrowing of the gap between the rich and the poor?

If we stick to the figures the answers are clear, unambiguous, and contrary to widely held beliefs. The statistics show no appreciable change in income shares for nearly twenty years. The heart of the story comes from data in U.S. Government publications available to all. The figures were obtained by ranking families from lowest to highest according to income and totaling the amount of income each group received. In 1960, the top 5 per cent made over $16,250, whereas the lowest 20 per cent made less $2800 (about $55 a week). During the thirties and the war years there was a distinct drop in the share of the income received by the upper-income groups. The share received by the wealthiest families dropped from 30 per cent of the total in 1929 to 21 per cent in 1944. Since that time it has not changed significantly.

Now let us look at the bottom of the income scale. In 1935, the poorest 20 per cent of families received only 4 per cent of the income. Their share rose to 5 per cent in 1944 and has remained at that level ever since. The stability of the shares received by each of the other fifths is equally striking.

These figures hardly support the picture that many Americans have been given about the equalization of incomes in our society. The changes that took place ended nearly twenty years ago and they largely involved a redistribution of income among families in the top and middle brackets.

The figures cited are for income before taxes. Since the wealthiest families pay a large share of the taxes, we might expect their share to be smaller on an after-tax basis. It is, but not by as much as one would guess. In recent years the wealthiest 5 per cent received 20 per cent of the income before taxes and about 18 per cent of the income after Federal individual income tax payments were deducted.

Are white-non-white differentials narrowing?

The narrowing of income differentials between whites and non-whites (mainly Negroes) is sometimes cited as evidence of a trend toward equalization. Surely one would expect a change here in view of the major relocation of the Negro population in recent years.

Migration and technological change during the past twenty years have altered the role of the non-white from a Southern farm wage worker or share-cropper to an industrial worker. Twenty years ago, four of every ten employed non-white males in the United States worked either as laborers or share-croppers on southern farms. At present, less than two of every ten are employed in agriculture and about half work as unskilled or semi-skilled workers at non-farm jobs.

The change in the occupational status of non-whites has been accompanied by a marked rise in educational attainment, proportionately far greater than for whites. In 1940, young white males averaged four years more of schooling than non-whites in the same age group. Today the gap has been narrowed to one and a half years.

Despite all these changes that have occurred in the past decade, the earnings differential between whites and non-whites has not changed. The average wage or salary income for non-white workers was about three-fifths of that received by the whites in 1950 and in 1960. Prior to 1950, there was a substantial reduction in the earnings gap between whites and non-whites; but this was largely due to war-induced shortages of unskilled labor and government regulations designed generally to raise the incomes of lower-paid workers.

Are occupational differences narrowing?

One of the most widely and strongly held views regarding income distribution concerns the narrowing of earnings differentials among occupations. The prevailing view holds that the decrease in the earnings gap between the skilled and unskilled in the United States is part of historical process that has been going on since the turn of the century.

Recent trends in income differentials between skilled and unskilled workers are represented in the average wages and salaries received during the year in the major occupation groups in which men are employed. Women are excluded because their earnings are highly influenced by the fact that a large proportion of them are intermittent workers who do not work at full-time jobs.

There was not too much variation among occupation groups in the rate of income growth during the entire 20-year period. But when we look at the growth rates for two different periods, 1939-50 and 1950-60, striking differences are revealed.

During the forties, the lower-paid occupations made the greatest relative gains in average income. Laborers and service workers (waiters, barbers, janitors and the like) had increases of about 180 per cent, craftsmen had increases of 160 per cent; and professional and managerial workers, the highest paid workers of all, had the lowest relative gains—96 per cent.

During the past decade the picture has been reversed. Laborers and service workers made the smallest relative gains, 39 per cent; craftsmen had increases of 60 per cent; and the professional and managerial workers had the greatest gains of all, 68 per cent. Evidently, the trend toward the narrowing of the income gap between the high-paid and the low-paid workers has stopped during the past decade and even seems to be moving in the opposite direction.

The facts show that our "social revolution" ended nearly twenty years ago; yet important segments of the American public, many of them highly placed Government officials and prominent educators, think and act as though it were a continuing process.

The stability of income distribution, particularly during the fifties, could be related to the fact that the decade was dominated by an administration that was committed to stability rather than change. The Kennedy Administration, on the other hand, has shown a keen awareness of the need to cope with our pockets of poverty.

The President has pressed for and obtained legislation intended to raise the levels of living of the poor; extension of unemployment insurance benefits, Federal aid to dependent children of the unemployed, liberalization of social security benefits, increase in the minimum wage and extension of its coverage, Federal aid to revitalize the economies of areas with large and persistent unemployment. These measures would also tend to reduce income inequality, other things being equal.

In opposition to the political factors that now seem to favor equalization, we face some very stubborn economic factors that seem to be headed in quite the other direction. For many years now unskilled workers have been a declining part of the American labor force. This fact has been documented over and over again; but during the past decade there appears to have been a significant new development.

In the decade 1940-50 and again in 1950-60 only one non-farm occupation group for men—laborers—declined in number, at a time when all other groups were increasing. Laborers had the greatest relative income gains during the forties when they were in short supply but the smallest relative gains during the fifties when their supply far exceeded the demand. Now the unskilled are finding it increasingly difficult to locate jobs and many who are employed live in constant fear of being replaced by machines.

It is now generally acknowledged that the American economy has been plagued by relatively high unemployment since late 1957. According to the Joint Congressional Economic Committee, which has studied the problem in some detail, it is still premature to attribute

AVERAGE WAGE OF WHITE AND NON-WHITE MEN

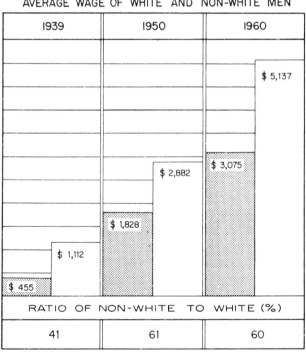

In 1939, the average non-white man's wage was only 41 per cent of the average white man's. By 1950 this had risen to 61. But the improvement stopped there; after another decade, the figure was only 60.

this unemployment to technological changes; but there can be no doubt that many thousands of unskilled workers have been permanently displaced by machines and that this trend will continue. Moreover, some economists disagree with the committee's view that our current difficulties in the employment field stem largely from the shortages in aggregate consumer demand rather than from technological changes in the economy.

It is conceivable, to many who have given the matter serious thought, that in the absence of remedial action, this nation may soon be faced with an increase in the disparity of incomes caused by the existence of a large block of untrained and unwanted men. Unless we are careful, we may then discover that our "social revolution" not only has been marking time for nearly twenty years, but is beginning to move backward.

MEN'S WAGES OR SALARIES BY OCCUPATION

$	PROFESSIONAL and MANAGERIAL WORKERS	CRAFTSMEN	SEMI-SKILLED FACTORY WORKERS	SERVICE WORKERS and LABORERS
6500	1960			
6000				
5500				
5000		1960		
4500				
4000			1960	
3500	1950			
3000		1950		
2500			1950	1960
2000				
1500	1939			1950
1000		1939		
500			1939	1939

PER CENT CHANGE

1939-60	230	316	325	290
1939-50	96	160	172	180
1950-60	68	60	56	39

The averages for each occupation are given. While all have gone up, the spread between occupation groups remains large. Furthermore, although in the forties the lowest-paid group made the largest percentage gain, in the next decade this group made the smallest gain.

Counting the Poor: Another Look at the Poverty Profile

Mollie Orshansky

U.S. Department of Health, Education, and Welfare

[Reprinted from the Social Security Bulletin, *January, 1965.]*

A REVOLUTION OF EXPECTATIONS has taken place in this country as well as abroad. There is now a conviction that everyone has the right to share in the good things of life. Yet there are still many who must watch America's parade of progress from the sidelines, as they wait for their turn—a turn that does not come. The legacy of poverty awaiting many of our children is the same that has been handed down to their parents, but in a time when the boon of prosperity is more general the taste of poverty is more bitter.

Now, however, the Nation is committed to a battle against poverty. And as part of planning the how, there is the task of identifying the whom. The initiation of corrective measures need not wait upon final determination of the most suitable criterion of poverty, but the interim standard adopted and the characteristics of the population thus described will be important in evaluating the effectiveness of the steps taken.

There is not, and indeed in a rapidly changing pluralistic society there cannot be, one standard universally accepted and uniformly applicable by which it can be decided who is poor. Almost inevitably a single criterion applied across the board must either leave out of the count some who should be there or include some who, all things considered, ought not be classed as indigent. There can be, however, agreement on some of the considerations to be taken into account in arriving at a standard. And if it is not possible to state unequivocally "how much is enough," it should be possible to assert with confidence how much, on an average, is too little. Whatever the level at which we peg the concept of "too little," the measure of income used should reflect at least roughly an equivalent level of living for individuals and families of different size and composition.

In such terms, it is the purpose of this paper to sketch a profile of poverty based on a particular income standard that makes allowance for the different needs of families with varying numbers of adults and children to support. It recognizes, too, that a family on a farm normally is able to manage on somewhat less cash income than a family living in a city. As an example, a family of father, mother, two young children, and no other relatives is assumed on the average to need a minimum of $1,860 today if living on a farm and $3,100 elsewhere. It should go without saying that, although such cutoff points have their place when the economic well-being of the population at large is being assessed, they do not necessarily apply with equal validity to each individual family in its own special setting.

The standard itself is admittedly arbitrary, but not unreasonable. It is based essentially on the amount of income remaining after allowance for an adequate diet at minimum cost. Under the criteria adopted, it is estimated that in 1963 a total of 7.2 million families and 5 million individuals living alone or with nonrelatives (excluding persons in institutions) lacked the wherewithal to live at anywhere near a tolerable level. Literally, for the 34½ million persons involved—15 million of them children under age 18 and 5 million persons aged 65 or older—everyday living implied choosing between an adequate diet of the most economical sort and some other necessity because there was not money enough to have both.

There are others in need not included in this count. Were one to add in the hidden poor, the 1.7 million elderly and the 1.1 million members of subfamilies—including 600,000 children—whose own income does not permit independent living at a minimum standard but who escape poverty by living in a household with relatives whose combined income is adequate for all, the number of poor rises to nearly 37.5 million persons.

The aggregate income available to the 7.2 million families and 5 million individuals in 1963 was only 60 percent as much as they needed, or about $11½ billion less than their estimated minimum requirements.

The Poverty Profile

From data reported to the Bureau of the Census in March 1964, it can be inferred that 1 in 7 of all families of two or more and almost half of all persons living alone or with nonrelatives had incomes too low in 1963 to enable them to eat even the minimal diet that could be expected to provide adequate nutrition and still have enough left over to pay for all other living essentials. Such a judgment is predicated on the assumption that, at current prices and current standards, an average family of four can achieve an adequate diet on about 70 cents a day per person for all food and an additional $1.40 for all other items—from housing and medical care to clothing and carfare.[1] For those dependent on a regular paycheck, such a budget would mean, for the family of four, total family earnings of $60 a week.

By almost any realistic definition, individuals and families with such income—who include more than a fifth of all our children—must be counted among our undoubted poor. A somewhat less conservative but by no means generous standard, calling for about 90 cents a day for food per person and a total weekly income of $77, would add 8.8 million adults and 6.8 million children to the roster. There is thus a total of 50 million persons—of whom 22 million are young children—who live within the bleak circle of poverty or at least hover around its edge. In these terms, though progress has been made, there are still from a fifth to a fourth of our citizens whose situation reminds us that all is not yet well in America.

Who are these people who tug at the national conscience? Are they all social casualties, visited by personal misfortune, like the woman left alone to raise a family? Are they persons who find little opportunity to earn their living, like the aged and the unemployed? Or are they perhaps mainly Negroes and members of other minority groups, living out the destiny of their years of discrimination? These groups, to be sure, are among the poorest of the poor, but they are not alone.

The population groups most vulnerable to the risk of inadequate income have long been identified and of late much publicized, but they make up only a small part of all the Nation's poor.

Families headed by a woman are subject to a risk of poverty three times that of units headed by a man, but they represent only a fourth of all persons in families classed as poor. Indeed, almost three-fourths of the poor families have a man as the head.

Children growing up without a father must get along on less than they need far more often than children living with both parents. In fact, two-thirds of them are in families with inadequate income. But two-thirds of all the children in the families called poor do live in a home with a man at the head.

---

[1] Estimates are based on a per capita average for all 4-person nonfarm families. Costs will average slightly more in small households and less in larger ones. A member of a 2-person family, for example, would need 74 cents a day for food and $2 a day for other items.

Many of our aged have inadequate incomes, but almost four-fifths of the poor families have someone under age 65 at the head. Even among persons who live alone, as do so many aged women, nearly half of all individuals classified as poor have not yet reached old age.

Nonwhite families suffer a poverty risk three times as great as white families do, but 7 out of 10 poor families are white.

And finally, in our work-oriented society, those who cannot or do not work must expect to be poorer than those who do. Yet more than half of all poor families report that the head currently has a job. More-over, half of these employed family heads, representing almost 30 per-cent of all the families called poor, have been holding down a full-time job for a whole year. In fact, of the 7.2 million poor families in 1963, 1 in every 6 (1.3 million) is the family of a white male worker who worked full time throughout the year. Yet this is the kind of family that in our present society has the best chance of escaping poverty.

All told, of the 15 million children under age 18 counted as poor, about 5¾ million were in the family of a man or woman who had a full-time job all during 1963.

Defining the Poverty Line

Poverty has many facets, not all reducible to money. Even in such terms alone, it will not be possible to obtain unanimous consent to a list of goods and services that make up the *sine qua non* and the dol-lars it takes to buy them. The difficulty is compounded in a country such as ours, which has long since passed the stage of struggle for sheer survival.

In many parts of the world, the overriding concern for a ma-jority of the populace every day is still "Can I live?" For the United States as a society, it is no longer whether but how. Although by the levels of living prevailing elsewhere, some of the poor in this country might be well-to-do, no one here today would settle for mere sub-sistence as the just due for himself or his neighbor, and even the poorest may claim more than bread. Yet as yesterday's luxuries become tomor-row's necessities, who can define for today how much is enough? And in a society that equates economic well-being with earnings, what is the floor for those whose earning capacity is limited or absent alto-gether, as it is for aged persons and children?

Available Standards for Food Adequacy

Despite the Nation's technological and social advance, or perhaps be-cause of it, there is no generally accepted standard of adequacy for essentials of living except food. Even for food, social conscience and custom dictate that there be not only sufficient quantity but sufficient variety to meet recommended nutritional goals and conform to customary eating patterns. Calories alone will not be enough.

Food plans prepared by the Department of Agriculture have for more than 30 years served as a guide for estimating costs of food needed by families of different composition. The plans represent a translation of the criteria of nutritional adequacy set forth by the National Research Council into quantities and types of food compatible with the preference of United States families, as revealed in food consumption studies. Plans are developed at varying levels of cost to suit the needs of families with different amounts to spend. All the plans, if strictly followed, can provide an acceptable and adequate diet, but— generally speaking—the lower the level of cost, the more restricted the kinds and qualities of food must be and the more the skill in marketing and food preparation that is required.[2]

Each plan specifies the required weekly quantities of foods in particular food groups for individuals of varying age and sex. The Department regularly publishes cost estimates at United States average prices based on the assumption that all meals are prepared at home from foods purchased at retail. Because no allowance is made for using any food from the home farm or garden, the cost estimates are not applicable to farm families without some adjustment, although the quantities presumably could be.

The low-cost plan, adapted to the food patterns of families in the lowest third of the income range, has for many years been used by welfare agencies as a basis for food allotments for needy families and others who wished to keep food costs down. Often, however, the actual food allowance for families receiving public assistance was less than that in the low-cost plan. Although spending as much as this food plan recommends by no means guarantees that diets will be adequate, families spending less are more likely to have diets falling below the recommended allowances for some important nutrients.

Recently the Department of Agriculture began to issue an "economy" food plan, costing only 75–80 percent as much as the basic low-cost plan, for "temporary or emergency use when funds are low." In January 1964, this plan suggested foods costing $4.60 a week per person, an average of only 22 cents a meal per person in a 4-person family.[3]

---

[2] See U.S. Department of Agriculture, *Family Food Plans and Food Costs*, Home Economics Research Report No. 20, November 1962.

[3] With recommended adjustments for family size, small families are allowed somewhat more and larger families somewhat less, and for all families the actual

For some family members, such as men and teen-age boys, the cost was higher; for others—young children and women, for example—it was less. The food plan as such includes no additional allowance for meals eaten out or other food eaten away from home. Meals eaten by family members at school or on the job, whether purchased or carried from home, must still come out of the same household food allowance.

The food costs for individuals according to this economy plan, at January 1964 prices, were used as the point of departure for determining the minimum total income requirement for families of different types. An additional set of poverty income points was computed, using the low-cost plan with its average per capita weekly cost of $5.90.

Income-Food Expenditure Relationship

It has long been accepted for individuals as for nations that the proportion of income allocated to the "necessaries," and in particular to food, is an indicator of economic well-being. A declining percentage has been associated with prosperity and higher income, and the rising percentage associated with lower income has been taken as an indicator of stringency.

The fact that larger households tend to spend a larger share of their income for food has not been so readily recognized as an indicator of economic pressure because of the assumed economy of scale. Yet, on the whole, larger families are less likely to have diets that satisfy the recommended allowances in essential nutrients. The dearth of data on expenditures of families classified by both size and income has made it difficult to assay the situation, and the fact that as families increase in size the age and sex distribution of the members changes too further obscures the picture.

In its 1955 study of household food consumption, the Department of Agriculture found that the diets of almost a fourth of the 2-person households but about half of the households with six or more members had less than the recommended amounts of calcium—a nutrient found mainly in milk products. Similarly, large households were

---

amounts of food suggested will vary with the sex and age of the members. Even in a 4-person family, the per capita cost will vary slightly from the figure cited, depending upon whether it includes teen-agers with high food requirements or a younger child or an aged member with food needs less than average.

Recent revisions in suggested food quantities to allow for changes -in the Recommended Dietary Allowances result in almost no change in the costs of the plans on the average. Foods for men of all ages and girls aged 9–12 cost slightly less than before, and foods for women under age 55 cost slightly more. (See *Family Economics Review* (U.S. Department of Agriculture), October 1964.)

twice as likely as small households to have diets lacking in ascorbic acid and two and a half times as likely to have diets short in protein. The latter situation is particularly striking because, though lack of protein is far less common in this country than deficiency in other nutrients, it is more telling. Diets too low in protein are more likely than other diets to have deficiencies in other essential nutrients also.[4]

It thus appears that what passes for "economy of scale" in the large family may in part reflect a lowering of dietary standards enforced by insufficient funds. Support for this thesis may be gained from the fact, illustrated later in this report, that families with large numbers of children do indeed have lower incomes than smaller families. Moreover, analysis of recent consumption data suggests that large families, given the opportunity, prefer to devote no larger a share of their income to food than do smaller families with the same per capita income.

The Agriculture Department evaluated family food consumption and dietary adequacy in a 1955 survey week and reported for all families of two or more—farm and nonfarm—an expenditure for food approximating one-third of money income after taxes.[5] Two-person nonfarm families used about 27 percent of their income for food, and families with three or more persons about 35 percent. A later study made in 1960–61 by the Bureau of Labor Statistics found for urban families that nearly a fourth of the family's income (after taxes) went for food. There is less variation by size of family than might have been anticipated, ranging between 22 percent and 28 percent, as Table 1 shows.

The data suggest that the declining income per person in the larger families may have been responsible for the different rate of spending as well as possibly more efficient utilization of food. Indeed, on more critical examination of the complete income-size distributions, it would appear that, given the same per capita income, the spending patterns appear to converge considerably.* Urban families in 1960–61, for example, spending on the average approximately every third of their available dollars for food, are estimated to have had incomes of approximately $1,000 per person when there were two in the family, $900 when there were three, $910 when there were four, $915 for five, and $800 for six or more.

---

[4]U.S. Department of Agriculture, Household Food Consumption Survey, 1955, *Dietary Evaluation of Food Used in Households in the United States*, Report No. 16, November 1961, and *Food Consumption and Dietary Levels of Households of Different Size, United States, by Region*, Report No. 17, January 1963.

[5]See U.S. Department of Agriculture, *Food Consumption and Dietary Levels of Households in the United States* (ARS626), August 1957.

* Illustrative tables omitted.

TABLE 1

Family size	USDA 1955, nonfarm[1]		BLS 1960-61, urban[2]	
	Average per capita income	Percent spent for food	Average per capita income	Percent spent for food
1	[3]	[3]	$2,967	23
2 or more, total	$1,328	33	1,886	22
2	2,036	27	2,750	22
3	1,603	31	2,302	22
4	1,299	35	1,854	24
5	1,067	36	1,512	26
6	837	40 }	1,944	28
7 or more	616	46 }		

[1] Derived from U.S. Department of Agriculture, Food Consumption Survey, 1955, Report No. 1, December 1956.

[2] Derived from Bureau of Labor Statistics, *Consumer Expenditures and Income,* Supplement 3, Part A, to BLS Report No. 237-38, July 1964.

[3] Because of the housekeeping eligibility requirement for this study, the single individuals included are not representative of all persons living alone.

Some of the difference in the results of the two studies cited may be attributed to differences in methodology. The questions employed by the Bureau of Labor Statistics to obtain the data on annual food outlays usually have yielded lower average expenditures than the more detailed item-by-item checklist of foods used in a week that serves as a questionnaire for the Agriculture Department. Moreover, since the Department studies are limited to families who have 10 or more meals at home during the survey week, they leave out some high food spenders represented in the BLS figures. On the other hand, the decreases undoubtedly reflect in part the general improvement in real income achieved by the Nation as a whole in the 6 years elapsed between the two studies.

For the present analysis, the earlier relationship was adopted as the basis for defining poverty—that is, an income less than three times the cost of the economy food plan (or alternatively the low-cost plan)— for families of three or more persons. For families with two members the ratio of 27 percent observed in that study was applied partly because it is generally acknowledged that a straight per capita income measure does not allow for the relatively larger fixed costs that small households face. Moreover, the more recent consumption curves themselves indicate that the 1- or 2-person families, who as a group are less homogeneous in composition, seem to be "out of line" with larger families with respect to the spending pattern.

For 1-person units, for whom the consumption data are hard to interpret because of the heavy representation of aged individuals not shown separately, the income cutoff at the low-cost level was taken at 72 percent of the estimated $2,480 for a couple, following BLS recent practice.[6] For the economy level, the income cutoff was assumed at 80 percent of the couple's requirement, on the premise that the lower the income the more difficult it would be for one person to cut expenses such as housing and utilities below the minimum for a couple.[7]

As stated earlier, for each family size several income points were developed in relation to the sex of the head and different combinations of adults and children. When weighted together in accordance with the distribution of families of these types in the current population,[*] they yield a set of assumed food expenditures and income that can be compared with the income of families of the same size who spend that amount per person for food, as estimated roughly from the 1960–61 consumption study.

It may be mentioned that the low-cost food plan criterion, derived correspondingly, can be taken as a rough measure of the results that would obtain if the income-food ratios in the BLS study were accepted as the guideline and applied to the lower food standard. Inasmuch as the economy plan for many families requires roughly three-fourths as much to buy as does the low-cost plan, multiplying by three the purchase requirement in the low-cost food plan yields approximately the same income point as multiplying the economy-plan cost by four.

---

[6] Willard Wirtz, statement in *Hearings Before the Ways and Means Committee, House of Representatives, Eighty-eighth Congress, on Medical Care for the Aged, November 18–22, 1963 and January 20–24, 1963.*

[7] See Mollie Orshansky, "Budget for an Elderly Couple," *Social Security Bulletin*, December 1960.

[*] Descriptive table omitted from original.

TABLE 2

	SSA poverty index— economy level (nonfarm)		BLS 1960-61 average (urban)[1]—
Family size	*Per capita food expense*	*Income*	*estimated income corresponding to economy food expenditure*
1....................	2	$1,540	2
2....................	$240	1,990	$1,560
3....................	270	2,440	2,475
4....................	260	3,130	3,120
5....................	245	3,685	3,600
6....................	230	4,135	4,020
7 or more..........	210	5,090	2

1 Derived from BLS Report 237-38, July 1964.
2 Not estimated.

The Farm-Nonfarm Adjustment

One additional adjustment was made to allow in some degree for the lesser needs of farm families for cash income. Farm families today buy much of their food, in contrast to the situation 40 or 50 years ago when they depended almost entirely on their own production. Yet it was still true in 1955 that about 40 percent of the food items consumed by all farm families—valued at prices paid by any families who did buy them—came from their home farm or garden. On the other hand, the food purchased represented—as it did for nonfarm families—a third of total cash income for the year after deductions for operating expenses.[8]

Farm families generally can count not only some of their food but most of their housing as part of the farm operation. Thus, it was assumed that a farm family would need 40 percent less net cash than a nonfarm family of the same size and composition.

The Resultant Standard

The poverty lines thus developed served to classify a representative Bureau of the Census population sample as of March 1964 for comparison of characteristics of poor and nonpoor units in terms of 1963 money income.[9] That is, for the farm and nonfarm population separately, unrelated individuals were classified by age and sex, and families by sex of head, total number of members, and number of related children under age 18. The income of each unit was then compared with the appropriate minimum. The households thus classified as poor and nonpoor were then analyzed for characteristics other than income.[10]

With the information on how the population is divided into units by size and number of children, it is possible to condense the 248 separate criteria into an abbreviated set for families of different size. As Table 3 indicates, the income cutoff points in the economy food plan

---

[8] See U.S. Department of Agriculture, Household Food Consumption Survey, 1955, *Food Production for Home Use by Households in the United States, by Region,* Report No. 12, January 1958, and *Farm Family Spending in the United States,* Agriculture Information Bulletin No. 192, June 1958.

[9] An earlier analysis related to 1961 income, along the same lines but restricted to families with children, was reported in the *Bulletin* for July 1963. For that earlier estimate, since family income data were available only by number of own children, not crossed with total number of persons, it was necessary to make arbitrary assumptions about the additional relatives. The present figures, based on a more refined income grid and incorporating 1960 Census data not previously available on characteristics of families and persons, represent not only an updating but, it is hoped, a refinement.

[10] Acknowledgement is made of the helpful assistance of Bureau of the Census staff in the preparation of the special tabulations for this purpose.

TABLE 3

Weighted average of poverty income criteria[1] for families of different composition, by household size, sex of head, and farm or nonfarm residence

Number of family members	Nonfarm			Farm			Nonfarm			Farm		
	Total	Male head	Female head	Total	Male head	Female head	Total	Male head	Female head	Total	Male head	Female head
	Weighted average of incomes at economy level						*Weighted average of incomes at low-cost level*					
1 (under age 65)	$1,580	$1,650	$1,525	$960	$990	$920	$1,885	$1,970	$1,820	$1,150	$1,185	$1,090
1 (aged 65 or over)	1,470	1,480	1,465	885	890	880	1,745	1,775	1,735	1,055	1,065	1,040
2 (under age 65)	2,050	2,065	1,975	1,240	1,240	1,180	2,715	2,740	2,570	1,640	1,645	1,540
2 (aged 65 or over)	1,850	1,855	1,845	1,110	1,110	1,120	2,460	2,470	2,420	1,480	1,480	1,465
3	2,440	2,455	2,350	1,410	1,410	1,395	3,160	3,170	3,070	1,890	1,895	1,835
4	3,130	3,130	3,115	1,925	1,925	1,865	4,005	4,010	3,920	2,410	2,410	2,375
5	3,685	3,685	3,660	2,210	2,210	2,220	4,675	4,680	4,595	2,815	2,815	2,795
6	4,135	4,135	4,110	2,500	2,495	2,530	5,250	5,255	5,141	3,165	3,165	3,165
7 or more	5,090	5,100	5,000	3,055	3,065	2,985	6,395	6,405	6,270	3,840	3,850	3,750

1 For definition of poverty criteria, see text.

for nonfarm units would range from $1,580 for a single person under age 65 to $5,090 for a family averaging eight members—that is, seven or more persons. At the low-cost level, the corresponding income range runs from $1,885 to $6,395. A nonfarm family of husband, wife, and two young children would need $3,100 or $3,980.

When applied to the Census income distributions the cutoff points are being related to income before income taxes, although they were derived on an after-tax basis. At the economy level the incomes are so low that for most families of more than two persons and for aged unrelated individuals no tax would be required. By contrast, the BLS "modest but adequate" budget for a similar family of four in autumn 1959 in 20 large cities ranged from $4,880 to $5,870, not including taxes, and from $5,370 to $6,570 with taxes included.[11]

How Adequate Is the Standard?

The measure of poverty thus developed is arbitrary. Few could call it too high. Many might find it too low. Assuming the homemaker is a good manager and has the time and skill to shop wisely, she must prepare nutritious, palatable meals on a budget that for herself, a husband, and two young children—an average family—would come to about 70 cents a day per person.

For a meal all four of them ate together, she could spend on the average only 95 cents, and to stay within her budget she must allow no more a day than a pound of meat, poultry, or fish altogether, barely enough for one small serving for each family member at one of the three meals. Eggs could fill out her family fare only to a limited degree because the plan allows less than 2 dozen a week for all uses in cooking and at the table, not even one to a person a day. And any food extras, such as milk at school for the children, or the coffee her husband might buy to supplement the lunch he carries to work, have to come out of the same food money or compete with the limited funds available for rent, clothing, medical care, and all other expenses. Studies indicate that, on the average, family members eating a meal away from home spend twice as much as the homemaker would spend for preparing one for them at home. The 20–25 cents allowed for a meal at home in the economy plan would not buy much even in the way of supplementation.

There is some evidence that families with very low income, particularly large families, cut their food bills below the economy plan

---

[11] Helen H. Lamale and Margaret S. Strotz, "The Interim City Worker's Family Budget," *Monthly Labor Review*, August 1960.

level—a level at which a nutritionally good diet, though possible, is hard to achieve. Indeed, a study of beneficiaries of old-age, survivors, and disability insurance—limited to 1- or 2-person families—found that only about 10 percent of those spending less than the low-cost plan (priced about a third higher than the economy plan) had meals furnishing the full recommended amounts of essential nutrients. Not more than 40 percent had even as much as two-thirds the amounts recommended. Only when food expenditures were as high as those in the low-cost plan, or better, did 90 percent of the diets include two-thirds of the recommended allowance of the nutrients, and 60 percent meet them in full.[12] Few housewives with greater resources—income and other—than most poor families have at their disposal could do better. Many might not do as well.

Varying the Reference Point

Much of the recent discussion of the poor has centered about an ad hoc definition adopted in 1963. Under this definition a family of two persons or more with income of less than $3,000 and one person alone with less than $1,500 were considered poor. At the time, a more refined poverty income test was believed to be desirable. The hope was expressed that, although the statistical magnitude of the problem would undoubtedly be altered by a different measure, "the analysis of the sources of poverty, and of the programs needed to cope with it, would remain substantially unchanged."[13] Since programs are selected on other than purely statistical considerations, this part of the statement is unchallenged. But at least the relative importance of various phases of the poverty question does depend on the criterion used.

The present analysis pivots about a standard of roughly $3,130 for a family of four persons (all types combined) and $1,540 for an unrelated individual—a level in itself not materially different from the earlier one. The standard assumes in addition that families with fewer than four persons will, on the average, require less and that larger families will need more, despite the fact that in actuality they do not always have incomes to correspond. The resulting count of the poor therefore includes fewer small families and more large ones, many of them with children. Moreover, the preceding standard treats farm and nonfarm families alike, but the one discussed here assumes a lower cash requirement for families receiving some food and housing without direct out-

---

[12] U.S. Department of Agriculture, *Food Consumption and Dietary Levels of Older Households in Rochester, New York,* by C. LeBovit and D. A. Baker (Home Economics Research Report No. 25), 1964.

[13] Council of Economic Advisors, *Annual Report 1964,* chapter 2.

lay, as part of a farming operation. Accordingly, farm families, despite their low cash income, have a somewhat smaller representation in the current count of the poor for 1963 than in the earlier statistic.

The gross number of the population counted as poor will reflect, in the main, the level of living used as the basis. In this respect the old definition and the present one are much alike: Twenty-eight and one-half million persons in families would be called poor today because their families have income less than $3,000; 29¾ million persons in families would be poor because their family income is considered too low in relation to the number it must support. What is more telling, however, is the composition of the groups selected, for in considerable measure they are not the same.

To the extent that families differing in composition tend also to differ in income, the power of the poverty line to approximate an equivalent measure of need determines how accurately the selected group reflects the economic well-being of families of different composition. It may be that the consistency of the measure of economic well-being applied to different types of families is even more important than the level itself.

Though one may question the merits of a food-income relationship alone as a poverty index, it probably does serve as an interim guide to equivalent levels of living among families in different situations. Additional variables could improve it, as, for example, allowance for geographic variables of community size and region, and indeed further study of the income-consumption patterns themselves. Even as it stands, however, this index is undoubtedly a better leveler than a single income applied across the board.

As a comparison of four different measures of poverty illustrates (table 4), the flat sum of $3,000 for a family and $1,500 for an individual would indicate that 33.4 million persons were living in poverty in 1963. One in 7 of them would be a farm resident, and 1 in 3 a child under age 18. The modification of this scale to allow $1,500 for the first person and $500 for every additional family member raises the number of the poor to 34.5 million, and the percent who are children to more than 40, but the ratio of 1 in 7 on a farm remains unchanged. Under the economy plan definition, the most complex and differentiated of the standards compared, there are 34.6 million poor—almost the same number as under the $500 per person modification of the single $3,000 standard—but the number of poor children, who now represent 43 percent of the population living in poverty, is 1 million greater. As would be expected, the proportion of the poor who live on farms is considerably lower, or only 1 in 11.

TABLE 4

Persons in poverty status in 1963, by alternative definitions
(In millions)

Type of unit	A[1]	B[2]	C[3]	D[4]	Total U.S. population
Total number of persons	33.4	34.0	34.5	34.6	187.2
Farm	4.9	6.4	5.1	3.2	12.6
Nonfarm	28.5	27.6	29.3	31.4	174.6
Unrelated individuals	4.9	[5]4.0	4.9	4.9	11.2
Farm	.2	1.4	.2	.1	.4
Nonfarm	4.7	2.6	4.7	4.8	10.8
Members of family units	28.5	30.0	29.6	29.7	176.0
Farm	4.7	5.0	4.9	3.1	12.2
Nonfarm	23.8	25.0	24.6	26.6	163.8
Children under age 18	10.8	15.7	14.1	15.0	68.8
Farm	1.8	2.4	2.1	1.5	4.8
Nonfarm	9.0	13.3	12.0	13.5	64.0

[1] Under $3,000 for family; under $1,500 for unrelated individuals (interim measure used by Council of Economic Advisers).
[2] Level below which no income tax is required, beginning in 1965.
[3] $1,500 for first person plus $500 for each additional person, up to $4,500. See testimony by Walter Heller on the Economic Opportunity Act, *Hearings Before the Subcommittee on the War on Poverty Program of the Committee on Education and Labor, House of Representatives, Eighty-eighth Congress, Second Session,* Part 1, page 30.
[4] Economy level of the poverty index developed by the Social Security Administration, by family size and farm-nonfarm residence, centering around $3,100 for 4 persons.
[5] Estimated; income-tax cutoff is $900; Census 1963 income data available only for total less than $1,000; this figure has been broken into less than $500 and $500-999 on basis of 1962 proportions.

Of particular significance is the incidence of poverty among different kinds of families. The uniform $3,000 test, which designated 9.3 million families as poor in 1962, by 1963 counted 8.8 million, or about 1 out of 5. By contrast, in 1963 the economy plan standard would tag only 1 in 7 families as poor, or 7.2 million all told. Although half the families poor by the $3,000 income test include no more than two members, 2-person units represent only a third of the families poor according to the economy level definition. In corresponding fashion, only 1 in 8 of the families with less than $3,000 had four or more children, but among those poor according to the economy level every fourth family had at least four children. Families with an aged head represented more than a third of all the families with less than $3,000 but only a fifth of those with incomes below the economy plan standard (table 5).

Clearly a profile of the poor that includes large numbers of farm families and aged couples may raise different questions and evoke different answers than when the group is characterized by relatively more

TABLE 5

Incidence of poverty by two measures: Families with 1963 incomes below $3,000 and below the economy level of the SSA poverty index, by specified characteristics

(Numbers in millions)

Characteristic	Total number of families	Poor— with incomes under $3,000[1]		Poor—with incomes below economy level[2]		
		Number	Percent of total	Number	Percent of total	Percentage distribution of all poor families
All families	47.4	8.8	19	7.2	15	100
Residence:						
Farm	3.1	1.3	43	.7	23	10
Nonfarm	44.3	7.5	17	6.5	15	90
Race of head:						
White	42.7	6.8	16	5.2	12	72
Nonwhite	4.7	2.0	43	2.0	42	28
Age of head:						
14-24	2.7	.8	30	.7	26	10
25-54	30.6	3.6	12	4.0	13	54
55-64	7.4	1.3	18	1.0	13	14
65 and over	6.7	3.1	45	1.5	24	22
Type of family:						
Husband-wife	41.3	6.2	15	5.0	12	70
Wife in paid labor force	13.4	1.0	8	.9	7	13
Wife not in paid labor force	27.9	5.2	19	4.1	15	57
Other male head	1.2	.3	23	.2	17	3
Female head	4.9	2.3	47	2.0	40	27
Number of persons in family:						
2	15.3	4.6	30	2.5	16	34
3	9.8	1.5	16	1.0	11	14
4	9.4	1.0	10	1.0	10	14
5	6.3	.7	11	.9	14	13
6	3.3	.4	12	.6	19	9
7 or more	3.3	.6	18	1.2	35	16
Number of related children under age 18:						
None	19.1	4.7	25	2.4	13	34
1	8.7	1.4	16	1.1	12	15
2	8.6	1.0	11	1.0	11	13
3	5.5	.7	14	1.0	17	14
4	2.9	.4	15	.6	23	9
5	1.4	.3	18	.5	36	7
6	1.2	.3	30	.6	49	8
Number of earners:						
None	3.7	2.8	76	2.0	53	27
1	20.8	3.9	19	3.3	16	46
2	17.3	1.8	10	1.5	9	21
3 or more	5.6	.3	6	.4	7	6

TABLE 5 (cont'd)

Incidence of poverty by two measures: Families with 1963 incomes below $3,000 and below the economy level of the SSA poverty index, by specified characteristics

(Numbers in millions)

Characteristic	Total number of families	Poor— with incomes under $3,000[1]		Poor—with incomes below economy level[2]		
		Number	Percent of total	Number	Percent of total	Percentage distribution of all poor families
Employment status and occupation of head:						
Not in labor force[3]	8.8	4.3	49	3.0	34	42
Unemployed	1.4	.4	28	.4	28	6
Employed	37.2	4.1	11	3.7	10	52
Professional, technical, and kindred workers	4.7	.1	3	.1	3	2
Farmers and farm managers .	1.8	.9	48	.5	29	8
Managers, officials, and proprietors (except farm) .	6.0	.4	6	.3	5	4
Clerical, sales, and kindred workers	4.9	.2	6	.2	4	3
Craftsmen, operatives, and kindred workers	14.5	1.1	8	1.2	8	17
Service workers, including private household	3.0	.7	23	.6	20	8
Laborers (except mine)	2.3	.7	33	.7	30	10
Work experience of head in 1963:[4]						
Worked in 1963	40.7	5.1	13	4.6	11	64
Worked at full-time jobs	37.9	3.8	10	3.6	10	50
50-52 weeks	30.7	2.1	7	2.0	7	28
Worked at part-time jobs . . .	2.8	1.4	49	1.0	36	14
Did not work in 1963	6.7	3.7	54	2.6	38	36

[1] Prepared by the Bureau of the Census from P-60, No. 43, *Income of Families and Persons in the U.S., 1963.*

[2] Derived from special tabulations by the Bureau of the Census for the Social Security Administration. For definitions of poverty criteria, see text.

[3] Includes approximately 900,000 family heads in the Armed Forces, of whom about 100,000 have incomes under $3,000.

[4] All work-experience data, including data for year-round, full-time workers, limited to civilian workers.

young nonfarm families—many of them with several children. Non-white families, generally larger than white families, account for about 2 million of the poor units by either definition. Because the total number of families counted among the poor by the economy standard is smaller, however, the nonwhite families make up a larger part of them. Because the measure of poverty for nonfarm unrelated individuals is almost the same under the economy level definition as under the earlier one—and 1-person households seldom live on a farm—characteristics of the 4.9 million unrelated persons now labeled poor are almost the same as those thus identified earlier (table 6).

TABLE 6

Incidence of poverty by two measures: Unrelated individuals with 1963 incomes below $1,500 and below the economy level of the SSA poverty index, by specified characteristics

(Numbers in millions)

Characteristic	Total number	Poor—with incomes under $1,500[1]		Poor—with incomes below economy level[2]		Percentage distribution of all poor unrelated individuals
		Number	Per-cent of total	Number	Per-cent of total	
All unrelated individuals ...	11.2	4.9	44	4.9	44	100
Residence:						
Nonfarm	10.8	4.7	43	4.7	44	97
Farm	.4	.2	67	.2	40	3
Race:						
White	9.7	4.1	42	4.1	42	83
Nonwhite	1.5	.8	56	.8	58	17
Age:						
14-24	1.0	.5	47	.5	48	10
25-64	5.9	1.8	31	1.9	56	38
65 and over	4.3	2.6	62	2.5	59	52
Sex:						
Male	4.3	1.4	33	1.4	34	30
Female	6.9	3.5	51	3.5	50	70
Earner status:						
Earner	7.0	1.8	26	1.8	26	37
Nonearner	4.2	3.1	75	3.1	74	63
Work experience in 1963[3]						
Worked in 1963	6.7	1.8	26	1.8	26	36
Worked at full-time jobs ...	5.5	1.1	20	1.2	21	23
50-52 weeks	3.7	.5	12	.5	13	10
Worked at part-time jobs ...	1.2	.7	55	.6	54	13
Did not work in 1963	4.5	3.1	72	3.9	80	64

[1] Prepared by Bureau of the Census from P-60, No. 43, *Income of Families and Persons in the U.S., 1963.*

[2] Derived from special tabulations by the Bureau of the Census for the Social Security Administration. For definition of poverty criteria, see text.

[3] All work-experience data, including data for year-round, full-time workers, limited to civilian workers.

The Income Deficit

Before elaborating further on who is poor and who is not, it may be well to assess the magnitude of the poverty complex in dollar terms. Just how much less than the aggregate estimated need is the actual income of the poor? Does it fall short by much or by little?

In the very rough terms that the selected income standard permits, it can be estimated that the 34.6 million persons identified as poor needed an aggregate money income of $28.8 billion in 1963 to cover their basic requirements. Their current income actually totaled about $17.3 billion, or only 60 percent of their estimated needs. Some of the deficit could have been—and no doubt was—offset by use of savings. By and large, however, it has been well documented that the low-income persons who could benefit most from such additions to their meager resources are least likely to have the advantage of them. And it is not usually the poor who have the rich relatives.

Unquestionably the income of the poor included the $4.7 billion paid under public assistance programs from Federal, State, and local funds during 1963. In December of that year such payments were going to a total of 7¾ million recipients. Not all persons who are poor receive assistance, but all persons receiving assistance are unquestionably poor. It cannot be said for sure how many of the poor were benefiting from other public income-support programs such as

TABLE 7

Income deficit of families and unrelated individuals below the economy level of the SSA poverty index, 1963[1]

Type of unit	Dollar deficit (in billions)			Percentage distribution		
	Total	Male head	Female head	Total	Male head	Female head
Total	$11.5	$6.4	$5.1	100.0	56.1	43.9
Unrelated individuals	3.1	1.0	2.1	27.2	8.5	18.7
Families with 2 or more members	8.4	5.4	3.0	72.8	47.6	25.2
With no children under age 18	1.8	1.4	.4	15.1	12.4	2.7
With children under age 18	6.6	4.0	2.6	57.7	35.2	22.5
1	1.0	.6	.4	8.5	4.9	3.6
2	1.0	.6	.4	8.9	5.2	3.7
3	1.3	.7	.6	11.7	6.2	5.5
4	1.0	.6	.4	9.1	5.8	3.3
5	1.0	.6	.3	8.5	5.6	2.9
6 or more	1.3	.9	.4	11.0	7.5	3.5

[1] For definition of poverty criteria, see text.

old-age, survivors, and disability insurance, unemployment insurance, veterans' payments, and the like.

Of the total deficit, about $5 billion represented the unmet needs of families headed by a woman. About three-fifths of the total ($6.6 billion) represented the shortage in income of families with children under age 18 and about 60 percent of this shortage was in the income of families with a man at the head (table 7). It is estimated that $600 million represented the deficit of poor persons on farms.

Even among the needy, there are some who are worse off than others, and in dollar terms the families consisting of a mother and young children must rank among the poorest. Such families as a group had less than half the money they needed, and the greater the number of children the greater the unmet need: Poor families with a female head and five or more children, including altogether about 1,650,000 children, as a group were living on income less by 59 percent than their minimum requirement. Of the total family units of this type in the population—that is, of all families with female head and five or more children—9 out of 10 were poor. As the following tabulation shows, for both male and female units, those families with the highest poverty rate—the families with several children—tended also to include the poorest poor.

TABLE 8

Income and family size: Median money income of nonfarm families, 1963, by number of members, number of children, and sex of head

Number of family members	Total	Number of related children under age 18						
		None	1	2	3	4	5	6 or more
Male head								
Total	$6,745	$6,045	$6,960	$7,290	$7,095	$7,080	$6,590	$5,765
2	5,400	5,415	(1)					
3	6,901	8,260	6,450	(1)				
4	7,490	11,410	8,810	7,000	(1)			
5	7,390	[2]12,570	9,640	8,680	6,900	(1)		
6	7,290	(1)	(1)	9,860	8,365	6,865	(1)	
7 or more	6,870	(1)	(1)	(1)	[2]10,770	8,430	6,590	5,765
Female head								
Total	$3,245	$4,585	$3,080	$2,940	$2,160	$2,260	[2]$1,660	[2]$2,230
2	3,340	3,955	2,115					
3	3,885	6,480	4,225	2,335				
4	3,151	(1)	[2]6,000	[2]3,230	1,940			
5	2,625	(1)	(1)	(1)	(1)	[2]2,050		
6	[2]2,120			(1)	(1)	(1)	[2]1,575	
7 or more	2,575			(1)	(1)	(1)	(1)	[2]2,230

[1] Not shown for fewer than 100,000 families.
[2] Base between 100,000 and 200,000.

For unrelated individuals, among whom are many aged persons poverty rates are high too, and their income deficits substantial (table 11).

Children and Poverty

Of all the persons in family units with income below the economy level (that is, disregarding for the moment persons living alone), half were

TABLE 9

Persons in poverty in 1963: Total number of persons in units with income below the economy level of the SSA poverty index, by sex of head and farm-nonfarm residence[1]

(In millions)

| Type of unit | Total | Sex of head | | Residence | |
		Male	Female	Farm	Non-farm
		Number of persons			
Total	34.6	23.5	11.1	3.2	31.4
Unrelated individuals	4.9	1.4	3.5	.1	4.8
Under age 65	2.4	.9	1.4	.1	2.3
Aged 65 or over	2.5	.5	2.1	([2])	2.5
Persons in families	29.7	22.1	7.6	3.1	26.6
With no children	5.3	4.4	.9	.6	4.7
With children	24.4	17.7	6.7	2.5	21.9
Adults	9.4	7.3	2.1	1.0	8.4
Children under age 18	15.0	10.4	4.6	1.5	13.5
Head year-round, full-time worker[3]	5.7	5.2	.5	([4])	([4])
Other	9.3	5.2	4.1	([4])	([4])
		Number of family units			
Total	12.1	6.7	5.4	0.9	11.2
Unrelated individuals	4.9	1.4	3.5	.2	4.7
Year-round, full-time workers	.5	.2	.3	([2])	([2])
Under age 65	.4	.2	.2	([2])	([2])
Aged 65 or over	.1	.2	.1	([2])	([2])
Other	4.4	1.2	3.2	([2])	([2])
Under age 65	1.9	.7	1.2	([2])	([2])
Aged 65 or over	2.5	.5	2.0	([2])	([2])
Families	7.2	5.2	2.0	.7	6.5
With no children	2.5	2.1	.4	.3	2.2
Head year-round, full-time worker[3]	.4	.4	([2])	([2])	([2])
Other	2.1	1.7	.4	([2])	([2])
With children	4.7	3.2	1.5	.4	4.3
Head year-round, full-time worker[3]	1.6	1.5	.1	([2])	([2])
Other	3.1	1.7	1.4	([2])	([2])

[1] For definition of poverty criteria, see text.
[2] Less than 50,000.
[3] One who worked primarily at full-time civilian jobs (35 hours or more a week) for 50 weeks or more during 1963. Year-round, full-time workers exclude all members of the Armed Forces. "Other" workers include members of the Armed Forces living off post or with their families on post.
[4] Not available.

TABLE 10

(Percent)

Type of unit	Male head		Female head	
	Incidence of poverty at economy level	Income of poor as proportion of required income	Incidence of poverty at economy level	Income of poor as proportion of required income
Total	14	64	46	53
Unrelated individual	34	57	50	58
Family	12	65	40	49
With no children	12	64	19	62
With children	12	65	55	47
1 or 2	8	68	42	53
3 or 4	14	66	72	45
5 or more	36	62	92	41

children under age 18. These 15 million youngsters represented more than 1 in 5 of all children living in families. Because poor families sometimes find it necessary to "double up" in order to cut down their living expenses, about 9 percent of the children in the poor families were designated as "related" rather than "own" children. In other words, they were not the children of the head of the family but the children of other relatives making their home with the family. Among the poor families with a woman at the head, one-seventh of the children were "related" rather than "own," and nearly a third of these related children were part of a subfamily consisting of a mother and children. Among poor families with a male head, 6 percent of the children in the households were children of a relative of the head.

A considerable number of subfamilies that include children are poor—a third of those with a father present and nearly three-fourths of those with only a mother. But from 50 percent to 60 percent of all subfamilies with inadequate income manage to escape poverty by living with relatives. Counting as poor the children in subfamilies whose own income is inadequate but who live as part of a larger family with a combined income above the poverty level would add 580,000 to the number of children whose parents are too poor to support them even at the economy level. Together with their parents, these children are part of a group of 1.1 million persons under age 65 not included in the current count of the poor, although they would be if they had to rely solely on their own income.

In contrast to this total of 15.6 million needy children, in December 1963 only 3.1 million children were receiving assistance in the form of aid to families with dependent children, the public program designed especially for them. Because some families stay on the assistance rolls less than a full year, 4 million to 4½ million children received aid during 1963.

Many children receive benefits from other public programs, such as old-age, survivors, and disability insurance and veterans' programs. It is not known at this writing how many of them are numbered among the poor or how many are in families with total income from all sources below the public assistance standards for their State.

Children in poor families with a man at the head are less likely than others to receive help. Such children number more than 10 million, but today the number of children with a father in the home who receive assistance in the form of aid to families with dependent children is less than 1 million, a ratio of not even 1 in 10.

Many of the families with children receiving public assistance undoubtedly swell the ranks of our poorest poor, because even by the limited standards of assistance of their own States—almost all of which allow less than the economy level of income—nearly half of the recipients have some unmet need. For a fourth of the families, according to a recent study, the unmet need came to as much as $30 a month or more.[14]

As would be expected—the larger the family, the more likely it is to include children. Indeed, among families of five or more, almost all have some children, and three-fourths have at least three.* The fewer adults in the family, the less opportunity there will be for additional earnings.

The statistics on family income that are generally available do not show detail by both family size and number of children. The figures presented in table 8 do show such data for 1963 for nonfarm families. It is readily apparent that no matter what the family size, the income decreases with increasing number of children at a rate that is not likely to be offset by the fact that children have lower income needs.

Accordingly not only do poverty rates among families vary with family size, but among families of a given size the chances of being poor vary in accordance with the number of children under age 18. The percentages below show the incidence of poverty—as defined by the Social Security Administration criterion at the economy level— among nonfarm families with specified number of children.

The sorry plight of the families with female head and children

---

[14] Gerald Kahn and Ellen J. Perkins, "Families Receiving AFDC: What Do They Have To Live On?" *Welfare in Review* (Welfare Administration), October 1964.
* Descriptive table omitted from original.

TABLE 11

The poverty matrix: Number of families and unrelated individuals (and total number of persons) below the economy level of the SSA poverty index,[1] by sex of head, number of children, and work experience of head in 1963
(Numbers in thousands)

Type of unit	U.S. population		The poor					Number of persons	
			Units						
	Number of units	Percent	Number	Percent	Poverty rate (percent)	Head year-round full-time worker[a]	Other head	Total	Children
All units	58,620	100.0	12,100	100.0	21	2,510	9,590	34,580	14,970
Unrelated individuals, total	11,180	19.1	4,890	40.4	44	480	4,410	4,890	....
Under age 65	6,910	11.8	2,360	19.5	34	400	1,960	2,360	....
Aged 65 or over	4,270	7.3	2,540	21.0	59	80	2,460	2,540	....
Families, total	47,440	80.9	7,210	59.6	15	2,030	5,180	29,690	14,970
With no children	19,120	32.6	2,460	20.3	13	370	2,080	5,340	....
With children	28,320	48.3	4,750	39.3	17	1,660	3,090	24,340	14,970
1	8,680	14.8	1,050	8.6	12	270	780	3,060	1,050
2	8,580	14.6	980	8.1	11	320	660	3,830	1,950
3	5,550	9.5	960	7.9	17	340	620	4,770	2,880
4	2,860	4.9	650	5.4	23	290	360	3,960	2,600
5	1,430	2.4	520	4.3	36	200	310	3,910	2,580
6 or more	1,210	2.1	600	5.0	49	240	370	4,810	3,910

Units with male head	46,830	79.9	6,670	55.1	14	2,090	4,580	23,500	10,420
Unrelated individuals	4,280	7.3	1,440	11.9	34	240	1,200	1,440	....
Under age 65	3,110	5.3	940	7.8	30	220	720	940	....
Aged 65 or over	1,170	2.0	500	4.2	43	20	480	500	....
Families	42,550	72.6	5,220	43.2	12	1,850	3,370	22,060	10,420
With no children	17,070	29.1	2,040	16.9	12	350	1,690	4,400	....
With children	25,480	43.5	3,180	26.3	12	1,500	1,680	17,660	10,420
1	7,650	13.0	650	5.4	9	240	420	2,160	650
2	7,830	13.4	620	5.1	8	280	340	2,630	1,230
3	5,070	8.6	620	5.2	12	300	320	3,280	1,870
4	2,600	4.4	460	3.8	18	270	180	2,920	1,820
5	1,280	2.2	380	3.2	30	180	200	3,070	1,920
6 or more	1,050	1.8	450	3.7	43	220	220	3,590	2,920
Units with female head	11,790	20.1	5,430	44.9	46	410	5,020	11,080	4,540
Unrelated individuals	6,910	11.8	3,450	28.5	50	240	3,210	3,450	....
Under age 65	3,800	6.5	1,410	11.7	37	180	1,240	1,410	....
Aged 65 or over	3,110	5.3	2,030	16.8	65	60	1,970	2,030	....
Families	4,880	8.3	1,980	16.4	41	180	1,800	7,630	4,540
With no children	2,050	3.5	420	3.4	19	20	390	940	....
With children	2,830	4.8	1,570	13.0	55	160	1,410	6,690	4,540
1	1,030	1.8	390	3.3	38	30	360	910	390
2	750	1.2	360	3.0	48	40	320	1,210	720
3	490	.8	340	2.8	70	40	300	1,490	1,010
4	260	.4	190	1.6	74	20	170	1,040	770
5	140	.2	130	1.1	91	20	110	840	660
6 or more	160	.3	150	1.3	93	10	140	1,220	990

[1] For definition of poverty criteria, see text.

[2] See footnote 3, table 9.

TABLE 12

Total number of family members	Children under age 18					
	None	1	2	3	4	5	6 or more
Families with male head:						
3	6	8	(1)	....	....	....	....
4	3	6	7	(1)	....	....	....
5	2	9	9	11	(1)	....	....
6	(1)	(1)	4	14	16	(1)	....
7 or more	(1)	(1)	(1)	10	22	30	42
Families with female head:						
2[2]	14	47	....	....	....	....	....
3	9	21	54	....	....	....	....
4	(1)	18	43	73	....	....	....

[1] Percentage not shown for base less than 100,000.
[2] Head under age 65.

is also evident. It needs no poverty line to explain why two-thirds of the children in such families must be considered poor.

An earlier report cited evidence that women in families without a husband present had more children than in those where the husband was still present.[15] Some of the poor families with children and a female head may well, at an earlier stage, have been members of a large household with a male head and inadequate income.

Finally, since the data both on income and on incidence of poverty relate to the number now in the family, there is an understatement of the relationship between large families and low income: Some of the families currently listed as having only one or two children undoubtedly will have more in the future or have others who are now past age 18 and may no longer be in the home. It is not likely that family income adjusts in equal measure. If anything, it may decline rather than increase as the family grows because it will be more difficult for the mother to work, and many of the families can escape poverty only by having the wife as well as the head in the labor force (table 16).

Age and Poverty

The figures in table 9 summarize the number of individuals and family units judged to be in poverty status in accordance with the economy level.

The total number of aged persons among the 34.6 million poor is about 5.2 million, or 1 in 7. Perhaps the poorest of the aged are

---

[15] See Mollie Orshansky, "Children of the Poor," *Social Security Bulletin,* July 1963.

elderly relatives living in the home of a younger family. Such elderly persons living in a family of which they were neither the head nor the wife of the head in March 1964 numbered about 2.5 million. There probably were a variety of reasons for their choice of living arrangements, but that financial stringency was a major factor is obvious: four-fifths of these elderly relatives had less than $1,500 in income of their own during 1963, the minimum required for an aged person to live alone. The vast majority of elderly persons designated as "other relatives" were living in a family with income above the poverty level.

Every second person living alone (or with nonrelatives) and classified as poor was aged 65 or older, and four-fifths of the aged poor were women. The low resources generally prevailing among this group mean that those who, by choice or necessity, live independently are likely to do so only at the most meager level, even if allowance is made for their using up any savings.[16]

The present analysis indicates that more than 40 percent of all aged men and nearly two-thirds of the aged women living by themselves in 1963 had income below the economy level. Only 1 in 4 of the aged women living alone had income above the low-cost level.

In summary, if to the 2.5 million aged persons living alone in poverty and the 2.7 million living in poor families as aged head, spouse, or relative are added the 1.7 million aged relatives too poor to get by on their own, but not included in the current count of the poor because the families they live with are above the economy level of the poverty index, the number of impoverished aged would rise to almost 7 million. Two-fifths of the population aged 65 or older (not in institutions) are thus presently subject to poverty, or escaping it only by virtue of living with more fortunate relatives.

Among poor individuals under age 65, poverty for some undoubtedly represented only a stage through which they were passing. The poverty rate was high among persons under age 25, half having incomes below the economy level, and dropped to about 1 in 4 for those aged 25–34 (table 16).

Among 2-person families, 16 percent of whom were poor by the economy level criterion, there was also a difference between the situation of those units approaching the last stage in the family cycle and those who were younger. Of all 2-person units, a third had a head aged 65 or older, but of those 2-person units called poor, half had an aged

---

[16] See Lenore A. Epstein, "Income of the Aged in 1962: First Findings of the 1963 Survey of the Aged," *Social Security Bulletin,* March 1964, and Janet Murray, "Potential Income From Assets . . .," *Social Security Bulletin,* December 1964.

TABLE 13

Family type	Male head		Female head	
	Total number of units (in thousands)	Per- cent poor	Total number of units (in thousands)	Per- cent poor
Two adults	13,026	14	1,557	22
Head under age 65	8,769	10	876	14
Head aged 65 or older	4,257	22	681	32
One adult, one child	87	(¹)	618	50

¹ Percentage not shown for base less than 100,000.

head. Presumably, some of the other units who were currently poor represented young couples who had decided not to delay marriage until they attained the better job status—and income—that they one day hoped to enjoy. But others consisted of a mother with a child, who were suffering the poverty that is likely to be the lot of the family with no man to provide support. Table 13 shows the rates of poverty, according to the economy level, among the different types of 2-person families.

Work and Poverty

The greater overall vulnerability of families headed by a woman is evidenced by the fact that such families, who number only 1 in 10 of all families in the country, account for nearly 1 in 3 of the Nation's poor. Although the inadequate income of the poor families with a female head may be attributed to the fact that few of the family heads are employed, this is not the reason among the families headed by a man. A majority of the men are working, but at jobs that do not pay enough to provide for their family needs. Moreover, of those not at work, most report themselves as out of the labor force altogether rather than unemployed. Yet the rate of unemployment reported by the poor was more than three times that among the heads of families above the poverty level (table 8).*

Current Employment Status

The employment status of the family heads in March 1964, when the income data were collected, was recorded as shown in table 14.

Detailed analysis of the data for white and nonwhite families will be reserved for a subsequent report, but some highlights seem pertinent here.

Despite the fact that unemployment generally is more prevalent among the nonwhite population than the white, among families whose

---

* Descriptive table omitted.

TABLE 14

Employment status of head, March 1964	Male head		Female head	
	Poor family	Nonpoor family	Poor family	Nonpoor family
Total	100	100	100	100
In labor force	67	88	33	60
Employed	60	85	29	57
Unemployed	6	3	4	3
Not in labor force	33	12	67	40

income marked them as poor there was no difference by race in the total proportion of the men currently looking for work. Among white and nonwhite male heads alike, 6 percent said they were out of a job. Indeed, since fewer among the white heads of families who are poor were in the labor force than was true among nonwhite heads of poor families, the rate of unemployment among those actually available for work was noticeably higher for the former group. What is more significant is that 73 percent of the nonwhite male heads of poor families were currently employed, and more than half of them—42 percent of all the poor—had been employed full time throughout 1963. Among male heads in white families with incomes below the economy level, only 56 percent were currently working, and no more than a third had been year-round full-time workers in 1963.

Unemployment for nonwhite workers is undeniably serious. But the concentration of nonwhite men in low-paying jobs at which any worker—white or nonwhite—is apt to earn too little to support a large family may be even more crucial in consigning their families to poverty at a rate three times that of their white fellow citizens.

In point of fact, the family of a nonwhite male is somewhat worse off in relation to that of a white male when both are working than when both are not, as table 15 suggests.

This difference does not come as a complete surprise. Earlier analysis of the income life cycle of the nonwhite man suggested that it is only when he and his white counterpart exchange their weekly pay

TABLE 15

Employment status of head, March 1964	Percent of families with male head with income below the economy level	
	White	Non-white
All families	10	34
Not in labor force	25	50
Unemployed	22	47
Employed	7	31
Year-round, full-time in 1963...............	5	23

TABLE 16

Incidence of poverty in 1963, according to SSA poverty index: Percent of families and unrelated individuals with 1963 income below specified level,[1] by specified characteristics and race of head

[Numbers in thousands: data are estimates derived from a survey of households and are therefore subject to sampling variability that may be relatively large where the size of the percentage or size of the total on which the percentage is based is small; as in all surveys, the figures are subject to errors of response and nonreporting]

Characteristic	All units			White			Nonwhite		
	Total number	Percent with incomes below—		Total number	Percent with incomes below—		Total number	Percent with incomes below—	
		Economy level	Low-cost level		Economy level	Low-cost level		Economy level	Low-cost level
Total	47,436	15.1	23.0	42,663	12.0	19.3	4,773	42.5	55.6
Residence:									
Nonfarm	44,343	14.6	22.4	39,854	11.6	18.7	4,489	41.2	54.3
Farm	3,093	23.0	31.8	2,809	18.9	27.2	284	62.3	75.5
Race of head:									
White	42,663	12.0	19.3	.....	.....	.....	.....	.....	.....
Nonwhite	4,773	42.5	55.6	.....	.....	.....	.....	.....	.....
Age of head:									
14-24	2,744	25.8	35.3	2,391	20.7	29.9	353	59.8	71.0
25-34	9,128	14.7	23.6	8,109	11.1	19.1	1,019	43.2	59.2
35-44	11,437	13.7	20.7	10,220	10.5	17.0	1,217	40.2	52.2
45-54	9,986	9.8	15.2	9,012	7.0	11.8	974	35.4	46.9
55-64	7,382	13.3	18.5	6,717	10.9	15.7	665	38.0	48.5
65 and over	6,759	23.5	36.9	6,214	20.9	33.9	545	52.6	70.4
Number of persons in family:									
2	15,287	16.1	24.3	13,917	14.4	22.3	1,370	33.0	44.7
3	9,808	10.6	16.5	8,906	8.7	13.6	902	29.0	44.8
4	9,435	10.3	15.9	8,678	7.6	12.6	757	41.9	53.9
5	6,268	14.5	22.1	5,718	11.4	18.2	550	45.2	59.9
6	3,324	19.1	30.9	2,908	14.2	26.1	416	53.8	65.0
7 or more	3,314	34.8	49.6	2,536	24.9	39.9	778	68.4	82.2

Families

Number of related children under age 18:									
None	19,119	12.7	20.1	17,607	11.5	18.5	1,512	26.8	39.3
1	8,682	12.1	17.7	7,771	9.6	18.4	911	32.8	45.6
2	8,579	11.3	17.5	7,824	8.3	13.8	755	42.5	56.1
3	5,554	17.4	26.8	5,030	14.0	22.5	524	48.2	66.2
4	2,863	22.8	34.8	2,476	16.8	29.1	387	60.7	70.5
5	1,429	35.8	53.0	1,145	27.2	44.7	284	73.6	89.6
6 or more	1,210	49.3	63.5	810	35.3	51.2	400	77.3	87.7
Region:									
Northeast	11,902	9.8	16.5	11,017	8.4	14.6	885	26.6	39.5
North Central	13,358	11.5	18.7	12,472	10.3	17.0	886	29.7	43.5
South	14,389	24.6	34.6	12,005	17.9	27.1	2,384	58.3	71.9
West	7,787	11.7	18.5	7,169	11.0	17.4	618	20.7	31.4
Type of family:									
Male head	42,554	12.3	20.0	38,866	10.2	17.3	3,688	34.1	48.2
Married, wife present	41,310	12.1	19.9	37,799	10.1	17.2	3,511	34.3	48.5
Wife in paid labor force	13,398	6.8	11.9	11,851	4.3	8.7	1,547	25.5	36.5
Wife not in paid labor force	27,912	14.6	23.6	25,948	12.6	21.0	1,964	41.3	58.0
Other marital status	1,243	17.0	23.4	1,067	14.5	20.1	177	[2]31.2	[2]42.6
Female head	4,882	40.1	49.3	3,797	31.2	40.1	1,085	70.8	80.5
Number of earners:									
None	3,695	53.4	70.2	3,242	49.2	66.9	453	83.9	93.9
1	20,832	15.7	24.7	18,976	12.5	20.7	1,856	48.5	64.5
2	17,306	8.7	14.4	15,484	6.3	11.3	1,822	28.8	39.8
3 or more	5,603	7.4	12.3	4,961	3.9	7.7	642	34.8	48.0
Employment status and occupation of head:									
Not in labor force[a]	8,757	34.4	47.9	7,673	30.0	43.7	1,084	65.4	77.6
Unemployed	1,427	28.3	39.9	1,190	23.8	34.5	237	53.4	70.2
Employed	37,252	10.0	16.4	33,800	7.5	13.1	3,452	34.5	47.8
Professional and technical workers	4,688	2.8	5.5	4,479	2.4	5.1	209	10.9	14.7
Farmers and farm managers	1,846	29.3	37.3	1,739	26.5	34.1	107	[2]77.0	[2]93.2
Managers, officials, and proprietors (except farm)	5,981	5.4	9.9	5,860	5.0	9.5	121	[2]22.2	[2]30.0
Clerical and sales workers	4,865	4.3	9.1	4,637	3.7	8.1	228	16.6	28.7
Craftsmen and foremen	7,102	5.5	11.1	6,704	4.5	9.7	398	21.3	32.3
Operatives	7,430	11.2	19.1	6,572	8.9	15.9	858	29.8	44.8
Service workers, including private household	2,996	20.1	29.8	2,184	12.1	19.9	812	40.2	54.8
Private household workers	285	63.8	70.0	95	[4]	[4]	190	[2]77.5	[2]83.1
Laborers (except mine)	2,344	29.9	43.2	1,625	21.1	33.8	719	50.0	64.4

See footnotes at end of table.

TABLE 16 (cont'd)

Incidence of poverty in 1963, according to SSA poverty index: Percent of families and unrelated individuals with 1963 income below specified level,[1] by specified characteristics and race of head

[Numbers in thousands: data are estimates derived from a survey of households and are therefore subject to sampling variability that may be relatively large where the size of the percentage or size of the total on which the percentage is based is small; as in all surveys, the figures are subject to errors of response and nonreporting]

Characteristic	All units			White			Nonwhite		
	Total number	Economy level	Low-cost level	Total number	Economy level	Low-cost level	Total number	Economy level	Low-cost level
Families									
Work experience of head:[5]									
Worked in 1963	40,753	11.3	18.2	36,791	8.6	14.8	3,962	36.9	50.4
Worked at full-time jobs	37,913	9.5	16.0	34,505	7.2	13.1	3,408	31.7	45.7
50-52 weeks	30,689	6.6	12.2	28,210	4.9	9.8	2,479	25.8	38.7
40-49 weeks	3,515	14.2	23.5	3,128	10.9	19.4	387	39.4	55.8
39 weeks or less	3,709	28.6	40.3	3,167	24.5	35.4	542	52.9	69.8
Worked at part-time jobs	2,840	36.2	47.9	2,286	28.5	40.7	554	67.9	79.2
50-52 weeks	1,065	30.0	40.6	868	22.4	32.0	197	[2]63.6	[2]78.8
49 weeks or less	1,775	39.9	52.3	1,418	32.3	46.0	357	70.3	79.3
Did not work in 1963	6,683	38.3	51.9	5,872	33.9	47.7	811	69.8	81.1
Ill or disabled	1,745	46.5	59.9	1,441	41.4	54.4	304	68.2	83.7
Keeping house	1,603	49.7	57.8	1,329	42.8	51.7	274	83.2	86.5
Going to school	77	...	...	68	...	...	9	...	...
Could not find work	202	49.3	60.5	154	[2]41.9	[2]53.8	48	...	...
Other	3,056	26.8	43.7	2,880	25.3	42.0	176	[2]52.7	[2]70.5
Unrelated individuals									
Total	11,182	43.9	49.8	9,719	41.8	48.0	1,463	57.5	61.7
Residence:									
Nonfarm	10,820	44.0	49.8	9,379	42.0	48.0	1,441	57.4	61.7
Farm	362	40.4	49.3	340	38.6	48.0	22	(4)	(4)

Race:									
White	9,719	41.8	48.0	...	...	...	...	...	...
Nonwhite	1,463	57.6	61.8	...	...	...	...	...	...
Age:									
14-24	989	47.6	49.9	873	45.5	47.6	116	²62.5	²65.9
25-34	995	26.3	28.6	792	23.3	25.2	203	38.7	42.7
35-44	1,000	23.6	25.4	785	19.9	21.8	215	37.1	39.6
45-54	1,575	30.5	35.3	1,308	25.9	30.2	267	52.0	59.5
55-64	2,332	39.3	43.4	2,024	34.9	39.3	308	67.8	70.4
65 and over	4,291	59.3	69.2	3,937	58.0	68.3	354	73.8	78.3
Sex:									
Male	4,275	33.7	39.4	3,591	31.3	37.3	684	46.1	50.0
Female	6,907	50.3	56.3	6,128	48.1	54.3	779	67.6	72.1
Region:									
Northeast	3,119	42.1	47.7	2,778	41.8	47.8	341	44.1	46.5
North Central	2,974	45.5	52.7	2,720	44.3	51.6	254	58.9	64.7
South	2,830	52.7	57.5	2,164	46.6	51.9	666	72.5	75.7
West	2,259	33.3	39.1	2,057	33.8	39.3	202	28.7	37.3
Earner status:									
Earner	6,978	26.0	30.4	5,992	23.0	27.4	986	43.8	49.0
Nonearner	4,204	73.8	82.0	3,727	72.2	81.2	477	85.7	88.0
Employment status and occupation:									
Not in labor force[3]	4,809	66.9	75.5	4,289	65.0	74.4	520	82.0	85.3
Unemployed	460	44.5	49.4	367	40.5	45.3	93	60.6	66.2
Employed	5,913	25.2	28.9	5,063	22.3	25.9	850	42.2	46.8
Professional and technical workers	1,234	28.5	30.8	1,159	28.4	30.7	75	35.6	40.0
Farmers and farm managers	131	²42.9	²46.9	121	²39.6	²44.0	10	(⁴)	(⁴)
Managers, officials and proprietors (except farm)	445	18.9	23.1	425	17.0	21.5	20	50.0	50.0
Clerical and sales workers	1,367	11.6	14.6	1,270	11.2	14.4	97	17.1	17.1
Craftsmen and foremen	301	5.8	7.5	289	6.0	7.8	12		
Operatives	866	14.4	17.6	727	11.4	14.0	139	29.8	36.5
Service workers, including private household	1,171	44.9	51.5	803	40.4	47.4	368	55.6	60.7
Private household workers	421	70.2	78.5	223	70.9	79.4	198	²69.4	²78.2
Laborers (except mine)	398	43.5	47.5	269	42.4	45.3	129	45.8	52.1

See footnotes at end of table.

TABLE 16 (cont'd)

Incidence of poverty in 1963, according to SSA poverty index: Percent of families and unrelated individuals with 1963 income below specified level,[1] by specified characteristics and race of head

[Numbers in thousands: data are estimates derived from a survey of households and are therefore subject to sampling variability that may be relatively large where the size of the percentage or size of the total on which the percentage is based is small; as in all surveys, the figures are subject to errors of response and nonreporting]

Characteristic	All units			White			Nonwhite		
	Total number	Percent with incomes below—		Total number	Percent with incomes below—		Total number	Percent with incomes below—	
		Economy level	Low-cost level		Economy level	Low-cost level		Economy level	Low-cost level
Work experience:[5]									
Worked in 1963	6,729	26.4	30.8	5,788	23.7	28.0	941	43.7	48.9
Worked at full-time jobs	5,564	20.8	23.9	4,864	19.2	22.1	700	32.4	38.0
50-52 weeks	3,719	12.8	15.6	3,294	11.5	13.9	425	22.3	29.1
40-49 weeks	744	22.9	25.9	650	21.6	24.5	94	(4)	(4)
39 weeks or less	1,101	46.1	50.6	920	44.9	50.0	181	53.9	55.3
Worked at part-time jobs	1,165	53.5	63.9	924	47.2	58.9	241	75.3	79.6
50-52 weeks	396	49.3	57.1	307	45.9	54.1	89	57.8	64.1
49 weeks or less	769	55.7	67.4	617	47.9	61.2	152	84.4	87.7
Did not work in 1963	4,453	70.4	78.5	3,931	68.7	77.5	522	82.7	85.0
Ill or disabled	974	79.8	86.4	747	76.6	84.9	227	87.2	88.4
Keeping house	2,076	71.5	79.8	1,941	70.8	79.5	135	84.8	84.8
Going to school	106	²88.6	²88.6	83	(4)	(4)	23	(4)	(4)
Could not find work	128	²83.3	²87.5	89	(4)	(4)	39	(4)	(4)
Unrelated individuals									
Other	1,169	57.6	68.0	1,071	56.8	67.0	98	...	...
Source of income:									
Earnings only	3,838	29.7	32.7	3,111	26.5	29.2	727	43.5	47.5
Earnings and other income	3,138	21.3	27.6	2,882	19.2	25.3	256	44.5	52.9
Other income only or no income	4,206	73.8	82.0	3,726	72.2	81.2	480	85.8	88.0

[1] For definition of poverty criteria, see text.
[2] Base between 100,000 and 200,000.
[3] Includes members of the Armed Forces.
[4] Not shown for fewer than 100,000 units.
[5] All work-experience data, including data for year-round, full-time workers, limited to civilian workers.

Source: Derived from tabulation of the Current Population Survey, March 1964, by the Bureau of the Census for the Social Security Administration.

envelope for a check from a public income-maintenance program that they begin to approach economic equality.[17] For most white families, retirement or other type of withdrawal from the labor force brings with it a marked decline in income. Some nonwhite families, however, are then actually not much worse off than when working.

Work Experience in 1963

Since it was the annual income for 1963 that determined whether the family would be ranked as poor, the work experience of the head in 1963 is even more relevant to the poverty profile than the employment status at the time of the Current Population Survey.

Among the male heads, only 1 in 3 of those in poor families was a full-time worker all during the year, compared with 3 in 4 of the heads in nonpoor families. Among the female heads, as would be expected, the proportion working full time was much smaller—a tenth among poor families and not a full four-tenths among the nonpoor. All told, the poor families headed by a man fully employed throughout 1963 included 5.2 million children under age 18 and those headed by a fully employed woman worker had half a million. Thus 2 in 5 of all the children growing up in poverty were in a family of a worker with a regular full-time job.

It is difficult to say which is the more striking statistic: that 6 percent of the families headed by a male year-round full-time worker were nevertheless poor, or that 25 percent of the families with a male head who did not have a full-time job all year were poor.

That a man risks poverty for his family when he does not or cannot work all the time might be expected, but to end the year with so inadequate an income, even when he has worked all week every week, must make his efforts seem hopeless.

Yet, with minimum wage provisions guaranteeing an annual income of only $2,600, and many workers entitled to not even this amount, it should not be too surprising that in 1963 there were 2 million families in poverty despite the fact that the head never was out of a job, as shown below.

Almost all the male heads who had worked full-time all year in 1963 were also currently employed in March 1964 in poor and nonpoor families alike. Among the women year-round full-time workers, only 80 percent of those at the head of families who were poor in terms of their 1963 income were still employed in the spring of the following year, compared with 96 percent of those not poor. Among 1.8 million

[17] Mollie Orshansky, "The Aged Negro and His Income," *Social Security Bulletin*, February 1964.

TABLE 17
(In millions)

Type of family	All families	Male head	Female head
Total number of poor families	7.2	5.2	2.0
With head a year-round, full-time worker	2.0	1.8	.2
White	1.4	1.3	.1
Nonwhite	.6	.5	.1
Other	5.2	3.4	1.8
White	2.7	2.6	1.1
Nonwhite	1.5	.8	.7

male heads of families who were poor despite their year-round full-time employment, more than a fifth gave their current occupation as farmers, an equal number were operatives, and nearly a fifth were laborers. Only 3 percent were professional or technical workers. By contrast, among the nonpoor, 1 in 7 of the male family heads working the year around at full-time jobs were currently employed as professional or technical workers and only 4 percent each were farmers or laborers.

Notwithstanding the current stress on more jobs, it is clear that at least for poor families headed by a full-time year-round worker—more than a fourth of the total—it is not so much that more jobs are required but better ones, if it is presumed that the head of the family will continue to be the main source of support and that there will continue to be as many large families. In less than a fifth of the poor families headed by a man working full time the year around was the wife in the paid labor force, and in only about two-fifths was there more than one earner. By contrast, in the corresponding group of nonpoor families, one-third of the wives were working or in the market for a job, and 55 percent of the families in all had at least one earner in addition to the head.*

Not even for the 5.2 million poor families with a head who worked less than a full year can jobs alone provide an answer. Among the poor, about two-thirds of the male heads who had worked part of the year or not at all in 1963 gave ill health or other reasons—including retirement—as the main reason, rather than an inability to find work. Of the female heads less than fully employed in 1963, about five-sixths gave household responsibilities as the reason; though fewer claimed ill health or disability, they nevertheless outnumbered those who said they

---

* Illustrative table omitted.

had been looking for work. Among the unrelated individuals, only 1 in 6 of the men and 1 in 14 of the women not working the year around gave unemployment as the chief reason. At best it will be difficult to find jobs that a large number of the underemployed heads of poor households can fill, as Table 18 indicates.

Occupation and Poverty

The chances of a family's being poor differ not only with the amount of employment of the head but also with the kind of work he does. This is a reflection of the different pay rates and lifetime earning patterns that workers at different trades can expect. It appears, however, that the association is compounded: Not only do certain occupations pay less well than others, but workers in those occupations tend to have larger families than the others. Thus an income unlikely to be high to begin with must be stretched to provide for more children rather than less.

Of families headed by a male year-round full-time worker and with income above the economy level, more than half had either no children under age 18 in the household or only one. Only 4 percent had more than four. By contrast, among the corresponding group of families with income less than the economy level, fewer than a third had no more than one child in the home and nearly a fourth had five or more.

The poverty rates for families with heads in different occupations (table 16) take on new meaning when ranked by a measure of

TABLE 18

| | Percentage distribution of units with income below economy level | | | |
| | Families | | Unrelated individuals | |
Work experience of head in 1963	Male head	Female head	Male	Female
Total	100	100	100	100
Worked all year...............	39	15	21	11
Full-time job	35	9	17	7
Part-time job	4	6	4	4
Worked part of the year	33	28	28	20
Looking for work	19	7	11	4
Ill, disabled	6	4	4	3
Keeping house	. . .	15	. . .	6
All other	8	2	13	7
Didn't work at all	28	58	51	69
Ill, disabled	12	10	20	14
Keeping house	. . .	41	. . .	43
Couldn't find work	1	2	4	2
All other	15	5	27	10

earnings potential. There is a cycle in family income as well as in family size, although the two patterns are not generally in perfect correspondence. On the assumption that for the average family it is mainly the earning capacity of the husband that sets the scale at which the family must live, the poverty rates for families of employed male heads by occupation have been arrayed according to the median earnings (in 1959) of men aged 35–44. This is the age at which, on the basis of cross-

TABLE 19

Occupation group	Median earnings of male workers aged 35-44[1]	Incidence of poverty among families with employed male head[2]	Percent of wives aged 35-44 of employed workers, with specified number of children ever born[3]		
			0-2	3	4 or more
White males:					
Professional and technical workers	$8,015	2	56	23	20
Managers, officials, proprietors, (except farm)	7,465	5	57	23	20
Sales workers	6,325	3	60	22	19
Craftsmen and foremen	5,795	4	54	21	25
Clerical and kindred workers	5,505	2	61	20	19
Operatives	5,075	9	52	20	27
Service workers	4,610	8	57	20	23
Nonfarm laborers	4,095	15	49	19	33
Farmers and farm managers	2,945	26	42	22	36
Farm laborers	2,020	43	35	17	48
Nonwhite males:					
Professional and technical workers	5,485	12	65	16	19
Managers, officials, proprietors (except farm)	4,655	21	57	16	27
Clerical and kindred workers	4,630	13	61	14	25
Sales workers	4,010	(4)	57	16	27
Craftsmen and foremen	3,885	21	52	13	35
Operatives	3,495	27	51	12	37
Service workers	2,970	25	57	13	30
Nonfarm laborers	2,825	45	48	11	41
Farm laborers	975	70	34	9	57
Farmers and farm managers	945	78	27	9	65

[1] In 1959.

[2] Currently employed family heads in March 1964, with 1963 family money income below the economy level in 1963.

[3] Wives of currently employed men at time of 1960 Decennial Census.

[4] Not available.

Source: *U.S. Census of Population, 1960: Occupation by Earnings and Education,* PC(2)-7B; *Women by Number of Children Ever Born,* PC(2)-3A; and Social Security Administration.

sectional data, earnings for the average worker in most occupations are at their peak. Two things are abundantly clear.

In general, the poverty rates for families of men in different occupations are inversely related to the median peak earnings—that is, the lower the average earnings at age 35–44, the greater the risk of poverty for the family. (In some instances, as among families of some of the proprietors, work of the wife and other adults may count as unpaid family labor rather than add earnings to the family income.) The size of the average family with children seems also to vary inversely with earning capacity, in terms of the number of children ever born to the wives aged 35–44 of men employed in these occupations.

Table 19 illustrates the patterns separately for white and nonwhite families with male head.

For many families a critical point in financial status may be the arrival of the fourth or fifth child. At all occupational levels (except among wives of professional and technical employees) the nonwhite family tends to be larger than the white, but on the average nonwhite families are at a lower economic level than white families in the same occupational class. A more accurate, or at least a narrower, occupational grouping would probably show less difference between the sizes of white and nonwhite families at equivalent economic levels.

Some of the differences in number of children are related to different patterns of age at first marriage. But even among women who married at the same age there remains evidence of a difference in life style among occupational groups, in terms of number of children ever born.

The discussion here centers on children ever born rather than the more common statistic of children present in the home. Use of the latter figure results in serious understatement of the total number of children in large families who may be subject to the risk of poverty before they reach adulthood.

Differences in the two statistics are greater for the low-income occupations, such as nonfarm laborers with their large families, than for high-income occupations, such as professional and technical workers with their smaller families. It appears to be the families with less income to look forward to in the first place who have more children.[18]

The statistics by occupation may throw light on the intergeneration cycle of poverty. It is not necessary here to repeat the admonition that education for our youngsters is a long step up in the escape from poverty. It is of importance, however, that in these days, when children generally are receiving more education than those a generation ago,

---

[18] See also Bureau of the Census, *Current Population Reports*, "Socioeconomic Characteristics of the Population: 1960," Series P-23, No. 12, July 31, 1964.

the degree of upward mobility is affected by social environment as indicated by the occupation as well as by the education of the father. According to a recent report, among children of men with the same educational attainment, those with fathers in white-collar jobs are much more likely than children of fathers in manual and service jobs or in farm jobs to acquire more years of school training than their parents.[19]

The statistics on occupation and poverty may have even further import. The work history of aged persons currently receiving public assistance might well show that many of the recipients (or the persons on whom they had depended for support) used to work at the same kinds of jobs currently held by many of the employed poor. Earnings too little to support a growing family are not likely to leave much margin for saving for old age. Moreover, such low earnings will bring entitlement to only minimal o.a.s.d.i. benefits.

Implications

The causes of poverty are many and varied. Because some groups in the population are more vulnerable, however, a cross-section of the poor will differ from one of the nonpoor, measure for measure. The mothers bringing up children without a father, the aged or disabled who cannot earn, and the Negro who may not be allowed to earn will, more often than the rest of us, know the dreary privation that denies them the good living that has become the hallmark of America.

But there are others thus set apart, without the handicap of discrimination or disability, who cannot even regard their plight as the logical consequence of being unemployed. There are millions of children in "normal" as well as broken homes who will lose out on their chance ever to strive as equals in this competitive society because they are denied now even the basic needs that money can buy. And finally there are the children yet to come, whose encounter with poverty can be predicted unless the situation is changed for those currently poor.

Neither the present circumstances nor the reasons for them are alike for all our impoverished millions, and the measures that can help reduce their number must likewise be many and varied. No single program, placing its major emphasis on the needs of one special group alone, will succeed. Any complex of programs that does not allow for the diversity of the many groups among the poor will to that degree leave the task undone. The poor have been counted many times. It remains now to count the ways by which to help them gain a new identity.

---

[19] Bureau of the Census, *Current Population Reports*, "Educational Change in a Generation," Series P-20, No. 132, Sept. 22, 1964.

[Author's Note]

Who Was Poor in 1966

[EXCERPTED FROM Research and Statistics Notes, *Social Security Administration, December 6, 1967.*]

By 1966 the income of the U.S. population had climbed to a new high. Even after allowing for higher prices, families averaged $5 in real income for every $4 available to them in 1959. But whereas a majority in the country were enjoying record-high incomes, a total of 29.7 million persons, or 1 out of every 7 noninstitutionalized Americans were in households with money incomes for the year below the poverty line. The poor were distributed throughout 11 million households, which contained one-sixth of all the Nation's children under age 18. Indeed, in 1966 as in 1959, such youngsters made up half of all the persons in poor families.

The Poverty Index

Between 1959 and 1966 both the income received by consumers and the prices of what they bought continued to climb but income went up faster. Inevitably then, the poverty thresholds, adjusted only for price change, were farther below general levels of income at the end of the period than at the outset. Median income of 4-person families in 1966 was $8,340, according to the Census Bureau—more than 2½ times the nonfarm poverty threshold of $3,335. In 1959, by contrast, median income for 4-person families was $6,070, about twice the poverty index cut-off line. In other words, the average income of 4-person families had increased by 37 percent but the poverty line by only 9 percent—or one-fourth as much. As a result, the poverty line for a nonfarm family of 4, which in 1959 averaged half the corresponding median income for families this size, by 1966 was 60 percent less than what the average family had. Many of the poor, of course, had incomes considerably under the poverty threshold. (See table 3) Because not only standards of living but the price lines of goods readily available tend to move upward with prevailing income, families poor in 1966 would find themselves more readily outbid and outspent than families tagged poor in 1959. To this extent comparing today's poor with those of the earlier year overstates the reduction in their number and understates the degree of relative deprivation.

The Poverty Gap in 1965

The latest statistics on the aggregate dollar amount by which poor households fell short of their estimated income need are for the year 1965 when the total poverty roster numbered 31.9 million persons, of whom 14 million were under age 18. At that time the total dollar poverty gap—the aggregate difference between required and actual income—stood at $11 billion. This represented an overall reduction of 20 percent since 1959, but now one-fifth of the gap represented unmet need of families with children and a female head as compared with one-sixth then. In contrast, the share of the total gap accounted for by families with children and a male head dropped from 37 percent in 1959 to 34 percent in 1965.

Differential Changes in Poverty 1959-66

In 1959, 24 percent of the Nation's households—counting as households both 1-person units and families of two or more persons—had so little income as to be counted poor; 7 years later it was just 17.8 percent with too little money income to support the number dependent on it. What is perhaps of greater significance than the general improvement is that, as already indicated, more of the poor in 1966 were persons of limited earning capacity or those whom age, home responsibilities, race discrimination or other factors kept out of the labor force altogether.

Children—particularly if in a home without a father—and old people are at a disadvantage compared with persons aged 18-64 when it comes to earning. The number of children under age 18 being reared in poverty went down from 16.7 million in 1959 to 12.5 million in 1966, but the number of near-poor dipped by only .4 million to reach 6.6 million by 1966. All told, even in 1966, after a continued run of prosperity and steadily rising family income, one-fourth of the Nation's children were in families living in poverty or hovering just above the poverty line.

Whereas the poverty rate among all persons aged 18-64 or older declined by more than one-third in the 7-year period, for the aged as a group it declined by only 13 percent. Children in a family with a female head were only 17 percent less likely to be poor in 1966 than in 1959; but for children in a home headed by a man the risk of poverty was 40 percent lower in 1966 than it had been earlier.

As a group, persons aged 65 or older were even worse off than the youngsters: those counted poor in 1966 numbered 5.4 million, the same as two years earlier, and only half a million less than the count of aged poor in 1959.

The number of poor families with a male head and children under age 18 went from 3.8 million to 2.4 million in 1966. But the 1½ million poor families headed by a female with children numbered almost as many as the number poor in 1959. Thus, though the total count of children in poverty was one-fourth less than 7 years earlier, the number poor in families with a female head was actually one-tenth higher than it had been formerly.

There was other evidence that economic growth had not helped all population groups in equal measure. The nonwhite population generally had fared less well than the white during the 1959-66 upswing, though by the end of the period it was making greater strides than at the beginning. To be sure, in 1966 it was 1 in 3 nonwhite families who were poor compared with 1 in 10 white, whereas in 1959 it was 1 in 2 nonwhite and 1 in 7 white families who were poor. But it is also a fact that nonwhites made up about one-third of the Nation's poor in 1966, compared with just over one-fourth in 1959—a widening disadvantage explained only in small part by the greater population growth among nonwhites.

It is clear that in the period since 1959, poverty, which never was a random affliction, has become even more selective, and some groups initially vulnerable are now even more so. There is still no all-embracing characterization that can encompass all the poor. Some are poor because they cannot work; others are poor even though they do. Most of the poor receive no assistance from public programs; others remain poor because they have no resources but the limited payments provided under such programs. And public programs to help the poor are in the main geared to serve those who cannot work at all or are temporarily out of a job. The man who works for a living but is not making it will normally find no avenue of aid.

TABLE 1

The Poor and Near Poor, 1966: Number and Percent of Persons in Households
Below SSA Poverty Level and Above that Level But Below Low-Income Level,
By Family Status and Sex and Color of Head
(Numbers in thousands)

Family status	All households					With male head					With female head				
	Total	Poor		Near poor		Total	Poor		Near poor		Total	Poor		Near poor	
		Number	Per-cent	Number	Per-cent		Number	Per-cent	Number	Per-cent		Number	Per-cent	Number	Per-cent
Total persons	193,415	29,657	15.3	15,150	7.8	168,536	18,952	11.2	13,031	7.7	24,878	10,704	43.0	2,119	8.5
In families	181,048	24,836	13.7	14,369	7.9	163,972	17,675	10.8	12,750	7.8	17,075	7,160	41.9	1,619	9.5
Head	49,922	6,086	12.4	3,554	7.3	43,750	4,276	9.8	3,061	7.0	5,171	1,810	35.0	492	9.5
Children under age 18	69,771	12,539	18.0	6,637	9.5	62,521	8,117	13.0	5,932	9.5	7,251	4,423	61.0	705	9.7
Other family members	62,355	6,211	10.0	4,178	6.7	57,701	5,282	9.2	3,757	6.5	4,653	927	19.9	422	9.1
Unrelated individuals	12,367	4,821	39.0	781	6.3	4,564	1,277	28.0	281	6.2	7,803	3,544	45.4	500	6.4
Under age 65	7,489	2,124	28.4	312	4.2	3,279	712	21.7	146	4.5	4,210	1,412	33.5	166	3.9
Aged 65 and over	4,878	2,697	55.3	469	9.6	1,285	565	44.0	135	10.5	3,593	2,132	59.3	334	9.3

White households

Total persons	170,384	20,313	11.9	12,278	7.2	151,265	13,417	8.9	10,651	7.0	19,120	6,896	36.1	1,627	8.5
In families	159,598	16,287	10.2	11,601	7.3	147,445	12,410	8.4	10,427	7.1	12,154	3,877	31.9	1,174	9.7
Head	44,016	4,375	9.9	2,968	6.7	40,006	3,264	8.2	2,586	6.5	4,010	1,111	27.7	382	9.5
Children under age 18	59,578	7,526	12.6	5,222	8.8	55,103	5,280	9.6	4,732	8.6	4,475	2,246	50.2	492	11.0
Other family members	56,004	4,386	7.8	3,411	6.1	52,336	3,866	7.4	3,109	5.9	3,669	521	14.2	300	8.2
Unrelated individuals	10,786	4,026	37.3	677	6.3	3,820	1,007	26.4	224	5.9	6,966	3,019	43.3	453	6.5
Under age 65	6,296	1,626	25.8	241	3.8	2,688	540	20.1	110	4.1	3,608	1,086	30.1	131	3.6
Aged 65 and over	4,490	2,400	53.5	436	9.7	1,132	467	41.3	114	10.1	3,358	1,933	57.6	322	9.6

Nonwhite households

Total persons	23,034	9,345	40.6	2,873	12.5	17,271	5,535	32.0	2,381	13.8	5,761	3,809	66.1	492	8.5
In families	21,450	8,549	39.9	2,768	12.9	16,527	5,265	31.9	2,323	14.1	4,921	3,283	66.7	445	9.0
Head	4,905	1,711	34.9	586	11.9	3,744	1,012	27.0	476	12.7	1,161	699	60.2	111	9.6
Children under age 18	10,193	5,014	49.2	1,413	13.9	7,419	2,837	38.2	1,201	16.2	2,776	2,177	78.4	213	7.7
Other family members	6,352	1,824	28.7	769	12.1	5,364	1,416	26.4	646	12.0	984	407	41.4	121	12.3
Unrelated individuals	1,584	796	50.3	105	6.6	744	270	36.3	58	7.8	840	526	62.6	47	5.6
Under age 65	1,196	499	41.7	72	6.0	592	172	29.1	37	6.3	604	327	54.1	35	5.8
Aged 65 and over	388	297	76.5	33	8.5	152	98	64.5	21	13.8	236	199	84.3	12	5.1

Source: Derived by the Social Security Administration from special tabulations by the Bureau of the Census from the Current Population Survey for March 1967.

TABLE 2

The Poor and Near Poor, 1966: Number and Percent of Persons in Households
Below SSA Poverty Level and Above that Level But Below Low-Income Level,
By Family Status and Sex of Head
(Numbers in thousands)

Age and family status	All households					With male head					With female head				
	Total	Poor Number	Per-cent	Near poor Number	Per-cent	Total	Poor Number	Per-cent	Near poor Number	Per-cent	Total	Poor Number	Per-cent	Near poor Number	Per-cent
Total persons	193,415	29,657	15.3	15,150	7.8	168,536	18,952	11.2	13,031	7.7	24,878	10,704	43.0	2,119	8.5
Living alone[1]															
Aged 14-21	12,367	4,821	39.0	781	6.3	4,564	1,277	28.0	281	6.2	7,803	3,544	45.4	500	6.4
Aged 22-64	690	378	54.8	43	6.2	280	141	50.4	27	9.6	409	237	57.9	16	3.9
Aged 65 and over	6,799	1,746	25.7	269	3.9	2,999	571	19.0	119	4.0	3,801	1,175	30.9	150	3.9
	4,878	2,697	55.3	469	9.6	1,285	565	44.0	135	10.5	3,593	2,132	59.3	334	9.3
In families	181,048	24,836	13.7	14,369	7.9	163,972	17,675	10.8	12,750	7.8	17,075	7,160	41.9	1,619	9.5
Children under age 18	69,771	12,539	18.0	6,637	9.5	62,522	8,117	13.0	5,931	9.5	7,251	4,423	61.0	706	9.7
Own children of head or spouse	66,319	11,307	17.0	6,258	9.4	60,183	7,472	12.4	5,652	9.4	6,137	3,835	62.5	605	9.9
Other related children	3,452	1,232	35.7	379	11.0	2,339	645	27.6	279	11.9	1,114	588	52.8	101	9.1
Under age 6	23,550	4,386	18.6	2,360	10.0	21,534	2,964	13.8	2,196	10.2	2,018	1,423	70.5	164	8.1
Aged 6-13	32,303	5,904	18.3	3,167	9.8	28,816	3,767	13.1	2,829	9.8	3,487	2,140	61.4	338	9.7
Aged 14-17	13,918	2,249	16.2	1,110	8.0	12,172	1,389	11.4	906	7.4	1,746	860	49.3	204	11.7
Aged 18-54[2]	83,502	7,968	9.5	5,081	6.1	76,749	5,855	7.6	4,484	5.8	6,751	2,112	31.3	594	8.8
Head	34,304	3,748	10.9	2,177	6.3	31,043	2,337	7.5	1,877	6.0	3,260	1,411	43.3	299	9.2
Wife	33,202	2,549	7.7	1,990	6.0	33,202	2,549	7.7	1,990	6.0	—	—	—	—	—

Never-married children aged 18-21	8,238	818	9.9	454	5.5	7,052	503	7.1	334	4.7	1,185	314	26.5	120	10.1
Other relatives	7,758	853	11.0	460	5.9	5,452	466	8.5	283	5.2	2,306	387	16.8	175	7.6
Aged 55-64	14,716	1,653	11.2	854	5.8	13,487	1,403	10.4	762	5.6	1,230	251	20.4	92	7.5
Head	7,689	800	10.4	381	5.0	6,900	635	9.2	329	4.8	790	166	21.0	52	6.6
Wife	5,803	685	11.3	386	6.7	5,803	685	11.8	386	6.7	—	—	—	—	—
Other relatives	1,224	168	13.3	87	7.1	784	83	10.6	47	6.0	440	85	19.3	40	9.1
Aged 65 and over	13,059	2,675	20.5	1,798	13.8	11,215	2,300	20.5	1,572	14.0	1,844	375	20.3	227	12.3
Head	6,929	1,538	22.2	996	14.4	5,806	1,304	22.5	855	14.7	1,122	234	20.9	141	12.6
Wife	3,548	835	23.5	594	16.7	3,548	835	23.5	594	16.7	—	—	—	—	—
Other relatives	2,582	302	11.7	208	8.1	1,861	161	8.7	123	6.6	722	141	19.5	86	11.9
Poor by own income	2,007	292	14.5	—	—	1,448	157	10.8	—	—	559	135	24.2	—	—
Not poor by own income[3]	573	10	1.7	—	—	412	4	1.0	—	—	163	6	3.7	—	—

[1]Excludes children under age 14 who live with a family to no member of which they are related. Income normally not reported for persons under 14.

[2]Includes heads, wives, and other ever-married relatives under age 18.

[3]An additional 100,000 of those not poor nevertheless had income below the near poor level. Thus the total number of aged other relatives with own income below the near poor level was 2.1 million; only 0.5 million lived in a poor or near poor family.

Source: Derived by the Social Security Administration from special tabulations by the Bureau of the Census from the Current Population Survey for March 1967.

TABLE 3

1966 Income of Families: Percentage Distribution of Poor and Nonpoor Families
By Amount of Income, by Sex of Head and Number of Children Under Age 18

Income	Total families	With no children	With children						
			Total	1 child	2 children	3 children	4 children	5 children	6 or more
Number (in thousands)	48,923	20,327	28,598	9,082	8,492	5,416	2,922	1,397	1,287
Total percent	100.0	100.0	100.0	100.0	100.0	100.0	100.0	100.0	100.0
			All families						
Under $1,000	2.3	2.4	2.3	.5	2.3	1.7	2.1	2.6	2.6
$1,000-1,499	2.3	3.2	1.6	2.0	1.4	1.2	1.0	2.1	2.5
$1,500-1,999	3.1	4.9	1.8	2.3	1.5	1.6	1.6	1.8	2.7
$2,000-2,499	3.4	4.9	2.3	2.4	2.0	2.1	2.1	2.4	5.9
$2,500-2,999	3.2	4.5	2.2	2.0	2.0	2.2	2.5	2.5	4.0
$3,000-3,499	3.5	4.3	3.0	3.0	2.4	2.6	3.5	3.7	5.9
$3,500-3,999	3.3	3.9	2.9	3.2	2.4	2.5	2.7	2.9	5.8
$4,000-4,999	7.1	7.5	6.8	6.8	6.0	6.0	7.8	8.4	11.1
$5,000-5,999	8.4	8.4	8.4	8.5	8.0	8.2	9.7	7.5	9.3
$6,000-6,999	9.4	8.0	10.3	9.3	11.2	10.1	10.2	12.0	11.0
$7,000-7,999	9.3	7.6	10.5	10.4	11.4	10.7	9.2	8.8	8.8
$8,000-8,999	8.1	6.9	9.0	8.7	9.2	9.5	9.2	9.0	7.1
$9,000-9,999	7.0	5.6	8.0	7.4	8.7	9.0	7.8	8.4	4.4
$10,000-11,999	11.2	9.7	12.3	12.3	12.3	13.7	12.1	11.3	8.1
$12,000-14,999	9.2	8.9	9.5	9.9	9.8	9.3	9.5	8.7	5.4
$15,000-24,999	7.5	7.3	7.6	7.9	7.9	7.6	7.2	7.0	3.8
$25,000 and over	1.7	1.9	1.6	1.4	1.4	2.0	1.9	1.0	1.7
Median income	$7,436	$6,740	$7,803	$7,776	$7,945	$8,108	$7,750	$7,467	$6,014

All poor families[1]

Number (in thousands)	6,086	2,206	3,880	844	869	695	544	390	541
Total percent	100.0	100.0	100.0	100.0	100.0	100.0	100.0	100.0	100.0
Under $1,000	18.9	22.7	16.7	26.7	22.3	13.6	11.4	9.6	6.1
$1,000-1,499	18.3	29.6	11.9	21.7	14.1	9.7	5.1	7.5	5.9
$1,500-1,999	22.5	38.7	13.4	24.1	14.3	12.3	8.6	6.5	6.5
$2,000-2,499	12.7	7.6	15.6	18.9	19.1	16.3	11.0	8.5	14.0
$2,500-2,999	7.8	1.1	11.6	5.6	14.7	16.5	13.6	9.0	9.6
$3,000-3,499	7.7	.4	11.9	2.1	12.2	16.7	17.6	13.2	14.0
$3,500-3,999	4.5	0	7.1	.2	2.0	12.1	11.9	9.8	12.9
$4,000-4,999	5.8	0	9.0	.2	1.1	2.0	17.1	25.1	24.4
$5,000 and over	1.8	0	2.8	.4	.1	.9	3.7	10.9	6.5
Median income	$1,784	$1,461	$2,257	$1,533	$1,976	$2,445	$3,005	$3,338	$3,283

All nonpoor families

Number (in thousands)	42,835	18,121	24,710	8,239	7,620	4,723	2,379	1,008	744
Total percent	100.0	100.0	100.0	100.0	100.0	100.0	100.0	100.0	100.0
Under $1,000	0	0	0	0	0	0	0	0	0
$1,000-1,499	0	0	0	0	0	0	0	0	0
$1,500-1,999	.3	.8	0	0	0	0	0	0	0
$2,000-2,499	2.0	4.5	.2	.7	0	0	0	0	0
$2,500-2,999	2.5	4.9	.7	1.7	.5	.1	0	0	0
$3,000-3,499	2.9	4.8	1.5	3.1	1.2	.6	.2	0	0
$3,500-3,999	3.1	4.4	2.2	3.5	2.5	1.1	.5	.3	.5
$4,000-4,999	7.3	8.5	6.4	7.5	6.6	6.5	5.7	2.0	1.5
$5,000-5,999	9.3	9.4	9.3	9.3	8.9	9.3	11.1	6.3	11.3
$6,000-6,999	10.7	9.0	11.9	10.3	12.5	11.6	12.5	16.6	18.9
$7,000-7,999	10.6	8.5	12.1	11.4	12.7	12.3	11.3	12.2	15.2
$8,000-8,999	9.3	7.8	10.4	9.6	10.2	10.9	11.3	12.5	12.2
$9,000-9,999	8.0	6.3	9.3	8.1	9.7	10.3	9.6	11.6	7.5
$10,000-11,999	12.8	10.9	14.2	13.6	13.7	15.7	14.9	15.6	14.0
$12,000-14,999	10.5	10.0	10.9	11.0	10.9	10.6	11.7	12.0	9.4
$15,000-24,999	8.5	8.2	8.8	8.8	8.8	8.7	8.8	9.6	6.6
$25,000 and over	2.0	2.1	1.8	1.6	1.6	2.4	2.3	1.4	3.0
Median income	$8,122	$7,441	$8,524	$8,269	$8,486	$8,782	$8,760	$9,017	$8,214

[1]Families with 1966 income below SSA poverty level.

Problems in the Definition and Measurement of Poverty

Martin Rein

Bryn Mawr College School of Social Work

[Paper for the International Seminar on Poverty, University of Essex, April 3-6, 1967.]

THE PROBLEMS of how to define and measure poverty cannot proceed until we clarify the conception of poverty we wish to employ. Three broad concepts of poverty can be identified. Poverty may be regarded as subsistence, inequality or externality. *Subsistence* is concerned with the minimum of provision needed to maintain health and working capacity. Its terms of reference are the capacity to survive and to maintain physical efficiency. *Inequality* is concerned with the relative position of income groups to each other. Poverty cannot be understood by isolating the poor and treating them as a special group. Society is seen as a series of stratified income layers and poverty is concerned with how the bottom layers fare relative to the rest of society. Hence, the concept of poverty must be seen in the context of society as a whole. The study of the poor then depends on an understanding of the level of living of the rich, since it is these conditions relative to each other that are critical in the conception of inequality. To understand the poor we must then study the affluent. *Externality* is concerned with the social consequences of poverty for the rest of society rather than in terms of the needs of the poor. The poverty line should serve "as an index of the disutility to the community of the persistence of poverty."[1]

People must not be allowed to become so poor that they offend or are hurtful to society. It is not so much the misery and plight of the poor but the discomfort and cost to the community which is crucial to this view of poverty. We have a problem of poverty to the extent that low income creates problems for those who are now poor. Poverty then is social problems which are correlated with low income. Hence only when income-conditioned problems are randomized can poverty be eliminated. To improve the level of living of the poor without reducing disutility to the rest of community, is insufficient.

---

[1]Eugene Smolensky, "Investment in the Education of the Poor: A Pessimistic Report," *American Economic Review*, Supplement LV, May 1966.

Each of these concepts presents numerous problems of definition and measurement. Should we define poverty only in terms of
economic insufficiency, economic inequality and economic disecono-
my, or should the definition be broadened to embrace non-economic
variables such as prestige, power and social services? For example,
Titmuss has insisted that "we cannot . . . delineate the new frontiers of
poverty unless we take account of the changing agents and characteristics of inequality."[2] Although the concept of poverty Titmuss holds
is that of inequality, he is posing the broader question that poverty is
more than the lack of income.

When a more encompassing view of poverty is accepted which
extends beyond the distribution of income, two critical issues emerge—
where to establish the cut-off points which separate the poor from the
non-poor, and which non-economic conditions should be taken into
account.

Paradoxically, we measure poverty in subsistence terms, but
the programs and policies we have evolved to reduce poverty in
America are based on a broader conception of the dimensions of
well-being for which no systematic statistical information is available.
These include the lack of accepted minima, or inequalities in the
distribution of power, education, and legal justice. These dimensions
of the level of living are not included in the goods and services
which make up a minimum personal market basket, on which the
measurement of poverty is based, because these items cannot be purchased by the individual with low income in the market. However,
little organized effort has been directed at conceptualizing and measuring a conception of poverty which is more closely related to the
programs we have developed, or at developing a program to reduce
poverty (cash transfers) which is more closely tied to the concept of
poverty we employ—the lack of minimum income for subsistence.

However, a small body of literature is being developed which
does attempt to spell out the non-economic dimensions of poverty.
Townsend, influenced by Titmuss, defines poverty as inequities in the
distribution of seven resources,[3] including income, capital assets,
occupational fringe benefits, current public services, and current private services, occupational and living environment and facilities. A

---

[2]Richard Titmuss, *Income Distribution and Social Change,* London,
George Allen and Unwin Ltd., 1962, p. 187.

[3]Peter Townsend, "Measures and Explanations of Poverty in High
Income and Low Income Countries: The Problems of Operationalizing the
Concepts of Development, Class and Poverty," a paper presented at the Interna-
tional Seminar on Poverty, University of Essex, April 3-6, 1967.

national study of poverty in England based on an empirical investigation of the distribution of these items is now being undertaken by Townsend and Abel-Smith. Miller and Rein, also influenced by Titmuss, have drawn up a somewhat different list of items which, in being more responsive to the American context, pays attention to the political, legal and educational components of well-being.[4]

But broadening the definition only confounds the problem of where to draw the cut-off points which distinguish those in poverty from the rest of the population. For a solution to this dilemma we return again to relative, absolute, and disutility conceptions of poverty. Are we interested in establishing standards which will enable us to define minimum powers, social honor, environmental health, and justice? Our search for such standards is illusory and no viable definition can be found which does not depend on inequalities in the distribution of these resources which comprise our level of living. Grigsby and Baratz suggest that the cut-off points may be established at that point or region where the relationship between income and social and personal problems is statistically randomized.[5] This formulation of where to establish the division between poor and non-poor draws on the externality conception of poverty, for it is concerned with the consequences of being poor or with the bottom of an income distribution.

The extensive reliance by governmental bodies such as the Office of Economic Opportunity and the Council of Economic Advisors on estimates of poverty which are based upon data concerning the cost of subsistence in the United States suggests that we have what is in effect an official American definition of poverty. As such, it deserves the closest scrutiny. This paper examines some of the problems inherent in the current "official" definition of poverty. Some attempt is made to place the analysis in a historical context, although no systematic historical review is attempted.

A Subsistence Definition of Poverty

A definition of poverty in terms of subsistence levels of living has had wide acceptance because it seems to accord with common sense and appears to be divorced from personal values of either harshness or compassion. It seeks to describe poverty objectively as lack of the

---

[4]S. M. Miller, Martin Rein, et al, "Poverty, Inequality and Conflict," *The Annals*, September 1967.

[5]William Grigsby and Merton Baratz, with Martin Rein, "Conceptualization and Measurement of Poverty," mimeo.

income needed to acquire the minimum necessities of life. Those who lack the necessities to sustain life are by definition poor. But how should "minimum" be defined? Agreement on the meaning of minimum is crucial to the development of standards which will permit the establishment of a dividing line separating the poor from the non-poor. Much of the history of the study of poverty can be understood as an effort to establish a non-subjective or "scientific" poverty line, the standard for which was equated with subsistence—the amount needed to sustain life. But like the search for the philosopher's stone, the efforts to discover an absolute and value-free definition of poverty based on the concept of subsistence proved abortive.

Rowntree was the first investigator to attempt a rigorous definition of poverty in subsistence terms (13). In his classic study of poverty in the city of York, he wrote:

> My primary poverty line represented the minimum sum on which physical efficiency could be maintained. It was a standard of bare subsistence rather than living. In calculating it the utmost economy was practised ... "A family living upon the scale allowed for in this estimate must ... be governed by the regulation, 'Nothing must be bought but that which is absolutely necessary for the maintenance of physical health, and what is bought must be of the plainest and most economical description'". (13, pp. 102-3)

Thus, a standard of bare subsistence could be supported if all human passions for frivolity, the relief of monotony, and even irresponsibility were ruthlessly suppressed. Only expenditures which provided physical health were permissible. The failure or the incapacity to conduct one's daily affairs according to these severe regulations brought the family into a state of secondary poverty. Secondary poverty existed when income was adequate to maintain a subsistence level, but the family failed to spend its income to purchase the necessities to sustain life and health. According to Rowntree, a defect of moral character or native intelligence, rather than an insufficiency of resources, distinguishes primary from secondary poverty. For his definition of "the minimum necessaries for the maintenance of mere physical efficiency," Rowntree drew upon the research of the American nutritionist, Atwater, who had devised a minimum diet based on research undertaken on American convicts. Atwater had estimated minimum caloric intake per day by determining the amount of food which was required to prevent prisoners from either gaining or losing weight. Estimating variations for men and women and determining the market value of the food which satisfied these minimum requirements, Rowntree arrived at a low-cost food plan which served as the basis for his definition of poverty (16, pp. 215 ff).

Present procedures for estimating minimum nutritional requirements have progressed beyond these primitive beginnings, but they
still depend on a judgment of nutritional need which takes into
account both actual consumption patterns and a definition of minimum caloric intake based on an independent assessment of nutritional
adequacy. The basic technique is operationalized in the U.S. Department of Agriculture's economy food plan which forms the basis for
several subsistence estimates of poverty. But the minimum amount of
money needed to achieve minimum nutritional standards tells us
nothing about the cost of clothing, shelter, and other items necessary
to maintain life. Some means of converting expenditure for food into
total expenditures is needed. Engel had observed in 1857 that there
was an inverse relationship between income and the percentage of
total expenditure spent for food. By examining the proportion of the
family budget spent for food in various income classes an Engel
coefficient[6] can be computed, which, when multiplied by food expenditure, provides an estimate of the total minimum budget required to
keep a family out of poverty.[7]

An alternative to an aggregate estimate of all non-food expenditures through the use of the Engel coefficient is the development of
an itemized budget for each consumption item necessary for subsistence—shelter, medical care, clothing, etc. This procedure assumes
that minimum requirements can be specified for each item and that
these can serve as cut-off points separating adequate consumption
from inadequate. To illustrate the procedure, we can consider how
minimum clothing needs may be defined.

During the 1930's, Dorothy Brady devised an imaginative
scheme based on the principle of income elasticity of demand where-
by the number of units of clothing purchased, rather than total
expenditures, was crucial. As income rises, a family reaches a critical
point where the number of additional units purchased declines and
the price paid per unit increases. That point is defined as the clothing
poverty line. For each consumption item a cut-off point which represents some combination of utilization pattern and arbitrary standard
of adequacy can be similarly determined, and the collection of points
becomes the basis for drawing a poverty line. In the case of clothing,

---

[6]For a discussion of Engel Coefficient, see (3).

[7]The Relationship can be expressed by the following equation: $C=ME$
where C is equal the cost of total consumption of a household, M equals
expenditures for a minimum food basket, and E equals the size of the Engel
coefficient. See (15).

with increased affluence the elasticity threshold is reached at a comparatively low income and thus is increasingly less useful in differentiating the poor from the non-poor, but the concept still has considerable merit.

As we might expect, there have been many attempts to define the minimum subsistence basket with reference not only to food essentials, but other necessities as well. Some of the earliest attempts to estimate minimum living costs, such as the studies undertaken by the Factory Investigating Commission of New York State in 1915, were based on estimates of the amount of money needed to achieve both an adequate diet and sanitary housing (5).[8] It proved very difficult, however, to establish rigorous standards of adequacy for any of the essentials of living except food. J. Murray Luck, analyzing the definition of poverty after World War II, put the matter as follows:

> The wants to be considered here are the recognized biological necessities—food and drink. Little will be said about housing. The need for shelter varies according to locale and to social custom: it cannot be accurately measured. Fuel is essential for survival in a cold environment, but this too is a regional and variable necessity. A similar consideration applies to clothing. The conventional biological definition of a necessity . . . excludes, except for reproduction, almost everything except food and water. (7, p. 15)

More recently, Orshansky has noted that "there is no generally acceptable standard of adequacy for essentials of living except food" (12, p. 5). Actually, as will be demonstrated below, even in the estimates of minimum food requirements, accepted standards are lacking. This fact raises a serious question as to the usefulness of any attempt to measure an absolute standard of adequacy which the term subsistence implies.

A Definition of Poverty Based on Nutritional Adequacy

Poverty is defined by the Social Security Administration (SSA) as nutritional inadequacy. This definition clearly implies some standard for determining the minimum cost of an adequate diet. During the depression the National Research Council undertook intensive work in developing a recommended dietary allowance which served as a basis for defining minimal nutritional requirements for calories and essential nutrients. All foods were sorted into eleven categories on the basis

---

[8]These studies grew out of an interest in determining how to estimate minimum wage requirements.

of the nutrients they contained. An estimate was then made of the quantities of food needed in each of these food groups, by individuals of different age and sex. As it turned out, if the recommended quantities of food were purchased in the most economical way and without regard to dietary habits, the cost of the food plan would be extremely low. Stigler, for example, estimated that if the minimum number of calories were purchased in the cheapest bulk market basket, the total cost to purchase the food needed for an adequate diet would come to about $40 per year in 1944 (14 p. 311 ff.). Even allowing for a tripling of prices since that date, the present cost would come to less than $120 per annum. Unfortunately, as Stigler sought to demonstrate by this calculation, persons in American society simply do not consume the lowest-cost food items. Thus, a realistic definition of poverty requires that attention be given to actual consumption patterns. "Even with food", Orshansky acknowledges, "social conscience and custom dictate that there be not only sufficient quantity but sufficient variety to meet recommended nutritional goals and conform to customary eating patterns. Calories alone will not be enough" (12). Yet food alone provides the best basis for measuring minimum requirements; however, the definition must therefore be based on both customary behavior and expert definition of nutritional adequacy.

Reflecting this fact, a household food consumption survey undertaken by the U.S. Department of Agriculture was divided into four levels of cost: economy, low, moderate, and liberal. The cost of a standard family food plan is developed at each of these levels. If, however, only prevailing consumption patterns were taken as a standard, without attention to an independent definition of adequacy, there would be no objective way of establishing a cut-off point which distinguishes an adequate from an inadequate diet. When the food plan was developed for each income group, therefore, it was based on expert judgment regarding an acceptable tradeoff between nutritional standards and consumption patterns (12, p. 5).

The SSA procedure for measuring poverty is based on the cost of USDA's "economy" food plan, which is adapted to the pattern of food expenditures of those in the lowest third of the income range. It is designed for "temporary or emergency use when funds are low" and costs about 75-80 percent of the low-cost plan (12, p. 6). It was adopted in about 1960 when a food plan was needed which was consistent with actual food budgets already developed for families receiving public assistance. The existing standards of welfare assistance served to define the food consumption needs of the poor.

In estimating costs, the Department of Agriculture assumed

that housewives make average choices within each food group and average prices are paid for each food item in the basket. Each year these average prices are adjusted for changes in the price level. It is further assumed that all family members under the plan prepare all of their food at home, including lunches which they may eat at work.

To determine the minimum total income requirements for a family an Engel coefficient is needed. A Department of Agriculture survey conducted in 1955 was used to determine the proportion of total family income among low-income family units that was spent for food (19). Actually, three different coefficients were used: 0.27 for two-person families; 0.33 for families of 3 or more; and for unattached individuals, a special estimate based on approximately 80 percent of the total requirements of a two-person family. The last is based on the assumption that when income is low, the cost of living for a single person is only slightly less than for a couple.

The SSA procedure for defining and measuring poverty is especially vulnerable to the criticism that when a choice among alternative estimating procedures was necessary the rationale for selection was arbitrary, but not necessarily unreasoned. The extent and character of this arbitrariness will be examined in four substantive areas: the size of the Engel coefficient; the diversity of nutritional need; the disparity between actual consumption patterns and expert judgment as to the ingredients of an adequate diet, and the insistence on an economical market basket.

The Size of the Engel Coefficient

The size of the Engel coefficient obviously affects estimates of the extent of poverty. However, an Engel coefficient is not used by the SSA to determine minimum budget requirements for persons living alone. The requirements of an unattached individual living alone are estimated indirectly as a proportion of the expenditures for a couple. The explanation offered is that "the consumption data are hard to interpret because of the heavy representation of aged individuals not shown separately" (12, p. 9). Although this procedure seems reasonable, there appears to be no firm evidence on which to estimate the needs of one aged person as a proportion of the needs of an aged couple. In an early report Orshansky notes that, "pending further research, the relationship of the cost of living for a single individual to that of a couple must remain something everyone talks about but about which little is known" (11, p. 31). The deficiency is serious, because, as Orshansky explains, the correction for single-person households is "by far the most important adjustment" (11, p. 28) which is necessary in making an estimate of the budgetary needs of the elderly persons. The extent of poverty among the aged could drop, perhaps sharply, if an estimate of 60 or 70 percent were used, instead of 80 percent (11, pp. 11-13).

If we consider the size of the coefficient used, even more serious objections can be raised to the procedures followed by SSA. As has been said, the lower the coefficient, the larger the number of impoverished. In estimating the income-food-expenditure relationship Orshansky had available two surveys, the Department of Agriculture consumption survey of 1955 (19), and a 1960-61 Bureau of Labor Statistics survey of urban families (18).

The BLS survey found that about 25 percent of the income of all families regardless of size goes for food, whereas the Agriculture survey found substantial variations by family size and an average expenditure for food of 33 percent for families with two or more members. The BLS data are based on interviewer estimates of annual outlays for food, while the Department of Agriculture figures are derived from a detailed checklist of foods consumed during the week in which the survey was held. The Social Security Administration used the Agriculture study. Haber criticizes this choice.

> It was suggested (by Orshansky) that the BLS study tended to understate food expenditures; but this would affect ratio figures only if it also tended to overstate or not similarly understate other expenditures. This was not demonstrated and since the study collected data on expenditures in all categories, not just food, there would seem to be an internal check on the relative figures. Furthermore, comparison of 1950 to 1960-61 BLS studies reflected a decline of 5.6 percent in the ratio within the same methodology. The earlier USDA figure is almost certain to be overstated. (2, p. 6)

Recalculating the poverty cut-off point with a coefficient of .30 rather than .33 for a four-person urban family and taking into account gross income rather than income after taxes, Haber arrives at a $3,474 poverty line "for the deceptive economy plan and a truer $4,263 for the low-cost plan," compared with a $3,130 line using Agriculture data (2, p. 7).

Rose Friedman also criticizes the "official" definition of poverty but on different grounds. Using estimates based on actual consumption and a higher Engel coefficient, she is able to cut the poverty population in half.

> The nutritive adequacy definition of poverty . . . gives an income of $2,200 as the poverty line for a nonfarm family of four. The cost of food implied by the $3,000 income for a family of four . . . is $5.00

per person per week. The amount actually spent for food, on the average, by a family of four with an income of $2,200 was over $6.00 per person per week, because the fraction of income spent on food at this level was about 60 percent and not 33 percent.

It should be emphasized that the difference between the Council's estimate that 20 percent of families were poor . . . and my estimate that 10 percent were poor results neither from a different basic criterion of poverty nor from the use of different data. Both use nutrition to separate the poor from the not-poor; both use the same standard of nutritive-adequacy; both use the same statistical data. (1, p. 35)

It is interesting to speculate on how political realities affect technical decisions. The first working definition of poverty used by the Council of Economic Advisors established the extent of American poverty at about 34 million persons, or roughly one-fifth of the population. More refined estimates, if they were to be politically acceptable, had to be consistent with CEA's estimate of the size of the problem. It was all right for a new definition to change the character of poverty, but not its size. As a consequence, technical decisions regarding definition of income or the size of the Engel coefficient or the choice of a survey on food consumption, all of which can significantly alter the estimated extent of poverty, have come to reflect not only our understanding of the meaning of subsistence but also the political views and realities which provide the framework for professional judgments.

What is important in all these controversies is not who is right and who is wrong but that even where presumably objective measures are available, the selection of minimum standards is of necessity arbitrary. This point is expanded upon in the following section.

The Diversity of Nutritional Need

Another example of abitrariness concerns the adjustments which are made for differential nutritional needs based on age and sex groupings, but not upon the level of activity. Adequate caloric intake comes to about 3,000 calories a day for a male age 18 to 64, while a child under ten requires 1,200 to 1,800 calories. However, the level of physical activity appears to be as important as age. A farmer, for example, may require as many as 4,500 calories.[9 and 10]

> Physical fitness is not a precisely definable condition. One has first to ask fitness for what? A bank clerk in the best of health might be

---

[9 and 10]These caloric estimates are discussed in (7, p. 15 ff.).

unfit to work on a trolley or in a coal mine. A woman able to bear two or three children without endangering her health might well prove unfit for the demands of motherhood in a society where families of seven or eight children were the rule. Secondly, standards of physical fitness vary over time, as well as between country and country . . . class and class. (8, pp 9-10)

Townsend estimates that when sedentary and manual occupations are compared, the number of calories needed per hour may differ from 30 to as much as 450. Since age and sex are taken into account in estimating minimal caloric need, one would think that the level of physical activity would be regarded as equally important, the more so because the poor are more likely than the non-poor to be employed in manual and unskilled jobs requiring physical exertion.

Townsend is sharply critical not only of the neglect of activity levels, but also of other factors involved in nutritional standards. In expressing his criticism, he offers an analysis of the formidable barriers to scientifically determined subsistence diets.

> There are real difficulties in estimating nutritional needs. The nutritionist has not subtly broken up the different needs of individuals; they have made overall estimates. These estimates are not even based on studies of the intake of persons in different occupations. Beyond a certain minimum (somewhere, perhaps, between 1,000 and 1,500 calories), the number of calories a man needs . . . depends upon the society in which he lives. Even his dietary needs depend upon climate, the kind of housing he lives in, the kind of job he has, and the kind of leisure activities he follows. In other words, estimates of need, even nutritional needs, cannot be absolute; they must be relative to the kind of society in which a man is living. (17, p. 15)

The estimates of caloric requirements at one time did take into account level of activity, but nutritionists have dropped this variable, perhaps because they were not primarily concerned with the problem of poverty. Caloric estimates lack the scientific rigor which is claimed for them, for they depend on global and aggregate judgments which underestimate the diversity of human need. But endless refinement of details is not the appropriate answer to the problem, the standards which emerge will become so complex and detailed as to add new dimensions of unreality. Moreover, there is no way of defining minimum levels of activity for work and leisure, even though caloric needs depend on energy spent.

These criticisms of estimates of caloric levels may seem somewhat overdrawn, since caloric requirements alone can be met quite cheaply. It is achieving a balance of vitamins, minerals, and other nutrients that is most problematic for the poor. Further, disagreements over minimum caloric requirements are not nearly so important as disagreements over what constitutes an adequate diet generally and whether minor deviations from prescribed diets affect performance—the capacity to learn and work. Still further, it is doubtful whether getting more refined estimates would affect the numbers of those in poverty to the same extent as does a change in the estimate of the size of the Engel coefficient. On the other hand, the issue of level of physical activity does highlight value problems by undermining the nutritionist claim for objectivity and by dramatizing the difficulties of measurement.

The Disparity Between Actual Behavior and Expert Judgment

An examination of actual consumption patterns reveals great variation among low-income families. On the average, families in the $2,999 income group in 1958 were spending more for food per person than the low-cost food plan of the Department of Agriculture calls for, but equally interesting was the fact that 28 percent of families were spending less than the amount suggested. Some of this spread is due simply to regional variations. In 1959, for example, the United States average weekly food consumption for a family consisting of a mother, father, and two children under age twelve was $24.00, but expenditures ranged from $19.80 in the South to $26.50 in the Northeast, a difference of 35 percent. (6, p. 5)[11]

There were also wide variations in expenditures by the aged. Orshansky estimates that there was a 20 percent spread in cost of living for the aged in the 20 largest cities and suburbs of the United States, ranging from $2,641 in Houston to $3,366 in Chicago. How these variations in the cost of living affect the cost of the low-cost food plan is by no means clear. On one hand, it is plausible to argue that at subsistence levels there is much less room for significant variations in actual budgets, and there is therefore little variability in actual expenditures. On the other hand, there are wide variations in actual expenditures for the income group which is expected to follow the low-cost food plan. If we consider one item—consumption of food at home—

---

[11]What is often overlooked is that migration between regions seems to affect food costs, because food consumption patterns are not instantly abandoned. A report on nutrition of Negroes states, "The food habits of Southern Negroes in the North . . . appear to be particularly erratic, with a substantial amount of money being spent to acquire Southern food which has a very limited nutritional value, such as fat-back and grits" (8, p. 163).

the range of expenditures seems to be impressively large, from $711 for an elderly couple in Houston to $900 in Boston.

These variations raise questions about the use of a single food plan to estimate poverty. Another reason for skepticism has to do with the fact that the economy food and low-cost plans assume an efficient housekeeper who secures an adequate diet for the family within the cost of the plan. This seems unlikely, partly because the low-income housewife is likely to be a less informed consumer and partly because the quality of the food she purchases may be inferior and higher priced in comparison with food purchased by higher-income shoppers. A recent study by the Bureau of Labor Statistics concluded that the poor pay more for food than consumers in higher-income areas, but that food stores do not charge more in low-income areas (10, p. 56). It is not that the poor are overcharged, but that they cannot exploit the economics of bulk purchase. For example, the poor tend to buy flour in two-pound rather than five-pound sacks, even though "the price for flour ranged from 14 percent a pound higher in New York to 35 percent higher in Chicago when purchased in two-pound sacks." Similar differentials hold for milk, sugar, and other food items (10, p. 56).[12]

In light of the above, it is not surprising to learn that many persons who have resources sufficient to live only at the level prescribed by the economy or low-cost food plan will also fail to meet a prescribed minimum diet. But to what extent should the experts be forced to revise their estimates of the cost of a minimum diet to reflect actual consumption patterns? If the budget needed to achieve minimum dietary adequacy is defined as less than what families apparently do spend to achieve this minimum, it is difficult to determine whether the experts are wrong in where they have placed the poverty line, or whether the prevailing pattern of consumption is an inappropriate criterion because the poor lack the capacity to consume. More important, to the extent that standards are based on actual consumption there is a circularity in the analysis (12, p. 8). Orshansky in a discussion with the author made a similar observation that there are no extrinsic standards for determining minimum nutritional needs.

The Economical Market Basket

The cost of the market basket of food items needed to prevent nutritional poverty is computed so that it is the most economic basket

---

[12]The study did not, however, examine why chain stores tend to stay out of low income areas.

possible. The concern for least cost is at conflict with the desire to take account of actual consumption patterns and introduces a note of unreality into the definition of the poverty line. Rowntree recognized this when he observed that "no housewife without a considerable knowledge of the nutritive value of different food-stuffs and considerable skill in cooking, would be likely to choose a menu at once so economically and so comparatively attractive as the one upon which I base my costs."[13] Orshansky makes the same observation, "the lower the level of cost, the more restricted the kinds and qualities of food must be and the more skill in marketing and food preparation is required."[14] But those in poverty clearly have the least skills in marketing, knowledge of nutrition, and resourcefulness in cooking to meet the stringent demands of economy. The failure to meet the nutritional standards set by the poverty budget is assumed to reflect the incapacity of the poor to consume, that is, secondary poverty. If the diet is to be based on actual consumption, and if it is to avoid building into its definition a confusion between primary and secondary poverty, then the standards of economy must be relaxed and a more realistic assumption of human error be accepted. The effect of this intrusion of reality into budgeting will be to raise the poverty level and increase the amount of poverty.

Summary

I have tried to demonstrate that the subsistence-level definition of poverty is arbitrary, circular, and relative. The definition of poverty based on nutritional requirements is dependent not only on expert definition but also on actual levels and patterns of living. Thus, no extrinsic standard to measure food adequacy is available and the subsistence definition of poverty is, therefore, circular. But this procedure imposes a number of arbitrary judgments which rob the nutritional approach of its claim that it is based on scientific rigor with minimum attention to value judgments. To take account of customary behavior requires that we know in advance the relevant income group which distinguishes the poor from the non-poor. Thus the procedure for measuring poverty is based on a circular argument from which it cannot retreat. The result is that those who hold different value judgments concerning how stringent or lenient the poverty standard should be, can use the same data to demonstrate that poverty is either a significant or trivial problem. All of the procedures in establishing a

---

[13]Rowntree, *Human Needs of Labour, op. cit.*, p. 112.
[14]Orshansky, *op. cit.*, p. 6.

tradeoff between consumption standards and expert judgment have an arbitrary quality which can be challenged by those who wish to see the standards of poverty defined more harshly or more leniently. On the other hand, the criterion that the budget should be *most* economical forces the expert to accept an unrealistic assumption of a no-waste budget, and extensive knowledge in marketing and cooking. An economical budget must be based on knowledge and skill which is least likely to be present in the low income groups we are concerned with. The result is that a stubborn and continuing ambiguity between primary and secondary poverty is built into the very procedures by which the minimum nutritional standard is determined. If we cannot distinguish between the capacity to consume and the adequacy of the resource base for consumption, there is no independent standard for questioning and revising expert judgment.

Almost every procedure in the subsistence-level definition of poverty can be reasonably challenged. The estimates are based on the consumption pattern of the entire low-income third instead of sub-groups of this population. The estimates of nutritional needs take age and sex into account but not physical activity. Average price and average consumption are used as the standard for constructing the low-cost food plan, rather than actual behavior. The economy food plan is an arbitrary derivative (approximately three-quarters) of the low-cost plan. We must conclude that subsistence measures of poverty cannot claim to rest solely on a technical or scientific definition of nutritional adequacy. Values, preferences, and political realities influence the definition of subsistence. Yet once a biological definition is abandoned and actual consumption is taken into account, no absolute measurement of poverty in subsistence terms is possible.[15] The other conceptions of poverty reviewed at the beginning of this paper deserve more attention and developments.

---

[15]In the light of these observations it is rather surprising to note Kolko's insistence on the validity of an absolute measure of subsistence. He asserts: "The maintenance budget is a synthesis of what families actually spend, modified to include what they must have to meet minimum health criteria. It is *not* a relative or changing standard such as that employed by 'social workers' (who) will call a person 'underprivileged' whose scale of living is considerably below the average'." Gabriel Kolko, *Wealth and Power in America* (New York: Frederick A. Prager, 1962), p. 96.

References

1. Friedman, Rose D. *Poverty: Definition and Perspective.* Washington, D.C., American Enterprise Institute for Public Policy Research, 1965.
2. Haber, Alan. "Poverty Budgets: How Much is Enough," *Poverty and Human Resources Abstracts,* I, No. 3 (1966). Ann Arbor.
3. Hobspawn, E. J. "Poverty," in *New International Encyclopedia of the Social Sciences* (forthcoming).
4. Kolko, Gabriel, *Wealth and Power in America.* New York, Frederick A. Prager, 1962.
5. Lamale, Helen H. "Changes in Concepts of Income Adequacy in the Last Century," *American Economic Review,* XLVII (May, 1958), 291-99.
6. "Low-Cost Food Plans—New Regional Estimates," Research and Statistics, No. 28, Social Security Administration, October, 1959.
7. Luck, J. Murray. *The War on Malnutrition and Poverty,* New York, Harper and Brothers, 1946.
8. Lynes, Tony. *National Assistance and National Prosperity.* Occasional Papers on Social Administration. Wellyn, Hertfordshire, England: Vedicite Press, 1962.
9. Mayer, Jean. "The Nutritional Status of American Negroes," *Nutrition Review,* XXIII, No. 6 (June, 1965).
10. *New York Times,* June 12, 1966.
11. Orshansky, Mollie. "Budget for an Elderly Couple: Interim Revision by the B.L.S.," *Social Security Bulletin,* XXIII, No. 12 (December, 1960) 20-26.
12. "Counting the Poor: Another Look at the Poverty Profile," *Social Security Bulletin,* XXVIII, No. 1 (January 1965), 3-29.
13. Rowntree, Benjamin S. *Poverty and Progress. A Second Social Survey of York.* London: Longmans, Green, 1941.
14. Stigler, George J. "The Cost of Subsistence," *Journal of Farm Economics,* XXVII (1945), 303-14.
15. Taira, Koji. *Country Report No. 6 on Japan.* International Trade Union Seminar on Low Income Groups and Methods of Dealing with their Problems, Social Affairs Division of the Organization for the Economic Co-operation and Development.
16. Townsend, Peter. "The Meaning of Poverty," *The British Journal of Sociology,* XVIII, No. 3 (September, 1962). 210-27.
17. ——. "The Scale and Meaning of Poverty in Contemporary Western Society," *Dependency and Poverty,* 1963-1964 Colloquim Series Paper, Brandeis University, July, 1965.
18. U.S. Bureau of Labor Statistics. *Consumer Expenditures and Income, Urban U.S. 1960-61.* Supplement 3-Part A to BLS Report 237-38, Table 29A, July 1964.
19. U.S. Department of Agriculture, Household Food Consumption Survey, 1955. *Dietary Evaluation of Food Used in Households in the United States.* Report No. 16, November, 1961.

Bibliography

1. Ben H. Bagdikian. *In the Midst of Plenty: A New Report on the Poor in America.* New York: Signet Books, 1964.

2. Robert H. Bremner. *From the Depths: The Discovery of Poverty in the United States.* New York University Press, 1956.

3. Wilbur J. Cohen and Eugenia Sullivan. "Poverty in the United States," *Health, Education and Welfare Indicators,* February, 1964.

4. Leo Fishman. *Poverty Amid Affluence.* New Haven: Yale University Press, 1966.

5. John Kenneth Galbraith. *The Affluent Society.* Boston: Houghton Mifflin Company, 1960.

6. Margaret S. Gordon (ed.), *Poverty in America.* San Francisco: Chandler Publishing Co., 1965.

7. Nathan Glazer. "Paradoxes of American Poverty," *Public Interest,* Fall 1965.

8. Allan Haber. "Poverty Budgets: How Much is Enough?" *Poverty and Human Resources Abstracts.* Vol. I, No. 3 (May-June 1966), pp. 5-22.

9. Michael Harrington. *The Other America—Poverty in the United States.* New York: The Macmillan Co., 1962.

10. Nat Hentoff. *The New Equality.* New York: The Viking Press, 1964.

11. Leon H. Keyserling. *Progress or Poverty: The United States at the Crossroads.* Washington, D.C.: Conference on Economic Progress, December, 1964.

12. Helen H. Lamale and Margaret S. Strotz. "The Interim City Worker's Family Budget," *Monthly Labor Review,* August, 1960.

13. Robert J. Lampman. *The Low Income Population and Economic Growth.* United States Congress, Joint Economic Committee, Study Paper Number 12, 86th Congress, First Session, December, 1959.

14. Herman P. Miller. "Changes in the Number and Composition of the Poor," *Poverty in America.* M. S. Gordon (ed.) San Francisco: Chandler Publishing Co., 1965, pp. 81-101.

15. Herman P. Miller. *Income of the American People.* New York: John Wiley and Sons, Inc., 1955.

16. Herman P. Miller (ed.). *Poverty—American Style.* Belmont, Calif.: Wadsworth Publishing Co., 1966.

17. Herman P. Miller. *Rich Man, Poor Man: A Study of Income Distribution in America.* New York: Crowell, 1964.

18. James N. Morgan, David H. Martin, Wilbur J. Cohen, and Harvey E. Brazer. *Income and Welfare in the United States.* New York: McGraw-Hill Book Co., Inc., 1962.

19. Mollie Orshansky. "Budget for an Elderly Couple. An Interim Revision by the Bureau of Labor Statistics," *Social Security Bulletin*, December, 1960.

20. Mollie Orshansky. "Recounting the Poor—A Five Year Review," *Social Security Bulletin*, April 1966, pp. 2-19.

21. Mollie Orshansky. "Who's Who Among the Poor: A Demographic View of Poverty," *Social Security Bulletin*, July 1965, pp. 3-33.

22. Charles E. Silberman. *Crisis in Black and White*. New York: Random House, 1964.

23. *Economic Report of the President*, Transmitted to the Congress, January 1964 and 1965 together with *The Annual Report of the Council of Economic Advisors*.

24. *Manpower Report of the President*, and *A Report on Manpower Requirements, Resources, Utilization and Training by the United States Department of Labor*, Transmitted to Congress, March, 1964 and March, 1965.

Chapter 2

Who Are the Poor?

Poverty is costly not only to the individual but also to society. Physical and mental disease, delinquency and crime, loss of productive capacity—all of these are part of the environment of poverty. But the most fundamental reason for declaring war on poverty is a moral one. This Nation and its institutions are founded upon the belief that each individual should have the opportunity to develop his capacity to the fullest. Those who are born into the world of poverty are not only deprived of most of the material comforts of life, but are also stunted in their emotional, intellectual, and social development, and thus effectively prevented from realizing their human potentialities. Past accomplishments in reducing the extent of poverty have been the result of combined efforts of all levels of government and of private groups. Similarly, the eventual elimination of poverty will call for a national effort involving a wide range of public and private measures to stimulate economic growth, wipe out discrimination, and increase opportunities by raising the educational, skill, health, and living levels of those Americans who have heretofore failed to share in the fruits of economic progress.

In order to attack the problem of poverty, it is essential to know who are the poor and what causes their poverty.

—From "Poverty in the United States" by Wilbur J. Cohen and Eugenia Sullivan, *Health, Education, and Welfare Indicators*, February, 1964.

RECENT ESTIMATES have focused on 30 million, 40 million, and even 50 million persons in the United States who are "poor"—who do not have enough money to buy an adequate living and have little opportunity to better themselves. Who are these people with inadequate incomes?

A 1967 government research and statistics note prepared by Mollie Orshansky cites the following:

> Included among the 45 million designated as poor or near-poor in 1966 were 18 to 28 percent of the nation's children and from 30 to 40 percent of the aged. Counted poor were nearly two in four of minority persons living on farms as against one in seven of the nonfarm population. The total with low incomes included 12 to 19

percent of the white population and 41 to 54 percent of the nonwhite. In 1966, households with a female head accounted for nearly one-half of all poverty units. In 1966, one in three of all poor children were minus a father in the home and the poverty rate among children in female-headed families was now four and a half times as high as families headed by a man.

In 1966 there were over 19 million children under age 18 among the persons defined as poor or near poor in this country. The infants born in the post-World War II baby boom have reached the critical 16 to 21 age group. Government officials have predicted that by 1970 there will be a million young people age 16 to 21 without jobs and with inadequate education and training unless the present trend is reversed.

Millions of workers constitute what has been called the "economic underworld of the by-passed." Many of them face the choice of a job at low level wages or no job at all. Many of them are not covered by the federal minimum wage and their poverty is due to the low rates of pay found most commonly in certain occupations. Others suffer irregular employment due to seasonal work, plant shutdowns, sickness or injury, discrimination and low bargaining power. Thousands have been bypassed by modern technological advances, unable because of outdated skills and meager education to get jobs. Some of these workers find that they are "too old" at age 40 or 50 to be reabsorbed in the labor force after their plant relocates or a machine takes over their old job. If they are lucky, they may find steady work, but in low paying, marginal industries at wage rates that are insufficient to meet their family needs.

Rural poverty has been described by Michael Harrington as "the poorest, lowest and meanest in the nation." The rural poor include farm laborers and migratory workers, ex-farmers, ex-coal miners, unemployed timber workers, reservation Indians. Migratory farm workers are among those rural workers having the most serious problems of income, health and education. One-and-a-half million rural farm families live on less than $250 a month; 2.8 million rural nonfarm families exist at the same income level. Over a million rural families have no more than $80 a month to pay for all their needs. A half-million rural youth between age 14 and 24 have never finished grade school. Their vision ends at the edge of a few acres of exhausted land.

The minority poor—Negroes, Puerto Ricans, Spanish-speaking Americans, American Indians—are hired last, paid less, and fired first. Nearly half the total Negro population in the United States—eight million—are poor. They number one-fifth of the country's total poverty stricken. Typically, wage rates for nonwhites are lower than for white workers, even when they work at the same jobs and have the same educational background. Negro college graduates can expect to earn only as much as white workers who leave school after the eighth grade, and white workers in their lifetime earn fifty percent more than Negroes and Puerto Ricans and one-third more than Spanish-speaking Americans. Fifty-three percent of New York City's Puerto Rican residents earned less than $4,000 in 1959; only eight percent earned more than $8,000. Three-fourths of Puerto Rican youth never enter high school. In the Southwest, three and a half million Spanish-speaking Americans face prejudice, inadequate education and language barriers. Of the half-million American Indians, among the hardest hit of this country's poverty stricken, 380,000 who live on or near reservations subsist on average family income one-fourth to one-third of the national average.

Death, desertion, divorce, and disability left almost five million fatherless families in the United States in 1962. Almost half live below the poverty-line. Many of the women heading multi-person households lack the education, training, and experience to get jobs with adequate incomes. Over eighty-five percent of the mothers receiving public assistance had not finished high school. They had worked as domestics, service workers and unskilled laborers; their chances of finding stable employment with adequate wage rates are remote.

But even among unattached individuals as distinct from multi-person households, sex is a factor in poverty. About thirty-eight percent of all women over age 14 are now in the labor force. Their median pay for full-time, year-round work is about sixty percent that of men. In addition, when jobs are scarce, they are more subject to unemployment. More than half of all single women live in poverty, contrasted to a little more than a third of all single men. Over a third of single women live on less than $1,000 a year, contrasted to slightly more than a fifth of the males.

Many of the aged poor have lived their lives in poverty and could not save enough throughout their working years to provide for independence after retirement. Half of the six and eight-tenths million heads of families over age 65 live on less than $3,000 a year. Half of these people support their families on less than $1,000 a year. Although the majority of older people are covered by Social Security, nearly two-thirds of the poorest aged—those living alone on incomes of less than $1,000 a year—are not covered by Social Security.

The people who live on incomes of under $3,000 a year are not a homogenous group. They include the young and the old, disabled and able-bodied, white and nonwhite, city and country dwellers. They include the employed, the underemployed, and the unemployed. They include those who were born in poverty and those who skidded into poverty through unemployment, sickness, disability, or advancing age. The majority of persons with inadequate incomes, however, share one common characteristic. Sixty-seven percent of our poorest live in families headed by persons who left school before eighth grade. A recent University of Michigan study revealed that fewer than two-fifths of the heads of poor families had gone beyond the educational attainment of their fathers. Only forty-five percent of the children in poor families finished high school compared to sixty-five percent of the children of all families. One-third of the children of the poor have less than a grade school education.

The findings of the President's Task Force on Manpower Conservation attested to the fact that poverty breeds poverty. The report of the Task Force, issued in January, 1964, found that one-third of this country's young people would fail to meet the standards for military services set by the Selective Service System. Poverty was the principal reason for their falling below the minimum mental and physical standards needed to be a private in the United States Army. About one-fifth of the young men refused on educational grounds from the service came from families which had received public assistance in the previous five years. Almost half came from families with six or more children. The fathers of more than half of these rejectees never finished grade school and four out of five of the rejectees had themselves dropped out of school.

Poverty, which cuts across many groups in our country, also is found in many different areas. In 1966 about one-half of all poor families—one-seventh of the white and two-thirds of the nonwhite—lived in Southern states. In the South over one-third of the nonwhite men who worked full-time in 1965 were poor, as were seven percent of the fully employed white males. About one-fourth of the white poor and two-fifths of the nonwhite poor live in urban areas. However, for the nation as a whole, the white poor outnumber the nonwhite even in central cities.

This chapter focuses on several groups of the poverty stricken in this country. Michael Harrington describes some of "the rejects" of our industrial society. Herbert Hill details the problems of racial ghettos in American cities. The characterisitics of the rural poor are discussed in an excerpt from a 1966 report by the President's Commission on Rural Poverty. Herman Miller analyzes the economic conditions of the Negro poor. The inadequacy of income for many of our aged citizens is focused on by Harold L. Sheppard. The economic problems of low-paid workers are reviewed in a statement by the Research Department of the A.F.L.-C.I.O. Finally, some economic and social characteristics of the Spanish-speaking peoples of the Southwest are presented in an article by Raymond F. Clapp.

The Rejects

Michael Harrington

League for Industrial Democracy

[Reprinted from Chapter 2 of The Other America: Poverty in the United States *(New York, 1963) by permission of The Macmillan Company. Copyright © 1962 Michael Harrington.]*

IN NEW YORK CITY, some of my friends call 80 Warren Street "the slave market."

It is a big building in downtown Manhattan. Its corridors have the littered, trampled air of a courthouse. They are lined with employment-agency offices. Some of these places list good-paying and highly skilled jobs. But many of them provide the work force for the economic underworld in the big city: the dishwashers and day workers, the fly-by-night jobs.

Early every morning, there is a great press of human beings in 80 Warren Street. It is made up of Puerto Ricans and Negroes, alcoholics, drifters, and disturbed people. Some of them will pay a flat fee (usually around 10 percent) for a day's work. They pay $0.50 for a $5.00 job and they are given the address of a luncheonette. If all goes well, they will make their wage. If not, they have a legal right to come back and get their half-dollar. But many of them don't know that, for they are people that are not familiar with laws and rights.

But perhaps the most depressing time at 80 Warren Street is in the afternoon. The jobs have all been handed out, yet the people still mill around. Some of them sit on benches in the larger offices. There is no real point to their waiting, yet they have nothing else to do. For some, it is probably a point of pride to be here, a feeling that they are somehow still looking for a job even if they know that there is no chance to get one until early in the morning.

Most of the people at 80 Warren Street were born poor. (The alcoholics are an exception.) They are incompetent as far as American society is concerned, lacking the education and the skills to get decent work. If they find steady employment, it will be in a sweatshop or a kitchen.

In a Chicago factory, another group of people are working. A year or so ago, they were in a union shop making good wages, with sick leave, pension rights, and vacations. Now they are making artificial Christmas trees at less than half the pay they had been receiving. They have no contract rights, and the foreman is absolute monarch. Permission is required if a worker wants to go to the bathroom. A few are fired every day for insubordination.

These are people who have become poor. They possess skills, and they once moved upward with the rest of the society. But now their jobs have been destroyed, and their skills have been rendered useless. In the process, they have been pushed down toward the poverty from whence they came. This particular group is Negro, and the chances of ever breaking through, of returning to the old conditions, are very slim. Yet their plight is not exclusively racial, for it is shared by all the semi-skilled and unskilled workers who are the victims of technological unemployment in the mass-production industries. They are involved in an interracial misery.

These people are the rejects of the affluent society. They never had the right skills in the first place, or they lost them when the rest of the economy advanced. They are the ones who make up a huge portion of the culture of poverty in the cities of America. They are to be counted in the millions.

❀ ❀ ❀

Each big city in the United States has an economic underworld. And often enough this phrase is a literal description: it refers to the kitchens and furnace rooms that are under the city; it tells of the place where tens of thousands of hidden people labor at impossible wages. Like the underworld of crime, the economic underworld is out of sight, clandestine.

The workers in the economic underworld are concentrated among the urban section of the more than 16,000,000 Americans denied coverage by the Minimum-Wage Law of 1961. They are domestic workers, hotel employees, bus boys, and dishwashers, and some of the people working in small retail stores. In the most recent Government figures, for example, hotel workers averaged $47.44 a week, laundry workers $46.45, general-merchandise employees $48.37, and workers in factories making work clothing $45.58.

This sector of the American economy has proved itself immune to progress. And one of the main reasons is that it is almost impossible to organize the workers of the economic underworld in their self-defense. They are at the mercy of unscrupulous employers (and, in the case of hospital workers, management might well be a board composed of the "best" people of the city who, in pursuing a charitable bent, participate in a conspiracy to exploit the most helpless citizens). They are cheated by crooked unions; they are used by racketeers.

In the late fifties I talked to some hospital workers in Chicago. They were walking a picket line, seeking union recognition. (They lost.) Most of them made about $30 a week and were the main support of their families. The hospital deducted several dollars a week for food that they ate on the job. But then, they had no choice in this matter. If they didn't take the food, they had to pay for it anyway.

When the union came, it found a work force at the point of desperation. A majority of them had signed up as soon as they had the chance. But, like most of the workers in the economic underworld, these women were hard to keep organized. Their dues were miniscule, and in effect they were being subsidized by the better-paid workers in the union. Their skills were so low that supervisory personnel could take over many of their functions during a strike. It required an enormous effort to reach them and to help them, and in this case it failed.

An extreme instance of this institutional poverty took place in Atlanta, Georgia, among hospital workers in mid-1960. Men who worked the dishwashing machines received $0.68 an hour; women kitchen helpers got $0.56; and the maids $0.55 an hour. If these people all put in the regular two thousand hours of work a year, they would receive just over $1,000 for their services.

The restaurants of the economic underworld are somewhat like the hospitals. The "hidden help" in the kitchen are an unstable group. They shift jobs rapidly. As a result, a union will sign up all the employees in a place, but before a union certification election can occur half of those who had joined will have moved on to other work. This means that it is extremely expensive for the labor movement to try to organize these workers: they are dispersed in small groups; they cannot pay for themselves; and they require constant servicing, checking, and rechecking to be sure that the new workers are brought into the union structure. . . .

When the hotels, the restaurants, the hospitals, and the sweatshops are added up, one confronts a section of the economy that employs millions and millions of workers. In retailing alone, there are 6,000,000 or 7,000,000 employees who are unorganized, and many of them are not covered by minimum wage. For instance, in 1961 the general-merchandise stores (with an average weekly wage of $48.37) counted over 1,250,000 employees. Those who made work clothes, averaging just over $45.00 a week, totaled some 300,000 citizens, most of them living in the other America of the poor.

Thus, in the society of abundance and high standards of living there is an economically backward sector which is incredibly capable of being exploited; it is unorganized, and in many cases without the protection of Federal law. It is in this area that the disabled, the retarded, and the minorities toil. In Los Angeles they might be Mexican-Americans, in the runaway shops of West Virginia or Pennsylvania, white Anglo-Saxon Protestants. All of them are poor; regardless of race, creed, or color, all of them are victims.

In the spring of 1961, American society faced up to the problem of the economic underworld. It decided that it was not worth solving. Since these workers cannot organize to help themselves, their only real hope for aid must be directed toward the intervention of the Federal Government. After the election of President Kennedy, this issue was joined in terms of a minimum-wage bill. The A.F.L.–C.I.O. proposed that minimum-wage coverage should be extended to about 6,500,000 new workers; the Administration proposed new coverage for a little better than 3,000,000 workers; the conservatives of the Dixiecrat-Republican coalition wanted to hold the figure down to about 1,000,000.

There was tremendous logrolling in Congress over the issue. In order to win support for the Administration approach, concessions were made. It does not take much political acumen to guess which human beings were conceded: the poor. The laundry workers (there are over 300,000 of them, and according to the most recent Bureau of Labor statistics figures they averaged $47.72 a week) and the hospital workers were dropped from the extension of coverage. The papers announced that over 3,000,000 new workers had been granted coverage—but they failed to note that a good number of them were already in well-paid industries and didn't need help.

In power politics, organized strength tells. So it was that America turned its back on the rejects in the economic underworld. As one reporter put it, "We've got the people who make $26 a day safely covered; it's the people making $26 a week who are left out." Once again, there is the irony that the welfare state benefits least those who need help most.

Racial Ghettos: The Crisis of American Cities
Herbert Hill
National Association for the Advancement of Colored People

[Excerpted with permission from Herbert Hill, "Demographic Change and Racial Ghettos: The Crisis of American Cities." Reprinted from Journal of Urban Law, *Winter 1966. With permission.]*

CURRENT CIVIL RIGHTS STRUGGLES are rooted in three major demographic developments of the American Negro community: accelerated growth, increasing mobility, and rapid urbanization. Almost half of the Negro population now lives in the North, but the response of American cities to this development has been a vast increase and rigidity in the pattern of residential segregation. Thus the Negro finds that he has left the segregated South for the segregated northern slum. The growth of housing segregation has been accompanied by an extension of the ghetto pattern in major cities together with vast urban blight and the decay of central city areas.

As a result of Negro population concentration in large cities and the movement of whites to the suburbs, the Negro is becoming strategically located to realize a growing potential of political power. However, racial segregation, poverty and exploitation are causing the emergence of a ghetto "underclass" profoundly alienated from the society. Federal, state and municipal agencies have directly encouraged segregation and the extension of racial ghettoes. The problem of urban redevelopment and the future of the cities is directly related to public policy on racial issues. There is now an urgent need for a new order of national priorities to fundamentally change the racial situation in the urban centers.

Negro Population Characteristics

The dual migration of Negroes from the rural South to the urban North and from the rural South to the urban South is one of the major demographic changes of our time with great social and political implications for the future of American society. In 1960, less than 60 percent of the nation's Negro population lived in the South. In 1965, only 53.6 percent of the Negro population lived below the Mason-Dixon line and if present trends continue a majority will be living in the North by 1970. Recent census studies indicate that the largest percentage increase in the Negro population was in the West, especially California. As of 1967, almost half of the total Negro population was living in the urban North and more than half of the southern Negro population was living in the growing urban industrial complexes of the South.

In 1960, 70 percent of the white population lived in cities and 73 percent of the country's Negro population lived in cities. In the North and West, nine in ten Negroes were urban residents and in the South, six in ten Negroes lived in cities.[1]

Over 15 percent of the Negro population of the South left the southern states during the 1940-50 decade and a greater number left during the 1950-60 decade.[2] As a result of these developments the

---

[1] U.S. Bureau of the Census, Census of Population: 1960, Vol. I, Pt. 1, U.S. Summ, Tables, 158, 233.

[2] U.S. Bureau of the Census, Current Population Reports, Population Estimates. Ser. P-25, No. 247, Table 4 (April 2, 1962).

Negro population of the United States is now more urban than the white population. In 1960, five of the six cities with the largest Negro population were in the North and West: New York, Chicago, Philadelphia, Detroit, Washington, D.C., and Los Angeles. Taken together, the San Francisco-Oakland Area in California has more Negroes than Birmingham, Alabama.[3] The American Negro has now become an urban dweller. Thus the rigid pattern of segregated city living is the central fact in the life of most colored citizens.

An interesting characteristic of Negro workers is that they are now more mobile than white workers on both a national and regional basis. While large numbers of Negro wage-earners move into northern urban areas seeking improved employment opportunities, and better educational and living facilities for their children, a significant number of southern Negro workers and their families seek a better life by moving to the rapidly growing industrial cities of the South. In a study of labor mobility in three southern states with large Negro populations—North Carolina, South Carolina, and Georgia—the authors conclude: the young are more mobile than the old, males are more mobile then females, and Negroes are more mobile than non-Negroes."[4]

The deteriorating economic and social conditions of the growing Negro population locked in the segregated slum ghettos of American cities is the source of increasing social discontent and strife.[5] However, the vast new urban population concentrations provide the basis for realistic efforts to end the traditional powerlessness of Negroes in American society. A study, sponsored by the University of Chicago's Population Research and Training Center, suggests the impact which rapidly growing Negro populations will have on Chicago and other major urban communities. The population

---

[3]U.S. Bureau of the Census, Current Population Reports, Ser. P.20, No. 104. Table 10 (Sept. 30, 1962); No. 113, Table 13 (Jan. 22, 1962); No. 118, Table 13 (Aug. 9, 1962); No. 127, Tables 1, 9 (Jan. 15, 1964); No. 134, Table 114 (Mar. 25, 1965).

[4]Bunting, Ashby & Prosper, Jr., "Labor Mobility in Three Southern States," *Ind. & Lab. Rel. Rev.* 432, 441 (1961).

[5]The meaning of the term "ghetto" has significantly changed since the 1920's when Louis Wirth and other sociologists used the word to describe a voluntary community of ethnic group concentration. Now it refers to an area of socially and economically deprived people belonging to a racial caste group suffering acute social disorganization and enforced segregation. The current residents of the ghetto remain outside the "opportunity structure" of the larger society. For a description of the earlier ghetto see Wirth, *The Ghetto* (1928).

study concluded that by 1974 Negroes will comprise at least 50 percent of Chicago's population.[6] Professor Philip M. Hauser, director of the center stated:

——by 1970 Negroes will equal or exceed the white population in at least a dozen major cities across the United States

——hundreds of thousands of white families will leave the cities for suburban areas so that by 1990 the suburban population will have doubled the 1960 census figure.[7]

The Report also notes that unless urgent measures are taken, the urban labor market may turn into a sea of unemployment and underemployment."[8]

Dr. Hauser made the following comment as he released the study: "The Negro will increasingly hold the balance of power in metropolitan centers. As he leaves the rural South for the urban North, he is becoming strategically located." Hauser noted that many other major urban centers face the prospect of eventually becoming "Negro cities." Hauser also predicted that more members of Congress and northern state legislatures will be Negro.[9]

The Negro protest against racism in the North is not new, but the intensity of the attack, the mass character, and sense of power of the movement, is a recent phenomenon. Its roots lie in the great migration North which has been steadily increasing during the last 30 years. From 1950 to 1960, 1.5 million Negroes left the South for North Central, and Northeastern areas. In 1900, only five percent of Negroes lived in the Northeast and six percent in North Central areas of the United States, but by 1960 the former area contained 15 percent non-whites and the latter 18 percent. In 1900, the South contained 87 percent of America's Negroes. By 1960 the percentage was down to 56 percent.[10]

The bulk of the migration represented an increase in the central cities of the twelve largest metropolitan areas: New York, Los

---

[6]Brogue & Dandekar, "Population Trends and Prospects for the Chicago-North-western Indiana Consolidated Metropolitan Area: 1960 to 1990" (Mar. 1962). The report noted that "Chicago City lost a total of almost 400,000 white residents in the decade and gained a total of 328,000 nonwhite residents in exchange." *Id.* at 7.

[7]Chicago *Sun Times*, Mar. 28, 1962, p. 3.

[8]Bogue & Dandekar, *supra* note 9, at 34.

[9]Chicago *Sun Times*, Mar. 28, 1962, p. 3. See also, Hauser, "Demographic Factors in the Integration of the Negro," 94 *Daedalus* 847 (1965).

[10]Housing and Home Finance Agency, *Our Nonwhite Population and Its Housing* 2 (July, 1963).

Angeles, Chicago, Philadelphia, Detroit, San Francisco, Oakland, Boston, Pittsburgh, St. Louis, Washington, D.C., Cleveland, and Baltimore. Combined, these cities hold 60 percent of the northern Negro population and 31 percent of the total Negro population.[11]

Between 1940 and 1960 the Negro population of Philadelphia doubled and is now 26.4 percent of the total population. In Detroit, during the same 20-year period, the Negro population more than tripled and is now almost 30 percent of the city's population. During this period the Negro population increased by 600 percent in Los Angeles County. Negroes make up 53.9 percent of the population in Washington, D.C., 37 percent of the population in New Orleans, La., 34.7 percent in Baltimore and 28.6 percent in Cleveland, Ohio.[12]

Beginning in 1900, in New York City, the proportion of Negroes to the total population increased in each successive decennial census. The absolute number also increased during each decade. By 1960, the number of Negro residents had multiplied in every borough of New York City ranging from nine times the 1900 population in Richmond to 69 times the 1900 population in the Bronx. In Manhattan, which has the largest concentration of New York City's Negroes, the 1960 Negro population was 11 times greater than that of 1900. In 1960, the Negro population in Brooklyn was 20 times greater than the Negro population in 1900, and in the Borough of Queens the Negro population was 56 times greater than the Negro population in 1900. The proportion of Negroes in the total population of Manhattan increased consistently from under 2 percent in 1900 to 24 percent in 1960, and in Brooklyn the Negro population increased substantially every ten years.[13]

> Rural southern Negroes were a large part of the population growth of Southern California during the 1950s and 1960s. While the California population grew 48 percent in ten years, the Negro portion of the population increased 91 percent; while the Caucasian population of Los Angeles County grew 40 percent the Negro portion grew 111 percent. Each month about a thousand Negroes were coming to Los Angeles County which now has more than half a million Negro Americans.[14]

---

[11]Silberman, "The City and the Negro," 73 *Fortune* 88, 88 (Mar. 1962).
[12]Clark, *Dark Ghetto* 24 (1965).
[13]Cromien, N.Y.C. Comm'n on Human Rights, *Negroes in New York City* (July 1961).
[14]Lillard, *Eden in Jeopardy* 39 (1966).

In 1910, eight out of ten Negroes resided in one of the 11 deep southern states, and over 90 percent of these Negroes resided in predominantly rural areas. Between 1940 and 1950 the Negro population increased two and one quarter times outside the South.[15] Thus, Negro migration to the northern states must be understood as an exodus from the South. According to the 1960 population census, of the 1,129,704 non-whites living in the New York Standard Metropolitan Statistical Area (SMSA) in 1960, more than 39,000 lived in North Carolina, South Carolina, Georgia, and Alabama in 1955. Similar migration took place in other northern cities. Nearly 19,000 Negroes moved from Mississippi to the Chicago SMSA between 1955 and 1960 and 3,555 Negroes left Alabama for Cleveland during the same period.[16]

In none of the ten northern cities with the largest colored populations was the percentage of southern-born Negroes less than 39 percent as in New York City. The highest percentage of southern-born Negroes was in Cleveland with 48 percent.

Keeping nearly perfect pace with the Negro migration has been the development of residential segregation. Negroes coming into northern cities have been forced to live in dilapidated dwellings with a very high density of population concentration.

In 1950, America's central cities held nearly 7,000,000 non-whites. By 1960, the number had increased 51 percent.[17] Whites, in contrast, were leaving the central city areas. While 52 percent of the white population lived in outlying suburban areas, 78 percent of non-whites lived in the central cities and only 22 percent were suburbanites.[18]

It is quite clear that as we enter the second half of the decade the non-white population, predominantly Negro, has come to make up an increasing percentage of our large cities' population. New York City's non-white population in 1960 was 1,141,000; 14.7 percent of the city's population. Between 1950 and 1960 the non-white population of Philadelphia, New York City, Detroit, Chicago, Cleveland, and Los Angeles increased by amounts between 41 and 97 percent. The pattern is the same for virtually all northern areas. City populations increased due to Negro migration, but whites left the cities during the

---

[15]Silberman, *supra* note 15, at 88.
[16]U.S. Bureau of Census, U.S. Census of Population: 1960, Mobility for Metropolitan Areas, PC(2)-2c, Table 3 (1963).
[17]*Our Nonwhite Population, op. cit. supra* note 14, table 7.
[18]*Id.*, at 3-4.

same years. Chicago, for example, has a 12.8 percent decrease in its white population during a period of large scale Negro in-migration.[19]

In Detroit, the crowding of Negroes into the urban core area did not keep pace with the exodus of whites to the suburbs. During the late 1950s and early 1960s there was an excess of available housing. This condition has now been changed by population influx, highway and school construction, and urban renewal demolition programs so that the quantity of housing available to low-income Negroes has, by 1966, become a critical problem. The fact that Detroit's housing crisis has been slower to develop may account, at least in part, for the absence of violent racial upheaval. As the housing market continues to tighten in the last half of this decade, a test of this hypothesis may occur.

If migrating Negroes had freedom of choice and the economic means to acquire adequate housing on a non-segregated basis, then it is possible that our large cities would be able to absorb their entry and provide decent living conditions. But the opposite has been the case. As *Fortune* editor Charles E. Silberman commented:

> when city officials talk about spreading slums, they are talking in the main about physical deterioration of the areas inhabited by Negroes. And when they talk about juvenile delinquency, or the burden of welfare payments, or any of a long list of city problems, officials are talking principally about the problems of Negro adjustment to city life. For the large city is not absorbing and urbanizing its new Negro residents rapidly enough; its slums are no longer acting as the incubator of a new middle class.[20]

Racial segregation now exists on a vast and growing scale. The masses of Negroes in the major cities of the North live in a rigidly segregated society.

The tensions of current northern race relations have their roots in the concentration of Negroes in segregated urban slums. The slums are expanding and are growing worse. Upon this continuing fact of residential segregation rests the interlocking problems of race and education, race and employment, and race and political power. Contemporary civil rights struggles are rooted in three major developments: the accelerated growth of the Negro population, the increasing mobility of the Negro population, and the rapid urbanization of the Negro population. The response of American cities to these interrelated developments has been a vast increase in the pattern of residen-

---

[19]*Id.*, table 7.
[20]Silberman, *supra* note 15, at 89.

tial segregation. The growth of housing segregation has been accompanied by an extension of school segregation, slums, exploitation, poverty, and social disorganization.[21]

Ghetto residents are the victims of consumer fraud and overpricing and pay exorbitant rentals for substandard housing.[22] An Associated Press survey of prices in seven areas of large supermarket stores in Connecticut stated that "people in low income neighborhoods—mainly Negroes—pay more for food." The results of the survey as reported on the front page of the Hartford *Courant*, August 15, 1966, under the headline "Poor Pay More for Food" quotes the manager of a food supermarket as saying: Negroes pay more for food because "they don't have the transportation to get to the shopping plazas. They have to pay what the local store is charging." The A.P. survey concluded that:

> The same groceries were found to cost considerably more in an independent market in a low income area than they did in a similar market in an upper income area. This despite the fact that the market in the richer neighborhood gave trading stamps, while the market in the predominantly Negro neighborhood did not.[23]

A survey made by the New York *Post* reported that, "Food in Harlem costs more than anywhere else in the city." The report stated that the price of a dozen eggs in Harlem was 20 cents higher than the city wide average and the price of butter 20 cents higher per pound. The same meat sold in Harlem for $1.69 a pound is sold elsewhere for $1.15 a pound.[24] Researchers for the Community Council of Greater New York in making the price survey discovered that the recent increase in living costs affects those with the lowest incomes more than other groups. In New York and elsewhere the poor pay more for goods and services than do other groups in the population.[25]

A recent study made by the Bureau of Labor Statistics concluded that: "For equivalent rents poor families get poorer housing than families with higher incomes. . . . Price collectors found that meat

---

[21]For a compelling analysis on the social consequences of housing segregation see Clark, *op. cit. supra* note 16; Paulsen & Kleiner, *Mental Illness in the Community*, Ch. 8 (1966).

[22]See, Caplovitz, *The Poor Pay More* (1963); Jacobs, "Keeping the Poor Poor," in *Economic Progress and Social Welfare* (Goodman ed., 1966).

[23]Hartford *Courant*, Aug. 15, 1966, p. 1.

[24]N.Y. *Post*, Aug. 29, 1966.

[25]Bluementhal, "Consumer Frauds Thrive in Ghettos," N.Y. *Times*, Aug. 20, 1966, p. 1.

and produce were not as fresh in poor areas and the stores were less clean and orderly." The BLS study also noted that poor families pay more for credit.[26] The Negro residents of the slum ghettos are experiencing a major crisis of unemployment and underemployment. The rate of unemployment among Negroes living in the Watts area of Los Angeles in the period immediately preceding the riots during the summer of 1965 was 34 percent. This figure exceeded the general rate of unemployment during the Great Depression of the 1930s which was between 22 and 26 percent.[27] In industrial Oakland, 34 percent of the city's 385,000 residents are Negro and 25 percent of Negro adult males are unemployed. Similarly high rates of unemployment in Negro ghettos are to be found in other cities.[28]

Of great significance is the fact that since 1951, the differential in the average income of Negro and white workers has been increasing. By December of 1951, the Negro median wage was approaching 57 percent of the white worker's average income. Since that time, however, the gap between the income of white and Negro workers has been growing steadily greater.[29]

Negroes make up the hard core of those in a permanent condition of poverty far out of proportion to their total numbers in the population. The "census" bureau reported on August 11, 1966 that 36 percent of the nation's non-white families had incomes last year of less than $3,000 and thus fell below the poverty line established by the federal government. By contrast only 14.4 percent of white families were living below the poverty line. The non-white median income

---

[26]Groom, "Prices in Poor Neighborhoods," 89 *Mo. Lab. Rev.* 1085, 87, 89 (1966).

[27]The rate of employment as determined by the Bureau of Labor Statistics is based upon the number of persons in the labor force actively seeking work. Unfortunately, official figures do not include the significant number of unemployed persons who have been driven out of the labor force as a result of long-term joblessness and who are no longer seeking employment. Thus, many thousands of older Negroes who have exhausted their unemployment insurance benefits as well as a large but undetermined number of young persons who have never entered the labor market in the first instance, are not included in official unemployment statistics which are regarded by many economists as a systematic understatement of true unemployment conditions. The problem of the "hidden unemployed" is especially acute in Negro slum ghettos.

[28]Hill, "Racial Inequality in Employment: The Patterns of Discrimination," 357 *Annals* 30(1965); Hill, "The Role of Law in Securing Equal Employment Opportunities: Legal Powers and Social Changes," 7 *Boston Coll. Ind. & Com. L. Rev.* 625 (1966).

[29]Miller, *Rich Man, Poor Man* 84-88 (1964).

was $3,971, while the median wage for white workers was almost twice as high at $7,170.[30]

On August 4, 1966, the Bureau of Labor Statistics issued a report indicating that Negro workers living in the ghetto are the major victims of a new economic development—the retreat of industry to the suburbs. The Bureau reported that the growing concentration of industry and business in the suburbs has added new economic pressures upon the status of the poor in major cities.

Data reveal that half of all new industrial buildings and stores built in the last 16 years were constructed outside the central city of the nation's metropolitan areas. "As a result many residents of the central city—whose incomes tend to be low—will find travel to and from work in the suburbs more expensive and time consuming," the Bureau said.

The Report stated that public transit costs increased at twice the rate during the last 16 years as the costs for owner operated automobiles. The Bureau of Labor Statistics concluded that, "tending to work and live in the central city, Negroes have median earnings considerably below those of suburban residents and are more apt to use public transportation."[31]

It has become evident that the political leadership of many municipalities prefers social welfare to social change thus helping to maintain and expand the Negro ghettos. Major cities, such as New York, Chicago, and others have increased the amount of money allocated for welfare programs, thereby merely providing a minimal subsistence life for the residents of the ghetto. All too frequently the projects of the so-called "war against poverty" are simply an extension of these welfare programs. Instead of making it possible—as would a real "war against poverty"—for the poor to exit out of their condition of permanent poverty, antipoverty programs are in most instances merely custodial operations by which public officials believe that they are purchasing racial peace.

This approach, however, only serves to increase the sense of hopelessness of those who live in the ghetto. The growing disturbances in ghetto areas must be understood as the revolt of the powerless against the hopelessness and despair of their lives. Ghetto life has led not only to growing alienation and withdrawal from society, but also to an increase in social pathology. Dr. Kenneth B. Clark has written that "The dark ghetto is institutionalized pathology; it is

---

[30]N.Y. *Times*, Aug. 15, 1966, p. 20.
[31]N.Y. *Daily News*, Aug. 15, 1966, § C, p. 7.

chronic, self-perpetuating pathology; and it is the futile attempt by those with power to confine that pathology so as to prevent the spread of its contagion to the 'larger community.' "[32] There is a most unfortunate tendency in American society to prefer the welfare approach as a substitute for economic innovation and social change. This is dramatically demonstrated in the tragic plight of the people of Appalachia who for more than a generation have lived in a permanent condition of welfare poverty and have been reduced to a state of welfare passivity.

Increases in municipal welfare budgets have been paralleled by increases in police budgets in those cities containing the major Negro ghettos. Municipalities are responding to the crisis of the ghetto by expanding the police power and by the establishment of so-called "special forces" concerned with riot control within the ghetto. There is some reason to believe, however, that those who live inside the Negro ghetto will in the future protest against the hopelessness of their condition outside of the ghetto where Negroes will not be the only victims.

What is urgently needed now is to literally wipe out the racial ghettos, to renovate some houses while demolishing the miles and miles of rat-infested, decaying slum dwellings, and through a vast new building program in the older blighted sections of large cities create a meaningful urban renewal program.

Every authority on housing problems knows that what now passes for urban renewal is a failure in the most fundamental social sense, because at the heart of all public housing programs is the unsettled question of racial segregation. In most instances these programs simply extend and perpetuate the Negro ghetto.

Together with the destruction of the slum ghetto, open occupancy in hitherto all-white residential areas must become a reality for Negro citizens. Unless the present pattern of segregated housing is eliminated and Negro citizens can escape from the ghetto, the blight of our central cities will increase and the ghettos will continue to expand. State and municipal civil rights laws have been of little value in eliminating the broad patterns of racial segregation in housing. The traditional forms of residential segregation remain impervious to such anti-discrimination statutes.[33]

---

[32]Clark, *op. cit, supra* note 16, at 81.

[33]For an examination of the operation of state anti-discrimination agencies see Hill, "20 Years of State Fair Employment Practice Commissions: A Critical Analysis with Recommendations," 14 *Buffalo L. Rev.* 22 (1964).

It is most unfortunate that the housing section of the Civil Rights Bill of 1966 has been rendered virtually meaningless. The housing section as amended by the House of Representatives would exempt most individual home sales, that is, at least 60 percent of the housing units in the nation. This would have little or no effect in breaking the Negro slum ghettos.

There has been a similar mutilation of the Demonstration Cities Act which would have established highly desirable social criteria for federal renewal programs in urban areas. The original Demonstration Cities Act proposed a $2.3 billion, 5-year program to upgrade slums in urban areas mostly populated by non-whites.[34] The Act finally adopted provides for a very limited $900 million, 2-year program.[35] The new authorizations amount to less than $10 per capita of urban population during the period of the program and will not significantly accelerate or give new social directions to current urban renewal programs.

However, if the racial ghettos are not destroyed, if Negro workers increasingly are forced into the ranks of the permanently underemployed and unemployed, if the social pathology of ghetto life is permitted to grow, and if there are not rapid and fundamental changes in the status of the urban Negro, especially the young people, then the future of American society is in jeopardy.

The People Left Behind: The Rural Poor

Report by the President's Commission on Rural Poverty

[Excerpted from The People Left Behind, *September, 1967.]*

IT IS A SHOCKING FACT that in the United States today, in what is the richest nation in history, close to 14 million rural Americans are poor, and a high proportion of them are destitute. By their poverty they are deprived of freedom to share in our economic abundance.

It may surprise most Americans to know that there is more poverty in rural America, proportionately, than in our cities. In metropolitan areas, one person in eight is poor, and in the suburbs the ratio

---

34H.R. 15890, Jan. 26, 1966 (original administration bill).
35S. 3708, enacted Sept. 1, 1966 (as amended).

is one in 15. But in rural areas one of every four persons is poor (table 1).

TABLE 1

Persons in Poverty, By Rural and Urban Residence, March 1965

Item	Persons at all income levels		Poor persons[1]		
	Number (millions)	Percent distribution	Number (millions)	Percent distribution	Percent poor
United States	189.9	100.0	33.7	100.0	17.7
Total rural	55.3	29.1	13.8	40.9	25.0
Farm	13.3	7.0	3.9	11.6	29.3
Nonfarm	42.0	22.1	9.9	29.4	23.6
Total urban	134.6	70.9	19.9	59.1	14.8
Small cities	27.1	14.3	6.4	19.0	23.6
Metropolitan areas	107.5	56.6	13.5	40.1	12.6
Central cities	58.6	30.8	10.2	30.3	17.4
Suburbs	48.9	25.8	3.3	9.8	6.7

[1]Income data relate to 1964. Poverty statistics presented here are preliminary estimates, based on the Social Security Administration poverty lines for urban and rural nonfarm, but using 85 percent rather than 70 percent as the farm-to-nonfarm ratio. The methods used in deriving this ratio and the above data are discussed in a technical report, to be published. Percentages may not add to 100 because of rounding.

Some 30 percent of our total population live in rural areas, but 40 percent of the nation's poor live there. Within this total there are nearly 3 million families, plus a million unattached persons.

Contrary to popular impression, all the rural poor do not live on farms, nor are all of them Negroes. Most live in small towns and villages. Only one in four of these rural families lives on a farm. And, of the 14 million rural poor, 11 million are white.

It is true that a higher proportion of Negroes than of whites are poor—three out of five rural nonwhite families are poor. They are heavily concentrated in some areas. In fact, 90 percent of them are clustered in the poorest counties in America. Low income white people are more widely scattered as well as more numerous.

Where Are the Rural Poor?

It has become popular to talk of "pockets of poverty." The truth is there are no such things as pockets of poverty. Poverty refuses to stay in pockets. But there are areas of heavy concentration of rural poor. And there is a continuing exodus to towns and cities.

Poor people live everywhere, including cities, but some areas and regions have such heavy concentrations of rural poverty that they stand out. Much of the South has a heavy concentration of rural poverty. Outside of the South, Indian reservations, noticeably in the Southwest and the upper Great Plains, contain distinct concentrations of the rural poor, along with New England and the upper Great Lakes.

Within the South several areas of rural poverty can be distinguished. Appalachia perhaps has become best known in recent years, but there is also the Coastal Plain to the east, the Ozarks to the west, the Black Belt of the Old South, and the Mexican-American concentrations along our southern border. Even within a state, distinct areas with high concentrations of poverty may be identified, as in the Delta and the hill country of Mississippi.

Symptoms of Poverty

Average family incomes are low in poverty areas, but there are many additional symptoms of poverty. A low level of formal schooling among adults parallels low income levels. Rural housing is dilapidated and in need of extensive repair or replacement. Relatively high proportions of children, youths, and the aged depend on those of working age. And the working-age population is less likely to be in the labor market, with the result that the burden of workers in supporting nonworkers is heavier than in more prosperous sections of America.

When a family's income is less than $3,000, that family is usually defined as poor. In the poverty areas of rural America, however, an income of $3,000 per family is the exception, not the rule. Of the poor families in these areas, more than 70 percent struggle along on less than $2,000 a year, and one family in every four exists, somehow, on less than $1,000 a year.[1]

Schooling in low income areas is as inadequate as incomes. Rural people generally have poorer schooling than city people, and rural poor people are severely handicapped by lack of education. Few

---

[1]Unpublished census data from 1966 Composite Survey of Economic Opportunity.

rural poor adults attain the general rural average of 8.8 years of school completed. Male farm laborers between 55 and 64 years of age and earning incomes of less than $1,000 average only 5 years of schooling.

Moreover, low educational levels seem to be self-perpetuating. If the head of a rural poor family has had little schooling, his sons are often handicapped in their efforts to get an education.[2]

It is especially difficult for rural people handicapped educationally to acquire new skills, or get new jobs, or otherwise adjust to a society increasingly urbanized. This is as true on the farm as in urban industry, for modern farming requires skills that the poorly educated lack. The less the schooling, the poorer the job and the lower the income.

Lacking in education, the rural poor either concentrate in low-paying jobs on the farm or elsewhere in rural areas, or swell the ranks of the unemployed and the underemployed.

Negroes, Indians, and Mexican Americans suffer even more than low income whites from unemployment and underemployment. Their schooling, as a rule, is even less than that of whites in the rural poverty areas. Negroes emerging from the share-cropper system often migrate to urban ghettos. Those who remain in rural areas are frequently unemployed, and when they do have jobs, they are found mostly in wage work; few become farm operators. Indians on reservations live in poverty, in the main, with few opportunities for work at well-paying jobs. Off the reservations Indians rarely find it possible to get a better paying job, if they find one at all.

At best, job opportunities in rural areas are scarce, and in many places they are getting scarcer year by year. For rural people living within commuting distance of nonfarm jobs, it is sometimes possible to combine farming with a variety of jobs off the farm, but in isolated areas the need for such opportunities is far greater than the supply. At that, even with every adult member of the family working, many families in rural poverty areas don't make enough for decent living.

In fact, some rural families make so little that their children are not only malnourished but literally starving, as a team of six physicians discovered on a 1967 survey in the rural South. The physicians summed up their findings in these words:

> In sum, we saw children who are hungry and who are sick—children for whom hunger is a daily fact of life and sickness, in many forms, an inevitability. We do not want to quibble over

---

[2]Current Population Reports, Series P-20, No. 132.

words, but "malnutrition" is not quite what we found; the boys and girls we saw were hungry—weak, in pain, sick; their lives are being shortened; they are, in fact, visibly and predictably losing their health, their energy, their spirits. They are suffering from hunger and disease and directly or indirectly they are dying from them— which is exactly what "starvation" means.

. . . It is unbelievable to us that a nation as rich as ours, with all its technological and scientific resources, has to permit thousands and thousands of children to go hungry, go sick, and die grim and premature death.[3]

Population Growth and Migration

Rural low income areas have lost population for a number of years, mainly through the exodus of rural farm people. From 1790 to the present, the nation's population has grown from about 4 million to nearly 200 million persons. In the process, it has switched from about 95 percent to 30 percent rural. As late as 1910 a third of the entire population was on farms, but this figure has dropped to only 6 percent. The more than 6,000 cities contained 125 million persons in 1960, or 70 percent of the total population.

The strictly rural areas, and areas with the lowest incomes, have the heaviest out-migration. Consider, for example, the counties classed as all rural—lacking a city (or place) of 2,500 or more popula- tion. By 1960, aside from the natural increase (births minus deaths) these counties had lost almost 2 million people, or 15 percent of their 1950 populations through migration. In contrast, the mainly urban counties (with 70 percent or more of their population in urban cen- ters) gained more than 5 million, or about 6 percent through mi- gration.

The poorest counties, with median family incomes of less than $2,000 in 1959, lost more than 600,000 persons—over a fourth of their 1950 population—through migration. In the Deep South, for example, a mass migration of Negroes, mainly to northern industrial centers, has helped reduce southern rural poverty at the expense of cities. At the same time, high income counties, with median family incomes of $7,500 or more in 1959, increased through migration by about 200,000 people.

Americans are well-known for their geographic and social mo- bility, and the freedom to be mobile is perhaps one of our most

---

[3]*Hungry Children. A Special Report.* Southern Regional Council. Atlanta, Ga.

cherished values. Many seek to escape rural poverty by moving from the farm or small town to larger cities and into non-farm work. But the fact remains that if one's origin is in agriculture, his chances of remaining there are relatively great. Given the low income levels of many farmers and farmworkers, the tendency to inherit one's occupation serves as an obstacle to an escape from poverty. Studies demonstrate that persons entering the labor market at the lowest income levels have the greatest difficulty in rising to better jobs and higher incomes. Many simply do not make the transition. Migration to a city is therefore no guarantee of escaping poverty, as the presence of millions of poverty-ridden ex-ruralites now in cities testifies.

More Children Than Income

The size of many low income families makes escape from poverty extremely difficult. The world over, large families have been traditional in rural areas, and the tradition lives on in rural America, especially in poverty areas. The result, of course, is that meager resources have to be stretched beyond the breaking point to feed, house, clothe, and educate the children.

The birth rate has been declining in the nation as a whole since 1957, but average number of births is still high in rural poverty areas. The 1960 statistics revealed that throughout the nation women 40 to 44 years of age had produced an average—statistically speaking—of 2.5 children each. In farm families with incomes of less than $2,000, the average was 3.7 for white mothers and 6.4 for nonwhites.

Persistence in rural America of the tradition favoring large families is understandable. The rural way of life, at one time, dictated the need for large families. Before machines and modern technology came along, the family farm needed children as potential workers. Religious beliefs buttressed the tradition. And society more or less expected and sanctioned large families.

To add to the burden, the households of low income people in rural areas often include several generations. This is partly from necessity, partly cultural inheritance. Rural people cling tenaciously to the custom of caring for the old folks at home. And when the children of friends and neighbors need a place to stay, they are taken in.

Then, when the youths and young adults of these households go to the city in search of jobs, those who are left have more dependents to support. The combination of few workers, low incomes, and more people to support creates a dependency problem that is acute.

The Residual Population

The mass exodus from low income rural areas in recent years has meant that those left behind are often worse off than before. Their chances of escaping from poverty, or avoiding deeper poverty, or even easing their burden have been reduced. Partly this is because the areas have too many old people and children for the working-age population to support. Partly it is because a smaller population, spread too sparsely, cannot support or build a strong, flexible social and economic superstructure in the area. Local governments, schools, and churches are dying from lack of support. And as local facilities and services continue to decline, the chances for redevelopment diminish.

Figures on the age of heads of households in rural poverty areas underline the hopelessness of the situation. In 1965, among low income families in these areas, one of every four heads of household was 65 years of age, or older. Contrast this with rural areas with adequate incomes. There, only about 7 percent of the heads of households were as old as 65. Nor is the picture brighter for heads of households who were younger but living in poverty areas. Of the age group 22 to 54, half were poor.

Employment

Nearly 800,000 rural adults between the ages of 20 and 64 are unemployed. Underemployment is also a serious problem for rural people: those who have jobs are 18 percent underemployed.[4]

The current situation in rural America is this: Employment in agriculture, forests, mines, and fisheries is declining faster than new jobs are being created in rural areas by construction, manufacturing, and service industries. At that, the rural unemployed get few of such new jobs as are created. They often don't know the job exists, they lack the skills needed, and they can't finance a move to a new job. So they remain poor.

Nationally, the unemployment rate has been running slightly under 4 percent. In rural areas the rate is much higher.

The seasonal nature of farmwork intensifies the problem. Not only is unemployment in agriculture about twice the annual average in nonagricultural industries, but the monthly employment rate also

---

[4]Unpublished data, based on 1960 Census, from Economic Research Service, U.S. Department of Agriculture.

fluctuates sharply. In July of 1966 the agricultural unemployment rate was 3.5 percent. But earlier in the year, in February and March, it was 11.6 percent. In nonagricultural industries the unemployment rate did not fluctuate by as much as one percentage point throughout 1966, and the average for the year stayed close to 3.4 percent.

As a matter of fact, the situation is a good deal worse than the figures on unemployment suggest. Official statistics count a rural resident as employed if he works part-time, or a few days a month. The truth, of course, is that he is often underemployed, and almost as badly off as if totally unemployed. We have evidence that underemployment is widespread in rural areas, and as acute a problem as unemployment.

Using 1960 census data the United States Department of Agriculture has estimated the amount of underemployment among employed rural residents.[5] The figure is 18.3 percent for all employed rural residents; 16.3 percent for males and 23.7 percent for females.

The rate of underemployment was 8.3 percent for rural non-farm males, and 20.4 percent for females. The rate of underemployment was highest among rural farm residents: 36.6 percent for females and 37.1 percent for males.

We find high rates of unemployment and underemployment among operators of small farms as well as among hired farmworkers and migratory laborers. Among rural people working in forests, mines, and fisheries, we find a pattern of irregular employment, low wages, and poor working conditions.

There aren't enough new jobs opening up in rural areas to wipe out rural unemployment or make a dent in rural poverty. Even where new jobs do appear, the applicant needs help in acquiring a new skill for the job, in adjusting to new working conditions, or in moving to a new location.

Some people in rural America are able to find new jobs and acquire new skills with little assistance. Some climb out of poverty unassisted by moving out of a poverty area or by shifting from farm to nonfarm occupations. But for many others the move from farm to city, or from farm to nonfarm job, merely transfers their problems and their poverty. Still others, because of age or family ties and the lack of employment, have to stay where they are, boxed in.

---

[5]Unpublished data from the Economic Research Service, U.S. Department of Agriculture.

Poverty and the Negro

Herman P. Miller

Bureau of the Census

[Excerpted with permission from Poverty Amidst Affluence, *Leo Fishman, ed., Yale University Press, 1966. Copyright © 1966 by Yale University.]*

So MUCH HAS BEEN SAID about Negro poverty these past few years that it is becoming increasingly difficult to say anything new or significant on the subject. It is common knowledge that Negroes are poorly housed, poorly educated, and discriminated against in many ways. It is also generally known that Negroes are over-represented in the bottom income groups, largely because they are either unqualified for the better jobs or because they often don't get them even when they are qualified. There would be little value in reciting once again the well-known facts about Negro disadvantage unless they could be put into an analytical framework which provides better insight into the historic causes of Negro poverty and the likely directions of future change. In attempting to do just that, I shall trace the role the Negro has played in the antipoverty program and explore the prospects for a narrowing of the economic gap between the races.

There are many who feel that a new day is dawning for the Negro in America. The passage of the Civil Rights Act, the enactment of the antipoverty program, the proposed expenditure of billions of additional dollars for education and training, and similar measures have raised hopes in some quarters that the day will soon come when the Negro and white worker will be able to compete for jobs on equal terms. However, some problem areas, in the absence of change, suggest caution rather than unbridled optimism regarding future prospects for a narrowing of the economic gap between whites and nonwhites.

Any objective evaluation of the economic position of Negroes in America would show that they have made tremendous progress. Negroes, once highly concentrated in sharecropping and farm labor, have now moved up to unskilled and semiskilled factory jobs. Appreciable numbers have even moved into white-collar employment. This change has raised the skills of the Negro labor force, it has increased their productivity, and it is in large measure responsible for the vast improvement in their level of living. If we take what is perhaps the single most important aspect of life that we attempt to measure, namely life expectancy itself, we find that the female Negro infant born in 1960 could expect to live 21 years longer than her mother born in 1920—a gain of nearly 50 percent in life expectancy in the relatively brief span of 40 years.

Not only are Negroes living longer, they are also living far better than ever before. Negro housing, for example, may still leave much to be desired; but, the proportion living in dilapidated houses was cut in half between 1950 and 1960. The real incomes of Negroes have also shown a remarkable rise. Between 1940 and 1960 the wages and salaries of the average male Negro worker rose from about $1,000 to about $3,000 (both figures measured in terms of 1960 dollars). In other words, there was a threefold increase in Negro purchasing power during this period.

History is important for societies but it counts for little in the reckoning of most individuals. If a man tells his wife that she is three times as well off as her grandmother was at the same age, she is not likely to be impressed. She regards it as much more significant if her neighbor has three times as much income as she herself has *now*. It is with the present and future that most people are concerned, not with the past. And, in considering the present, our position relative to others is most important. The Negro's lot is improving but so is that of the white. The critical question in many minds is whether the gap between the races is narrowing.

Tom Kahn, who was Bayard Rustin's assistant in organizing the 1963 March on Washington, recently wrote:[1]

> It takes a lot of running to stand still on the treadmill of this technologically advancing society. When you know you're running hard and everyone tells you you're moving at a fast clip, and yet the scenery around you remains the same, the most appropriate word to describe your reactions is . . . frustration.

Yet, the fact is that the Negro has not been standing still and the scenery around him has been changing most dramatically. He has had tremendous increases in all aspects of life for which objective measures are available. The only reason many Negroes feel they are standing still is that the whites too have had these gains, and in many areas the gap between the races does not appear to be narrowing.

Role of the Negro In the War on Poverty

The war on poverty has many causes, and it would be unwise and incorrect to simplify too much. The high rate of unemployment for

---

[1]Tom Kahn, "Problems of the Negro Movement," *Dissent* (Winter 1964), p. 111.

nearly a decade was undoubtedly a major factor in initiating the new program, as was the threat of continued or perhaps even increased unemployment caused by automation. Nor can we forget the contributions of latter-day muckrakers like Michael Harrington or the happy circumstance that we had an action-minded President, who first proposed the war on poverty in the fall of 1963. While all these factors are important—and there were others too—I am inclined to agree with Nathan Glazer that racial tension "is undoubtedly the chief reason why poverty has become a major issue in this country."[2]

A casual glance at the statistics on poverty will show that 2.0 million of the 7.2 million poor families are nonwhite. On this basis, one might conclude that nonwhites constitute only a small fraction (about one-fourth) of the poor. Indeed, one astute scholar who should and does know better came to this very conclusion not too long ago. In a commencement address at Lincoln University in 1964, Gunnar Myrdal said, "Though the Negro people account for a disproportionately large number of the poor and the disadvantaged in the American nation, the poor among the Negroes nevertheless constitute only a minority of the subdued 'underclass' in the United States, perhaps 25 per cent or a little more depending on where the line is drawn."[3] A close examination of the facts will show that the Negro is much more prominent among the poor than this figure suggests.

The total number of poor families includes 1.5 million aged families, who today represent a more or less passive element among the poor. During the depression, the aged were very active as a pressure group for social reform. The movement that organized around Townsend was perhaps the most striking example of their activity. Although there still are some important pressure groups among them, the aged appear to be much less forceful and effective today than they were 30 years ago. If the aged poor are removed from the total, we find that nonwhites constitute one-third (33 per cent) of the poor under 65 years old. Even this number understates the importance of the Negro as a component of the poor, because it includes many persons who are only temporarily poor, and they are more likely to be white than nonwhite. An unpublished Census Bureau tabulation shows that about three-fourths of the nonwhite families with incomes under $3,000 one year are also likely to have

[2]Nathan Glazer, "A Sociologist's View of Poverty," *Poverty in America,* edited by Margaret S. Gordon (San Francisco: Chandler, 1965), p. 20.

[3]Gunnar Myrdal, *Challenge to Affluence* (New York: Vintage Books, 1965), p. 178.

incomes of the same amount the following year, as compared with only 60 per cent of the white families. On this basis, it seems likely that the proportion of chronically poor families that are nonwhite is likely to be closer to 40 per cent than to 28 per cent, as the raw unadjusted data show.

With these figures in mind, we can better appreciate the role of the Negro in shaping the new antipoverty program with its emphasis on education, training, and rehabilitation rather than money hand-outs. During the thirties, Negroes were largely tucked away in the rural South, where they worked for the most part as subsistence farmers or sharecroppers. Although their need then was as great as, and perhaps even greater than, that of other segments of the population, they operated largely as passive agents in the war on poverty waged at that time. During the depression the unions and their leaders sparked the drive against poverty. The target was income maintenance to combat the effects of unemployment. The unions organized the millions of unskilled workers; they marched, sang, and struck. They were the prime movers in obtaining passage of the social security laws that characterized the antipoverty measures of the depression.

Today it is primarily the Negro leadership that is focusing attention on the poor. Negroes have been particularly hard hit by the rapid economic changes in recent years. Unemployment rates for Negroes, especially Negro youth, have been painfully high for nearly a decade. For some years we suffered under the delusion that the next turn in the business cycle or a tax cut might clear things up; but it is quite apparent now that the dislocations for some segments of the population, the Negro in particular, are much deeper than that.

The recent riots in several major Northern cities suggest that there is a large dissident element among Negro youth that does not need government statistics to tell them they are being by-passed by society, as were their fathers and grandfathers before them. They are aware of the existence of job vacancies for delivery boys, bus boys, handymen, and other menial tasks, but they are not inclined to flock to them. Their attitude is summarized by Bayard Rustin, who stated recently, "To want a Cadillac is not un-American; to push a cart in the garment center is."[4] There is one major difference between these boys and their forebears: Negro youth today will not stand idly by. In all regions of the country, a revolution is in progress—a revolution that demands rights, dignity, and jobs.

[4]Bayard Rustin, "From Protest to Politics," *Commentary* (February 1965), p. 27.

This revolution may in large measure be responsible for the war on poverty today. President Johnson summed up the matter very neatly when he stated in his message on voting legislation:[5]

> The real hero of this struggle is the American Negro. His actions and protests—his courage to risk safety and even life—have awakened the conscience of the nation. His demonstrations have been designed to call attention to injustice, to provoke change and stir reform. . . . And who among us can say we would have made the same progress were it not for his persistent bravery, and his faith in American democracy.

The rural poor, the aged poor, and even the poor hillbillies in Appalachia and the Ozarks could not arouse the nation to their urgent needs. They continued to suffer indignities of body, mind, and spirit year after year in quiet desperation while they lived in hovels and their children were poorly educated. Action came only recently. It followed a prolonged period of marches, sit-ins, and other forms of protest by the Negro community. There is no reason to believe that the war on poverty and these protest activities are unrelated.

Who Are the Nonwhite Poor?

The Council of Economic Advisers, in its study of poverty, used an income of $3,000 as the poverty line for a family of two or more persons and $1,500 for an individual living alone or with nonrelatives. The failure to take various factors such as size of family, age of family head, and farm residence into account was recognized as a serious shortcoming of the data at the time they were prepared; however, it was not then possible to make more refined estimates. As the data in Table 5.1 illustrate, it is now possible to do so, on the basis of the retabulation by the Department of Health, Education, and Welfare of the Census Bureau's statistics for 1963 using a flexible poverty line.

The basic procedure in preparing the revised estimates employed the use of an economy budget developed by the Department of Agriculture. This budget specifies in great detail the weekly quantities of foods needed by men, women, and children in various age groups in order to maintain nutritional adequacy. Using the quantities specified in the budget and food prices published by the Department of Agriculture, annual estimates were prepared for 124 different types of families classified by farm and nonfarm residence, age and sex of

---

[5]House of Representatives, 89th Congress, 1st Session, "Message from the President of the United States Relative to the Right to Vote," March 15, 1965, p. 5.

TABLE 5.1

Selected Characteristics of Nonwhite Families in Poverty Status in 1963
By Alternative Definitions
(in millions)

Selected Characteristics	All Families	Economy Budget[a]		Income Under $3,000[b]	
		Number	Per cent of total	Number	Per cent of total
Total	4.8	2.0	43	2.0	43
Residence					
Farm	0.4	0.2	62	0.2	79
Nonfarm	4.4	1.8	41	1.8	40
Region					
Northeast	0.9	0.2	27	0.2	26
North Central	0.9	0.3	30	0.3	32
South	2.4	1.4	58	1.4	59
West	0.6	0.1	21	0.1	19
Age of head					
14 to 24 years	0.4	0.2	60	0.2	63
25 to 64 years	3.9	1.5	39	1.4	37
65 years and over	0.5	0.3	53	0.4	73
Type of family					
Male head	3.7	1.3	34	1.3	34
Female head	1.1	0.7	71	0.7	73
Size of family					
2 persons	1.4	0.5	33	0.7	50
3 - 5 persons	2.2	0.8	38	0.8	39
6 or more persons	1.2	0.7	62	0.5	42
Employment status of head					
Not in labor force	1.1	0.8	65	0.8	72
Unemployed	0.2	0.1	53	0.1	43
Employed	3.5	1.1	35	1.1	34
Work experience of head in 1963					
Worked in 1963	4.0	1.5	37	1.4	36
Worked at full-time jobs	3.4	1.1	32	1.0	31
50 - 52 weeks	2.5	0.6	26	0.6	24
Worked at part-time jobs	0.6	0.4	68	0.4	70
Did not work	0.8	0.5	70	0.6	77

[a]Economy level of the poverty index developed by the Social Security Administration by family size and farm vs. nonfarm residence, centering around $3,100 for a nonfarm family of four persons.

[b]Interim measure used by Council of Economic Advisers--under $3,000 for families of two or more persons.

Source: Figures for all families and for number in "economy budget" column are taken from Mollie Orshansky, "Counting the Poor: Another Look at the Poverty Profile," *Social Security Bulletin*, January 1965, Table 8. Figures for number with incomes under $3,000 are based on unpublished data of the Bureau of the Census.

head, and number of children. These annual food costs were converted to incomes on the basis of assumed relationships between food expenditures and total income. Families of three or more persons were assumed to be in poverty if their income was less than 33 per cent of the cost of an economy food budget. In other words, the poverty line for these families was obtained by multiplying the cost of the food budget by a factor of three,[6] a reasonable relationship between income and food expenditures based on data derived from the 1960 Survey of Consumer Expenditures.[7] A ratio of 27 per cent was used for two-person families; unrelated individuals were assumed to need 80 per cent of the requirement for a couple "on the premise that the lower the income the more difficult it would be for one person to cut expenses such as housing and utilities below the minimum for a couple."[8] The estimates for farm families are based on the assumption that they would need 40 per cent less cash income than nonfarm families of the same size and type since many farmers receive part of their food and most of their housing without cash payment.

The dollar values used as the poverty line ranged from about $1,100 for an elderly couple living on a farm to $5,100 for a nonfarm family with seven or more persons. A nonfarm family of four persons was assumed to need $3,130, which allows about 70 cents daily per person for an adequate diet, and an additional $1.40 per person for all other needs—housing, clothing, medical care, transportation, etc. The poverty lines for other family types were designed to provide equivalent levels of living. Using these dollar values, retabulations were made of the March 1964 Current Population Survey, in which the income reported for each family was compared with the income "required" by that family. If the reported income was below the required amount for that family type, the family was classified as poor. Families identified as poor on this basis were then retabulated according to various characteristics.

There is little difference in the results produced by the two different concepts of poverty—the flat $3,000 poverty line used by the Council of Economic Advisers and the flexible poverty line used by

---

[6]Mollie Orshansky, "Counting the Poor: Another Look at the Poverty Profile," *Social Security Bull.* (January 1965).

[7]Helen Lamale, "Expenditure Patterns of Low-Consumption Families," *1964 Proceedings of Business and Economic Statistics Section*, American Statistical Assoc., p. 440.

[8]Orshansky, *op. cit.*

HEW. The overall number of nonwhite families classified as poor is virtually identical and the distribution by various characteristics is also much the same. The analysis will therefore proceed in terms of the $3,000 criterion, since that will facilitate the use of the voluminous 1960 Census data available on the subject.[9] Following are some of the highlights regarding nonwhite poverty suggested by these data.

Geographic Distribution

Nonwhite poverty is a geographic problem to a much greater extent than is commonly realized. About one-half of all nonwhite families live in the South, where incomes in general, and for nonwhites in particular, lag far behind the rest of the nation. Nearly 60 per cent of the Southern nonwhite families are in poverty as compared with rates that are only half as high in the rest of the nation. Because nonwhite families are concentrated in the South, where they receive low incomes, about 70 per cent of all nonwhites in poverty are located in that region.

The Negro sharecropper, who once figured prominently in the ranks of the poor, has dwindled in absolute and relative numbers. At present, only about one-sixth of all Negro families in the South live on farms—about one-quarter of a million. Negro poverty today, even in the South, is much more concentrated in the cities and in rural hamlets than on the farms.

Negro poverty in the North and West is located almost entirely in the big urban centers like New York, Chicago, Philadelphia, and Detroit. Old age does not appear to be a major cause of Negro poverty. Much more important are family instability, unemployment, and low rates of pay.

According to any reasonable assumptions regarding rates of out-migration, over half of all Negroes will still be living in the South by 1980. The expected relatively high rates of out-migration are likely to be offset by the high fertility of those who remain. As a result, the geographic distribution of the Negro population does not shift as much as the figures on migration might suggest. In view of the intensity of feeling manifested by Southern whites on racial matters, it is hard to believe that Negroes in this region will receive to any great extent either the training they need or the opportunity to move into more promising jobs. We are, however, living in an age of rapid

---

[9]There are many different kinds of poverty—economic, cultural, spiritual, etc. Only economic poverty is considered here.

change and must not dismiss the possibility of a vast upheaval that will change the whole political structure in the South. The possibility of this kind of transformation is far greater today than it was only six months ago. At the same time, the ingenuity of the Southern white in thwarting the political aspirations of the Negro should not be underestimated. Only time will tell how the position of the Southern Negro will change, but it would be well not to expect too much. The President has wisely cautioned that after the new voting bill is passed "the people of Selma . . . must still live and work together. And when the attention of the nation has gone elsewhere they must try to heal the wounds and to build a new community."[10] It is at this point that the real tests will come.

The Family Structure

The matriarchal structure of nonwhite family life is well known and its relation to poverty is obvious. There are proportionately more than twice as many broken families among nonwhites as among whites. The women who head these families, particularly among the nonwhites, start childrearing early, often under very difficult circumstances. They lack the training to get a good job, and they have the dual burden of being both mother and father to their children. Under these circumstances it is not surprising that families headed by women have a very high incidence of poverty and that a large proportion of the poor nonwhite families are of this type.

In the Northern states, only one-fifth of the nonwhite husband-wife families were in poverty as compared with three-fifths of the broken families. Because of the very difficult circumstances faced by families headed by women in the North, they constituted one-half of all poor nonwhite families in the region.

The generally lower incomes in the South, particularly for nonwhites, produced a higher incidence of poverty for married couples as well as for broken families. In the South, about half of the nonwhite married couples and about 80 per cent of the broken families were in poverty. These figures suggest that in the North a married nonwhite couple stands an excellent chance of having an income above the poverty line; nonwhite married couples in the South and broken families in all regions are much less likely to have an adequate income.

---

[10] "Message from the President of the United States Relative to the Right to Vote," *op. cit.*, p. 6.

Employment Status Related to Income

Although psychological factors are often stressed in discussions of nonwhite poverty, about one million families—half the total classified as poor—were headed by full-time workers. About 600,000 of these families were headed by a person who worked full-time throughout the year, and 400,000 were headed by full-time workers who experienced some unemployment. Nearly half of these workers were employed as laborers or as service workers (domestics, janitors, gas station attendants, porters, etc.); another large block worked as semiskilled factory workers. These facts suggest that low wages and unemployment account for much of the poverty for nonwhites, as they do for whites. Retraining might get some of these low-paid family heads into more lucrative types of employment. For the great majority, however, it is not at all clear how they will be brought above the poverty line without some form of wage or income subsidization.

Increases in the coverage and the amount of the minimum wage are often suggested as antipoverty tools for the low-paid worker. Although this technique has understandable appeal, there is by no means unanimity of opinion—even among liberal economists—that it will do the job. Sar Levitan, an eminent authority in this field, wrote recently that there is a "need for exercising caution in considering any further increases in minimum wages over the next few years, assuming the continuation of recent trends in overall productivity and consumer prices." He expresses some concern about the disemployment effects of an increase in the minimum wage at present and concludes that there is a question "whether the low paying jobs would exist at all if minimum rates were raised above levels justified by the productivity of the affected workers."[11]

Occupational Gap Between the Races

One of the important reasons for Negro poverty and discontent today is the Negroes' failure to move into the better-paying jobs in any large numbers. While none can deny that the Negro worker has gained in employment during the past 50 years in an *absolute* sense, he has not moved ahead relative to the white worker. It is of some significance therefore to examine the patterns of occupational change in the past to see what must be done if the Negro worker is to bridge the occupational gap.

---

[11]Sar A. Levitan, *Programs in Aid of the Poor* (Kalamazoo: W. E. Upjohn Institute, 1965).

Census data show that by 1910 the white labor force had already completed much of the transition from agriculture to industry. In the decennial census taken that year, only one-fourth of white workers were employed in farming; another one-fourth worked in white-collar jobs; and the remaining half were more or less equally divided among craftsmen, factory operatives, and nonfarm laborers or service workers (see Table 5.2). In that same year, the Negro labor force was split 50–50 between farming and nonfarm work. The farmers were, of course, largely Southern sharecroppers or laborers working and living under the most miserable conditions, even by contemporary standards. Those who were not working as farmers were employed largely as service workers (i.e. domestics, waiters, bootblacks) and as nonfarm laborers largely on railroads and construction gangs. Relatively few (only 5 per cent) had even risen to the point of semiskilled factory work, and even fewer (only 3 per cent) worked as craftsmen or white-collar workers.[12]

The next fifty years witnessed a dramatic movement out of agriculture for both whites and Negroes. The proportion of white workers dropped from 28 per cent at the turn of the century to only about 7 per cent at present. In the case of the nonwhites the shift away from farming was even more dramatic. The 50 per cent estimate for 1910 dropped to only 10 per cent. The frequent cry of some economists for greater mobility as a solution to rural poverty has certainly been heeded by the Negro. He has shown tremendous mobility and energy in search of economic opportunity, often against overwhelming odds. The displacement of Negroes from farming has largely been absorbed by the manual and service trades, although in recent years, opportunities for nonwhites in white-collar employment have been growing in importance.

A close examination of the decennial census data provides better insight than we have had before into the way the transformation of the Negro labor force took place. In each decade, as new industries and occupations developed, it was the white worker who moved in first. According to one analysis, "White workers capture the newly growing fields in which labor resources are scarce, pay levels are good, prospects for advancement are bright, the technology is most advanced, and working conditions the most modern."[13] They leave in their wake jobs in the older industries that are less desirable

---

[12]Dale Hiestand, *Economic Growth and Employment Opportunities for Minorities* (New York: Columbia University Press, 1964), p. 42.
[13]*Ibid.*, p. 114.

TABLE 5.2

Percentage Distribution of White and Negro Labor Force, By Occupational Field, 1910-60

	1910		1920		1930		1940		1950		1960	
	White	*Negro*	*White*	*Negro*	*White*	*Negro*	*White*	*Negro*	*White*	*Negro*	*White*	*Negro*
All sectors	100.0	100.0	100.0	100.0	100.0	100.0	100.0[a]	100.0[a]	100.0[a]	100.0[a]	100.0	100.0
Nonfarm	72.0	49.6	76.0	53.4	80.6	63.9	82.3	66.6	81.6	79.5	92.7	88.7
White-collar sector	23.8	3.0	27.8	3.6	33.0	4.6	35.7	6.0	39.9	10.2	46.5	15.4
Professional and technical workers	4.8	1.4	5.3	1.5	6.5	2.1	8.0	2.7	8.6	3.4	12.2	4.7
Proprietors, managers, and officials	7.4	.8	7.4	.8	8.3	1.0	9.0	1.3	9.8	2.0	11.5	2.3
Clerical and sales workers	11.6	.8	15.1	1.3	18.2	1.5	18.7	2.0	21.5	4.8	22.8	8.4
Manual and service sector	48.2	46.6	48.2	49.8	47.6	59.3	46.6	60.6	47.7	69.3	46.2	73.3
Skilled workers and foremen	13.0	2.5	14.5	3.0	14.2	3.2	12.2	3.0	14.4	5.5	13.8	5.7
Semiskilled workers and operatives	16.1	5.4	16.8	7.3	17.2	9.4	19.0	10.3	20.3	18.3	17.8	20.7
Laborers	14.3	17.4	13.4	20.8	11.7	21.6	6.1	14.3	5.0	15.7	4.4	14.1
Service workers	4.8	21.3	3.5	18.7	4.5	25.1	9.3	33.0	8.0	29.8	10.2	32.8
Farm	28.0	50.4	24.1	46.6	19.4	36.1	16.7	32.8	11.1	19.0	7.3	11.3

[a]Sum of items does not equal 100 per cent because some failed to report an occupation.

Source: Dale L. Hiestand, *Economic Growth and Employment Opportunities for Minorities* (New York: Columbia University Press, 1964), p. 42.

because the pay is not as good, nor are the prospects for advancement. Moreover, many of the jobs left behind by the whites are in industries dominated by an old technology, which, when replaced, would be likely to require reduced manpower.

Thus, in every decade, the newest and best opportunities available to the Negroes were often quite vulnerable. The jobs deserted by the whites were invariably better than the ones at which Negroes were employed at the time, but they were, nonetheless, not the jobs with the bright futures. This pattern of occupational change is, as we shall see, of great significance in assessing the prospects of the Negro. It suggests that if the Negro is ever to approach occupational equality with whites he must seek out and somehow gain admittance to the "frontier area of occupational expansion." If he continues to get only jobs that the white has left over, he may never bridge the occupational gap. Indeed some would argue that if the Negro follows the traditional pattern of occupational mobility, he may find himself in a tighter and tighter job squeeze because the employment that would have normally been handed down to him is being automated.

It must be granted on the basis of the empirical evidence that the absolute employment position of the Negro worker has improved considerably in the past fifty years. But, has the relative gap between whites and Negroes changed? In the work previously referred to, Hiestand constructed an occupational index that permits this type of comparison to be made.[14] He first separated the white and Negro workers for each year into seven occupational groups: professional, managerial, clerical and sales, skilled, semi-skilled, unskilled, and agriculture. A weight was then assigned to each occupation roughly indicative of the relative earning power for that kind of work. The actual weights used were the median incomes reported in the 1950 Census for workers who were employed throughout the year. A weighted index for each year was then constructed by multiplying the proportion of workers in each occupation by the weight and summing the results for all seven occupation groups. This operation was performed separately for white and Negro men and women. The ratio of the Negro to the white index computed for each year shows the relative occupational position of Negroes to whites.

In the case of men, the index shows no significant change between 1910 and 1940. There was some slight improvement in the relative occupational position of Negro men during the past twenty years; but this is entirely due to their movement out of the South.

---

[14]*Ibid.*, p. 51.

Indexes which have been constructed on a state-by-state basis show that there were very few significant changes in the occupational distribution of Negro males relative to whites in the past twenty years.[15]

The relative occupational distribution of Negro women relative to whites also was about the same in 1940 as it was in 1910. As in the case of the males, there appears to have been some improvement in the relative occupational position of Negro women during the past twenty years, but this change also may be primarily due to their movement out of the South with its very limited opportunities for Negro employment, rather than to any general upgrading of the kinds of jobs open to Negroes.

The weight of the evidence therefore indicates that although there has been considerable occupational improvement for Negro workers during the past fifty years in an absolute sense, the position of Negroes relative to whites has not changed much. Having established these facts, we may now turn to an examination of their meaning, particularly with respect to assessing their significance for future trends in Negro employment (and income). Here we must tread with care because, as so many forecasters have discovered to their regret, past is not necessarily prologue.

Future Possibilities

It seems clear from the data that the gap between whites and non-whites will not be narrowed if the traditional patterns of occupational change are maintained. In order to catch up with the whites, Negro workers will have to be propelled into promising new jobs in new industries instead of drifting into the old jobs in the dying industries, as in the past. This change will come about for Negroes only if two conditions are met. They must obtain the education and training required for the new jobs, and the barriers to their entry into the better-paying fields must be lowered. The prospects that both of these conditions will be met in the near future are not very good. It is unrealistic to talk about bridging the occupational gap in the modern world when one-fourth of the Negro youth in their early twenties have not gone beyond the eighth grade and over half have not completed high school. There is not much that people with so little education can be trained to do in our complex economy.

---

[15]U.S. Senate, *Hearings before the Committee on Labor and Public Welfare on Bills Relating to Equal Employment Opportunities* (Washington, D.C.: Government Printing Office, 1963), p. 323.

Moreover, there is little evidence that society is willing to make the huge investments in education and training that are required if the Negro is ever to be able to compete on equal terms with the white in the labor market. Most attempts to provide effective school integration have met with hostility and "foot-dragging." Even in the prosperous North there has been more lip service than action in the improvement of the quality of education in deprived areas. Now at last we are beginning to talk seriously about pouring billions of additional dollars into education in low-income areas. It remains to be seen, however, if the money will in fact be appropriated and if it will result in better education.

Finally, we come to just plain discrimination, which may be the hardest of all obstacles to overcome because it is so deeply imbedded in our culture. As previously noted, about 60 per cent of the Negroes still live in the South and, according to any reasonable assumptions regarding rates of out-migration, over half of them will still be in that region by 1980. In view of the intensity of feeling that has been manifested by the Southern whites on racial matters, it is hard to believe that in the foreseeable future Negroes in this region will receive to any great extent either the training they need or the opportunity to move into the more promising jobs.

In the face of these and many other factors, there is little reason to be optimistic about the possibility of narrowing the occupational gap between the races in the near future. There are, however, offsetting forces that provide some hope. At present, there is probably less discrimination against Negroes than at any previous time in our history. It is also likely that discrimination will tend to decrease with time because of the strong pressures being exerted by the federal government. These efforts should create new opportunities for Negro employment in federal, state, and local governments, in private companies doing contract work for the federal government, and in other companies that will be under social pressure to liberalize their employment practices.

At the same time that the prospects for Negroes to obtain skilled employment have been increasing, the attitudes of some Negro leaders have been undergoing a change. Historically, the civil rights movement has focused attention largely on efforts designed to publicize the plight of the Negro and to promote integration. This emphasis led to the March on Washington, demonstrations, sit-ins, picketing, and other activities that were instrumental in promoting passage of the civil rights and antipoverty legislation. More recently it was the drive for voting rights in Selma, Alabama, that captured the headlines and the public imagination. In the background, however, there are signs that attention in some quarters is now shifting to other areas such as the fight for better jobs, education, and housing, with only secondary emphasis on questions like integration. This attitude was clearly expressed by Bayard Rustin when he said recently, "We have got to lift the school problem from integration to that of quality schools; which has to include, we say, integration secondarily."[16]

This is not to say that the fight for rights and political power is being abandoned. On the contrary, recent events suggest that they are being intensified, if anything. At the same time, however, there seems to be a growing recognition of the need to develop the skills and other qualities that are needed by Negro workers in order to take full advantage of the job opportunities that may arise. As Nathan Glazer has pointed out very effectively in a recent article, the legislative gains that have been made by Negroes in the past few years make it possible and perhaps even necessary for contemporary leaders of the civil rights movement to return to the fundamental policies outlined by Booker T. Washington at the turn of the century. According to Glazer,[17] Booker T. Washington

> saw that the Negro had been denuded by slavery of the qualities necessary for building an independent and satisfying life. Primarily what concerned him . . . was the devaluation of work produced by slavery, for he felt that independent and productive work was the basis of racial respect. But Washington also assumed that the Negroes, as they gained in education and income, would be enfranchised and would be able to play a major role in politics and in the shaping of their own fate. He fought desperately against the movement to disenfranchise Negroes in the South in the 1890's. When this movement succeeded, and Jim Crow began to fasten its bonds on the Negro people, he was left with half a program. The other half became the program of protest.

Glazer then goes on to state that "we now have a situation which corresponds . . . to the one Booker T. Washington first saw as his major task, the building up of the economic and social foundations of the Negro community."

So long as the Negro could see no reasonable prospect for advancement beyond the most menial jobs, he was behaving more or

---

[16]"The Negro Revolution—Where Shall It Go Now?," *Dissent* (Summer 1964), p. 282.
[17]Book review by Nathan Glazer in *Commentary* (October 1964), pp. 77-79.

less rationally in assigning a low value to education, saving, and the other fruitful avenues to advancement. Limited opportunities for employment in the professional fields forced Negroes to concentrate on those areas where there was a Negro market for their services—preaching, teaching, and social work. Because of their concentration in these low-paid fields the average Negro college graduate, even today, can expect to earn less over a lifetime than the white who does not go beyond the eighth grade. In view of facts such as these, who could argue with the young school dropout who might feel what James Baldwin has expressed so well in the following words: "It is not to be wondered at that if . . . studying is going to prepare him to be a porter or an elevator boy—or his teacher—well, then, to hell with it."

But we now have a chance to change all of this. Whether in fact we will depends upon two things: the extent to which our society opens up and takes the Negro in as a full-fledged participating member; and the extent to which the Negro is prepared to move in should the opportunities present themselves. Only time will tell whether we can succeed in getting both of these forces to move in the right direction at the right time.

The Poverty of Aging

Harold L. Sheppard

Upjohn Institute for Employment Research

[*Reprinted with permission of The Macmillan Company from* Poverty as a Public Issue, *edited by Ben Seligman. Copyright © The Free Press, a Division of the Macmillan Company 1965.*]

THE STATUS of a society's aged may well be taken as a measure of the degree to which that society has met the problem of poverty in general. When the aged have "reached the end of the road" or the "home stretch in the race of life" in one condition or another, we have some indication of the institutions and actions taken by the general community prior to that period which affect the outcome of individual life careers.

To begin with, the problem of the aged is essentially one associated with the emergence of a modern, industrialized society. Such societies have far greater proportions of their populations over the age of sixty-five than do traditionally underdeveloped ones. At the same time, despite a greater proportion of older persons, these societies use a smaller proportion of their older members in their active labor force. The reasons are obvious, having to do with the increased (and increasing) longevity due to the improved practice of medicine, public health, and sanitation, with improved living and working conditions, and the like, as well as with the reduction in manpower hours required to produce goods and services.

More people are living to be "old," absolutely and proportionately, as compared to our own past, and as compared to other existing societies. Moreover, people are living beyond the age where they are needed in the labor force. Even within the United States today, the relation between industrialism and the age-occupation distribution is clear, as shown by the fact that the proportion of the aged male segment of the labor force engaged in agriculture is about two-and-a-half times the proportion of males of all ages in agricultural occupations.

The problems of poverty among the aged stem also from the fact that an increasing number of the sixty-five plus population are becoming definitely "aged," and within this upper-age bracket among the old, say, seventy-five and over, women will predominate, especially husbandless women with low incomes. By 1980 one-fifth of all the sixty-five-plus population will be females aged seventy-five and over. Employment is clearly out of the question for the vast majority of such individuals, men included. Retirement becomes the vital variable in the poverty condition of the aged, and the longer the average person lives in retirement, the greater are his or her chances of becoming impoverished. The radical decline in labor-force participation among the aged, from a rate of 70 per cent for men in 1890 to less than one-third in 1960 (including even part-time workers), is not due merely to the rising numbers of the very old among the aged. Even in the sixty-five to sixty-nine group, employment as a source of income is declining. For example, the labor-force participation rate, including part-time work, dropped for the sixty-five- to sixty-nine-year-old males from 57 per cent in 1954 to about 45 per cent in 1960. We can expect this rate to continue to decline in years to come.

Employment as a source of income for the total aged population of sixty-five and older is a status enjoyed only by about one-fifth of that population. The median income of all two-person families with aged heads (including those employed) is about $2500: this means that more than one-half of such families are below the poverty line of $3000. The median income of all aged persons living alone is about

$1000; this means that more than one-half of aged individuals living alone—most of them women—are below the poverty line of $1500.

It is striking to note that there is little in the way of public thinking—and even in the official documents of our government agencies—that adequately conveys what may be called the dynamic and longitudinal facets of the phenomena involved. For example, the typical statistical presentations will tell us that the aged in 1960 had improved in their economic status, say, over 1950. The imagery here is that of a boat—labeled A-G-E-D—floating in a canal, through a series of locks that raise or lower the boat from one point in space to another point in space. To mix the image a bit, space represents time.

But this primitive model has very little to do with reality. One of the things we should be looking at, for example, is the following: what happens to a group of people, say, aged fifty-five to sixty-five in 1950 by the time they live to the year 1960, when they become at least sixty-five, and, at most, seventy-five years of age? That is the basic question, in my opinion.

The question usually asked is: are the aged of 1960 any better off, or worse off, than the aged of 1950? The first query pertains to the life career pattern of given individuals insofar as they experience relative deprivation over time, that is, relative to their earlier income. The second question, and the answers to it, shed light on how well the society has fared in assuring the aged of one era a decent standard of living as compared with the aged of another era.

To quote from the 1961 *Report of the Senate Subcommittee on Problems of the Aged and Aging,*

> . . . one major flaw characterizes much of the ordinary discussion about the income status of our aged citizens. This is the failure to reckon with the dynamic nature of the problem. For example, when it is said . . . that the median money income of aged family heads as a percentage of the median income of all families dropped from 60 per cent in 1949 to 52 per cent in 1959, there seems to be a tacit assumption that the aged of 1959 are the same people as those aged in 1949, but they are not exactly the same. The 4.8 million men and 5.5 million women aged 65 to 74 in 1960 were not "aged" in 1950, for example.
>
> The crucial question is, what change takes place in the incomes of a given age group as it moves into retirement status? When we say that between 1949 and 1959 the income of the male "aged" increased 55 per cent, we are really not talking about the same intact population. In reality, the median income of men aged 55 to 64 in 1949 was $2366, but by 1959 the same men (minus those who died, etc.) experienced not an increase in their median income but a decrease.

More specifically, the best data available on this point are provided by the Bureau of the Census, in its January 1961 report on 1959 incomes. The median income of men born in March 1895 and earlier was $1710 in 1949; 10 years later, the median income of the *same* group had *decreased* 8 per cent, to $1576. These figures, moreover, are in current dollars and not constant ones: an analysis using constant 1959 dollars would reveal that this group of men suffered an approximate 33 per cent *decrease* in real income from 1949 to 1959, while during the same period of time the real median income for men aged 24 to 34 in 1949 *increased* by approximately 57 per cent; for men aged 34 to 44 in 1949, the increase was approximately 34 per cent.

The same analysis can be applied to the changes in assets and savings. In all of these trends, it is important to recognize another aspect that is too often neglected, namely, the effect of rising expectations in the general population—expectations which do not automatically abate upon retirement. This aspect further aggravates the problem of an adequate income for future generations of retired Americans. An increasing number of such persons will be more insistent on an adequate level of living than past generations of retirees. The younger Americans of today will carry into their own retirement of tomorrow many expectations and aspirations that cannot be met if their retired income status is no better than that of the aged of the present time.[1]

Another point I want to make relates to the controversial document issued by the Ad Hoc Committee on the Triple Revolution, in which it is argued that modern technology increasingly requires a smaller and smaller proportion of the population to create and provide goods and services, and that therefore we should abandon the social institutions and mechanisms that require employment in an occupation as a condition for obtaining food, clothing, housing, and other services—with money as the primary intermediary between em ployment and these ends. One does not have to accept this radical suggestion for the total population's problems to see its relevance to the problems of the retired aged.

The point should be obvious; namely, that if there is any class of human beings to which the Triple Revolution applies it is the group of aged Americans who are retired. Indeed, we have already accepted the principle of income and material support without the intermediary of employment—although many students of gerontology would hasten to add that we only tolerate this principle meagerly and that we apply it begrudgingly and in a miserly fashion.

A third point is less controversial, perhaps, but more concrete and immediate, with consequences for the problem of future poverty among the aged of tomorrow, all of us included. The University of Michigan study[2] (by Morgan, Cohen, Brazer, and David) reveals that out of 1967 spending units headed by nonretired persons aged thirty or over:

136, or 6 per cent will have no pensions.

1098, or 55 per cent will have social security only.

710, or 39 per cent will have social security *and* private pensions.

Some signs of possible poverty to come may be gleaned from the following findings, also from The University of Michigan study. They suggest the lack of advance preparation for old-age security:

1. Spending units who have had less than $500 in the bank for the past five years are more likely than not to report they will get along during retirement.

2. Nine per cent of heads between 30 and 45 see hard times in old age. Sixteen per cent of heads older than 45 see hard times in old age.

3. Assurance of financing of medical care during retirement is low.

4. More than one third of middle-aged and over ([45+] have less than $5,000 assets of any kind.

5. About one half of non-retired people said they are now doing nothing or cannot do anything to add to retirement income. (This includes many who nevertheless are covered by social security.)

TABLE 1

Median Income of Men, by Age, for the United States:
1959 and 1949
(in current dollars)

Age	1959	1949	Index (35 to 44 Years=100)	
			1959	*1949*
Total	$3996	$2346	75	79
14 to 24 years	1131	1112	21	39
14 to 19 years	411	410	8	14
20 to 24 years	2612	1726	49	58
25 to 34 years	4747	2754	89	93
35 to 44 years	5320	2951	100	100
45 to 54 years	4852	2751	91	93
55 to 64 years	4190	2751	79	80
65 years and over	1576	1016	30	34

Source: Bureau of the Census.

TABLE 2

Median Income of Men in 1959 and 1949,
by Period of Birth, for the United States
(in current dollars)

Period of Birth	Median Income In: 1959	Median Income In: 1949	Per Cent Change, 1949 to 1959
April 1925 to March 1935	$4747	$1112	327
April 1915 to March 1925	5320	2754	93
April 1905 to March 1915	4852	2951	64
April 1895 to March 1905	4190	2751	52
March 1895 and earlier	1576	1710	-8

Source: Bureau of the Census.

The authors go on to comment that

> ... aside from the automatic and largely compulsory retirement systems, and the accumulation of equity in a home, most people are making little other provision for retirement. The vast increase in retirement systems, particularly the Federal social security system, makes this less of a problem than it has been in the past. The question remains whether people, most of whom expect to retire by the time they are seventy years old, will find themselves dissatisfied with their economic situation when they retire.

The aged of today have had a lifetime in which to accumulate savings and other wealth, but their highest incomes in that working lifetime were not adequate to assure subsequent years of well-being. There is no assurance that the aged of 1975 or beyond will have had much improvement in the same conditions affecting the working lives of the aged of 1964.

Roughly 70 per cent of the nonretired (aged thirty or more) heads of spending units in The University of Michigan study indicate that they plan retirement after the age of sixty-five, or do not plan to retire at all. It will be interesting, in the decades ahead, to observe the actual behavior of today's working population, determining whether they retire at the age they planned, and how any discrepancy between planned and actual retirement age affects their economic status. Table 7, which reveals the savings experience of people already retired, suggests to some extent what might be expected for those who plan, as compared to those who do not plan to retire.

TABLE 3

Highest Income Head Ever Earned

	Aged	Nonwhite[1]	All Poor Families	All Families
	(percentages)			
$ 1- 949	13	19	14	4
950-1949	18	19	18	5
1950-2949	18	17	18	7
2950-4949	10	25	21	22
4950-7449	2	6	9	33
7450+	1	0	3	21
Not ascertained	38	14	17	8
Never worked	28	2	12	4
Mean highest income ever earned	$2230	$2490	$2949	
Mean budget requirement	$2401	$4144	$3676	
Number of families	137	128	755	2800

Source: *Income and Welfare in the United States,* by J. Morgan et al, p. 200. Copyright 1962 by McGraw-Hill Book Company. Used by permission of McGraw-Hill Book Company.

[1]Excludes aged, disabled, single with children, those who worked less than 49 weeks in 1959 but usually employed.

TABLE 4

Hospitalization Insurance

	Aged	Nonwhite[1]	All Poor Families	All Families
	(percentages)			
Everyone in s.u.[2] covered	21	39	32	63
Someone covered	3	8	5	6
No one covered	74	51	62	30
Not ascertained	2	2	1	1

Source: *Ibid.*, p. 204.
[1]See previous table.
[2]"Spending unit."

TABLE 5

Types of Poor Families, by Regions (1959)

Region	*Aged*	*Nonwhite*[1]	*All Poor Families*	*All Families*
		(percentages)		
Northeast	23	4	16	23
North Central	27	12	23	29
South	41	83	51	33
West	9	1	10	15

Source: *Ibid.*
[1]Excluding groups cited in above tables.

TABLE 6

Planned Retirement Age Within Earning Potential
(Percentage Distribution of Nonretired Spending Unit
Heads Thirty and Older)

	Earning Potential of Spending Unit Heads					
			White Nonfarmers By Education			
Planned Retirement Age	*Nonw.*	*W. Farmers*	*0-11*	*12*	*Some College*	*All Non-retired S.U. Hds. 30 & Older*
	(percentages)					
30 to 59	4	4	4	5	9	5
60 to 64	9	8	9	11	14	11
65 to 70	40	27	48	51	43	46
71 and over	1	0	1	1	2	1
Not ascertained	14	17	13	11	10	12
Do not plan to retire	32	44	25	21	22	25
Number of s.u. heads	270	155	748	399	382	1967

Source: *Ibid.*

TABLE 7

Experience of Those Who Are Already Retired

Amount of Dissaving Since Retirement	Whether Head's Retirement Was Planned		
	Planned	Not Planned	Total
Had savings at retirement; have used less than ¼	14	6	9
¼ to ½	4	8	7
½ to ¾	3	6	4
more than ¾	6	20	15
amount not ascertained	9	6	7
Have not dissaved; had no savings at retirement time, have none now	51	37	42
Have saved since retirement	13	17	16
Number	104	177	304

Source: *Income and Welfare in the United States*, by J. Morgan et al, p. 200. Copyright 1962 by McGraw-Hill Book Company. Used by permission of McGraw-Hill Book Company.

According to The University of Michigan findings, 40 per cent of all families in the United States (with thirty-year or older heads and nonretired) are covered by private pensions. By contrast, 11 per cent of poor families (with thirty-year or older heads and nonretired) are so covered. *There is no guarantee that all of these will actually retire with a private pension.* We can only be certain regarding percentages now covered by Social Security and other government pensions: 93 per cent of all families, and 84 per cent of all poor families will have some form of Social Security benefit. This is apart from the question of the adequacy of such anticipated retirement incomes. But no one knows for sure how many of the persons now working for companies with private pension plans (40 per cent) will actually have a pension when they retire. Some estimates indicate that perhaps a maximum of one-half will be so fortunate—this, again, apart from the question of the adequacy of such retirement income.

The significance of these observations for those Americans now in their last working years, and for those working poor in general, can be seen in the following statements by the authors of The University of Michigan study:

> For persons fifty-five and older, the question of resources for the future is particularly critical. The incidence of both illness and unemployment increases for that age group, and the availability of a cushion of savings or insurance is important. . . .

Neither the past earning experience nor the assets of the poor suggest that a large fraction were much better off in the recent past than they were in 1959. Their present level of savings and their rights to health insurance and pensions suggest that many will be worse off in the future. None of the poor can afford sickness or injury. Some will be unable to retire because they have no pension rights. This substantial long-term poverty suggests the need for an examination of the transmission of poverty from one generation to the next.[3]

For anyone to assert that today's retired aged should have saved while they were working—and presumably on a voluntary basis—is an indication of indifference or ignorance of economic facts. It is true that most people, for reasons of unawareness or lack of emotions concerning their future as retirees, make few if any private decisions that will improve such futures. But economic growth generally means that incomes and purchasing power improve in the process of growth, at least for those still contributing to the economy through employment. While so engaged when younger and employed, the aged of any given generation had to spend most of their wages and salaries merely to attain a decent standard of living. If they were able to save at all, it was generally very little, certainly, in terms of future retired status needs. Furthermore, it has been argued that if the labor force were to engage in extensive private savings while employed in order to assure major improvements in its members' future retirement incomes, the withdrawal of current purchasing power would constitute an irretrievable economic shock to the Gross National Product; such excessive savings would result in widespread and persistent unemployment. If all this is correct, then, it might be further claimed that the employed nonretired population owes much of its present income and living levels to the currently nonemployed retired population, and that therefore the latter group should be rewarded (or supported) to an extent much greater than is currently sanctioned under present social policy.

The poverty of the aged, therefore, can be attributed partly to a social system which still insists on current employment as the basic requirement for human well-being, even though the technology does not have need for the labor of an increasing number of men and women in the upper age brackets. Moreover, there is every indication that the "entry age" into the status of retirement will continue to decline. The irony is that this decline is due partly to the pressures of younger workers trying to eliminate competitors for jobs. This is one of the social consequences of automation and cybernation, at least in certain industries and certain occupations.

At the upper end of the "old age continuum," more and more Americans will be able to live to the ages of seventy-five, eighty, and even older. In this connection, while the total aged population, that is, the sixty-five-plus group, will increase between 1960 and 1975 by about 33 per cent, the size of the population eighty-five and older will increase, according to current estimates, by nearly 80 per cent! Medical science is adding years to life; medical politics is helping to add poverty to these years.

Unlike other disadvantaged groups in the recent past and in the present, the aged have now very little power to effectuate any significant change in the current pattern of distributing wealth and income. There are some minor exceptions, and these are usually in local situations, not on the national level. Essentially, this lack of power is due to the fact that the masses of the aged, unlike farmers, workers, or ethnic minority groups, do not coalesce as a self-identifying group. Many of the *statistical* conditions for political effectiveness—including population size, income figures, and even percentages of total voting-age population—are present and seem to be emerging more definitely. But the *sociopsychological* conditions are not present. One fact alone is worth repeating here:

> . . . in every presidential election since 1948 (except for 1956 when Eisenhower's qualities seemed to have affected all age groups) the older voters have shown a greater preference for the Republican candidates than have the young voters. In 1960 voters over 65 were the only age group that voted just as strongly Republican in 1960 as they had in 1965. . . .[4]

And the Republican Party, at the present time at least, is the party least likely to support any basic departure from contemporary public policy regarding the poverty status of the aged.

Given the fact that the only tool of bargaining power the retired aged would have is the vote—not their power to withhold their labor (which is nonexistent)—I doubt that any significant improvement in their poverty status will be achieved, short of a major revolution in the moral sentiments of the rest of the population.

Monthly Social Security benefits, which average about $80 for a male retiree, and about $125 for a retired couple, and which most retired Americans now receive in varying amounts, up to about $130 per month for a male retiree, are obviously much too low to provide any immunity from poverty for most retired Americans. Only a small percentage of Social Security beneficiaries receive private pensions. It is also estimated that, for some time to come, recipients of Old-Age Assistance will continue to number about 2 million.

The basic solution, consequently, for the poverty problem among the aged lies in major increases in public benefits, which, of course, would require larger contributions from those Americans now working and from their employers, either in the form of a higher percentage of the present taxable income, or by raising the ceiling on that taxable income, which is $4800. Private pensions will not, in the next several decades, offer the basic solution, and the Social Security system, which was created in order to provide a floor of old-age security, is, for most Americans, a floor under water. An additional form of improvement in the poverty status of older Americans would consist of a meaningful program of health care insurance financed through Social Security, but current proposals by the administration, even if passed, will probably be of such a restrictive nature that only a meager change will have been accomplished.

We cannot ignore the fact that nonemployment—retirement— is the crucial factor in the poverty status of the aged. Taking just married couples with at least one member aged sixty-five or older (a population group which is, on the average, better off than nonmarried aged males and females); about half of these couples have an earner. Of those with no earners, 60 per cent, involving about 3 million individuals, had 1959 incomes of less than $2000, well below the poverty line of $3000. We can expect nonearners to increase, both among couples and nonmarried individuals, as population and medical and industrial technology trends continue to exert their impact on the size and proportion of the aged groups not in the labor force. Present programs for assuring adequate retirement income and the outlook for any improvements offer very little assurance of significant progress for future generations of old Americans, especially if we consider the expectations and changing definitions of adequate standards of living within our own society.

There is a comfortable myth that many people entertain about the aged, to the effect that older persons do not need as much money as younger persons. This myth is presumably supported by citations of facts, namely, that older persons typically spend relatively less on clothing and household goods than younger families, relatively more on food and medical care. The facts do show that older persons spend less than younger persons, but from such facts a logical leap is made to the conclusion that the aged therefore *need* less income. The same sort of evasive logic has been used to sanction the low incomes of other segments of the poverty population: Negroes don't need as much money as whites since they require but enough money to buy low-cost food items such as chittlins and fatback and turnip greens;

they are happy with hand-me-down clothes and two dresses and one pair of shoes.

The answer to this myth should be obvious, namely, that since older persons typically *receive* less income, they *spend* less, just like younger persons who have low incomes. In an analysis of consumer patterns of aged spending units, Sidney Goldstein has shown that:

> The data for the higher income group (among the aged) suggest that those older units who continue to have high incomes continue to follow their earlier patterns of consumption. Only when their income level is markedly reduced, with the resulting need to spend relatively more for the more essential categories of consumer goods and services, are old family units forced to make sharp changes in the patterns of expenditures to which they are accustomed.[5]

I do not think that we can truly point with pride to our system of old-age insurance as having accomplished its original purpose of assuring adequate income to the aged. OASI payments amount to no more than 2 per cent of our GNP. If we add all other types of federal programs, the expenditures for the elderly might amount to 4 per cent, for a population segment that is about 9 per cent of the total population. It is evident that our incomes and the national economy can afford to sustain a decision to provide the retired aged with truly minimal incomes of, say, $3000 per couple, and $1500 per unmarried individual, because "the resulting increase in payments will incur no withdrawals of income, since the nature of the need for funds by the elderly insures that the increased . . . payments will be spent on consumption needs rather than take the form of savings by the elderly."[6]

Whether we will move, in a significant degree, to provide nonpoverty incomes to our aged depends, therefore, not on the ability of the economy, but rather on the willingness of the nation to share the benefits of an expanding economy with the aged. Historically, the ratio of nonproductive to productive persons has been declining (until very recently), although the aged make up an increasing part of the nonproductive population. The resultant increasing productivity allows us room for increasing supports for the aged (which, of course, raises the basic problem of full-employment policies), the proportion of national income now devoted to the aged being nowhere near the proportion that the aged represent in the total population.

Much of the data and reasoning in the foregoing argument point to a possible development usually not confronted—namely, that we may be witnessing certain trends and policies that will create a poverty class that did not always live in conditions of poverty. This possible development goes against the popularly accepted notion that poverty is bred by poverty. But the extension of life in retirement, emerging as a result of increased longevity and also as a result of the gradual lowering of the retirement age, coupled with severely lagging adjustments in levels of retirement income to rising costs (apart from rising living standards), should be expected to provide the conditions for the emergence of such a population group in coming decades—one that lives for 10 to 20 years in poverty *after* having lived for 60 to 65 years in relatively comfortable circumstances.[7]

Notes

1. *Report of Senate Subcommittee on Problems of the Aged and Aging* (Washington, D.C.: Government Printing Office, 1961), pp. 71-72.
2. *Income and Welfare in the United States* (New York: McGraw-Hill Book Co., 1962).
3. *Ibid.,* p. 205.
4. Angus Campbell, "Social and Psychological Determinants of Voting Behavior," in *Politics of Age,* edited by Wilma Donahue and Clark Tibbitts (Ann Arbor: University of Michigan Press, 1962), p. 93.
5. "Consumer Patterns of Older Spending Units," *Journal of Gerontology,* July, 1959, p. 332.
6. Herbert E. Striner, "The Capacity of the Economy to Support Older People," in *Aging and the Economy,* edited by Harold L. Orbach and Clark Tibbitts (Ann Arbor: University of Michigan Press, 1963), p. 27.
7. Existing data are not organized systematically and adequately to verify this proposition insofar as certain segments of today's retired aged are concerned. However, I do know of fragmentary evidence to this effect: for example, of seventeen public-assistance cases in the caseload of one social worker acquaintance, six of them are elderly women who were daughters of an equal number of wealthy families in the past. All of them are over the age of seventy-five.

The Low-Paid Worker

A.F.L.–C.I.O. Department of Research

[Reprinted by permission from "The Wage-Hour Law—A Lift Out of Poverty"
in the A.F.L.–C.I.O. American Federationist, August 1964.]

MASS POVERTY, one of the most serious domestic problems of the 1930s, has been greatly reduced with the help of federal minimum wage and hour protection. On January 8, 1964, President Lyndon B. Johnson called the nation to a renewed war against poverty, pointing out that in the 1960s, one-fifth of all American families had incomes too small to meet their basic needs. To be meaningful, this new war on poverty also must include an attack on low wages and long hours through improvements in the Fair Labor Standards Act.

The fall in worker purchasing power, which led to lower demand for goods and services and reduced employment opportunities, was of great concern during the depression of the 1930s. Passage of the Fair Labor Standards Act was aimed at maintaining worker purchasing power and curbing the vicious downward spiral of wage cuts which bred unemployment.

In the 25 years since passage of the Act, it has proved to be an important stabilizing factor in maintaining the purchasing power of those workers covered by the Act. To maintain this safeguard, the gap between average wages and the minimum wage must now be narrowed.

The Act placed a floor under wages. This wage floor has needed periodic adjustment to reflect changing economic conditions and increased living costs. Such improvements were made in 1949, 1955 and 1961. Today, the Act again needs to be adjusted upward to reflect current conditions.

FLSA Coverage Incomplete

There is a total of approximately 69 million people at work in the United States. Of these 69 million people, 25 million are in such groups as the self-employed, government workers, executives, professionals or outside salesmen. That leaves 44 million other wage and salary earners.

The Fair Labor Standards Act at present, however, applies to only 29 million of the 44 million workers. About 15 million wage and salary earners are excluded from the law's protection by special exemptions and by an unduly narrow definition of covered interstate commerce. Many of these excluded wage earners suffer very low wages and poor working conditions. The Act excludes 3.3 million retail trade workers, more than 4 million employes in the services, particularly hotels, laundries and hospitals; approximately 2.5 million domestic service workers and about 2 million in agriculture.

In addition, there are special groups of workers still excluded from the minimum wage law—workers in small logging operations, some processing of farm products, cotton ginning and theaters.

Most of the exclusions date from the Act's original adoption in 1938.

Restaurants

Over 1.5 million non-supervisory workers in restaurants and other food service enterprises are excluded from the minimum wage and overtime provisions of the Fair Labor Standards Act. The June 1963 U. S. Labor Department survey of wages paid these workers reported average hourly earnings of $1.14. In the South, the average was only 80 cents an hour— half of the $1.58 average paid in the West.

The average wage hides the even lower wages paid to tens of thousands of these workers. Nearly one-fourth of these workers—300,000 —were paid less than 75 cents an hour.

Contrary to popular belief, a large majority of employes in restaurants do not receive tips.

Of more than 1 million people surveyed in the restaurant field by the Labor Department, only one-third were waiters and waitresses. Others were chefs, cooks, bakers, dishwashers, porters, cashiers, hostesses and others. These workers received no supplement to their low wage scales and tipped employes, too, should be guaranteed a minimum wage and decent workweek.

The fact that many union contracts provide minimums substantially above $1.25 shows the industry could adjust to coverage.

Nearly a fifth of all restaurant employes are already guaranteed a minimum wage of $1.15 or more an hour by state minimum wage laws. Thus the industry plainly is able to adjust to a legal minimum wage level.

The impact on the total wage bill of bringing workers up to the present $1.25 minimum wage would be nearly 25 percent. However, since labor costs are only 22 percent of total sales, the maximum impact would amount to only 5 percent of the sales dollar or a little more than many existing state sales taxes.

Long working hours are another problem in this industry. One-third of all restaurant workers now work 48 or more hours each week. Thousands of additional fulltime jobs could be made available by extending maximum hours coverage to restaurant workers. Elimination

THE LABOR FORCE AND FEDERAL WAGE-HOUR COVERAGE

Each complete symbol equals 1,000,000 workers.

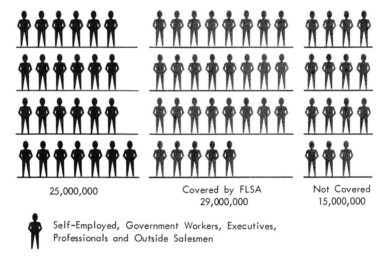

| 25,000,000 | Covered by FLSA
29,000,000 | Not Covered
15,000,000 |

Self-Employed, Government Workers, Executives,
Professionals and Outside Salesmen

Wage and Salary Workers Excluding
Supervisory and Others

Source: Based on 1962 estimates of W.H. & P.C.
U.S. Department of Labor

of excessive hours worked in these establishments would be sufficient to provide as many as 30,000 additional fulltime job opportunities.

Hotels

There are 489,000 non-supervisory workers in hotels and motels excluded from minimum wage and overtime provisions of the Fair Labor Standards Act. Average hourly earnings of these workers are $1.17, according to the June 1963 Labor Department survey. Again, southern wages were much lower—with an average of only 85 cents an hour.

The average doesn't tell us about the very low wages in this industry. Nearly 10 percent—34,000—are paid less than 50 cents an hour. Other surveys made by the Labor Department show who some of these workers are. For example, chambermaids in New Orleans averaged only 50 cents an hour in July 1961. In 1948, these chambermaids had an average of 29 cents an hour, so their wages had increased 21 cents over this 13-year period while the federal minimum wage increased 60 cents during the same time period.

Those earning less than $1.25 in hotels and motels in 1963 comprised 61 percent of the non-supervisory employes. Raising the earnings of these workers to $1.25 would have a 22 percent impact upon the hourly wage bill. Since labor costs account for only 20 percent of hotel receipts, the maximum total impact on the sales price would be about 4 to 8 percent.

This industry, with $3 billion in annual sales, also has shown it can accommodate itself to decent minimum wages. Union contracts in various parts of the country provide for conditions substantially above the federal minimum. Approximately 20 percent of all hotel and motel employes are now protected by state minimum wage rates of $1.15 or more.

Long hours are also an unwholesome feature of the hotel and motel industry. Thirty percent of the employes work 48 hours or more a week. By extending the Fair Labor Standards Act to the 489,000 workers in this industry and curtailing their hours to 40, as many as 25,000 additional fulltime jobs could be made available.

Laundries

The 513,000 non-supervisory laundry and cleaning workers need the protection of the federal minimum wage and hour law. This is another low-wage industry, with average hourly earnings of $1.26, according to the June 1963 Labor Department survey. In the South, the average hourly earnings were only 95 cents.

Wages paid laundry workers are particularly oppressive. More than half the workers are paid less than $1.25 an hour. About 40,000 of these workers earn less than 75 cents an hour. The hundred lowest-paid employes, according to the survey, all of whom were in large establishments with annual sales of $250,000 or more, were paid less than 35 cents an hour—an outrageous condition in the 1960s.

Other Labor Department studies show that average hourly earnings for bundle wrappers in Memphis increased only 11 cents—from 47 to 58 cents an hour—between 1951 and 1963. During the same time period, the federal minimum wage rose 50 cents an hour.

Raising of laundry and cleaning worker wages to $1.25 an hour would mean a 13 percent increase in the hourly wage bill. The labor costs in this industry are about 46 percent, meaning the maximum impact would be no more than 6 percent on the sales dollar. A few workers in this industry have already gained substantial increases in recent years—indicating the country's ability to adjust to higher wages.

In Newark, N. J., average hourly earnings rose from $1.31 to $1.48 between 1961 and 1963, an increase of 13 percent.

Coverage of laundry workers by the Fair Labor Standards Act is feasible. Already 17,000 non-supervisory laundry workers are protected by the Act since they are employed in laundries selling across state lines or servicing primarily manufacturing plants. Most union contracts also have minimums of at least $1.25 an hour. Eight states have minimum wage rates for laundry and cleaning workers of at least $1.25 an hour.

Overtime protection is also needed by laundry workers. One-fourth of them work more than 44 hours a week.

Hospitals

About 700,000 non-supervisory, non-professional workers are employed in non-governmental hospitals. In 1963, the Labor Department surveys showed that one-fourth of the non-supervisory non-professional employes studied were paid less than $1.25 an hour.

Many of these workers are engaged in the same type work as employes unprotected in some of these previously mentioned industries. Among the lowest-paid hospital employes are kitchen helpers, dishwashers, porters, maids and laundry workers. The earnings of some of these hospital employes are as low as those found in surveys of restaurants, hotels and laundries.

Retail Workers

About 3.3 million retail employes, in addition to restaurant workers, are still excluded from protection because of the high dollar volume standards established for coverage of retail employes. In 1961, minimum wage protection was extended to about 2 million retail workers employed by firms with annual gross sales of $1 million or more, provided the particular store at which they worked had sales of $250,000 or more.

The 1962 Labor Department surveys showed that, whereas the newly-protected workers had a floor placed under their earnings and a ceiling on their hours, conditions of the unprotected workers did not substantially improve. Tens of thousands of these workers, excluded from FLSA coverage, still were paid less than $1 an hour.

Farm Workers

The nearly 2 million Americans who work for wages in agriculture are among the most oppressed workers excluded from coverage. Average hourly earnings of farm workers were 89 cents an hour in May 1963 and the majority of these workers were employed much less than a full year. Nearly half of the farm workers earned less than 75 cents an hour. For some 75,000 workers, their earnings were less than 30 cents an hour.

Congressional studies of the plight of migratory farm laborers

FEDERAL WAGE-HOUR COVERAGE BY INDUSTRY

Each complete figure equals 10%
of non-supervisory workers covered.

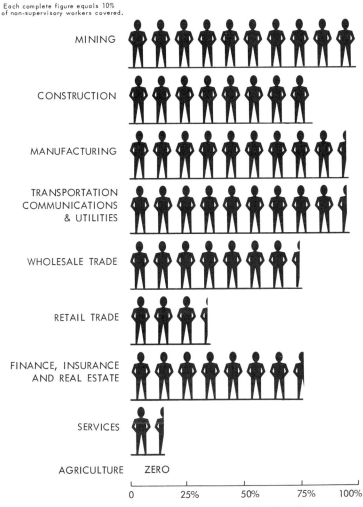

Source: Based on 1962 estimates of Wage-Hour and Public Contracts
Divisions, U.S. Department of Labor.

has shown the need and destitution of these workers who toil in an industry heavily subsidized by the federal government. In addition, their low wages undermine the standards of family farms.

Minimum wages of $1.25 an hour have been set in a number of union contracts. Two states also have placed farmworkers under their minimum wage laws. Even the federal government has established minimum wages for some farm workers--such as those in the sugar fields and foreign farm laborers.

Long hours have been a traditional curse of farm work. In spite of the vast increase of mechanization, large numbers of farm workers still work more than the typical industrial workweek. In a 1962 survey, the Agriculture Department found that 45 percent of the farm laborers worked more than 44 hours a week.

Logging

About 87,000 employes of small logging operations are now excluded from the Act's protection. Logging camp and sawmill employes working for an employer with less than 13 employes are unprotected. Thus 87,000 out of 340,000 logging and sawmill employes are presently exempted from the Act.

The 1963 Labor Department survey showed that thousands of these woodsmen were paid less than $1.25 an hour. Many of these workers are in areas of the country plagued by poverty, such as parts of Appalachia, northern Wisconsin, Michigan and Minnesota.

MILLIONS UNPROTECTED BY FEDERAL WAGE-HOUR LAW

Restaurants			
Hotels & Motels			
Laundries			
Hospitals			
Farm Workers			
Retail Workers*			
Theatres			
Loggers			
Millions of Workers	1	2	3

*Not covered by 1961 extension of coverage to giant retail and department stores.

Source: Based on estimates of Wage-Hour and Public Contracts Divisions, U.S. Department of Labor.

According to the government survey, 52 percent of the workers in small non-integrated logging establishments in the South were earning less than $1.25 an hour in 1963. Raising their wages to $1.25 would have a 6.6 percent impact on the hourly wage bill. Labor costs represent about one-fourth of the total value of the industry's shipments. Thus the maximum impact in the lowest wage areas would only be about 1.5 percent on the sales dollar.

When the $1.25 minimum wage went into effect for sawmill and planing mill workers in larger operations covered by FLSA, 73 percent of those working in the South received wage increases to $1.25. The industry met this requirement and continued to prosper. Certainly the industry can adjust to covering those workers now excluded.

Overtime protection is also needed for workers in this industry. The Labor Department survey showed that 15 percent of the employes in small logging operations worked more than 40 hours a week.

Agricultural Processing Workers

Agricultural processing workers and cotton ginning employes are enmeshed in a hodgepodge of exemptions. The minimum wage and maximum hours exemptions applying to such workers should be eliminated. The great majority of agricultural processing workers are already covered without any serious problems and the exclusions should be dropped.

An example of the hodgepodge of exemptions is a worker at a grain elevator that (a) is not located in a place of 2,500 or more population or within a mile of such place and (b) has not received 95 percent of the grain from within 50 miles of the elevator. However, for the storing of commodities other than grain and soybeans, a 20-mile test applies. For cotton ginning, a 10-mile test applies. A tobacco warehouse has to be within 50 miles of its source to be exempt.

Miscellaneous

About 130,000 motion picture theatre employes are presently excluded. The 1962 Labor Department survey of wages in Washington, D. C., showed that 40 percent of the men who work in theatres were paid less than $1 an hour. Other amusement and service workers are similarly ill-paid.

Extension of Hours Protection

Many workers who are covered by the federal minimum wage provisions are still exempt from the overtime provisions of the Fair Labor Standards Act.

Local transit employes and gas station attendants at stations with annual sales of $250,000 were covered by the 1961 amendments, but only by the minimum wage provisions. Also, the 1961 amendments continued the hours exemption for truck drivers and railroad employes under the nominal jurisdiction of the Interstate Commerce Commission.

There is no rational reason for continuing these exemptions. High unemployment calls for a reduction in hours so more workers can share in the available employment opportunities.

Agricultural processing employes have been plagued with duplicating and overlapping overtime exemptions, all applying to the same industry. The Labor Department reported that "differences in the extent of the exemption period available for the various industries are not related to length of season or length of workweek." These unjustified exemptions should be removed.

Spanish-Americans of the Southwest

Raymond F. Clapp

Department of Health, Education, and Welfare

[From Welfare in Review, Vol. 4, No. 1, January, 1966.]

THE SPANISH-AMERICAN POPULATION has had a long history in this country. Colonization of what is now the Southwest was started more than three centuries ago when this entire area, along with Mexico, was part of Spain's vast overseas empire. Santa Fe was an important urban settlement in 1609. By 1790 the white population of the Southwest was practically all Spanish and included an estimated 23,000 persons, distributed as follows in areas which later became the States of Arizona, 1,000; California, 1,100; New Mexico, 15,000; and Texas, 6,000.[1]

Now, more than 350 years later, the Spanish-American population in the Southwest numbers 3,465,000 persons—12 percent of the population of the five States under study. The total 1960 population of the five States was 29,300,000, of whom "Anglos" represented 79

---

[1]Report of the "1932 Report of the Committee on Linguistic and National Stocks in the Population of the United States," representing the American Council of Learned Societies. Cited by Herschel T. Manuel in "Spanish Speaking Children in the Southwest," 1965.

percent, Negroes 7 percent and all other nonwhite persons, 2 percent. White persons, other than those identified as Spanish-Americans, are commonly referred to in the Southwest as "Anglos", and that term will be used in this report when Spanish-Americans are compared with other whites. The study excludes "braceros," Mexican residents who enter the United States under contract for a limited time to work as farm laborers and then return to Mexico.

Because Spanish-Americans comprise a group that is classified with other whites, few statisticians outside the Southwest, and not even many within that area, have attempted to identify this group in their social data. In most census tabulations they are included with other whites. It is, however, in the special Census volume, "White Persons of Spanish Surname,"[2] that the most meaningful data have been found. Our preliminary report is essentially an analysis of the statistics presented in this valuable document.

Related Census data referring to other ethnic groups have also been utilized. As an example, we may consider the Negro population. In the United States as a whole 20,488,000 nonwhites were enumerated, of whom 18,848,619, or 92 percent were Negro. Because the Negro is so predominant in the nonwhite population outside the West, it has become the practice of many statisticians to equate nonwhite data with Negroes and to disregard other races in gathering their information. Fortunately, the Census Bureau has not ignored this fact, nor have we in this study. Two Census Subject Reports entitled "Non-White Population by Race"[3]—covering Negroes, Japanese, Chinese, and Filipinos—and "Puerto Ricans in the United States,"[4] have proved invaluable and permit a comparison of many of the characteristics of these ethnic groups with Spanish-Americans.

Education

In education, as measured in median number of years completed by the adult population, the Spanish-American ranks as low as, or below, any other ethnic group identified and tabulated by the Census except the American Indian woman (Table 1).

The group most nearly comparable to the Spanish-American in the Southwest, in numbers and in economic and educational status, is the Negro. For this reason a series of tabulations comparing Spanish-American with Negro groups in the five-State area has been prepared for this article.

---

[2]Subject Report PC(2)IB 1960 U.S. Census.
[3]Subject Report PC(2)IC 1960 U.S. Census.
[4]Subject Report PC (2) ID 1960 U.S. Census.

TABLE 1

Years of School Completed

Sex	White Persons of Spanish Surnames in 5 Southwestern States[1]	Puerto Rican Birth and Parentage - U.S.	Nonwhite persons in the West			Nonwhite persons in California	
			Negro	American Indian	Chinese	Japanese	Filipino
Total males 14 years old and over	8.1	8.4	10.3	8.2	11.3	12.4	8.7
Total females 14 years old and over	8.2	8.2	10.6	8.1	11.8	12.3	11.5

[1] Median years of school completed by persons aged 14 and over of selected ethnic groups in the Southwest and West from various 1960 U.S. Census reports.

In school enrollment of males aged 14 years and over, when compared to all males aged 14-24 inclusive, the Spanish-American ratio is 33.3 percent, the Negro 34.9 percent (Table 2).

TABLE 2

School Enrollment

Sex and Age	Spanish-American	Negro
Males		
Number of males age 14-24	312,080	168,255
Number of males age 14 and over enrolled in school	103,954	58,680
Ratio of enrollees to males age 14-24	33.3	34.9
Females		
Number of females age 14-24	313,988	171,168
Number of females age 14 and over enrolled in school	111,744	67,177
Ratio of enrollees to females age 14-24	35.6	39.2

Source: U.S. Census, 1960. Subject Reports PC(2)-1B, Tables 2 and 6; PC(2)-1C; Table 50.

Male Unemployment

Unemployment runs high among Spanish-American men—almost twice that of the "Anglos." However, unemployment among Negro men is slightly higher and among American Indians considerably higher than that for Spanish-Americans.

In 1960, the ratio of unemployed Spanish-American men seeking work to the total male civilian labor force was 8 percent, as compared with 4.5 percent for "Anglos" in the same five-State area. For Negro men it was 9.7, for the American Indian 18.4 percent. Other racial and ethnic groups range from a male unemployment ratio of 2.6 percent for the Japanese to 4.0 percent for the Chinese (Table 3).

TABLE 3

Unemployment: By Sex and Ethnic Group

	Male			Female		
Ethnic group	Civilian labor force	Number unemployed	Percent unemployed	Labor force	Number Unemployed	Percent unemployed
Spanish-Americans in 5 Southwestern States	801,045	64,277	8.0	295,417	28,512	9.7
Negroes in 5 Southwestern States	470,986	45,694	9.7	321,201	27,741	8.6
Persons of Puerto Rican birth and parentage in whole United States	214,279	20,365	9.5	102,640	11,281	11.0
American Indians in the West	43,324	7,991	18.4	17,362	2,378	13.7
Chinese in the West	43,625	1,753	4.0	19,783	882	4.5
Japanese in California	45,210	1,191	2.6	26,507	820	3.1
Filipinos in California	24,008	1,871	7.8	4,586	626	13.7
Anglos in 5 Southwestern States	6,027,385	269,754	4.5	2,907,536	147,444	5.1

Source: U.S. Census 1960: Reports PC(2)1B, 1C and 1D and Volume 1.

Figure 1

Household Composition

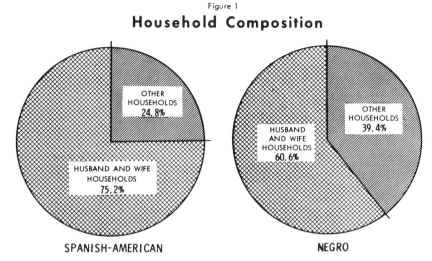

SPANISH-AMERICAN   NEGRO

Source: "U.S. Census of the Population: 1960." Subject Report: PC(2)1B, Table 3: Social Characteristics of White Persons of Spanish Surname. PC(2)1C, Table 50: Social Characteristics of the Negro Population.

In these calculations the labor force is defined as all employed persons except armed forces personnel, plus all persons unemployed but seeking employment.

Household Composition

The majority of Spanish-Americans are found to have a relatively cohesive family life: 75 percent of their households have both husband and wife present, as compared with 61 percent of Negro households (Figure 1). Based upon the number of household heads, Spanish-American households average 4.31 persons and Negro households, 3.51. Nonrelatives are found less frequently in Spanish-American than in Negro households, with a ratio of only one non-relative to 50 Spanish-American homes, and 1 to 10 Negro homes (Table 4).

In the five-State area under study, there were 630,000 Spanish-American children under age 6 (calculated from Figure 2), and 268,000 Spanish-American mothers with one or more natural children of this age under their care who were neither employed nor seeking employment (Table 5), a ratio of 243 such children to 100 such mothers (Figure 3). In the same area there were 364,000 Negro children under age 6, and 106,000 Negro mothers, neither employed nor seeking employment, caring for one or more children of this age, a ratio of 334 such children to 100 such mothers. Obviously, not all preschool children were with a mother who was free of outside

TABLE 4

Households

	Spanish-American			
Relationship	Number	Per household[1]	Number	Per household[1]
Persons in household	3,369,651	4.31	2,097,772	3.51
Head	775,844	1.00	598,084	1.00
Wife (husband present)	583,232	0.75	362,699	.61
Children and other relatives	1,972,598	2.54	1,077,756	1.80
Non-relatives	37,977	0.02	59,233	.10

[1]Based on number of household heads.
Sources: Census Subject Report PC(2)1B. Table 3.
Census Subject Report PC(2)1C. Table 50.

Figure 2
Age Distribution
Spanish-Americans and Negroes in the Southwest
All White Persons in the United States

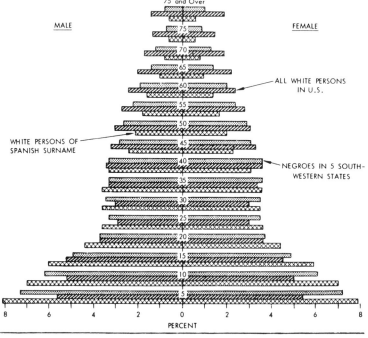

Source: "U.S. Census of Population: 1960." Subject Report: "Persons of Spanish Surname," PC(2)-1B, Table 6: Economic Characteristics of White Persons of Spanish Surname. PC(2)-1C, Table 55: Economic Characteristics of the Negro Population.

TABLE 5

Employment Status

Sex	Spanish-American		Negro	
	Number	*Percent*	*Number*	*Percent*
Males				
Total males, 14 years and over	1,056,904	100.0	679,627	100.0
Labor force	819,271	77.5	504,963	74.3
Armed Forces	18,226	1.7	33,977	5.0
Civilian labor force	801,045	75.8	470,986	69.3
Employed	736,768	69.7	425,292	62.6
Unemployed	64,277	6.1	45,694	6.7
Not in labor force	237,633	22.5	174,664	25.7
Inmate of institution	21,650	2.0	23,415	3.4
Enrolled in school	103,954	9.8	58,680	8.6
Other, under 65 years old	63,294	6.0	51,850	7.6
Other, 65 years old and over	48,735	4.6	40,719	6.0
Females				
Total females 14 years and over	1,027,276	100.0	726,520	100.0
Labor force	295,417	28.8	321,201	44.2
Employed	266,655	26.0	292,698	40.3
Unemployed	28,512	2.8	27,741	3.8
Not in labor force	731,859	71.2	405,319	55.8
Inmate of institution	5,593	0.5	5,042	0.7
Enrolled in school	111,744	10.9	67,177	9.2
Other, under 65 years old	551,149	53.7	274,136	37.7
With own children under 6 years old	267,844	26.1	106,374	14.6
Other, 65 years old and over	63,373	6.2	58,964	8.1

Source: U.S. Census, 1960: Subject Reports PC(2)1B Table 6 and PC(2)1C Table 55.

employment, but it seems reasonable to assume that the Spanish-American child receives this type of care more often than the Negro child. It also seems likely, from the higher proportion of husband-wife households, that the Spanish-American child more often lives in a home with both parents present than does the Negro child.

The importance of this condition is emphasized by Figure 2, the population pyramid, which depicts the high proportion of younger children in the Spanish-American population. The extent to which young children are in two-parent homes with a mother who is not working and therefore unable to provide supplementary income is an important factor in the welfare of the Spanish-American family.

Figure 3

Employment Status
Spanish-Americans and Negroes in the Southwest

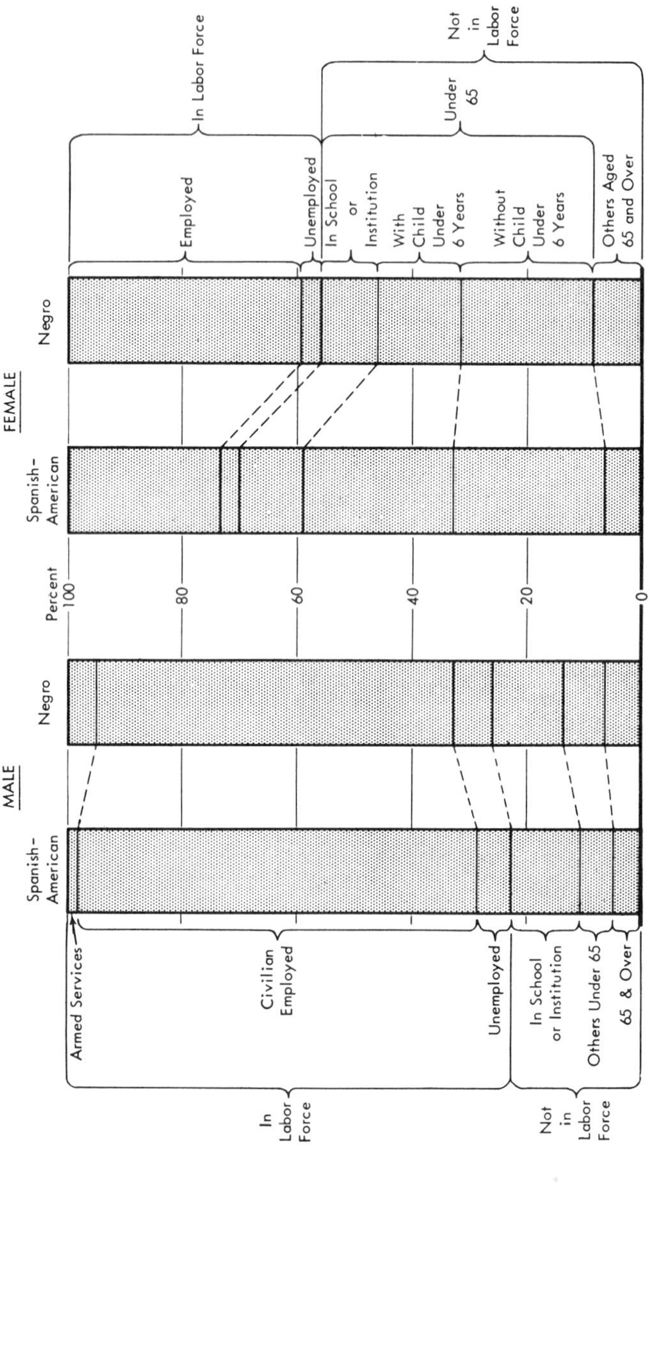

Source: "U.S. Census of the Population: 1960," Vol. 1, "Characteristics of the Population," parts 4,6,7,33 and 45, Table 58: Occupation Group of Employed Persons. Subject Report: PC(2)1B, Table 6: Economic Characteristics of White Persons of Spanish Surname and PC(2)1C, Table 55: Economic Characteristics of the Negro Population.

The high birth rate of Spanish-Americans, evidenced by this age distribution, is accompanied by a relatively high death rate among adults, as indicated by the rapidly shrinking upper levels of the Spanish-American pyramid. This condition points to the need for inquiry into the adequacy of medical care.

Employment Status of Men

Employment and related indices are generally similar for Negro and Spanish-American males. At the time of the 1960 Census, the proportion of all males aged 14 and over who were in the armed forces was 5.0 percent for Negroes, about three times the 1.7 percent for Spanish-Americans. In the civilian sector, however, we find that about 70 percent of Spanish-American men over age 14 and 63 percent of Negro men over that age were employed. Unemployment in Figure 3 and Table 5 is calculated as a percentage of the total population aged 14 and over.

Only 2 percent of Spanish-American males were in institutions, compared to 3.4 percent of the Negro men; 9.8 percent of all Spanish-American males aged 14 and over were enrolled in school and 8.6 percent of the Negro men.

In addition to the above categories, another 10.6 percent of the Spanish-American males and 13.6 percent of the Negro males were out of the labor force, that is, neither at work nor looking for work. In evaluating these comparisons, it should be kept in mind that a substantially larger proportion of the Spanish-American males are under age 35 than the Negro males and that conversely an appreciably higher proportion of the Negro males are over 40 than of the Spanish-American males. This would help to explain, at least in part, the higher rates of school enrollment of Spanish-American persons 14 and over —both male and female—and lower proportions in institutions and of "others not in the labor force."

Employment Status of Women

The employment pattern of Negro women is very different from that of Spanish-American women (Figure 3). Of all Negro women aged 14 and over, 40 percent were employed at the time of the 1960 Census. This is more than half again the 26 percent of the Spanish-American women who were employed. Conversely, 71 percent of Spanish-American women were neither employed nor seeking employment, in comparison with 56 percent of Negro women. Those unemployed and looking for work represented 3 percent of all Spanish-American females and 4 percent of all Negro females. Of those women in the civilian labor force, that is, either at work or looking for work, 9.7 percent of the Spanish-American women were unemployed, and 8.6 percent of the Negro women. Women aged 14 to 65 who were neither in the labor force nor enrolled in school, nor in institutions, comprised over half (53.7 percent) of all Spanish-American women of this age range, but little more than one-third (37.7 percent) of Negro women of this group.

Spanish-American women, not in the labor force and caring for their own children under 6 years of age, represented 26 percent of all Spanish-Americans aged 14 and over, while Negro women in this category represented less than 15 percent of all Negroes 14 years of age and over.

Male Occupational Distribution

The Bureau of the Census has developed a hierarchy of occupations with professional, technical and managerial at the top and service and labor at the bottom. Figure 4 and Table 6 represent the relative distribution of employment of men and women in the two groups under analysis, together with that of the "Anglos."

It can be seen that, as a group, Spanish-American men on the average enjoy a somewhat higher place in the occupational hierarchy than Negro men, but a considerably lower position than Anglo men. Of the Spanish-American men in employment, 19 percent were found in the professional and clerical occupations, while 14 percent of Negro men and 47 percent of Anglo men were employed in these occupations. Craftsmen and operatives included 39 percent of Spanish-American, 32 percent of Negro, and 37 percent of Anglo men. The Spanish-American, with 16 percent working as farm laborers and foremen, greatly exceeded the Negro (5 percent), and the Anglo (2 percent) men in this category. In service occupations were found 19 percent of the Negro men, 7 percent of the Spanish-Americans, and 5 percent of the Anglos; and in laboring jobs, 22 percent of the Negro, 14 percent of the Spanish-American, and 5 percent of the Anglo men.

Female Occupational Distribution

The pattern of female occupations, as with the male pattern, differs substantially among the Anglo, Spanish-American and Negro women. But the extent of the differences in the three groups is much greater for the women than for the men.

In professional, technical, clerical and sales were found 67

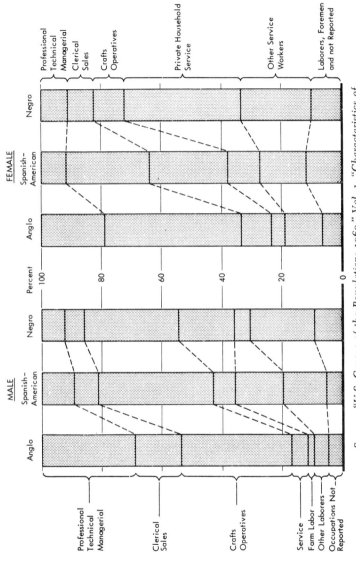

Figure 4

Occupational Distribution
By Sex and Selected Ethnic Groups

MALE

FEMALE

Source: "U.S. Census of the Population: 1960," Vol. 1, "Characteristics of the Population," parts 4,6,7,33 and 45, Table 133; Income in 1959 of Persons by Race. Subject Report: PC(2)1B, Table 6: Economic Characteristics of White Persons of Spanish Surname and PC(2)1C, Table 55: Economic Characteristics of the Negro Population.

TABLE 6

Occupational Distribution[1]

Occupation-Males	White persons of Spanish surname		Negroes		Anglos	
	Number	Percent	Number	Percent	Number	Percent
Total males employed	736,768	[2]100.0	425,292	[2]100.0	5,757,627	[2]100.0
Professional and technical; farmers and farm managers; managers, officials, and proprietors, except farm	77,407	10.5	31,976	7.5	1,810,036	31.4
Clerical, sales, and kindred workers	58,799	8.0	26,513	6.2	878,678	15.3
Craftsmen, foremen, operatives, and kindred workers	285,075	38.7	134,387	31.6	2,126,815	36.9
Service workers, including private household	53,627	7.3	79,569	18.7	295,049	5.1
Farm laborers and foremen	117,688	16.0	21,247	5.0	118,115	2.1
Laborers, except farm and mine	106,409	14.4	92,520	21.8	271,376	4.7
Occupation not reported	37,763	5.1	39,080	9.2	257,558	4.5

Occupation-Females

Total females employed	266,655	[2]100.0	292,698	[2]100.0	2,760,342	[2]100.0
Professional and technical; farmers and farm managers; managers, officials, and proprietors, except farm	21,909	8.2	25,874	8.8	591,163	21.4
Clerical, sales and kindred workers	74,545	28.0	25,105	8.6	1,264,801	45.8
Craftsmen, foremen, operatives, and kindred workers	69,485	26.1	29,996	10.2	273,955	9.9
Private household workers	28,514	10.7	113,947	38.9	119,890	4.3
Service workers, except private household	41,189	15.4	68,491	23.4	341,609	12.4
Farm laborers and foremen; laborers, except farm and mine; occupation not reported	31,013	11.6	29,285	10.0	168,924	6.1

[1]Includes Arizona, California, Colorado, New Mexico, and Texas.

[2]Percentages may not add to 100.0 due to rounding.

Source: U.S. Bureau of the Census. U.S. Census of the Population: 1960. Subject Reports; Persons of Spanish Surname. Final Report PC(2)-1B, Table 6. Subject Reports; Nonwhite Population by Race, Final Report PC(2)-1C, Table 55. Vol. 1, Characteristics of the Population. Parts 4,6,7,33 and 45, Table 58.

percent of the Anglo, 36 percent of the Spanish-American, and only 17 percent of the Negro employed women. Women employed as craftsmen and operatives totalled 26 percent of employed Spanish-Americans, and 10 percent of both Negro and Anglo women. Private household work accounted for 39 percent of Negro employment, 11 percent of Spanish-American employment and 4 percent of Anglo employment.

Annual Income

Consistent with the occupational advantage of Spanish-American over Negro males, the income distribution was also more favorable for the Spanish-American group. Figure 5, however, indicates the low income distribution for both groups as compared with Anglo males. For instance, total income in 1959 was below $3,000 for 31.8 percent of the Anglos, but 52.8 percent of the Spanish-Americans, and 59 percent of

Figure 5

Income Distribution

White Anglo, Spanish-American and Negro Males in the Southwest-1959

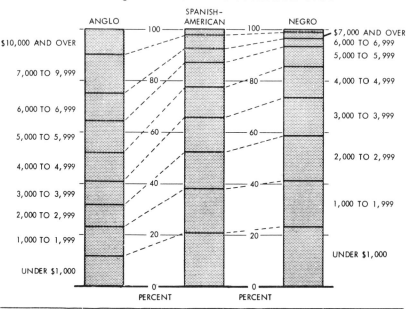

Source: "U.S. Census of the Population: 1960," Subject Report: PC(2)1B, Table 1: Nativity, Parentage and Country of Origin of White Persons of Spanish Surname.

the Negro men in the five Southwestern States earned less than $3,000. At the other end of the distribution, annual income of $7,000 or more was reported by 24.5 percent of Anglo men, but only 6.9 percent of Spanish-American men, and 2.8 percent of Negro men earned $7,000 or above.

Nativity, Parentage, Country of Origin

Of all Spanish-Americans in the Southwest, according to the 1960 Census, 84.6 percent were born in the United States. Only 15.4 percent were born elsewhere: the majority, 13.5 percent, in Mexico, and only 1.9 percent in other countries (Figure 6, Table 7). Of the total Spanish-American population, 54.8 percent were native-born of native parentage, and 29.8 percent, of Mexican parentage.

Data from the most recent census, from earlier census tabulations, and from migration records support the conclusion that a high proportion of the Spanish-American group under study migrated from Mexico or are descendants of such migrants.

Figure 6

Nativity, Parentage, Country of Origin

Spanish-Americans in the Southwest-1960

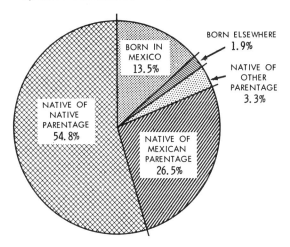

Source: "U.S. Census of the Population: 1960." Subject Report: PC(2)1B, Table 1: Urban and Rural Residents of White Persons of Spanish Surname PC(2)1C, Table 55: Economic Characteristics of the Negro Population. "U.S. Census of the Population: 1950." Special Report: PE(2)3C, Table 2: White Persons of Spanish Surname, and PE38, Table 15: Age of the Negro Population, Urban and Rural.

TABLE 7

Nativity and Parentage: Spanish-Americans

Total	3,464,999	100.0
Native born	2,930,185	84.6
Native parentage	1,894,402	54.8
Foreign or mixed parentage	1,030,783	29.8
Mexican parentage	917,614	26.5
Other	113,167	3.3
Foreign born	534,814	15.4
In Mexico	468,684	13.5
Elsewhere	66,130	1.9

Source: U.S. Census, 1960, Subject Report PC(2) 1B Table 1.

Urban-Rural Residence

Much the same as other Americans throughout the Nation, Spanish-Americans are tending to concentrate in urban areas in the Southwest. This is also true of the Negroes of this area (Figure 7).

Next Steps

Findings to date indicate that Spanish-Americans rate lowest in education as it is measured by years of school completed. To be explored further in the literature is the extent to which members of this group continue to hold to Spanish as the language of home and community and how this practice limits learning in a land where English is so vitally important.

The fact that Spanish-Americans have to a considerable degree found their way into technical, clerical and skilled occupations offers promise for their further escalation, as opportunities are afforded them. The relative cohesiveness of Spanish-American families would also seem to be reassuring for the future progress of this group.

But many Spanish-Americans have far to go. This is conclusively demonstrated by the fact that 53 percent of Spanish-American men had incomes of less than $3,000 in 1959. Given the preponderance of large young families and the apparent tendency of Spanish-American mothers to stay out of the work force when their children are young, it seems unlikely that this low income could be increased to any meaningful degree without increasing substantially the earning capacity and opportunity of the men.

With a substantial proportion of incomes below the poverty line figure, the problems of Spanish-Americans are further compound-

Figure 7
Urban and Rural Residence
Spanish-Americans and Negroes
in the Southwest

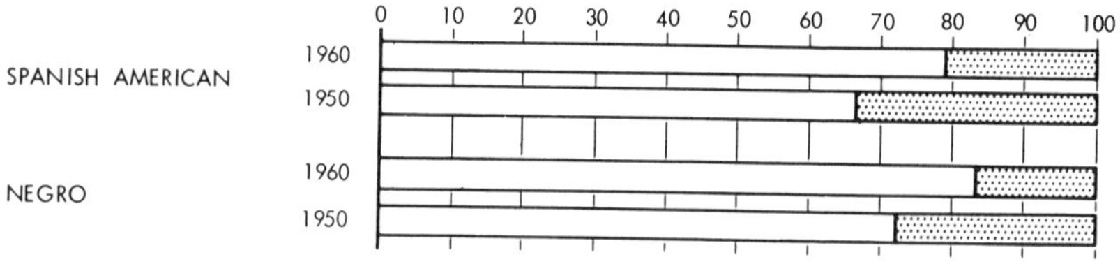

	0	10	20	30	40	50	60	70	80	90	100
SPANISH AMERICAN	1960										
	1950										
NEGRO	1960										
	1950										

ETHNIC GROUP	YEAR	URBAN	RURAL	TOTAL
SPANISH - AMERICAN	1960	79.1	20.9	100.0
SPANISH - AMERICAN	1950	66.4	33.6	100.0
NEGRO	1960	83.5	16.5	100.0
NEGRO	1950	72.4	27.6	100.0

URBAN [   ]

RURAL [::::]

Source: "U.S. Census of the Population: 1960." Vol. 1, PC(1)-1B, U.S. Summary, Table 47: Age by Color and Sex for the U.S. Subject Reports: PC(2)1B, "Persons of Spanish Surname," Table 2: Age of White Persons of Spanish Surname; PC(2)-1C, Nonwhite Population by Race, Table 50: Social Characteristics of the Negro Population.

ed by the fact that their education is limited. At the same time, it is not a simple matter to extend necessary services to this group since they tend to live apart from the mainstream of American life.

Whatever programs may be suggested to help meet the needs of this largely underprivileged group will depend on the outcome of continued analysis of relevant information.

Selected Bibliography

1. Sydney E. Bernard. "Poverty, Public Assistance and the Low Income," in *The One Parent Family in the United States*. Robert Bell, Ed. (in press).

2. Donald J. Bogue. *Skid Row in American Cities*. Chicago: Community and Family Study Center at the University of Chicago, 1963.

3. M. Elaine Burgess and Daniel O. Price. *An American Dependency Challenge*. Chicago: American Public Welfare Association, 1963.

4. Harry M. Caudill. *Night Comes to the Cumberlands: A Biography of a Depressed Area*. Boston: Little Brown and Company, 1963.

5. Kenneth Clark. *Dark Ghetto*. New York: Harper and Row, 1965.

6. Laurie D. Cummings. "The Employed Poor: Their Characteristics and Occupations," *Monthly Labor Review*, July 1964.

7. "The Negro American," *Daedalus*. Entire issues, Fall 1965, and Winter 1966.

8. Richard Elman. *Poorhouse State: the American Way of Life on Public Assistance*. New York: Pantheon, 1966.

9. Lenore A. Epstein. "Income of the Aged in 1962: First Findings of the 1963 Survey of the Aged," *Social Security Bulletin*, March, 1964.

10. Richard Greenberg. *Problems Related to Unemployment in the Vicinity of Hazard, Kentucky*. New York: Committee of Miners, 1963.

11. Harlem Youth Opportunities Unlimited. *Youth in the Ghetto*. New York: HARYOU, 1964.

12. Vivian W. Henderson. *The Economic Status of Negroes: in the Nation and in the South*. Atlanta, Georgia: Southern Regional Council, 1963.

13. Herbert Hill. *No Harvest for the Reaper*. New York: National Association for the Advancement of Colored People, 1960.

14. Sar A. Levitan. *Federal Aid to Depressed Areas: An Evaluation of the Area Redevelopment Administration*. Baltimore: Johns Hopkins Press, 1964.

15. Edgar May. *The Wasted Americans*. New York: Harper and Row, 1963.

16. Truman E. Moore, *The Slaves We Rent*. New York: Random House, 1965.

17. Mollie Orshansky and Thomas Karter. *Economic and Social Status of the Negro in the United States*. New York: National Urban League, 1961.

18. Thomas F. Pettigrew. *A Profile of the Negro American*. Princeton: D. Van Nostrand Co., 1964.

19. President's Council on Aging. *The Older American*. Washington, D. C.: Government Printing Office, 1963.

20. President's Task Force on Manpower Conservation. *One-Third of a Nation: A Report on Young Men Found Unqualified for Military Service,* 1964.

21. Arthur M. Ross and Herbert Hill, (eds.). *Employment, Race and Poverty.* New York: Harcourt, Brace and World, 1967.

22. Alvin L. Schorr. *Poor Kids.* New York: Basic Books, 1966.

23. United States Congress, Senate Subcommittee on Migratory Labor of the Committee on Labor and Public Welfare. *The Migrant Farm Worker in America: Background Data in the United States Today.* Washington: Government Printing Office, 1963.

24. United States Department of Agriculture, Economic Research Service. *Economic, Social, and Demographic Characteristics of Spanish-American Wage Workers on U. S. Farms,* Agricultural Economic Report Number 27, March, 1963.

Chapter 3

Poverty and the Political Economy

The growth of a "Pressure Group State," generated by more massive concentrations of interlocking economic, managerial and self-regarding professional power, points . . . towards more inequality; towards the restriction of social rights and liberties and the muffling of social protest among a large section of the population. The growing conservatism of professionalism, of the imposed inequalities resulting from the decisions of congeries of social power . . . [raises] the fundamental problem of reinterpreting social equality and personal liberty in the conditions of a new age and a changed society.

—Richard M. Titmuss. *Essays on "The Welfare State,"* London: Unwin University Books, 1963.

SOCIOLOGICAL AND ECONOMIC DESCRIPTIONS of the poor identify a variety of "negative risk factors" associated with poverty: low education, mental deficiency, colored skin, old age, poor health, large or unstable families, and rural background. These in turn are related to "negative personality characteristics": apathy, hopelessness, rejection of the work ethic and chronic dependency. It is easy to jump from this descriptive accumulation of negative characteristics to the notion that the *cause* of poverty therefore lies with the poor themselves. The next "logical" step is to see the remedy to poverty in "correcting" the poor, particularly improving their education and providing special social services to enable better social adjustment.

The problem of causation must be approached differently. It is true that the situation of economic marginality and deprivation is, in some cases, associated with personal attributes which limit an individual's ability to take advantage of social opportunity. And, in a clinical sense, these personal attributes—the so-called "culture of poverty"—must be altered if an individual's full potential is to be released. However:

(1) For most poor people, the attribution of these negative per-

sonality factors is totally inappropriate. Far from being slothful and hopeless and chronically dependent, they work harder, longer and under more trying conditions than do most Americans. They have aspirations for their families, if no longer for themselves, further above their present status than do most Americans; and they are bitterly resistant to charity, paternalistic social services and imputations of inferior social worth.

(2) These negative characteristics, even where they do apply, do not have functional autonomy. They derive from a restricted environment and are largely a defensive adaptation to environmental stress, powerlessness and objective deprivation. When hard experience undercuts expectations, aspirations are soon brought down into line.

(3) Negative personal characteristics rarely produce poverty. People who start poor tend to stay poor; poverty produces poverty. Poor people who do not start poor become poor only rarely because of low motivation, a preference for the dole, mental illness or the like. They become poor because they are subjected to the action of external forces which deprive them of adequate income: job shortages, enforced retirement, accidental disability, or obligation to care for dependent children.

In each case, the lack of opportunities, and not the ability of the poor to take advantage of opportunities, is the factor limiting mobility. The question of causation must focus on those forces outside the control of the poor which limit their opportunity for economic well-being. These are the forces which determine the availability of jobs and skill training, wage scales, size of transfer payments, availability of credit, race discrimination, etc. They are part of the total functioning of the American political economy.

Political economy concerns the allocation of economic and community resources. It involves both impersonal social and economic processes and the conscious decisions of political and economic units. The poor in America are groups which, by and large, receive the smallest share of the nation's economic resources and the least adequate community resources. They have the weakest voice in the decision-making processes which govern resource allocation.

Furthermore, the poor are excluded from the main institutions of the political economy: they do not have organized lobbies; they are low political participators; and in urban areas, their neighborhoods tend to be dominated by patronage machines. They are not organized in labor unions and usually their jobs are not even protected by the legislative minimums of wages and working conditions won by more strongly organized workers. They are rarely represented on public bodies: school boards, welfare departments, urban renewal planning committees, utility regulatory commissions and even antipoverty program boards. The dictum of democracy—that the people should have voice in the decisions which affect their lives—is imperfectly realized for affluent America, but for the poor it is so much empty rhetoric. This chapter will explore several aspects of the political economy of poverty: the relationship between politics and the welfare system that introduces both intentional and unintentional restrictions to a meaningful service delivery system to the poor (Cloward and Piven); the interaction of race discrimination and changing labor demands to create a virtual class exclusion of the mass of Negroes from the economy (Kahn); trends in automation which decrease the availability of low-skill jobs and increase the required investment in the labor force (Killingsworth); the wage-depressing effects of high competition in labor intensive, low-skill industries (Bluestone); and the conditions of automation and concentration which are eroding the economic position of the small farmer (Bennett).

While these topics highlight certain key factors in the social causation of poverty, by no means do they cover all aspects of the relation between poverty and the ongoing processes of the affluent society. There are at least five additional features of the American political economy that have relevance to the political economy of poverty.

One: Defense Spending and Poverty

The massive defense budget preempts fifty to sixty percent of federal funds for nonconsumable goods thereby imposing sharp limits on resources available for social investment. The budget concentrates job demands in high skill areas, creating a skilled technician group. It subsidizes extensive research and development by universities and corporations thereby accelerating technological change and eroding the existing occupational structure. It creates community dependency on defense production and consequent community disruption and social hardship with changes in procurement patterns. It concentrates defense profits in relatively few business units, giving them an inordinate investment in the status quo. Such effects of a massive defense budget have certain consequences for the political economy of poverty. The engineer in an affluent defense industry in San Diego has a vested interest in the perseverance of current resource allocation. The career military officer and the company that has a heavy investment in defense work will also favor the current resource allocation. These people will not favor change in resource allocation at the expense of their own interests but may use social and political power at their command to retain the status quo.

Two: Cold War Ideology and Poverty

The prevailing political posture of "domestic unity in the face of communist threat" generates and reinforces a social and political climate where there is a distrust of social experimentation, innovation, and planning. A strong reactionary current in this country, partly generated by the Cold War and partly by historical process, has made a mystique of free enterpise, individualism, private property, states rights and profits and rendered as virtually un-American any discussion of major economic reform (e.g. national economic planning, some regulation of private economic power or the development of a comprehensive base of income, medical and welfare benefits). In this climate, the fundamental changes needed for a concerted attack on the roots of poverty are apt to be opposed by national, state and local interest groups. The range of alternatives for action are, thus, severely restricted and considerable effort must be expended for small social gains. It is this climate also that generates a distrust of the social reformer or the dissenter and his voice is muted by the threatened or real pressures that these interest groups can bring to play on him.

Three: Corporate Power and Poverty

Competition among large corporate structures with new patterns of corporate consolidation, product change, scientific management and market domination have resulted in increased pressures to reduce operating costs. This pressure manifests itself in an acceleration of technological change and a twist in labor demand away from the low-skilled and manual worker toward higher skilled, service and professional workers. These patterns concentrate the gains from governmental demand stimulating policies in highly capitalized markets, with relatively little job-creating benefit for low-skilled workers. They also invest some corporate structures with an inordinate degree of influence in establishing market conditions that are detrimental to the reduction of poverty. Such influence usually is exerted in a climate where the prime consideration is profit motivated actions with substantial social costs and consequences. The end result is to create major concentrations of political influence which have effective veto power over tax reform measures that can be used as a means of financing federal or local social investment programs.

Four: Community Power Structure and Poverty

In most communities the limits on policy alternatives and political action are effectively set by an informal coalition of economic leaders and some segment of the formal political leadership. This group usually exerts some control over the mass media of the community through direct business pressures and informal protest measures. At the day-to-day "grass roots" level, there usually exist mechanisms to maintain social stability and protect property and financial interests. These tend to involve a close working relationship between public officials, local merchants, real estate interests and other forms of organized community power. Groups pressing disruptive demands, whether for redress of individual grievances or broad social betterment are faced with the organized power of the community—power which is wielded in the name of the public welfare but which serves to protect the private interests of the privileged. In some cases this power is used subtly and only the community intimate can recognize its form of expression. In other cases, as in Selma, Alabama, the power is used overtly and its form of expression is easily recognizable.

Five: Conservative Coalition and Poverty

The Congress for the last twenty-five years has been dominated by a working coalition of Southern Democrats and Conservative Republicans which has blocked or forced major revision in nearly every item of proposed social welfare legislation and has exerted major influence in the structure and staffing of regulatory agencies. This coalition, in turn, serves as the congressional voice for the major lobbies of conservative economic and social policy: the National Association of Manufacturers, the Chamber of Commerce, the American Medical Association, the National Farm Bureau Federation and other economic interest groups. In turn, they find their public platform through heavily financed campaigns in the major mass media and in professional-business associations which share their political and social views.

This range of topics has not been subject to systematic research, at least in terms of their effects on the generation and possible elimination of poverty. They involve, needless to say, issues of great scope and high controversy. It is a mark of our intellectual deficit that these unresearched topics will probably have far greater consequences in the war on poverty than many of the issues to which social science has given its most careful attention.

Politics, the Welfare System, and Poverty

Richard A. Cloward and Frances Fox Piven

Columbia University School of Social Work

[Paper prepared for Columbia University School of Social Work Arden House Conference on, "The Role of Government in Promoting Social Change," Harriman, New York, November 18-21, 1965.]

THE GROWTH of the bureaucracies of the welfare state has meant the diminished influence of low-income people in public spheres. This has come about in two ways: first, the bureaucracies have intruded upon and altered processes of public decision so that low-income groups have fewer occasions for exercising influence and fewer effective means of doing so; and second, the bureaucracies have come to exert powerful and inhibiting controls on the low-income people who are their clients.

In response to the critics who point to these propensities of the public bureaucracies, several recent federal programs have made special provisions for citizen participation. It is our contention that such measures fail to offset the conditions which permit bureaucratic usurpation of power. Not only is citizen participation by and large a ritual conducted at the discretion of the public agencies, but it tends to become another vehicle for the extension of bureaucratic control.

Political leaders obviously must strive to accommodate groups that will provide them with the votes to win elections. To this extent, the flow of influence is upward. Programs for public benefits, however, are not simple electoral decisions to be made and reconsidered by a new polling of electoral sentiments. They are ensconced in bureaucratic complexes which are the domain of experts and professionals, masters of the special knowledge and techniques considered necessary to run the public agencies and administer the public benefits. Whole spheres of decision are made within these agencies, or in deference to their advice. The professional bureaucracies represent a new system of public action, only occasionally subject to electoral control.

The bureaucracies are exposed to direct control by broad constituencies only at periodic formal junctures: elections, budget hearings, or public referenda on appropriations. And at those points at which they are vulnerable, public agencies are themselves able to exert powerful counter-influence in electoral decisions. They bring to bear on their own behalf the weight of their acknowledged (but obscure) expertise and their great organizational capability, as well as a host of supportive liaisons formed with political leaders and other organizations in the public and private sectors.

The low-income clientele whom the bureaucracies are charged to serve, to placate, and to contain are a special source of sensitivity to them. Any disruption or assertiveness on the part of clients, to the extent that it is visible, will put in jeopardy the support of groups and organizations that watch over the public agencies. The bureaucracies therefore manipulate the benefits and services on which their clients come to depend in such a way as to control their behavior. In this way, governmental benefit systems have become a powerful source of control over low-income people, used to ensure the conforming client behaviors which the bureaucracies require both for internal stability and in order to maintain electoral support. Through these processes, the bureaucracies come to serve as the filter of power, selectively accommodating the alert, the organized, and the influential, but containing the low-income groups which, by depending on public benefits, fall under bureaucratic control.

Our central proposition is that the public bureaucracies strive chiefly to maintain the conditions necessary for their stability and expansion. They are essentially neutral, aligned with neither class nor party, except as such alignments serve jurisdictional claims or determine the availability of necessary resources. They distribute public benefits in response to organizational requirements, adjusting the distribution to maintain and enlarge the flow of organizational resources. The influence of any group upon them ultimately depends on its role in this process—either contributing resources and supporting jurisdictional claims, or threatening the attainment of these objectives. Public agencies strive to maintain themselves with the least possible internal stress and change and therefore try to use their organizational capacity to limit both the occasion and the extent of their vulnerability to outside groups. Organizational equilibrium and enhancement are, in short, the compelling forces in bureaucratic action.

In this paper we will discuss three sets of tactics by which the bureaucracies pursue these goals: tactics of organizational consolidation and coalition; tactics of political accommodation; and tactics of low-income client control.

Tactics of Organizational Consolidation and Coalition

When by legislative mandate we establish an agency and charge it with the distribution of some public benefit, we vest in it powerful resources by which to influence electoral decisions, other organizations, and its own clientele. These resources consist of the technical expertise with which the agency is credited, the benefits it is charged with distributing, and control of its own elaborate organizational structures and processes. These resources are employed by the public agency to protect and extend its jurisdiction in the following ways.*

The Consolidation of Expertise

Acknowledgement of expertise is a component of the political mandate initially granted to the public agency. It is inherent in political acceptance of technical definitions of problems and solutions, and also in political reliance on complex bureaucratic structures to carry out these solutions.

The expertise that is initially acknowledged by political mandate is itself used by public agencies to extend and consolidate the need for expertise. To acknowledge expertise in a given area is to grant authority. By its nature, expertise is obscure and its appropriate boundaries cannot easily be judged by the non-expert. It is therefore difficult to contain the propensities of expert-bureaucrats to elaborate still further the specialized knowledge and technique required in the recognition of and solution of problems.

There seems to be a tendency, moreover, toward the coalition of expertise, both within and among organizations. Problems are interpreted not only as highly technical but as multifaceted; thus they require the application of a variety of expert skills. Consequently, the public bureaucracies come increasingly to be staffed by coalitions made up of experts from a variety of professions. A non-expert trying to appraise the claims of the professional bureaucrats has virtually no recourse once the importance of expertise is acknowledged, but to turn to other experts. A competitive pluralism among organizations and professions provides some counter to bureaucratic influence, not only by fostering alternative programs but by fostering alternative experts whose opinions may be a basis for evaluating and controlling given programs. Coalitions of experts, by contrast, constitute monopolies on expertise which foreclose alternative appraisals, confronting electoral leaders, the general public, special-interest constituents and competing organizations with a virtually impenetrable professional phalanx.

---

*We use "jurisdiction" to include the various ways in which an agency's operations are limited by legislative or administrative mandate. There are obviously any number of dimensions according to which jurisdiction can be defined: area, population (or "target group"), duration of operation, and a host of criteria limiting the kind of benefits or expertise allowed the agency and the manner or occasion of application.

The Consolidation of Benefits

The professional bureaucracies are vested with control over the distribution of various benefits, presumably to serve some public purpose. Benefits are also inducements or sanctions and therefore are a resource for influence which the agencies control. We have referred to the bureaucratic capacity to distribute benefits which, by serving the purposes of electoral leaders, may procure political support for the bureaucracies. We will subsequently show how the use of benefits as inducements or sanctions also ensures client behavior, which are consonant with the agency's larger political concerns.

In seeking to extend and entrench their jurisdictions, professional bureaucracies reveal a tendency to expand organizational control to a variety of benefits. The emphasis on "multifaceted" problems leads not only to the formation of coalitions of experts under one organizational structure but to the consolidation of a range of benefits within the same structure. The "multiproblem" family is thus said to require a variety of both experts and benefits; thus the web of experts and benefits becomes more intricate with the "saturation" and "comprehensive" approaches to a social problem.

This tendency is everywhere discernible in social welfare services. The schools include a variety of guidance counselors, psychologists, and physicians in their coalition of experts and they dispense the benefits over which these experts have jurisdiction. Public housing authorities sponsor a host of special programs and services involving many different professionals and many diverse facilities.* With each repeated discovery of the persistence of problems in service, the professionals make their bid for more experts and benefits, co-opting new and different varieties along the way.

The Joining of Benefits and Expertise

A third tactic of the professional bureaucracies is to link expertise to benefits so that benefits are conditional on the use of expertise. In this way the importance of benefits tends to accrue to expertise and

---

*Most commentators see such expansion as reform. Writing about housing, Wolf Von Eckhardt notes approvingly that "Mrs. Marie C. McGuire, head of the public housing agencies, reports that there are 19,000 community service programs—such as scouting, health care, homemaking, arts and crafts, and literacy training—concentrated in public housing projects throughout the nation. These programs attract 2.6 million people a month ... they are on the side of good community design, social awareness and social integration" ("The Department of Headaches," *New Republic*, November 6, 1965, p. 20).

conversely, the discretion inherent in expertise is employed in the distribution of benefits. We are told that public housing is of little value without social service; that welfare cash assistance must be accompanied by "rehabilitation" programs; that education requires therapeutic and guidance specialists.

The legislation of a benefit ordinarily implies political acknowledgement of a collective problem which the new benefit is intended to ameliorate. Distribution of the benefit is therefore important to the political collectivity. When that distribution is defined as requiring expert skills, expertise gains importance, and experts acquire influence in confrontations with electoral leaders and public groups. And, as will be shown later, a similar use is made of benefits in dealing with clients, for whom benefits are especially critical.

The linkage of expertise and benefits extends the discretion of the professional bureaucracies. Discretion is inherent in expertise; the mystique of esoteric knowledge and technique shields the bureaucratic management of benefits from easy review by political leaders or public groups and from the assertions of client claimants. In this connection, it is interesting to note that those now ensconced in the government bureaucracies—educators, social workers, vocational counselors—are members of the less authoritative and prestigeful professions. Bureaucratic control over benefits and bureaucratic obfuscation of practice lend these professions a complement of authority and prestige. They are thus able to claim critical functions in the public sector in their bid for full professional recognition.

These are some of the tactics by which professional bureaucracies extend and consolidate the resources with which they are initially endowed by public mandate. Concretely these tactics can be recognized in the characteristic efforts of the bureaucracies to "coordinate" different organizational and professional activities, to form "comprehensive" programs, and to unify organizational jurisdictions—always under the banner of increased effectiveness and efficiency.

Once they are charged with the distribution of a class of benefits, and once their technical and organizational capabilities are acknowledged, the bureaucracies employ these assets in subsequent confrontations with political leaders, electoral groups, and other organizations. Their control of technical and organizational expertise permits public agencies to remove themselves from scrutiny and at the same time to form for public view all-embracing but esoteric legitimations of their operations. Ultimately they succeed in these tactics, of course, only because the functions they perform by distributing benefits have come to be regarded as essential to the society.

Tactics of Political Accommodation

For their initial public mandate and for subsequent public allocations, the bureaucracies depend on political decisions. They require the support of political leaders. They also require at least the tacit support of those organized forces in the community that are able to watch over governmental policies and to threaten intervention in political decisions. The agencies must therefore bring their distinctive capabilities to bear in inducing supportive responses and discouraging action which might subvert agency jurisdiction.

Political Leaders

New welfare programs are typically legislated when political leaders are confronted with mounting concern among their electoral constituencies, often in response to some form of social disruption. With newspapers and civic groups in the lead, there is a call for action on some issue which has come to be defined as a public problem. The politician looks for a solution which will placate public concern without jostling any groups on whose support he relies. He tries to find a solution which will appear to be forceful and yet will avoid controversy. The general electorate should feel unduly offended in neither their purses nor their sentiments. Nor should the solution activate and engage any new groups in the fray by threatening their particular interests.

The task in any political proposal is to find that course of public action which minimizes conflict and reflects the broadest possible agreement among those alerted by the issue. Welfare problems bring into public focus the poor, the minorities, or the deviants, groups which are not themselves part of the middle-class political consensus and whose cause is as likely to arouse the wrath of some as it is the pity of others. To invent a solution to a welfare problem is not easy. It is vastly facilitated, however, by the professional bureaucracies.

What to the politician is a disturbance in his constituency and a threat to his majority becomes for the professional bureaucrat an opportunity to extend his public mandate, his resources, and his jurisdiction. The agencies are ready for liaison with the political leader. They bring to that liaison the capacity to convert political problems into technical problems. Issues which are rooted in group conflict, which have been framed as "who gets what," are transmuted into issues of method and framed in terms of a technology. That the technology is obscure is largely an advantage; the germinal political issue of "who gets what" is thereby also obscured. Moreover, the authority and prestige of expertise, and the faith in science and progress which it calls forth, are added to the political equation and made still more compelling by the complexity of the proposal. Indeed, the ultimate public action may be a program of research and demonstration to devise or advance the necessary technology.

Once a new program is initiated, the public agencies and their political allies continue in close symbiotic relationship. Politicians rely on professionals for information and recommendations regarding policies which are increasingly esoteric and complex. The bureaucracies, in filling this function, are in turn closely responsive to the concerns of their political patrons.

In this kind of partnership between political leaders and the public agencies, there is clearly gain to be had for both sides. The politicians are able to offer to their constituencies programs which inspire confidence and assuage conflict by their very technicism. The bureaucracies, for their part, are extended and made more powerful. This, too, is an advantage for politicians, for when public action is contained within bureaucratic spheres, it is less likely to produce politically disruptive change.

Peer Organizations

Government and private spheres have experienced a parallel growth of large, rationalized organizations. The bureaucracies are vulnerable to these organizational peers which have the resources to maintain a steady watch over the complex activities of public agencies, to decipher the implications of these activities, and to threaten to exercise comparable influence in electoral processes.

Large, rationalized organizations are able to keep abreast of the maze of actual and proposed legislation and procedures, and exploit many formal and informal occasions for negotiations and bargaining. They have the ability to generate public issues; they have access to the press and the political parties and can call on other organizations with whom they have regular liaisons. In addition, the technical capability of other organizations and their programatic cooperation are often valuable assets to the public agencies.

Consequently, public agencies strive to form liaisons with organizational peers, public and private, accommodating them in ways designed to ensure their support or at least to avoid attack. A planning commission deals with other municipal agencies and with organizations of realtors and homeowners; a board of education deals with teachers' unions and parents' associations; and social welfare agencies deal with each other, with professional societies and philanthropic federations.

Tactics to Control Clients

The bureaucracies employ their distinctive capabilities to make certain of client acquiescence in agency actions, and to prevent any public display of assertiveness by low-income clients which may reflect on the agency and put in jeopardy the support of other community groups. As a consequence, the political influence of low-income people has been diminished by their involvement as clients of the agencies of the welfare state. Benefits are formed and distributed in ways which inhibit the development of client groups capable of collective action, which in turn limit the capacity of low-income people to exert influence in the electoral system. Ordinarily a group gains influence because it organizes for the collective application of its resources, whether the tactics it employs are negotiation, block voting, or disruption. The working classes were organized through the political machines in the residential areas where they lived and through the unions in the factories where they worked. They were able to improve their position in part by political influence through which they secured governmental regulation of economic institutions. Today's poor, by contrast, not only have little leverage as workers in economic spheres but have few organizational resources for influencing government and they are increasingly cast into a relationship with the institutions of the welfare state which entrenches and reinforces their powerlessness.

Benefits Which Discourage Interaction

Public benefits to the contemporary poor inhibit the emergence of collective low-income power in two ways. First, benefits are of a kind which isolates low-income people from major social roles, particularly occupational roles. Second, benefits are designed as individual benefits and the manner in which they are distributed discourages the aggregation of clients.

Isolative benefits. In general, group interests are expressed politically by organizations developed around the major roles which people perform, and principally around economic roles. Regular participation in an institutional role makes possible the tacit organization of people—or rather of their contributions—as a concomitant of role performance. Thus political interest groups are typically associations of tradesmen or professionals or homeowners. Less obviously, civic associations seem to prosper when they are closely linked to economic roles.

Similarly, the power of organized labor depends on the role of workers in economic institutions, and on the factory as a context for building regular and stable union organization. As a consequence, most of the social welfare innovations of the last few decades have reinforced the occupational role, ensuring economic stability and a higher standard of living for people employed in preferred occupations. The welfare state has come to be the bulwark against downward mobility from the working class for the temporarily unemployed, the survivors of deceased workers, and the old. Through organization in occupational roles workers not only gained leverage in private enterprise but came, through the unions, to exert influence in securing various government benefits for the working classes.

The client categories by which public bureaucracies define eligibility for benefits, however, are not coterminous with regular role categories in the social structure. Rather these categories define people by "non-roles": clients are school dropouts, broken families, or unemployables. Eligibility for benefits is thus established by inability to gain access to or to maintain educational roles, occupational roles, family roles, and the like. Consequently, people receiving benefits cannot associate with their status as clients any set of common rights and obligations derived from other major social roles. Nor are people likely to form groups as clients when to do so is to collectively acknowledge and label themselves by the role failure which the client status represents. Finally, and perhaps most important, benefits of this kind, by isolating people from major social roles, also isolate them from major institutional spheres, from the mainstream of social and economic life. Clients do not gain the influence which can be derived from regular participation in major institutions. They remain separated from the leverage inherent in regular role performance and without the opportunity for organizing that leverage which an institutional context provides.

Individual benefits. Another important characteristic of benefits to the poor is that they apply to individuals rather than to groups and so constitute no inducement for the formation of groups. Nor does the manner in which benefits are distributed tend to aggregate people, a means by which latent incentives for organization might be activated. The right to bargain collectively, for example, was a benefit *to an organization* and therefore an inducement to organize, provided by legislation to those workers who were not yet unionized. No comparable inducement flows out of the benefits provided to the contemporary poor.

At least embryonic organizations must exist before influence can be directed to secure benefits which nurture organizations. The emerging labor movement produced a leadership that was in a position to recognize organizational concerns and to press management and government for the benefits which enhanced the unions as organizations. By contrast, the contemporary poor are disorganized. What influence they have in electoral processes is not exerted for organizing benefits. The working classes were already partially unionized when they pressed for legislation giving them the right to bargain collectively; so were the Negroes of the South when they demanded legislation empowering them to vote. For the most part, today's poor are atomized. Aggregate action, when it occurs, takes form as waves of unrest and disruption—as in the recent uprisings in the ghettos of the North—from which no leadership comes forth. The poor are placated with individual benefits and, by receiving them, remain unorganized.

Tactics to Counter Collective Action

Low-income groups occasionally emerge in the context of public benefit systems. In some instances benefits simply cannot be managed by individualized distribution (e.g., education and large-scale housing); in other instances bureaucratic action unites people who are already loosely affiliated by imposing on them a common deprivation, uncompensated by benefits (e.g., slum clearance). Such low-income groups are not likely to join the ranks of organized constituents with whom the bureaucracies form accommodating relations. Bureaucratic responsiveness to low-income groups incurs the risk of arousing hostile forces in the community and of eventually undermining electoral support for the bureaucracies. This risk has to do not only with the substance of these responses to the low-income groups but with the very fact of engaging in reciprocal relations with the poor.* Low-income groups can themselves offer the bureaucracies little significant support in a wider community context. Moreover, the bureaucracies have certain capabilities for containing and directing such groups which provide an alternative to accommodation.

Containment and direction are in fact, the strategy which the bureaucracies typically employ in response to low-income groups which impinge upon them. For this strategy they are uniquely equipped by their capacity to manipulate information and benefits.

---

*See Georg Simmel's essay on "The Poor" (*Social Problems*, Fall 1965, pp. 118-140) for a dilineation of the sociological bases for the exclusion of the poor from participation in the administration of public assistance.

First, the bureaucracies can withhold or dispense information about their own procedures which low-income groups require in order to formulate any challenge to bureaucratic action. This is in part a consequence of the highly complex and technical maze of bureaucratic regulation and practice. It also has to do with the fact that most bureaucratic activity is not visible from the vantage point of clients, and even less so from the vantage point of low-income protest groups, which are outside the system entirely. Complexity and obscurity are, as we have noted, an asset in many contests in which bureaucracies strive for influence. Bureaucrats are not likely to take the initiative in so structuring and advertising their actions as to encourage surveillance by anyone, and especially not by low-income groups whose claims will generate controversy or strain their supportive liaisons.

The second major tactic which bureaucracies employ in controlling and directing low-income groups is the manipulation of benefits. When such groups are formed among clients, the bureaucracies are able to offer peripheral benefits as incentives for conformity and to threaten the withdrawal or curtailment of essential benefits as punishment for dissent.

Thus, housing programs seem occasionally to provide a context for the formation of groups among low-income people. In the public housing program, for example, low-income people were necessarily aggregated in the course of receiving benefits simply because housing was provided in large projects. The project structure was dictated by other considerations having to do with administrative efficiency and political acceptability (Note the recent alarm over the rent-supplement proposal, which might have subsidized low-income tenants to live in middle-class areas). Not long after World War II, and rather early in its bureaucratic life, the New York public Housing Authority was confronted with militant tenant groups in several of its projects. Not only were these groups taking active positions on public-housing matters, but they appeared to have a politically radical character of some notoriety. The Housing Authority reacted by prohibiting the use of project facilities by tenant organizations.

Not only the withdrawal of benefits, but also the proffering of benefits can work to weaken low-income groups. This is, of course, a more likely tactic when the bureaucracies confront groups of people who are not yet beneficiaries. When tenants in some of the slum buildings of New York organized "no heat, no hot water" protests, the housing agencies responded by selectively redressing only the most vigorous tenant complaints. With much publicity, the agencies seemed to bring to bear their total armory of legal enforcement and rehabilitation aids, but only on a few star buildings. Tenant leadership was turned aside and the protests were deflated, but the grievances of most slum dwellers remained unanswered.

Public action in urban renewal has occasioned some of the most stubborn and aggressive low-income group protests of recent years. These groups were composed of residents in areas scheduled for renewal. Confronted with the stress of upheaval, the loss of neighborhood, and the prospect of greatly increased rentals,[1] these people were the hardest hit by the costs of renewal but were not to receive the benefits provided by the new developments. They were people already together in neighborhoods, united by a common deprivation or threat of deprivation to the neighborhood, and in no significant way appeased by any benefits. The new developments included chiefly high-rental housing; slum clearance was no boon to slum dwellers for whom it meant mainly dislocation.

The adamancy of these local protest groups often threatened to disrupt urban renewal projects. The agencies countered with programs for "community participation," consisting largely in the careful advertisement of renewal plans to resident groups and the active initiation of local leaders at an early stage in order to "educate" and win them to the plans. Thus programs for directed community participation were developed to offset the spontaneous, but disruptive, participation of local protest groups. At the same time, many of the facts of renewal (e.g., the numbers to be displaced and the relocation alternatives available) continued to be concealed and sometimes appeared to be simply fabricated.

Tactics of Political Socialization

Governmental benefit systems are also structures for political socialization.[2] Low-income people are drawn into these systems as recipients. They are attracted by the promise of benefits, and once in the system, they remain tied to it by the benefits they receive. These benefits are typically not vested by law or conferred as a matter of unambiguous right; they are proffered at the discretion of the professional bureaucracy. They can be employed as threats and rewards to

---

[1] For review of problems in relocation see Chester Hartman, "The Housing of Relocated Families," *Journal of the American Institute of Planners*, November 1964, pp. 266-286.

[2] For a general discussion of the political power inherent in public benefits see Charles Reich, "The New Property," *Yale Law Review*, Vol. 73, No. 5, April 1964.

influence client attitudes and ensure conforming client behavior. Access to resources which people require—money, housing, education—is made conditional on acceptable behavior, including often acquiescence to professional counseling or therapy. The threatened denial of essential benefits is a powerful sanction to control client behavior.

Conditional benefits. All public bureaucracies require some measure of discretion in the distribution of benefits, for no mandates can be so precise and inclusive as to provide firm guidelines for all the varied circumstances presented for decisions. All bureaucracies tend to expand that discretion by elaborating technical expertise and organizational complexity. When recipients of a program are primarily low-income people, several circumstances combine to support the further enlargement of bureaucratic discretion.

The initial establishment of a public agency is a consequence of a collective political decision in which low-income people are not likely to have been very forceful, and surely not forceful as organized political actors. The framing of statutes establishing public benefits for low-income people typically reflects the attitudes of other groups which *are* effective political proponents. These include the middle-class groups whose attitudes dominate political consensus, the bureaucracies, and the professional associations linked to the bureaucracies. Such proponents prefer to vest discretion in the public functionaries who deal with the poor rather than to establish these benefits as a right, to which the poor are entitled.[3]

The dominant view of the poor among the American middle class is that they are defective, morally as well as in other ways, and are likely to take advantage of public beneficence. And public agency personnel feel themselves constrained by the constant threat of arousing powerful community forces to employ criteria in defining eligibility for benefits which go beyond objective economic need and take account of widely held invidious definitions of the poor. The New York City Welfare Department, for example, enjoins its investigators to discourage malingering, reminding them in its manual that "the denial or withdrawal of assistance is as constructive a factor as the granting of assistance, both to the client and to the community."

The threat of community opposition is real, as attested by the recurrent attacks upon welfare departments and public housing au-

---

[3]The New York City Public Housing Authority, for example, is not governed by formulated regulations in selecting tenants. Nor have successive reforms impelled by professional and civic organizations moved in this direction. Instead, a maze of criteria establishing priorities and ineligibility has been developed, to be applied largely at the discretion of the agency functionaries.

thorities for allegedly fostering immorality and degeneracy among their clients. Accordingly, the administrators of these agencies employ the discretion allowed to them in an array of investigatory and policing practices intended to ensure that the recipients or potential recipients of benefits will be publicly regarded as "worthy" of the sums and services dispensed to them. Public housing functionaries maintain surveillance over the morals of their tenants, employing their own police forces and their own quasi-judicial procedures, made potent by the threat of eviction and virtually unrestrained by laws or regulations protecting the rights of tenants. In New York City, the project managers have even developed a system of tenant "fines" which are imposed for all manner of behavior which the manager regards as bad tenancy. Similarly, public welfare departments invest enormous organizational energy in the initial determination of a client's worthiness and eligibility for the dole. Once approved, the recipient is the object of constant surveillance to make sure he continues to meet these conditions. The most striking example of such practice is the "post-midnight raid" to which mothers receiving ADC grants are subjected in order to catch by surprise a man who may be on the premises.

The ambiguity surrounding the nature of client rights pertains also to procedures for appeal from agency decisions. It is not clear with many benefits whether an aggrieved person has the right to do anything more than complain. By and large, appeals procedures are not defined in legislation. With appeals, as with the initial dispensing of benefits, bureaucratic discretion over low-income clients is supported because it permits practices which accommodate to the invidious attitudes toward the poor held by dominant groups in the community.

The professionals who staff the bureaucracies are a second factor in reinforcing bureaucratic discretion over clients. Professionals generally tend to view the problems of low-income people as resulting from defects in socialization. Remedies for these defects are said to require exposure to professional services, and the discretion inherent in professional services is often employed to make judgments about the dispensing of benefits on which low-income people depend.

The third circumstance which expands bureaucratic discretion in dealing with clients is the general tendency of the bureaucracies to coordinate and consolidate their functions. In an earlier era of private charity, the poor could solicit cash relief or other benefits from one or another private agency, never entirely and finally subject to the judgment of any one. Now they confront one comprehensive welfare bureaucracy from whose decision they have no recourse. Even private agencies have developed mechanisms for maintaining broad supervision of their clientele. The Social Service Exchange, for example, is a device for comprehensive surveillance, designed in part to identify low-income people who shop around for services.

Proposals for bureaucratic reform seem inevitably to involve reorganization to establish more comprehensive jurisdiction over one category of clients or another, and to call for extension of the professionalization of staff and services. Through years of controversy regarding housing-code enforcement practices in New York City, reformers have repeatedly recommended consolidation of all housing agencies. Whether consolidation will in fact improve the condition of the low-income plaintiff remains questionable. Conflicting and overlapping jurisdictions may be administratively inefficient, but they give the low-income tenant some alternative course of action when, as has frequently been the case, his complaint is not heeded by a given agency. Similarly, the improvement of bureaucratic services means greater professionalization of staff and the extension of professional services and discretion. For example, in reform of criminal practices it is argued that probation officers should be social workers, surveillance should be therapeutic, and therapeutic evaluations should be the basis for criminal sentencing.

That the discretion derived from systems of conditional benefits is a source of enormous power over low-income people is self-evident. For people on public welfare, their very livelihood, however meager, is at stake; for the public-housing tenant it may be his only chance for a decent dwelling; to the family of the child confronted with the possibility of school suspension it is the only chance to give their offspring an education and indeed a future livelihood. There are few institutionalized safeguards against the exercise of discretion by government agencies which distribute conditional benefits to the poor. The laws which establish these benefits are vague and administrative procedures are complex and ambiguous.

Political desocialization. Exposure to bureaucratic discretion leads to political desocialization. First, bureaucratic procedures reflect the premise that the poor have few rights. Recipients of benefits are not apprized of procedures but are continually confronted with apparently arbitrary actions. Bureaucratic procedures are also punitive, reflecting the premise that the poor are unworthy and the constant fear that the client will lapse into sloth and chicanery. Such procedures in fact make people into what they are already said to be, for when their rights are ignored, men do indeed live by their wits, evading what is capricious and arbitrary or lapsing into apathy. Thus the clients of the welfare state come to live in fear, moving to control their fate not by political action, but by evasion and ultimately by acquiescence. In this way, welfare programs debilitate and demoralize;

the attitudes and ways of life into which clients are forced inhibit their effective participation in even ordinary social roles and surely inhibit political activism.

Secondly, clients are often socialized to particular forms of political participation through the exposure to professional services which receiving benefits entails. Professional service is an opportunity for educating clients in political beliefs and modes of political participation that are consonant with the views of the middle-class majority.[4]

For example, public-housing tenants who use recreational facilities are required to submit to supervision by agents of the housing authority and recreation becomes an occasion for political education. In the case described earlier, the New York Public Housing Authority continued to suffer publicly after eliminating tenant organizations, not so much for the radicalism of tenants as for their ostensibly antisocial behavior. The right-wing press launched periodic exposés of crime, delinquency, and abuse of property in the projects. In time, the Authority developed a more sophisticated strategy than simple fiat for the containment of tenants: it undertook to form its own tenant organizations, linking these to various community services and dominating them through staff organizers. Tenants were encouraged to participate in recreational and self-help programs such as project beautification, consumer education, and household skills,[5] and were steered away from actions troublesome to the Authority.

Whether the professional bureaucrat is a caseworker, a guidance counselor, an educator, a recreational expert, or a community organizer, and whether the program is a youth employment agency or a "Headstart" operation, the professional is the agent of socialization, and the program is the vehicle for socialization, as to the legitimacy of existing political arrangements and the propriety of middle-class political styles. The consequences of this socialization are clear. Established institutional arrangements are endorsed, their democratic character is

---

[4]The use of professional service as a means of control is by no means limited to government bureaucracies. The industrial counseling profession, for example, seems to owe its genesis to the functions it serves for management in allaying worker discontent, a use of counseling first made evident in the Mayo studies.

[5]One of the most notorious public-housing projects in the country, the Pruitt-Igoe project in St. Louis, is now undergoing major rehabilitation and reform. In this, the Housing Authority, "aware that fiscal rehabilitation may only provide 'something else to break' has a series of programs underway to involve the tenant in the process" (James Bailey, "The Case History of a Failure," *Architectural Forum*, December 1965).

asserted, and middle-class styles of formalized participation and negotiation are inculcated. These beliefs leave no role for the conflict and protest which often characterize lower-class activism; indeed, they even make conflict and protest immoral. But today's unorganized poor have few of the resources needed for middle-class styles of participation and negotiation. They have little to bargain with and so are partners to no one's negotiations. And by becoming educated in the beliefs and strategies of action appropriate only for groups in higher economic strata, they are rendered ineffective.

To summarize, we see no evidence that government's involvement of the poor will generate a force for social change by nurturing their political capabilities or by activating them with the promise of benefits. Rather, governmental programs for the poor are likely to diminish whatever collective political vitality the poor still exhibit.

Future prospects for social change will be increasingly shaped by the expansionist forces of the public bureaucracies. How low-income people fare through this expansion will depend on the extent and kinds of benefits distributed by the bueaucracies. These benefits have been formed chiefly in accommodation to the middle-class consensus on which the bureaucracies depend for support. At the same time, public benefits have been designed to placate unrest among the poor and to deflect any political articulation of this unrest.

Under these conditions, ths best the poor can expect are programs such as those generated by the Office of Economic Opportunity, programs that impart to them the skills through which they may be integrated into occupational roles. At worst, they will get more programs such as public assistance which further isolate them—while controlling them—from major social roles in the society. If future programs do successfully impart competitive skills, the bureaucracies, in pursuing their own enhancement, may thereby succeed in raising many low-income people into the middle class. In this way the clients of the bureaucracy can one by one join the middle-class political majority and public benefits can indeed be said to increase their political influence. It will have done so, however, at the price of diminishing the ranks and therefore the influence of those who are still in the lower class. Thus the social change accomplished by bureaucratic expansion will not challenge the middle-class consensus as to appropriate forms of political participation and will not enlarge the capacity of the dispossessed to influence their environment. In particular, it will not enlarge the capacity of the poor to influence the public bureaucracies upon which they depend. This is the path marked out by public benefit systems which act to reinforce the existing alignment of influence.

The Economics of Inequality

Tom Kahn

League for Industrial Democracy

[Excerpted from the monograph, The Economics of Equality by Tom Kahn (New York, 1964) by permission from the League for Industrial Democracy.]

The relative economic position of the Negro is declining. In part this is due to overt racial discrimination, but mainly to his membership in an economic class to which he has been bound by centuries of exploitation. The position of this class is deteriorating because of technological developments which are revolutionizing the structure of the labor force. More precisely, it results from the failure to evolve sweeping national policies to meet the economic and social problems thrown up by the technological revolution. Since the economic future of the Negro is inseparable from that of his economic class, the civil rights movement must mobilize behind radical programs for the abolition of poverty and unemployment, thus infusing "the other America" with the dynamic and spirit of the Negro revolt. Failing this, persistent economic inequalities will undermine the drive toward legal and social equality.

The Treadmill

Running fast to stand still is essentially the position in which the Negro finds himself today. If the segregated lunch-counter is a hollow relic of the *ancient régime*, one which would inevitably topple at an early stage in the civil rights revolution, the more fundamental, institutional forms of discrimination are more securely rooted in our economic system. And current trends in that system imperil the Negro's economic future.

What emerges from the statistics on jobs and income are the following trends:

1. There is a widening *dollar gap* between Negroes and whites.

2. The *relative* income gap between Negroes and whites has remained virtually constant over the past decade.

3. The unemployment gap between Negroes and whites has been widening.

4. The industries and occupations where the Negro made his greatest gains have either declined or shown relatively little growth over the past decade.

5. Negroes constitute a growing percentage of all workers in most of the declining job categories.

Widening Dollar Gap

The median Negro family income is $3,233, or 54% of the white family's $5,835. Approximately two out of every three Negro families subsist on less than $4,000 annually—and are therefore poor or deprived—as compared with 27.7% of the white families. Only one out of five Negro families earns $6,000 or more, as compared with one out of two white families. In the whole country there are only 6,000 Negro families that can boast of incomes of $25,000 or more.

These figures tell us where the Negro is today, but they become more meaningful when compared to the 1945 figures, as Table 1 shows.

TABLE 1

Percent Distribution of Income of Families by Color for United States, 1945-1961

Total Money Income Level	1945		1961		Percent Change in Ratio Over 1945	
	White	Nonwhite	White	Nonwhite	White	Nonwhite
Under $4,000	75.5	90.1	27.7	60.2	− 63.3	− 33.1
$4,000-$5,999	16.8	6.1	22.4	19.7	+ 33.3	+223.0
$6,000 and over....	7.7	3.8	49.9	20.1	+548.0	+429.0
Total	100.0	100.0	100.0	100.0		

Source: U.S. Department of Commerce, *Current Population Reports*, Consumers Income, Series P-60, No. 2, March 2, 1948 and No. 38, August 28, 1962.

Notice that between 1945 and 1961, the percentage ratio of whites who escaped from the below $4,000 category (63.3%) is almost double that for Negroes (33.1%), despite the fact that a larger percentage of Negroes were in that category in 1945 (90.1% as against 75.5% of white families). Similarly, whites entered the $6,000-and-over category at a faster rate than Negroes.

On the other hand, the percentage increase of Negro families entering the $4,000–$5,999 category seems very impressive when compared with the figures for whites. But the percentage gain is great only because the starting figure was so low.

Fisk economist Vivian Henderson emphasizes that while

relative growth in wage and salary income of Negroes since 1940 has been greater than that of whites . . . the absolute, or *dollar*, difference has widened considerably. . . . People spend and save dollars. It is this dollar difference that counts. Pronouncements regarding economic progress which are confined to acceleration concepts and percentage change obscure the real predicament—*Negroes are losing ground rapidly in gaining dollar parity with whites.* The "dollar gap" trend . . . means very simply that earnings are increasing for whites at a faster pace than for Negroes. [*The Economic Status of Negroes,* Southern Regional Council, pp. 12–13.]

One aspect of the earning gap is particularly astonishing. When we compare the lifetime earnings of Negro and white males by education (Table 2), we find that the Negro who finishes four years of college will earn less than a white with only eight years of elementary school.

TABLE 2

Male Lifetime Earnings by Race and Education
(in thousands)

Highest Grade Completed	White	Negro	Negro As % of White
Elementary School			
Less Than 8 Years	$157	$ 95	61
8 Years	191	123	64
High School			
1 to 3 Years	221	132	60
4 Years	253	151	60
College			
1 to 3 Years	301	162	54
4 Years	395	185	47
5 Years or More	466	246	53
Average	241	122	51

Source: Employment and Earnings, Bureau of Labor Statistics, Feb. 1964.

Relative Income Gap

Not only is the dollar gap widening, but the *relative* income gap has remained virtually constant for almost a decade. While the figures reported by statisticians vary slightly, they point to the conclusion of Herman P. Miller of the Census Bureau:

In the last decade . . . there has been no change in income differential between [Negroes and whites]. The median pay of the Negro worker has remained stuck at about 55% of the white [*N.Y. Times,* Aug. 12, 1963].

The Negro's *relative* income gains were actually registered between 1940 and 1954, when Negro family median income jumped from 37% to 56% of the white figure.

Behind this gain was World War II (not the New Deal, after eight years of which 25% of the Negro work force was still unemployed as against 13% of the white). War production created a shortage not only of skilled workers, but of semiskilled and unskilled workers as well.

Consequently, thousands of Negroes left the rural South and poured into the factories. Protected by a federal FEPC, needed by an expanding economy, and absorbed in large numbers into the CIO, they won higher wages than the farms could offer. Many acquired new skills. The base of the Negro lower middle class was considerably expanded.

After Congress killed FEPC in 1946, job discrimination surged up and many of the newly acquired skills were lost to the Negro community through lack of use. Still, in the relatively prosperous post-war years, the unemployment rate among Negroes was only about 60% higher than the white rate. *Since 1954 it has been at least 200% higher.*

The point to be stressed here is that the Negro's income gains were the result of peculiar employment opportunities that no longer exist. In part, as Michael Harrington has observed, these gains were due to "economic geography rather than the workings of the society." They reflect the shift of rural Negroes to cities and Southern Negroes to the North. In these cases, the people involved increased their income by going into a more prosperous section of the economy as a whole. But within each area—Northern city, Southern city, agriculture —*their relative position remained the same: at the bottom.*

Thus, masses of Negroes entered industrial production but were concentrated in unskilled and semiskilled jobs. And these are precisely the jobs now being destroyed by automation. The "bottom" is falling out of society; it is no longer needed.

"Invisible Army of the Unemployed"

Just as the dollar gap between Negroes and whites has been widening, so has the unemployment gap, as Figure 1 indicates. Whereas the unemployment rate from 1947 to 1953 never exceeded 8.5% for Negroes and 4.6% for whites, now it stands at 12.4% and 5.9% respectively. Not only have there been rising levels of unemployment since 1954, but— and this is of strategic importance—the Negro-white unemployment gap has tended to widen in times of high unemployment and narrow in times of low unemployment. Historically the Negro fares better, absolutely and relatively, the closer the economy is to full employment.

Both tendencies—rising unemployment and a widening unemployment gap—come into sharper focus if we replace the official figures with more realistic ones which take into account what Professor Killingsworth (see preceding article) has called the "invisible army of unemployed"—"people forced out of the labor market some time ago who are willing and able to work, but have become too discouraged to search for jobs" and are therefore not counted as part of the labor force by the government. Professor Killingsworth carefully calculated the size

FIGURE 1: NEGRO AND OVER-ALL UNEMPLOYMENT RATES, 1947–1963

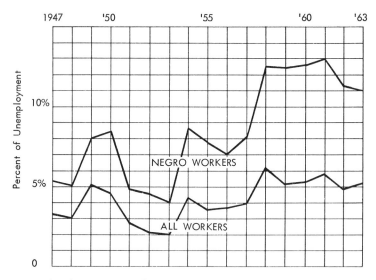

Estimates based on statistics of U. S. Department of Commerce, Bureau of the Census, and other sources.

of this "invisible army" at 1½ million. They would raise the national unemployment rate to 8.8%. Gunnar Myrdal, the eminent Swedish economist, likewise taking into account the number of persons who would re-enter the labor force if jobs opened up, put the figure at 9%.

While Killingsworth has not made a racial breakdown of the "invisible army," he emphasized that its members are educationally disadvantaged. A disproportionate number are undoubtedly Negroes, many of whom support themselves in the ghettos by means they are not likely to report to census takers. Labor economists believe the real Negro unemployment rate is probably close to 20%. In the words of the *New York Times*, "Unemployment of these proportions, were it general, would be a national catastrophe."

The Under-class

Especially ominous is the long-term unemployment rate among Negroes. For the long-term unemployed tend also to be the most frequently hit by unemployment, and the longer they are unemployed the less chance they have of ever finding jobs. They make up a swelling "under-class" that is daily becoming economically more obsolete. This "under-class" is composed mainly of Negroes, males 65 and over, young men, farm laborers, those in unskilled occupations and those with less

FIGURE 2: LONG-TERM UNEMPLOYMENT, 1953—1962
(15 weeks or more)

Source: U.S. Bureau of Labor Statistics   *January–June, seasonally adjusted.

than 12 years of schooling. For all of them, unemployment is worsening in frequency and duration. The mass unemployment of the thirties has yielded to a new "under-class" unemployment.

The seriousness of the problem is illustrated in Figure 2, which shows that since 1953 the long-term unemployed have been constituting *an increasing percentage of the total unemployed*. This means that a growing section of the work force is being more or less permanently detached from the economy and sinking into the "under-class."

Within this "under-class," Negro representation is mounting. Vivian Henderson reports that

> in September, 1958, the average duration of unemployment for Negroes was 17.8 weeks and for white workers 13.3 weeks. The average length of unemployment in September, 1962, for Negroes was 18 weeks while that for whites had dropped to 13 weeks. Negroes accounted for about 25% of all the long-term unemployed, but for only about 11% of the labor force. About 29% of the very long term unemployed in September, 1962, were Negroes compared with 21% in September, 1961. Long-term joblessness among Negroes results from discrimination in hiring and inadequate training and inadequate manpower development. [*op. cit.*, p. 16.]

Generally, the long-term unemployed are more likely to be the victims of technological change, while the short-term unemployed may be seasonal lay-offs, retrainees, or seekers of better jobs. What percentage of long-term joblessness among Negroes is attributable to discrimination *per se* and what percentage to inadequate training is difficult to state with precision.

The role of discrimination is clearest in the areas of income and occupational distribution of Negro college graduates. Lack of training certainly cannot explain the figures in Table 2. Nor can it satisfactorily explain why only 5% of Negro college men become proprietors, managers, or officials as compared with 22% of white college men; or why Negroes with some college training are found in service and laborer jobs in numbers five times greater than whites with similar training. It absolutely cannot explain why 10% of Negro women who finish college end up as domestics! Here is an obvious waste of skills that can be ascribed only to blatant discrimination and segregation.

On the other hand, college graduates constitute only 3.5% of the non-white population, and they are not usually to be found in the ranks of the long-term unemployed. In fact, because of skilled manpower shortages, educated Negroes are likely to make the most rapid progress in the period ahead.

For the vast majority of Negroes, however, an economic crisis is in the offing. And overt discrimination seems less a part of it than the weight of centuries of past discrimination combining with portentous economic forces that are themselves color-blind. *It is as if racism, having put the Negro in his economic "place," stepped aside to watch technology destroy that place.*

Changing Labor Force

As indicated above, most of the Negroes' economic gains in recent years were made in the period 1940–1953 and reflect their movement out of agriculture into mining, manufacturing, and construction, where they took up unskilled and semiskilled jobs. These blue-collar jobs in the goods-producing industries paid better than the unskilled and semiskilled jobs in the service-producing industries. But they were also the jobs most hit by automation and technological change.

As Table 3 shows, the past decade has witnessed a decline of 339,000 jobs in the goods-producing industries and an increase of 7.3 million jobs in the service-producing industries.

But these figures reveal only part of the impact of the technological revolution on the work force. Customarily, goods-producing jobs are considered blue-collar and service-producing jobs are considered white-collar. The fact is that *within* the goods-producing industries there has been a dramatic increase in the number of white-collar jobs and an even more dramatic loss of blue-collar jobs.

TABLE 3
The Shift in Non-Farm Jobs 1953-1963
(in thousands)

	1953	1963	Gain	Loss
Goods-Producing				
Mining	866	634		232
Construction	2,623	3,030	407 [1]	
Manufacturing	17,549	17,035		514
	21,038	20,699		339
Service-Producing				
Transportation, Public Utilities	4,290	3,913		377
Wholesale Trade	2,727	3,143	416	
Retail Trade	7,520	8,721	1,201	
Finance, Insurance, & Real Estate	2,146	2,866	720	
Miscellaneous Services	5,867	8,297	2,430 [2]	
Federal Government	2,305	2,358	53	
State, Local	4,340	7,177	2,837	
	29,195	36,475	7,280	

[1] Most of this increase was made by 1957; since then the number of construction jobs has remained fairly static.
[2] A high proportion of these jobs is part-time.
Source: *Employment and Earnings*, U.S. Bureau of Labor Statistics, Feb. 1964.

In manufacturing, for example, 1.6 million blue-collar (production and maintenance) jobs have been obliterated in this decade while more than one million white-collar (non-production) jobs have been added. The blue-collar decline is also evident in the service-producing industries. Note that the only service-producing jobs that declined since 1953 were in transportation and utilities (especially in railroading).

Thus the growth in white-collar jobs resulted not only from the expansion of the service industries, but also from the application of technology to the productive process itself. The economic revolution wrought by these developments became fully evident in the mid-1950s when the number of white-collar workers exceeded the number of blue-collar workers for the first time in history.* The decrease in the agricultural work force is also evident. As a consequence of agricultural mechanization, more than 1.5 million farm jobs have been wiped out since 1953.

It is against this background that the economic position of the Negro must be viewed. Figure 3 shows the percentage of whites and non-whites in each of the occupational categories. Notice the disproportionate concentration of Negroes in blue-collar and service jobs. (These service jobs are not to be confused with white-collar jobs *in service-producing* industries.)

---

* Illustrative table omitted.

FIGURE 3: OCCUPATIONAL BREAKDOWN BY RACE

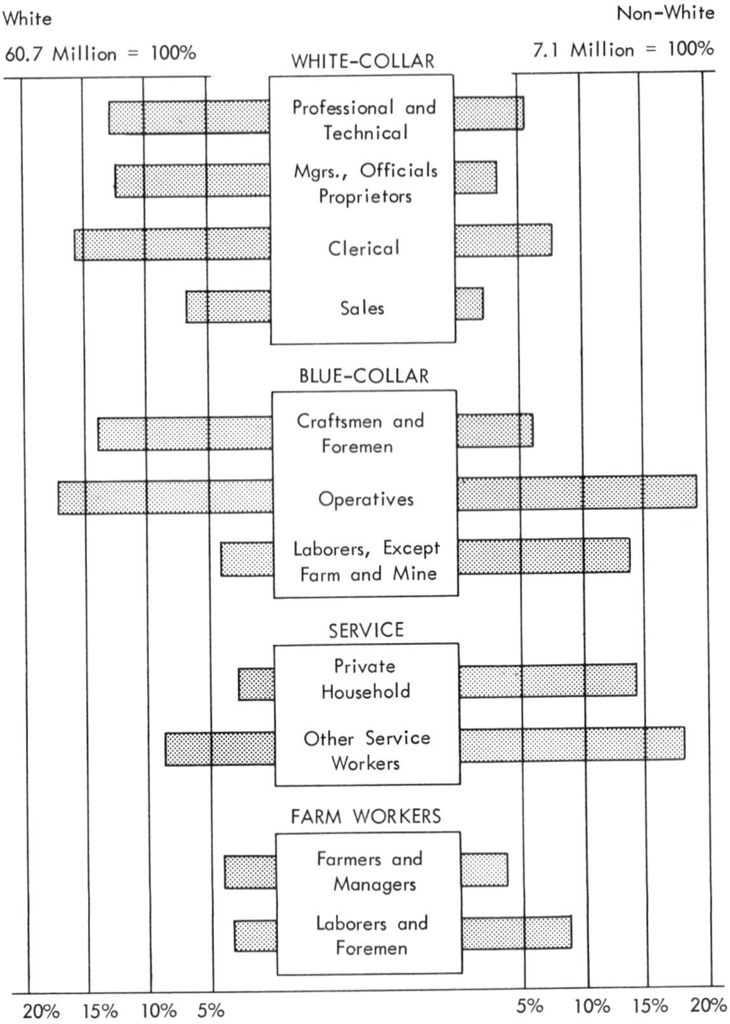

White		Non-White
60.7 Million = 100%		7.1 Million = 100%

WHITE-COLLAR

Professional and Technical

Mgrs., Officials Proprietors

Clerical

Sales

BLUE-COLLAR

Craftsmen and Foremen

Operatives

Laborers, Except Farm and Mine

SERVICE

Private Household

Other Service Workers

FARM WORKERS

Farmers and Managers

Laborers and Foremen

20% 15% 10% 5%   5% 10% 15% 20%

Source: U.S. Bureau of Labor Statistics

That these jobs are becoming increasingly marginal to the economy becomes clear when we examine Figure 4, which shows the rate of unemployment in each occupation. Note that the occupations in which unemployment is highest—for example, laborers, operatives, and "other service workers"—are precisely the occupations in which Negroes are most heavily concentrated. Conversely, the occupations with the

FIGURE 4: UNEMPLOYMENT BY OCCUPATION

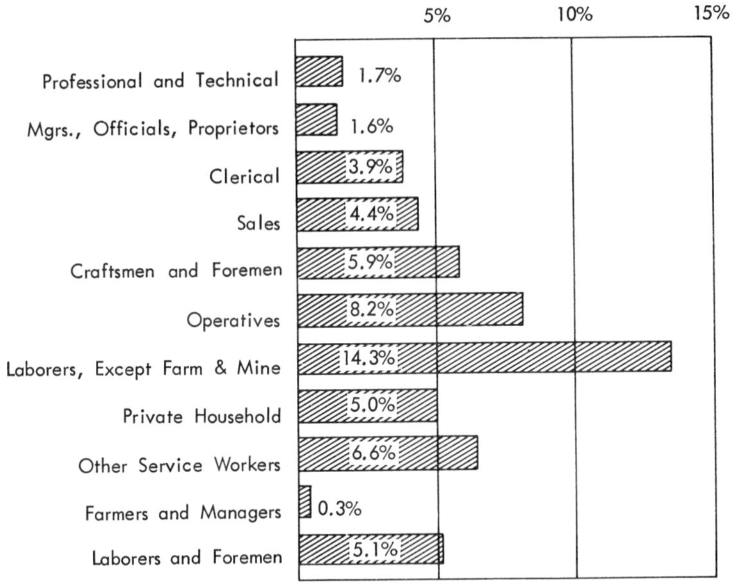

	5%	10%	15%
Professional and Technical	1.7%		
Mgrs., Officials, Proprietors	1.6%		
Clerical	3.9%		
Sales	4.4%		
Craftsmen and Foremen	5.9%		
Operatives	8.2%		
Laborers, Except Farm & Mine	14.3%		
Private Household	5.0%		
Other Service Workers	6.6%		
Farmers and Managers	0.3%		
Laborers and Foremen	5.1%		

Source: U.S. Bureau of Labor Statistics

lowest unemployment rates—for example, managers, officials, and proprietors—are those in which Negroes are least concentrated. Taken together, Figures 3 and 4 suggest that if Negroes suddenly changed their skin color but not their occupations, their unemployment rate would still be far above the national average.

Further study reveals that while the national trend is toward a white-collar labor force, the percentage of Negroes in blue-collar jobs is increasing. Thus, while the percentage of white males in blue-collar jobs *fell* from 53% in 1950 to 50% in 1960, the percentage for Negroes rose from 64% to 67%. And the greater part of this increase was in the "laborer" category. These are the figures for Negro *males*. More shocking are those for Negro females, an increasing percentage of whom are now in *blue-collar* jobs (15% in 1950, 17.2% in 1962; corresponding figures for white women are 22.3% and 17.3%).

The percentage of Negroes in white-collar jobs is also increasing, though in percentage points whites gained more than Negroes in professional and technical jobs. Most of the Negroes' gains were in clerical jobs where wages are generally lower than in manufacturing. It is precisely in the professional and technical field that the job market is expanding most rapidly. Herman Miller concludes, "In most states, the nonwhite male now has about the same occupational distribution relative to whites that he had in 1940 and 1950."

But unless this occupational distribution is radically altered, disaster looms for the Negro. Not only will the unemployment gap widen because of increasing automation in categories where Negroes are concentrated, but so will the dollar gap. As Henderson summarizes,

> Whites are acquiring the highest paying jobs in the higher occupational classifications. The benefits of general economic expansion and technology, therefore, have only trickled down to the Negroes, putting more of them into wage and salary jobs. These benefits automatically produced high acceleration in income change, but were restricted tightly to lower occupational classifications. Thus, despite the unprecedented growth of income among Negroes and the percentage gains made, the fact remains that *income progress of Negroes has leveled off*. The percentage of Negro families in lower income brackets is twice as high as whites, and *the differential in earnings of whites and Negroes continues to widen*, largely offsetting percentage gains. Accordingly, it is still difficult for Negroes to purchase health, education and the amenities of life on the same level as other members of the population. [*op. cit.*, pp. 12–13. Italics added.]

Not only are Negroes trapped in declining and stagnant job categories; *they constitute a growing percentage of the total workers in these categories*. Of all laborers (except farm and mine), Negroes were 27.6% in 1960 as against 21.2% in 1940; among operatives and kindred workers, Negroes constituted 11.6% as against 6.1%; among clerical workers, 6.7% as against 1.6%. While Negroes constituted a larger percentage of farm laborers and foremen in 1960 (23.6%) than in 1940 (22.5%), they make up a decreasing percentage of farmers and farm managers (8.6% as against 13.1%). The reason for this, of course, is agricultural mechanization, which has hit Negroes hardest. Between 1940 and 1959, the drop in the number of American farms was 39%, but the number of farms owned or operated by Negroes was cut more than one-half, from over 700,000 to less than 300,000. (Only 23% of Southern Negro farm workers own their own farms as contrasted with 60% of white farm workers. On the other hand, almost half of all tenant farmers and over 65% of all sharecroppers are Negroes.)

The Talk of Progress

To sum up, then, the decline in the relative economic position of the Negro is evident in the widening dollar and unemployment gaps between Negroes and whites, stagnation of the relative income gap, erosion of the job categories in which Negroes are concentrated, and the increasing segregation of Negroes in the declining job categories.

Underlying these trends are basic changes in the structure of the total labor force. The rising productivity caused by technological advances has reduced the number of workers required to produce the goods and services we need. While the effect of automation will become increasingly widespread, the blue-collar production and maintenance jobs are hardest hit. Paralleling the erosion of unskilled and semiskilled jobs is the growth of white-collar jobs and a mounting demand for skilled labor, where manpower shortages already exist. Because of centuries of discrimination and exploitation Negroes have been disproportionately concentrated in the unskilled and semiskilled jobs now being obliterated and lack the training demanded by the new skilled jobs. Even if every racial barrier were immediately torn down, the mass of Negroes would still face a disastrous economic future.

Nothing even vaguely resembling a "master plan" has been set in motion to eliminate the twin problems of racial inequality and technological unemployment. Because current government programs do not cope with the economic revolution, deepening structural unemployment frustrates the efforts of Negroes to enter the job market even when discriminatory barriers are eliminated. Thus, even if existing apprenticeship openings were fully integrated, Negro unemployment rates would remain intolerably high. Neither "equal opportunity" nor "preferential treatment" can solve the problems of Negro unemployment within the framework of a private economy which has failed to generate jobs over the past decade. To accept this framework is necessarily to accept a form of economic tokenism which benefits relatively few Negroes, and not those most in need.

Causes and Cures

In an article against "discrimination in reverse," Secretary of Labor Wirtz cited the "three causes of minority group unemployment":

1. "The present shortage of jobs in the economy as a whole for *all* workers."

2. "Unquestionably the fact of lesser qualifications" among minority groups.

3. "The harsh ugly fact of discrimination." ["Toward Equal Opportunity," *American Child*, Nov., 1963.]

These remarks are an excellent point of departure for an evaluation of government programs in the field.

Federal Training and Education Programs

The Manpower Development and Training Act of 1962 sought to retrain 400,000 workers within three years. A bill extending the program and adding 93,000 workers was signed by President Johnson in December, 1963. As Dan Schulder, of the Manpower Development and Training Agency, told a Washington Conference in November, 1963,

> MDTA programs in the South in the first 8 months of operation have trained only 234 Negroes, according to the report of the Civil Rights Commission. That figure represents only 11% of the total MDTA trainees, while Negro unemployment in the South is 30%. Further, training has been offered to Negroes in only a few of the occupations provided by the Commission. In the clerical and sales categories, 90% of the Negroes were trained as stenograph-typists. In the service category, such jobs as tailoring, typewriter-repairing were available to most of the Negroes. Others were trained as waiters and waitresses. [!]

Under the original terms of the Act, one-third of the applicants under 25 were rejected on grounds of illiteracy—an added handicap for Southern Negroes, who have a disproportionately high illiteracy rate.* Racist state officials are a stumbling block, since the states are responsible for approving the training programs. Mississippi has no program under way because the state refuses to offer assurances that the program would be administered on a nonracial basis. Finally,

> the Act states that people cannot be accepted for training without "reasonable expectation of employment"; in the South this provision can be interpreted to mean that since a white man will not want to hire a Negro for any job but a "Negro job" (cleaning, digging), there is not reasonable expectation of employment.

In short, the Federal retraining program is not only inadequate to begin with, but it is also forced to accommodate to the dominant political and economic patterns within the states.

Apprenticeships

NAACP Labor Secretary Herbert Hill estimated in 1960 that Negroes make up only 1.69% of the total number of apprentices in the economy. This is the result of generations of systematic exclusions of Negroes

---

* There are 8 million "functional illiterates" in the U.S., i.e., persons who have completed fewer than 4 years of school. The illiteracy rate among Negroes is four times that of whites. It has been estimated that one out of every 10 Negro men in the U.S. is completely illiterate.

from skilled trades. The segregationist practices of the craft unions are well-known and among the ugliest chapters in labor history. They are now under fire from the AFL–CIO itself.

However, the struggle against discrimination in apprenticeship programs, though vital, cannot solve the problem of Negro employment. Such discrimination is not a major cause of the present high levels of Negro unemployment. As A. Philip Randolph has pointed out,

> We complain because the building trades have no room for Negroes; but the real trouble now is that these unions are designed for profit through scarcity. If the crafts were open to us, that could not, in the present economy, create more than 40,000 jobs. (*Testimony before the Committee on Employment and Manpower,* July 25, 1963.)

From California the note is echoed by William Becker of the Jewish Labor Committee:

> It is not enough to prohibit discrimination in the apprenticeship programs which receive government assistance. It is important to take steps to provide for *more* apprenticeship training programs and *more* opportunities for the employment of apprentices. Equal opportunity is important.

The point here is that the effort to secure apprenticeship openings for Negroes is inevitably conditioned by the total number of apprenticeship openings available. When that number is relatively small, proportional representation for Negroes in the entire population of apprentices can be achieved only at the expense of white workers. It requires an idealized faith in the altruism of insecure white workers to believe for a moment that Negro workers could win their objectives under such circumstances. Labor unions must share the blame for the historical development of discrimination in apprenticeship programs, but the scarcity of apprenticeships results from the state of the national economy—from the changing structure of the work force. For this the labor movement bears little responsibility. Business and government must carry the brunt. FEPC's effectiveness depends on how much room it has to operate in. If the job market is expanding, then FEPC can bring widespread results. In itself, however, FEPC does not affect the job market. Moreover, FEPC outlaws discrimination at the *point of hiring*. It cannot deal with past discrimination which has impeded the acquisition of the skills required for the most rapidly expanding job opportunities. Thus the "equal opportunity" principle is only a principle and not a formula for jobs. Even the most rigorously enforced FEPC would be inadequate to this end, as inadequate as "equal opportunity" in apprenticeship programs.

The operational sterility of the "equal opportunity" principle has given rise to the "preferential treatment" slogan. Other terms have been coined—"compensatory hiring," "positive discrimination," the "doctrine of the debt," etc.—all meaning essentially the same thing.

Corporate Orientation

The moral objections to "preferential treatment" have on the whole been flabby and pious. The real deficiencies in "preferential treatment" are on another level.

The real question is, what are the limitations on private economic action, to reduce the differentials in Negro employment, education, and housing? Who will benefit from "preferential treatment" in the absence of basic, government-spearheaded economic reform? Without such reform, can there be full employment—and can there be fair employment without full employment?

So long as we have class unemployment and Negroes are disproportionately concentrated in the lower job categories, only full employment can keep them engaged in the economy. This is not a notion to which one either subscribes or doesn't subscribe. It's an implacable economic reality which would not obtain if Negroes had the same job distribution as whites. Preferential treatment cannot substantially alter this distribution in the context of a stagnant economy.

But If No Job Exists?

A Negro cannot be given preference over a white if no jobs exist for either of them. The demand for preferential treatment has been unsuccessful where labor supply exceeds labor demand (as in the New York construction industry). This is the situation confronted by workers with the least education because of the inadequate expansion of the unskilled and semiskilled occupations for which they are qualified.

Preferential treatment has benefited those Negroes who can qualify for the more skilled occupations. These are the occupations that are expanding most rapidly. The more education and training they require, the more they are characterized by an excess of labor demand over labor supply. Professional and technical occupations—the fastest growing part of the labor force—will expand 40% in the '60's, as compared with 15% for semiskilled jobs and no growth at all in unskilled jobs.

To list the companies most commonly associated with "preferential treatment" policies is to indicate expanding industries in need of skilled manpower.

For the 3.5% of the adult Negro population with college degrees, for the 240,000 Negroes presently enrolled in colleges and professional schools, and for numbers of Negro high-school graduates, preferential treatment could quicken the pace of their absorption into the occupations that are expanding with technological progress.

Not only do these Negroes constitute a relatively small portion of the Negro population; they are also the least disadvantaged. Their incomes are higher, their unemployment rates lower. Preferential treatment is the most militant demand of the "black bourgeoisie."

Meanwhile, there is the danger that the emphasis on preferential treatment sows the illusion that Negroes can make progress in a declining economy, and diverts attention from the real nature of the unemployment problem. Moreover, while one may scoff at the abstract arguments against preferential treatment used by middle-class liberals, one cannot dismiss the fears it arouses among white workers, especially those whose own economic positions are marginal.

Preferential treatment, at least in the context of the present economic order, does not go to the root of the Negro's job problem. The great majority of the Negro population is trapped in the lower educational categories. As the figure below indicates, members of these categories have the highest unemployment rates and these rates will increase even more as cybernation's conquest of our economy places mounting premiums on skilled labor.

Thus Daniel Bell predicts that:

> By 1970 with the demand for unskilled labor shrinking, relative to the total labor force, and the substantial majority of workers in white-collar or highly skilled blue-collar jobs, the relative disproportion between whites and Negroes in the low-skilled and service jobs—despite a rise in the levels of Negro education—may be even greater. For while the levels of Negro education are rising they are not rising fast enough.

Failure of the Private Economy

There are three possible—but not mutually exclusive—solutions:

1. Massive education and training to qualify Negroes for the expanding occupations;

2. Planned creation of unskilled and semiskilled jobs for which Negroes are already qualified;

3. Direct financial relief.

None of these approaches, taken singly or in combination, can be seriously entrusted to the private economy; they are simply not natural functions of the profit motive.

Whichever approach is taken, the private economy has little to offer. Take education, for example. Corporations may contribute to higher education, from which they reap the most immediate rewards. Elementary and secondary education, however, depend on real estate taxes for their basic revenue. These generally regressive taxes are among the costs which business enterprises seek to *reduce* when selecting sites. Yet expansion and reform of the elementary and secondary school systems is indispensable for raising the educational status of the general Negro community.

Moreover, while expanding sections of the private economy may apply preferential treatment in the acquisition and training of needed white-collar workers, they are not concerned with *creating* jobs of the kind that the mass of Negro workers could readily assume. These jobs can be performed more profitably by machines.

The purpose of business, if we need to be reminded, is to make profit, not jobs. The two don't necessarily go together.

The fact is that the demand for labor in the total private economy has remained virtually constant in recent years. Between World War II and 1957, nearly a million new jobs were created each year. Since then, fewer then 500,000 have been generated. But even these figures do not tell the full story. In the past ten years, most of the net jobs-increase in private industries was in part-time work. By contrast, state and local government jobs have risen by more than 2.5 million. There could be no more devastating answer to the champions of "free enterprise" who flail against "big government."

The failure of the private economy to generate jobs must be measured against future needs. It has been estimated that 30 million jobs must be created by 1970 to offset technological displacement and to absorb the 26 million young workers who will be added to the labor force. If the total economy continues to open new jobs at the present rate, unemployment will reach eleven million in 1970.

Corporate Profits

Side by side with rising unemployment are rising corporate profits. Largely because of automation, *productivity* (output per man-hour) increased 20.2% between 1956 and 1962. This means that private industry could produce more with fewer workers, thereby saving on labor costs. But the increase in workers' purchasing power in this period was only 15.2%. As Figure 5 shows, the disparity is even greater for manufacturing workers, many of whom are Negroes.

Thus the cost savings resulting from higher productivity have not been passed on to the consumer through lower prices or to workers through commensurately higher wages. They have gone into corporate profits, which reached a record $26.8 billion after taxes in the second quarter of last year.

FIGURE 5: LAG OF REAL WAGES BEHIND ADVANCING PRODUCTIVITY

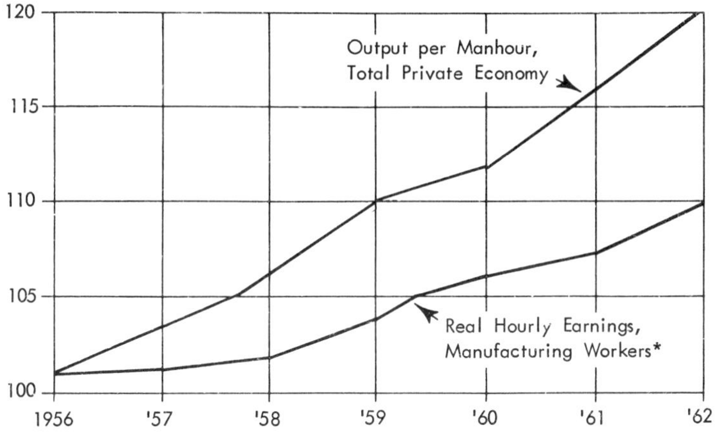

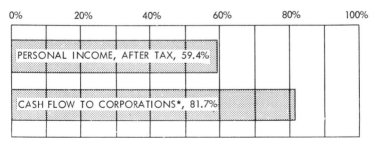

120

Output per Manhour,
Total Private Economy

115

110

105

Real Hourly Earnings,
Manufacturing Workers*

100

1956   '57   '58   '59   '60   '61   '62

*Hourly earnings, including payroll fringe benefits, adjusted for changes in the Consumer Price Index. Earnings figures exclude non-payroll fringes, such as pension and health-welfare plans.
Source: U.S. Bureau of Labor Statistics.

This imbalance in our economy is revealed even more dramatically in Figure 6. In the past ten years, the rise of personal income has lagged far behind the cash-flow to corporations.

One result of this trend is the growing concentration of the nation's wealth in fewer hands. The share held by the richest 1% grew from 24.2% in 1953 to 28% in 1961; the number of millionaires leaped from 27,000 to 100,000. Meanwhile, the share of the 60% of all families at the bottom of the economic ladder has gone down.

FIGURE 6: LAG IN RISE OF PERSONAL INCOME BEHIND
CASH FLOW TO CORPORATIONS 1953-1963.

0%   20%   40%   60%   80%   100%

PERSONAL INCOME, AFTER TAX, 59.4%

CASH FLOW TO CORPORATIONS*, 81.7%

* Corporate profits and depreciation allowances after payment of all costs, taxes, and rising dividends to stockholders.
Source: U.S. Department of Commerce

Production Lag

Because real wages have not kept pace with productivity and profit, the ability of consumers to purchase goods and services has fallen behind our capacity to produce those goods and services. One way to prevent inadequate purchasing power from putting the brakes on production would be to produce at maximum capacity and distribute goods and services on the basis of need. Our economic system is based on production for profit, however, and production has therefore been limited to the demands of the market. Corporate profits keep soaring because many large corporations can do better by maintaining high profit margins on a smaller volume of production than by lowering margins in hopes of raising volume.

The overall result, as Figure 7 shows, is a growing gap between actual and potential national production. This gap between the economy's actual performance and its growing potential to produce amounted to $63 billion in 1963. Were it not for our "permanent war economy"—which does not produce goods for use—the gap would be even greater. In any case, this untapped reservoir of wealth, if exploited in the interest of the society at large, could go a long way toward lifting living standards, improving education and health facilities, clearing slums, and reducing poverty.

There is every reason to believe that the gap between actual and potential production will widen in the years ahead as automation boosts

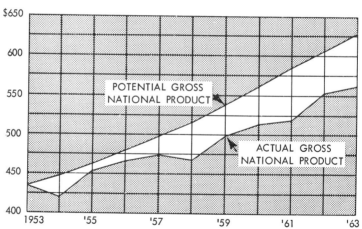

FIGURE 7: GROWING GAP BETWEEN ACTUAL AND POTENTIAL NATIONAL PRODUCTION (in billions of 1962 dollars)

AFL–CIO Estimate
Source: Council of Economic Affairs and AFL–CIO Research Department

productivity. Furthermore, it is unlikely that social altruism will dethrone the profit motive in the private economy and prompt decisions to close the gap by increasing production for the purpose of waging war on poverty. It is equally unlikely that a private economy characterized by high profits and high unemployment can undertake a "Marshall Plan" that would substantially improve the living conditions of the majority of Negroes. This is a social responsibility. It rests with government, which is ultimately entrusted with the national welfare. The exercise of this responsibility is therefore a political, not a private, decision.*

Automation, Jobs, and Manpower

Charles C. Killingsworth

Michigan State University

[*Excerpted, by permission, from testimony given before the Senate Subcommittee on Employment and Manpower, September 20, 1963.*]

ON THE SAME DAY the *New York Times* carried two news stories which seem to typify the continuing discussion of automation. The headline over one story read, "Automation Hailed as Creator of Jobs." The headline over the other story read, "Electronic 'Brains' Already Setting Type and Keeping Books on Three Newspapers—Employees Uneasy Over Jobs."

Does automation create jobs or does it destroy them? In the view of a great many people, that important question has been conclusively answered, and it is a waste of time to debate it further. Unfortunately, however, there is still strong disagreement as to what that conclusive answer is. The great majority of professional economists today agree that we simply cannot have any such thing as permanent technological unemployment. A prominent economist recently remarked that those who dispute that proposition are simply challenging the main stream of economic thought. On the other hand, voices are heard in the land disputing the proposition that automation creates jobs. Labor leaders, among others, point to such examples as the elimination of tens of thousands of elevator operator jobs in New York City alone as a concrete result of automation, and they view with alarm the appearance of such revolutionary innovations as automatic typesetting.

---

* This does not mean that private enterprise can play no role in a domestic "Marshall Plan." It can play an important role in housing, for example. But government priming and leadership in setting goals is essential.

This sharp conflict between the excessively general assertion and the excessively specific example has seriously hampered the search for solutions to problems of automation and employment. It is hard to agree on solutions when there is no agreement on what the problems are.

(I) What is automation?

(II) How is automation different from earlier kinds of technological changes?

(III) What are the effects of automation on jobs?

I. What Is Automation?

So many definitions of automation have been offered that a number of thoughtful people have concluded that the word has no fixed meaning— that it is simply an emotion-laden slogan which responsible discussion should avoid. Undoubtedly the term is frequently used very loosely, and misused, in popular discussion. But I insist that the word, "automation," is a useful and necessary addition to the language because— in careful usage—it identifies a distinguishable and significant development in modern technology.

The word was originally coined, I believe, simply as a short-cut way of saying, "automatic operation." And that is still an acceptable way to define the word. Many of the more elaborate definitions that have been offered have really attempted to describe particular applications, or particular techniques used to achieve automatic operation. An examination of the fundamental concepts involved in modern automatic systems will, I believe, provide the basis for a more comprehensive and illuminating definition of the term.

Let us take as an example a complex petroleum refining unit which is completely controlled by an electronic computer. One such unit is located at Port Arthur, Texas. This unit is a multi-million dollar installation, several stories tall and with miles of pipes and wires connecting a great variety of vessels and other equipment. It processes several million gallons of raw material daily. Although human operators are still assigned to the control room, they are little more than "witnesses." The entire operation is constantly monitored, and the necessary adjustments are made by the computer without human assistance.

The basic elements required for automatic operation are by no means new. And examples of automatic systems of various kinds can be found even in the ancient world. But the explosive growth of scientific knowledge in the last two decades and our successes in applying this new knowledge have greatly affected the elements of automation. Measuring instruments have multiplied in numbers and kinds and they have become incredibly sensitive and reliable. Powered controls have become more versatile and powerful. We have a burgeoning young science of communication and control, called cybernetics, which makes it possible to rig up the measuring instruments to transmit great quantities of information in the form of electric pulses, and to rig up the computer to generate instructions which produce the desired response in the controls. Most significant of all is the development of the computer, which has an infallible memory and the capability to duplicate at lightning speed some kinds of human thought processes.

"Automation is the mechanization of sensory, control, and thought processes."

Not all applications of automation techniques involve all three of these elements; i.e., sensory, control, and thought processes. As I will develop further at a later point, automation is a matter of degree. But even the completely automatic refining unit is by no means a unique example. There are several such units in the petroleum industry. The same basic technique is employed in the construction of several automatic chemical plants which are now in operation; in automatic power-plants; and in computer-controlled steel rolling mills, to cite a few other examples. Some important kinds of automation do not include a computer in the system. For example, "Detroit automation" involves huge compound metalworking machines which have their instructions designed into them; the raw material on which they work is fairly uniform, and they are used for long production runs, so that the kind of flexibility and adaptability which a computer provides are not needed. But the transfer machines do incorporate measuring instruments and powered controls, and they utilize some of the principles of cybernetics to achieve a high degree of self-regulation.

II. How Is Automation Different from Earlier Technological Changes?

I now turn to my second basic question. A great many people today argue that automation is essentially no different from earlier technological developments like the assembly line. In my opinion, this argument is a source of error. The magnitude of the error is revealed, I believe, by a consideration, first, of the changed economic environment of today, and second, of some intrinsic characteristics of automation which make it different from such developments as the assembly line.

The economic environment in the United States today is far different from what it was when the steam engine, electric power, the assembly line and other major technological changes of the past appeared. Today, we live in a rather fully developed mass-consumption society. Let me illustrate the point by reference to data on one important economic barometer: automobile registrations.* The year when Henry Ford introduced his revolutionary idea of a moving assembly line was 1913. In that year, the automobile industry was in its early adolescence—a period of explosive growth and great potential for further growth. The country had only about a million automobiles registered in that year, which was 1 car for every 100 people in the country. The assembly line greatly increased productivity in Ford's factory; direct labor requirements were cut by 90 percent on the assembly line. But sales increased enormously: the number of cars registered increased tenfold in the 10 years following 1913, and most of them were Fords. By 1923, there was 1 car for every 10 people. So the rapidly growing market for cars enabled Ford to employ more workers despite his labor-saving inventions. It should be added that the growth of the market was stimulated by Ford's big price cuts.

Compare that 1913 situation with the situation in the 1950's, when the transfer machine—"Detroit automation"—made its appearance. This new device in some major installations typically achieved direct labor savings of about 90 percent—about the same as the assembly line. But in the 1950's we had an automobile industry which had completed the rapid growth phase of its development. There were already 40 million cars registered in the United States, which was 1 car for every 4 persons. The market was not completely saturated, but the growth potential was much more limited than it was in 1913. In the decade of the fifties (the most prosperous period this country had seen up to that time), the total number of automobile registrations continued to climb. But the growth in 10 years was 50 percent, compared with the increase of 1,000 percent in the 10 years following 1913. We moved from one car for each four persons in 1950 to one for three in 1960.

I think that this comparison illustrates a point of fundamental importance. When a major laborsaving invention is introduced in an industry which is in its rapid growth stage—its adolescence—the invention may help to spur further rapid growth, especially through price cuts, and total employment in the industry may increase substantially. This is the historical pattern which prompts many people to argue that "machines make jobs." But the fact is that when an industry has reached maturity—for example, when there is already one car for each three people—it just is not possible to achieve further dramatic increases in sales, even with the largest price cuts within the realm of reason. The improved productivity made possible by laborsaving machines simply enables the industry to keep up with the normal growth of the market

---

* Illustrative chart omitted.

while employing fewer production workers. This is what happened in a number of our major industries in the 1950's.

Look across the whole range of consumer goods and you will see that our mass consumption society has done a highly effective job of supplying the wants of the great majority of consumers.[1] About 99.5 percent of the homes that are wired for electricity have electric refrigerators; 93 percent have television sets; 83 percent have electric washing machines; and we have even more radios than homes. The only sharply rising sales curve in the consumer durables field today is that of the electric can opener industry. The electric toothbrush and electric hairbrush industries are starting to grow rapidly, too. But the growth of employment in these new "industries" will not offset the declines in the older, larger consumer goods industries.

The doctrine that "machines make jobs," to the extent that it rests on research rather than faith, is drawn primarily from studies of the periods 1899–1937 and 1899–1953. These were mainly years when the growth potential of most markets for goods was still very great. I think that it is a major source of error to assume that the markets of our great mass-production industries will grow at the same prodigious rate in the 2d half of the 20th century that they achieved in the 1st half. Without that kind of growth rate, the doctrine that "machines make jobs" will surely be as obsolete as the model T.

We can get some perspective on our present situation by considering the basic causes for the booming prosperity which most of Western Europe and Japan are now enjoying. Those countries are in the early growth stages of the mass-consumption society. Their ratios of automobiles to population, electric refrigerators to houses, and so on, are generally comparable to our ratios in the 1920's (or earlier). At their present rates of growth, it will be several decades before they achieve our degree of saturation of markets. So automation is having a different impact there.

---

[1] I am not unaware of the "vast unmet needs" (to use the familiar phrase) in such fields as education and housing. I have more to say about education below. The housing needs are found almost entirely in "the other America"—the 20 or 30 percent of the population with incomes so low that these people do not realistically provide a market for anything more than the barest essentials. Unless their incomes rise dramatically—and there is no apparent reason to expect this to happen—their housing and other needs will remain unmet. This is not, of course, a situation which we should complacently accept; but we are not doing very much about it. The point here is the elementary one that in our society "vast unmet needs" do not equal vast markets without purchasing power in the hands of those who have the needs.

I do not mean to suggest that all consumer markets in the United States are approaching saturation and that consumers will soon be buying only replacements for what they already have. One of the few things that we can predict with reasonable certainty in economics is that as consumers' incomes rise, their spending will rise, too. But our history reveals some longrun changes in the patterns of consumer spending. These changes have an important effect on patterns of employment. The recent decline of employment in the goods-producing industries accompanies the long-term rise in employment in the service-producing industries—banking, trade, health care, education, and Government. This slow shift in emphasis from the production of goods to the production of services appears to be characteristic of the mature stage of a mass-consumption society. The United States is the only country in the world in which the jobs in services outnumber the jobs in goods industries.

Will the growth of jobs in the services offset the loss of jobs in goods industries? This kind of offset is possible, but by no means inevitable. We cannot safely accept the convenient assumption of economic theory that all labor is homogeneous, and the conclusion that only inertia or ignorance can impede the free flow of laborers from one industry to another as the patterns of consumer spending change. The displaced assembly line worker may be readily adaptable to work in a filling station; he may be much less acceptable as a clerk in a department store; and, without years of training, he cannot qualify as a teacher or a nurse. Adapting the labor force to changes in the supply of jobs is a matter of crucial importance in our society today. I will return to this point shortly.

The economic environment today is so different from that of 40 or 50 years ago that simply more of the same kinds of technological change that we experienced in the first half of the century would have a different impact now. But automation differs in some respects from most of the earlier technological changes.

One major difference is the much broader applicability of automation. Computer technology in particular seems likely to invade almost every area of industrial activity.

A related difference is that automation appears to be spreading more rapidly than most major technological changes of the past.[2]

_____

[2] If automation is spreading as rapidly as I think, why don't our productivity figures show substantial increase? In the first place, the rate of improvement in output per man-hour has been somewhat higher in recent years than the long-run trend (about at the level of the 1920's, in fact). In the second place, as I have already suggested, most automation installations require a very large investment of

A third characteristic of automation techniques is that, to a much greater extent than past technologies, they are the product of the laboratory scientist rather than the production man. In other words, the importance of pure science as a source of invention has greatly increased. In the Nation as a whole, about 20 percent of our productive capacity is idle. The automatic refining unit and the automatic steel mill were not invented because of an urgent demand for vastly larger quantities of oil and steel. These inventions were the byproduct of the very rapid growth of scientific knowledge in our generation. In the last half of the century, we are often finding that "invention is the mother of necessity."

Last, automation has effects on the structure of demand for labor which are different from those of earlier technological developments.

III. What Are the Effects of Automation on Jobs?

Automation, especially in its advanced forms, fundamentally changes the man-machine relation. There are two major results. One is a great reduction in the number of simple, repetitive jobs where all you need is your five senses and an untrained mind. The other result is a great increase in the number of jobs involved in designing, engineering, programing and administering these automatic production systems. Industry needs many more scientists, engineers, mathematicians, and other highly trained people, and many fewer blue-collar workers.

Between 1957 and 1962 in manufacturing, production workers declined by nearly a million, while nonproduction workers increased by about a third of a million. Moreover, what happened from 1957 to 1962 was the continuation of a postwar trend. Throughout the 1920's, the ratio between production and nonproduction workers in manufacturing fluctuated between narrow limits at around 19 or 20 percent. The great depression and World War II temporarily affected the ratio; at the outset of the depression, the blue-collar workers were laid off before the white-collar workers were, and in the war salesmen and clerks were drafted while blue-collar workers were added. By about 1951, the prewar ratio of about one white-collar worker to four blue-collar workers had been reestablished. But as automation gathered momentum during the 1950's, the ratio continued to change. It is now at about 26 percent and the trend is still strongly upward. Generally, the most highly automated industries have the highest ratio of white-

---

man-hours in preparatory work; charging these man-hours against current output undoubtedly results in an understatement of the current rate of productivity improvement. The operation of the economy at considerably less than optimum levels of output has also helped to hold down the productivity figures.

collar workers. In chemicals and petroleum, for example, the ratio is 40 percent.

In an economy in which so many patterns are changing rapidly, broad averages and grand totals may conceal more than they reveal. I think that this is especially true of the effects of automation and the concomitant changes of today. Let us take as an example the figures showing total civilian employment since 1949. Those figures clearly reveal the persistent upward trend in total employment—from 58 million jobs in 1949 to more than 68 million in 1963. This great increase is another piece of evidence often cited by those who claim that "machines make jobs." But there is another side to this coin. Unemployment crept upward during the latter part of this period—first two notches up, then one notch down, and then another two notches up. In 1951–53, the average was about a 3 percent rate of unemployment. In 1962–63, the average has been almost double that, or between 5½ and 6 percent.

It is not self-evident from these figures that any part of this creeping unemployment problem is due to automation or other basic changes in the patterns of the economy. There is eminent authority to the contrary. The President's Council of Economic Advisers has repeatedly declared that automation and "structural unemployment" are not responsible for the gradual creep of unemployment above the 4-percent level of 1957. For example, the 1963 report of the Council includes the following passage (p. 25):

"The problems of structural unemployment—of imperfect adaptation of jobs and workers—are persistent and serious, and they are thrown into bold relief by the prolonged lack of sufficient job opportunities over the past 5 years. *But these problems of adaptation have not constituted a greater cause of unemployment in recent years than in earlier periods.* The source of the higher employment rates in recent years, even in periods of cyclical expansion, lies not in labor market imbalance, but in the markets for goods and services." [Emphasis not in original.]

I think that it can be demonstrated that the Council is the victim of a half-truth. The lagging growth rate is only a part of the problem, and it may not be the most important part. It gives woefully inadequate attention to what I regard as a key aspect of the unemployment problem of the 1960's; namely, labor market imbalance.

Let me preface my analysis with a brief restatement of my argument to this point. The fundamental effect of automation on the labor market is to "twist" the pattern of demand—that is, it pushes down the demand for workers with little training while pushing up the demand for workers with large amounts of training. The shift from goods to services is a second major factor which twists the labor market in the same way. There are some low-skilled, blue-collar jobs in service-producing industries; but the most rapidly growing parts of the service sector are health care and education, both of which require a heavy preponderance of highly trained people.

These changing patterns of demand for labor would not create labor market imbalance, however, unless changes in the supply of labor lagged behind. We turn now to the figures which show that such a lag has in fact developed.

Table 1 shows the relationship between rates of unemployment and levels of education of males 18 and over in 2 years—1950 and 1962.

The overall unemployment rate was substantially the same in both years—6.2 in 1950, and 6.0 in 1962. But there was a redistribution

TABLE 1
Education and unemployment, April 1950 and March 1962
(males, 18 and over)

	Unemployment rates		Percentage change,
Years of school completed	*1950*	*1962*	*1950 to 1962*
0 to 7	8.4	9.2	+9.5
8	6.6	7.5	+13.6
9 to 11	6.9	7.8	+13.0
12	4.6	4.8	+4.3
13 to 15	4.1	4.0	−2.4
16 or more	2.2	1.4	−36.4
All groups	6.2	6.0	−3.2

of unemployment between these 2 years. The unemployment rates at the top of the educational attainment ladder went down, while the rates at the middle and lower rungs of the ladder went up substantially. The most significant figure in this table, I think, is the one showing the very large decrease in the unemployment rate of college graduates.

In a sense, these unemployment figures are only the part of the iceberg that is above the water. For a better understanding of their significance, we must consider also the changes in demand and supply that took place at the various educational levels between 1950 and 1962. Chart 1 shows (for males 18 and over) the percentage changes in the supply of labor (labor force), in the demand for labor (employment), and in unemployment rates at various levels of educational attainment between 1950 and 1962. The left-hand bars show labor force changes, the center bars show employment changes, and the right-hand bars show unemployment rate changes. The three bars at the far right of the chart show these changes for all groups combined; these aggregates obviously conceal some differences between educational levels which are of cardinal importance.

268   Poverty in America

CHART 1

THE CHANGING STRUCTURE OF LABOR FORCE,
EMPLOYMENT AND UNEMPLOYMENT, 1950 TO 1962
(males, 18 and older)

PERCENTAGE OF CHANGE

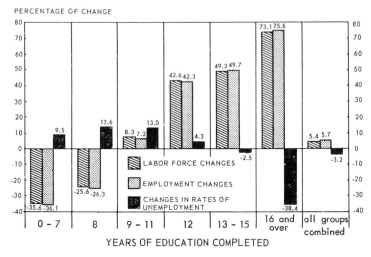

YEARS OF EDUCATION COMPLETED

The bars for the 0 to 7 years of education group show that the number of this group in the labor force declined very greatly from 1950 to 1962; but the jobs held by this group declined even more, so that its unemployment rate went up. The experience of the group with 16 or more years of education was particularly striking. The supply of men in this group increased by 75 percent, but the jobs for them increased even more than that, so that their unemployment rate went down by more than a third.

It is important to note that all of the improvement in the unemployment situation in 1962, as compared with 1950, was concentrated in the elite group of our labor force—the approximately 20 percent with college training. In all of the other categories, which have about 80 percent of the labor force, unemployment rates were substantially higher in 1962 than in 1950. These figures, I contend, substantiate the thesis that the patterns of demand for labor have been twisted faster than the patterns of supply have changed, and that as a result we had a substantially greater degree of labor market imbalance in 1962 than in 1950.

But these figures do not fully reveal the power of the labor market twist. The "labor force" enumeration includes (with minor exceptions) only those who say that they have jobs or that they have actively sought work in the week preceding the survey. Those who have been out of work so long that they have given up hope and are no longer "actively seeking" work—but who would take a job if one were available—are simply not counted either as unemployed or as a member of the labor force. The percentage of a given category of the total population that is "in the labor force" (under the foregoing definition) is expressed as the "labor force participation rate." It seems probable that worsening employment prospects for a particular group over a long period would force down the labor force participation rate—i.e., would squeeze a number of people out of the labor market altogether, in the sense that they would give up the continuing, active search for jobs. Conversely, it seems probable that improving employment prospects would tend to pull more people into the labor market and thus to raise the labor force participation rate. These two trends are indeed observable since 1950. The squeezing out of people at the lower end of the educational ladder and the pulling in of people at the upper end is another manifestation of the labor market twist. Table 2 presents the pertinent figures for males.

TABLE 2

Labor Force Participation Rates and Educational Attainment,
April 1950 and March 1962 (males, 18 and over)

	Labor force participation rates		Percentage change in rate, 1950
Years of school completed	1950	1962	to 1962
0 to 4	74.6	58.2	−22.0
5 to 7	85.0	74.6	−14.4
8	88.1	78.2	−12.7
9 to 11	92.1	88.8	−3.9
12	94.0	90.7	−3.7
13 to 15	79.6	83.0	+5.4
16 or more	92.1	92.3	+0.2
All groups	87.6	83.5	−4.7

Source: The 1950 population data are taken from the 1950 census. The 1962 figures are from unpublished data supplied by the U.S. Bureau of Labor Statistics.

This table tells us that the participation rates at the lower end of the educational scale, which were already relatively low in 1950, had gone much lower by 1962. At the other end of the scale, participation rates had gone up by 1962. Some of the decline in participation rates at the lower end of the scale is due to higher average ages, with a larger proportion in this group (as compared with upper groups) attaining age 65 and voluntarily retiring. But that is by no means the whole story. A detailed comparison by age group as well as by educational level shows that declines occurred at almost every age level in the noncollege category, while there was a rise in participation rates for a majority of the age groups of men with college training.

The important point that I want to make with these figures is that in all likelihood the official unemployment statistics substantially understate the size of the labor surplus of men with limited education. If we found jobs for most of those now officially reported as unemployed, the news of improving opportunities would undoubtedly bring back into the labor force many men who are not now counted as members of it. Unfortunately, we cannot count on the same flexibility of supply at the top of the educational scale. Even the most extreme pressures of demand cannot pull the participation rate much above 98 or 99 percent, which is the current rate in some college-trained age groups.

Our overall unemployment rate has now been above 5 percent for more than 5 years, and we cannot be sure what effects a substantial increase in spending by consumers, businesses and Government (i.e., an increase in aggregate demand) would have on the patterns of employment, unemployment, and labor force participation just discussed. Many respected economists believe, as one of them once put it, that the hard core of unemployment is made of ice, not rock, and that it would melt away if overall demand rose high enough. This line of reasoning assumes (either implicitly or sometimes explicitly) that no serious bottlenecks of labor supply would appear before the achievement of the overall unemployment rate of 4 percent. I seriously question the validity of this critically important assumption under the labor market conditions of today and the foreseeable future.

The benefits of a decline in the overall rate of unemployment appear to be quite unevenly distributed among the educational attainment groups that we have been considering. The year 1957 was the last one in which we had an unemployment rate as low as 4 percent. It is instructive to see how the patterns of unemployment changed from 1950, when the overall rate was above 6 percent, to 1957, and then again to 1962, which had about the same overall rate as 1950. This comparison is made in two forms in Table 3. This table shows the actual unemployment rates for the various educational attainment groups in those 3 years, and it also expresses the unemployment rate for each group in each of the 3 years as a ratio of the rate for all of the other groups combined. (Thus, the 0 to 7 years of education group had an unemployment rate about 50 percent higher than all other groups combined in 1950; its rate was more than double the rate for all other groups in 1957; and its rate was 70 percent higher in 1962.)

Clearly, unemployment at the bottom of the educational scale was relatively unresponsive to general increases in the demand for labor, while there was very strong responsiveness at the top of the educational scale. The percentage unemployment rate for college graduates in 1957

TABLE 3
Actual and Relative Unemployment Rates by Educational Attainment,
April 1950, March 1957, and March 1962 (males, 18 and over)

Years of school completed	Unemployment rates					
	Actual percentages			Relative[1]		
	1950	1957	1962	1950	1957	1962
0 to 7	8.4	6.9	9.2	154	203	170
8	6.6	4.4	7.5	108	110	132
9 to 11	6.9	4.7	7.3	115	120	142
12	4.6	3.0	4.8	70	67	75
13 to 15	4.1	2.7	4.0	64	64	65
16 or more	2.2	.6	1.4	34	14	21
All groups	6.2	4.1	6.0	([1])	([1])	([1])

[1] The relative unemployment rate is the ratio between the percentage unemployment rate for a given educational attainment group and the percentage unemployment rate for all other groups at the same point in time.

merits close attention. It was an almost incredible o.6 percent. I have queried the experts in the Bureau of Labor Statistics on this figure, and they assure me that they have no less confidence in it than in the other 1957 figures. Surely a figure as low as that represents what is sometimes called "overfull" employment—i.e., demand which seriously exceeds supply.

Bear in mind that the unemployment rates for the lower educational attainment groups (those with 80 percent of the men) are now higher than in 1950, and that the unemployment rate for college graduates is now substantially lower than in 1950. Also bear in mind that the labor force participation rate figures strongly suggest a large and growing "reserve army"—which is not counted among the unemployed—at the lower educational levels, and that there is no evidence of any such reserve of college-trained men. Finally, bear in mind the differences between the lower end of the educational scale and the upper end in responsiveness to overall decreases in the unemployment rate.

When you put all of these considerations together, I believe that you are ineluctably led to the conclusion that long before we could get down to an overall unemployment rate as low as 4 percent, we would have a severe shortage of workers at the top of the educational ladder. This shortage would be a bottleneck to further expansion of employment. I cannot pinpoint the level at which the bottleneck would begin to seriously impede expansion; but, on the basis of the relationships revealed by Table 3, it seems reasonable to believe that we could not get very far below a 5-percent overall unemployment level without hitting that bottleneck.

IV. Conclusion

The most fundamental conclusion that emerges from my analysis is that automation and the changing pattern of consumer wants have greatly increased the importance of investment in human beings as a factor in economic growth. More investment in plant and equipment, without very large increases in our investment in human beings, seems certain to enlarge the surplus of underdeveloped manpower and to create a shortage of the highly developed manpower needed to design, install, and man modern production facilities.

The Manpower Development and Training Act is aptly named, soundly conceived, and well administered. This program was not originally intended to provide general literacy training as such. Experience under the Act has shown how essential literacy training is as a prerequisite for specific occupational training. But I doubt that even the most enthusiastic supporters of the Manpower Development and Training Act program (and I count myself among them) would argue that its present or projected size is really commensurate with the size of the job to be done. We ought to be thinking in terms of helping two or three times as many people as this program is now expected to reach. Money is not the limiting factor in the development of the Manpower Development and Training Act program. The real shortage in most areas, I believe, is trained manpower—specifically, qualified instructors and program administrators. It would be pointless to double or triple the appropriations for the program if the extra money could not be spent, and I doubt that it could be. Here we have an example of a present shortage of highly trained manpower, a shortage that limits the possibility of investment to remedy the educational deficiencies of the past.

Let us consider another, somewhat similar example. As we have all heard over and over again, the outlook for high school dropouts is bleak indeed. But here again dollars alone are not the answer. We need many more highly skilled teachers, counselors, and social workers. These, too, are in very short supply. Many other present shortages of highly trained manpower, in the private sector of the economy as well as in the public, could be cited. Unquestionably these shortages would be intensified and new ones would appear if we moved closer to full utilization of our economic potential.

To my mind, the greatest shortcoming of the administration's program for reducing unemployment is the failure to recognize the crucial need to break the trained manpower bottleneck. More important, even the largest appropriations for higher education within the realm of remote possibility would leave virtually untouched the most difficult aspect of the financing of higher education. That is the investment that the student, or his parents, must make in his subsistence costs during 4 or more years of training. For most students today, the minimum cost is $5,000.

To put a complex matter briefly, we must find a fundamentally new approach to the financing of at least this important part of the cost of higher education. We must make it as easy for an individual to finance his own investment in higher education as it is for him to finance the purchase of a home.

And we don't have all the time in the world. Human history has been described as a race between education and catastrophe. In the past dozen years, education has been falling behind in that race.

Lower-Income Workers and Marginal Industries

Barry Bluestone
The University of Michigan

POVERTY STEREOTYPES of the ADC mother, the aged, the infirm, the small farmer, the handicapped, the unemployed, and the undereducated often mask the fact that nearly a third of all families living in poverty in 1964 were headed by a person who worked 50-52 weeks a year at a full-time job and that over a tenth of all persons living alone in that year were in this position—fully employed yet unable to free themselves from impoverishment. Unlike the unemployed or those who have dropped from the labor force, the existence of the working poor is less documented and their plight is less understood. Yet their problems are more complex than most, for the working poor are not simply the result of singular causes—sickness, illiteracy, lack of jobs, discrimination, or bad luck. Rather the working poor are the product of a confrontation between individuals with little opportunity and economic markets with little realized potential. To understand the individuals who are America's working poor—to know their educational, familial, and historical characteristics—is not sufficient to explain the persistence of employed indigents. To fully understand poverty employment is to understand the dynamics of the marketplace and the concatenation of product and labor market forces which produce the structure of wages and jobs in the nation.

For many of the working poor the trials of poverty must indeed be oppressive. To toil at a sweatshop job, reminiscent of the Nineteenth Century, for up to 60 hours a week every week of the year is the cruel fate of many working poor. For their meager reward the working poor spend nearly half of their waking hours at jobs often arduous, numbingly repetitious, and devoid of opportunity for occupational mobility. In the best of times, when the economy is booming all around them, they can hope for full work weeks and wage increases which may keep pace with inflation. In the worst of times, the fear of losing their pittance of a wage constantly haunts them. Whether the economy comes up heads or tails, the working poor always lose.

Who Are the Working Poor?

Poverty itself does not allow easy definition even when reduced to pure quantitative terms. Official government statistics have traditionally placed the poverty "line" at or around $3,000 a year for a family of four; to be precise, $3,130 in 1964.[1] The exact poverty line depends primarily on family size and geographical location, and in one form is computed on the basis of family needs allowing for a minimal "economy" diet, housing, clothing, and other bare necessities. However, calculated in this manner (or in any other finite way, for that matter), the poverty "line" should not be taken too seriously. To assume that once a family has surpassed the poverty line by a few dollars it has left the world of poverty is nonsense. Impoverishment is a state of existence rather than a notch on some economic measuring rod.

In this light poverty must be considered on a *relative* rather than an *absolute* scale. Compared with the standard of living in the underdeveloped countries of the world, the American "poor" fare quite well, and indeed, the average impoverished citizen of the 1960's materially surpasses the living standard of his counterpart of the last century. Yet compared with today's average factory worker, let alone professionals, wealthy entrepreneurs and capitalists, the employed poor are indeed impoverished since they share in so little of the total economic product. In dealing with the "working poor" it is especially necessary to consider the level of their wages not only in absolute terms (i.e. at a $3,000 level), but also in relative terms to the wage distribution or wage-level in all industry.

---

[1] Office of Economic Opportunity, *Dimensions of Poverty,* December 1965, p. 8.

The concept of the "working poor," like poverty, is not clear-cut. In the few studies undertaken of low-wage occupations and industries, the "working poor" have been narrowly defined as those who work 50-52 weeks a year at a full-time job, yet remain within the ranks of the impoverished. Difficulty with this definition arises from the large number of individuals in the labor force who hold one job yet are employed only 45-50 weeks annually or who work an average of 35-38 hours a week rather than a full American standard of forty. Millions of other workers earn a poverty wage at a full-time job, but are not counted in the traditional definition of working poor because, with secondary workers in the family, their family income is brought above the poverty threshold.

It is convenient when speaking of aggregates to narrowly define the working poor, but when dealing with individual industries and occupations, statistics which include all low-wage earners are needed to analyze the factors which produce low-paying jobs and the "working poor" in America. In dealing with low-wage industries it is further necessary to pay some attention to *non*-low-wage industries. This is especially true when attempting to isolate the characteristics and causes of low-paying industry. It is also necessary since some high-wage industries have low-wage segments which should not be overlooked. Likewise, some knowledge of poverty segments within individual occupations aids in understanding the working poor and the causes of their condition.

The Aggregate Picture

In 1963, *8.5 million* people in the United States worked throughout the year at a full-time job, yet earned less than $3,000 for their effort.[2] Of these, 2,072,000 were family breadwinners and an additional 1.1 million were unrelated individuals.

The working poor made up then, and continue to make up, a sizeable fraction of the total labor force. Of all full-time working family heads in 1963, 6.9 percent earned a poverty wage. In addition, 30 percent of all unrelated individuals earned a working poor annual income. (See Table 1)

As a segment of the indigent of America, the number who work full-time is substantial. In 1963, one-fifth of all families in the United States were counted as poor, but of these, more than one in four had a full-time working breadwinner. Indeed, in the majority of

---

[2]Mollie Orshansky, "More about the Poor in 1964," *Social Security Bulletin*, May 1966, p. 5ff.

TABLE 1

Income and Work Experience of Family Heads, Unrelated Individuals, and Males and Females, 1963
(In thousands)

Work experience	Household — All family heads — Total	Income less than $3,000 Number	Percent	Household — Unrelated individuals — Total	Income less than $3,000 Number	Percent	Sex — Male — Total	Income less than $3,000 Number	Percent	Sex — Female — Total	Income less than $3,000 Number	Percent
Total[1]	47,436	8,776	18.5	11,182	7,358	65.8	51,039	15,127	29.6	32,188	22,313	69.3
Worked during year	39,894	5,027	12.6	6,698	3,249	48.5	35,685	5,782	16.2	14,993	7,287	48.6
Worked 50-52 weeks	31,071	2,546	8.2	4,081	1,428	35.0	33,587	4,105	12.2	11,862	4,398	37.1
Full-time job	30,027	2,072	6.9	3,690	1,107	30.0	—	—	—	—	—	—
Part-time job	1,044	474	45.8	391	321	82.1	—	—	—	—	—	—
Did not work	6,346	3,548	54.2	4,473	4,160	93.0	2,098	1,677	79.9	3,132	2,889	92.2
Total	100.0	—	—	100.0	—	—	100.0	—	—	100.0	—	—
Worked during year	84.1	—	—	59.9	—	—	69.9	—	—	46.6	—	—
Worked 50-52 weeks	65.5	—	—	36.5	—	—	65.8	—	—	36.9	—	—
Full-time job	63.3	—	—	33.0	—	—	—	—	—	—	—	—
Part-time job	2.2	—	—	3.5	—	—	—	—	—	—	—	—
Did not work	13.8	—	—	40.0	—	—	4.1	—	—	9.7	—	—

[1]Members of the Armed Forces covered by the survey are included in the total but are not shown separately by work experience.

Note: Inquiry on consumer income, survey for the month of March; data on work experience based on February survey.

From: Laurie D. Cummings, "The Employed Poor: Their Characteristics and Occupations," *Monthly Labor Review*, LXXXVIII, July 1965, p. 829.

Source: *Current Population Reports: Consumer Income*, "Income of Families and Persons in the United States: 1963," P-60, No. 43, September 29, 1964, tables 11 and 28 (U.S. Bureau of the Census).

poor families in that year, at least one person was working either part-time or full-time all year long.[3] The men and women (family heads) who worked full-time, all year in 1964 and yet received a poverty wage were the parents of a full two-fifths of the nation's poor children. Nine out of ten such families were headed by men.[4]

Agriculture possesses the highest incidence of poverty in America, but other sectors of the economy account for the substantial majority of employed poor. Although most hired farm workers were not employed full-time in 1965, 400,000 were counted as such by the government. They earned an average of $2,791 for a full year's work, averaging 327 days per year.[5]

In 1963, 30 percent of the employed heads of poor families were in agriculture, forestry, and fisheries.[*] The remaining bulk (70 percent) of employed poor family heads were primarily in urban occupations and industries.[6] (see Table 2)

> 15 percent were in manufacturing
> 15 percent were in retail trade
> 10 percent were in personal services
> 9 percent were in construction
> 21 percent were in miscellaneous other non-agricultural employment

It is interesting to note that the first four sectors (manufacturing, retail trade, personal services, and construction) claim four out of ten jobs among all working men and one-half of all women's jobs in the aggregate economy.

In terms of occupation, the bulk of working poor are operatives, service workers, laborers, and farmers. Sales workers, clerical employees, and private household workers make up another 12 percent of the working poor. In general the skill requirements for working poor jobs are below average, yet are the same as the requirements for many high wage industry jobs in manufacturing.

Characteristics of the Working Poor

Who are the working poor and why have particular individuals been doomed to poverty jobs?

---

[3]Laurie D. Cummings, "The Employed Poor: Their Characteristics and Occupations," *Monthly Labor Review,* Vol. 88, July 1965, p. 828.
[4]*Ibid.*
[5]U.S. Department of Labor, *Manpower Report of the President,* 1967, p. 108.
[*]This includes income-in-kind as part of the poverty income.
[6]Cummings, *op. cit.,* p. 828.

TABLE 2

Industry and Occupational Group of Employed
Heads of Poor Families, 1963

Industry	Percent distri- bution	Occupational Group	Percent distri- bution
Total, employed	100	Total, not self-employed	100
Agriculture, forestry, and		Professional, technical and	
fisheries	30	kindred workers	3
Mining	1	Managers, officials, and	
Construction	9	proprietors, except farm	2
Manufacturing	15	Clerical and kindred workers	4
Transportation, communi-		Sales workers	3
cation, and other public		Craftsmen, foremen, and	
utilities	4	kindred workers	9
Wholesale trade	3	Operatives and kindred	
Retail trade	14	workers	18
Finance, insurance, and		Private household workers	5
real estate	2	Service workers, except	
Business and repair services	3	private household workers	13
Personal services	10	Laborers, except farm and	
Entertainment and recreation		mine	12
services	1	Farmers and farm managers	23
Professional and related services	6	Farm laborers and	
Government	2	foremen	8

Note: Because of rounding, sums of individual items may not equal totals.
Source: *Current Population Reports: Consumer Income*, "Income of Families and
Persons in the United States: 1963," Series P-60, No. 43, September 29, 1964, tables 9
and 10 (U.S. Bureau of the Census).
From: Laurie D. Cummings, "The Employed Poor: Their Characteristics and Occu-
pations," *Monthly Labor Review*, LXXXVIII, July, 1965, p. 830.

Race. Approximately one-third of working poor families are non-
white.[7] Yet roughly equal percentages of white and non-white poor
are full-time workers.[8] (Approximately 30 percent of impoverished
white families and 30 percent of impoverished non-white families are
members of the working poor. Nearly one/tenth of all poor white
unrelated individuals are employed full-time; the same fraction holds
for all non-white unrelated individuals.[9]) However, when one considers male heads of household only, the story changes drastically. Sev-
enty-three percent of the non-white male heads of poor families were

[7]Cummings, *op. cit.*, p. 828.
[8]Orshansky, *op. cit.*, pp. 12-13.
[9]Orshansky, *op. cit.*, pp. 12-13.

employed in 1963 and more than half of them (42 percent) worked full-time all year long. Yet for indigent white male bread-winners, the percentages were much smaller. Only 56 percent worked at all that year and no more than a third were full-time workers.[10]

For the U.S. labor force as a whole, a disproportionately large number of Negroes are in low-wage jobs, but Negro women nevertheless fare relatively better than their male counterparts. Whereas Negro women comprise *one out of eight* working women, they comprise *one out of six* women in low-wage occupations, a pretty sad picture in itself. However, for Negro men the situation is intolerable; whereas they comprise but *one/twelfth* of the non-agricultural male workforce, they hold *one out of four* low-wage jobs! For the Negro male, the "normal" job is often a low-paying one. For identical amounts of education the Negro male can expect to earn only about 60 percent of the earnings of his white counterpart.[11]

Although recently some inroads have been made into eliminating racial discrimination in hiring practices and in internal firm mobility, discrimination remains rampant, striking at the non-white male most acutely. Undesirable jobs at low pay are all too often the only employment offered non-whites. Discrimination and lower educational opportunity for non-whites result in the high unemployment rate, as well as the high percentage of full-time non-white working poor and the extremely high proportion of all low-wage jobs held by Negro men and women.

Nevertheless, white workers, because of their greater numbers, predominate numerically in almost all low-wage occupations and industries.[12] Race discrimination and lower educational opportunities for non-whites play major roles in the allocation of poverty jobs, but whites are not automatically immune to the worst jobs America has to offer.

Age. One might expect to find the working poor to be clustered in the younger and older age groups—those under 25 and over 55—for those are the age groups with the lowest incomes. But this is not so. In 1964, over half of all unrelated individuals among the working poor were between the ages of 25 and 54, and for family heads the

---

[10]Mollie Orshansky, "Counting the Poor: Another Look at the Poverty Profile," in L. Ferman, J. Kornbluh, and A. Haber, eds. *Poverty in America,* University of Michigan Press, Ann Arbor, 1965, p. 70.
Democracy, New York, 1964.
[11]Tom Kahn, "The Economics of Equality," League for Industrial Democracy, New York, 1964.
[12]Cummings, p. 831.

percentage was even larger with over three-fourths of them in the prime age group.[13] Two-thirds of the women and one-half of the men in low-wage occupations were in like situation.[14] This compares favorably with the non-agricultural civilian labor force. By and large, the working poor are healthy and of prime age.

Sex. Women are particularly likely to have jobs paying low wages. Although women compose only one-third of the labor force, they account for more than one-half of those with incomes below $3,000. More than one-third of *all* full-time employed women reported incomes under $3,000 in 1963 while only one out of eight men did so.[15] Yet, of all families among the working poor, 90 percent of them are headed by men. And in almost a fifth of these male-headed households where the wife was present, the wife also worked at least part-time. Still for some of these families with two wage earners, the sum total of their effort failed to raise the family income above the poverty threshold![16]

TABLE 3

Median Incomes of Heads of Families
and Their Educational Attainments, 1961

Education Level	White	Non-white
Elementary	$4,378	$2,539
Less than 8 years	3,656	2,294
8 years	4,911	3,338
High School	6,186	3,863
1 to 3 years	5,882	3,449
4 years	6,390	4,559
College	8,288	6,444
1 to 3 years	7,344	5,525
4 years or more	9,315	7,875

Source: U.S. Bureau of Census

[13]Orshansky, "More about the Poor in 1964," p. 8.
[14]Cummings, p. 831.
[15]*Ibid.,* p. 828.
[16]Dawn Wachtel, *The Working Poor,* Institute of Labor and Industrial Relations, The University of Michigan and Wayne State University, Ann Arbor, 1967.

Education. It is a well known fact that income highly correlates with education.

In a similar vein, correlation *between* broad occupational groups and education appears extremely high. Professionals, on the average, are better educated than clerical workers and accordingly receive higher incomes. Foremen and craftsmen are generally more educated than operatives and laborers and again, the difference is reflected in higher earnings for the more educated.

Yet *within* occupational categories the relationship between the education of the worker and his wage rate is not so clear. Operatives in the high-wage industries appear to possess almost the same educational histories as many of their occupational equivalents who work for poverty incomes either in the same industry (located possibly in a different region of the country) or in different industries. Delehanty and Evans found that among operative occupations in manufacturing industry the difference in educational attainment between most workers in low-wage groups and those in above poverty-line wage operations stood at less than .6 of a year in 1963, the median years of school completed being 9.6 for all operatives.[17] They also found that the six major poverty wage clerical occupations divide into three equal groups with educational levels which bracket the over-all median.[18] And of the 29 service worker occupations, 21 fall into the low-wage category, but the educational level of workers in 15 of these 21 either exceeds or is not more than one-half year below the 9.7 year median educational level for all service employees.[19] Consequently, we cannot easily characterize the working poor as illiterate, unschooled, or for that matter, educationally inferior to workers in comparable occupations in high-wage industries. Education can explain why engineers earn more than janitors, but it cannot alone explain why a janitor in one industry fares so much better than one in the low-wage sector.

Skill. Although education usually serves as a proxy for job skill, the two are not perfectly interchangeable, and agility and speed on a repetitious operation are not necessarily the by-products of school attendance. Nevertheless, it appears safe to assume that the conclusion regarding education and low-wage occupations can be extended to

---

[17]George E. Delehanty and Robert Evans, Jr., "Low-Wage Employment: An Inventory and an Assessment," Northwestern University, mimeographed, n.d., p. 33.

[18]*Ibid.,* p. 32.

[19]*Ibid.,* p. 33

job skills. There is little reason to believe that an assembler in the high-wage auto industry is more skilled than the operative in a Southern sawmill or textile plant, or that the former who is paid by the hour is any speedier than the latter who works at a piece-rate.

Geographical Location. The working poor are located in every state in the union, but the heaviest concentration of employed poor is found in the South. In 1964 over half of all working poor families and a third of all fully-employed unrelated individuals lived in southern states. Altogether, in that year, the families of the working poor represented 12.4 percent of all southern families, while they represented only 5.8 percent in the North Central region, 4.2 percent in the West, and only 3.3 percent in the Northeast.[20]   Employed impoverished unrelated individuals fared even more poorly than families, accounting for 18 percent of all working unrelated individuals in the South.

Aside from the South where the working poor are in greatest proportions, there are isolated "pockets of poverty" like the Ozark Plateau, the Down East section of the eastern coastline, and the cutover region of the Upper Great Lakes which include some of the full-time working poor and greater numbers of poor part-time workers and the unemployed. Many of the working poor are concentrated in the ghettos of northern and western industrial cities where they work in marginal industries. Yet, again we beg the question if we conclude that the working poor can be explained in terms of the region from which they originate, since there is nothing theoretically inherent in the geography which should make one region less well-paying than another. It becomes necessary to focus on the product and labor market characteristics in the regions where low wages are concentrated.

Labor Mobility. One would expect that workers in low-wage occupations and industries would be eager to seek improvement in their lot by moving to high-wage areas of the country. To some extent empirical studies appear to substantiate this expectation, for there is a close relationship between median income levels and state migration patterns. Between 1950 and 1960, the poorest 13 states had an average net out-migration of 7 percent while the 13 richest states had an average net in-migration rate of 6 percent.[21] We also know that while the quit rate for all manufacturing industry in November 1966 was

---

[20]Orshansky, "More about the Poor in 1964," pp. 8, 14.

[21]Gerald G. Somers and Glen G. Cain, *Geographic Mobility and the Reduction of Poverty,* Office of Economic Opportunity, July 1965, p. 3.

2.1 per 100 employees, it stood at 3.1 for manufacturing industries with average wages under $2.25 per hour.[22]

This movement, however, is not necessarily associated with poor workers who need better wages. Rather, geographical mobility rates are associated with education, age, and race, and in general, migration rates are higher for people with more education and for people in younger age groups. Workers in their twenties have the highest migration rates (19-22 percent) while the rates decline progressively with each succeeding age category, falling below 4 percent in the 60-64 age group.[23]

Yet, even mobility does not necessarily indicate escape from poverty. Although low-wage industries have greater labor quit rates than industries which pay higher wages, the high mobility of persons in low-wage jobs is not solely a reflection of job improvement. The results of two studies of within-year mobility, conducted by the Bureau of Labor Statistics in 1955 and 1961, indicate that workers in low-wage occupations improved their situations through changing jobs only about as often as workers in higher-paid occupations. Of all mobile persons, 33.7 percent reported that their move improved their economic status. The three low-wage occupations, operatives, service workers, and laborers, reported improvement from their move in 37.9, 36.7, and 23.8 percent of the cases respectively.[24]

The lack of mobility of the working poor, and moreover, the inefficacy of mobility, account for a good measure of the continuing poverty of low-wage industry workers. While some refuse to move to higher wage industries because of ties to family and region, many others cannot move because they lack the wherewithal to meet the expenses of resettlement. For many, movement to another area appears risky, especially if it means forfeiture of an already existing full-time job, albeit one which pays but a low wage. Furthermore the economic climate may be such that industries in high-wage areas have few jobs open for newcomers and because of fixed wage floors refuse to expand employment. Educational requirements pose another barrier for the employed poor who possess the will to advance to higher wage areas, but lack the educational background to change occupations. In any case, wherever mobility of the working poor is restricted—whether due to personal preference, economic environment, educational inad-

---

[22]Calculated from Table D-2, p. 81 in *Employment and Earnings Statistics*, U.S. Department of Labor, Vol. 13, No. 1, January 1967.

[23]Somers and Cain, *op. cit.*, p. 6.

[24]Delehanty and Evans, *op. cit.*, p. 44.

equacy, or discrimination—the opportunity for escaping from working poverty is reduced.

General characteristics of the working poor give some indication of the people most likely to be members of the employed poor, but alone do not afford an explanation of low-wage employment. The employed poor are found predominantly in low-skill jobs requiring less education and training than most occupations. Nevertheless, thousands, if not millions, of workers in comparable trades who possess little more skill or education earn incomes well in excess of the working poor. Women and non-whites are especially prone to low-wage employment, yet nothing inherent in their sex or race accounts for their disproportionate numbers among the employed poor. Furthermore, the working poor are not primarily senior citizens or untrained youth whose productivity is reduced by age or inexperience. Only lack of mobility appears to give some systematic explanation to the individuals who are working poor. Employed in low-wage industry, they are unable or unwilling to move to higher wage employment in low-skill occupations either because of discrimination, the risk and expense of changing jobs, or personal preference for home.

Thus, although we know something at this point of who is most likely destined for poverty employment—the under-educated, the immobile, the non-white, women, and those who live in the South— we have little indication of what produces low-wage jobs in the first place. The explanation that people are paid low wages because they are inherently unproductive and only worth a low-wage to the producer falls under too many diverse circumstances to be of value as a general theory of low-wage employment. Instead, attention must be turned to the product and labor markets of low-wage industry in order to understand the existence of poverty income jobs and the root causes of the working poor.

Low-Wage Industries

The working poor, as expected, are not spread evenly throughout all industries. Rather, employed indigents are concentrated in a number of industries, which, for one reason or another, have failed to provide a living wage for many of their employees. Isolating these industries from all others provides some insight into the characteristics of low-wage firms.

As a first approximation we can isolate industries which have a relatively low average wage for all non-supervisory personnel, $2.25 per hour or below. Other criteria could be substituted for this breaking point, but these, with little variance, would result in the same general conclusions about the characteristics of low-wage industries and firms. Nonetheless, labor surveys show that an industry with an average wage near $2.25 can be expected to have a sizable number of working poor in its employ. Of course, industries below this level can be expected to have even larger numbers of impoverished full-time workers.

When this average wage criterion is utilized we find that mining and construction industries are relatively free of poverty employment, showing no two or three-digit Standard Industrial Code (SIC) sectors falling below the breaking point in 1966.[25] Likewise, the transportation and public utilities industries indicate average wages well above the low-wage line. However, when we turn to manufacturing, the working poor begin to appear in the statistics. Of the broad 21 two-digit industrial classifications in manufacturing, six are low-paying and 30 of the 119 separately government listed three-digit industries fall below our criterion. Eight of these are in durable manufacturing; 22 in non-durables. More than half of these are in the textile and clothing industries and none are in the heavy goods industry.

Although no wholesale trade industries fall into the low-wage category, ten of the 13 listed retail trade industries and five of the seven two-digit retail classifications fall well below the low-wage line. In the realm of finance, insurance, and real estate, only the banking

TABLE 4

Low Wage Industrial Sectors

Industrial Sector	Number of three-digit industries	Number of low-wage three-digit industries
Mining and Construction	12	0
Manufacturing	119	30
(Durable goods)	65	8
(Non-durable goods)	54	22
Transportation & Public Utilities	10	0
Wholesale Trade	8	0
Retail Trade	13	10
Finance, Insurance & Real Estate		
(Two-digit industries)	4	1
Services and Miscellaneous	3	2

Source: *Employment and Earnings Statistics,* Volume 13, No. 1, January, 1967.

---

[25]*Employment and Earnings Statistics,* Table C-2, p. 60, U.S. Department of Labor, Vol. 13, No. 1, January 1967.

industry has an overall average wage which puts it in the poverty employment category. Finally, in turning to the services sector we find two of the three listed three-digit industries paying well below the low-wage threshold.

To achieve a more accurate picture of the employed poor, it is necessary, however, to investigate earnings distributions within and between industries rather than average hourly wages. Table 5 shows the percentage of employees in certain selected manufacturing and retail trade industries who earn a low wage.*

Characteristics of Low-Wage Industries

A "character" sketch similar to that of low-wage workers applied to low-wage industries permits some insight into the dynamics of the low-wage sector of the economy. While it may not allow a perfect understanding of all low-wage jobs, it does unveil the economic and social forces conducive to the persistence of poverty employment within the confines of a materially affluent society.

Growth Rate of Average Hourly Earnings. Delehanty and Evans report that between 1958 and 1963, the gain in average hourly earnings in

---

*Table 5 was calculated using the *Industry Wage Surveys* of the Bureau of Labor Statistics, Department of Labor. Because the *Industry Wage Surveys* were produced over a number of years it is necessary to standardize the poverty "line" in order to produce comparable results for different industries. This was done by resorting to a *relative* poverty line concept based on the average gross earnings of production workers on all manufacturing payrolls, 1955-66. (From *Employment and Earnings Statistics,* January, 1967) Somewhat arbitrarily the poverty criterion was defined as average straight-time weekly or hourly earnings of *60 percent or less* of the above-mentioned national manufacturing average.

The average group earnings of production workers was taken as a standard for two major reasons: (1) Most low-wage employment in the United States appears in manufacturing, retail trade, and the low-skill services. Rather than take an average wage representing all employment in the United States, the manufacturing average seems best to represent the potential wage for "low-wage" industry and at the same time an income which is considered "adequate" by American living standards. (2) This statistic is easily collected, accurate, and highly representative of a large segment of American jobs.

The 60 percent criterion was chosen in connection with the manufacturing earnings figures so as to result in a poverty line comparable to the "official" government poverty figures for the 1960's. A higher or lower percentage could, of course, be used if the government poverty threshold is felt inadequate or over-sufficient. Indeed both the standardized group and the percentage criterion can be altered either to yield the same poverty thresholds or different poverty levels depending on preference.

Using the criteria outlined above, the annual poverty line for the years 1955-66 is presented opposite.

all manufacturing was 17 percent, while the gain in low-wage industries was limited to 13.6.[26] Over a longer period, 1953 to 1963, the median increase for low-wage two-digit industries was only 30 percent while the median in other manufacturing industry exceeded 45. The differential in wage growth rates is also reflected in the relative changes in wages in broader employment categories. (See Table 6). Between 1947 and 1966, wages in non-durable goods and retail trade rose less rapidly than wages in all manufacturing, and overall, low-wage industries within manufacturing produced the smallest gains both relatively and absolutely.

Rather than closing, the earnings gap between low-wage industries and most high wage industries appears to be growing. Relative to the average worker in society, the working poor wage-earner is more poor today than he was 20 years ago, and although some workers in low-wage industries have escaped absolute poverty in the sense that they have broken through the artificial $3,000 threshold, their income position, relatively speaking, has deteriorated. Small decreases in the percentage of low-wage employment among industries in re-

Average Earnings of Production Workers on Manufacturing Payrolls

			Poverty Line (60% Criterion)		
Year	AWE	AHE	AWE	AHE	Annual Income
1955	$ 75.70	$1.86	$45.50	$1.11	$2,270
1956	78.78	1.95	47.20	1.17	2,360
1957	81.59	2.05	49.00	1.23	2,450
1958	82.71	2.11	49.60	1.26	2,490
1959	88.26	2.19	53.00	1.31	2,640
1960	89.72	2.26	53.90	1.36	2,690
1961	92.34	2.32	55.40	1.39	2,760
1962	96.56	2.39	58.10	1.43	2,910
1963	99.63	2.46	59.70	1.48	2,980
1964	102.97	2.53	61.70	1.52	3,090
1965	107.53	2.61	64.50	1.57	3,220
1966	112.19	2.71	67.20	1.63	3,360

Using the "Poverty Line" Average Hourly Earnings (Column 5), the percentage of below-poverty line employees in an industry is calculated. For each industry this is calculated for total employment, male employment, and female employment. For some industries, wage surveys were completed for two or more years. In these industries it is possible to consider the persistence of poverty wages.

If an absolute rather than relative standard of poverty is preferred, the poverty threshold for different years can be fabricated by choosing a base year poverty line and correcting for changes in the consumer price index. This, however, will not significantly alter the listing or relative positions of the low-wage industries.

[26]Delehanty and Evans, *op. cit.*, p. 9.

TABLE 5

Percent of Low-wage Employment in Selected Industries, 1961-1966

Industry	Year	Total Empl.	AHE*	%L.W.*	Male Empl.	AHE	%L.W.	Female Empl.	AHE	%L.W.
Southern Sawmills & Planing Mills	1962	110,726	$1.25	88.2	—	—	—	—	—	—
Nursing Homes & Related Facilities	1965	172,637	1.19	86.3	19,636	1.31	—	153,001	1.17	—
Work Clothing	1961	51,594	1.24	77.1	6,134	1.48	54.2	45,460	1.21	81.2
	1964	57,669	1.43	72.8	6,998	1.61	—	50,671	1.40	—
Children's Hosiery Mills	1962	17,181	1.33	76.9	3,900	1.47	57.1	13,281	1.29	84.3
	1964	17,364	1.46	67.3	3,974	1.58	47.7	13,390	1.42	73.0
Men's & Boy's Shirts	1961	93,190	1.26	75.5	8,844	1.47	55.2	84,346	1.24	77.8
	1964	96,935	1.45	70.4	8,962	1.63	53.4	87,973	1.43	73.2
Laundries & Cleaning Services	1963	418,883	1.26	75.4	96,744	1.62	45.8	322,139	1.16	83.7
	1966	397,715	1.44	72.5	88,091	1.81	45.3	309,624	1.33	80.6
Men's Hosiery Mills	1962	24,039	1.37	71.7	6,775	1.52	48.5	17,264	1.31	80.8
	1964	21,223	1.47	65.2	5,656	1.62	44.4	15,567	1.42	77.7
Synthetic Textiles	1963	84,214	1.57	55.5	51,389	1.63	43.2	32,825	1.47	66.3
Cigar Manufacturing	1961	21,562	1.39	55.4	4,721	1.48	52.3	16,841	1.37	55.3
	1964	21,675	1.54	50.7	5,249	1.61	52.8	16,426	1.52	47.3
Cotton Textiles	1963	225,655	1.53	54.5	140,117	1.56	40.1	85,538	1.47	61.4
	1965	219,477	1.74	35.1	136,641	1.78	35.1	82,836	1.67	40.2
Wood Household Furniture	1962	106,193	1.57	50.8	95,540	1.58	49.3	10,653	1.43	66.2
	1965	120,000	1.71	48.1	106,810	1.73	49.0	13,190	1.55	66.8
Footwear	1962	182,449	1.64	49.3	75,303	1.88	32.8	107,146	1.47	56.9
	1965	173,804	1.77	50.6	70,597	2.02	34.7	103,207	1.60	61.4
Women's Hosiery Mills	1962	45,663	1.55	50.0	11,550	1.83	25.8	34,113	1.46	53.3
	1964	44,325	1.62	45.0	10,257	1.84	26.8	34,068	1.56	50.3
Fertilizer Manufacture	1962	26,150	1.67	41.7	—	—	—	—	—	—
	1966	25,484	1.90	38.8	—	—	—	—	—	—

Industry	Year									
Hospitals (excl. Federal)	1966	1,781,300	1.86	41.2	360,000	1.98	34.6	1,421,000	1.82	49.2
Candy & Other Confectionery	1965	49,736	1.87	34.2	20,872	2.11	19.1	28,864	1.69	45.3
Brick & Structural Clay Tile	1964	23,274	1.91	33.9	23,164	1.91	33.5	110	1.29	94.5
Wool Textiles: Wool, Yarn, & Broadwoven Fabric Mills-Worsted	1962	19,599	1.59	32.7	8,863	1.68	25.8	10,736	1.51	38.3
Wool Textiles: Scouring & Combing Plants	1962	4,069	1.64	23.1	3,396	1.67	20.5	673	1.54	42.9
	1966	4,041	1.92	12.4	3,255	1.96	11.5	786	1.76	16.0
Wool Textiles: Wool, Yarn & Broadwoven Fabric Mills-Wool (Worsted & Wool)	1962	30,971	1.70	22.3	20,396	1.73	19.6	10,575	1.64	26.1
	1966	41,765	1.90	15.8	23,800	1.97	12.2	17,965	1.81	20.7
Structural Clay Products	1964	51,324	2.08	20.8	47,577	2.10	19.9	3,747	1.78	32.2
Miscellaneous Plastic Products	1964	109,482	1.95	19.9	65,939	2.15	9.2	43,543	1.65	36.0
Men's & Bcy's Suits & Coats	1963	92,116	2.12	19.5	30,154	2.59	7.8	61,962	1.88	25.1
Wool Textiles: Dyeing & Finishing Plants	1962	4,744	1.82	16.9	3,649	1.92	10.2	1,095	1.51	39.9
	1966	3,559	2.12	7.7	2,702	2.22	5.1	857	1.80	15.7
Textile Dyeing & Finishing	1966	54,774	1.96	16.7	45,523	2.02	12.9	9,251	1.68	35.7
Meat Packing	1963	131,965	2.69	10.0	114,770	2.72	8.5	17,195	2.47	19.8
Leather Tanning & Finishing	1963	25,493	2.13	9.9	23,200	2.16	8.6	2,293	1.80	23.2
Flour & Other Grain Mill Products	1961	15,984	2.22	9.4	15,398	2.23	9.2	586	1.91	17.2
Fabricated Structural Steel	1964	55,429	2.50	6.6	—	—	—	—	—	—
Motor Vehicle Parts	1963	186,684	2.59	6.1	151,756	2.72	3.0	34,928	2.01	19.5
Communications	1961	599,108	2.67	5.9	258,505	—	—	340,603	—	—
Paints & Varnishes	1961	28,340	2.23	5.0	26,819	2.25	4.5	1,521	1.78	12.9
	1965	31,147	2.56	4.7	29,684	2.58	4.6	1,463	2.09	9.7
Electric & Gas Utilities: Nonsupervisory Office Workers	1962	115,187	2.42	4.7	—	—	—	—	—	—
Nonsupervisory Physical Workers	1962	290,115	2.86	1.2	—	—	—	—	—	—
Iron & Steel Foundries	1962	152,928	2.50	2.2	151,071	2.50	2.2	1,857	2.06	6.0
Pressed or Blown Glass & Glassware	1964	81,748	2.31	2.1	54,629	2.46	2.1	27,119	1.99	2.7

TABLE 5 (cont.)

Industry	Year									
Synthetic Fibers	1966	62,407	2.45	.7	43,996	2.53	.6	18,411	2.27	.7
Pulp, Paper, & Paperboard	1962	166,769	2.35	.5	160,614	2.37	.5	6,155	1.95	.9
West Coast Sawmilling	1964	83,250	2.66	0.0	——	——	——	——	——	——
Motor Vehicles	1963	460,798	2.90	0.0	——	——	——	——	——	——
Basic Iron & Steel	1962	484,600	3.17	0.0	——	——	——	——	——	——
Cigarette Manufacturing	1965	31,507	2.51	0.0	19,519	2.58	——	14,988	2.38	——
RETAIL TRADE										
Limited Price Variety Stores	1965	277,100	1.31	87.9	35,600	1.59	69.8	241,500	1.27	90.5
Eating & Drinking Places	1963	1,286,708	1.14	79.4	542,654	1.41	62.4	744,054	.95	90.2
Hotels & Motels	1963	416,289	1.17	76.1	197,223	1.32	65.4	214,066	1.04	85.9
Drug & Proprietory Stores	1965	371,800	1.56	71.3	149,800	1.88	61.1	222,000	1.36	78.1
Gasoline Service Stations	1965	476,100	1.52	66.7	460,000	1.52	66.7	16,000	1.37	67.9
Apparel & Accessory Stores	1965	582,100	1.70	59.7	180,200	2.06	40.5	401,900	1.52	68.3
Department Stores	1965	1,019,300	1.75	59.6	298,200	2.22	34.9	721,100	1.54	69.9
Miscellaneous Retail Stores	1965	968,200	1.75	58.0	539,900	1.97	47.2	428,300	1.44	71.7
Retail Food Stores	1965	1,366,800	1.91	47.6	895,300	2.03	42.9	471,500	1.66	56.5
Building Material, Hardware, & Farm Equipment Dealers	1965	488,900	1.98	39.4	412,800	2.03	37.3	76,100	1.67	50.9
Furniture, House Furnishings & Household Appliances	1965	363,900	2.10	38.4	258,800	2.24	31.9	105,100	1.67	54.2
Motor Vehicle Dealers	1965	604,400	2.40	28.7	541,200	2.46	27.6	63,200	1.83	38.5

Source: Industry Wage Surveys, Bureau of Labor Statistics, Department of Labor (1961-1966).

* AHE = Average Hourly Earnings   L.W. = Low Wage

TABLE 6

Changes in Employment and Wages of Production or Non-Supervisory Workers on Payrolls of Selected Industries

	Employment		%Change in Employment	Average Hourly Earnings		%Change in AHE	%Change in Wage (All Mfg.=100)
	1947	1966		1947	1966		
Mining	871,000	488,000	-43.0	$1.47	$3.05	108	88
Construction	1,759,000	2,789,000	+58.5	1.54	3.87	149	122
All Manufacturing	12,990,000	14,202,000	+ 9.4	1.22	2.71	122	100
Durable Manufacturing	7,028,000	8,305,000	+18.2	1.88	2.89	133	109
High Wage Durable							
Primary Metals	1,114,000	1,081,300	- 2.9	1.39	3.28	136	111
Machinery	1,087,000	1,313,800	+20.8	1.34	3.08	129	106
Transportation Equipment	1,039,000	1,357,100	+30.6	1.44	3.33	131	107
Low Wage Durable							
Lumber and Wood Products	783,000	543,500	-30.6	1.09	2.27	108	88
Furniture and Fixtures	296,000	378,600	+28.0	1.10	2.20	100	83
Miscellaneous Manufacture	367,000	352,000	- 4.1	1.11	2.22	100	83
Non-Durable Manufacturing	5,962,000	5,897,000	- 1.1	1.14	2.45	115	94
High Wage Non-Durable							
Paper and Allied Products	406,000	521,900	+28.6	1.15	2.75	139	114
Printing and Publishing	487,000	652,500	+34.0	1.48	3.16	113	93
Petroleum and Related Products	170,000	113,900	-33.0	1.50	3.41	127	105
Low Wage Non-Durable							
Textile Mill Products	1,220,000	848,200	-30.6	1.04	1.96	88	72
Apparel and Related Products	1,047,000	1,240,100	+18.4	1.16	1.89	63	52
Leather and Leather Products	374,000	312,900	-16.3	1.04	1.94	87	71
Retail Trade	6,595,000	9,761,000	+48.0	.90	1.91	112	92
Wholesale Trade	2,165,000	2,928,000	+39.9	1.22	2.73	123	101

Source: Manpower Report of the President, 1967, Tables C-3 and C-6, pp. 250, 253.

cent years (See Table 5) reflect a minor reduction in absolute working poverty, but camouflage the fact that wage increases have not
been spread throughout the industry. Rather, wage dispersion within
the low-wage industries has been reduced, possibly due to upward
pressure on lowest wages because of broader coverage of minimum
wage laws.

Demand for Labor in Low-wage Industry. All things equal, industries
with increasing demand for labor are generally expected to have
wages increasing at a faster pace than those where labor demand has
slackened. Yet in this regard, empirical evidence on low-wage industry appears equivocal. While a number of low-wage industries have
had steadily declining employment consistent with slow rather than
rapid wage advance, other low-wage industries have had relatively
high employment growth rates.

Lumber and wood products, textile mill products, leather and
leather goods, laundries and cleaning services, and footwear are prime
examples of the declining low-wage industry. On the other hand,
apparel and related products, furniture and fixtures, and above all,
retail trade, contradict the expectation as all of these have had healthy
advances in employment without eliminating their poverty wage
scales. A number of industries have had large decreases in employment yet have not fallen prey to low-wages. Over the last two
decades both mining and primary metal industries have had absolute
decreases in non-supervisory production personnel yet have managed
to keep wages at a high level. Indeed primary metal industries have
increased wages at a rate in excess of the average for all manufacturing firms. Obviously all things have not been equal in the economy
and hence, other factors must be called upon to explain the dimensions of low-wage industry.

Productivity of Low-wage Industries. When the productivity of a firm
increases, presumably wages can be raised, profits can be increased,
prices can be lowered, or a combination of the three can occur. In
oligopolistic industries, productivity has been rising fairly steadily and
the result, at least in part, has been expanding wages and profit
margins, often at the same, or higher, growth rate as the productivity
rate. When low-wage manufacturing industries are investigated, they
are found, on the average, to possess productivity growth rates consistent with the gains in the rest of manufacturing. Using the ratio of the
Federal Reserve Board's "Production Index" divided by total employment as a measure of productivity for the years 1958-1963, Delehanty
and Evans found a 26 percent median increase in productivity for
low-wage two-digit manufacturing classifications. For the remaining

manufacturing sectors, the median increase was slightly *less*, 25 percent. Nevertheless, absolute productivity in the low-wage sectors was
found to be well below that in non-low-wage industries. The value-
added per production worker man/hour in the low-wage sectors was
only $3.63 while in other manufacturing industry the median was more
than double, $8.17.[27]

The low absolute productivity of labor in low-wage industry, no
matter whether the cause is too little complementary capital or inefficient management, partly explains the low level of wages in the
poverty industries. But the productivity gains in low-wage industry
are not reflected in the relative wage rate changes in low-wage industry. Rather than contributing to higher wages, productivity increases
are either being absorbed into broader profit margins or otherwise into
lower prices due to raging competition. Productivity, then, cannot
alone explain the plight of the low-wage industry and its poverty-
stricken workforce.

Profits. Periodically, it is suggested that poverty wages are the result of
employee exploitation by profit-grubbing monopolistic firms. Indeed, firms maintaining influence in labor markets can artificially
reduce wages below the return due to workers based on their productivity and thereby accrue higher money profits for the company. In
some low-wage industries where the local labor market is at the mercy
of a company town, no doubt exploitation of this kind is practiced. Yet
in general, the evidence points to low-profit margins in the bulk of
low-wage industry.

Using Stigler's study of capital and the return on capital in
manufacturing, Delehanty and Evans computed the median rates of
return (profit margins) over the years 1948 to 1957 for both all
manufacturing and an isolated set of low-wage industries. The median
for the former was 7.33 percent while for low-wage industry, the
median was limited to 5.75 percent, a considerably smaller profit
margin.[28] More recent data from the Federal Trade and the Securi-
ties and Exchange Commissions gave comparable results, although
they showed a declining relative and absolute gap in the profit margin
between all manufacturing and the low-wage sector.[29] Some wage
exploitation may be occurring in a few specific industries; nevertheless, the low-profit margins recorded here and reported in addition by
Gus Tyler[30] of the International Ladies' Garment Workers Union

[27]*Ibid.*, p. 11.
[28]*Ibid.*, p. 13.
[29]*Ibid.*, p. 14.
[30]Gus Tyler, "Marginal Industries, Low Wages, and High Risks,"
Dissent, Summer 1961, pp. 321-325.

lead us to believe that individual low-wage industries, by and large, have had little success in attempting wage exploitation. The working poor are being exploited by the economy as a whole rather than by the individual firms employing them.

Concentration and Competition. The degree of market concentration in an industry or conversely market competition determines the ability of a firm to administer prices rather than be forced through economic pressure to submit to the ensuing set of market prices. When product market competition is fierce, because of a plethora of small firms competing where none can control the market, productivity increases tend to resolve into lower commodity prices rather than higher profit margins or higher wages. In contrast to mammoth oligopolistic industries which can set prices without fear of open price conflict, many relatively small firms which produce the same commodity cannot match the wages of the titans. Wage increases in manufacturing giants can be passed along at rates equal to productivity, while the competitive firm is often forced to lower prices rather than increase profits or wages. In some cases, the oligopolistic firm may be forced to raise wages even above productivity gains, paying for this by cutting into monopoly profits or by boosting the price of their products. The highly competitive firm is rarely in such a position.

Data from Kaysen and from Delehanty and Evans point to the much lower concentration ratios in the low-wage industries.[31,32] For instance, the latter found that of the 1,132 five-digit product classes in all manufacturing, 23 percent were such that the four largest producers for each product made 60 percent or more of the total output. Prime examples are the industrial titans of automobile, steel, rubber, and aluminum. Among low-wage industry, however, only 9 percent of the product classes were produced in highly concentrated industries. Clearly the degree of competitiveness among the low-wage industries is greater than that for the rest of manufacturing, and the same generally holds, probably even to a greater extent, for retail trade and services, both low wage sectors.

This analysis appears to account for the disparity between productivity and wage gains in the low-wage sector versus the better paying industries. While productivity in low-wage industries has kept

---

[31]Carl Kaysen and Donald F. Turner, *Antitrust Policy: An Economic and Legal Analysis,* Howard University Press, Cambridge, 1959. (See appendices.)

[32]Delehanty and Evans, *op. cit.,* pp. 19-20.

pace or in some cases has exceeded the rest of industry, wages and profits have not risen as quickly because of the raging price competition in the low-wage sector not present in the rest of the economy.

Nonetheless, a highly concentrated industry per se does not guarantee a higher wage scale, for there is nothing inherent in the size of a firm or in the absence of product market competition which accounts for better wages. Rather, oligopoly provides what might be called a "permissive economic environment" within which other forces can more easily work for higher wages.[33] Needless to say, such an economic climate is non-existent for the frail, competitive, often low-wage, firm. A permissive economic environment entails capital-intensive production possibilities, the ability to set prices based on product demand conditions, high public visibility, low firm entry, and the opportunity for strong unionism.

Utilization of Capital. Where each worker has a great deal of machinery at his command, output per man will be large and the wage bill correspondingly, will be a small fraction of the total costs incurred by the producer. Such wages will have a tendency to be higher than where production is labor-intensive. Furthermore, resistence to wage increases will be less in the capital-intensive industry since wages make up a small part of operating costs.

Data on manufacturing production functions in the United States give adequate evidence to support the hypothesis that low-wage industries in general are less capital-intensive than more lucrative industries.[34] In four of six low-wage manufacturing industry classifications the extent of capital available was significantly related to the wage level.[35] In most cases, the correlation was also significant between the size of the firm and the amount of capital per worker. In both cases the same results certainly must extend to retail trade and services.

Part of the low-wage pattern found in labor intensive firms is no doubt due to unexploited economies of scale and to the fact that small wage increases, let alone large, add considerably to total operating costs of small firms which are weak in capital. Hence, the lack of capital in the low-wage firm accounts for some of the growing gap in relative incomes between the average worker and the working poor.

---

[33]Harold M. Levinson, "Unionism, Concentration, and Wage Changes: Toward a Unified Theory," *Determining Forces in Collective Wage Bargaining,* John Wiley and Sons, New York, 1967.

[34]George H. Hildebrand and Ta-Chung Liu, *Manufacturing Production Functions in the United States, 1957.* (As used in Delehanty and Evans.)

[35]Delchanty and Evans, p. 23.

Product Demand. Although there is little data on the demand for different products, it is plausible to posit that the demand for many low-wage industry commodities is quite elastic due to product substitutes and foreign competition. Only recently is foreign competition in the heavy goods industry beginning to dent domestic sales and prices in the high wage sector. In textiles, miscellaneous manufacturing, watches and clocks and apparel, foreign competition has been fierce and in some cases has not completely destroyed a comparatively inefficient domestic industry only because of restrictive tariffs.

To the extent that a product has inelastic demand, wages can be raised at the expense of higher prices, as in the automobile industry. But where demand is highly elastic, a small increase in price reduces the demand precipitously. When cigar prices rise, smokers switch to pipes and cigarettes; when domestic textile prices rise, fashions turn to imported fabrics. Consequently, the low-wage firm has little recourse to a price increase as a means of boosting wages or profit margins for that matter. If the firm faces an elastic demand, it runs itself out of the market when it raises prices too high. The choice for workers in this industry becomes not low wages or high wages, but low-wages or no wages. In the bituminous coal industry for example, the choice was against paying low wages to a multitude of coal-miners. Instead, the industry was mechanized, prices remained competitive but a great part of the workforce was eliminated. Many were thrown out of lifelong work, but those who survived the cut received an adequate wage for their continuing toil.

Public Visibility. When General Motors Corporation announces net profits in excess of 20 percent per year, employs over 400,000 workers, and controls prices in a $20 billion-plus industry, the nation cannot help but take notice. The same holds for other major industries in the country. But the near invisible low-wage sector of the economy escapes the constant public scrutiny to which the industrial giants are subjected. A large firm can hardly escape paying relatively high wages even if there is little internal pressure from its workforce. The small "invisible" firm, on the other hand, often avoids the sharp eye of the government inspector and the acute sensitivities of an aroused public opinion. Consequently, low wages and poor working conditions have a much better chance of survival in the industries of the working poor. Similarly, laws are so drawn as to exclude many workers in the low-wage sector. As late as 1963, for instance, minimum wage laws excluded from coverage over one and one-half million restaurant workers, 489,000 hotel and motel employees, over a half million laundry workers, 700,000 hospital workers, over three million retail clerks, and, in addition, millions of farmers and thousands of loggers and agricultural processing workers.[36] Ironically, the minimum wage law covers *all* auto, steel, rubber, and aluminum workers where the average wage is over twice the minimum and literally no one earns below one and a half times the legal minimum wage.

Unionization. Although low-wage industry is not as highly unionized as high-wage manufacturing, it is not totally unorganized. Unions exist in many low-wage industries, but they are beset by a number of nearly insurmountable hurdles brought on by the characteristics of most low-wage industry. The same barriers account for the sectors of low-wage industry devoid of unionization.

There is nothing inherent in the nature of oligopolistic industrial giants which explains, not their ability, but their actual granting of higher wages. If we are to fully understand the causes of high wages and, consequently, those of low-wages and working-poor jobs, it is necessary to include the all important dimension of unionization.

A number of studies over the past few years have shown that greater rates of wage increases have been strongly associated with (1) a relatively high degree of oligopoly, (2) high profit rates, and (3) strong unions.[37] Yet these forces do not act independently, but rather bear systematic relation to each other. High product market concentration and high profits provide the footing for a "permissive economic environment" in which strong unions can reap economic and social rewards for their members. Where an industry is inhabited by a few massive price-setting, highly mechanized, non-competitive, publicly visible, and highly profitable firms, entry of new firms is highly improbable and, indeed, quite rare. The needed initial resources are too vast to be accumulated by a newcomer. Consequently, unions, once they have become established, are relatively secure and free from the competition forced on them by an unorganized sector in the industry. Free to press for higher wages without fear of eliminating jobs by pricing their firm's product above unorganized competition, the union can demand their share of productivity and productivity gains, which in a capital-intensive industry are usually relatively high. With the industry held up to the inspection of both government and the public, the industry is doubly careful to refrain from "inappropri-

---

[36]AFL-CIO, "The Low-Paid Worker," *American Federationist,* August, 1964.

[37]See Arthur Ross and William Goldner, "Forces Affecting Interindustry Wage Structure," *Quarterly Journal of Economics,* Vol. 64, No. 2, May 1950, pp. 254-305; William G. Bowen, *Wage Behavior in the Postwar Period,* Princeton, 1960; Harold M. Levinson, *op. cit.*

TABLE 7
Proportion of Wage Earners Under Union Agreements in 1962

Manufacturing Industries

75-100 per cent	50-75 per cent	25-50 per cent	under 25 per cent
Agricultural equipment	Chemicals	Cotton shirts and dresses	(None)
Aircraft	Furniture	Food, except meat packing	
Aluminum	Instruments	Hosiery	
Automobile	Jewelry and silverware	Luggage and handbags	
Brewery	Leather and shoes	Lumber	
Coats and suits	Machinery, except electrical	Textiles	
Dyeing and finishing	Metal products		
Electrical machinery	Millinery and hats		
Fur	Paper and pulp		
Glass and glassware	Printing and publishing		
Meat packing	Steel products		
Ordnance	Tobacco products		
Petroleum and coal products	Woolen and worsted textile		
Railroad equipment			
Rubber			
Shipbuilding			
Steel, basic			
Stone and clay			

Nonmanufacturing Industries

75-100 per cent	50-75 per cent	25-50 per cent	under 25 per cent
Actors and musicians	Bus lines, intercity	Newspaper offices	Agriculture
Airline pilots and mechanics	Technicians, radio and motion picture	Barber shops	Beauty shops
Bus and streetcar, local	Light and power	Cleaning and Dyeing	Clerical
Coal mining	City bus and streetcar lines	Hotels	Laundries
Construction		Taxicabs	Restaurants
Longshoring		Wholesale trade	Retail trade
Maritime			
Metal mining			
Motion-picture production			
Railroads			
Telephone and telegraph			
Trucking			

Source: Florence Peterson, *American Labor Unions: What They Are and How They Work*, 2nd. ed., Harper and Row, New York, 1963, p. 150.

ate" activities viz-a-viz their employees and their union. The high profits of the titans of industry present a choice target for union wage demands when bargaining sessions open.

In some high-wage industries, the product market nevertheless fails to be characterized by oligopolistic, highly profitable firms. High wages in these industries can usually be explained by the ability of the market to self-regulate entry or for unions to tightly control firm entry themselves. This is usually due to the "spatial" characteristics of the industry. The coal industry located in Appalachia is controlled in this way by the United Mine Workers. The Teamsters Union which operates in a highly competitive industry, nevertheless reaps high wages for its members since it is able to control entry through over-the-road spatial agreements.

Consequently, we can conclude that most industries which are capital intensive, highly profitable, and free from raging competition have the *ability* to raise wages with relatively less pain and effort than other industry. Furthermore, it is precisely this economic environment which provides the most suitable conditions for strong unions. They can tackle the ability of their industries to pay high wages and turn it, through collective bargaining and the threat of collective action, into real wage advances for their members. In other industries where unions can control entry and organize the whole market, high wages are also possible, although sometimes, as in the bituminous coal case, at the expense of eliminating many jobs.

In the low-wage sector, we have found nearly the opposite conditions. And, indeed, to a great extent, the low-wage industries represent the end result of a "repressive economic environment." Absolute productivity is well below that of all industry; less capital is utilized in production; profit rates are smaller, and most importantly, competition flourishes. The ability of many low-wage industries to pay adequate wages without drastically cutting employment is seriously open to question. Furthermore, the repressive environment decidedly stymies union organization and the pressure of unions for higher wages. Where an industry is so established that entry is free and open to new, unorganized firms, we can expect weak unions and most probably low-wages. Where industries are marked by easy entry, fierce national and international competition, highly elastic product demand, low profits, and low productivity, we can almost be assured of two things: if a union exists at all, it is bound to be weak and ineffective, and there will surely be large numbers of working poor. Such is the case in textiles, apparel and related products, cigar manufacturing, fertilizer manufacture, and so forth. Many of the same characteristics are found in agriculture and the retail and service trades.

The same characteristics do not always apply to all industries which pay low wages and employ America's working poor. Some fail to pay higher wages because of foreign competition, watches and clocks for instance. Some, such as nursing care and retail trade, fail primarily because of low advances in productivity. Others fail for the most part due to one or more of these factors plus elastic demand for the product, e.g. cigar manufacturing.* Most fail, however, because of the competitiveness of their product markets.

It is interesting to note that precisely where the market approaches its theoretical best—in the firms furthest from monopoly and closest to laissez faire—the market cannot supply jobs adequate enough to feed a man's family satisfactorily. In part, this arises because of the fact that the marginal industry exists in an economy alongside of oligopolies. As Gus Tyler has put it most eloquently,

> Just as small industry must lose out to oligopoly in the struggle for the market, so too, must the worker in the competitive, mobile, low-profit trades lose his standing relative to the worker in the mechanized, immobile, high-profit industries.
>
> The 25 percent profit return on original investment not uncommon in steel and autos as contrasted with the 1 percent profit in garments does not derive from an inherent virtue of metal over fabrics, but from the monopoly character of the former and the competitive character of the latter. The workers in the latter industries suffer although many of them possess skills as great or even greater than those required in the basic industries.[38]

The inadequate incomes of most of the working poor are not of their own making. If we are to blame them for anything it must be for not having the good fortune to complete an education topped off by a college degree. Rather we must blame the economic system which in too many instances provides less than an adequate job for those of adequate talents. In dealing with the working poor it is not enough to deal with the problems of individuals—too little schooling, not enough

---

*Note that no working poor are in the cigarette industry although over one/half of all cigar workers are paid low wages. This is mostly due to the fact that cigarette manufacture is capital-intensive, oligopolistic, highly profitable, strongly unionized, and faces an inelastic market for its product. In the cigar industry the conditions are reversed.

[38]Tyler, *op. cit.*, pp. 323-324.

training, inadequate housing and filthy neighborhoods, no hope, and no political power. We must also find solutions for the economic system which continues to propel a poverty wage sector right into the decade of the '70's.

What Can Be Done

The vogue solution to the poverty of those able to work, but either unemployed or low-paid, has been to inject a dose of retraining and subsequently place the individual back into the labor force presumably now equipped to function in America's high speed economy. Yet it should be clear that for many of the working poor (and many of the unemployed) the problem is not so much due to a lack of preparation on the part of the individual, but due to the inability of a section of the economy to furnish an adequate wage for what is adequate work. Manpower retraining is needed for those who can benefit by progressing to better paying occupations. But it cannot attack the root causes of low-wage jobs, which given their existence, will inevitably fall to those least able to take advantage of the affluent sectors of the economy.

To effectively attack and successfully vanquish low-wage jobs requires a combination of measures emanating from the government and the trade union movement.

(1) Minimum wage legislation must continue to be broadened and raised. Those industries uncovered to date by such legislation must be included and the minimum must be raised to at least $2.00 per hour. This will assure those working in any industry an above-poverty line income, yet will still, unfortunately, leave many with inadequate incomes.

(2) The Congress must act to repeal Section 14(b) of the Taft-Hartley Act in order to eliminate the legally sanctioned open shop plaguing union organization. This section of the law has been most effective in the South in preventing unions from forming, and without national support for union organizing, those regions where unionization is needed most will fare the worst.

(3) The trade union movement must take a major offensive in eradicating poverty wage scales. In many ways, the movement itself has supplied the climate within which the non-organized sector has wallowed. By raising wages some unions have decreased employment in their industries. Those displaced from the high-wage industries are subsequently added to the pool of those seeking employment and consequently wages in the non-organized sector are forced down due to the added competition for remaining jobs.

Furthermore, unions have had at least some effect in terms of creating inflation. While having little impact on the unionized sector due to strong collective bargaining and cost of living arrangements, inflation has taken a great toll from the real incomes of those working in the unorganized unprotected sectors. Consequently, in this sense, unions in America have a long standing debt to the unorganized. Using their resources the trade union movement is in the position to pay that debt and raise the working poor from their miserable existence. Trade unions must organize the unorganized and aid new unions financially and otherwise in taking on the tasks of organization.

(4) Finally, it must be made clear, that the raising of wages to adequate levels in many present low-wage industries will necessarily entail cutbacks in employment, sometimes of drastic proportions. It thus becomes necessary to assure all those who have worked and would work if jobs were available a guaranteed minimum income provided as a matter of right. Recent discussions of negative income tax proposals and children's allowances must be seen as crucial to the whole matter of the working poor and a solution to the question of poverty in America. If an industry cannot pay an adequate wage, serious thought is necessary as to whether that industry should be permitted to survive at the cost of maintaining its workers at a poverty level. If the industry is crucial, it may be deemed necessary to subsidize it so that it can pay decent wages without decreasing its production. Otherwise such inefficient industries or individual firms within an industry should be forced to meet the minimum standards for wages and working conditions or leave the market. The end result of such a program will be to reduce competition and reduce the repressiveness of the economic environment. It should not be the workers who suffer for the inefficient operation of these sectors or the consequent reduction in employment as they are forced from the market.

In short, our commitment must be to a complete abolition of low wages and to the assurance of an adequate job for all Americans. Furthermore, we must be willing to guarantee a minimum standard of living to those displaced because of frictional alterations in low-wage industries.

The Condition of Farm Workers

Fay Bennett

National Sharecroppers Fund

[Excerpted from the 1963, 1964, 1967 Annual Reports of the National Sharecroppers Fund with permission from the Fund.]

AMERICAN AGRICULTURE ought to be the greatest success story in the whole historical saga of the United States as a land of wealth and opportunity. In 1910, one American farm worker could produce enough food and fiber to meet the needs of seven people. The next half-century saw a continuous rise in the national standard of living, and by 1966 when the average American was consuming a great deal more, a single farm worker could produce enough for nearly 40 persons.

Yet when pockets of poverty in our affluent society are uncovered, the largest single area of distress turns out to be the farm economy. Nearly half of the nation's 3,300,000 farm families have incomes below $3,000. Probably three-fourths of the 800,000 rural families whose chief income is from wages live below the poverty level.

As productivity per worker has soared, two things have happened: First, far fewer workers are needed. Second, the capitalization costs of these technical productive miracles are rising beyond the reach of many present and potential farm owners. Farm workers and working farmers alike are being displaced.

Concentration of Control: Wealth vs. Poverty

There were 5.4 million farms in 1950. These were reduced to 4.8 million in 1954; to 3.7 million in 1959. Between 1959 and 1960 an estimated 370,000 more, involving over a million people, have given up. Two-thirds (about two million) of the families who stayed on their farms earned less than $1,000 a year from both farm and non-farm work.

Only 21.5 percent of U.S. farms have sales of $10,000 or more, which the Department of Agriculture estimates will return a minimum family income of $2,500. But it takes $4,000 "to place the multiperson family above poverty in the American context today," according to the Conference on Economic Progress and other authorities. At the other end, only 2.7 percent of the farms have sales of $40,000 or more. They control 20 percent of all farm land and 14 percent of all cropland harvested, and profit from more than 30 percent of all farm products sold.

Rural Poverty

The poor live everywhere, but an estimated 40 percent of the poverty in the United States is in rural areas, against 30 percent of the total population. In the rural South, 90 percent of the rural Negro poor are clustered in the nation's poorest counties. A continuing stream of people searching for a better life migrate from these areas to the cities. The annual outmigration from agriculture exceeded a million in the 1950-60 decade; it averaged almost 800,000 annually from 1960 to 1965.

About one out of every six Southern farm operators is Negro. Less than one-third own or even rent their own farms; about 40 percent are sharecroppers, and the rest are tenant farmers.

The average size white-operated commercial farm in the South is about 382 acres; the average non-white commercial farm 56 acres. The average value of land and buildings is $37,816 for whites, and $7,328 for non-whites. The average value of products sold is $10,396 for whites and $3,029 for non-whites. Displacement, greater in the South than elsewhere, is proportionately greater among Negro farmers. In the last decade the South has lost half its Negro-operated farms. The number of tenants, both Negro and white, dropped about 45 percent and the number of sharecroppers about 55 percent.

Hunger in America

In May 1967, five doctors toured a six-county area in Mississippi and returned to shock the nation with reports of malnutrition approaching starvation, disease and disability which could have been remedied with earlier help, and children whose lives had been stunted before they were school age. Subsequent investigation by the *National Observer* made clear that the hunger crisis is nationwide, in Iowa as well as Alabama. Efforts were made by the Department of Agriculture to increase the number of areas covered by surplus food distribution programs and the price of food stamps was lowered for the poorest as a result of public reaction; OEO legislation was amended to authorize a special food fund for the hungry, but appropriations are in doubt. The needed effort to rush food free was not forthcoming and when 1967 ended, children were still going hungry.

Housing

More than a million rural homes are dilapidated; many are unsafe and beyond repair. That is 27 percent of all rural dwellings, contrasted with 14 percent in urban areas. In the southern states, only 36.5 percent of farm and 47.2 percent of nonfarm rural dwellings are sound and contain all plumbing facilities. What this means for the majority is a common pump up the road, shared by many families; unsanitary privies, windows without screens, walls and floors with cracks, no central heating. It means bitter cold and constant danger of fire in winter; insect-borne disease the year-round. For farm workers and migrants it may be worse: a duck coop, an automobile, a tent.

Health

Ill health is natural in the context of poor housing, low income, and hunger. Although 30 percent of the population dwell in rural areas, only 12 percent of physicians and 18 percent of nurses are located there. One fourth of the poor have never seen a dentist. The inaccessibility of health and medical care means an additional expense in travel and working time lost for rural people, many of whom cannot afford medical fees at all. Rural people are more apt to have chronic or disabling conditions than urban people. They have a higher rate of injury and accident. Agriculture regularly ranks third among major industries in work-related accidental deaths. Surveys of health conditions among migrants find them worse off. They have, for example, an influenza and pneumonia mortality rate twice as high as the national average. There are estimates of more than 5,000 with untreated tuberculosis, and more than 16,000 expectant mothers who will not have prenatal care. Three fifths of the counties identified as migrant home base or work areas are not yet touched by Migrant Health Act services.

Most of the Poor are White

Although a larger percentage of Negroes live in poverty, a larger number of whites are poor. A recent Department of Agriculture report on *White Americans in Rural Poverty* reveals that of 9.65 million families living in poverty in 1960, 6.1 million lived in nonmetropolitan areas and, even excluding Spanish Americans, 80 percent of them were white. Of all farm families in poverty, 85 percent are white. Even if rural nonfarm population is counted, the figure drops only to about 75 percent. All rural areas have been shortchanged on government benefits including antipoverty programs. But because of their lack of organization, poor whites have benefited even less than poor Negroes from the gains made in recent years.

Education

One reason those who leave the land are apt to find life as dismal in urban ghettos as in rural isolation is the poor level of rural education; they lack the skills needed for employment. In 1960 there were still 700,000 adults in rural areas who had never enrolled in school; 3.1 million with less than five years schooling who are functional illiterates; more than 19 million who had not completed high school. In 1960, more than 2.3 million rural youth left school before graduating, nearly 200,000 of them before they had completed fifth grade. The worst situation is in the deep South states, and the most poorly educated people of all are the outmigrants and their children. Of those 25 and older, about half have not gone beyond eighth grade.

Declining Work Opportunities

The decline in the number of farms in this century has been continuous. In the decade 1950-60 alone, the number dropped from 5.4 million to 3.7 million. A third of those who made their living on the land had to turn elsewhere. The decline in the number of hired workers tells a different story. While their number dropped from 3.4 million in 1910 to 1.8 in 1962, their role in the total farm work force rose from 24.9 to 27.3 percent, as independent farmers, tenants, and sharecroppers became hired workers on the large corporate farms that have developed.

The number of migrants is never known with exactness, but it is declining each year. The official 1962 estimate (probably much too low) was about 380,000, plus half that many foreign contract workers. Somewhere between a million and a million and a half people still follow the crops each year.

Mechanization and Unemployment

The greatest decline in work opportunities is still in cotton. It is hard to distinguish between underemployment and unemployment, but the manpower of between one-quarter and one-half million persons is being replaced. In cotton, as in many other crops, this is due not only to the mechanization of harvesting, the time when the peak number of workers is used. It also includes use of chemicals and other agents (such as geese) to destroy weeds; this cuts off work in another part of the year.

The very size and shape of our fruits and vegetables is under continuous adaptation to meet the needs of the developing harvest machines. The list seems endless. Cranberries are now 95 percent mechanized and so are snap beans in most states. Tomatoes and cucumbers are two or three years away from complete mechanization. An electric fan which blows grapefruit from trees was 99 percent successful in tests; if leaf damage does not hurt next year's crop, grapefruit will be almost entirely mechanically picked within two years. In every part of the country and in nearly every crop, the advance is steady.

Each change eliminates some farm jobs. In 1962, 271,000 farm workers reported their major occupation as "unemployment." Many of these displaced workers are settling in sprawling rural fringes of the cities to seek nonfarm work which becomes more scarce all the time. The number of unskilled jobs in the national economy is steadily declining, and farm workers have less of the educational qualifications necessary for acquiring new skills than any other group in the country. The median years of school completed by male farm workers 18 years and older was 7.7 in 1959, not significantly more than the 7.6 it had been twenty years before. Of adult migrants 25 years and older, 34 percent have had less than five years' schooling, and their children are repeating the cycle.

Hired Farm Workers

Nearly 2.8 million people worked on farms for cash wages during 1966, the last year for which full records are available. This represented a decline of 11.7 percent from 1965. Casual laborers, who worked less than 25 days, numbered about 1.1 million and noncasual workers about 1.6 million. Of these, 32 percent were young people 14 to 17 years of age, nearly three fourths of them boys. Nearly half (47 percent) of the total lived in the South, 8 percent in the Northeast, 19 percent in Northcentral states, and 26 percent in the West. The total number of foreign workers was 23,600, up 100 from the preceding year, with about 12,000 of them working at peak employment periods. Half the nation's farmers do not hire any workers at all, and 89 percent of all expenditures for hired labor in 1964 were on the 29 percent of farms that sold products valued at $10,000 or more.

Income

For an average 85 days of farm work, hired farm workers earned $731 in cash wages in 1966. The 1.6 million noncasual workers average 138 days and earned $1,188. The 1.1 million casual workers averaged 63 days of work and earned $521. Domestic migratory workers averaged 121 days of work and earned $1,307. About 1.7 million people did farm work only; they averaged 104 days' work and earned $894. Those who were employed at both farm and nonfarm work averaged 109 days of nonfarm and 55 days of farm work with average earnings of $1,880.

Productivity

One farm worker can now supply the food and fiber needs of 40 persons, compared with 23 in 1957-59. Between 1965 and 1966, output per manhour rose 4.7 percent for the farm sector as against 2.4 for the nonfarm sector of the economy. Mechanization and the use of chemicals continued to increase, and experiments continue, for instance, to develop square tomatoes and to increase the "dropability" of citrus fruit by Vitamin C injections.

Migrant Children

The most neglected children of America, it was reported at April 1963, hearings on farm workers legislation, are those 50,000 migrant children who are six years old and less. Too young to work in the fields (although some are so employed at the age of 5 or 6), they are either left locked up in the shack that serves as home, perhaps in the care of a scarcely older child, or taken to the fields to sleep in trucks or play in the dust under a blazing sun.

At least another hundred thousand children of school age follow the crops with their parents. The Fair Labor Standards Act provides a 16-year minimum age for their employment in agriculture during school hours but no minimum age outside of school hours. Local crop and harvest "vacations" make it legal to bring them out of the classroom at peak seasons. Yet the Department of Labor, with limited inspection facilities, found 6,712 children illegally employed in the fields in 1962. Of those who were migrants, 72 percent were below their normal school grade.

Eighty percent of the migrant family heads reported in 1966 that no children under 14 traveled with them; 20 percent reported that a total of 140,000 children did. An estimated 50,000 are on the road between October and May when other children are in school, and larger numbers miss school time at the beginning and the end of school semesters. Aside from the educational loss and health hazards faced by these children, they, like adult workers, suffer a disproportionately large number of work-related accidents. In an 18-month study (1964-65) of work injuries to minors under 18 reported by 28 states, 10.9 percent, or 1,849, were to minors working in agriculture.

The Secretary of Labor, under new authorization from Congress in 1967, now bans minors from some hazardous occupations in agriculture. But children in agriculture still do not have as much protection under the Fair Labor Standards Act as other children.

Organization of Farm Workers

Efforts to unionize farm workers continued in California, Florida, Louisiana, Texas, and some midwestern states, but the United Farm Workers Organizing Committee, AFL-CIO, in California is as yet the only organization strong enough to have made substantial gains. After winning contracts with several wine grape growers, UFWOC turned to Giumarra Vineyards, the country's largest table grape producer, employing 2,500 workers at peak. Giumarra refused to negotiate, and the union launched a nationwide consumer boycott, which still continues early in 1968. UFWOC activity in Texas was concentrated in Starr County, home of thousands of migrants. This effort brought organized opposition including arrests and judicial repression; and violence against the strikers by Texas Rangers aroused national concern. Repeated spontaneous strike action in Florida indicated strong desire by workers there for unionization. Obreros Unidos was organized in Wisconsin, chiefly among Texas migrants, and Michigan and Ohio also saw organizing activities.

Legislation

Securing coverage for farm workers under the National Labor Relations Act was the prime concern in 1967; the pending bills, S.8 and H.R. 4769, are expected to be reported favorably to the floor in both houses during the 1968 session, and strong public support will be needed to win final passage of this measure. Other pending legislation needing public support provides for coverage of farm workers under unemployment compensation and further restriction of child labor in agriculture under the Fair Labor Standards Act.

Cooperative Developments

Poor farmers are finding that their newly organized co-ops are mutually beneficial and new co-ops are being developed. But they face many problems: lack of funds for hiring trained management; lack of programs to train co-op members and boards for their roles in the co-ops; and sometimes local opposition. Yet despite the problems, the co-ops progress. South West Alabama Farmers Cooperative Association (SWAFCA), a ten-county, 1,000-member farmer co-op, marketed one million pounds of produce during the first year. A three-county co-op was organized in South Carolina and expects to serve at least 500 members, including small farmers in neighboring counties. The Southern Cooperative Development Program, organized by the low-income co-ops, received foundation support to hire community organizers to assist co-ops in four states and to train their management and board members. The Southern Federation of Cooperatives, an alliance of these low-income co-ops in the South, continued to grow and provide more services to its members. In addition, the co-op movement spread from the farms to industry, and the poor organized garment factory co-ops in Georgia and Alabama.

Government Programs

Farmers Home Administration. More than 3.2 million rural people were aided by credit from the Farmers Home Administration during fiscal 1967. Economic opportunity loans totaled $32.2 million and benefited 16,453 low-income rural families and 382 cooperatives serving low-income people. $300.3 million were borrowed by 64,946 family farmers to improve farming operations and finance operating costs, and $260 million in farm ownership loans went to 13,987 borrowers. A total of $442.1 million for housing construction and improvement included $6.5 million for farm labor housing and $19 million for senior citizen projects. Although funds for the poor continue to increase annually, they are still only a small fraction of FHA commitments. The 10 percent across-the-board budgetary cut in funds for 1968 made at the President's request will hurt the rural poor disproportionately.

Extension Service. In the deep south states, the Cooperative (state-federal) Extension Service's potential aid to poor farmers and rural people has been greatly handicapped by continuing discriminatory policies. A 1966 report of the Georgia Advisory Commission indicated that compliance with the Civil Rights Act there was more formal than actual. Segregation had been technically eliminated in lines of supervision and work, with staff located in the same building. But Negro agents had separate offices and were confined mostly to working with Negro clientele. Most were assigned to "work with low-income groups" although there was no job description and no program to match, and no whites were assigned to this category. Of 130 professional workers only 7 were Negro, none with the same title as a white. This pattern is duplicated in other states.

Office of Economic Opportunity. Rural areas received an average 32 percent of OEO funds in fiscal 1967. By programs, the rural share breaks down: Neighborhood Youth Corps, $113 million, 34 percent;

Job Corps, $84 million, 40 percent; Operation Mainstream (the Nelson Amendment), $23 million, 100 percent; Title V Work Experience, $30 million, 30 percent, VISTA, $13 million, 52 percent. Rural areas received $207 million, or 27 percent, for Title II Community Action Programs for fiscal 1967. Title III's specifically rural funds totaled $65 million, including $33 million for migrant programs and $24 million for rural loans. The National Advisory Commission on Rural Poverty has commented that the 40 percent of the nation's poor in rural areas need more than 40 percent of the funds because of the higher average cost of serving people in low-population density areas, yet they are still receiving less than one third of the funds available.

Welfare and Social Security. Although nearly half the estimated U.S. poverty—urban and rural—is in the southern states, public assistance payments there run less than one fourth of total U.S. payments. All the southern states are among the 21 that are forfeiting $106 million a year available in federal payments to dependent children because they will not pay enough to raise the combined (state and federal) minimum to $32 a month. Federal payments are related to state per capita income and form the largest share of payments in all southern states. For instance, of the Mississippi $9.30 per month per child, $1.55 is state money and $7.75 is federal; if the payment were $32, the federal share would be $24.10. Mississippi is at present losing $18.1 million a year in potential federal funds for children. Restrictive legislation and administrative actions that keep poor people from public assistance to which they are entitled are being challenged increasingly in the courts. Residence requirements have been ruled unconstitutional in several lower courts. Removal from welfare because of the birth of an illegitimate child has been challenged successfully in Alabama; "substitute father" (another man in house) and "available work" restrictions are also under legal attack.

A government analysis released in April 1967, showed that less than 1 percent of the 7.3 million Americans on public welfare (only about 50,000) would be capable of supporting themselves if they could find jobs. Of the 7.3 million total, 2.1 million, mostly women, are 65 or older, with a median age of 72; 700,000 are blind or otherwise severely handicapped; 3.5 million are children whose parents cannot support them. The remaining million are parents of those children, about 900,000 mothers and 150,000 fathers; of the 150,000 two-thirds are incapacitated. Local surveys have shown repeatedly that many who should be receiving assistance are not; and that the rate of assistance is below the poverty level and often below the state's own subsistence standard. For instance, the Alabama standard of living for a single adult living alone under the Old Age Assistance program is $124.85 a month; but payment in the state is a maximum of $82, 66 percent of the minimal.

Subsidies. It is now admitted that the major beneficiaries of the agricultural subsidy policy have been the large producers. Senate hearings on Department of Agriculture appropriations in 1967 revealed that as much as $2.8 million was paid to a single farm in 1966 and that nine farms each received more than $1 million in benefits. A report prepared for the National Advisory Commission on Rural Poverty studied the distribution of benefits of the various farm commodity programs for selected years since 1960 and found that

> the 10 percent of rice producers with the smallest payments received only 0.1 percent ($1 in every $1,000) of rice program benefits. The 10 percent with the largest payments received 48 percent of the total. In wheat, the comparable figures were 1.5 percent to the 10 percent at the bottom and 44 percent to the 10 percent at the top. In cotton it was less than 1 percent contrasted with 50 percent (and the top 1 percent received 21 percent of the benefits); and in sugar cane, 0.4 percent contrasted with nearly 75 percent.

Despite increasing public awareness of the problem of poverty in America, the needs of the sharecropper, the small farmer, the migrant, and other farm workers and low-income rural people continue to be neglected. The job of speaking out for them remains urgent.

Selected Bibliography

1. Alan B. Batchelder. "Decline in the Relative Income of Negro Men," *Quarterly Journal of Economics*, August 1964.

2. A. A. Berle. *American Economic Republic*. New York: Harcourt, Brace and World, 1963.

3. Herman D. Bloch. "Some Effects of Discrimination in Employment," *American Journal of Economics and Sociology*, 25 (January 1966).

4. Conference on Economic Progress. *The Toll of Rising Interest Rates: The One Great Waste in the Federal Budget*. Washington: The Conference, 1964.

5. Alan Haber, "The American Underclass," *Poverty and Human Resources Abstracts*. Vol. II, No. 3, pp. 5-19.

6. Dale L. Hiestand. *Economic Growth and Employment Opportunities for Minorities*. New York: Columbia University Press, 1964.

7. Herbert Hill. "Racial Inequality in Employment: The Patterns of Discrimination," *Annals of the American Academy of Political and Social Science*, February, 1965.

8. Paul Jacobs. *Prelude to Riot*. New York: Random House, 1968.

9. Gabriel Kolko. *Wealth and Power in America: An Analysis of Social Class and Income Distribution*. New York: Praeger, 1962.

10. Herbert Krosney. *Beyond Welfare: Poverty in the Supercity*. New York: Holt, Rinehart and Winston, 1966.

11. Robert J. Lampman. *How Much Does the American System of Transfers Benefit the Poor?* Madison: Institute for Research on Poverty, University of Wisconsin, 1966.

12. Ray Marshall. *The Negro and Organized Labor*. New York: John Wiley and Sons, 1965.

13. Donald Michael. *Cybernation: The Silent Conquest*. Santa Barbara: Center for the Study of Democratic Institutions, 1962.

14. S. M. Miller. "The Politics of Poverty," *Dissent*, Spring, 1964.

15. Gunnar Myrdal. *Challenge to Affluence*. New York: Pantheon, 1962.

16. Bernard Nossiter. *The Mythmakers: An Essay in Power and Wealth*. Boston: Houghton-Mifflin, 1964.

17. *Nation's Manpower Revolution*. Hearings Before the Subcommittee on Manpower and Employment of the Committee on Labor and Public Welfare, United States Senate, Pts. I–X and Subcommittee Report, 1963–64.

18. National Advisory Committee on Farm Labor. *Agribusiness and Its Workers*. New York: The Committee, 1964.

19. Arthur M. Ross. *Unemployment and the American Economy*. New York: Wiley, 1964.

20. Tax Foundation. *Allocation of the Tax Burden by Income Class*. New York: The Foundation, 1960.

21. Richard M. Titmuss, *Income Distribution and Social Change*. London: George Allen and Unwin, 1962.

22. Don Villarejo. "Stock Ownership and Control of American Corporations," *New University Thought*, Pts. I, II, III, 1961.

23. Arnold R. Weber. "The Rich and the Poor: Employment in An Age of Automation," *Social Service Review*, 37 (September, 1963).

24. William Appelman Williams. *The Great Evasion*. Chicago: Quadrangle Press, 1964.

25. Carl Wittman and Tom Hayden. *An Interracial Movement of the Poor.* Ann Arbor, Mich.: Economic Research and Action Project, 1964.

Chapter 4

Sustaining Conditions of Poverty

There remains an unseen America, a land of limited opportunity and restricted choice. In it live nearly 10 million families who try to find shelter, feed and clothe their children, stave off disease and malnutrition, and somehow build a better life on less than $60 a week. Almost two-thirds of these families struggle to get along on less than $40 a week.

These are the people behind the American looking glass. There are nearly 35 million of them. Being poor is not a choice for these millions; it is a rigid way of life. It is handed down from generation to generation in a cycle of inadequate education, inadequate homes, inadequate jobs, and stunted ambitions. It is a peculiar axiom of poverty that the poor are poor because they earn little, and they also earn little because they are poor. For the rebel who seeks a way out of this closed cycle, there is little help. The communities of the poor generally have the poorest schools, the scarcest opportunities for training. The poor citizen lacks organization, endures sometimes arbitrary impingement on his rights by courts and law enforcement agencies; cannot make his protest heard or has stopped protesting. A spirit of defeatism often pervades his life and remains the only legacy for his children.

If the American economy can be compared to a 20-story luxury apartment house where even the ground floor tenants share the comforts, then this one-fifth of our population inhabits a sub-basement, out of sight, and almost out of mind.

—From "The War on Poverty," A Congressional Presentation, March 17, 1964, prepared under the direction of Sargent Shriver, special assistant to the President.

THE POOR ARE CAUGHT UP in what Alvin Schorr, in *Slums and Social Insecurity,* has called "a syndrome of mutually reinforcing handicaps." On a day-to-day basis a poor person faces a vicious cycle of disabling circumstances in the way social and economic institutions are conceived, developed, and operated.

By the sustaining conditions of poverty, we are referring to the institutional structures and social relationships in American society that prevent the poor from gaining access to adequate financial resources and social rewards. There are at least five such factors in our society that act to sustain poverty: (1) ecological and demographic trends; (2) the limited opportunity structure for the poor; (3) patterns of racial discrimination; (4) deficiencies in community resources for the poor; and (5) agency-client relationships.

One: Ecological and Demographic Trends

One of the most pronounced trends in the last twenty years has been the "suburban drift." The affluent have fled the cities in ever greater numbers to live in the suburbs. The results of this movement have been deeply felt by the poor who remain in the core of urban areas. First, a reduced tax base limits the educational investment of the community. Deteriorated school facilities, inadequate supplies, ill-equipped or unqualified teaching staffs handicap the children who need special educational resources.

The spatial ghettoization of the poor is a second consequence of this suburban drift. Indeed, the poor may be so physically and socially distant that for all practical purposes they are invisible. Their social participation patterns are sharply limited. Their children grow up in a social environment lacking the educational, recreational, and social advantages offered to children of higher income families.

Urban renewal patterns also help reinforce the financial problems of the poor. Slum clearance programs have replaced the slum dwellings of the poor with higher-cost housing which low-income families can't afford. The poor are concentrated in ever-shrinking land areas of slum housing. Urban renewal may also mean an uprooting of the poverty-stricken from their familiar social and physical environment into new neighborhoods among strangers where housing may be more expensive and where living conditions may be more crowded and disorganized than ever before.

Two: the Opportunity Structure for the Poor

Poverty is also sustained by a limited opportunity structure for those persons who have inadequate incomes. The undereducated, the underskilled, the Negro and the aged worker are at a competitive disadvantage in the labor market. They must accept the job opportunities that have been rejected by others—unstable, low-paying work which is generally unprotected by the institutional safeguards of better paying jobs. Many of these jobs are economically exploitive; some of them easily lend themselves to mechanization or automation with the result that even this meager opportunity structure for the marginal worker in low-paid employment is shrinking, making predictability in economic and social life difficult, if not impossible.

Three: Patterns of Racial Discrimination

About twenty-five percent of the poverty-stricken are members of minority groups. Their exclusion from the economic and social opportunities of the society needs no documentation. The Negro, for example, may be denied entrance to the job, or training for the job, or residence in an area where jobs are available. The opening of new plants with job opportunities in a suburban area does the Negro, or Spanish-American, or Puerto Rican little good if he is residentially chained to the center city ghetto where travel to a distant job involves heavy costs in transportation time and money. The perseverance of these patterns of discriminatory practices reinforces the poverty of the minority group member and hampers his movement toward full participation in the society.

Four: Deficiencies in Community Resources for the Poor

The poor are not only deficient in money, but also in obtaining the special resources of the community. This process is most strikingly seen in their lack of access to adequate medical care, housing, credit, and legal aid.

Health: United States National Health Survey statistics have shown that the poor get sick more frequently, take longer to recover, seek and receive less medical, dental, and hospital treatment, and suffer far more disabling consequences than persons with higher incomes. One reason is that persons with incomes under $4,000 spend half as much money on medical care than those in the higher income brackets. Yet, four times the number of people in the lower income group find their major activities limited by chronic ailments than do persons with family incomes over $7,000.

The poor can't afford adequate health protection. Only one-third of families with incomes under $2,000 have health insurance compared with three-quarters of all American families. The hospitalization rate for poor Negroes is twenty times lower than for the population as a whole. Unequal access to medical care is reflected in the higher morbidity and mortality rates in low-income states and in low-income neighborhoods of major cities. For example, one-third of the pregnant women in cities with populations over 100,000 are medically indigent, a 1962 United States Health, Education and Welfare study revealed. Increasing numbers receive little or no prenatal care although prenatal care is a major preventable cause of premature births and mental retardation. Reflecting the high concentration of poverty, four times as many Negro as white women die in childbirth.

Recent studies have also shown that mental illness is often a product of the strains and stresses of poverty. Robert E. Clark found in 1949 that unskilled and semi-skilled workers were six times more likely to be hospitalized for psychoses than professional or managerial personnel. In *Social Class and Mental Illness* (New York: John Wiley & Sons, Inc., 1958), Hollingshead and Redlich found that three times as many persons in the poorest group studied in New Haven, Connecticut, had psychiatric illnesses than did persons in upper income groups. Yet three times as much money had been spent on the mentally ill at the top of the income ladder than on those at the bottom rung.

Overcrowded and inefficient public clinics, vast and impersonal city hospitals, understaffed and overpopulated mental institutions—all of these compound the suffering of the low-income ill. Having the breadwinner become sick or disabled is a tragedy in any family, but for the poor, unprotected by savings and medical insurance, it may be a disaster.

Housing: Lack of access to good housing also sustains poverty. In *The Other America*, Michael Harrington has written, "The slum, with its dense life, hammers away at the individual. . . . It is as if human beings dilapidate along with the tenements in which they live." Rentals for slum housing are frequently higher than the rent paid by higher income groups for better housing. But beyond that, better housing may be closed to the poor because of discrimination—racial discrimination against non-whites and, in addition, social discrimination against the life styles of the poor, black or white.

Slum housing problems are also aggravated by the problems of absentee ownership. The slum landlord reaps a high return on his property due to the high demand for his facilities and his low investment in maintaining even adequate living conditions. Few of the poor ever get to see the owners of their homes; the insensitivity of the rental agent to their problems is widely known.

The poor may pay for their housing by sacrificing quality and accepting minimum living standards, or by living with other family units to extend their housing budgets, or by borrowing money from other budget items. The end result is the same: the development of a complex web that makes it increasingly difficult for the poor to leave not only the slums, but the complex net of poverty in which they are caught.

Credit: Failure to gain access to reliable commercial credit sources may also keep the poor in a state of financial crisis. In the area of purchasing power, people with inadequate incomes face formidable obstacles in getting even normal value out of the little money they have. They become poorer for the ironic reason that they don't have enough money.

Lacking the ready cash to shop at discount stores, and lacking the stable employment records to open charge accounts at large downtown stores, most low-income families buy their durables from neighborhood dealers and door-to-door peddlers. These merchants frequently cover their risk of extending credit to low-income families by exorbitant markups on low-quality merchandise.

Dependent on credit, lacking shopping sophistication, the poor are more vulnerable to high pressure salesmen who attempt to convert them from cash to credit customers. Their shopping difficulties are compounded by other merchandising practices: bait advertising, erroneous information about costs or credit charges, faulty or repossessed merchandise sold to them as new. As a result, many low-income families encounter serious consumer difficulties: legal pressures because of missed payments, repossession of goods, garnishment of salary or threats of garnishment. Their heavy credit obligations may reach crisis proportions when their income is suddenly reduced through unemployment or ill health. Certainly, the failure to establish reliable commercial credit prevents the poverty-stricken from obtaining adequate goods and services.

Legal aid: The poor are also disadvantaged in their access to legal services. As United States Attorney General Nicholas Katzenbach stated in a recent government conference on legal aid for the poor, "For a poor person to hold rights in theory satisfies only the theory. . . . Unknown, unasserted rights are no rights at all."

Yet from the attitude of the corner policeman to the institutional maze of legal technicalities and details, the poor face a network of legal problems which frequently leads to unequal protection of their individual freedom, curtailment of their social entitlements, and unequal access to the protection of law. Lack of knowledge of their legal prerogatives and lack of legal aid compound their legal problems. In turn, this increases their vulnerability to fines, garnishments, jailings, and other sanctions of the law which further reduces their income through suspensions, firings, and even blacklisting from the chances of getting a steady job.

Thousands whose public assistance is revoked or reduced have no ideas of their legal rights of appeal. Large numbers must honor contract obligations with finance companies even though the merchandise for which they pay has never been delivered or fails to work. Many have their purchases repossessed after months of payment with no idea that they are entitled to get their equity returned.

It has been pointed out that there are two legal systems in family law—one for those with money, and one for those without. A poor person who applies to a legal aid society for help in obtaining a divorce must frequently follow the agency's prescribed procedures to attempt a marital reconciliation. Persons who have money may just hire a lawyer and get a divorce.

Professor Monroe G. Paulsen of Columbia University Law School told a recent government conference on legal aid to the poor, "It seems rather too bad to require something of indigents that is not required of those with means. . . . This kind of notion, I believe, runs through a great many of the legal institutions which the poor must use. . . . To me, however, it is an unhappy thought because it contributes to what I believe to be one of the most difficult aspects of dealing with poverty: the existence of an attitude on the part of the poor that they are clients rather than citizens, an attitude unhappily reflected in the minds of many who deal with them."

Thus there are many deficiencies in access to community services. The very access that the higher income groups take for granted may involve either a closed door or a long wait for the poor. Invariably, the poor may have to accept inferior substitutes for these services, or go without.

Five: Agency-Client Relationships

The poverty-stricken are related to the society through a network of contacts with social agencies that offer specialized services to the poor (e.g., child care centers, family service agencies, legal aid societies, and public welfare agencies). There are two apparent handicaps to these agency-client relationships which block avenues of aid to the poor in their efforts to cope with problems of poverty. First, inadequate financial resources and personnel limit the amount of resources an agency can offer to its clients. Social work agencies compete with a network of other interest groups for a share of the charity dollar. All too often, the formula for distributing community charity money is outdated; frequently, agencies that are *relatively* unimportant in poverty reduction obtain the lion's share of community financial resources. In addition, the resources needed to meet the complex and heterogeneous needs of the poverty problem are not easily understood. The result is that funding for agency services to the poor tends to fall short of that needed for adequate personnel and programs.

A second handicap to good agency-client relationships is the pessimism and bureaucratic rigidity that overwhelms many of these social agencies. For example, the case worker in a welfare agency is frequently overworked, underpaid, and undertrained. His case load, which may range from two hundred to three hundred clients, may include a mixture of the indigent, the aged, ADC mothers, and special problem cases. As a result, the agency may indirectly foster the development of *structured dependency* from their clients. Activities of the poor may be controlled and monitored for more efficient record-keeping purposes and these efforts may take precedence over other service and rehabilitation activities that could help the client to more effectively handle his problems. In such a climate, the client is intentionally or unintentionally encouraged to be dependent on the agency worker and to accept his judgment of the situation. Consequently, the poor may develop an attitude of pessimism or even hostility to the agency worker who may come to symbolize his frustrations and bitterness rather than to represent an avenue of help or the alleviation of basic problems.

These, then, are some of the major sustaining causes of poverty. There are others that could be briefly mentioned: the lag that inevitably occurs between the social needs of the poor and the legislation that develops to serve these needs; the lack of socially developed mechanisms to provide services to families or individuals making the transition from rural to urban areas; and finally, the perseverance of old social, economic, and educational institutions in the face of change. An elimination of the sustaining conditions of poverty will require a critical self-examination of American life, particularly those institutional structures and social relationships that directly and indirectly affect the poor.

In this chapter Cloward and Elman explore the defaults of the society in safeguarding the rights of the poor and some of the difficulties low-income persons meet in their relationships with welfare agencies. David Caplovitz describes the many consumer problems faced by low-income customers in dealing with the marketing system in poverty neighborhoods. The relationship between housing codes, taxes, and substandard housing is analyzed by Alvin L. Schorr, who also discusses the public and private dimensions of how the poor pay for their housing. Major urban school issues and some suggestions for their possible solution are reviewed by Patricia C. Sexton. Finally, the problems of rural schooling, health, and housing are highlighted in this excerpt from the President's Commission on Rural Poverty report.

Social Justice for the Poor

Richard A. Cloward and Richard M. Elman

Columbia University School of Social Work

[Excerpted with permission from the articles "An Ombudsman for the Poor?" and "How Rights Can Be Secured," The Nation, February 28, 1966, pp. 230-35, and March 7, 1966, pp. 264-68.]

AMERICANS THINK of justice primarily in connection with agencies of law enforcement, for such agencies have drastic powers, even over life itself. But at a time when the United States Supreme Court is upholding the right to counsel in criminal proceedings of all kinds and otherwise curbing infringements of individual liberties by law-enforcement agencies, it needs to be said that many other government agencies have only slightly less drastic powers, especially over low-income people. It is no small matter that a person may be arbitrarily defined as ineligible for public relief, no small matter that he may be arbitrarily evicted from a public-housing project. There are few institutionalized safeguards against the potentially unjust exercise of power by governmental "poor agencies," and virtually no place where low-income people can turn for assistance in availing themselves of the channels of redress that do exist.

In America, we continue to define poverty as resulting from all manner of personal devils which must be exorcised with commensurate autos-da-fé. England, by contrast, has moved far beyond the Elizabethan "poor-law" concepts which still dominate much of America's orientation toward the impoverished. Our welfare state is accordingly characterized by a lawlessness, a discrimination by class and race, a disregard for human rights and dignity, and a niggardliness that are recurrent, often routine, if not institutionalized. And if our social-welfare system is regularly unjust, it is because American public opinion about the poor makes it so.

There is a plethora of evidence to support this view. For one thing, America spends as small a proportion of its tax dollar on social-welfare programs as any other major social-welfare nation in the West; furthermore, if the changing value of the dollar is taken into account, we spend little more now than two decades ago. For another, the notion that our welfare programs are chiefly for the poor is a persisting fiction. In fact, most of the economic innovations of the last few decades have not substantially aided those for whom poverty is a desperate and constant condition. Social security payments, for example, mostly benefit working-class persons, and not all of them at that.

The regularly unemployed poor have not, to cite another example, gotten unemployment compensation, for one must have been employed to become eligible. Although this measure may protect a good many working-class people from the worst consequences of unemployment (at least temporarily), it is no great boon to the unemployable or the chronically unemployed. In retrospect, it seems fair to say that the chief function of this benefit is to enable the temporarily unemployed person to avoid the "means" or "poverty" test required of the chronically poor, who struggle daily to establish and maintain eligibility for the dole. Unlike the applicant for public assistance, who is obliged to divest himself of many assets while on relief, the working-class person can obtain economic benefits without having his insurance, savings and automobile attached. Working-class groups have not only increased their share in the fruits of the institution of private property through union organization; they have also understood the necessity of finding ways to secure themselves against such tides of economic misfortune as might thrust them back. The programs of the welfare state are one among many mechanisms by which these groups insure the continuity of their status.

Legislation for the poor, by contrast, makes benefits available to as few as possible, and then only under the most trying and degrading conditions. The New Deal established a huge public-welfare program under federal-state-local auspices, but great numbers of our poorest citizens are even now systematically excluded. Every state in the Union has passed laws withholding public-welfare benefits from persons not residents in the state for some specified period of time. In Michigan, for example, some public benefits are available only to people who have lived in the state for five of the nine years preceding application. For decades, residency provisions have penalized the poorest elements in the society, especially rural migrants within our borders and those crossing from Puerto Rico. Efforts to repeal these laws have been stubbornly resisted. New York—perhaps the most liberal state and certainly one of the wealthiest—has barely resisted the temptation to promulgate a more stringent residence law: such legislation has actually reached the governor during the past decade but was vetoed.

Residence laws probably violate the constitutional right to cross state boundaries without penalty. They are not the only examples of legislation governing "poor agencies" which are of questionable constitutionality. Issues of "equal protection" are constantly posed in the welfare structure. One is the requirement that self-supporting relatives (who already pay income taxes to support social-welfare programs) be taxed again to support their indigent kin. "Relative-responsibility" laws have been successfully reversed in some state courts, under the "equal-protection" clause of the Constitution, but no cases have yet reached the federal courts where more binding precedents could be established.

Efforts to secure liberalizing legislation founder much of the time, for powerful groups across the country are working to make the social-welfare apparatus even worse. At various times, it has been proposed that desertion be declared a federal offense if a family is receiving public assistance, that sterilization of welfare recipients who continue to bear illegitimate children be made mandatory, and that conviction for a felony be made grounds to deny any form of assistance. Even at a time when many wonder whether automation will not throw huge numbers into enforced idleness, programs of work relief which verge on peonage are continually being put forth. Although many of these proposals never pass into law, a good many do. A number of states, for example, have ceilings on public-welfare grants to penalize large families, ostensibly to depress the birth rate among the poor. In two states, Nebraska and Iowa, courts have declared these laws to be violations of "equal protection" on the ground that the child in a large family needs to eat as much as the child in a small family.

That the legislative framework of our social-welfare system is becoming more humane is, therefore, open to debate. Gains can be pointed to, but there are setbacks; and it must be recognized that some of the most regressive legislation has been passed in recent years. In the late fifties and early sixties, for example, a number of states passed "suitable-home laws" in response to public outrage over disclosures of high rates of illegitimacy on public-welfare case loads. Louisiana passed a law that any woman who had had illegitimate children while on welfare could be denied further aid, and more than 20,000 mothers and children were immediately struck from the rolls. Other legislatures, as in Florida, gave mothers a choice: surrender your illegitimate children for placement (i.e., institutionalization) or be dropped from the rolls. Thousands of mothers elected to give up assistance rather than their children, and the Florida Department of Welfare, calculating to the second decimal place the millions saved, put itself before the public in subsequent annual reports as a model of administrative efficiency and moral virtue. But in Michigan, where a similar law was passed, mothers who chose to leave the rolls found that the state was determined to get their children anyway: after living for a few months in absolute poverty, they were brought into court on charges of physical neglect, and the children were forcibly removed from their homes.

A characteristic of our welfare state is that administrative practice is almost always worse than statute. Broad grants of discretion in doling out benefits are given to administrators because there is no consensus at the legislative level concerning concepts of social welfare. Some measure of discretion is inevitable for no set of statutes can provide firm guidelines for all the varied circumstances that will be presented for decision. Legislators assume that those who carry out the laws will be reasonable and prudent men, possessed of common sense if not of the uncommon sense to divine the intent of vague and ambiguous statutes. But in areas as controversial as social welfare, the language of statutes may be purposely vague, since greater specificity would reveal more sharply the differences among contending political groups and would thereby foreclose the possibility of any legislation at all. The task of explicating the statutes then falls upon the welfare bureaucracies, so that the political struggle shifts from the legislature to the arenas of administration.

The struggle to control the discretion of the administrator is, for the low-income person, an unequal one. Those he confronts are organized and powerful, whether taxpayers' associations, newspapers, civic groups, professional societies or political actors. They have the resources to maintain constant watch over agency practices, the knowledge to frame issues and put forward policies, and the power to influence and activate sectors of the populace in behalf of these policies. Lacking comparable weapons, the low-income person is merely a refugee from a battle that alternately rages and dies down, shifting from one area of his existence to another. Whether the field of battle is his morals (if in public housing), or his willingness to work (if on public welfare), he is its victim.

Housing for the poor is an instructive case in the operation of administrative discretion. Faced with far more applicants than can be accommodated, housing officials have had to make choices. In the process they have come to be only incidentally concerned about the need of applicants. They have established elaborate screening techniques to rebuff the unworthy, what ever their need, thereby erecting defenses against the continual charge that public moneys are being used to subsidize immorality. Applicants can thus be rejected (and quite regularly are) if they have illegitimate or retarded children, have been separated from a spouse two or more times, are alcoholic, or display what is defined as obnoxious behavior at the application interview. Families on welfare with illegitimate children are shunned—a curious policy by which eligibility for one meager public benefit disqualifies a family for another. And so it is that agencies established to dispense money and other material benefits become guardians of public morality.

But the chief characteristic of public agencies serving the poor is not the punitive use of lawful discretion: it is the exercise of unlawful discretion—the promulgation of administrative rules and procedures which undoubtedly violate either constitutional provisions or the immediate statutes governing departments. No more vivid evidence can be cited of the enormous impact of political pressures upon these agencies. The most flagrant example in a history of flagrant abuses is the "after-midnight raid" on ADC mothers—an unannounced visit, without benefit of warrant, in which a home is searched for male attire that might be taken as evidence that a man (whether husband or not) is available and presumably capable of providing support, or for some suggestion of immoral activities or child neglect, any of which might justify terminating benefits. (During the past summer, candidates for office in Nassau County—both the Democrat and the Republican-Liberal—asserted the right of the district attorney's office to make such raids; the Conservative candidate denounced the practice.) These actions surely violate constitutional prohibitions against illegal search and seizure. They are, nevertheless, conducted by virtually every welfare department in the country. When an Oakland, Calif., welfare worker refused to take part in a raid in January, 1962, he was dismissed for insubordination, and is now suing for reinstatement through the appeals courts of that state. At one stage of the proceedings, the state argued that people taking public assistance waive certain rights, not the least being the right to privacy.

Another instance of lawless discretion is revealed in the way relative-responsibility statutes are applied (assuming for the moment that they are constitutional). Laws in each state designate the categories of relatives who are to be considered responsible, but administrators expand on legislative intent by instructing staff to seek out additional categories of relatives (and even friends) as potential "financial resources." When such sources of support are located, the applicant may be denied assistance, or his grant may be arbitrarily reduced by an amount presumed to be available elsewhere.

Or consider the administration of New York's "welfare-abuses law," passage of which followed hard on the Newburgh controversy. This statute, a residency law, provides that a person may be denied benefits *only* if it can be shown that he came into the state for the express purpose of securing them. It stipulates that the burden of proof is on the local welfare department, and that emergency relief must be granted pending a factual determination on the issue of motive. As a practical matter, however, the mere fact that an applicant is from out of state is often taken as prima facie evidence of intent to collect welfare. Many thousands of families have been illegally disqualified since passage of the law in 1962.

But administrative lawlessness is not limited to matters of initial eligibility for benefits. Once on the welfare rolls, recipients in need of special grants of many kinds—for winter clothing, furniture, apartment security, for example—frequently fail to secure them. There are at least three reasons. The law states that requests for all grants must be investigated, frequently by a home visit, and overburdened departments cannot always spare the manpower. In addition, under pressure to conserve funds, departments often ignore requests for special grants. Finally, because of high turnover, public-welfare employees frequently do not themselves know what benefits the applicants are entitled to and how these can be obtained for them. For instance, welfare recipients in New York who live in rat-infested buildings can receive a so-called "rat allowance" to cover the cost of keeping their lights burning all night long; few welfare workers seem to know about special grants of this kind and few clients are told of them. By such practices, welfare clients are routinely deprived of substantial cash entitlements.

In America, then, all faces are turned against the welfare apparatus. Everyone seeks to secure the release of the poor from what is defined as the bondage of "welfare colonialism" or from the psychological entrapment allegedly induced by prolonged dependence on the dole. Only the strategies differ: conservatives would make welfare practices more punitive than they are to deter men from dependency; liberals would lift the poor from dependency by equipping them to become economically competitive. Even the crusade against poverty is a crusade against public welfare; Mr. Shriver has repeatedly stressed that the Office of Economic Opportunity does not sanction "handouts."

Concepts of economic individualism also permeate the civil rights movement. The movement calls upon Americans to strike down historic barriers to individual achievement such that the poor may rise, one by one, into higher economic strata. The Negro is said to want to share in America's wealth on the same idealized terms and by the same idealized means as other groups. Thus consumer boycotts have been organized primarily to enlarge opportunities for the employment of individual Negroes, especially in white-collar positions. Out of deference to this ideology, "compensatory programs" in education and "quotas" in employment have not been pressed hard, for they seem antithetical to a social order based on the theory of open competition and individual merit. This same way of thinking accounts in no small part for the fervor with which so many now embrace the philosophy of the Office of Economic Opportunity—especially as it is symbolized in skills-investment programs like preschool education and youth-employment training. The great mass of poor whose daily lives are controlled by the "poor agencies" thus have neither defenders nor have they organized to defend themselves.

Group conflicts, along both class and racial lines, are deeper the closer one gets to the local community. In recent years, disputes about integration in education, employment and housing have evoked bitter antagonism at the local level, and local officials have been virtually immobilized because of apparently irreconcilable differences among their constituents. By and large, federal perspectives on social welfare have been more liberal; most local practices would be much more punitive were it not for pressures from federal agencies. At a time when the Congress has been passing historic civil rights legislation, state bodies have been passing residence laws and suitable-home laws, not to speak of regressive laws in other categories, which partly reflect growing racial tensions. In New York, mounting pressure for an unqualified residence law stems from the in-migration of both Negroes and Puerto Ricans, for the high proportion of these groups on welfare rolls makes them vulnerable to attack by conservative political interests. As the Negro continues to strike at the roots of historic patterns of class and racial dominance, tensions will undoubtedly mount, and further punitive social-welfare legislation and practices at the local level may result. Professional ideology is rooted in political ideology. Reflecting the values of their culture, American professional groups have not argued for the rights of the poor or for the legitimacy of dependency. Rather they have said that introducing better-trained personnel into the welfare apparatus will eliminate moralistic punitive practices and supplant them by scientific, rehabilitative ones. But whether strategies are puritanical or professional, the poor are still to be lifted from dependency in spite of themselves. Rehabilitative services should, of course, be extended to those who can use them, but submitting to such technical services should not be made a condition for access to economic and other material benefits; and that is how professionals have always seen it. Public housing, for example, now employs many kinds of professionals. If management finds the behavior of a tenant objectionable, he may be required to accept some form of therapy upon pain of eviction. Professionals have thus become new agents in an enveloping fabric of bureaucratic control of the poor and are, if only unwittingly, part of the problem that needs correcting. When an unwed mother makes application for public housing in New York City for herself and her children, to cite a further example, she is routinely referred to what the Housing Authority calls its "social consultation unit." There professionals employ their higher skills to make a determination of her "suitability"—not her need—for residence in a public project. Thus the rights of the poor are jeopardized as much by those who find legitimacy for their practices in the sciences as by those who find it in the scriptures.

The notion that the poor should participate in the decisions affecting their dependency is not novel. In the depression years, the Workers' Alliance—a union of relief clients and relief workers—performed this important function in New York City. The Alliance staged sit-ins at welfare offices, mass demonstrations and letter-writing campaigns, and succeeded in securing improved benefits for its members.

Recently, groups under diverse sponsorships and in scattered localities have begun to organize around welfare issues. In some cases, as in Syracuse or Washington, they have been organized by professional social workers, using OEO funds. In Newark, Cleveland, Detroit, some parts of the South and elsewhere, they have been organized by newly emergent radical groups, principally SNCC and SDS. One would be hard put to describe these sporadic efforts as a movement, or even a potential movement. They have been isolated efforts to adjust individual grievances through protest.

In some instances, efforts have been made to establish procedures comparable to collective bargaining. If this process is to succeed, it must attract expert allies. A short time ago, for example, a group of Lower East Side Negro and Puerto Rican ADC mothers, represented by an attorney and a social worker, held a meeting with the Commissioner of Welfare to negotiate grievances. The immediate aim of this Committee of Welfare Families, organized through Mobilization for Youth, was to force the Welfare Department to supply its members with winter clothing. The Committee first notified the Commissioner that it had unsuccessfully made formal requests to the appropriate welfare investigators for the necessary cash grants. It threatened to picket if the Commissioner refused a hearing. The Commissioner agreed to a meeting with the Committee, and subsequently negotiated a formal grievance procedure with them. But, throughout the negotiations, the Commissioner continued to insist upon the traditional prerogative to investigate assertions of individual need, rather than to accept the validity of the Committee's assertions. While acceding to the principle of collective bargaining, he reaffirmed the right of the Department to conduct confidential interviews with clients, unimpeded by the presence of other Committee members, lawyers, social workers or translators. "Why should a discussion on why our members are not receiving the winter clothing which is due them contain so much 'confidential' information?," the Committee wrote to the Commissioner recently. And they went on: "If Mrs. John Doe is told by her investigator that her coat received in 1959 or 1960 should last '5 to 8 years,' or if a Mrs. Rodriguez is told that her investigator is too busy with 'more important things, and I don't know when I can get around to see you,' is all this 'confidential'?" Despite bureaucratic tactics of resistance, these efforts at reform—however faltering and few—are needed in a society whose social-welfare apparatus has always had its way with the poor.

And, finally, it should be said that new legislation—such as the proposed plan for a federally sponsored "guaranteed minimum income" —would solve most of the problems cited in this article, for it would eliminate their source. Nor should anyone mourn the passing of the local public-assistance agency, if that ever comes to pass. One reason for developing vigorous programs to protect individual rights—whether by information dissemination, advocacy, legal testing or collective action—is to dramatize the need for a new way to distribute income by revealing just how bad is the way that now prevails.

The Merchant and the Low-Income Consumer

David Caplovitz

Columbia University

[Reprinted from Chapter 2* of The Poor Pay More: Consumer Practices of Low-Income Families *by David Caplovitz (New York, 1963) by permission of The Free Press of Glencoe, A Division of The Macmillan Company. Copyright © 1963.]*

THE VISITOR TO EAST HARLEM cannot fail to notice the sixty or so furniture and appliance stores that mark the area, mostly around Third Avenue and 125th Street. At first this may seem surprising. After all, this is obviously a low-income area. Many of the residents are on relief. Many are employed in seasonal work and in marginal industries, such as the garment industry, which are the first to feel the effects of a recession in the economy. On the face of it, residents of the area would seem unable to afford the merchandise offered for sale in these stores.

That merchants nevertheless find it profitable to locate in these areas attests to a commonly overlooked fact: low-income families, like those of higher income, are consumers of many major durables. The popular image of the American as striving for the material possessions which bestow upon him both comfort and prestige in the eyes of his fellows does not hold only for the ever-increasing middle class. The cultural pressures to buy major durables reach low- as well as middle-income families. In some ways, consumption may take on even more significance for low-income families than for those in higher classes. Since many have small prospect of greatly improving their low social standing through occupational mobility, they are apt to turn to consumption as at least one sphere in which they can make some progress toward the American dream of success. If the upper strata that were observed by Veblen engaged in conspicuous consumption to symbolize their social superiority, it might be said that the lower classes today are apt to engage in *compensatory consumption*. Appliances, automobiles, and the dream of a home of their own can become compensations for blocked social mobility.[1]

---

* This chapter is based in part on an unpublished research report by Wolfram Arendt and Murray Caylay.

[1] I am indebted to Robert K. Merton for suggesting the apt phrase "compensatory consumption." The idea expressed by this term figures prominently in the writings of Robert S. Lynd. Observing the workers in Middletown, Lynd noted that their declining opportunities for occupational advancement and even

The dilemma of the low-income consumer lies in these facts. He is trained by society (and his position in it) to want the symbols and appurtenances of the "good life" at the same time that he lacks the means needed to fulfill these socially induced wants. People with small incomes lack not only the ready cash for consuming major durables but are also poorly qualified for that growing substitute for available cash—credit. Their low income, their negligible savings, their job insecurity all contribute to their being poor credit risks. Moreover, many low-income families in New York City are fairly recent migrants from the South or from Puerto Rico and so do not have other requisites of good credit, such as long-term residence at the same address and friends who meet the credit requirements and are willing to vouch for them.[2]

Not having enough cash and credit would seem to create a sufficient problem for low-income consumers. But they have other limitations as well. They tend to lack the information and training needed

---

the depression did not make them class-conscious. Instead, their aspirations shifted to the realm of consumption.

Fascinated by a rising standard of living offered them on every hand on the installment plan, they [the working class] do not readily segregate themselves from the rest of the city. They want what Middletown wants, so long as it gives them their great symbol of advancement—an automobile. Car ownership stands to them for a large share of the "American dream"; they cling to it as they cling to self respect, and it was not unusual to see a family drive up to the relief commissary in 1935 to stand in line for its four or five dollar weekly food dole. [The Lynds go on to quote a union official:] It's easy to see why our workers don't think much about joining unions. So long as they have a car and can borrow or steal a gallon of gas, they'll ride around and pay no attention to labor organization. . . . [Robert S. Lynd and Helen Merrill Lynd, *Middletown in Transition* (New York: Harcourt, Brace and Co., 1937), p. 26. See also pp. 447–448.] It should be noted that the Lynds identify the installment plan as the mechanism through which workers are able to realize their consumption aspirations. Similar observations are to be found in *Knowledge for What?* (Princeton University Press: 1939), pp. 91, 198. Lynd's student, Eli Chinoy, also makes use of the idea of compensatory consumption in his study of automobile workers. He found that when confronted with the impossibility of rising to the ranks of management, workers shifted their aspirations from the occupational to the consumption sphere. "With their wants constantly stimulated by high powered advertising, they measure their success by what they are able to buy." Eli Chinoy, "Aspirations of Automobile Workers," *American Journal of Sociology*, 57 (1952), 453–459. For further discussion of the political implications of this process, see Daniel Bell, "Work and Its Discontents" in *The End of Ideology* (New York: The Free Press of Glencoe, 1960), pp. 246 ff.

[2] A frequent practice in extending credit to poor risks is to have cosigners who will make good the debt should the original borrower default. The new arrivals are apt to be disadvantaged by their greater difficulty in finding cosigners.

to be effective consumers in a bureaucratic society. Partly because of their limited education and partly because as migrants from more traditional societies they are unfamiliar with urban culture, they are not apt to follow the announcements of sales in the newspapers, to engage in comparative shopping, to know their way around the major department stores and bargain centers, to know how to evaluate the advice of salesmen—practices necessary for some degree of sophistication in the realm of consumption. The institution of credit introduces special complex requirements for intelligent consumption. Because of the diverse and frequently misleading ways in which charges for credit are stated, even the highly-educated consumer has difficulty knowing which set of terms is most economical.[3]

These characteristics of the low-income consumer—his socially supported want for major durables, his small funds, his poor credit position, his lack of shopping sophistication—constitute the conditions under which durables are marketed in low-income areas. To understand the paradox set by the many stores selling high-cost durables in these areas it is necessary to know how the merchants adapt to these conditions. Clearly the normal marketing arrangements, based on a model of the "adequate" consumer (the consumer with funds, credit, and shopping sophistication), cannot prevail if these merchants are to stay in business.

On the basis of interviews with fourteen of these merchants, the broad outlines of this marketing system can be described. This picture, in turn, provides a backdrop for the more detailed examination in later chapters of the marketing relationship from the viewpoint of the consumer.

Merchandising in a Low-Income Area

The key to the marketing system in low-income areas lies in special adaptations of the institution of credit. The many merchants who locate

---

[3] Professor Samuel S. Myers of Morgan State College has studied the credit terms of major department stores and appliance outlets in Baltimore. Visiting the ten most popular stores, he priced the same model of TV set and gathered information on down-payments and credit terms. He found that the cash price was practically the same in the various stores, but that there were wide variations in the credit terms leading to sizeable differences in the final cost to the consumer. (Based on personal communication with Professor Myers.)

In his statement to the Douglas Committee considering the "Truth in Interest" bill, George Katona presented findings from the consumer surveys carried out by the Survey Research Center of The University of Michigan. These studies show that people with high income and substantial education are no better informed about the costs of credit than people of low income and little education.

in these areas and find it profitable to do so are prepared to offer credit in spite of the high risks involved. Moreover, their credit is tailored to the particular needs of the low-income consumer. All kinds of durable goods can be obtained in this market at terms not too different from the slogan, "a dollar down, a dollar a week." The consumer can buy furniture, a TV set, a stereophonic phonograph, or, if he is so minded, a combination phonograph-TV set, if not for a dollar a week then for only a few dollars a week. In practically every one of these stores, the availability of "easy credit" is announced to the customer in both English and Spanish by large signs in the windows and sometimes by neon signs over the doorways. Of the fourteen merchants interviewed, twelve claimed that from 75 to 90 percent of their business consisted of credit and the other two said that credit made up half their business. That these merchants extend credit to their customers does not, of course, explain how they stay in business. They still face the problem of dealing with their risks.

The Markup and Quality of Goods

It might at first seem that the merchant would solve his problem by charging high rates of interest on the credit he extends. But the law in New York State now regulates the amount that can be charged for credit, and most of these merchants claim they use installment contracts which conform to the law. The fact is that they do not always use these contracts. Some merchants will give customers only a card on which payments are noted. In these transactions the cost of credit and the cash price are not specified as the law requires. The customer peddlers, whom we shall soon meet, seldom use installment contracts. In all these cases the consumer has no idea of how much he is paying for credit, for the cost of credit is not differentiated from the cost of the product.

Although credit charges are now regulated by law, no law regulates the merchant's markup on his goods. East Harlem is known to the merchants of furniture and appliances in New York City as the area in which pricing is done by "numbers." We first heard of the "number" system from a woman who had been employed as a bookkeeper in such a store. She illustrated a "one number" item by writing down a hypothetical wholesale price and then adding the same figure to it, a 100 percent markup. Her frequent references to "two number" and "three number" prices indicated that prices are never less than "one number," and are often more.

The system of pricing in the low-income market differs from that in the bureaucratic market of the downtown stores in another respect:

in East Harlem there are hardly any "one price" stores. In keeping with a multi-price policy, price tags are conspicuously absent from the merchandise. The customer has to ask, "how much?," and the answer he gets will depend on several things. If the merchant considers him a poor risk, if he thinks the customer is naïve, or if the customer was referred to him by another merchant or a peddler to whom he must pay a comission, the price will be higher. The fact that prices can be affected by "referrals" calls attention to another peculiarity of the low-income market, what the merchants call the "T.O." system.

Anyone closely familiar with sales practices in a large retailing establishment probably understands the meaning of "T.O." When a salesman is confronted with a customer who is not responding to the "sales pitch," he will call over another salesman, signal the nature of the situation by whispering, "this is a T.O.," and then introduce him to the customer as the "assistant manager."[4] In East Harlem, as the interviewers learned, T.O.'s extend beyond the store. When a merchant finds himself with a customer who seems to be a greater risk than he is prepared to accept, he does not send the customer away. Instead, he will tell the customer that he happens to be out of the item he wants, but that it can be obtained at the store of his "friend" or "cousin," just a few blocks away. The merchant will then take the customer to a storekeeper with a less conservative credit policy.[5] The second merchant fully understands that his colleague expects a commission and takes this into account in fixing the price.[6] As a result, the customer who happens to walk into the "wrong" store ends up paying more. In essence, he is being charged for the service of having his credit potential matched with the risk policy of a merchant.

---

[4] The initials stand for "turn over." The "assistant manager" is ready to make a small concession to the customer, who is usually so flattered by this gesture that he offers no further resistance to the sale. For further descriptions of the "T.O.," see Cecil L. French, "Correlates of Success in Retail Selling," *American Journal of Sociology*, 66 (September, 1960), 128–134; and Erving Goffman, *Presentation of Self in Everyday Life* (New York: Doubleday, Anchor Books, 1959), pp. 178–180.

[5] The interviewers found that the stores closer to the main shopping area of 125th Street generally had more conservative credit policies than those somewhat farther away. This was indicated by the percentage of credit sales the merchants reported as defaults. The higher-rental stores near 125th Street reported default rates of 5 and 6 percent, those six or seven blocks away, as high as 20 percent.

[6] The referring merchant does not receive his commission right away. Whether he gets it at all depends upon the customer's payment record. He will keep a record of his referrals and check on them after several months. When the merchant who has made the sale has received a certain percentage of the payments, he will give the referring merchant his commission.

As for the merchandise sold in these stores, the interviewers noticed that the furniture on display was of obviously poor quality. Most of all, they were struck by the absence of well-known brands of appliances in most of the stores. To find out about the sales of better-known brands, they initially asked about the volume of sales of "high-price lines." But this question had little meaning for the merchants, because high prices were being charged for the low-quality goods in evidence. The question had to be rephrased in terms of "high *quality*" merchandise or, as the merchants themselves refer to such goods, "custom lines." To quote from the report of these interviews:

> It became apparent that the question raised a problem of communication. We were familiar with the prices generally charged for high quality lines and began to notice that the same prices were charged for much lower quality merchandise. The markup was obviously quite different from that in other areas. The local merchants said that the sale of "custom" merchandise was limited by a slow turnover. In fact, a comparable markup on the higher quality lines would make the final price so prohibitively high that they could not be moved at all. A lower markup would be inconsistent with the risk and would result in such small profits that the business could not be continued.

The high markup on low-quality goods is thus a major device used by the merchants to protect themselves against the risks of their credit business. This policy represents a marked departure from the "normal" marketing situation. In the "normal" market, competition between merchants results in a pricing policy roughly commensurate with the quality of the goods. It is apparent, then, that these merchants do not see themselves competing with stores outside the neighborhood. This results in the irony that the people who can least afford the goods they buy are required to pay high prices relative to quality, thus receiving a comparatively low return for their consumer dollar.

In large part, these merchants have a "captive" market because their customers do not meet the economic requirements of consumers in the larger, bureaucratic marketplace. But also, they can sell inferior goods at high prices because, in their own words, the customers are not "price and quality conscious." Interviewers found that the merchants perceive their customers as unsophisticated shoppers. One merchant rather cynically explained that the amount of goods sold a customer depends not on the customer but on the merchant's willingness to extend him credit. If the merchant is willing to accept great risk, he can sell the customer almost as much as he cares to. Another merchant, commenting on the buying habits of the customer, said, "People do not shop in this area. Each person who comes into the store wants to buy something and is a potential customer. It is just up to who catches him."

The notion of "who catches him" is rather important in this economy. Merchants compete not so much in price or quality, but in getting customers to the store on other grounds. (Some of these gathering techniques will shortly be described.)

Another merchant commented rather grudgingly that the Negroes were beginning to show signs of greater sophistication by "shopping around." Presumably this practice is not followed by the newer migrants to the area.

But although the merchants are ready to exploit the naïveté of their traditionalistic customers, it is important to point out that they also cater to the customer's traditionalism. As a result of the heavy influx of Puerto Ricans into the area, many of these stores now employ Puerto Rican salesmen. The customers who enter these stores need not be concerned about possible embarrassment because of their broken English or their poor dress. On the contrary, these merchants are adept at making the customer feel at ease, as a personal experience will testify.

> Visiting the area and stopping occasionally to read the ads in the windows, I happened to pause before an appliance store. A salesman promptly emerged and said, "I know, I bet you're looking for a nice TV set. Come inside. We've got lots of nice ones." Finding myself thrust into the role of customer, I followed him into the store and listened to his sales-pitch. Part way through his talk, he asked my name. I hesitated a moment and then provided him with a fictitious last name, at which point he said, "No, no—no last names. What's your first name? . . . Ah, Dave; I'm Irv. We only care about first names here." When I was ready to leave after making some excuse about having to think things over, he handed me his card. Like most business cards of employees, this one had the name and address of the enterprise in large type and in small type the name of the salesman. But instead of his full name, there appeared only the amiable, "Irv."

As this episode indicates, the merchants in this low-income area are ready to personalize their services. To consumers from a more traditional society, unaccustomed to the impersonality of the bureaucratic market, this may be no small matter.

So far, we have reviewed the elements of the system of exchange that comprise the low-income market. For the consumer, these are the availability of merchandise, the "easy" installments, and the reassurance of dealing with merchants who make them feel at home. In return, the merchant reserves for himself the right to sell low-quality merchandise at exorbitant prices.

But the high markup on goods does not insure that the business will be profitable. No matter what he charges, the merchant can remain in business only if customers actually pay. In this market, the customer's intention and ability to pay—the assumptions underlying any credit system—cannot be taken for granted. Techniques for insuring continuity of payments are a fundamental part of this distinctive economy.

Formal Controls

When the merchant uses an installment contract, he has recourse to legal controls over his customers. But as we shall see, legal controls are not sufficient to cope with the merchant's problem and they are seldom used.

Liens Against Property and Wages.—The merchant can, of course, sue the defaulting customer. By winning a court judgment, he can have the customer's property attached. Should this fail to satisfy the debt, he can take the further step of having the customer's salary garnisheed.[7] But these devices are not fully adequate for several reasons. Not all customers have property of value or regular jobs. Furthermore, their employers will not hesitate to fire them rather than submit to the nuisance of a garnishment. But since the customer knows he may lose his job if he is garnisheed, the mere threat of garnishment is sometimes enough to insure regularity of payments.[8] The main limitation with legal controls, however, is that the merchant who uses them repeatedly runs the risk of forfeiting good will in the neighborhood.

Repossession.—Under the law, the merchant can, of course, repossess his merchandise, should the customer default on payments. But repossession, according to the merchants, is rare. They claim that the merchandise receives such heavy use as to become practically worthless in a short time. And no doubt the shoddy merchandise will not stand much use, heavy or light. One merchant said that he will occasionally repossess an item, not to regain his equity, but to punish a customer he feels is trying to cheat him.

Discounting Paper.—The concern with good will places a limitation on the use of another legal practice open to merchants for minimizing their risk: the sale of their contracts to a credit agency at a discount. By selling his contracts to one of the licensed finance companies, the merchant can realize an immediate return on his investment.

---

[7] It is of some interest that the low-income families we interviewed were all familiar with the word "garnishee." This may well be one word in the language that the poorly educated are more likely to know than the better educated.

[8] Welfare families cannot, of course, be garnisheed, and more than half the merchants reported that they sell to them. But the merchants can threaten to disclose the credit purchase to the welfare authorities. Since recipients of welfare funds are not supposed to buy on credit, this threat exerts powerful pressure on the family.

The problem with this technique is that the merchant loses control over his customer. As an impersonal, bureaucratic organization, the credit agency has recourse only to legal controls. Should the customer miss a payment, the credit agency will take the matter to court. But in the customer's mind, his contract exists with the merchant, not with the credit agency. Consequently, the legal actions taken against him reflect upon the merchant, and so good will is not preserved after all.

For this reason, the merchant is reluctant to "sell his paper," particularly if he has reason to believe that the customer will miss some payments. When he does sell some of his contracts at a discount, his motive is not to reduce risk, but rather to obtain working capital. Since so much of his capital is tied up in credit transactions, he frequently finds it necessary to make such sales. Oddly enough, he is apt to sell his better "paper," that is, the contracts of customers who pay regularly, for he wants to avoid incurring the ill will of customers. This practice also has its drawbacks for the merchant. Competitors can find out from the credit agencies which customers pay regularly and then try to lure them away from the original merchant. Some merchants reported that in order to retain control over their customers, they will buy back contracts from credit agencies they suspect are giving information to competitors.[9]

Credit Association Ratings.—All credit merchants report their bad debtors to the credit association to which they belong. The merchants interviewed said that they always consult the "skip lists" of their association before extending credit to a new customer.[10] In this way they can avoid at least the customers known to be bad risks. This form of control tends to be effective in the long run because the customers find that they are unable to obtain credit until they have made good on their past debts. During the interviews with them, some consumers mentioned this need to restore their credit rating as the reason why they were paying off debts in spite of their belief that they had been cheated.

---

[9] Not all merchants are particularly concerned with good will. A few specialize in extending credit to the worst risks, customers turned away by most other merchants. These men will try to collect as much as they can on their accounts during the year and then will sell all their outstanding accounts to a finance company. As a result, the most inadequate consumers are apt to meet with the bureaucratic controls employed by the finance company. For a description of how bill collectors operate, see Hillel Black, *Buy Now, Pay Later* (New York: William Morrow and Co., 1961), chap. 4.

[10] See *Ibid.*, chap. 3, for a description of the world's largest credit association, the one serving most of the stores in the New York City area.

But these various formal techniques of control are not sufficient to cope with the merchant's problem of risk. He also depends heavily on informal and personal techniques of control.

Informal Controls

The merchant starts from the premise that most of his customers are honest people who intend to pay but have difficulty managing their money. Missed payments are seen as more often due to poor management and to emergencies than to dishonesty. The merchants anticipate that their customers will miss some payments and they rely on informal controls to insure that payments are eventually made.

All the merchants described their credit business as operating on a "fifteen-month year." This means that they expect the customer to miss about one of every four payments and they compute the markup accordingly. Unlike the credit companies, which insist upon regular payments and add service charges for late payments, the neighborhood merchant is prepared to extend "flexible" credit. Should the customer miss an occasional payment or should he be short on another, the merchant considers this a normal part of his business.

To insure the close personal control necessary for this system of credit, the merchant frequently draws up a contract calling for weekly payments which the customer usually brings to the store. This serves several functions for the merchant. To begin with, the sum of money represented by a weekly payment is relatively small and so helps to create the illusion of "easy credit." Customers are apt to think more of the size of the payments than of the cost of the item or the length of the contract.

More importantly, the frequent contact of a weekly-payment system enables the merchant to get to know his customer. He learns when the customer receives his pay check, when his rent is due, who his friends are, when job layoffs, illnesses, and other emergencies occur—in short, all sorts of information which allow him to interpret the reason for a missed payment. Some merchants reported that when they know the customer has missed a payment for a legitimate reason such as illness or a job layoff, they will send a sympathetic note and offer the customer a gift (an inexpensive lamp or wall picture) when payments are resumed. This procedure, they say, frequently brings the customer back with his missed payments.

The short interval between payments also functions to give the merchant an early warning when something is amiss. His chances of locating the delinquent customer are that much greater. Furthermore, the merchant can keep tabs on a delinquent customer through his knowledge of the latter's friends, relatives, neighbors, and associates, who are also apt to be customers of his. In this way, still another informal device, the existing network of social relations, is utilized by the neighborhood merchant in conducting his business.[11]

The weekly-payment system also provides the merchant with the opportunity to sell other items to the customer. When the first purchase is almost paid for, the merchant will try to persuade the customer to make another. Having the customer in the store, where he can look at the merchandise, makes the next sale that much easier. This system of successive sales is, of course, an ideal arrangement—for the merchant. As a result, the customer remains continuously in debt to him. The pattern is somewhat reminiscent of the Southern sharecropper's relation to the company store. And since a number of customers grew up in more traditional environments with just such economies, they may find the arrangement acceptable. The practice of buying from peddlers, found to be common in these low-income areas, also involves the principle of continuous indebtedness. The urban low-income economy, then, is in some respects like the sharecropper system; it might almost be called an "urban sharecropper system." [12]

The Customer Peddlers

Characteristic of the comparatively traditional and personal form of the low-income economy is the important role played in it by the door-to-door credit salesman, the customer peddler. The study of merchants found that these peddlers are not necessarily competitors of the store-owners. Almost all merchants make use of peddlers in the great competition for customers. The merchants tend to regard peddlers as necessary evils who add greatly to the final cost of purchases. But they need them because in their view, customers are too ignorant, frightened, or lazy to come to the stores themselves. Thus, the merchants' apparent contempt for peddlers does not bar them from employing outdoor sales-

---

[11] The merchant's access to these networks of social relations is not entirely independent of economic considerations. Just as merchants who refer customers receive commissions, so customers who recommend others are often given commissions. Frequently, this is why a customer will urge his friends to deal with a particular merchant.

[12] The local merchants are not the only ones promoting continuous debt. The coupon books issued by banks and finance companies which underwrite installment contracts contain notices in the middle announcing that the consumer can, if he wishes, refinance the loan. The consumer is told, in effect, that he is a good risk because presumably he has regularly paid half the installments and that he need not wait until he has made the last payment before borrowing more money.

men (or "canvassers," as they describe the peddlers who work for one store or another). Even the merchants who are themselves reluctant to hire canvassers find they must do so in order to meet the competition. The peddler's main function for the merchant, then, is getting the customer to the store, and if he will not come, getting the store to the customer. But this is not his only function.

Much more than the storekeeper, the peddler operates on the basis of a personal relationship with the customer. By going to the customer's home, he gets to know the entire family; he sees the condition of the home and he comes to know the family's habits and wants. From this vantage point he is better able than the merchant to evaluate the customer as a credit risk. Since many of the merchant's potential customers lack the standard credentials of credit, such as having a permanent job, the merchant needs some other basis for discriminating between good and bad risks. If the peddler, who has come to know the family, is ready to vouch for the customer, the merchant will be ready to make the transaction. In short, the peddler acts as a fiduciary agent, a Dun and Bradstreet for the poor, telling the merchant which family is likely to meet its obligations and which is not.

Not all peddlers are employed by stores. Many are independent enterprisers (who may have started as canvassers for stores).[13] A number of the independent peddlers have accumulated enough capital to supply their customers with major durables. These are the elite peddlers, known as "dealers," who buy appliances and furniture from local merchants at a "wholesale" price, and then sell them on credit to their customers. In these transactions, the peddler either takes the customer to the store or sends the customer to the store with his card on which he has written some such message as "Please give Mr. Jones a TV set."[14] The merchant then sells the customer the TV set at a price much higher than he would ordinarily charge. The "dealer" is generally given two months to pay the merchant the "wholesale" price, and meanwhile he

---

[13] A systematic study of local merchants and peddlers would probably find that a typical career pattern is to start as a canvasser, become a self-employed peddler, and finally a storekeeper.

[14] According to a former customer peddler, now in the furniture business, the peddlers' message will either read "Please *give* Mr. Jones . . ." or "Please let Mr. Jones *pick out* . . ." In the former case, the customer is given the merchandise right away; in the latter, it is set aside for him until the peddler says that it is all right to let the customer have it. The peddler uses the second form when his customer is already heavily in debt to him and he wants to be certain that the customer will agree to the higher weekly payments that will be necessary.

takes over the responsibility of collecting from his customer. Some "dealers" are so successful that they employ canvassers in their own right.[15] And some merchants do so much business with "dealers" that they come to think of themselves as "wholesalers" even though they are fully prepared to do their own retail business.

Independent peddlers without much capital also have economic relations with local merchants. They act as brokers, directing their customers to neighborhood stores that will extend them credit. And for this service they of course receive a commission. In these transactions, it is the merchant who accepts the risks and assumes the responsibility for collecting payments. The peddler who acts as a broker performs the same function as the merchant in the T.O. system. He knows which merchants will accept great risk and which will not, and directs his customers accordingly.

There are, then, three kinds of customer peddlers operating in these low-income neighborhoods who cooperate with local merchants: the canvassers who are employed directly by the stores; the small entrepreneurs who act as brokers; and the more successful entrepreneurs who operate as "dealers." A fourth type of peddler consists of salesmen representing large companies not necessarily located in the neighborhood. These men are, for the most part, canvassers for firms specializing in a particular commodity, e.g., encyclopedias, vacuum cleaners, or pots and pans. They differ from the other peddlers by specializing in what they sell and by depending more on contracts and legal controls. This type of peddler, in particular, can cause a good deal of trouble for the low-income consumer.

Peddlers thus aid the local merchants by finding customers, evaluating them as credit risks, and helping in the collection of payments. And as the merchants themselves point out, these services add greatly to the cost of the goods. One storekeeper said that peddlers are apt to charge five and six times the amount the store charges for relatively inexpensive purchases. Pointing to a religious picture which he sells for $5, he maintained that peddlers sell it for as much as $30. And he estimated that the peddler adds 30 to 50 percent to the final sales price of appliances and furniture.

---

[15] One tiny store in the area, with little merchandise in evidence, is reported to employ over a hundred canvassers. The owner would not consent to an interview, but the student-observers did notice that this apparently small merchant kept some four or five bookkeepers at work in a back room. The owner is obviously a "dealer" whose store is his office. As a "dealer," he has no interest in maintaining stock and displays for street trade.

Unethical and Illegal Practices

The interviewers uncovered some evidence that some local merchants engage in the illegal practice of selling reconditioned furniture and appliances as new. Of course, no merchant would admit that he did this himself, but five of them hinted that their competitors engaged in this practice.[16] Several of the consumers we interviewed were quite certain that they had been victimized in this way.

One unethical, if not illegal, activity widely practiced by stores is "bait" advertising with its concomitant, the "switch sale." In the competition for customers, merchants depend heavily upon advertising displays in their windows which announce furniture or appliances at unusually low prices. The customer may enter the store assuming that the low offer in the window signifies a reasonably low price line. Under severe pressure, the storekeeper may even be prepared to sell the merchandise at the advertised price, for not to do so would be against the law. What most often happens, however, is that the unsuspecting customer is convinced by the salesman that he doesn't really want the goods advertised in the window and is then persuaded to buy a smaller amount of more expensive goods. Generally, not much persuasion is necessary. The most popular "bait ad" is the announcement of three rooms of furniture for "only $149" or "only $199." The customer who inquires about this bargain is shown a bedroom set consisting of two cheap and (sometimes deliberately) chipped bureaus and one bed frame. He learns that the spring and mattress are not included in the advertised price, but can be had for another $75 or $100. The living-room set in these "specials" consists of a fragile-looking sofa and one unmatching chair.[17]

The frequent success of this kind of exploitation, known in the trade as the "switch sale," is reflected in this comment by one merchant: "I don't know how they do it. They advertise three rooms of furniture for $149 and the customers swarm in. *They end up buying a $400 bedroom set for $600 and none of us can believe how easy it is to make these sales.*"

In sum, a fairly intricate system of sales-and-credit has evolved in response to the distinctive situation of the low-income consumer and the local merchant. It is a system heavily slanted in the direction

---

[16] Events are sometimes more telling than words. During an interview with a merchant, the interviewer volunteered to help several men who were carrying bed frames into the store. The owner excitedly told him not to help because he might get paint on his hands.

[17] In one store in which I inspected this special offer, I was told by the salesman that he would find a chair that was a "fairly close match."

of a traditional economy in which informal, personal ties play a major part in the transaction. At the same time it is connected to impersonal bureaucratic agencies through the instrument of the installment contract. Should the informal system break down, credit companies, courts of law, and agencies of law enforcement come to play a part.

The system is not only different from the larger, more formal economy; in some respects it is a *deviant* system in which practices that violate prevailing moral standards are commonplace. As Merton has pointed out in his analysis of the political machine, the persistence of deviant social structures can only be understood when their social functions (as well as dysfunctions) are taken into account.[18] The basic function of the low-income marketing system is to provide consumer goods to people who fail to meet the requirements of the more legitimate, bureaucratic market, or who choose to exclude themselves from the larger market because they do not feel comfortable in it. As we have seen, the system is extraordinarily flexible. Almost no one—however great a risk—is turned away. Various mechanisms sift and sort customers according to their credit risk and match them with merchants ready to sell them the goods they want. Even the family on welfare is permitted to maintain its self-respect by consuming in much the same way as do its social peers who happen not to be on welfare. Whether the system, with its patently exploitative features, can be seriously altered without the emergence of more legitimate institutions to perform its functions, is a question to be considered at length.

Housing Codes, Taxes, and Slums*

Alvin L. Schorr

U. S. Department of Health, Education, and Welfare

[Reprinted from Chapter 4 of Slums and Social Insecurity *by Alvin L. Schorr (Washington, D.C., 1963).]*

WIDESPREAD FAILURE to attempt to enforce housing codes is one of the reasons that so much housing is now substandard. Housing codes are a key element of successful rehabilitation programs. Yet, in current circumstances, it is not at all certain that they can be or will be broadly enforced. When violations become a public scandal, the laws may be

---

[18] Robert K. Merton, *Social Theory and Social Structure*, rev. ed. (New York: The Free Press of Glencoe, 1957), pp. 71–82.

* Biographical footnotes have been omitted.

enforced with some effect. (In the past decade, slum fires in Baltimore, Brooklyn, Chicago, and Cleveland, killing 15, touched off, respectively, a new ordinance, a grand jury investigation, an angry article in a national magazine, and an enforcement campaign.) But where public attention is not engaged, violations are endemic.

Why is it so difficult to enforce codes? Why do they not work effectively? These questions have many overlapping answers. Codes are antiquated and unclear. Penalties embodied in the law are slight. Owners find it cheaper to pay occasional fines than to make repairs. Municipal enforcement staff is likely to be undermanned. Political interests may not support or may actively sabotage enforcement efforts. Those who must move because of crowding or because buildings are condemned cannot find even equivalent housing. Absentee owners cannot, without a good deal of trouble, be put under sufficient pressure to produce results. Resident owners may not have the resources to make improvements. Tenants may resist enforcement because it means rent rises or that some must move. Even with momentarily successful enforcement, in the long run industry, highways, and other blighting influences take their toll.

Some of the remedies for these difficulties are obvious; some that are less obvious are being developed. A sustained, effective enforcement program requires a clear law, an adequately manned enforcement body with defined responsibility and support from city hall. In addition, Baltimore has pioneered the use of a housing court, a court thoroughly familiar with housing practices that has special counseling services at its disposal. It has been suggested that there should be special organizations to take over and rehabilitate properties that a city forces onto the market. Attention has focused on methods for dealing with recalcitrant landlords. It has been suggested that any building should be condemned and torn down if the cost of repairs is equivalent to 50 percent of its "true" value. New York City now has the power to seize buildings, make repairs that are necessary to meet minimum requirements, and recapture the cost out of rent collections.[1]

---

[1] Prior to this, the statute permitted "the Department of Buildings to declare a building a public nuisance; let out contracts for repairs to be made and . . . maintain a suit against the owner to recover the amount of the expense. Such a procedure is so unsatisfactory as to preclude its use. . . . It is . . . an open invitation to the unscrupulous owner to milk the profits from the property, have the city make necessary repairs, and through legal maneuvering make it exceedingly difficult for the city to recoup expenditures." Letter from Peter J. Reidy, Commissioner of the Department of Buildings, the City of New York, to Frank P. Zeidler, Mar. 2, 1961.

For thoughtful descriptions of the problems that interfere with enforcement and for proposals for remedies, see *Guiding Metropolitan Growth, Residential Re-*

One cannot review the problems of code enforcement and the solutions that are proposed without concluding that they are superficial, if grave, symptoms of a deeper maladjustment. The hard fact is that profitmaking incentives run counter—so far as the maintenance of housing is concerned—to the best interests of the poor. Tax laws and condemnation procedures combine with the peculiarly vulnerable situation of those who are poor to pay the most profit for the worst housing. Where enforcement is pitted day by day against the businessman's incentive to make profit, enforcement is bound to be in trouble.

Factors that operate in this fashion are the municipal property tax, the capital gains tax, the basis for calculating value in condemnation, and the depreciation allowance. The property tax, as it is based upon valuation, increases as property is improved. Any number of observers and some studies testify that such a basis for a tax leads to neglect of property. A more touching bit of testimony is an information bulletin offered to homeowners by the government of Dayton, Ohio. "Protect your home!" it reads. "Home Maintenance Does Not Increase Your Taxes." Obviously, the possibility of a tax rise deters not only those who are interested in profit, but some who might be improving their own homes as well.

The capital gains tax may have a somewhat similar effect. If the owner's income tax bracket is high, his interest centers on ultimate resale value. Though resale value in other property may depend on maintenance, in low-income neighborhoods it is likely to depend on the value of the land and on the net income that is being produced. Thus, the profit lies in holding on while the land becomes valuable and, secondarily, in current income. Neither of these incentives need involve maintenance of a building. Condemnation procedures provide one of the reasons that income production determines resale value. Even though income is not a consideration in setting the property tax, it is recognized as a factor in negotiating payment upon condemnation. Thus, for this reason too, money spent on maintenance brings little cash benefit. The most deteriorated property may eventually be disposed of to the city at a profit.[2]

The depreciation allowance provides a further element that influences the maintenance of housing. In Federal income tax the depreciation allowance treats real estate like machinery and equipment. A

---

habilitation: Private Profits and Public Purposes, The Human Side of Urban Renewal, and *Making Urban Renewal More Effective.*

[2] Summarizing the opinions of "outstanding authorities" in the investment field, Arthur M. Weimer writes: "Most investors . . . recognize that renewal programs . . . have the effect of bailing out the owners of various properties and of shoring up the expectations of the owners of many near-in properties."

high percentage may be written off in early years and declining percentages subsequently. Though a single owner may not receive credit for more than his own cost, upon resale the property may be depreciated all over again. The point of largest profit, therefore, is in the early years. After 6 or 8 years, if tax cost is a consideration for the owner, it becomes profitable to sell and purchase a new property.[3] This effect may seem to operate in the opposite direction from the effect, just cited, of the capital gains tax, which leads to holding on to property for increase in value. The two provisions have in common, however, that they return no profit for the cost of maintaining or improving center-city property. Maximum profit lies in manipulating tax and financial matters quite unrelated to building maintenance. It lies also in securing high short-term profit: this translates into securing the most tenants that are feasible in the space available, with the lowest possible expenditure.

In practice, the effect of these financial incentives turns out approximately as follows:

> One of the great problems of slum ownership is the fact that slum properties have changed hands many times during their life and each person has expected to make a profit from the sale. The tendency therefore is to raise the price of the building and to seek ever-increasing rents at the same time the physical value of the building is deteriorating. As a building gets older and the price the latest owner pays for it represents more and more profit taking in successive sales, the latest owner must crowd more and more tenants in a dying building to meet his costs, thus hastening its dilapidation. . . . The latest owner may possess what is little or more than a pile of bricks and kindling wood, but he presumes the building has a high residual value. If he is lucky,

---

[3] That rapid turnover of real estate is one result of the depreciation allowance was, in effect, agreed upon in hearings before the House Ways and Means Committee. The administration had proposed that profit on the sale of real estate be treated as ordinary (not capital gains) income to the extent of past depreciation. Speaking for the proposal, Dan Throop Smith, professor of finance at Harvard University, asked that it apply especially to real estate. "The opportunities for manipulation," he said, "are particularly great in buildings, where properties can be and are bought, depreciated and sold by a succession of owners in a way that is not feasible for most machinery and equipment." Speaking against the administration proposal, Richard H. Swesnick, of the National Association of Real Estate Boards, said: ". . . Owners would be unwilling to sell real estate except in distress or other highly unusual circumstances, and purchasers would be unwilling to acquire new real property which, as a practical matter, they would have to treat as a permanent investment." Obviously other issues are involved, but the point here is that there is agreement from diverse sources that the depreciation allowance produces rapid turnover.

the local government will come along and buy him out at an inflated price for some public work or a slum clearance project.[4]

As buildings are subdivided, crowded, and more deteriorated, they become well nigh impossible to maintain. Moreover, it becomes impractical to try to maintain neighboring houses. They too become a profitable investment and slum development spirals. If the city steps in and tries to enforce codes strictly, some owners will be able to make no profit at all. They paid too high a price and counted on overcrowding. If it is suggested that the municipality take the houses over, paying for their reasonable value, it develops that this is less than the current owner paid for it. Why pick on him? Once begun, the cycle is not readily interrupted.

The significance of these forces cannot be overestimated. The maintenance of existing housing is far more important to poor families than the building of new housing. Programs to rehabilitate existing housing will be token remedies unless the underlying processes can be made healthy. There are not enough, and there cannot be enough, housing inspectors in the country to assure code enforcement against the tidal forces that present public policies establish.

How the Poor Are Housed*

Alvin L. Schorr

U. S. Department of Health, Education, and Welfare

[Reprinted from Chapter 5 of Slums and Social Insecurity *by Alvin L. Schorr (Washington, D.C., 1963).]*

How do poor families pay for housing? The question has dimensions that are private and public. As a private matter, the question is answerable in terms of budget management and family arrangements. As a public matter, one answers in terms of specific public programs or of the concept that housing filters down to the poor as those who are better off move on to better housing. All national programs intended

---

[4] Zeidler, Frank P. *Making Urban Renewal More Effective.* A series of twelve reports dated August 1, 1960 to July 1, 1961, to the American Institute for Municipal Research, Education, and Training, Inc., Washington, D.C., p. 32.

* Biographical footnotes have been omitted.

to sustain income and insure against such risks as old age are, in a certain sense, devices to provide housing (et cetera) to those who might otherwise be poor. However, most of these programs place in the beneficiary's hand money which he has, in one manner or another, earned. He is in the same situation as any wage earner, so far as housing is concerned. (If his benefits are inadequate, he is in the same situation as other people.) Two national programs, public assistance and public housing, incorporate a means test and intervene directly in the housing of the poor. They will merit special attention when we come to the public dimension of the provision of housing to the poor.

The Private Dimension

The poor pay for housing, first, in its poor quality. Reflection will show that this is a theme that lies just under the surface of most of our discussion. Whether they own or rent, it is the poor families who tend to occupy the country's substandard housing. In 1956 half of those with income less than $2,000 lived in housing that was dilapidated or lacked plumbing.

This is a rough measure. We have not taken into account size of family. Moreover, current income counts several kinds of people as if they were the same: the rich man who has taken a temporary loss, the retired man who once had more income, and the man who is chronically poor. The first man is likely to be able to spend out of savings and conceivably the retired man too, but hardly the man who has never had a decent income. Nevertheless, the rough measure makes it clear that some who are poor acquire standard housing. They do not acquire it by accident. Analysis of the Chicago population shows that the poor in standard dwellings "typically" pay more rent than those in substandard dwellings. Even those who do not manage standard housing make sacrifices for the quality that they do achieve.

One step that poor families take is to allocate a high percentage of their income to housing. We have already noted a tendency for those who relocate from cleared areas to spend more for improved housing. In 1956 the great majority of families with incomes under $2,000 spent 30 percent or more of their income on rent. On the other hand, of families with incomes between $8,000 and $10,000 the great majority spent less than 15 percent. We have suggested that current income is not always a good indication of a family's financial circumstances. However, relating the amount a family spends to the cost of its housing gives a similar picture. In 1950 urban families with incomes under $1,000 a year spent 26 percent of their total outlay for housing. Families from $1,000 to $2,000 spent 22 percent; from $2,000 to $3,000, 18 percent; and so on.

What would a suitable yardstick be? For most cities the BLS city worker's family budget allocates to housing something less than 20 percent of the total.[1] Moreover, the BLS budget totals are over twice as high as the level of poverty. One would assume that if, out of incomes already lower than adequate, more than 20 percent is allocated to housing, increased deprivation will be felt in other areas of the budget. A depression study in Stockton, England, concluded that higher rents had led to malnutrition. A study reported by Elizabeth Wood came to a more refined conclusion. The study addressed itself to the question, "Can a family pay one-third of its income for rent and yet have enough left to nourish the family?" The conclusion: ". . . under such conditions fathers and children were sufficiently well-nourished, but mothers tended to be undernourished." The same point is made in reverse by a District of Columbia study of 81 families living in public housing who presented rent payment problems. Of the families who presented rent problems, "28 percent had spent their rent money for clothing and other unmet needs of their children."[2]

One possibility is clear—to pay for adequate shelter by settling for inadequate food and clothing. In many cases, the family must be governed not by a deliberate choice to favor housing but by the way inadequate money gets spent. Under sustained pressure, costs that are fixed and regular are met and those that seem stretchable or postponable—food, clothing, recreation, medical care—are not met. In any case, the consequences of spending more than 20 percent for housing do not seem healthy. It is anybody's guess how much lower than 20 percent a rule of thumb for poor families ought to be. Certainly, so far as public decisions are concerned, 20 percent should be regarded as a maximum rather than an average housing expenditure for poor families.

Income for income, naturally, the pressure to make some adjustment to housing needs is felt most by large families. If figures can reflect a sense of strain, perhaps those that follow suggest the financial pressure that builds up in the budget management of a large, low-income family. The table is based on the rents paid by families of varying size before and after relocation. The report covers 1,373 families in 9 cities that did not substantially assist with relocation; rentals reported for 5 cities that did assist show a similar pattern.

---

[1] One city, 15 percent; 2 cities, 16 percent; 6 cities, 17 percent; 4 cities, 19 percent; 5 cities, 20 percent; and 2 cities, 21 percent. The BLS budget includes the cost of rent and heat. The *1956 National Housing Inventory* figures above and the 1950 figures based on the *Survey of Consumer Expenditures* also represent the "gross" cost of housing.

[2] 21 percent had failed to receive support money due them; 18 percent presented budget management problems; 33 percent failed for miscellaneous reasons.

Average Monthly Rentals Before and After Relocation
[By family size, 9 cities, 1955–58]

Number of persons in family	Rent before relocation	Rent after relocation	Rent increase
2	$30.35	$34.81	$4.46
3	32.35	36.23	3.88
4	34.45	37.96	3.51
5	36.50	39.07	2.57

Does it force these data to suggest that these small but consistent differences indicate the degree to which any increased cost must be resisted? Relocation means that all the families must pay more. The larger the family, the less, by a matter of pennies, it can accede to the pressure for higher cost.

What steps do the large families take? Reviewing the *1950 Survey of Consumer Expenditures*, Louis Winnick concludes about the average large family: "They obtain more housing space and, at the same time, maintain or even increase the budgets devoted to other consumer goods." However, poor large families are not able to bring this off. They spend more in total for food and for clothing. To balance the increase, they spend less in total for housing, household operation, and medical care. (This confirms a conclusion we had already reached.) How do the higher income families manage to maintain their spending for other items while obtaining more space? Apparently they do it by sacrificing the physical quality of the housing. (We have seen that poor families are familiar with this tactic too.) So far as ownership is concerned, for example, small families tend to have houses that are worth more, compared to their incomes, than large families. Thus, relative values are lower for the larger families despite the fact that they have more space. Larger families generally try to gain some advantage by purchasing rather than renting, but lower incomes tend to close off this possibility. Poor large families do not, like other large families, show a markedly higher tendency to own than smaller families.

To return to speaking of poor families in general, an additional strategy has now been suggested. Any family, large or small, may think of purchase as a way to secure more housing for its money.[3] Obviously, however, low income restricts the opportunity to buy. Almost 60 percent of the dwellings in metropolitan areas are now owned by the families in them. But in the lowest fifth of the income distribution, in Chicago, 20 percent of the families owned homes. Of urban families

---

[3] The question of ownership versus rental is not determined simply on financial grounds.

receiving aid to families with dependent children, predominantly with incomes under $2,000 a year, 17 percent own homes. For those families that manage it, buying a house involves them in the same tactic as committing a high percentage of income to housing. When a poor family buys a house, it is almost always valued at three times or more the family's income. By contrast, families with incomes over $6,000 tend to pay 1.5 to 2 times their income.[4] Further, buying reduces the flexibility with which a family can meet other contingencies—illness, unemployment, and so forth.

The purchase of housing, though it is not usually thought of in the same terms, is a form of going into debt. Poor families may not receive more short-term credit than families with more income (because it will be refused), but the struggle to buy on credit or borrow money is an everyday fact of life. Borrowed money may be applied directly to rent or it may buy clothing because clothing money went for rent—the effect is the same. The use of credit to pay for housing produces the problems that have just been noted—a future commitment to sacrifice something tomorrow to pay for today's housing and limited flexibility in the face of emergencies. Moreover, the poor family pays a premium for credit. A study of the buying patterns of families in several public housing projects notes some of the problems associated with credit:

> Because of their poor credit potential, many of these families are restricted in where they can shop for durables. . . . They do not shop in department stores and discount houses. Instead they depend upon chain stores, neighborhood merchants and door-to-door peddlers—in short, merchants who are prepared to extend credit to poor risks. The dependence upon such credit means that they pay high prices for appliances.

---

[4] These observations are based on the relation of current income to value, and may be somewhat influenced by families who had purchased homes some time before and whose incomes had declined. However, figures taken at the point of purchase of FHA-insured homes show a similar trend. In 1959 those with incomes under $3,600 bought new homes valued at over 3 times their income or existing homes valued at 2.5 times their income. The ratio of value to income in 1959 shows a steady fall as family income rises.

The values cited in relation to income may understate the poor family's disadvantage in buying a house. If a family with larger income has made a larger downpayment, their monthly payment is reduced even more. Moreover, the owner with more income is likely to secure better lending terms. Some low-income families, at the other extreme, find themselves buying under lease-purchase, with inflated monthly payments and very little chance indeed of eventually obtaining title to the property.

. . . Because of their poor education and relatively young age, and because many are recent migrants to the city, they tend to be naïve shoppers, vulnerable to the lure of "easy credit." . . . Perhaps as many as a third of the families have suffered at the hands of unscrupulous salesmen.[5]

The strategies that are open to poor families are not limited to trying to shift about small sums of money. Analysis of the living arrangements of the aged in the United States indicates that, when help for the old person is needed, the poor tend to pool living arrangements. The plight of the poor "is so difficult that they must select the most efficient way of sharing, which is living together." An attempt to understand crowding among Negroes in Chicago produces a somewhat similar observation:

> Doubling-up of families and sharing the dwelling with nonrelatives probably account for the relatively large household size in the non-white population; and such doubling-up and sharing of dwellings are themselves probably means by which nonwhites pool incomes in order to compete for housing.

Smaller studies produce supporting evidence. In sum, one tactic for providing housing is to share space beyond the immediate family and to pool available money.

On the other hand, apparently there is a point of surrender, when adequate housing comes to seem impossible and families break apart. Studying a group of families who were being required to relocate, the Department of Public Welfare of the District of Columbia reported:

> . . . We found some who had already accepted separation as a partial answer. Other families were on the verge of breaking up when it appeared that it would no longer be possible to maintain a common home.[6]

This strategy, if one can call it that, has been of special concern to child welfare agencies. Of 11,500 children in foster care in New York City at one point, 750 could have gone home "at once" if adequate low-cost housing had been available. ". . . 112 children might not have been placed at all had adequate housing with supportive services been available at the point of placement." A study of women committed to the

---

[5] Caplovitz, David, with the assistance of Louis Lieberman. *The Consumer Behavior of Low Income Families.* Columbia University Bureau of Applied Social Research, New York, 1961, pp. 197–98.

[6] Department of Public Welfare, Public Assistance Division. "Report of the Advisory Committee of the Service to Displaced Families to the Director of Public Welfare at the Expiration of the Six Months Trial Period," March 21, 1960 to September 20, 1960. Washington, D.C., November 1, 1960, mimeographed.

New Jersey Reformatory for Women on charges of child neglect found that close to 50 percent "had been living in housing that could only be described as dangerous and not fit for human habitation. . . . Mother after mother described the feeling of discouragement and frustration that came after hours of house-hunting with no success." Says this study in conclusion:

> Grossly inadequate housing was a serious problem to more than 60 percent of these families. This factor was particularly pertinent to the large family groups. A community that cannot provide decent housing and does not exercise adequate control to protect families from exploitation and from living in dangerous situations certainly runs the risk of increasing the neglect problem.[7]

The figures vary from study to study, but all make a similar point. Despite a national policy that is, perhaps, 50 years old,[8] economic need is still an effective force in separating children from their families. Chief among the specific mechanisms that operate in financial need is inability to find adequate housing.

Obviously, families also seek in a variety of ways to *improve* their income. One device that has consequences for family arrangements is to send an additional member of the family to work. Of the group of families cited earlier who left public housing to purchase homes, 7 percent had originally had more than one member of the family working. When interviewed in their own homes not long afterward, 32 percent had more than one worker. The rate at which married women work appears to confirm this finding. On the whole, women tend not to work when they have preschool children in the home. But couples with less than $2,000 income show a marked tendency for the wife to work, if they have preschool children and if they do not. Presumably the wife's income is the only income or it is a necessary supplement to bring family income even to this low level. . . .

Public Housing.—Public housing is not a single program, historically; it is a single vessel that has been used for diverse public purposes.

[7] Hancock, Claire R. *A Study of Protective Services and the Problem of Neglect of Children in New Jersey, 1958.* Report of project sponsored by the New Jersey State Board of Child Welfare, Department of Institutions and Agencies, conducted June 1957–January 1958.

[8] Among the conclusions of the White House Conference on Children in 1909: "Home life is the highest and finest product of civilization. It is the great molding force of mind and of character. Children should not be deprived of it except for urgent and compelling reasons. . . . Except in unusual circumstances, the home should not be broken up for reasons of poverty, but only for consideration of inefficiency or immorality."

In the 1930's, public housing was intended for families who voluntarily sought to improve their housing but could not afford private rentals. This group was not regarded as dependent. Indeed, some housing authorities limited the number of public assistance recipients they would accept and others would not admit any. In the 1940's, the program was redirected to provide housing for war workers. Following the Housing Act of 1949, public housing was oriented again to poor families—with a difference. Partly because postwar amendments gave priority to families having the most urgent housing need, to the aged, and to those displaced by urban renewal, this third generation in public housing contains a high concentration of depressed, untutored, and dependent families.

It would be misleading to speak of the development of the program as if all the crucial changes were made by Congress. If public housing is the vessel, perhaps Congress is the vintner, but one must ask about the grape and the palate of the taster. The recipe for populating a city, of which we have spoken, concentrates Negroes in public housing as in slums. Segregation is not entirely new, of course, but since 1954 it has become a more open insult. To the extent that public housing found its sites chiefly in land cleared for renewal, large areas were devoted exclusively to public housing (St. Louis is an example). To the extent that the growing suburbs successfully resisted public housing, they confined it to the city core. Meanwhile, as between 1935 and 1960, there was a greater proportion of Americans who had never experienced poverty personally or were trying to forget it. They contributed to a more critical, if not pious, public view of public housing. Thus, a conjunction of social and economic trends leads to the setting apart of families in public housing.

As is so often the case, internal problems of policy and administration aggravate a difficult situation. Authorities have been widely criticized for poor housing design—too much standardization, too high densities, lack of imagination, and disregard of informal social patterns. The Commissioner of Public Housing took note of the criticism in a letter to local authorities.

> What the localities need [she said in part] is a loosening of regulations by Washington, and that we will do. There are so many regulations about square footage and the space between buildings, for example, that the result is the same housing in Maine and in southern California.[9]

---

[9] *New York Times.* "New Ideas Sought in Public Housing," November 26, 1961.

Housing that was tending to be concentrated in terms of people had taken on, as well, an institutional appearance. Further, tenants must leave public housing if their income exceeds a permissible maximum.[10] In effect, those families must leave who achieve at least limited success and who might provide variety and leadership in the housing developments. The struggle of housing authorities to find remedies may itself create a problem. As a number of tenants have the most primitive understanding of housing, regulations and penalties proliferate: Windows must be shut in the winter . . . a fine if drains are plugged without good reason . . . eviction for an illegitimate pregnancy . . . and so forth. Some tenants find this to be precisely a confirmation of their greatest anxiety, that they were being offered decent housing in exchange for their independence. The stage is set for mutual suspicion between tenant and manager, with relationships inside a housing development diverging increasingly from those that are typical in private housing.[11]

The alteration in its population also leads to a financial problem for public housing. Tenants' income (in constant dollars) has remained level in the past decade, but each year the tenants' income falls further below the median for the country. That is, in 1955 the median net income of families admitted to public housing was 46.5 percent of the median income of all families in the United States. In 1961, it was less than 40 percent. Consequently, the rents that may be collected from tenants do not rise as rapidly as maintenance costs. Between 1950 and 1958 monthly receipts from rent increased by 25 percent (from $28.93 to $36.50 per unit per month), but expenditures increased by 52 percent (from $21.32 to $32.50). Not unexpectedly, then, the Federal contribution to local housing authorities has been moving steadily toward its permissible maximum. With the overall Federal contribution reaching 87 percent of the maximum in fiscal year 1961, some local housing authorities would find themselves still with substantial leeway and others with rather little.

Public housing is faced with grave problems which go to the heart of its ability to remain solvent and shape the kind of housing, in the sense of total social and physical environment, that it is able to

---

[10] The Housing Act of 1961 permits local housing authorities to retain over-income families for a limited period if it can be shown that standard private housing is not available to them.

[11] A study of management policies in public housing concludes that ". . . the imposing of numerous controls on tenant behavior has tended to intensify the misunderstandings which arise between tenants and managers."

TABLE 1

Percentage of 3- and 4-Person Families in Total Population and
Moving Into Public Housing, 1960

Income for year	Percentage of total population	Percentage of all families moving into public housing
Under $1,500	5.8	11.7
$1,500 to $4,000	18.7	83.7

Sources: *Current Population Reports*, table 5, and *Families Moving Into Low-Rent Housing, Calendar Year 1960*, table 6.

provide.[12] What are the consequences for tenants? The first and perhaps the most serious consequence is that public housing is not available to more than a small proportion of the low-income families. Though the Housing Act of 1949 authorized 810,000 units, that authorization is as yet far from exhausted. There are in all something over half a million units—roughly 1 percent of the housing supply. If public housing were limited to the lowest incomes, with current resources it could house 2 million of the 32 million we have defined as poor. As it reaches above the very lowest incomes, it houses even a smaller percentage of the poor than these figures indicate. Consequently there are waiting lists of people eligible for public housing. In the District of Columbia, the number of families awaiting admission has at times exceeded the total number of housing units.

Since public housing must look to its receipts, it tends to exclude families with the lowest incomes who cannot pay minimum rents. Table 1 sets numbers to this observation. That is, the bulk of families entering public housing have incomes under $4,000 a year. Among the families having less than $4,000, in the total population roughly one in four has under $1,500 income. But only one in eight of those who move into public housing has less than $1,500.[13] Families may be excluded as undesirable, too. Though such exclusions would doubtless diminish if there were more public housing, they represent an effort to maintain a degree of acceptability among tenants. On the other hand, when

---

[12] Not all of the problems have been touched on here. For a careful description of policy and financial developments, see the "working paper" by Warren Jay Vinton for the Conference on Housing the Economically and Socially Disadvantaged Groups in the Population. For a development of the meaning of the change in tenant population, see "Public Housing and Mrs. McGee."

[13] Perhaps half of the families with less than $1,500 income who move into public housing are public assistance recipients. The non-recipient with very low income is therefore represented in a very small proportion indeed.

careful study was made of 82 families excluded as undesirables in New York City, the decision was reversed for 33 of the families. Other reviews have produced higher percentages of reversal. In addition to the limited capacity of the program, we have already noted that many presumably eligible families are not willing to live in public housing. Their reluctance must arise, to some degree, from the program's current difficulties, but it also represents a feeling about living in a managed— particularly, in a Government-managed—community. As early as 1946, a local study reported that only a third of those eligible were willing to live in public housing. In sum, public housing is limited by its quantity, its fixity upon the middle range of low incomes, and by management and tenant views of acceptability.

Americans are often more attentive to the tempo and direction of a trend than to the underlying facts. Because we are preoccupied with the problems and movement of public housing, we may conceivably overlook the function it is performing. When they are asked, the majority of families who live in public housing say that they like it. They appreciate its facilities; their general morale is higher than it was in substandard housing. One must, of course, take into account that those who would object most to public housing never enter it, or they leave.[14] Nevertheless, for those who take up tenancy, public housing represents a considerable improvement in physical surroundings. Moreover, the aspects of the environment which are offensive to some families may be secondary or even functional for others. Kurt W. Back finds that two types of people move into public housing, those who seek to use it as a vehicle for change and those who see it as an end in itself. Of the latter, he writes:

> In general, the tenants form the weaker and more vulnerable part of the [public housing] population. They have less income, less secure income, and are more likely to represent broken homes. In a very real way they need the protection afforded by government action, and many of them received some government aid. These people apparently look on government housing as a type of institutional support, which they need.[15]

Thus, public housing performs at least acceptably for those poor families who see it as an improved, somewhat protected environment. Presumably, it offers their children a better start than they might otherwise

---

[14] The rate of moveouts, though it signals difficulty in some places, is not strikingly high compared with general population mobility. It is lower overall than the moveout rate for rental housing insured by FHA.

[15] Back, Kurt W. *Slums, Projects, and People: Social Psychological Problems of Relocation in Puerto Rico.* Durham, N.C.: Duke University Press, 1962, p. 102.

have had. Analysis of turnover statistics suggests that others use public housing as a way station to improved housing. In this sense, too, public housing serves the prevention of poverty.

Thus, strictly managed housing may suit one family—or at least not trouble it—and trouble others very much. Public housing is pressed, if it is going to serve families with any precision, to define its objectives and to alter policies to further these objectives. At least three choices are open: (1) A real estate operation for the respectable poor—the purely poor. (2) A rehabilitative program for the seriously dependent and troubled poor. (3) A greatly enlarged and altered program, at least in part deinstitutionalized, with a variety of kinds of housing opportunities. In the absence of a settled decision to seek the third course and of the legislation that would make it possible, local housing authorities are moving slowly, in most cases with pronounced reluctance, toward rehabilitative programs. Under present circumstances the families who are entering public housing make such a course inevitable. Not only are the families isolated and segregated; increasing numbers are aged, many receive public assistance, and many are in broken families. They cannot be abandoned to their problems; they must be served. Moreover, when they are not served, buildings deteriorate, delinquencies occur, and deprived youngsters grow into disabled adults. It becomes plain that neglect is expensive. . . .

How does public housing serve the poor? It serves some of them, a small minority of them. Those it serves, does it serve them well? Some of them, only some of them.

Public Assistance.—People who do not have enough money for decent living may be helped by public assistance. Major assistance programs, representing a partnership of Federal and State Governments, are addressed to children in family homes, to the aged, the blind, and the disabled. Some States and localities also provide general assistance for needy people not eligible under the categorical programs. In accordance with the Social Security Act, assistance in the Federal-State programs is given to recipients in money, without stipulating how it must be spent.[16] As this practice suggests, the intent of the legislation was to provide funds for subsistence, without public intrusion into the choices that must be made in family management. Public assistance agencies have, therefore, tended to refrain from dealing directly with

---

[16] However, payments may be made on behalf of a recipient to a person or organization providing medical or other remedial care. In aid to families with dependent children, in a limited number of cases where it is in the children's interest, the entire payment may be turned over to a third party to spend on behalf of the recipient family.

landlords. But assistance provides the means for securing housing. When recipients have difficulty in securing adequate housing, assistance agencies are perforce involved in their clients' problems. At the beginning of 1962, over 7 million people were receiving assistance. Though less directly than public housing, to be sure, public assistance is the largest national program concerned with the housing needs of the poor. It is important, therefore, to ask about the quality of housing that assistance recipients secure and about the welfare department's influence upon it.

Although information about the quality of recipients' housing has not been systematically collected, it is clear that the quality is poor. Data about plumbing facilities in Table 2 suggest how the housing of recipients compares with that of the general population. It may not be surprising that assistance recipients, having the lowest incomes, are worse off than the average. However, it is an impressive figure that 4 out of 10 aged recipients and 3 out of 10 recipient families with dependent children manage without each of these basic facilities. One can guess at the proportions of their dwellings that are dilapidated and deteriorated. Measures of crowding suggest that over time assistance recipients are not improving their housing at the same rate as the general population. In the decade from 1950 to 1960, the median number of persons per room in the AFDC household declined from 1.0 to 0.94. In the same period, the national median declined from 0.75 to 0.59. That the median number of persons per room in the AFDC household is now 0.94 means that almost half the families are crowded. One in five of the AFDC families are "critically overcrowded," living in households in which there are 1.5 persons or more per room.

TABLE 2

Plumbing Facilities Available in 1960, to Total U.S. Population, to Recipients of Aid to Families With Dependent Children, and of Old Age Assistance

	Total U.S. population, percent having	Aid to families with dependent children, percent of recipients having	Old-age assistance, percent of recipients having
Hot and cold running water inside structure	87	70	60
Exclusive use of a flush toilet	87	72 [1]	59

[1] Includes a small number having a bath or shower but no flush toilet.

Sources: *1960 Census of Housing, Characteristics and Financial Circumstances of Recipients of Old-Age Assistance 1960*, and a national study of aid to families with dependent children.

Special State and city studies provide a more intimate appraisal of the housing of public assistance recipients. Florida reviewed 13,000 cases of aid to families with dependent children to determine whether the homes were suitable for children. The study noted "excessively high rents for unspeakably inadequate slum homes." A survey of recipient families with dependent children in the State of Maine found that four out of five did not have central heating. The report concludes:

> Over half [of AFDC families] do not have what most Americans take for granted: central heating and all three of the essential plumbing facilities, running water, bath, and exclusive use of a toilet. About a third . . . are overcrowded and many others lack privacy because of a need to share a living arrangement with relatives and non-relatives.[17]

There are variations in the numbers and the degree of detachment with which other studies report. But the same basic situation has been documented for Chicago; Atlanta; Baltimore; Washington, D.C.; Philadelphia; Westchester County, N.Y.; and Alexandria, Va. Occasionally a study inquires specifically into the housing of recipients who would have special difficulty in finding housing—for example, families with unmarried mothers. The findings are predictable. Of over 3,000 illegitimate children who were receiving AFDC, Cleveland reported that 10 percent were living in public housing. The remaining 90 percent lived in housing that was "overcrowded and substandard. . . . The majority live in neighborhoods that are rooming house areas and slums." A similar study in New York City found a quarter of the married mothers and half of the unmarried mothers living in "rooming houses considered undesirable for family living."

The repetition of percentages about crowding and sanitary facilities may fail to convey what caseworkers see and recipients experience. The Commissioner of Welfare in New York City quotes a caseworker as follows:

> In this six-story building, converted into furnished rooms, filth prevails throughout—filled garbage cans without covers line the hallways with the surplus refuse spilling over; roaches and rats abound; broken flooring, plumbing, windows, lighting fixtures and plaster are observable throughout. The average room size [occupied by a family] is 13x15 with two beds, a dresser, two chairs, a table, a refrigerator and a closet, as the standard equipment supplied by the landlord. One community kitchen is used by seven families. Twelve toilets are intermittently in service on six floors. There is no lock on the door from the street and

---

[17] Romanyshyn, John M. *Aid to Dependent Children in Maine.* State of Maine Department of Health and Welfare, June 1960, p. 10.

vagrants, including drug addicts and alcoholics, often wander in to sleep in the unlocked kitchens and bathrooms. This is the abode of thirty families and 105 children. . . .[18]

One has to ask how such conditions occur for so many people in programs intended to maintain health and decency and to strengthen family life. It goes without saying that, by the nature of the problem that makes recipients of them, some families are handicapped in finding and maintaining decent housing. Old age, physical disability, and a broken marriage or no marriage may each, in its own way, make a family poor tenants. But there are simpler, more powerful causes of the problem.

Fundamentally, the amount of money paid to recipients of public assistance in most places is not enough to pay for proper housing and the other elements of a healthful and decent budget. Payments under the Federal-State programs are, in all cases, based on an assessment of actual need. In making the assessment and determining the payment, however, a number of policies and practices are interposed to reduce the amount of assistance that is paid to a family. First, the basic amounts allowed for budget items are likely not to be realistically related to costs. The cost of rent or mortgage payments is not estimated in stand-ard amounts by States; it is budgeted in relation to the actual payment. Seventeen States budget rentals "as paid" by the client or as paid for reasonable or modest housing. But 35 States budget rentals only "as paid *to a maximum.*" In an attempt to assess the realism of other budget items, in 1958 State standard allowances for food for a single man (OAA) and for a family of four (AFDC) were compared with the U. S. Depart-ment of Agriculture low-cost food plan. For the old-age assistance case, only Arizona budgeted an amount for food as great as the U. S. Depart-ment of Agriculture standard. For the family with dependent children, only Florida and Michigan matched the Department of Agriculture standard. Thus, it is clear in the initial calculation of need that real minimum costs will not be met.

Second, regardless of the amount of money that States determine to be needed, they may apply a maximum to the overall amount of the payment. About two-thirds of the States apply a maximum of some sort to payments in each of the Federal-State programs. In consequence, 29 percent of OAA recipients in 1960 received less than they had been de-termined to need by the State's own standards. The median amount of the deficit was over $9 a month. Forty-eight percent of AFDC families in

---

[18] Dumpson, James R. "The Human Side of Urban Renewal," *The Wel-farer,* Vol. XIII, No. 10, October 1960, pp. 1, 4.

1958 received less than they had been determined to need. The average amount of the deficit was nearly $39 a month. A third practice that reduces the assistance payment is to impute income to a client, whether or not he receives it. Twenty-four States impute income—when there is a relative who is responsible to help, when a court orders a support payment to a family, or if a parent has refused available employment. Such policies are intended to encourage client or family responsibility but, as there may never actually be payment or earnings, the effect is frequently confined to reducing the amount of assistance. Finally, payments may be reduced simply because of human error. It is a curious fact, turned up by regular audits, that the majority of errors that are evident in public assistance records result in *under*payments to recipients. It is difficult to account for this, except to suppose that in administering complicated regulations some caseworkers are leaning far over backwards indeed to avoid overpayment. In simplest outline, these are the steps by which payments which are in principal minimally adequate become something less—or a great deal less—than adequate.

We have already looked at the dilemma in which the family with less than enough money finds itself. In addition, recipients are more than ordinarily likely to suffer [for housing purposes] from being Negro, in broken families, and having several children. The fact of being a recipient may itself lead landlords to refuse to rent. Less than enough money is, one might say, sufficient handicap. The compounding of the problem by other handicaps means that most recipients will not find decent housing unless they are somehow protected or aided. In fact, welfare departments are moving to assist with housing. Their motivations are several: the desperate circumstances of some recipients, the patent exploitation of others, and the cost of paying for hotels or institutional care simply because reasonable housing cannot be found. In general, three courses are open to welfare departments. They may provide counsel and other aids to clients. They may turn to public housing for their recipients. They may ally themselves with other community forces to eliminate substandard housing and superstandard charges for it. . . .

The issues that exist between public housing and public assistance are predictable byproducts of the convergence of two independent programs. The provision of more effective service by public assistance to its clients in public housing should assist in resolving these issues. But with or without issues, public housing is the one dependable resource to which public assistance may turn for acceptable housing for recipients. The help that it finds is limited chiefly because the quantity of public housing is limited.

The final course open in attempting to assist recipients is for welfare departments to ally themselves with other community forces to eliminate substandard housing and exorbitant rents. Though welfare departments are widely privy to violations of housing codes, they do not routinely press the appropriate municipal departments for enforcement. The studies of housing codes in Philadelphia and New York State that were touched upon earlier criticize welfare departments for failing to offer cooperation. It is unlikely that the failure arises from a lack of concern. Whether they have wished to be involved in providing decent housing or not, it looms up as a major problem confronting welfare administrators. Moreover, with funds for assistance chronically short, it nags at one's nerves to know that a portion of the money that is available goes into the exchequers of profiteers. In their experience in reporting violations, however, welfare departments have discovered how little they can expect in the way of result. They discover, with a certain immediacy, the powerful forces that operate against code enforcement. Depending upon the local situation, they may abandon reporting violations entirely or report the more dramatic ones—but without hope or followup.

From time to time, welfare administrators make ceremonial statements urging enforcement upon other executive officials and legislatures. For practical results, however, some appear to be looking to their own ability to put pressure on landlords. When negotiations with a landlord fail, they may assist the recipient to move. This constitutes effective pressure only in the comparatively few communities where housing is readily available. In 1962 New York State passed a law permitting public welfare officials to withhold welfare rent payments from seriously substandard dwellings. About the same time, welfare workers in Chicago were advising their clients to withhold rent payments in such dwellings.[19] Recipients were, in due course, evicted by their landlords but were able to find other housing. Since the welfare department does not pay rent in arrears, the cost to slum landlords was substantial. Moreover, the city corporation counsel filed suit against landlords at the same time to force them to correct code violations. An "SRO" program in New York City was even more forceful. The housing authority and welfare and real estate departments collaborated in the enforcement of an ordinance prohibiting family occupancy of single rooms. (SRO stands for "single room occupancy" as well as its more customary,

---

[19] In turn, the welfare department withholds rent money from the client. Where Federal money is involved, regulations would require clarity that the recipient was acting on his own behalf, not under compulsion by the welfare department.

entirely relevant meaning.) The city took legal possession of a number of houses that were conspicuous offenders and were largely tenanted by assistance recipients. The houses were cleared and adequate dwellings located for the tenants. . . .

How does public assistance serve in providing housing for poor people? It leaves many in poor housing and some in desperately poor housing. Basically, its failure is a failure to provide recipients with enough money to pay for decent housing. Because of this failure, public assistance is pressed to offer special aids and protection for its clients. These help, to some degree, but to larger degree are frustrated by limitations of available housing and inability to force legal maintenance of housing. Because public assistance has not historically regarded itself as a provider of housing, agencies may also fail to invest their fullest energies in the securing of housing.

Two old studies suggest the direction and pace with which public assistance has moved in relation to housing. A U.S. Children's Bureau study of Mothers' Aid (a predecessor to AFDC) in 10 representative communities in 1928 reports:

> Except in one large city, where housing conditions left much to be desired, the families were for the most part in decent, sanitary dwellings or flats in respectable neighborhoods; many were in comfortable one-family houses, and a considerable number had flower gardens. If families were found living in too congested quarters, under insanitary conditions, or in neighborhoods where morality was questionable, the courts required them—or the agencies persuaded them—to move to better locations.[20]

In 1940, the U.S. Housing Authority and the Social Security Board reviewed common areas of their programs. Among their conclusions:

> . . . it is apparent that relief and public assistance families are inadequately housed. . . . It is estimated that 50 to 90 percent of such families occupy the *worst* kind of shelter.
>   . . . Inadequate housing is related to inadequate income with but few exceptions.
>   . . . There are no *generally accepted* basic standards of the quantity and quality of housing considered a minimum essential for every family.[21]

---

[20] Bogue, Mary F. *Administration of Mothers' Aid in Ten Localities*, U.S. Department of Labor, Children's Bureau, Publication No. 184, 1928, p. 15.

[21] U.S. Housing Authority in Cooperation with the Social Security Board. *Housing and Welfare*, Federal Works Agency, Washington, D.C., May, 1940, pp. 6 and 7.

So far as the housing of public assistance recipients is concerned, the direction between 1928 and 1940 was downward. The recommendations that followed from the findings of the 1940 study are obvious: adequate payments, applying objective standards to recipients' housing, regular reporting of the quality of recipients' housing, more public housing to use for assistance recipients. Prescriptions that were plain when the Social Security Act was new have yet to be acted upon.

Can Poor Families Be Housed?

If one reflects upon the ways in which poor families pay for housing in their private lives and upon the ways in which public policies assist them, it is possible to perceive a discrepancy. The private and the public dimensions are out of balance. Poor people pay for housing as a total effort, out of their food and out of the fabric of their lives together. The effects of the struggle are experienced without Sabbath and without holiday. But public efforts to assist them are directed only to a minority. Out of those who are reached, many are helped meagerly, subject to conditions that may be relevant, irrelevant, or even self-defeating.

In public efforts to provide housing we have so far relied chiefly upon stimulation and subsidy of private industry. The results, for those with incomes over $5,000 or $6,000, have been respectable. Recent legislation attempts to extend the impact of such activity to lower incomes. The problem has so far appeared to be one of interesting builders and developers in such a market. It appears likely that some gains will be made. But it must be evident that the problem of the poor will not be met in this manner. We have referred to the reasons; they require only to be brought together.

First, though special incentives for low-income building and contraction of demand in the middle-income market may lead to more builder interest in low-cost housing than heretofore, it is unlikely that interest will reach down to the families with $2,500 incomes. High risks, limited profits, and other difficulties that have discouraged business from building for families with $5,000 incomes will seem insuperable at half those incomes.

Second, it is not unreasonable that builders and banks should take pause. A family of four with less than $2,500 income is not able to buy a house or pay a rent that provides a profit on it, no matter how low the interest rate on the mortgage. The family's income is not adequate to its need for food, clothing, and other necessary items—even if it were paying no rent at all.

Third, inducing low-income families to pay 25 or 30 percent of their incomes carries a heavy risk of its own and is not sound public policy. The housing that is bought at the expense of food or medical care is dearly bought.

This is not to say that we are unable to provide decent housing for all American families. Public housing and public assistance provide avenues for decent housing, providing that the serious limitations of these programs are corrected. Small-scale experiments of other sorts are being tried. A number involve public subsidy to those who provide housing for low-income families, with purchasers or tenants making such payments as they can afford. There has been recurrent consideration of the possibility of providing a direct subsidy to low-income families to be used for purchasing or renting standard housing. Such a proposal was considered by the Senate Subcommittee on Housing and Urban Redevelopment headed by Senator Robert A. Taft. Reporting in 1945, the subcommittee rejected direct subsidies, mainly because they might flow to substandard housing. There was also objection to channeling such funds through public assistance agencies. After more than a decade of experience with urban renewal, attention has been turning again to the possibility of providing a direct subsidy to poor families. A number of schemes have been put forward that provide protections against misuse; nor would subsidies necessarily be furnished through public assistance agencies.

We can indeed shape a program that will provide "a decent home and a suitable living environment for every American family." Such a program need not appear to be favoritism. On the contrary, aids that have so far been devised (income tax advantages, mortgage insurance) reach middle- and upper-income families with special effect. Resources and techniques are available to right the balance.

City Schools

Patricia Cayo Sexton

New York University

[Reprinted with permission from The Annals of the American Academy of Political and Social Science, *March 1964.]*

To TALK ABOUT URBAN EDUCATION is to talk about an old fallen phrase in such disrepute during two postwar decades that it has hidden out from scholarly journals like a furtive sex criminal. The phrase "class struggle" now appears in black tie and softened aliases as "slum and suburb," "inequalities," problems of the "disadvantaged," of the "culturally deprived," of "integration." However Americanized or blurred the new image may appear, the basic fact seems simple enough: a remarkable "class struggle" now rattles our nation's schools and the scene of sharpest conflict is the city. Southern cities—and New York—were the scenes of first eruptions, but now almost every northern city, and many suburbs, are feeling the new tremors.

A high-ranking official in New Rochelle, New York, put it in these words: "It's not just race in our schools . . . it's class warfare!" Class conflict, of course, is not the only issue in city schools. There is ethnic conflict and the special status of Negroes—and of Puerto Ricans and other identifiable groups—at the bottom end of the ladder and the special Rickover pressure-cooked conformism and prestige-college frenzy at the upper end.[1] Nor are the sides in the conflict always clearly formed. But, usually, when the chaff and wheat are separated, what is left is the "haves" in one pile and "have-nots" in another, with some impurities in each—middle-class white "liberals," for example, who support some Negro demands and white have-nots who oppose them. Banfield and Wilson claim four important cleavages in city politics: (1) haves and have-nots, (2) suburbanites and the central city, (3) ethnic and racial groups, (4) political parties.[2] A reduction to more basic outlines might show that the first category would, with some slippage, cover the other three. Indeed, the authors acknowledge as much when they say: "These tend to cut across each other and, in general, to become one fundamental cleavage separating two opposed conceptions of the public interest."[3] When they refer to ". . . The fundamental cleavage between the public-regarding Anglo-Saxon Protestant, middle-class ethos and the private-regarding lower-class, immigrant ethos," they seem to refer, though the phrase is unspoken, to one aspect of the class struggle.[4]

---

[1] Rickover supporters in the Council on Basic Education voice some misgivings about the Admiral's program to restrict higher education to an elite.

[2] Edward C. Banfield and James Q. Wilson, *City Politics* (Cambridge, Mass.: Harvard University Press and MIT Press, 1963).

[3] *Ibid.*, p. 35.

[4] *Ibid.*, p. 329. Their ascription of a "public-regarding" ethos to the middle class and a "private-regarding" one to the "lower class" seems an extraordinary and questionable reversal of the usual association of the middle class with private efforts and the lower class with public efforts. It is most puzzling when contrasted with their summary statement: "If in the old days [of lower class ward politics] specific material inducements were illegally given as bribes to favored individuals, now much bigger ones are legally given to a different class of favored individuals . . ." (p. 340).

Other major urban school issues exist—finances, bureaucracy, and the unionization of teachers, among others—and may seem, on the surface, unrelated to class conflict. At second glance, the shortage of school funds can be seen as a product of the antitax ideology of haves. The behemoth bureaucracies may be seen everywhere as more accessible to and influenced by haves, and the decentralization of administration—to which New York's Superintendent Gross and others have devoted themselves—may be seen as a partial response to the growing arousal of have-not groups. The unionization of city teachers may be seen as a response to the hitherto rather rigid conservative control of school systems and the new thrust of liberalism in the cities and the schools, released by have-not votes and agitation, as well as a defense against the difficult conditions in have-not schools.[5]

Levels of Conflict

The class struggle in the schools and the struggle for power which is part of it are carried on at many levels. In some cases, it seems least visible under the spotlight—on the school boards. Through liberal and have-not activity, some city school boards are now composed of middle-class moderates who are more inclined to represent the educational interests of have-nots than were their more conservative predecessors. Some big-city boards, as New York's, seem exemplary public servants, superior in purpose and competence to higher political bodies. Their efforts on behalf of have-nots are limited by several personal as well as external characteristics: they are haves, a quality that usually though not invariably limits zeal and identity with have-nots; they are moderates in contrast to those leading the more militant have-not groups. Among the limits set by school systems are: (1) the traditional conservative reluctance of boards to interfere in the operations of the bureaucracy; (2) the inertia and resistance of the bureaucracy to pressure from the board; (3) the usual tendency to become defensive of "their system" and to take criticisms of the system as personal affronts; (4) influences from middle-class interests which are usually more insistent and weighty than have-not pressure; (5) interference from outside groups—such as the unprecedented threat of the Northcentral Associa-

---

[5] In New York and Chicago especially, the popular political issues of "bossism" and "machine politics" have been referred to the school arena. In New York, 110 Livingston Street (the Board of Education headquarters) has appeared to many as the school equivalent of "city hall," the one place you "can't beat" and with which you often cannot even communicate. Now a proposal is being considered to divide the city schools into several fairly autonomous geographic units in order to scatter the shots at "city hall" and provide easier access.

tion to withdraw accreditation from the Chicago schools if the school board insisted on a step which forced Superintendent Willis into further desegregation. The external limits on the situation, however, seem more determining: (1) the difficulty of the job to be done, (2) the lack of sufficient money to do the job.

Services to have-nots within the city system, therefore, are limited by these conservative factors: (1) the moderate position of most liberal board members and the insufficiency of zeal or identification to drive home the grievances of have-nots; (2) conservatism and resistance within the bureaucracy; (3) conservative influence which acts to shut off funds to the schools.

In the movement of the class struggle from one end of the continuum, where a small elite holds total power, to the other extreme, where have-nots share proportionate influence, there are many points of compromise, and public officials tend to pursue ever more liberal ends and means. The white liberals who sit on some city boards may begin to push for more rapid change or may be replaced soon by representatives who will.

The claim that the city and its school system are so constrained by outside conservatism, especially at the state level, that they can do little seems largely true, though partially exaggerated. Too often outside interference is made an excuse for inertia. City schools have not given adequate service to have-nots largely because the have-nots were underrepresented in decision-making positions. As cities go, New York's school board seems unusually enlightened, appointed as it is by a relatively responsive mayor and served by two unusually alert citizen groups—the Public Education Association and the United Parents Association. Yet a nine-member board includes only one Negro and no Puerto Rican, although these groups together compose 40 percent of the city's public school enrollment. Nor is there any blue-collar worker or person of modest means or position on the board, but, then, such individuals are rare specimens on city boards. One trade unionist, himself a university graduate and member of a professional union, sits on the board. Of some 777 top officials in the system—board members, superintendents, and principals—it appears that only six are Negroes, 0.8 per cent of the total.[6]

Although it is sometimes asserted that the interest-group identity of board members does not affect their decision-making, what may be more nearly the case, given present knowledge of group dynamics,

[6] Daniel Griffiths and Others, *Teacher Mobility in New York City* (New York, 1963).

is that the group interests of the lone have-not representative may be submerged in a board's moderate consensus.

Perhaps the "equality lag" within city systems may be more directly attributable to deficiencies in have-not organization than to lack of good faith among liberals and board members. Many cities could nearly be "possessed" by Negroes who approach a majority in some cases, but Negroes do not vote their numerical strength and may be evicted from the city limits by urban renewal before they catch up with their potential. Nor do labor unions use their full authority in school affairs. A major weakness of have-nots is their limited understanding of power, who has it and how to get it; they also lack the time, money, and organization often needed to purchase it.[7]

Beyond the City Limits

Local class conflict seems only a dim reflection of a larger conflict. The main drama of class conflict and thrust of conservatism are seen in full dimension in a larger arena—at the federal and state levels. The national scene cannot be ignored in any consideration of the city school situation. Only at this level does there appear a possibility of releasing the funds needed to support high-quality education and the high-level job opportunity that goes with it. The claim that federal aid to education is the *only* school issue and that other concerns are simply distractions is given substantial support by any cursory study of city school budgets and revenue limitations.[8]

Nationally, the conflict seems shaped by at least two major factors:

(1) The congressional system is biased against have-nots and their representatives. The bias results from at least two forms of conservative manipulation: (a) manipulation of rural and small-town interests, North and South, and, through them, congressional apportionment

---

[7] Banfield and Wilson, *op. cit.*, p. 282: "Organized labor—even if it includes in its ranks the majority of all the adult citizens in the community—is generally regarded as a 'special interest' which must be 'represented'; businessmen, on the other hand, are often regarded, not as 'representing business' as a 'special interest,' but as serving the community as a whole. Businessmen, in Peter Clark's term, often are viewed as 'symbols of civic legitimacy.' Labor leaders rarely have this symbolic quality, but must contend with whatever stigma attaches to being from a lower-class background and associated with a special-interest group. . . . Labor is handicapped not only by having imputed to it less civic virtue but also by a shortage of money and organizational skills."

[8] This seems to suggest that social scientists could much more profitably study the political mechanisms by which such aid could be released rather than the often esoteric and "academic" studies of culture, personality, and the like which now tend overly to occupy many who are concerned with have-nots.

and votes; (b) the additional manipulation of southern rural conservatism—which is given unusual congressional power by the committee seniority system—through the exchange of votes on the race issue.

The superior effective power of haves at this top level serves to block federal legislation in general but specifically those measures that might ensure rapid economic growth through federal expenditures, full employment, and the extension of power to have-nots—measures that would give significant relief to the city's distress. More directly relevant, it has blocked any substantial aid to urban areas and held up the transfer of political power from rural to urban areas.[9]

Moreover, largely by the manipulation of conflicting religious interests, this coalition has prevented the passage of the federal aid that seems indispensable to urban schools. At the same time, it has continued, through extension programs, copious aid to rural education.

(2) Seriously deprived have-nots have failed to enter their full power into the political arena.

The State

If direct federal aid seems distant and the aid formula unlikely to provide much assistance to the cities, fiscal aid from the state may be closer at hand, depending upon how quickly reapportionment will be enforced in the states. New York City received $197 in school aid for each student in its public schools in 1961–1962, while the average in the rest of the state was $314. Miami, Florida paid $47 million in state taxes in one recent year and got back only $1.5 million in grants-in-aid. With sympathetic legislatures, cities may be able to call on other revenues, including an income tax on suburbanites working in the city such as has been adopted in Philadelphia and Detroit.

Inequalities

The consequences of local, state, and national class conflict are seen in the school inequalities and class-biased training given to children even within the most liberal city systems. Only in the past few years has the concern of some unionists, academicians, liberals, and many Negroes brought the full range of inequities to public attention. The "spoils" of the city school, limited as they are by outside controls, are usually divided according to the crude formula "them as has gets." Only now

---

[9] The assumption that a proper apportioning of representatives, giving a proper share to the city's suburban areas, will result in an accretion of power to haves may not be warranted inasmuch as have-nots are also being rapidly suburbanized yet, contrary to expectation, seem to be maintaining their political identity.

in some cities is there any insistence on the more radical "compensatory" formula—"to each according to need."

Documentary evidence about class inequalities, past and present, is now weighty. My own study of one large city school system, *Education and Income*, describes the various forms of class inequities within one system.[10] I will refer here only to a few facts about Chicago and New York (not the cities of my study). In 1955, following Dr. Kenneth Clark's demand for attention to Negro schools, an "outside" study found that Negro and Puerto Rican schools in New York City were generally inferior to "Other" schools.[11] In a group of Negro and Puerto Rican schools (the X Group), 50.3 percent of teachers were on tenure, compared to 78.2 percent in the "Other" group (the Y Group); 18.1 percent in the X group and only 8.3 percent in the Y group were "permanent substitutes." On the average, facilities in Group X schools were older, less adequate, and more poorly maintained than Y schools. The costs of operating Y schools were higher than costs in X schools. Though the New York Board of Education now claims that Negro and Puerto Rican schools are equal or superior to "Other" schools, Dr. Kenneth Clark still says Harlem schools reflect "a consistent pattern of criminal neglect."

In the absence of cost-accounting, comparative expenditures in have and have-not schools in New York cannot be checked. Certainly efforts are being made by New York schools to provide better education for deprived minorities, especially in "certain" schools where extra services tend to be over-concentrated, but the schools still do not seem to approach full equality, and the cost estimates do not measure the *full* cost of education—the differences in nursery and kindergarten education, the last two years of high school missed by the low-income dropout, and the costs of higher education—not to mention the low-quality and segregated "ability" tracks into which have-not children are often placed.

Though New York permitted an outside study of school inequalities in 1954, the Chicago Superintendent of Schools, Benjamin Willis, has only in the past year agreed to a three-man study committee of which he will be a member. In 1962 John E. Coons, Northwestern University law professor, prepared for the United States Commission on Civil Rights a report on segregated schools in Chicago.[12] Ten schools

---

[10] Patricia Cayo Sexton, *Education and Income* (New York: Viking Press, 1961).

[11] *The Status of the Public School Education of Negro and Puerto Rican Children in New York City*, October, 1955.

[12] John E. Coons, *Civil Rights USA, Chicago, 1962*, A Report to the United States Commission on Civil Rights.

in each of three groups were selected—white, integrated, Negro—and the findings were as follows:

1961–1962	*White*	*Integrated*	*Negro*
Number of pupils per classrooms	30.95	34.95	46.8
Appropriation per pupil	$342	$320	$269
Number of uncertified teachers	12%	23%	27%
Average number of books per pupil	5.0	3.5	2.5

In 1963 a *Handbook of Chicago School Segregation* claimed that 1961 appropriations for school operating expenses were almost 25 percent greater per pupil in white than in Negro schools, that teacher salaries were 18 percent higher, that nonteaching operating expenses— clerical and maintenance, salaries, supplies, textbooks—were 50 percent higher, and that only 3 percent of Chicago's Negro population finishes college.[13]

The reluctance of Chicago schools to move as far as New York on the race issue seems to derive from at least these sources: (1) the centralization of power in the Chicago system, parallel to the centralization of civic power in the person of the mayor; (2) the praise of Dr. Conant—probably the most influential person in American education— for Mr. Willis and the Chicago method and his concurrent criticism of the New York method; (3) the presence in New York of large numbers of unusually concerned and articulate white middle-class liberals; (4) the inordinate influence in Chicago schools and civic affairs of State Street, tax-conscious financial interests; (5) the past failures of have-not organization in Chicago.

An example of influential conservatism in relation to have-nots and the schools is seen in this passage from the Chicago *Tribune:* "Let's Throw the Slobs out of School":[14]

> The ignoramuses have had their chance. It is time to make them responsible for their actions. . . . Sweep through the school house with a fiery broom. Remove the deadwood, the troublemakers, the no-goods, the thugs. . . .
>
> [The teacher can tell on the first day] which students are the dis-

---

[13] *Handbook of Chicago School Segregation, 1963,* compiled and edited by the Education Committee, Coordinating Council of Community Organizations, August 1963.

[14] Reprint from *Chicago Tribune Magazine,* "Let's Throw the Slobs out of School," as it appears in *Human Events,* September 21, 1963, a weekly magazine distributed to social-studies classes in schools throughout the nation.

satisfied, the misfits, the illitearate [*sic*], undeserving, *non compos* nincompoops. We have become the victims of the great transcendental fraud, a deceit put upon us by a generation of psychiatrists, guidance counselors, and psychologists, none of whom spends any more time in the classroom dealing with these apes than he has to.

Despite the fact that median income in Chicago is higher than in New York, Chicago in one recent year spent $410 per pupil while New York spent $761.52.[15]

Inequalities and the compensatory formula now being advocated —reverse inequality—produce only one kind of conflict, one which may be more easily resolved than other disputes because it involves simply the redistribution of money. The "concept" of equality itself seems far less susceptible to change—the notion that, with proper attention, the abilities of have-not children may prove roughly equal to those of haves and that, therefore, they should not be separated, sent off at an early age on different tracks, or given disproportionate access to higher education.

In New York City, fiscal inequality, segregation, and the "concept" of inequality resulted in the following racial distribution of recent graduating classes in New York's special high schools for "gifted children" drawn from the whole city:

	Negroes	*Puerto Ricans*	*Others*
Bronx High School of Science	14	2	863
Stuyvesant High School	23	2	629
High School of Music and Art	45	12	638
Brooklyn Technical School	22	6	907

In one recent year, Negroes and Puerto Ricans were about 14 percent of the graduating class in the city's academic high schools and about 50 percent in the city's vocational high schools. In the vocational schools, Negroes and Puerto Ricans tend to be heavily concentrated in inferior manual trade schools and seriously underrepresented in the technical schools. For example, in a class of 361 in the aviation school (a high-level technical school), 26 were Negroes, 51 were Puerto Ricans, 284 were "Others." In the class at the New York printing school, 4 were

---

[15] While 21.3 percent of Chicago's population have incomes over $10,000 annually, only 18.5 percent of New Yorkers are in this category. In Chicago, 26.3 percent of whites are in this bracket and only 8.7 percent of Negroes; at the same time, 9.9 percent of whites and 28.4 percent of Negroes have incomes less than $3,000 per year.

Negroes, 16 were Puerto Ricans, and 183 were "Others." At the Clara Barton school for hospital workers, Negroes were a clear majority. Vocational schools have been "tightening standards" recently and sending minorities to "academic" schools where, if neglected, they may be no better off.

Higher Education

A developing conflict centers on higher education. Though ethnic records are not kept, one expert estimate is that about 2 percent of students at the University of the City of New York (formerly the city's free colleges) are Negro. One branch of the University is located at the edge of Harlem and is more integrated and accessible to Negroes than other branches, yet less than 5 percent Negro enrollment is reported there.

In New York, Negroes tend to fall between the free city colleges and the dominant and expensive private universities (New York University, Columbia, and their like). They can neither qualify for the former nor afford the latter. Needs tests are not applied to city-college admissions, and free tuition is extended to the affluent with an 85 high school average and denied the impoverished with an 84 average; enrollments are reported to be now predominantly middle class.[16]

Some critics now say that the only equitable system of tuition charges, in all types of institutions, is a sliding scale based on ability to pay. New York does not have a single state university; what is called the University of the State of New York is simply a scattered collection, mainly in nonurban areas, of teachers colleges, agricultural schools, a few technical schools.[17] Recently, the state gave a 40 percent subsidy to New York's city colleges, converted by some graduate offerings into the University of the City of New York. The importance of federal funds to education is seen in federal research and development investments in California and the pervading effect such funds have had in underwriting and stimulating growth of educational institutions there.

---

[16] A recent admissions change at the city university from sole reliance on high school averages to inclusion of college boards scores is expected further to lighten the skin of enrollees. The Board of Higher Education, however, is now discussing a change of admissions standards to accommodate more Negroes.

[17] California spent $33 million on community and junior colleges in 1961–1962 and $214 million on other types of higher education. New York State spent $5.7 million on community and junior colleges and $111 million on other types of higher education. M. M. Chambers, Joint Office of Institutional Research, "Appropriations of State Funds for Operating Expenses of Higher Education, 1961–62," Washington, D. C., January 1962.

New York City's effort through the years to provide free college education and to compensate for the void at the state level has been extraordinary. No other city appears to have made any comparable effort. Still the city seems not to have deployed its college resources equitably, and the gathering debate over the city colleges suggests a conflict of view—or interest—between the city's have-nots and its numerous liberal middle class.[18]

The compilation and release of information about ethnic and social class enrollments in institutions of higher education, as well as the postsecondary experiences of students, appear to be the first step out of the college inequities which have, in turn, imposed inequities on lower educational levels. Equality of opportunity in higher education will probably come only through a national network of community colleges—low in cost and located within easy commuting distance—and available to all "average"-or-above students who want further education.[19] Perhaps Britain's proposed experiment with televised university instruction will provide an alternative, or supplementary model, to the community college.

Class and Ethnic Roles

Within the city itself, at least these elements seem to have some separate, though often overlapping, identity: (1) Negroes; (2) labor unions; (3) white have-nots; (4) white liberals; (5) the Jewish community; (6) the Catholic community; (7) business organizations and their allies in city silk-stocking areas.

The roles and activities of these groups in relation to the schools have never been adequately defined, but impressionistic observation seems to indicate the following outlines: The main white support for civil rights in the past several decades has unquestionably come from the leadership within the labor and Jewish communities—with some major assists from middle-class liberal and church groups, particularly in the last several years. The rank-and-file within the labor-union and

---

[18] None of the New York Board of Education's three community colleges (where admissions standards are such that Negroes can, and often do, qualify) are located in Negro areas. One is now scheduled for Manhattan, but the tentative location is between 23rd and 42nd streets, a white area—one of the few in Manhattan. One high ranking public-school official is quoted as saying "the municipal colleges are not equipped to operate vestibule courses for students who have to be civilized."

[19] The so-called "Russell Report" (Columbia Teachers College) to the Michigan legislature reported that the college enrollments by area rose and fell in proportion to the distance from the state's colleges.

Jewish communities, more personally threatened by Negroes, have tended to lag some distance behind on civil rights.[20]

In the schools, the class and ethnic lines are distinct, even though less clearly drawn than in the larger community. Some political allies of Negroes have been largely outside the school conflict: unions and large numbers of white have-nots, notably the Poles, Italians, and Irish who have tended to use parochial schools. Some feel it is fortunate that these have-not groups have tended to be outside the public school controversy; others feel that the parochial-public school separation has worked hardships on the public schools and delayed a crisis that would, in the long run, be beneficial to the public schools. Union leaders have been less involved in the schools than in other political affairs because of what seems to be a rather basic alienation from the schools and frequently because of their own parochial background. They have, however, supported school expansion, improvement, financing, and their organized political power, as in New York, has given important direct assistance to the schools and to the claims of Negroes on the schools.

The organized business community has traditionally opposed tax increases for public education, the leadership in these groups usually residing in the suburbs where they have provided ample funds for good schools. Powerful real-estate groups have opposed property taxes as well as school and housing integration. The "swing" group has been the Jewish community and, to some extent, the white liberal. The Jewish community, even middle and upper income, has consistently given solid support to the public schools,[21] but its own heavy stress on education and the fact that it is one of the largest remaining white middle-class groups within many cities have produced some ambivalence in its role and some conflict in unexpected places. The confrontation of these two allies in the city public schools is a source of growing distress to both groups. Because the Jewish community has tended to remain in the city and to use the public schools, it is generally contiguous, geographically

---

[20] On general political and economic issues, class lines seem quite clearly drawn: Negroes, unions, white have-nots, and a preponderance of the Jewish community appear on the have-not side, and the organized business, middle-class, and upper-class groups on the have side. Strangely, perhaps, and to some large extent understandably, Negroes chose two groups closest to them politically for their first-line offense: unions and the Jewish community. Both were vulnerable, having made continuing proclamations, accompanied by considerable effort, on behalf of equality and brotherhood, yet having done much less than their best to provide equality for Negroes within their own jurisdictions.

[21] In Detroit, a recent school-tax election was won, informed observers report, by majorities rolled up in the Negro and Jewish precincts.

and emphatically, with the Negro community and located in the middle of the integration cross fire.[22] Negroes point to Jewish predominance in the "better" high schools, the top "ability" groups, the free city colleges, and in public school administration. In many of the "integrating" areas of the city, the two groups have joined in open conflict, though in other areas they have integrated without friction. Thus, the Jewish community, because it has not fled like others from the city, often finds itself in the same situation as the labor movement with regard to Negroes: competition within a family of mutual interest for a scarcity of opportunities—in the schools in one case and in the job market in the other.[23] Perhaps for this reason, among others, the International Ladies Garment Workers Union has been a particularly sensitive target.[24]

Acculturation and Integration

The urban schools now confront the most difficult task they have attempted. Never before has a major *racial* minority been integrated into a nation's school or society. In fact, such integration within a dominantly non-Latin European population is unprecedented in history, the Soviets having settled their racial affairs by geographic separation.

The urban school, whose heavy job has always been the acculturation of immigrant and foreign-speaking ethnic groups, is now taking its first large bite of racial acculturation, as a giant reptile tries to swallow a whole animal. The city is accustomed to educating the immigrant:

---

[22] If the Jewish community is represented in the schools in proportion to its numbers in the population (one quarter of the New York population), then together with Negroes and Puerto Ricans (40 percent) it would represent at least 65 percent of public school enrollments.

[23] On the nine-man New York City school board, three representatives are traditionally selected for each of the three religious communities: Catholic, Protestant, Jewish. Though the Jewish community is represented by three board members, plus a Jewish-Unitarian superintendent of schools, the Negro and Puerto Rican communities, who constitute 40 percent of the public school population, have only one representative (a Negro) on the board.

[24] The Negro struggle seems to have an interacting effect on other have-not groups. In Detroit, the civil-rights movement is supported by the auto workers' union. In battle-torn Chicago, where the class struggle appears in its more primitive form, unembellished by righteous platitudes, the school board seems to have had two lone dissenters on equality and class issues: a steelworker representative (the only unionist on the board) and a Negro (another Negro member has consistently voted with the more conservative majority). The civil-rights drive, however, comes at a time when white workers feel insecure about jobs and their place in society and fear Negro competition in an already glutted job market. In areas of the nation where white have-nots are not organized (as in the South) and therefore do not have this broad view, racial conflict among have-nots is maximum.

In New York City in 1960, 48.6 percent of the population was either foreign-born or had at least one foreign-born parent; in Chicago, the figure was 35.9; in Detroit, 32.2; in San Francisco, 43.5. But the Negro group is unique in these respects: (1) it is the largest "immigrant" group of low-income, public-school-using Protestants (many other recent immigrations having skirted the public schools); (2) it is the first large racial minority to come to the city schools and the first large group with non-Western origins; (3) it has had a unique history of educational and social deprivation.

The active demand of Negro parents for integration perhaps cannot be fully appeased. Negro—and Puerto Rican—students are approaching a majority in many city public schools and any demand for total, one-for-one integration—which few would make—may be impossible in view of the increasing shortage of white public school students. Rather large-scale integration seems possible, however, as New York City is now beginning to demonstrate. Perhaps the issue will finally be settled by integrated urban renewal, or by setting up superschools and superservices in Negro areas—such as the Amidon school in Washington, D. C.—that will attract white students into Negro areas. Mainly, the urban school integration movement has served the latent function of calling attention to Negro education and arousing concern over the quality of Negro schools. The hope is held by many that, if Negro schools are improved, Negroes will not be so eager to integrate.

Among the newer racial demands in urban schools are: (1) compensatory treatment to balance past inequities; (2) "reverse" integration of schools and the busing of whites into Negro schools in order to "equalize" sacrifice (in New York, the demand has been for compulsory busing of both groups; on this most controversial point, Dr. Kenneth Clark has objected that Harlem schools are not fit either for Negroes or for whites and that busing should be "out" only); (3) heterogeneous grouping to scatter Negroes throughout the school population in any given school, rather than segregating them into slow-moving, homogeneous "ability" groups. In New York City and elsewhere, homogeneous grouping has proceeded so far that children in some places are "ability grouped" in kindergarten, based on whether or not they have been to nursery school; these groups, starting almost in the cradle, tend to perpetuate themselves throughout the child's school life.

Some Ways Out

In this author's view, major breakthroughs in urban education may come via any or all of the numerous possible routes.

Outside the school, the possibilities include: (1) a political break-

through of have-nots at the congressional and state legislative levels;
(2) increasing civil-rights activity and pressure; (3) organization of
have-nots at the following levels: political community, ethnic (civil
rights), on the job (union), out of a job (unemployed); (4) federal aid
programs—either through direct federal aid or around this bottleneck
and through special funds, job retraining, Health, Education, and Welfare funds, urban-renewal domestic peace corps, vocational education;
(5) massive infusions of voluntary aid to the schools and assistance
from private foundations.

Inside the schools, the break-through might come from such
sources as: (1) massive enlargement of college opportunities through
the introduction of new funds or new methods of teaching; (2) technological innovation in public school, especially educational television;
(3) the unionization of teachers and the arousal of the professional
group with the greatest stake in improved schools (organized teachers,
it has been demonstrated in New York City, can have an electric effect
on the schools, attracting qualified teachers through improved salaries
and working conditions, reduced class size, improved curriculum, and
quality of school administration and instruction); (4) decentralization
of city school systems to encourage greater participation of have-nots
and clearer and closer channels of communication.[25]

Recent months have seen a spectacular burst of citizen interest
in the schools, perhaps unparalleled by anything in the history of public
education. Women's clubs, youth groups, civil-rights organizations, settlement houses, churches, local government, private funds, and foundations have taken up "tutorials" in deprived areas, and the more imaginative and energetic groups have moved out from there into community
organization. The intrusion of nonschool groups into the learning process
has injected some new excited spirit into the institutional drabness.

Accompanying this new citizen concern with the "disadvantaged"
is a new wave of interest among educators, writers, and scholars in the
problems of poverty and equality, a current that has in recent months
washed over previous concentration on the "gifted" and almost swept
the word out of the educator's vocabulary.

Another source of backdoor assistance to the schools will be the
decongestion of cities—a desperate need of New York especially—by:
(1) the natural attrition of a suburban-bound, affluent population, and
a Negro population pushing ever outward; (2) the forced decentraliza-

---

[25] In New York, the new community school boards, serving as advisory
groups, have already geometrically increased the flow of new ideas, spirit, and
activity into the schools from the local communities and cleared the clogged lines
of communication.

tion of urban renewal, thinning out populations and bringing back into central areas a more taxable balance of middle and lower income groups. Renewal, intelligently, humanely, and artfully carried on, has the potential, of course to remake urban life—by decentralizing, rebuilding, rehabilitating, and creating a truly heterogeneous class and ethnic community.

The Rural Poor: Education, Health and Housing
Report of the President's Commission on Rural Poverty

[Excerpted from The People Left Behind, *September, 1967.]*

THERE WERE more than 700,000 adults in rural America in 1960 who had never enrolled in school. About 3.1 million had less than 5 years of schooling and are classified as functional illiterates. More than 19 million had not completed high school.

This pool of adults with low levels of educational achievement is being fed by a stream of rural youth. More than 2.3 million rural youth aged 14 through 24 dropped out of school before graduating in 1960. About 8.7 percent of them—some 199,000—completed less than 5 years of schooling.

Rural adults and youth are the product of an educational system that has historically short-changed rural people. The extent to which rural people have been denied equality of educational opportunity is evident from both the products of the educational system and the resources that go into the system. On both counts, the quality of rural education ranks low.

Low levels of educational achievement of rural adults give some indication of the poor quality of education in the recent and distant past. In 1960, the average years of schooling for the urban population 25 years of age and over in the United States was 11.1. This compares with 9.5 years for rural nonfarm and 8.8 years for rural farm people. Only 11 percent of the rural adult population had any college education compared with 19 percent of the urban population.

While rural youth are getting a better education than their parents, the level of educational achievement is still lower than for urban youth. Twenty-eight percent of rural nonfarm youth and 23 percent of rural farm youth aged 14 to 24 in 1960 dropped out before graduating. This compares with 21 percent for urban youth.

Not only do rural students drop out sooner, but the percentage of those who go to college after completing high school is much lower than for urban youth. In 1960, about twice as high a proportion of urban as rural youth were enrolled in college.

Those who enroll in college have a hard time competing with students from urban schools. A study of students entering Iowa State University, for example, from urban and rural backgrounds showed that rural students scored lower on entrance examinations and more often had deficiencies in preparation that had to be made up.

The ingredients of any educational system include teachers, buildings, facilities, curriculum, and programs. Their quality in rural schools, compared to urban schools, is low.

Because of low teacher salaries, rural schools are not able to attract and hold the better teachers. Small communities have fewer high school teachers with five or more years of college and more elementary teachers without a college diploma. The percentage of rural teachers not properly certified is about twice as high as for urban teachers.

Failure of rural schools to attract and hold good teachers is also related to the poor facilities in many rural schools. In spite of considerable consolidation of school units, rural schools in general are smaller and less well equipped than urban schools. There are still about 10,000 one-room schools in this country—mostly in rural America. Vast improvements have been made, but some of these small schools still have outdoor privies and are without running water.

Those facilities that are generally associated with scholastic achievement are notably short in rural schools. A recent study, sponsored by the Office of Education in response to the Civil Rights Act of 1964, and referred to as the Coleman Report, indicated, for example, that fewer rural schools have science and language laboratories. The report showed discrepancies in many other physical facilities generally associated with a good school by today's standards.

Rural Schools and Poor People

Bringing the quality of rural schooling up to the level of urban areas would greatly improve the educational opportunities of the rural poor. This alone, however, will not solve the educational problems of economically deprived students. An even larger disparity in quality of schooling exists within rural areas than between rural and urban areas. Some of the most modern schools in the country exist in rural areas. They are in sharp contrast to the one- and two-room schools that are scattered across the landscape. The "poor schools" most often are associated with poor people and poor communities.

The more fundamental problem with respect to the education of the rural poor is the failure of even the better schools to meet their unique educational needs. It was concluded in the Coleman Report that ". . . whatever may be the combination of nonschool factors—poverty, community attitudes, low educational level of parents—which put minority children at a disadvantage in verbal and nonverbal skills when they enter the first grade, the fact is the schools have not overcome it." It was found that the gap in achievement scores between minority students and white students actually widened as the grade level increased.

A very significant finding of the Coleman study is that factors associated with the individual student were more important in explaining differences in educational achievement than factors associated with the schools. For example, all of the "school factors" combined, such as the training of teachers and quality of facilities, were not as important in explaining differences in achievement scores as the student's attitude regarding the amount of control one has over his or her destiny. Students, regardless of race, who had a strong conviction that they could control their future achieved at a higher rate than those who did not. The importance of this finding is illustrated by the fact that the variability among individual pupils within the same school was about four times greater than the variability among pupils between schools.

The big challenge facing the educational system is to develop the capacity of schools to cope with differences among students from varying social and economic backgrounds. Too many people associated with rural schools view students from deprived homes and communities as unwilling or unable to learn. There are many studies and demonstrations that disprove these theories. There are many public school systems that can be looked to as examples of what can be done. The failure of the rural school system to serve adequately the special needs of disadvantaged students is associated with many factors. A big one is lack of knowledge on how to deal with their unique problems. However, many schools need freedom from local pressure and support from outside the community as much as they need new technicians.

Health Status

This Commission is profoundly disturbed by the health problems of low-income people in rural America. Nowhere in the United States is the need for health service so acute, and nowhere is it so inadequate.

The statistical evidence is overwhelming yet the statistics barely suggest the inequity and the discrimination against the rural poor in medical and dental care and in modern health services.

We have failed miserably to protect the health of low-income people in rural areas. The health service they get is not only inadequate in extent but seriously deficient in quality. It is badly organized, underfinanced, rarely related to the needs of the individual or the family. Such health service as there is too often is discriminatory in terms of race and income and heedless of the dignity of the individual.

This Commission is strongly of the opinion that comprehensive, continuous health service of the highest quality should be accessible to all Americans regardless of race, income, and place of residence. The recommendations offered in this report are designed to help achieve that goal.

First, however, consider the facts that describe the problem. We begin with the facts of infant mortality. They underscore the situation in rural America as few things could.

In 1964, one-third of the 1,343 maternal deaths in the United States were mothers in rural areas and small towns of less than 10,000 inhabitants located outside of metropolitan counties. The maternal mortality rate of 40.9 per 100,000 live births in these largely nonurbanized areas was much higher than the national average of 33 deaths per 100,000. The lowest maternal death rate, 25 per 100,000, prevailed in the largely suburban areas surrounding the nation's great cities.

The evidence is clear that there is a definite relationship between illness and income. We know that the progressive nature of illness ultimately interferes with normal productive activity and results in reduced income. We also know that poverty and its associated conditions—inadequate nutrition, unsanitary living conditions, and other effects of poverty—result in frequent and long illness which in turn results in inability to work.

Limitation of activity due to chronic illness is more prevalent among the poor than among the rich. This relationship is even more pronounced when chronic illness affects the person's ability to work at a job, to do housework, or to go to school. Regardless of income, rural residents, especially the elderly, are much more likely to have disabling chronic health conditions than their urban counterparts. Rural persons also have higher rates of injuries than urban residents, have more days of restricted activity, and lose more days from work due to illness and injury than their urban counterparts. The injury rate from motor vehicle accidents is highest among rural nonfarm residents. Rural farm residents have the highest rate of injuries caused by work-related accidents. Accident death rates are higher among rural than among urban people. In 1963, rural residents accounted for 3 out of 5 deaths caused by accidents.

Because the rural poor do not have easy access to appropriate health services early in the illness, the result is much greater disability.

Available data on services provided by physicians and dentists clearly show that the poor are less likely than those with higher incomes to receive adequate medical care. The lack of medical care is most acute among the children of the poor.

Regardless of income, rural farm residents average fewer physician visits per person—consultation with a physician or services provided by a nurse or other person under the physician's supervision—than rural nonfarm and urban residents. Rural residents, especially the children of the rural poor, are less likely to have used the services of a physician during the year than their urban counterparts. And relatively more rural residents than urban residents have never seen a physician.

Although three-fourths of the people in the United States have some kind of health insurance coverage to protect them against the cost of medical care, unfortunately the poor who need it most do not have such protection. About one-third of the persons in families with incomes of less than $2,000 have health insurance compared with nine-tenths of the persons with incomes of $10,000 or more. Regardless of income, the rate of insurance coverage is lowest for rural farm residents, a fact which partially reflects differences in patterns of employment between urban and rural areas. The proportion of persons with insurance protection is lowest for the rural poor on southern farms.

Health Manpower and Facilities

The scarcity of health manpower and facilities in the low-income rural areas is alarming and is not likely to be corrected overnight. Although about 30 percent of our population still lives in rural areas, only 12 percent of our physicians, 18 percent of our nurses, 14 percent of our pharmacists, 8 percent of our pediatricians, and less than 4 percent of our psychiatrists are located in rural areas.

Because of continued population growth, advances in medical knowledge, and overall improvements in the opportunities of the people, the demand for health services and, therefore, for health personnel to provide the services, will continue to increase. Existing shortages of doctors, dentists, nurses, and other health personnel are likely to last for some time. Shortages of hospital beds and high quality extended care facilities—such as nursing homes and other homes for the aged, chronic disease hospitals, and geriatric hospitals—also are not likely to be corrected in a short time. Needless to say, the strain will be felt most in rural areas of the nation.

Health personnel tend to concentrate in metropolitan areas and to specialize. The number of physicians per 100,000 population is 53 in isolated rural areas compared with 195 in large metropolitan centers. The isolated counties are conspicuously lacking in specialists and physicians employed by hospitals and industry. Hence, the continuing decline in the ratio of general practitioners to population during the last decade becomes more critical for rural areas than urban because rural people depend on general practitioners more than on specialists.

Despite an increase in the number of dentists, the ratio of dentists to population has declined during the past decade. The ratio of dentists to population ranges from 69 per 100,000 persons in large metropolitan areas to only 27 in the isolated rural areas. The nurse-population ratio ranges from over 300 per 100,000 persons in urban centers to 126 per 100,000 in the isolated rural areas of the country.

In recent years the operation of the Federal-State hospital construction program under the Hill-Burton Act of 1946 has increased the number of hospitals in rural areas. However, with the rapid population growth the ratio of the number of beds in general hospitals to the nation's population has increased very little.

Although quality of hospital care cannot be measured solely by the number of beds, we do know that the size of the hospital to some extent reflects the services available. The larger hospitals are better staffed with technical personnel and specialists and are generally better equipped. But rural people have to depend largely on the smaller hospitals. In these small hospitals in the outlying areas, free, organized outpatient departments are seldom found.

Historically, the States have had responsibility for the care of the mentally ill and the mentally retarded. However, mental hospital standards vary from State to State. In each of the four most urbanized States the ratio of mental hospital beds "acceptable" to the State supervising agency exceeds 30 per 1,000 population. In the four most rural States, this ratio is lower than 3 per 1,000. The staffing problems in these hospitals are even more acute. The result is that senile and other psychotic patients from rural areas usually end up in seriously substandard facilities. Often patients remain in mental hospitals because of a lack of extended care facilities in the community.

Many of these patients are elderly, and suffer from physical illness which results in psychiatric disorders. Often when these physical illnesses receive appropriate medical or surgical treatment, the psychiatric disorder disappears.

Outpatient psychiatric clinics for rural children and youth are often the only mental health resource available in rural areas. In 1961 only 4 percent of clinics serving children and youth in the nation were located in rural areas. The 35 States without any rural clinics had around 65 percent of the rural children. Rural clinics provided only 1.5 percent of the total clinic manhours of service per week. More of the rural clinics are operated on a part-time basis and have smaller staff than urban clinics. These data are not surprising considering the very heavy concentration of psychiatrists in the large metropolitan areas.

The more affluent rural residents can and often do obtain medical services in the hospitals in distant cities. However, distance continues to be a problem for the rural poor who lack the ready means of transportation, financial resources, and the medical awareness needed to obtain medical and surgical services in the large city hospitals.

To make matters worse for the poor living in the isolated rural areas of the country, services have become increasingly centralized so that availability of transportation and of time to take advantage of these services becomes an additional problem. Dispersion of hospitals and clinics is necessary. However, in rural areas population density is not high enough to make feasible the operation of well-staffed hospitals.

Rural Housing

Decent housing is an urgent need of the rural poor. They live in dilapidated, drafty, ramshackle houses that are cold and wet in winter, leaky and steaming hot in the summer. Running water, inside toilets and screened windows are the exception rather than the rule.

Mrs. Willie Anderson, wife of a migrant farm-worker, testifying before this Commission in Tucson, Ariz., described the shacks for migrant farm laborers near a small town in California as follows:

> The houses were raggedy. It would come a dust storm, the wind would blow, and everything in the house would shake, and the dust would blow in through all the cracks. It was just bad.
>
> . . . Most of the people . . . just like ourselves before we moved, they don't know what it is to get up and turn a faucet on and get hot water; and they don't know what it is to get into a bathtub in a bathroom, you know, and take a bath. They have to heat their water on the stove and take a bath in a tin tub. They don't know what it is to have heat in their house. . . .

Census data show these conditions are all too typical:
- In 1960, 27 percent of occupied rural housing was classified as substandard—deteriorating or dilapidated—compared with 14 percent for urban areas.
- Of the 9.2 million substandard occupied housing units in the nation, 3.9 million were in rural areas.
- More than a million rural homes are dilapidated—structurally unsafe for human occupancy. Many of these homes are beyond repair.
- Less than 1 in 4 occupied rural farm dwellings have water piped into their homes.

● About 30 percent of all rural families still use the traditional privy.

● Fewer than half of all rural homes have central heating. Most rural homes are heated by kerosene-, gas-, wood-, or coal-burning stoves. The result is uneven heating and an ever-present danger of fire.

● Nearly 60 percent of all rural families with incomes of less than $2,000 lived in houses that were dilapidated or lacked complete plumbing.

Rural families who rent are twice as likely to occupy substandard housing as families who own their homes. Twenty percent of rural owner-occupied units were substandard, as compared with 42 percent of the renter-occupied units. Although less than 29 percent of rural housing was renter-occupied, families that rented housing occupied more than half of all dilapidated housing.

A disproportionate number of the elderly occupy substandard housing in rural areas.

The South has the highest proportion of substandard housing in the country (table 1).

TABLE 1

Percent of Rural Dwellings That Were Sound and
Had All Plumbing Facilities, United States, 1960

[Percent]

Region	Rural farm	Rural nonfarm	Rural, total
South	36.5	47.2	44.8
North Central	58.9	60.3	59.9
Northeast	64.9	71.3	70.8
West	69.7	65.4	66.1

SOURCE: U.S. Census of Housing, 1960 – U.S. Summary (table 2).

This is not surprising, for this region has the lowest per capita income, the lowest median family income, the largest families, and the largest proportion of the nonwhite population who are especially disadvantaged.

For eight southeastern counties in Kentucky, substandard housing in the rural communities ranged from 66 percent to 74 percent of the total of all rural housing.

In West Virginia, a State whose population is 60 percent rural, "two-thirds of rural nonfarm dwellings are dilapidated, or lacking in sanitary facilities, or both."

Nonwhites occupy, proportionately, far more substandard housing than whites. Among the nonwhites, Negroes (who make up 92 percent of the nonwhite population nationally, and 98 percent in the South) occupy the largest share of the rural substandard housing. Among rural households with a nonwhite head, 31 percent (more than 360,000) of the housing units were dilapidated, in contrast with 5 percent for households with a white head. In addition, more than 400,000 houses occupied by a family with nonwhite head were deteriorating. Less than 40 percent of nonwhite families had water piped into the home; less than 7 percent had central heating. Owner-occupancy among nonwhites was approximately three-fifths the rate among whites, while renter-occupancy was twice as high:

Color of household head	Owner-occupancy (percent)	Renter-occupancy (percent)
White	73.3	26.7
Nonwhite	45.7	54.3

The deplorable condition of rural housing is a matter of neglect and discrimination. The rural poor simply cannot provide adequate housing for themselves out of their meager earnings; nor have they shared equitably in Federal housing programs. Not until 1961 were funds appropriated for public housing for the rural poor.

If the problem is to be solved, a multifaceted program must be instituted. New programs must be developed to increase the supply of housing for renter and owner-occupied housing.

It is the firm conviction of the Commission that the complexity of the problems of rural poverty preclude the success of a single program or approach. Programs addressed to immediate needs will not erase the underlying conditions creating and perpetuating rural poverty. Programs addressed to these conditions will not immediately help the poor.

The Commission is convinced that the abolition of rural poverty in the United States, perhaps for the first time in any nation, is completely feasible. The nation has the economic resources and the technical means for doing this. What it has lacked, thus far, has been the will. The Commission rejects the view that poverty, in so rich a nation, is inevitable for any large group of its citizens.

Selected Bibliography

1. Junius L. Allison. "Poverty and the Administration of Justice in the Criminal Courts," *Journal of Criminal Law, Criminology, and Police Science*, 55 (June, 1964).

2. Odin W. Anderson, Patricia Collette, and Jacob J. Feldman. *Changes in Family Medical Care Expenditures and Voluntary Health Insurance: A Five Year Resurvey*. Cambridge: Harvard University Press, 1963.

3. Edgar S. and Jean C. Cahn. "The War on Poverty: A Civilian Perspective." *Yale Law Journal*, 73 (July, 1964).

4. David Caplovitz. *The Poor Pay More*. New York: The Free Press of Glencoe, A Division of the Macmillan Company, 1963.

5. James S. Coleman. *Equality of Educational Opportunity*. Washington, D.C.: Government Printing Office, 1966.

6. James B. Conant. *Slums and Suburbs: A Commentary on Schools in Metropolitan Areas*. New York: McGraw Hill Book Co., Inc., 1961.

7. Leonard J. Duhl, Ed. *The Urban Condition: People and Policies in the Metropolis*. New York: Basic Books, Inc., 1963.

8. Arthur J. Goldberg. "Equal Justice for the Poor, Too," *New York Times Magazine Section*, March 15, 1964.

9. George and Eunice Grier. *Equality and Beyond. Housing Goals in the Great Society*. Chicago: Quadrangle Books, 1966.

10. August B. Hollingshead and Frederick C. Redlich. *Social Class and Mental Illness; A Community Study*. New York: John Wiley and Sons, Inc., 1958.

11. Elenor Hunt. "Infant Mortality and Poverty Areas," *Welfare in Review* 5, No. 7 (August-September 1967).

12. Philip S. Laurence and Robert B. Fuchsberg. "Medical Care and Family Income," *Health, Education and Welfare Indicators*, May, 1964.

13. National Commission on Technology, Automation and Economic Progress. *Technology and the American Economy*. Washington, D.C.: Government Printing Office, February, 1966.

14. Henry A. Passow, Ed. *Education in Depressed Areas*. New York: Columbia University Press, 1963.

15. Ellen J. Perkins. "Unmet Need in Public Assistance," *Social Security Bulletin*, April, 1960.

16. Robert M. Guion. "Employment Tests and Discriminatory Hiring." *Industrial Relations*, February 1966.

17. Charles A. Reich. "Midnight Welfare Searches and the Social Security Act," *Yale Law Review*, 72 (May, 1963).

18. Alvin L. Schorr. *Slums and Social Insecurity: An Appraisal of the Effectiveness of Housing Policies in Helping to Eliminate Poverty in the United States*, Research Report Number 1, Division of Research and Statistics, Social Security Administration, United States Department of Health, Education and Welfare, Washington, D.C.: Government Printing Office, 1963.

19. Patricia C. Sexton. *Education and Income*. New York: Viking, 1961.

20. United States Department of Health, Education and Welfare, Welfare Administration. *The Extension of Legal Services to the Poor*. Conference Proceedings, Washington, D.C.: The Administration, 1964.

21. Jacobus TenBrock (ed.) *The Law of the Poor*. San Francisco: Chandler Publishing Co., 1966.

22. Elizabeth Wickendan. *Poverty and the Law—The Constitutional Rights of Assistance Recipients*. New York: The National Social Welfare Assembly, 1962.

23. Daniel Wilner, et al. *The Housing Environment and Family Life*. Baltimore: Johns Hopkins Press, 1962.

Chapter 5

The Values of the Poor

The underprivileged worker lives in a different economic and social environment from that in which the skilled and the middle-class workers live. Therefore the behavior that he learns, the habits that are stimulated and maintained by his cultural group, are different also. The individuals of these different socioeconomic statuses and cultures are reacting to different realistic situations and psychological drives. Therefore their values and their social goals are different. Therefore, the behavior of the underprivileged worker, which the boss regards as "unsocialized" or "ignorant," or "lazy," or "unmotivated" is really behavior learned from the socioeconomic and cultural environments of these workers. In a realistic view, we must recognize it to be perfectly normal, a sensible response to the conditions of their lives.

—From "The Motivation of the Underprivileged Worker" by Allison Davis. Reprinted from *Industry and Society*, William Foote Whyte, ed., New York: McGraw-Hill Book Co., 1946.

ONE READS A GOOD DEAL nowadays both in the popular and scholarly publications about a "culture of poverty." The thesis is presented that there exist neighborhoods, hamlets or larger geographical units where there is an organized social life with a distinctive set of assumptions and beliefs called "lower class values." The logical consequence of this thesis is to suggest a social grouping that (1) does not share the basic assumptions of everyday life of the larger society and (2) has undergone a set of experiences that is different from other groups in the community. The "culture of poverty" is regarded as an adaptive series of responses peculiar to the problems of low-income people. This is an interesting thesis and deserves comment, if for no other reason than the fact that assumptions about a culture of poverty become guidelines for programs to reduce poverty.

Three points can be made about the "culture of poverty" thesis. First, as Hylan Lewis has noted, present-day social science abounds with the uncritical and loose usage of the culture concept. There is reference to a "culture of the uninvolved," to a "culture of violence" and to a "culture of unemployment." The term *culture* is widely applied to numerous dimensions and components of aggregates, groups and persons. One common fallacy is to confuse *culture* with *class*. In a *culture* context we speak of norms and values which regulate behavior in some form of *organized social grouping*. In a *class* context, we refer to certain attitudes and motives that are *common to a category of individuals* sharing the same life chance or economic resources. In the latter case, workers may have the same beliefs but as a function of sharing like economic experiences rather than being socialized into certain beliefs in an organized social grouping. The offspring of the poor are not socialized into a *different* set of beliefs and assumptions about life but they are exposed at an early age to the lack and unpredictableness of economic resources and this exposure may be the important fact in structuring the irreducible assumptions about life. Thus, the cycle of poverty may refer to the intergenerational exposure to certain kinds of economic problems rather than exposure to a particular set of values and beliefs.

The second point to be made about a "culture of poverty" thesis is its utility as an explanatory variable in the behavior of the poor. The existence of a certain set of beliefs or behaviors tells us nothing about *why* these exist among the poor in contrast to other beliefs or behaviors. If we examine critically the explanations of poverty in the intellectual history of the western world, we observe a progression of stereotypes rather than logical, empirically-based explanations. Early explanations explain poverty as a failure to obtain salvation or as punishment for original sin. This explanation was replaced by a biologistic explanation —the poor have low intellectual endowment or physiological defects; or the poor are the "losers" in the natural ordering of society that follows the social Darwinist's struggle for survival. The "culture of poverty" explanation, largely proposed and championed by American intellectuals in the post World War I period, was essentially the replacement of previous stereotypes by others. Granted that the culture hypothesis is more intellectually satisfying than religious or biological explanations, has the case been proven that the behavior and values of the poor are reflections of culture rather than class?

Finally, a "culture of poverty" hypothesis must inevitably raise the question of the utility and worthiness of lower-class values in solving the poverty problem. Do we try to stamp out the values of the poor and try to socialize them to middle class values or do we try to strengthen what exists and respect the uniqueness and inviolability of cultural values? Is the solution to poverty to be found within the value framework of the poor or the value framework of the more affluent groups in the society? If we assume that the poor have the "wrong" values, the solution might be educational programs for the poor that emphasize the emergence of new values. On the other hand, if the assumption is that values reflect differentials in life chance, some effort would have to be made to change the opportunity structure. It may very well be that an anti-poverty program might emphasize both approaches.

In this chapter, Walter B. Miller presents a description of the main themes in lower-class culture, emphasizing the distinctiveness of those values. Oscar Lewis attempts to draw conceptual boundary lines around the culture of poverty. S. M. Miller and his associates examine some common stereotyped notions about the values of the poor. Hylan Lewis examines the distinction between behavior based on the culture of poverty and behavior based on the economic position of the poor. Finally, Herbert Gans discusses the existence of a lower-class subculture and its relationship to the opportunity structure.

Focal Concerns of Lower-Class Culture

Walter B. Miller

Brandeis University School of Social Work

[Excerpted from the article, "Lower Class Culture as a Generating Milieu of Gang Delinquency" from the Journal of Social Issues, *March 1958, by permission of The Society for the Psychological Study of Social Issues, and the author.]*

THERE IS A SUBSTANTIAL SEGMENT of present-day American society whose way of life, values, and characteristic patterns of behavior are the product of a distinctive cultural system which may be termed "lower class." Evidence indicates that this cultural system is becoming increasingly distinctive, and that the size of the group which shares this tradition is increasing.[1] The lower class way of life, in common with that of all

---

[1] Between 40 and 60 percent of all Americans are directly influenced by lower class culture, with about 15 percent, or twenty-five million, comprising the "hard core" lower class group—defined primarily by its use of the "female-based" household as the basic form of child-rearing unit and of the "serial monogamy" mating pattern as the primary form of marriage. The term "lower class culture" as used here refers most specifically to the way of life of the "hard core" group; systematic research in this area would probably reveal at least four to six major subtypes of lower class culture, for some of which the "concerns" presented here would be differently weighted, especially for those subtypes in which "law-abiding" behavior has a high overt valuation. It is impossible within the compass of this short paper to make the finer intracultural distinctions which a more accurate presentation would require.

distinctive cultural groups, is characterized by a set of focal concerns—areas or issues which command widespread and persistent attention and a high degree of emotional involvement. The specific concerns cited here, while by no means confined to the American lower classes, constitute a distinctive *patterning* of concerns which differs significantly, both in rank order and weighting from that of American middle class culture. The following chart presents a highly schematic and simplified listing

CHART 1

FOCAL CONCERNS OF LOWER CLASS CULTURE

Area	*Perceived Alternatives* *(state, quality, condition)*	
1. *Trouble:*	law-abiding behavior	law-violating behavior
2. *Toughness:*	physical prowess, skill; "masculinity"; fearlessness, bravery, daring	weakness, ineptitude; effeminacy; timidity, cowardice, caution
3. *Smartness:*	ability to outsmart, dupe, "con"; gaining money by "wits"; shrewdness, adroitness in repartee	gullibility, "con-ability"; gaining money by hard work; slowness, dull-wittedness, verbal maladroitness
4. *Excitement:*	thrill; risk, danger; change, activity	boredom; "deadness," safeness; sameness, passivity
5. *Fate:*	favored by fortune, being "lucky"	ill-omened, being "unlucky"
6. *Autonomy:*	freedom from external constraint; freedom from superordinate authority; independence	presence of external constraint; presence of strong authority; dependency, being "cared for"

of six of the major concerns of lower class culture. Each is conceived as a "dimension" within which a fairly wide and varied range of alternative behavior patterns may be followed by different individuals under different situations. They are listed roughly in order of the degree of *explicit* attention accorded each, and, in this sense represent a weighted ranking of concerns. The "perceived alternatives" represent polar positions which define certain parameters within each dimension. As will be explained in more detail, it is necessary in relating the influence of these "concerns" to the motivation of delinquent behavior to specify *which* of its aspects it is oriented to, whether orientation is *overt* or *covert, positive* (conforming to or seeking the aspect), or *negative* (rejecting or seeking to avoid the aspect).

The concept "focal concern" is used here in preference to the concept "value" for several interrelated reasons: (1) It is more readily derivable from direct field observation. (2) It is descriptively neutral—permitting independent consideration of positive and negative valences as varying under different conditions, whereas "value" carries a built-in positive valence. (3) It makes possible more refined analysis of subcultural differences, since it reflects actual behavior, whereas "value" tends to wash out intracultural differences since it is colored by notions of the "official" ideal.

Trouble: Concern over "trouble" is a dominant feature of lower class culture. The concept has various shades of meaning; "trouble" in one of its aspects represents a situation or a kind of behavior which results in unwelcome or complicating involvement with official authorities or agencies of middle class society. "Getting into trouble" and "staying out of trouble" represent major issues for male and female, adults and children. For men, "trouble" frequently involves fighting or sexual adventures while drinking; for women, sexual involvement with disadvantageous consequences. Expressed desire to avoid behavior which violates moral or legal norms is often based less on an explicit commitment to "official" moral or legal standards than on a desire to avoid "getting into trouble," e.g., the complicating consequences of the action.

The dominant concern over "trouble" involves a distinction of critical importance for the lower class community—that between "law-abiding" and "non-law-abiding" behavior. There is a high degree of sensitivity as to where each person stands in relation to these two classes of activity. Whereas in the middle class community a major dimension for evaluating a person's status is "achievement" and its external symbols, in the lower class, personal status is very frequently gauged along the law-abiding-non-law-abiding dimension. A mother will evaluate the suitability of her daughter's boyfriend less on the basis of his achievement potential than on the basis of his innate "trouble" potential. This sensitive awareness of the opposition of "trouble-producing" and "non-trouble-producing" behavior represents both a major basis for deriving status distinctions, and an internalized conflict potential for the individual.

As in the case of other focal concerns, which of two perceived alternatives—"law-abiding" or "non-law-abiding"—is valued varies according to the individual and the circumstances; in many instances there is an overt commitment to the "law-abiding" alternative, but a covert commitment to the "non-law-abiding." In certain situations, "getting into trouble" is overtly recognized as prestige-conferring; for example, membership in certain adult and adolescent primary groupings ("gangs") is contingent on having demonstrated an explicit commitment to the law-violating alternative. It is most important to note that the choice between "law-abiding" and "non-law-abiding" behavior is still a choice *within* lower class culture; the distinction between the policeman and the criminal, the outlaw and the sheriff, involves primarily this one dimension; in other respects they have a high community of interests. Not infrequently brothers raised in an identical cultural milieu will become police and criminals respectively.

For a substantial segment of the lower class population "getting into trouble" is not in itself overtly defined as prestige-conferring, but is implicitly recognized as a means to other valued ends, e.g., the covertly valued desire to be "cared for" and subject to external constraint, or the overtly valued state of excitement or risk. Very frequently "getting into trouble" is multi-functional, and achieves several sets of valued ends.

Toughness: The concept of "toughness" in lower class culture represents a compound combination of qualities or states. Among its most important components are physical prowess, evidenced both by demonstrated possession of strength and endurance and athletic skill; "masculinity," symbolized by a distinctive complex of acts and avoidances (bodily tatooing; absence of sentimentality; non-concern with "art," "literature," conceptualization of women as conquest objects, etc.); and bravery in the face of physical threat. The model for the "tough guy"— hard, fearless, undemonstrative, skilled in physical combat—is represented by the movie gangster of the thirties, the "private eye," and the movie cowboy.

The genesis of the intense concern over "toughness" in lower class culture is probably related to the fact that a significant proportion of lower class males are reared in a predominantly female household, and lack a consistently present male figure with whom to identify and from whom to learn essential components of a "male" role. Since women serve as a primary object of identification during pre-adolescent years, the almost obsessive lower class concern with "masculinity" probably resembles a type of compulsive reaction-formation. A concern over homosexuality runs like a persistent thread through lower class culture. This is manifested by the institutionalized practice of baiting "queers," often accompanied by violent physical attacks, an expressed contempt for "softness" or frills, and the use of the local term for "homosexual" as a generalized pejorative epithet (e.g., higher class individuals or upwardly mobile peers are frequently characterized as "fags" or "queers"). The distinction between "overt" and "covert" orientation to aspects of an area of concern is especially important in regard to "toughness." A positive overt evaluation of behavior defined as "effeminate" would be out of the question for a lower class male; however, built into lower class culture is a range of devices which permit men to adopt behaviors and concerns which in other cultural milieux fall within the province of women, and at the same time to be defined as "tough" and manly. For example, lower class men can be professional short-order cooks in a diner and still be regarded as "tough." The highly intimate circumstances of the street corner gang involve the recurrent expression of strongly affectionate feelings towards other men. Such expressions, however, are disguised as their opposite, taking the form of ostensibly aggressive verbal and physical interaction (kidding, "ranking," roughhousing, etc.).

Smartness: "Smartness," as conceptualized in lower class culture, involves the capacity to outsmart, outfox, outwit, dupe, "take," "con" another or others, and the concomitant capacity to avoid being outwitted, "taken," or duped oneself. In its essence, smartness involves the capacity to achieve a valued entity—material goods, personal status—through a maximum use of mental agility and a minimum use of physical effort. This capacity has an extremely long tradition in lower class culture, and is highly valued. Lower class culture can be characterized as "non-intellectual" only if intellectualism is defined specifically in terms of control over a particular body of formally learned knowledge involving "culture" (art, literature, "good" music, etc.), a generalized perspective on the past and present conditions of our own and other societies, and other areas of knowledge imparted by formal educational institutions. This particular type of mental attainment is, in general, overtly disvalued and frequently associated with effeminacy; "smartness" in the lower class sense, however, is highly valued.

The lower class child learns and practices the use of this skill in the street corner situation. Individuals continually practice duping and outwitting one another through recurrent card games and other forms of gambling, mutual exchange of insults, and "testing" for mutual "conability." Those who demonstrate competence in this skill are accorded considerable prestige. Leadership roles in the corner group are frequently allocated according to demonstrated capacity in the two areas of "smartness" and "toughness"; the ideal leader combines both, but the "smart" leader is often accorded more prestige than the "tough" one—reflecting a general lower class respect for "brains" in the "smartness" sense.[2]

The model of the "smart" person is represented in popular media by the card shark, the professional gambler, the "con" artist, the promoter. A conceptual distinction is made between two kinds of people:

---

[2] The "brains-brawn" set of capacities are often paired in lower class folk lore or accounts of lower class life, e.g., "Brer Fox" and "Brer Bear" in the Uncle Remus stories, or George and Lennie in "Of Mice and Men."

"suckers," easy marks, "lushes," dupes, who work for their money and are legitimate targets of exploitation; and sharp operators, the "brainy" ones, who live by their wits and "getting" from the suckers by mental adroitness.

Involved in the syndrome of capacities related to "smartness" is a dominant emphasis in lower class culture on ingenious aggressive repartee. This skill, learned and practiced in the context of the corner group, ranges in form from the widely prevalent semi-ritualized teasing, kidding, razzing, "ranking," so characteristic of male peer group interaction, to the highly ritualized type of mutual insult interchange known as "the dirty dozens," "the dozens," "playing house," and other terms. This highly patterned cultural form is practiced on its most advanced level in adult male Negro society, but less polished variants are found throughout lower class culture—practiced, for example, by white children, male and female as young as four or five. In essence, "doin' the dozens" involves two antagonists who vie with each other in the exchange of increasingly inflammatory insults, with incestuous and perverted sexual relations with the mother a dominant theme. In this form of insult interchange, as well as on other less ritualized occasions for joking, semiserious, and serious mutual invective, a very high premium is placed on ingenuity, hair-trigger responsiveness, inventiveness, and the acute exercise of mental faculties.

Excitement: For many lower class individuals the rhythm of life fluctuates between periods of relatively routine or repetitive activity and sought situations of great emotional stimulation. Many of the most characteristic features of lower class life are related to the search for excitement or "thrill." Involved here are the highly prevalent use of alcohol by both sexes and the widespread use of gambling of all kinds—playing the numbers, betting on horse races, dice, cards. The quest for excitement finds what is perhaps its most vivid expression in the highly patterned practice of the recurrent "night on the town." This practice, designated by various terms in different areas ("honky-tonkin'"; "goin' out on the town"; "bar hoppin'"), involves a patterned set of activities in which alcohol, music, and sexual adventuring are major components. A group or individual sets out to "make the rounds" of various bars or night clubs. Drinking continues progressively throughout the evening. Men seek to "pick up" women, and women play the risky game of entertaining sexual advances. Fights between men involving women, gambling, and claims of physical prowess, in various combinations, are frequent consequences of a night of making the rounds. The explosive potential of this type of adventuring with sex and aggression, frequently leading to "trouble," is semi-explicitly sought by the individual. Since there is always a good likelihood that being out on the town will eventuate in fights, etc., the practice involves elements of sought risk and desired danger.

Counterbalancing the "flirting with danger" aspect of the "excitement" concern is the prevalence in lower class culture of other well established patterns of activity which involve long periods of relative inaction, or passivity. The term "hanging out" in lower class culture refers to extended periods of standing around, often with peer mates, doing what is defined as "nothing," "shooting the breeze," etc. A definite periodicity exists in the pattern of activity relating to the two aspects of the "excitement" dimension. For many lower class individuals the venture into the high risk world of alcohol, sex, and fighting occurs regularly once a week, with interim periods devoted to accommodating to possible consequences of these periods, along with recurrent resolves not to become so involved again.

Fate: Related to the quest for excitement is the concern with fate, fortune, or luck. Here also a distinction is made between two states— being "lucky" or "in luck," and being unlucky or jinxed. Many lower class individuals feel that their lives are subject to a set of forces over which they have relatively little control. These are not directly equated with the supernatural forces of formally organized religion, but relate more to a concept of "destiny," or man as a pawn of magical powers. Not infrequently this often implicit world view is associated with a conception of the ultimate futility of directed effort towards a goal: if the cards are right, or the dice good to you, or if your lucky number comes up, things will go your way; if luck is against you, it's not worth trying. The concept of performing semi-magical rituals so that one's "luck will change" is prevalent; one hopes that as a result he will move from the state of being "unlucky" to that of being "lucky." The element of fantasy plays an important part in this area. Related to and complementing the notion that "only suckers work" (Smartness) is the idea that once things start going your way, relatively independent of your own effort, all good things will come to you. Achieving great material rewards (big cars, big houses, a roll of cash to flash in a fancy night club), valued in lower class as well as in other parts of American culture, is a recurrent theme in lower class fantasy and folk lore; the cocaine dreams of Willie the Weeper or Minnie the Moocher present the components of this fantasy in vivid detail.

The prevalence in the lower class community of many forms of gambling, mentioned in connection with the "excitement" dimension, is also relevant here. Through cards and pool which involve skill, and thus both "toughness" and "smartness"; or through race horse betting, involving "smartness"; or through playing the numbers, involving predominantly "luck," one may make a big killing with a minimum of directed and persistent effort within conventional occupational channels. Gambling in its many forms illustrates the fact that many of the persistent features of lower class culture are multi-functional—serving a range of desired ends at the same time. Describing some of the incentives behind gambling has involved mention of all of the focal concerns cited so far— Toughness, Smartness, and Excitement, in addition to Fate.

Autonomy: The extent and nature of control over the behavior of the individual—an important concern in most cultures—has a special significance and is distinctively patterned in lower class culture. The discrepancy between what is overtly valued and what is covertly sought is particularly striking in this area. On the overt level there is a strong and frequently expressed resentment of the idea of external controls, restrictions on behavior, and unjust or coercive authority. "No one's gonna push *me* around," or "I'm gonna tell him he can take the job and shove it. . . ." are commonly expressed sentiments. Similar explicit attitudes are maintained to systems of behavior-restricting rules, insofar as these are perceived as representing the injunctions, and bearing the sanctions of superordinate authority. In addition, in lower class culture a close conceptual connection is made between "authority" and "nurturance." To be restrictively or firmly controlled is to be cared for. Thus the overtly negative evaluation of superordinate authority frequently extends as well to nurturance, care, or protection. The desire for personal independence is often expressed in such terms as "I don't need *nobody* to take care of me. I can take care of myself!" Actual patterns of behavior, however, reveal a marked discrepancy between expressed sentiment and what is covertly valued. Many lower class people appear to seek out highly restrictive social environments wherein stringent external controls are maintained over their behavior. Such institutions as the armed forces, the mental hospital, the disciplinary school, the prison or correctional institution, provide environments which incorporate a strict and detailed set of rules defining and limiting behavior, and enforced by an authority system which controls and applies coercive sanctions for deviance from these rules. While under the jurisdiction of such systems, the lower class person generally expresses to his peers continual resentment of the coercive, unjust, and arbitrary exercise of authority. Having been released, or having escaped from these milieux, however, he will often act in such a way as to insure recommitment, or choose recommitment voluntarily after a temporary period of "freedom."

Lower class patients in mental hospitals will exercise considerable ingenuity to insure continued commitment while voicing the desire to get out; delinquent boys will frequently "run" from a correctional institution to activate efforts to return them; to be caught and returned means that one is cared for. Since "being controlled" is equated with "being cared for," attempts are frequently made to "test" the severity or strictness of superordinate authority to see if it remains firm. If intended or executed rebellion produces swift and firm punitive sanctions, the individual is reassured, at the same time that he is complaining bitterly at the injustice of being caught and punished. Some environmental milieux, having been tested in this fashion for the "firmness" of their coercive sanctions, are rejected, ostensibly for being too strict, actually for not being strict enough. This is frequently so in the case of "problematic" behavior by lower class youngsters in the public schools, which generally cannot command the coercive controls implicitly sought by the individual.

A similar discrepancy between what is overtly and covertly desired is found in the area of dependence-independence. The pose of tough rebellious independence often assumed by the lower class person frequently conceals powerful dependency cravings. These are manifested primarily by obliquely expressed resentment when "care" is not forthcoming rather than by expressed satisfaction when it is. The concern over autonomy-dependency is related both to "trouble" and "fate." Insofar as the lower class individual feels that his behavior is controlled by forces which often propel him into "trouble" in the face of an explicit determination to avoid it, there is an implied appeal to "save me from myself." A solution appears to lie in arranging things so that his behavior will be coercively restricted by an externally imposed set of controls strong enough to forcibly restrain his inexplicable inclination to get in trouble. The periodicity observed in connection with the "excitement" dimension is also relevant here; after involvement in trouble-producing behavior (assault, sexual adventure, a "drunk"), the individual will actively seek a locus of imposed control (his wife, prison, a restrictive job); after a given period of subjection to this control, resentment against it mounts, leading to a "break away" and a search for involvement in further "trouble."

It would be possible to develop in considerable detail the processes by which the commission of a range of illegal acts is either explicitly supported by, implicitly demanded by, or not materially inhibited by factors relating to the focal concerns of lower class culture. In place of such a development, the following three statements condense in general terms the operations of these processes:

1. *Following cultural practices which comprise essential elements of the total life pattern of lower class culture automatically violates certain legal norms.*

2. *In instances where alternate avenues to similar objectives are available, the non-law-abiding avenue frequently provides a relatively greater and more immediate return for a relatively smaller investment of energy.*

3. *The "demanded" response to certain situations recurrently engendered within lower class culture involves the commission of illegal acts.*

A large body of systematically interrelated attitudes, practices, behaviors, and values characteristic of lower class culture are designed to support and maintain the basic features of the lower class way of life. In areas where these differ from features of middle class culture, action oriented to the achievement and maintenance of the lower class system may violate norms of middle class culture and be perceived as deliberately non-conforming or malicious by an observer strongly cathected to middle class norms. This does not mean, however, that violation of the middle class norm is the dominant component of motivation; it is a by-product of action primarily oriented to the lower class system. The standards of lower class culture cannot be seen merely as a reverse function of middle class culture—as middle class standards "turned upside down"; lower class culture is a distinctive tradition many centuries old with an integrity of its own.

The Culture of Poverty

Oscar Lewis

University of Illinois

[Reprinted from Scientific American, *October, 1966.* © *1966 by Oscar Lewis. An expanded version of this article appears in* La Vida, *by Oscar Lewis, reprinted by permission of Random House, Inc.]*

POVERTY AND the so-called war against it provide a principal theme for the domestic program of the present Administration. In the midst of a population that enjoys unexampled material well-being—with the average annual family income exceeding $7,000—it is officially acknowledged that some 18 million families, numbering more than 50 million individuals, live below the $3,000 "poverty line." Toward the improvement of the lot of these people some $1,600 million of Federal funds are directly allocated through the Office of Economic Opportunity, and many hundreds of millions of additional dollars flow indirectly through expanded Federal expenditures in the fields of health, education, welfare and urban affairs.

Along with the increase in activity on behalf of the poor indicated by these figures there has come a parallel expansion of publication in the social sciences on the subject of poverty. The new writings advance the same two opposed evaluations of the poor that are to be found in literature, in proverbs and in popular sayings throughout recorded history. Just as the poor have been pronounced blessed, virtuous, upright, serene, independent, honest, kind and happy, so contemporary students stress their great and neglected capacity for self-help, leadership and community organization. Conversely, as the poor have been characterized as shiftless, mean, sordid, violent, evil and criminal, so other students point to the irreversibly destructive effects of poverty on individual character and emphasize the corresponding need to keep guidance and control of poverty projects in the hands of duly constituted authorities. This clash of viewpoints reflects in part the infighting for political control of the program between Federal and local officials. The confusion results also from the tendency to focus study and attention on the personality of the individual victim of poverty rather than on the slum community and family and from the consequent failure to distinguish between poverty and what I have called the culture of poverty.

The phrase is a catchy one and is used and misused with some frequency in the current literature. In my writings it is the label for a specific conceptual model that describes in positive terms a subculture of Western society with its own structure and rationale, a way of life handed on from generation to generation along family lines. The culture of poverty is not just a matter of deprivation or disorganization, a term signifying the absence of something. It is a culture in the traditional anthropological sense in that it provides human beings with a design for living, with a ready-made set of solutions for human problems, and so serves a significant adaptive function. This style of life transcends national boundaries and regional and rural-urban differences within nations. Whenever it occurs, its practitioners exhibit remarkable similarity in the structure of their families, in interpersonal relations, in spending habits, in their value systems and in their orientation in time.

Not nearly enough is known about this important complex of human behavior. My own concept of it has evolved as my work has progressed and remains subject to amendment by my own further work and that of others. The scarcity of literature on the culture of poverty is a measure of the gap in communication that exists between the very poor and the middle-class personnel—social scientists, social workers, teachers, physicians, priests and others—who bear the major responsibility for carrying out the antipoverty programs. Much of the behavior accepted in the culture of poverty goes counter to cherished ideals of the larger society. In writing about "multiproblem" families social scientists thus often stress their instability, their lack of order, direction and organization. Yet, as I have observed them, their behavior seems clearly patterned and reasonably predictable. I am more often struck by the inexorable repetitiousness and the iron entrenchment of their lifeways.

The concept of the culture of poverty may help to correct misapprehensions that have ascribed some behavior patterns of ethnic, national or regional groups as distinctive characteristics. For example, a high incidence of common-law marriage and of households headed by women has been thought to be distinctive of Negro family life in this country and has been attributed to the Negro's historical experience of slavery. In actuality it turns out that such households express essential traits of the culture of poverty and are found among diverse peoples in many parts of the world and among peoples that have had no history of slavery. Although it is now possible to assert such generalizations, there is still much to be learned about this difficult and affecting subject. The absence of intensive anthropological studies of poor families in a wide variety of national contexts—particularly the lack of such studies in socialist countries—remains a serious handicap to the formulation of dependable cross-cultural constants of the culture of poverty.

My studies of poverty and family life have centered largely in Mexico. On occasion some of my Mexican friends have suggested delicately that I turn to a study of poverty in my own country. As a first step in this direction I am currently engaged in a study of Puerto Rican families. Over the past three years my staff and I have been assembling data on 100 representative families in four slums of Greater San Juan and some 50 families of their relatives in New York City.

Our methods combine the traditional technique of sociology, anthropology and psychology. This includes a battery of 19 questionnaires, the administration of which requires 12 hours per informant. They cover the residence and employment history of each adult; family relations; income and expenditure; complete inventory of household and personal possessions; friendship patterns, particularly the *compadrazgo*, or godparent, relationship that serves as a kind of informal social security for the children of these families and establishes special obligations among the adults; recreational patterns, health and medical history; politics; religion; world view and "cosmopolitanism." Open-end interviews and psychological tests (such as the thematic apperception test, the Rorschach test and the sentence-completion test) are administered to a sampling of this population.

All this work serves to establish the context for close-range study of a selected few families. Because the family is a small social system, it lends itself to the holistic approach of anthropology. Whole-family studies bridge the gap between the conceptual extremes of the culture at one pole and of the individual at the other, making possible observation of both culture and personality as they are inter-related in real life. In a large metropolis such as San Juan or New York the family is the natural unit of study.

Ideally our objective is the naturalistic observation of the life of "our" families, with a minimum of intervention. Such intensive study, however, necessarily involves the establishment of deep personal ties. My assistants include two Mexicans whose families I had studied; their "Mexican's-eye view" of the Puerto Rican slum has helped to point up the similarities and differences between the Mexican and Puerto Rican subcultures. We have spent many hours attending family parties, wakes and baptisms, responding to emergency calls, taking people to the hospital, getting them out of jail, filling out applications for them, hunting apartments with them, helping them to get jobs or to get on relief. With each member of these families we conduct tape-recorded interviews, taking down their life stories and their answers to questions on a wide variety of topics. For the ordering of our material we undertake to reconstruct, by close interrogation, the history of a week or more of consecutive days in the lives of each family, and we observe and record complete days as they unfold. The first volume to issue from this study is to be published next month under the title of *La Vida, a Puerto Rican Family in the Culture of Poverty —San Juan and New York* (Random House).

There are many poor people in the world. Indeed, the poverty of the two-thirds of the world's population who live in the under-developed countries has been rightly called "the problem of problems." But not all of them by any means live in the culture of poverty. For this way of life to come into being and flourish it seems clear that certain preconditions must be met.

The setting is a cash economy, with wage labor and production for profit and with a persistently high rate of unemployment and underemployment, at low wages, for unskilled labor. The society fails to provide social, political and economic organization, on either a voluntary basis or by government imposition, for the low-income population. There is a bilateral kinship system centered on the nuclear progenitive family, as distinguished from the unilateral extended kinship system of lineage and clan. The dominant class asserts a set of values that prizes thrift and the accumulation of wealth and property, stresses the possibility of upward mobility and explains low economic status as the result of individual personal inadequacy and inferiority.

Where these conditions prevail, the way of life that develops among some of the poor is the culture of poverty. That is why I have described it as a subculture of the Western social order. It is both an adaptation and a reaction of the poor to their marginal position in a class-stratified, highly individuated, capitalistic society. It represents an effort to cope with feelings of hopelessness and despair that arise from the realization by the members of the marginal communities in these societies of the improbability of their achieving success in terms of the prevailing values and goals. Many of the traits of the culture of poverty can be viewed as local, spontaneous attempts to meet needs not served in the case of the poor by the institutions and agencies of the larger society because the poor are not eligible for such service, cannot afford it or are ignorant and suspicious.

Once the culture of poverty has come into existence it tends to perpetuate itself. By the time slum children are six or seven they have usually absorbed the basic attitudes and values of their subculture. Thereafter they are psychologically unready to take full advantage of changing conditions or improving opportunities that may develop in their lifetime.

My studies have identified some 70 traits that characterize the culture of poverty. The principal ones may be described in four dimensions of the system: the relationship between the subculture and the larger society; the nature of the slum community; the nature of the family, and the attitudes, values and character structure of the individual.

The disengagement, the nonintegration, of the poor with respect to the major institutions of society is a crucial element in the culture of poverty. It reflects the combined effect of a variety of factors including poverty, to begin with, but also segregation and discrimination, fear, suspicion and apathy and the development of alternative institutions and procedures in the slum community. The people do not belong to labor unions or political parties and make little use of banks, hospitals, department stores or museums. Such involvement as there is in the institutions of the larger society—in the jails, the army and the public welfare system—does little to suppress the traits of the culture of poverty. A relief system that barely keeps people alive perpetuates rather than eliminates poverty and the pervading sense of hopelessness.

People in a culture of poverty produce little wealth and receive little in return. Chronic unemployment and underemployment, low wages, lack of property, lack of savings, absence of food reserves in the home and chronic shortage of cash imprison the family and the individual in a vicious circle. Thus for lack of cash the slum householder makes frequent purchases of small quantities of food at higher prices. The slum economy turns inward; it shows a high incidence of pawning of personal goods, borrowing at usurious rates of interest, informal credit arrangements among neighbors, use of secondhand clothing and furniture.

There is awareness of middle-class values. People talk about them and even claim some of them as their own. On the whole, however, they do not live by them. They will declare that marriage by law, by the church or by both is the ideal form of marriage, but few will marry. For men who have no steady jobs, no property and no prospect of wealth to pass on to their children, who live in the present without expectations of the future, who want to avoid the expense and legal difficulties involved in marriage and divorce, a free union or consensual marriage makes good sense. The women, for their part, will turn down offers of marriage from men who are likely to be immature, punishing and generally unreliable. They feel that a consensual union gives them some of the freedom and flexibility men have. By not giving the fathers of their children legal status as husbands, the women have a stronger claim on the children. They also maintain exclusive rights to their own property.

Along with disengagement from the larger society, there is a hostility to the basic institutions of what are regarded as the dominant classes. There is hatred of the police, mistrust of government and of those in high positions and a cynicism that extends to the church. The culture of poverty thus holds a certain potential for protest and for entrainment in political movements aimed against the existing order.

With its poor housing and overcrowding, the community of the culture of poverty is high in gregariousness, but it has a minimum of organization beyond the nuclear and extended family. Occasionally slum dwellers come together in temporary informal groupings; neighborhood gangs that cut across slum settlements represent a considerable advance beyond the zero point of the continuum I have in mind. It is the low level of organization that gives the culture of poverty its marginal and anomalous quality in our highly organized society. Most primitive peoples have achieved a higher degree of sociocultural organization than contemporary urban slum dwellers. This is not to say that there may not be a sense of community and *esprit de corps* in a slum neighborhood. In fact, where slums are isolated from their surroundings by enclosing walls or other physical barriers, where rents are low and residence is stable and where the population constitutes a distinct ethnic, racial or language group, the sense of community may approach that of a village. In Mexico City and San Juan such territoriality is engendered by the scarcity of low-cost housing outside of established slum areas. In South Africa it is actively enforced by the *apartheid* that confines rural migrants to prescribed locations.

The family in the culture of poverty does not cherish childhood as a specially prolonged and protected stage in the life cycle. Initiation into sex comes early. With the instability of consensual marriage the family tends to be mother-centered and tied more closely to the mother's extended family. The female head of the house is given to authoritarian rule. In spite of much verbal emphasis on family solidarity, sibling rivalry for the limited supply of goods and maternal affection is intense. There is little privacy.

The individual who grows up in this culture has a strong feeling of fatalism, helplessness, dependence and inferiority. These traits, so often remarked in the current literature as characteristic of the American Negro, I found equally strong in slum dwellers of Mexico City and San Juan, who are not segregated or discriminated against as a distinct ethnic or racial group. Other traits include a high incidence of weak ego structure, orality and confusion of sexual identification, all reflecting maternal deprivation; a strong present-time orientation with relatively little disposition to defer gratification and plan for the future, and a high tolerance for psychological pathology of all kinds. There is widespread belief in male superiority and among the men a strong preoccupation with *machismo*, their masculinity.

Provincial and local in outlook, with little sense of history, these people know only their own neighborhood and their own way of life. Usually they do not have the knowledge, the vision or the ideology to see the similarities between their troubles and those of their counterparts elsewhere in the world. They are not class-conscious, although they are sensitive indeed to symbols of status.

The distinction between poverty and the culture of poverty is basic to the model described here. There are numerous examples of poor people whose way of life I would not characterize as belonging to this subculture. Many primitive and preliterate peoples that have been studied by anthropologists suffer dire poverty attributable to low technology or thin resources or both. Yet even the simplest of these peoples have a high degree of social organization and a relatively integrated, satisfying and self-sufficient culture.

In India the destitute lower-caste peoples—such as the Chamars, the leatherworkers, and the Bhangis, the sweepers—remain integrated in the larger society and have their own panchayat institutions of self-government. Their panchayats and their extended unilateral kinship systems, or clans, cut across village lines, giving them a strong sense of identity and continuity. In my studies of these peoples I found no culture of poverty to go with their poverty.

The Jews of eastern Europe were a poor urban people, often confined to ghettos. Yet they did not have many traits of the culture of poverty. They had a tradition of literacy that placed great value on learning; they formed many voluntary associations and adhered with devotion to the central community organization around the rabbi, and they had a religion that taught them they were the chosen people.

I would cite also a fourth, somewhat speculative example of poverty dissociated from the culture of poverty. On the basis of limited direct observation in one country—Cuba—and from indirect evidence, I am inclined to believe the culture of poverty does not exist in socialist countries. In 1947 I undertook a study of a slum in Havana. Recently I had an opportunity to revisit the same slum and some of the same families. The physical aspect of the place had changed little, except for a beautiful new nursery school. The people were as poor as before, but I was impressed to find much less of the feelings of despair and apathy, so symptomatic of the culture of poverty in the urban slums of the U.S. The slum was now highly organized, with block committees, educational committees, party committees. The people had found a new sense of power and importance in a doctrine that glorified the lower class as the hope of humanity, and they were armed. I was told by one Cuban official that the Castro government had practically eliminated delinquency by giving arms to the delinquents!

Evidently the Castro regime—revising Marx and Engels—did not write off the so-called *lumpenproletariat* as an inherently reactionary and antirevolutionary force but rather found in them a revolutionary potential and utilized it. Frantz Fanon, in his book *The Wretched of the Earth,* makes a similar evaluation of their role in the Algerian revolution: "It is within this mass of humanity, this people of the shantytowns, at the core of the *lumpenproletariat,* that the rebellion will find its urban spearhead. For the *lumpenproletariat*, that horde of starving men, uprooted from their tribe and from their clan, constitutes one of the most spontaneous and most radically revolutionary forces of a colonized people."

It is true that I have found little revolutionary spirit or radical ideology among low-income Puerto Ricans. Most of the families I studied were politically conservative, about half of them favoring the Statehood Republican Party, which provides opposition on the right to the Popular Democratic Party that dominates the politics of the commonwealth. It seems to me, therefore, that disposition for protest among people living in the culture of poverty will vary considerably according to the national context and historical circumstances. In contrast to Algeria, the independence movement in Puerto Rico has found little popular support. In Mexico, where the cause of independence carried long ago, there is no longer any such movement to stir the dwellers in the new and old slums of the capital city.

Yet it would seem that any movement—be it religious, pacifist or revolutionary—that organizes and gives hope to the poor and effectively promotes a sense of solidarity with larger groups must effectively destroy the psychological and social core of the culture of poverty. In this connection, I suspect that the civil rights movement among American Negroes has of itself done more to improve their self-image and self-respect than such economic gains as it has won although, without doubt, the two kinds of progress are mutually reinforcing. In the culture of poverty of the American Negro the additional disadvantage of racial discrimination has generated a potential for revolutionary protest and organization that is absent in the slums of San Juan and Mexico City and, for that matter, among the poor whites in the South.

If it is true, as I suspect, that the culture of poverty flourishes and is endemic to the free-enterprise, pre-welfare-state stage of capitalism, then it is also endemic in colonial societies. The most likely candidates for the culture of poverty would be the people who come from the lower strata of a rapidly changing society and who are already partially alienated from it. Accordingly the subculture is likely to be found where imperial conquest has smashed the native social and economic structure and held the natives, perhaps for generations, in servile status, or where feudalism is yielding to capitalism in the later evolution of a colonial economy. Landless rural workers who migrate to the cities, as in Latin America, can be expected to fall into this way of life more readily than migrants from stable peasant villages with a well-organized traditional culture, as in India. It remains to be seen, however, whether the culture of poverty has not already begun to develop in the slums of Bombay and Calcutta. Compared with Latin America also, the strong corporate nature of many African tribal societies may tend to inhibit or delay the formation of a full-blown culture of poverty in the new towns and cities of that continent. In South Africa the institutionalization of repression and discrimination under *apartheid* may also have begun to promote an immunizing sense of identity and group consciousness among the African Negroes.

One must therefore keep the dynamic aspects of human institutions forward in observing and assessing the evidence for the presence, the waxing or the waning of this subculture. Measured on the dimension of relationship to the larger society, some slum dwellers may have a warmer identification with their national tradition even though they suffer deeper poverty than members of a similar community in another country. In Mexico City a high percentage of our respondents, including those with little or no formal schooling, knew of Cuauhtémoc, Hidalgo, Father Morelos, Juárez, Díaz, Zapata, Carranza and Cárdenas. In San Juan the names of Rámon Power, José de Diego, Baldorioty de Castro, Rámon Betances, Nemesio Canales, Lloréns Torres rang no bell; a few could tell about the late Albizu Campos. For the lower-income Puerto Rican, however, history begins with Muñoz Rivera and ends with his son Muñoz Marín.

The national context can make a big difference in the play of the crucial traits of fatalism and hopelessness. Given the advanced technology, the high level of literacy, the all-pervasive reach of the media of mass communications and the relatively high aspirations of all sectors of the population, even the poorest and most marginal communities of the U.S. must aspire to a larger future than the slum dwellers of Ecuador and Peru, where the actual possibilities are more limited and where an authoritarian social order persists in city and country. Among the 50 million U.S. citizens now more or less officially certified as poor, I would guess that about 20 percent live in a culture of poverty. The largest numbers in this group are made up of Negroes, Puerto Ricans, Mexicans, American Indians and Southern poor whites. In these figures there is some reassurance for those concerned, because it is much more difficult to undo the culture of poverty than to cure poverty itself.

Middle-class people—this would certainly include most social scientists—tend to concentrate on the negative aspects of the culture of poverty. They attach a minus sign to such traits as present-time orientation and readiness to indulge impulses. I do not intend to idealize or romanticize the culture of poverty—"it is easier to praise poverty than to live in it." Yet the positive aspects of these traits must not be overlooked. Living in the present may develop a capacity for spontaneity, for the enjoyment of the sensual, which is often blunted in the middle-class, future-oriented man. Indeed, I am often struck by the analogies that can be drawn between the mores of the very rich— of the "jet set" and "café society"—and the culture of the very poor. Yet it is, on the whole, a comparatively superficial culture. There is in it much pathos, suffering and emptiness. It does not provide much support or satisfaction; its pervading mistrust magnifies individual helplessness and isolation. Indeed, poverty of culture is one of the crucial traits of the culture of poverty.

The concept of the culture of poverty provides a generalization that may help to unify and explain a number of phenomena hitherto viewed as peculiar to certain racial, national or regional groups. Problems we think of as being distinctively our own or distinctively Negro (or as typifying any other ethnic group) prove to be endemic in countries where there are no segregated ethnic minority groups. If it follows that the elimination of physical poverty may not by itself eliminate the culture of poverty, then an understanding of the sub-culture may contribute to the design of measures specific to that purpose.

What is the future of the culture of poverty? In considering this question one must distinguish between those countries in which it represents a relatively small segment of the population and those in which it constitutes a large one. In the U.S. the major solution proposed by social workers dealing with the "hard core" poor has been slowly to raise their level of living and incorporate them in the middle class. Wherever possible, psychiatric treatment is prescribed.

In underdeveloped countries where great masses of people live in the culture of poverty, such a social-work solution does not seem feasible. The local psychiatrists have all they can do to care for their own growing middle class. In those countries the people with a culture of poverty may seek a more revolutionary solution. By creating basic structural changes in society, by redistributing wealth, by organizing the poor and giving them a sense of belonging, of power and of leadership, revolutions frequently succeed in abolishing some of the basic characteristics of the culture of poverty even when they do not succeed in curing poverty itself.

Poverty and Self-Indulgence: A Critique of the Non-Deferred Gratification Pattern

S. M. Miller, *Ford Foundation*
Frank Riessman, *New York University*
Arthur A. Seagull, *Michigan State University*

The history of this article is an interesting commentary on the development and dissemination of ideas. The basic outline of its concerns first appeared in Frank Riessman's unpublished doctoral dissertation, Class Differences in Attitudes Towards Participation and Leadership, *Columbia University, 1955. Miller and Riessman developed the ideas in a series of papers; one "The Critique of the Non-Deferred Gratification Image of the Worker" (1956), was exclusively devoted to the non-deferred gratification pattern. They were never able to find an academic journal willing to publish it. The article was privately circulated until the editors of this volume asked to publish it. Meanwhile, Arthur A. Seagull had worked with Miller and did his dissertation,* The Ability to Delay Gratification, *Syracuse University, 1964, on an experiment involving a test of the deferred pattern. Consequently, we were able to expand the article. One moral of this tale is that not only has the interest in poverty led to new work but that it also has disinterred neglected studies.*

THE OUTPOURING OF SOCIAL SCIENCE LITERATURE on social class differences has led to efforts to develop general themes which codify the scattered data and provide ways of thinking about class dynamics. One such theme is that of the deferred gratification pattern, which is thought to provide the basis for the social and economic advance of the middle classes. Its presumed absence in the non-middle classes is regarded as a barrier to improvement among this population, and, for some, an explanation of why the poor are poor.

In the absence of competing explanations of the varied data, the deferred gratification pattern (DGP) has been in the first rank of principles explaining "lower class behavior." Indeed, it is probably the most frequently used element in discussion of lower class life. The recent attention to poverty has renewed interest in the DGP. Our feeling is that it is a thin reed on which to hang analyses of behavior and that logical examination of the concept and appraisal of empirical materials do not confirm its usefulness as an all-explanatory theme.

While we believe that the DGP concern does point to some important problem areas, we do not have confidence that it is a satisfactory summation of the data, nor that it can be mechanically applied to interpret low income life. Since it affects social policy we believe it must be closely appraised.

The Concept of the DGP

The DGP is frequently discussed in the negative—that is, the characteristics which result from its absence in low income life. Schneider and Lysgaard[1] have provided the most compact summation of the non-deferred gratification pattern. They have concluded that in contrast with middle class life, lower class life is characterized by an inability to defer gratification by "impulse following" rather than "impulse renunciation." The catalogue of lower class, "impulse-following" non-deferred gratification behavior includes: "relative readiness to engage in physical violence, free sexual expression (as through intercourse), minimum pursuit of education, low aspiration level, failure of parents to identify the class of their children's playmates, free spending, little emphasis on being 'well-mannered and obedient,' and short time dependence of parents." On the other hand, "Middle class persons feel that they *should* save, postpone, and renounce a variety of gratifications."[2]

Allison Davis' approach[3] is central to the notion of ability to de-

---

[1] Louis Schneider and Sverre Lysgaard, "The Deferred Gratification Patterns: A Preliminary Study," *American Sociological Review*, 18 (April, 1953), pp. 142–49. We place a heavy emphasis on this article because it is a thoughtful effort to integrate a variety of studies.

[2] Sverre Lysgaard, "Social Stratification and the Deferred Pattern," *Proceedings*, World Congress of Sociology, Liege, International Sociological Association, 1953, p. 142.

[3] Allison Davis, *Social Class Influences Upon Learning*, Cambridge: Harvard University Press, 1949; Allison Davis and Robert J. Havighurst, "Social Class and Color Differences in Child-Rearing," *American Sociological Review*, II, 1946, pp. 698–710; Allison Davis, "Child Rearing and the Class Structure of American Society," in *The Family in Democratic Society*, Anniversary Papers of the Community Service Society of New York, New York: Columbia University Press, 1949.

lay, or its concomitant, "impulse renunciation." Davis felt that starting with early child rearing practices there was less emphasis on impulse control among lower class parents than middle class parents. He felt that, "Generalizing from the evidence . . . we would say the middle class children are subjected earlier and more consistently to the influences which make a child an orderly, conscientious, responsible and tame person."[4]

Considering the behavior of lower income adults, Davis stated that their propensity for choosing immediate reward was an adaptive response to the slum environment. "The lower class people look upon life as a recurrent series of depressions and peaks with regard to gratification of their basic needs. In their lives it is all or nothing. . . . The learned fears of deprivation drive lower class people to get all they can of other physical gratification, 'while the getting is good.' "[5]

The middle classes are believed to be distinguished by the presence and significant operation of the ability to defer gratification, to accept later rewards instead of immediate satisfactions, to bank their impulses, and to plan effectively for the future. The non-middle classes are believed to be characterized by the absence of these abilities. To some extent, then, the DGP statements are relative statements: the middle classes have more of the deferred patterns than do other classes (the upper classes are usually ignored in these discussions). Consequently, an examination must not only weigh the existence of these patterns among the poor but the degree of deficiency when compared with the middle classes.[6]

It is important to realize that an undertone of the DGP analysis is that the pattern is not temporary nor easily overcome. Indeed, the assumption is that the ability or inability to defer gratification is deeply embedded in the personality dynamics of the individual, performing an

---

[4] Davis and Havighurst, *op. cit.*, p. 707.

[5] Davis, *Social-Class Influence Upon Learning*, p. 27.

[6] We shall not discuss the social value of the deferred gratification patterns and the possible individual and social prices exacted by them. The avidly melancholy voice of Paul Goodman has been raised in question of the pain of impulse-renunciation. Indeed, some of those who pioneered the concept of deferred gratification like Allison Davis, were extremely critical of the price the middle classes paid for their impulse-renunciation, though feeling that it would be well for the less affluent to pay this price in order to advance. Nor do we question whether the DGP is a sine qua non for the development of occupational skills although we doubt that it is. See S. M. Miller, "Dropouts—A Political Problem," in David Schreiber, ed., *The School Dropout*, Washington: National Education Association, 1964.

important role in the psychodynamic economy. The picture seems to be that the DGP or the non-DGP are developed through early life experience: they become incorporated in the personality and are relatively impervious to situational factors. We hasten to add that not all who espouse the DGP approach share the psychodynamic orientation or the notion of relative fixity. Perhaps, it is only ambiguous presentations which lead us to believe that most do.

Who Are the Non-Deferrers?

One of the difficulties in the discussion of the DGP is that the world is divided frequently into the middle classes and the non-middle classes. All in the middle classes are possessors of the ability to defer gratification, and those of the non-middle classes are bereft of this ability. Obviously, even among those who believe strongly in the dichotomous distribution of the deferring attributes, it is recognized at some level that it is not a 100 percent against a 0 percent distribution problem. Central tendencies are what are basically assumed—although some writing does not imply this—so that some middle class individuals do not possess the DGP and some non-middle class persons do.

Beyond the blurring of the distribution problem is the lumping of all who do not possess middle-level income or white collar jobs into the non-middle classes, frequently called "the lower class." We have previously indicated the inadequacy of lumping together regularly employed, skilled, blue-collar workers with irregularly employed, low-skill service workers.[7]

More recently it has been pointed out that there is considerable internal differentiation among those at the lower-income end of the lower class. Four sub-groups among the newly rediscovered poor have been denoted: the stable poor, the strained poor, the copers/skidders, and the unstable poor.[8] It is our suspicion that the kinds of attitudes and behavior which have been subsumed under the DGP term are most

---

[7] S. M. Miller and Frank Riessman, "The Working-Class Subculture: A New View," *Social Problems*, 1961. Reprinted in Arthur Shostak and William Gomberg, eds., *Blue Collar World*, Englewood Cliffs: Prentice-Hall, Inc., 1964, and in Frank Riessman, *The Culturally Deprived Child*, New York: Harper and Row, 1962.

[8] S. M. Miller, "The American Lower Classes: A Typological Approach," *Social Research*, 1964. Reprinted in Frank Riessman, Jerome Cohen and Arthur Pearl, eds. *Mental Health of the Poor*, New York: Free Press, 1964; in Shostak and Gomberg, *op. cit.*; in Shostak and Gomberg, eds., *Perspectives on Urban Poverty*, Englewood Cliffs: Prentice-Hall, Inc., 1965.

likely to be found among the unstable poor. It is misleading, then, to write as though all the poor have the same outlook as the unstable poor and will be benefited by the same social policies as might aid the unstable poor.

Since most analyses of attitudes and behaviors do not make fine distinctions within the poor or the lower classes, what might be real differences between the unstable poor and other groups of poor, near-poor and the middle classes do not appear in the available data.[9] Nevertheless, while we believe that some DGP elements may be more characteristic [10] of the unstable poor, we do not find the DGP concept a fully adequate way of understanding the behavior of the poor and of other non-middle class groups.

In investigations with no immediate middle-class comparison groups or in more general statements about the absence of the DGP among the poor, the middle classes are frequently explicitly or implicitly imaged in an out-moded way. They are regarded as delighting in hard work, frugally and carefully planning and budgeting every activity and expenditure, abjuring debt, and constantly foregoing the indulgence of present gain in order to reap future rewards. It is hard to recognize this "Protestant Ethic" pattern in the new middle classes possessed by "other direction" and pursuing the consumption euphoria of today. The rise of consumer debt among the middle classes, the refrain of "not being able to make ends meet" despite affluent income levels, the competition between work and the coffee break, suggest that important changes have taken place in many sections of the middle classes, or that the middle classes were never quite as described. Consequently, the comparisons with the middle classes are frequently of the actual behavior of the poor with "official norms rather than actual practice"

---

[9] Unfortunately the absence of refined social-class categories means that data on "the lower class" may in some studies we cite refer mainly to the upper working classes. We reluctantly and tacitly accept this group in the discussion of "the poor," because of difficulties in developing principles to include or exclude studies. Since the cited studies are used in buttressing the DGP position, we feel it important to raise questions about them.

We have used interchangeably terms like the non-middle classes, "the poor," "the lower classes," to refer to the groups which are being contrasted with the middle classes.

[10] By using "more" we mean to imply that the comparison is with the middle classes and that the unstable poor may not be "typically" characterized by these attributes. While more of the unstable may have these attributes, these practices may not characterize the overwhelming majority.

of the better-off.[11] Some official middle class norms may have changed as well, compounding the irreality of the comparison.

The Logical Basis of the DGP

Before proceeding to evaluate research on the class distribution of the DGP, it is important to note some problems in the formulation of this mode of analysis. In order for a valid interclass comparison to be made, certain conditions must be met:

1. *The two class groups must equally value the satisfaction that is being deferred.* If the object is less valued by the low income group, then obviously the interest in making immediate sacrifices is less.

2. *The two class groups must have an equal understanding and opportunity to defer an immediate gain for a future reward.* If one group is not presented with or is not aware of the opportunities of future gain, then we cannot infer from the fact that it has not deferred that it is unwilling to do so.

3. *The two class groups must suffer equally from the deferment.* If one class has many more other satisfactions, then it is difficult to equate the impact of the deferment. Or, if the penalty of postponement is greater for one of the groups, the comparison falls down.

4. *The two class groups must have the same probability of achieving the gratification at the end of the deferment period.* If one group has less risk than the other or has more confidence that the gratification will be forthcoming, then the comparison is not valid. Objective and subjective risk must be comparable.

Clearly, no research meets these conditions. Indeed, it is probably impossible in real life to find circumstances under which these conditions prevail in groups differently situated in the social structure. It was these doubts that made us first ponder the usefulness of the DGP. In most situations talked about in relation to the DGP, middle class or higher income groupings are more likely than lower-income groupings to value the object that is deferred (sometimes because they know more about it; sometimes because of value choices); or they are likely to suffer less from a deferment of gratification (largely because they have alternative rewards), or they are much more likely to be sure of getting the reward at the end of the deferment period.

---

[11] S. M. Miller and Frank Riessman, *op. cit.,* p. 90. For changes in child-rearing practices in the middle classes, see Urie Bronfenbrenner, "Socialization and Social Class through Time and Space," in Eleanor E. Maccoby, Theodore M. Newcomb, and Eugene L. Hartley, eds., *Readings in Social Psychology,* New York: Henry Holt & Company, 1958.

Furthermore, it is important to recognize that the same act can have quite different meanings and implications in the different settings of middle class and working class life. Deferment or non-deferment in the same situation may have different motivations in different groups. Caution must be exercised in order to avoid analyzing the behavior of the poor in terms of middle class experience without consideration of alternative explanations.

Nevertheless, class differences do exist. That one would expect differences between classes in their approach to life would seem incontrovertible, given differences in income, housing, education, and opportunities for upward mobility. It remains to be seen whether viewing these differences from a framework of "the ability to defer or to delay gratification," is helpful.

In our limited space, we cannot review every study that touches upon the DGP. We shall cite studies which question the appropriateness of the non-DGP for describing the behavior and attitudes of the poor. In a few studies, the investigators do not conclude that their data support the self-indulgence theme; in others, the investigators do conclude that their results support the non-DGP idea, but their data can be differently interpreted.[12]

We believe that data have been fairly consistently interpreted as supporting the non-DGP even where the results have been ambiguous. One purpose of this paper, therefore, is to free us to look in a more rounded way at the data and studies. By raising questions of interpretation, perhaps we shall begin to think of other alternative modes of analysis.

Spending and Savings

The ability to save—"to put money away for that rainy day," to forego the satisfactions of the immediate purchase, to resist "impulse buying"— are important elements in the DGP.[13] Schneider and Lysgaard studied the DGP by asking 2,500 high school students whether they thought that their parents had saved money to give them a start in life. In the middle class, over 80 percent thought that their parents had saved for them, as contrasted to over 70 percent in the non-middle class groups, be-

---

[12] In citing studies we do not wish to imply that the investigator himself necessarily believes in the value of the DGP analyses. Rather, his work has been interpreted as supporting evidence.

[13] This paragraph and the two following are based on Frank Riessman, *Workers' Attitude Towards Participation and Leadership, op. cit.*, pp. 94–96. In this analysis we have refrained from making methodological criticisms of studies.

cause differences were not controlled in the study. Although statistically significant, this difference between the upper and lower groups is not great when differences in income and hence available amounts for saving are considered. The non-middle class families—at least in the eyes of their children—were making efforts to help their children. And such efforts may have required more organization than in the middle class families of higher income.[14]

These findings of Schneider and Lysgaard are presented by them, however, to buttress the position that workers cannot defer gratifications as evidenced by the lower percentage reporting savings. Yet the same findings can be interpreted as indicating a restriction of consumption in order to save despite the obstacles of comparatively lower incomes.

Schneider and Lysgaard also observed class differences in response to the question, "If you won a big prize, say two thousand dollars, what would you do with it?" Again there is a small difference in the percentages of non-middle class and middle class students who indicate that they would "save most of it." They report this difference as indicative of less deferred gratification ability on the part of the worker. But over 65 percent of both class groups state that they would "save most of it," and the absolute class difference is less than 5 percent. Certainly, this small difference could be expected in terms of the likelihood that a larger proportion of the lower income group would need to spend more of its funds on direct economic necessities.

The difficulties of interpreting data are well revealed in William F. Whyte's findings that the corner boy shares his money with his friends.[15] Schneider and Lysgaard infer that ". . . the corner boys must share their money with others and *avoid* middle class thrift." (Italics ours.) This is considered to be an illustration of a negative attitude toward deferring gratifications. But since money shared with others is unavailable for personal gratification, sharing might be considered under the rubric of "renunciation," and hence a delay of gratification, although there may be some gain in status.

To infer a distinctive value or attitude pattern from this kind of data seems somewhat questionable. Particularly is this so in the light of the report of McConnell who described the "savings" orientation of

---

[14] The importance of impulse-buying among the middle classes suggests that the propensity to defer and save receives great competition from the propensity to consume even among the better off.

[15] William F. Whyte, *Street Corner Society,* Chicago: University of Chicago Press, 1958.

the blue-collar worker as "defensive savings" for a "rainy day" rather than as one focused toward status ascent.[16] This observation suggests that the savings practices of workers may fit into a different pattern than that of middle class individuals. Therefore, their low rate of savings may not be affected by the same psychological focus which would presumably be important among non-saving middle class individuals.

School

Schneider and Lysgaard interpret the fact that working class and lower class adolescents leave school earlier as evidence of their inability to defer gratification. Ely Chinoy has well expressed this point of view:

> The quick surrender of working class youth to the difficulties they face is not necessarily forced or unwilling. Although they are encouraged to focus their aspirations into a long future and to make present sacrifices for the sake of eventual rewards, they are chiefly concerned with immediate gratifications. They may verbally profess to be concerned with occupational success and advancement (as did fourteen working class boys who were interviewed), but they are likely to be more interested in "having a good time" or "having fun." They want to "go out," to have girl friends, to travel, to own a car or a motorcycle.[17]

While of course it is true that working class adolescents as a whole leave school earlier than do middle class youth, the question is whether the interpretation of this behavior is adequate. In addition to the school leaving statistics, at least three other items have to be considered:

1. The school situation, less enjoyable for the non-middle class youth than for the middle class youth because of its middle class structuring, teacher expectations, and utilization of class biased intelligence tests, is not comparable for the two—the strain of school is probably greater on the working class youth;[18]

2. Economic necessity undoubtedly contributes to the disproportionate withdrawal from school;

3. Lower income youth are, at least implicitly, being contrasted with the presumably deferred gratification middle class adolescent. A question therefore has to be raised as to whether today the latter typically give up spending money, good times, girl friends, travel, or a

---

[16] John McConnell, *The Evolution of Social Classes*, Washington: American Council on Public Affairs, 1942, pp. 144 ff.

[17] Ely Chinoy, *Automobile Workers and the American Dream*, New York, Doubleday and Company, 1955, p. 113.

[18] Riessman, *The Culturally Deprived Child*, *passim*.

car in order to go to school or college. Stern has asserted that certain schools are "fountains of knowledge where the students come to drink," i.e., enjoy themselves.[19]

The motivation of the behavior of an individual cannot be fully understood unless attention is paid to the particular pressures on him and to the means and resources available to him in a physical, financial and cultural sense. The imputed contrast between middle class and working class youth has to be studied in terms of these factors. For example, Beilin concludes that college education was the culmination of a desire of the working class student, and hence a gratification rather than a postponement. In his questionnaire study, he found no relationship between ability to delay gratification and upward mobility in his lower class sample.[20]

It is important to gather objective data concerning class differences in the area of education. Without a doubt, real class differences exist in attitude, dropout rate, and college attendance. One must be cautious, however, in ascribing a solitary motivation to a particular behavior, since individuals may react in an identical manner for very different reasons.

Sexual Experience

It is widely believed that differences between social classes in the amount of pre-marital sexual intercourse mirror differing ability to postpone immediate gratification and control "impulse following." The free and unrestrained sexual activity of non-middle class adolescents and adults is contrasted with that of their middle class counterparts. Allison Davis has presented a concise portrait:

> Like physical aggression, sexual relationships and motivation are far more direct and uninhibited in lower class adolescents. The most striking departure from the usual middle class motivation is that in much lower class life, sexual drive and behavior in children are not regarded as inherently taboo and evil.
>
> At an early age the child learns of common-law marriages, and extramarital relationships by men and women in his own family. He sees

---

[19] G. G. Stern, "Characteristics of the Intellectual Climate in College Environments," *Harvard Educational Review*, 33, 1963, pp. 5–41.

[20] Harry Beilin, "The Pattern of Postponability and Its Relation to Social Class and Mobility," *Journal of Social Psychology*, 44, 1956, pp. 33–48. Unfortunately, Beilin defined "lower socio-economic group as those subjects 'whose fathers were in the lower middle class or below' (in such classification schemes as Warner's." Cf. Murray Straus, "Deferred Gratification, Social Class, and the Achievement Syndrome," *American Sociological Review*, 27, 1962, pp. 326–335.

his father disappear to live with other women, or he sees other men visit his mother or married sisters. Although none of his siblings may be illegitimate, the chances are very high that sooner or later his father and mother will accuse each other of having illegitimate children, or that at least one of his brothers or sisters will have a child outside of marriage. In his play group, girls and boys discuss sexual relations frankly at the age of eleven or twelve, and he gains status with them by beginning intercourse early.[21]

The Kinsey data are often cited to support the notion that the worker is sexually promiscuous and unable to defer gratifications.[22] While there are many limitations to the Kinsey studies which we cannot enter into here, it is worth noting, if the Kinsey material is to be offered in evidence, that much of it is self-contradictory, and that much of it does not support the usual interpretation of workers' sexual behavior.

For example, Schneider and Lysgaard cite the Kinsey reports as supporting the conclusion that "relatively 'lower' class persons indulge considerably in premarital intercourse; 'upper' class persons show relative deferment of gratification in this section of behavior."[23] Schneider and Lysgaard omit, however, from the Kinsey reference the report that middle class males pet and masturbate more. Apparently, Schneider and Lysgaard do not consider the middle class pre-marital pattern of erotic involvement without intercourse as a sexual experience, although Kinsey emphasized that this is itself a middle class attitude:

> The conflict [about sexual morality] is obviously one between two systems of mores, between two cultural patterns, only one of which seems right to a person who accepts the tradition of the group in which he has been raised. With the better educated groups, intercourse versus petting is a question of morals. For the lower level, it is a problem of understanding how a mentally normal individual can engage in such highly erotic activity as petting and still refrain from actual intercourse.[24]

The investigator's definition of what constitutes sexual experience is a crucial variable in determining whether a difference will be noted in the ability of either class to delay, and not the subject's behavior

---

[21] Allison Davis, "Socialization and Adolescent Personality," in Guy E. Swanson and Theodore H. Newcomb and Eugene Hartley, eds., *Readings in Social Psychology*, New York, Henry Holt and Company, 1955.

[22] A. C. Kinsey and others, *Sexual Behavior in the Human Male*, Philadelphia: W. B. Saunders, 1948. A. C. Kinsey and others, *Sexual Behavior in the Human Female*, Philadelphia: W. B. Saunders, 1953.

[23] Schneider and Lysgaard, *op. cit.*, p. 143.

[24] Kinsey, et al., *Sexual Behavior in the Human Male*, p. 541.

per se. Non-middle class and middle class males differ more in their manner of achieving sexual gratification than in the amount of sexual experience achieved, considering all sources.[25]

Even when using intercourse as the only criterion for sexual gratification, much of the data is contradictory and does not support the usual interpretation of the sexual behavior of the low income population:

1. While Kinsey reports that non-middle class males engaged in considerably more pre-marital intercourse than middle class males, no such class difference is reported for the females.

2. Kinsey finds that the middle class engaged in fellatio and cunnilungus to a much greater extent than did the non-middle class. He reported the latter as expressing disgust at these practices which are also violations of professed middle class mores. Thus, lower-income people avoided and condemned sexual practices which were not infrequent among middle class males, although they are counter to the usual middle class prescriptions.

3. Kinsey's data on nudity show that working class people are less likely to have intercourse without clothes than is true of middle class males.

Furthermore, according to Maccoby and Gibbs, lower class parents are much less likely to permit their children to walk around naked in the house, and they are also less likely to appear unclothed before their children.[26] What this means is not entirely clear, but we may tentatively hypothesize that it is related to problems of crowded living conditions and to some concern for the development of children's ideas with regard to sex.

The data on masturbation, to some extent, lend support to this hypothesis. The studies of Maccoby and Gibbs reveal that non-middle class families, far from encouraging indulgence of the child's sexual play with himself, are more concerned than are middle class parents to prevent sexual play. Now, this effort may be undesirable, but it certainly does not indicate any easy indulgence of the impulses of the

---

[25] In Kinsey's large sample, lower class males reported more premarital and extra-marital intercourse in the early years of marriage, and more intercourse with prostitutes, than did middle class males. Middle class males reported premarital petting and masturbation, and more extra-marital intercourse later in marriage. Can class-linked personality traits be legitimately inferred from these differences in sexual behavior when the definition of sexual experience is itself class related?

[26] Eleanor Maccoby, Patricia K. Gibbs, et al., "Methods of Child-Rearing in Two Social Classes," in William E. Martin and Celia Burns Stendler, eds., *Readings in Child Development*, New York: Harcourt, Brace and Company, 1954, pp. 380–96.

child. The low-income child is much more likely to be punished for masturbatory acts than is the middle class child (whose parents may be more attuned to the contemporary demands of permissive up-bringing).

Kinsey's data on adolescents and adults, which indicate less masturbation on the part of the lower class, could be interpreted in terms of the latter's greater outlet in sexual intercourse. The definite inhibition of masturbatory behavior in childhood on the part of the lower class cannot, however, be as easily explained in terms of the usual image of sexual "freedom." Moreover, the attitudes toward masturbation developed in childhood may provide a more adequate explanation of adolescent and adult rates of masturbation in the lower class.

Further evidence of the intricate regulation of working class sexual life rather than its unrestricted "freedom" is found in Whyte's analysis of the slum sex code of Cornerville.[27] Some have taken his study to reveal sexual licentiousness on the part of the Italian working class youth whom he describes. Yet, as the term "the slum sex code" suggests, their sexual behavior is strongly regulated by codes and traditions. As Whyte points out, it is clearly taboo to have intercourse with "good girls," i.e., virgins and relatives of friends. What kind of intimacy is acceptable and with whom is governed by strong community norms.

The data on illegitimacy have also been misunderstood. The presumption is that non-middle class populations have higher rates than middle class; this empirical observation is used by some to support the notion of easy sexual indulgence by the lower classes. Both the reports of data and their interpretation are questionable.

Early research sampled only public clinics and hospitals; the conclusion was that unwed mothers tended to come from lower socio-economic levels and from broken homes. When a more representative sample was employed, including private physicians and hospitals, Vincent concluded that, contrary to earlier beliefs, "the unwed mothers . . . were not predominantly of low socio-economic status, nor even predominantly of any particular socio-economic stratum."[28]

Furthermore, the illegitimacy rate by itself cannot be considered a behavioral measure of inability to delay, without controlling for "rate

---

[27] William F. Whyte, "A Slum Sex Code," *American Journal of Sociology,* XLIX, 1943, pp. 24–31, reprinted in Reinhard Bendix and Seymour M. Lipset, eds., *Class, Status and Power,* Glencoe: Free Press, 1953. We are indebted to David Matza for bringing to our attention the misleading interpretation of the Whyte data.

[28] Clark E. Vincent, *Unmarried Mothers.* Glencoe: Free Press, 1961, p. 64.

of illicit coitus"[29] and differential knowledge of contraceptive methods between classes.[30]

Knowledge of class-linked sexual behavior does not lend itself to an easy summary. But the limited evidence that we have brought together should question the facile acceptance of the notion that the sexual practices and outlook of the non-middle classes clearly support the DGP interpretation.[31]

Ability to Delay

We have examined some of the case studies and questionnaire investigations on the ability to delay gratification. We shall now survey some of the relevant experimental literature on class differences in the ability to delay gratification.[32]

Mahrer found that the expectancy that the "social agent" (E) actually would keep his word about bringing a delayed reward was an important cue for the choice of delayed or immediate reward.[33] His subjects were working class grade school children. He manipulated the level of their expectancy for reward in three different experimental groups by promising a delayed reward on each of four training trials, though keeping his promise none of the time in one group (low ex-

---

[29] *Ibid.*

[30] The importance of viewing alternative explanatory possibilities is shown in Cavan's explanation of why lower income groups have large families. (Ruth Cavan, *The American Family*, New York: Thomas Y. Crowell Company, 1953, pp. 182 ff.) In a sophisticated sociological discussion she reviews the effects of the larger number of Catholics in the non-middle classes, the expense and self-discipline involved in using contraceptives, the asset value of children as early wage earners (which, incidentally, is quite a long range deferred gratification view), and the lesser financial burdens that low-income children impose upon their families compared to the funds expended on middle class children. Some of the reasons stated by Cavan for large, low-income families are undoubtedly correct, but other, unmentioned reasons also exist. For example, the significance of the family as a crucial cooperative unit for many low-income groups is overlooked or the possibility of a positive feeling towards children and a desire to have a "big family" as a way of life.

[31] Lee Rainwater, *And the Poor Get Children*, Chicago: Quadrangle Books, 1960.

[32] Because of space limitations, we do not discuss the experimental literature or temporal orientation. In any case, the connection between temporal orientation and ability to defer gratification is not clear-cut. Cf. Levon H. Melikian, "Preference for Delayed Reinforcement: An Experimental Study Among Palestinian Arab Refugee Children," *Journal of Social Psychology*, 50, 1959, pp. 81–86; Walter Mischel, "Preference for Delayed Reinforcement and Social Responsibility," *Journal of Abnormal Social Psychology*, 1961, pp. 1–7. The discussion borrows from Seagull, *op. cit.*

[33] Mahrer, A. R., "The Role of Expectancy in Delayed Reinforcement," *Journal of Experimental Psychology*, 42, 1956, pp. 101–106.

pectancy); twice in the second group (moderate expectancy); and all four times in the third group (high expectancy). The fifth trial (test trial) was a choice between two toys—a less valued toy to be had immediately or a more valued one obtainable after a day's delay.

He found that the "high expectancy" group differed significantly from the other two groups in choice of "delayed reinforcement." His results supported the position, at least for working class children, that it was the situation rather than the personality which determined whether they chose delayed or immediate reward.

He also found that neither the low, moderate, or high expectancy groups generalized from their experience with the E of the training trials (Ea) to a different E (Eb). ". . . the effects of training with Ea failed to generalize to Eb. Instead there were uniform reactions to Eb independent of the kind of training with Ea. . . . The implication is that delayed reinforcement behavior in general depends not only on the value of the reinforcements, but also on the expectancy for the occurrence of delayed reinforcement as related to the social agent involved."[34]

Such a position militates against uniform interpretations of the ability to delay as a class-linked personality variable, since it was clear that the choice of reward was determined by the particular interaction with the experimenter.

Shybut used a composite measure to explore the relationship between the ability to delay and certain psychological and demographic variables, including several measures relating to social class.[35] The first two components were behavioral measures—a vote for a "record hop" within a week, or a "band dance" with a well-known and much-liked band a month from the testing; and a "thank you ticket" worth 25c, 35c, or 50c in merchandise at a store, depending on how long the subject delayed cashing in the ticket. The third, a projective measure, was an essay about their personal reaction to obtaining a large windfall of money. A "Delayed Gratification Index" (DGI) was constructed from the responses to the three measures.

There was no significant relationship between the DGI and socio-economic level as defined by any of the following criteria: paternal occupation, family income, an index of the number of people per room at home, or paternal education. Thus, on a well constructed, composite measure there was no indication that socio-economic classes differed in ability to delay. Ethnic groups, "Anglos" and "Non-Anglos" (Indians)

---

[34] *Ibid*, p. 105.
[35] Shybut, J., *Delayed Gratification: A Study of Its Measurement and Its Relationship to Certain Behavioral, Psychological and Demographical Variables,* Unpublished Master's thesis, University of Colorado, 1963.

did, however, differ, the Non-Anglos having a significantly higher DGI than the Anglos.

Seagull[36] investigated Mischel's hypothesis that the choice of delayed gratification might depend on the degree of trust the subject has for the *E*, rather than on the class affiliation. Children were given Mischel's choice between one bar of candy now or two bars in a week.[37] For the second and third sessions, however, the classrooms were randomly assigned to a trust condition (that *E* kept his promise about bringing the candy) and a Mistrust condition (where *E* did not). After the promise was kept or broken, the children again chose to delay or not.

The results were clear cut. The first week, when there was no experimental manipulation, no differences appeared between children from any social classes, or between white or Negro children. The second and third session, there was a large and significant difference between the Trust and Mistrust conditions in choice of delayed reward in the expected direction. It should be noted that there was no indication of a differential rate of sensitivity to trust or mistrust, since the rate of change was the same to or from a delay reward choice for the different social groups.

Thus, for those children whose socio-economic level was definable, there were no differences in ability to delay on the choice presented, while the differences in choice when they could trust the *E* or not were very large and significant.

The situational variable, then, rather than class affiliation determined the ability to delay. Though there are many other populations and choice stimuli to be sampled, the data do not support the hypothesis that the ability to delay is class-linked at least over the whole range of subjects and situations.

Conclusion

The studies that we have reviewed do not instill confidence in the sweeping conclusions of the DGP. Obviously, our interpretations of data can be questioned. Our intention is not to foreclose discussion on the usefulness of the DGP concept, but to encourage study of it and competing explanations.

---

[36] Seagull, *op. cit.*

[37] Walter Mischel's work has been influential. See his "Preference for Delayed Reinforcement: An Experimental Study of a Cultural Observation, *Journal of Abnormal Social Psychology*, 56, 1958, pp. 57–61; "Delay of Gratification, Need for Achievement and Acquiescence in Another Culture," *Journal of Abnormal and Social Psychology*, 62, 1961, pp. 543–552; "Father-absence and Delay of Gratification," *Journal of Abnormal and Social Psychology*, 63, 1961, pp. 116–124; "Reward as a Function of Age, Intelligence, and Length of Delay Interval," *Journal of Abnormal and Social Psychology*, 64, 1962, pp. 425–431.

We do feel that many lower-income people have a shorter time perspective than do many middle-income persons. The shorter time outlook may handicap many of the poor. But we are not sure that the shorter time perspective is *always* linked with an inability to defer gratification. More importantly, we do not view all those who seem to be unable to defer gratification as so psychodynamically constrained that the ability to delay is unavailable to them. For some, this is undoubtedly true. But for others, situations which offer perceived hope do lead to postponement and planning.[38] They may not be able to overcome all the obstacles which face them, but they are not locked into self-indulgence.

The experimental studies on the importance of trust underline the significance of situational rather than psychodynamic variables. The former perspective leads us to provide situations which do, in truth, offer chances of payoff for postponement. Furthermore, by emphasizing nonpersonality variables, we have the possibilities of helping individuals to *learn* the kinds of patterns that may be important for their well-being. We do not doubt, for example, that lower income youth could have school experiences which work toward expanding the time in which the youth expect to get a return for their activities.

Many studies show that educational level is the major variable explaining different social class behavioral/attitudinal patterns. This conclusion suggests that we are not dealing with outlooks that have an immutable quality; rather, they are affected by knowledge, and understanding. They are subject, consequently, to influences and change.

The DGP emphasis leads to social policies which emphasize "rehabilitation" rather than expanding opportunity. Some of the poor obviously need "rehabilitation" in order to take advantage of opportunity. For others, opportunity may reduce the need for "rehabilitation."

Our objections to the DGP emphasis do not rest with its social policy implications. At the level of social science analysis, the verdict on the DGP is "not proved." It is not adequate as the major, and sometimes sole, variable in explanations of the behavior of the poor. By recognizing the limitations as well as the insights of DGP approach, we might move to search for alternative or supplementary explanations of the attitudes and behavior of that large slice of the American population who are not in the middle classes.

---

[38] For a sophisticated approach to a situational analysis see the important article by Louis Kriesberg, "The Relationship Between Socio-Economic Rank and Behavior," *Social Problems*, 10, 1963, pp. 334–53; also in the Reprint Series of the Syracuse University Youth Development Center.

Child Rearing Among Low-Income Families

Hylan Lewis

Howard University

[Excerpted from Child Rearing Among Low Income Families. *Child Rearing Project, Health and Welfare Council of the National Capital Area. Washington, D.C.: The Washington Center for Metropolitan Studies, 1961.]*

MY COLLEAGUES AND I have been engaged in a field project with the operating title: "Child Rearing Practices Among Low Income Families in the District of Columbia." The focus of the project is on the relationships between the conditions of life in poorer families, and child neglect, parental inadequacy, and dependency. Stated simply, the aims in this phase of a planned two-part project are, first, to find out how different kinds of low-income families in different kinds of community situations are guiding the development of children; and, second, to discover what kinds of community programs involving the voluntary participation of lower income families are practicable.

This project, representing as it does a union of social science and social welfare techniques and experiences, is a pragmatic operation. It exists to provide a service for those who are confronted with practical, harsh, immediate problems.

While the central interest is in child rearing practices and community settings among low income "problem" families, material has been obtained, for comparative purposes, on low income families without "problems" and on "adequate" income families.

As of May, 1961, field observations had been made on a total of sixty-six families, of which fifty-seven are low income families, forty-nine non-white and eight white. Twenty-six, or slightly less than one-half of the low income families in the study population, are currently active with public welfare agencies; sixteen of these are families with Aid to Dependent Children grants.*

Field workers have been trained to observe and to report on people in their natural settings. The purpose is to get material in depth, to see as well as to listen.

The field documents illustrate wide variety in the concrete human

---

* The number of field contacts with families ranges from one to twenty-seven. The average number of contacts with low-income families was more than nine; the average number of hours of contact for these families was twelve.

styles of low income families. The fact that these documents were obtained indicates, among other things, an impressive willingness of these low income family heads to share their experiences over extended periods of time. One of the mothers volunteered that she was pleased to be "a part of a larger study," of a project that is "doing something that might be of help to other families like mine, so that they might not have to go through all the things we have been through."

My present purpose is not to summarize project accomplishments or findings—in fact, the analysis of the field materials is far from being completed; rather, it is to share some propositions and reflections that we think have relevance for family and child welfare programs, and for understanding the contemporary poor.

In general, our materials confirm the findings of other students that among low income families, unguided, unplanned influences outside of the family or household are relatively more important, and affect the socialization of the child relatively earlier, than among higher or adequate income families. Our initial analysis of the field materials has resulted further in a series of propositions about family and community influences on child rearing among low income families.

Among the propositions that we wish to share here are some that have to do with (1) parental control in low income families, (2) the relationship between the family values and the actual behavior of lower income parents, and (3) the quality of life in low income neighborhoods.

In many families studied, the effects of external influences are reflected in the strikingly early appearance of cut-off points in parental control and emotional support—in the falling off of parents' confidence in their ability, as well as in their will, to control and give attention to their children.

For practical purposes—and this reminds us of the recent news story about the seven-year-old veteran of vandalism and breaking in—the immediate point is that changes in parents' control, and in their self-estimates of ability to control, occur sometimes when the children are as young as five and six. In these instances I am talking about now, the factors associated with potential and actual child neglect are different from those in which neglect and inadequate care of infants and very young children are related to parental rejection. This latter type of situation is well understood, of course.

Here we are talking about the mothers who are not basically rejecting of, or hostile to, their children. Characteristically, for such mothers the care and control of younger children is not perceived as a real problem: the mothers show confidence, warmth, and ability to exercise effective control. As children grow older there seems to be a cut-off point at which parents express impotence and bafflement. Although there are anxieties, the fate of these growing children is often written off as out of parents' hands. There recurs in the records a mixture of hope and resignation: "I do hope they don't get in trouble. I tried to raise them right." "The Lord will have to look out for them." "I'm glad mine are little. I kinda hate to see them grow up. At least I can do something for them now."

Additional factors that seem to have something to do with the cut-off points are the size of the family and expectations about the child's work role. Mothers in low income, large family situations frequently set training and discipline goals in keeping with needs or demands for assistance in the household and in the care of other children; these goals are unrealistic in relation to growing children who are exposed progressively to extra-family influences. When mothers in such family situations fail to achieve their specific and immediate child rearing goals related to household functioning, they exhibit discouragement and bafflement. They describe their inability to cope with external factors which they say have stronger pulls on their children than maternal demands for good manners, respect, floor scrubbing, and supervision of the younger children.

A staff member's comments on some of the generalizations current about class factors in parental control should be considered:

> There is current in much of the literature on child rearing a belief that mature status for the child is granted relatively early on the lower socio-economic levels. Much is made of the idea that middle and upper class children envy the "freedom" of their lower class contemporaries. Our field materials suggest that this apparent freedom of the children in lower income families is not necessarily "granted." Frequently, it appears to be wrested from begrudging parents or parental substitutes.

The fact that the loss of parental control occurs so early in many of these families, whether due to parental abdication or the revolt of children, should be juxtaposed with the fact that the adolescent period is the socially accepted or expected period of revolt.

Much popular thinking, reinforced by some earlier studies, stresses presumed or demonstrated class differences in child rearing values. Our field materials suggest that the low income parents in this study group, whether they are adequate or inadequate, dependent or not dependent, tend to show greater conformity to, and convergence with, middle class family and child rearing standards in what they say they want (or would like to want) for their children and themselves, than in their actual child rearing behavior. This is evident in much of the material examined in relation to parental concerns and controls, self-appraisals of child rearing behavior, education of children, sex, marriage, and illegitimacy.

In both categories of low income families, the dependent and the non-dependent, are found parents who show a high degree of interest in children's health, education, and welfare. The persistence of positive concern, and of the willingness to sacrifice for children, despite deprivation and trouble, are features of the child rearing behavior of a good proportion of the low income families observed.

As other studies have shown, the low income mothers of this study group have relatively high educational aspirations for their children, and, above all, they want better housing and neighborhoods. The persistent themes are: "getting a good education," "getting enough education," "getting a good job." A staff member points out, however, that what constitutes a good job, or sufficient education, is not always specified.

> There is lack of knowledge or clarity as to how children are to obtain the goals projected; and there is very little indication that the parents know what to do themselves in order to motivate children. On the contrary, what seems to be an underlying theme is expressed in various ways in the idea that "you can lead a horse to water. . . ." There is communicated a combination of realism and pessimism, a kind of wise weariness that may appear to belie the very educational or career goals they express for at least some of their children.

Acute dissatisfactions cluster around housing, and the lack of proper places for children to play. Examples are:

> The first step I'm striving for is better housing . . . I just want to get out of all of this.

> The one thing I want, it's a backyard fenced in so my children don't play out in the street. I hope and pray some day to do better. But what can I do now?

> I would like a comfortable home for them, if I could give them anything.

> So we have the will, we're just waiting for the way. (With reference to moving out of the area.)

In the observations of parents in our study group of low income families, we have distinguished three varieties of parents classified according to concern: (1) those with high concern who demonstrated it in their behavior; (2) those with considerable verbal concern, but who exhibited inconsistent or contradictory behavior; and (3) those who expressed little or no concern and who are extremely neglectful.

The first type consists of parents whose high concern is exhibited in actions related to the welfare of children, in contrast to verbalizations. Working with what they have, they show high "copability," self-reliance, and self-respect. The way in which they face problems—that is, react to outside impersonal forces—indicates good mental health in this sense of the term.

The second type of parents includes those who are inconsistent in their concern and exhibit a borderline degree of parental control. They tend to be highly self-centered and demanding. Characteristically, parents of this type are persons who themselves recall unsatisfactory or deprived childhoods. They are reported as having difficulty in accepting the child as an individual. They tend to be impatient and they apply discipline inconsistently.

Parents of the third classification are the central adult figures in the classic picture of child neglect—children who suffer undernourishment, untreated physical ailments, exposure to violence, harsh treatment, and arbitrary punishment. There is a tendency among the parents who show a very low degree of concern and few parental strengths to use their children as scapegoats. Dependent and lacking in self-reliance themselves, they seem to resent their children for being dependent on them. They are rated low in self-confidence and self-esteem. It is probable that a good proportion of Junior Village children come from this type of parent.

The most inadequate and neglectful parents are the most reluctant to talk about the specifics of child rearing. Even the most neglectful parents, however, ascribe no virtue to inadequacy or neglectful behavior in themselves or in others, or to neighborhood disorganization. If there is any suggestion of approval of neglectful behavior or accentuation of the negative, it smacks of perverseness, defiance, bravado, or desperation of the "I-don't-care" type. The following field document illustrates this:

> When a neighbor commented to a mother that one of the mother's four children appeared to have a bad cold, the mother, referring to herself, calmly said, "Her mother don't care!" At the neighbor's expression of surprise that she would say such a thing, the mother, bridling at the implied criticism, countered with, "Well, that's the way it is so I might as well tell the truth."

In every category of low income families observed there are differences in hopes and expectations of changes for the better, and in the parents' estimates of resources they think they have, or can find, to effect changes in themselves. In other words, there are cutting points also in the optimism and confidence of many parents about the futures of their families—and in the belief that their efforts alone might affect them. This cut-off point in parental optimism and confidence is something that emerges, as one of the most insidious and eroding processes affecting child rearing. Confidence that is continuing, even though mixed or fluctuating, as much as anything, distinguishes low income families that are not now marked by neglect or dependency, from those that are "clinically" dependent or neglectful.

The "multi-problem" or "hard core" cases of inadequacy, dependency, and neglect are, to use medical terminology, "clinical cases," with unknown or varying potential for rehabilitation. As in types of heart disease and cancer, when the condition becomes known or public, it is frequently too late; prognosis for these cases is poor. "Clinical" dependency, that which is known to public and private agencies and health and welfare institutions, is costly, and provokes concern beyond the numbers involved.

Although it is necessary and important to seek improved ways of rehabilitation or containment, the long-range dividends are likely to be greater from research and demonstration programs that seek to identify and work with the highly vulnerable families, not yet publicly dependent or neglectful; that is, to examine the "pre-clinical" and "sub-clinical" aspects of dependency and neglect.

While there is a statistical relationship between illegitimacy and poverty, it is necessary to get behind the gross statistics, and to be discriminating in our judgments and conclusions. For example, any interpretation or programming based on the assumption that there is a distinctive population of unwed mothers, or that unwed mothers would rather be unwed, flies in the face of the facts.

Our materials support three propositions. First, the belief is not valid that broad categories of people, such as lower income groups, newcomers, and certain ethnic minorities, are not troubled about illegitimacy. Second, birth in wedlock is an important value; but in any given instance, it might be pre-empted by another important value, or its realization thwarted by practical considerations. Third, for program purposes, the salient values and practices related to illegitimacy are those reflected in the affirming of family support for the mother and child, "taking them in," or having and keeping the child in the face of possible community disapproval.

Pregnancy out of wedlock, particularly the first pregnancy, is commonly referred to as a "mistake." Identifying with her pregnant daughter, the mother of ten children differed with her husband who wanted to put his daughter out; she said:

> I told him she ain't the first one who ever made a mistake and I was going to let her stay right here with me. I told Esther we would take

care of her through this one, but no more babies before you're married. I did this because I had made a mistake and got pregnant and I could understand how anybody could make a mistake, at least once.

The idea of one's mistake being "human" or even a "right" is also heard. Not unmindful of the fact that she did not marry until her second pregnancy, another mother said:

Everybody has a right to one mistake, but two out of wedlock children are no mistake—and three—the girl's just beyond herself!

The acceptance of the "first mistake" does not imply, however, that there is no emotional upheaval on the part of the parents.

A grandmother, learning in court that her granddaughter's "mistake" had occurred in their own living room, said: "I just knew I was going to die. I had tried so hard." A white mother who considered the possibility of her daughter's becoming pregnant decided:

I don't know. Maybe I almost would have lost my mind, but I would not turn her out. I just could not do it. I certainly would take care of the baby. I would not permit the baby to be put for adoption.

A Negro mother of eight children concurred, saying:

I know it would hurt me an awful lot. But I wouldn't put her out. A real mother wouldn't do that. But it would really hurt me . . . I would not do that. But I wouldn't place the baby for adoption even though I have so many children.

The field materials indicate a great deal of popular misunderstanding and some myth about the sex behavior and propensities of lower income families and individuals from these families. There is a striking incidence of parental shame and embarrassment about sex. (We seriously doubt that this last is in itself a class trait, unique to this category of the population.)

Sex education is found to be a family matter to a very limited degree. Vague warnings and prohibitions constitute the bulk of sex training. Behavior and expressions of many mothers in relation to children's curiosity about sex are reminiscent of a Victorian attitude. Their evasions are reinforced by dismissal of talk about sex as "bad" and "nasty." A mother in her early twenties who lives with her family in a housing project said:

We knew nothing about sex the whole time we were growing up. Sex was hush-hush. It was like the Dark Ages. It was sad. It really was.

A forty-two-year-old white mother of five children said:

No, we would never talk about such things to my mother. We had too much respect for her.

A thirty-one-year-old mother in a housing project said:

> All my mother said to me was, "Tell your sister," when I started menstruating; and to this day that is all she said to me.

For the mothers in general, the onset of the menstrual cycle was the point at which the silence was broken by vague admonitions about keeping away from boys.

> My mother told me about "ministrating." She never told me about sex, nothing about a man and she say—after I got up the nerve to ask her— "You fool around with a boy, you get a baby" and that was all!

> My mother didn't talk to me when I was growing up. She would say, "If something happens to you, will you please let me know?" I used to wonder what she was talking about, but that's all she would say.

The woman whose mother referred her to her sister for explanation was told by the sister to read aloud a passage on menstruation from a medical book. She drew the conclusion that conception could occur automatically and was therefore expecting to become pregnant momentarily.

A young woman who married at eighteen said that she became pregnant three months later and, although she knew by then where the baby was, she was puzzled about how it was going to get out of her stomach.

The key problem, as in previous generations, seems to be embarrassment in talking about sex. Even some of the mothers who said they wanted to bring their children up differently, mentioned difficulty in overcoming this embarrassment. One of the mothers, when pressed for an explanation of why she said that she often got her sister to talk to her children, said:

> It was the way I was raised. I had a very strict mother and she never came out and talked to me about it and when they came to me I just couldn't.

This embarrassment in discussing any aspect of sex appeared to be widespread. A wife whose three children were born out of wedlock, blushed when any aspect of sex was mentioned, and said she "doesn't believe in that nasty talk."

Despite embarrassment and ambivalence, what to do about the sex training of children and the recognized threat of illegitimacy was seen as an acute dilemma by a good proportion of the low income mothers. Two of the more poignant examples are the mother who brought home condoms from the drugstore to explain their use to her twelve year old daughter, and another mother who requested a diaphragm from the birth control clinic for her fourteen year old daughter.

An important commentary on the matter of sex and illegitimacy among low income groups was the avidity with which women in four mothers' groups entered into a discussion of problems in these areas. A staff report said about these meetings:

> One got the impression of people anxious to share and exchange views and to learn. Tempers were riled, anxieties expressed, and personal confidences shared in brisk and lively sessions. . . . What was of particular importance was that so much interest was evidenced, even though it was clearly understood that our prime interest was in learning what they had to say and not in telling them what to do. Their reaction suggests that there is much more that can be done in this area on an educational level.

In spite of the fact that many homes do not have fathers or husbands, the lower income male and father is a key figure in gaining an understanding of child rearing in the lower income or dependent family. Of particular importance is the man's ability to support and stand for the family—to play the economic and social role wished of him, particularly by wives, mothers, and children. Some of the implications of this are suggested in the field document that describes a mother of six children chiding her husband for being afraid and not showing aggressiveness in looking for a second job to increase the family income. Showing his pay stub, she said: "This looks like a receipt for a woman's paycheck instead of a man's."

Although the analysis of our data is incomplete, the materials suggest that neither the quality of life in most low income neighborhoods nor the child rearing behaviors of low income families is to be interpreted as generated by, or guided by, what one student calls "a cultural system in its own right—with an integrity of its own." The behavior observed in these varying low income families does not represent the kind of organization or cohesion suggested by these phrases. Rather it appears as a broad spectrum of pragmatic adjustments to external and internal stresses and deprivations. In any event, programming might best focus on the facts of deprivation and the varied responses, rather than on presumably organized values that represent a preferred or chosen way of life.

Many low income families appear here as, in fact, the frustrated victims of what are thought of as middle class values, behavior, and aspirations. That this has its implications for child rearing is suggested in the separate comments of two mothers who blamed their parents for their childhood deprivations. "I don't think my parents should have sacrificed us to get a house." "My father ought not to have sacrificed us for a car."

Probably one of the more important contributions that can be made to thinking and research about the people who have in common the one trait of poverty is the stressing of the difference between the hard-core, "undeserving" poor—and the hard luck, "deserving" poor, as Dr. Thomas Gladwin did recently in a paper before the National Conference on Social Welfare. One of our difficulties is that this has not been done often or consistently enough; and one of the reasons is the false assumption about, or the image of, a homogeneous lower class culture. What many people mistakenly describe or imagine to be the attributes of the lower class, seem actually, to be the traits of a small segment, the so-called hard-core, of the whole category.

One danger from this confusion is that attempts to change or to penalize the hard core "undeserving" poor might divert our attention from, and unduly penalize a segment of, the poor population whose explicit behavior, if not values and preferences, is a result of not enough money, not enough work. Their exposure to harsh social, economic, and political realities can be a chronic and recurrent condition which they would rather not have to ameliorate or rationalize in the same terms that the hard core poor apparently do. We should not forget that money and work are sorely needed by many poor who are deserving by any test.

There are some assumptions about the contiguousness, the communication, the potentials for community organization among the hard core poor that need to be further examined in a number of different settings. Is there a community, a network, of the hard-core poor? Or do they exist in the cracks and crevices of larger communities of the poor and the more affluent? The practical point here is that the chronically dependent and not-yet dependent poor often live side-by-side in the same neighborhood or area; but often that is all that they do, or want to do together. Much community organization and block work assumes that, because they live in the same neighborhood or area, this in itself provides or connotes a sound basis for developing a more viable and organized community. The truth is that in our slums there are likely to be wide gaps between the hard core poor and the other core—the more respectable and deserving poor as it were. Too frequently the conventional community organization approach is geared to getting the respectable and non-respectable poor together. This represents built-in frustration. One frequent result is that all poor are written off, or condemned as hard-to-reach, because they will not cooperate, either with each other or the block organizers.

Even if homogeneous, continuing communities of the hard-core poor did exist in the past, the chances of finding them today are getting slimmer because of urban renewal, slum clearing, highway construction, etc. The chances are greater now that the poor people of all kinds will be scattered; they will live nearer and be more visible to us non-poor and not-so-poor people.

The lack of identification of the non-hard-core poor with the hard-core poor is graphically depicted in the following excerpts from two staff memos:

> Is there a representative Upton Square resident? In a sense there is not, since individuality and idiosyncrasies of character flourish here as they do not, at present, in conformist middle-class society.
>
> . . . we find a recurrent, underlying theme throughout a great deal of the "family" data, a theme which is corroborated by some of the generalized "participant-observations" . . . the reference is to the perception of "undesirable, anti-social behavior," not necessarily from the point of view of the broader society, but rather from the point of view of the milieu in question. These are frequently attributed to some vague, almost undefinable group called "the others" or those "others." Thus parents interviewed refer constantly, or almost so, to the "fussin" and "fightin," the bad language, and "cussin" and the "bad" manners of other families, of other children.
>
> The universe of the "winehead," the pimp and the whore seems to lie somewhere else than in the bosom of the household in question.

The first phase of our overall project concerned with child rearing among the poor has demonstrated, among other things, that all three types of lower income families—the "subclinical," the "pre-clinical," and the "clinical" dependents—are accessible for program participation. The willingness of families to cooperate appears to be related to an initial approach that stressed the contributions the families can make to a project larger than themselves—a project that they think will contribute something to the improving of child rearing—for themselves, if possible, for others certainly. Our experience shows the improving of child rearing to be a basic human value that is not confined by class lines, despite the fact that what some people themselves do about it, or are able to do about it, or even have the will to do about it, varies. As much as anything, the reasons we give for this variability have major consequences for social welfare practices and policy.

With your permission I will let four mothers sound the closing notes. Each one says something different about this "business of raising."

The first two comment on the neighborhoods in which they live; the second two tell about what they hope for their children.

The first said:

> I don't like the people here, because every place I live they just are wineheads and drink too much and use this bad cursing all the time.

The second mother had just moved into another area:

The home owners don't pay much attention to you. But among those who live near me, people are all equals. They're all scuffling just like me. They ain't got nothing but a little furniture and nobody thinks she's any better than anybody else.

A young mother with several children, and now without a husband in the home, said with resignation:

Like I said, you can't make no plans. I know I can't make no plans for myself until my children grow up and marry. Then I will be old. I have never thought too much about making any plans at all. I know I am going to have Welfare help until my children are able to look out for themselves. Maybe after that I can plan something for myself, but sometimes I don't see no use in trying to make plans because something is always happening to upset you.

And finally, with a restrained upbeat, the fourth said:

When there are children, you usually have to watch out, because if you don't you'll have too many. And without education . . . and luck . . . you can't support your children. So that's why you should try to show your children that going to school and finishing school is for their good. Not so that you can hold up your head and brag and say, "That's my child. . . ." Because this world is getting weaker and wiser and it's going to take two parents to try and show a child the facts of life and the facts of marriage.

Subcultures and Class

Herbert J. Gans

[Reprinted from Chapter 11 of The Urban Villagers *(New York, 1962) by permission of The Free Press of Glencoe, A Division of the Macmillan Company. Copyright © 1962.]*

A Description of Working-Class, Lower-Class, and Middle-Class Subcultures

THE IDENTIFICATION OF THE PEER GROUP SOCIETY as a class phenomenon makes it possible to suggest some propositions about the working class that will distinguish it both from the lower and middle classes. These propositions rest on a specific definition of class.

Class can be defined in many ways, depending on the theoretical, methodological, and political orientation of the researcher.[1] Some sociologists have argued that class is a heuristic concept, nominalist in nature, which serves as a methodological device to summarize real differences between people in income, occupation, education, and related characteristics. Other sociologists have viewed classes as real aggregates of people who share some characteristics and group interests, who favor each other in social relationships, and who exhibit varying degrees of group consciousness. In the latter category, one school of sociologists has explained class mainly on the basis of occupational characteristics, on the assumption that work determines access to income, power, and status, and that it has considerable influence on an individual's behavior patterns.

Others see classes as more than occupational aggregates, that is, as strata in the larger society, each of which consists of somewhat—but not entirely—distinctive social relationships, behavior patterns, and attitudes. The strata thus are composed of subcultures and subsocial structures. For the sake of brevity, however, I shall henceforth describe them only as subcultures. While occupation, education, income, and other such factors help to distinguish the subcultures, the exact role of these factors is thought to be an empirical question. The strata are defined as subcultures on the assumption that relationships, behavior patterns, and attitudes are related parts of a social and cultural system. The word "system" must be used carefully, however, for many similarities and overlaps exist between them. Moreover, these systems are quite open, and movement between them is possible, though—as I shall try to show—not always easy. Considerable variation also exists within each stratum, for social mobility and other processes create innumerable combinations of behavior patterns.[2]

The heuristic conception of class, not being very productive for social theory, need not concern us here. The two remaining ones each have some advantages and disadvantages. The occupational conception is most useful for understanding societies in the early stages of industrialization, when unemployment is great, and when an individual's job is both a determinant of and an index to his way of life. But in a highly

---

[1] The comments that follow are a highly oversimplified description of the various points of view, and serve only to introduce the hypotheses about class that follow below. More sophisticated discussions of the major "schools" in the study of class are available in Bernard Barber, *Social Stratification*, New York: Harcourt, Brace and World, 1957; Milton M. Gordon, *Social Class in American Sociology*, Durham: Duke University Press, 1958.

[2] Even so, studies of status inconsistency have shown that many of these combinations create marginality both in social position and cultural allegiances.

industrialized society with considerable occupational variation and much freedom of choice in jobs—as well as in other ways of life—too great a concern with occupation, or any other single factor, is likely to lead the researcher astray. For instance, when a blue-collar worker earns more than a white-collar one, and can live by the values of the middle class, it would be a mistake to classify him as working class. Similarly, when a white-collar worker lives like a blue-collar one, even in a middle-class neighborhood, one should not consider him middle class.

The great advantage of the subcultural conception is that it makes no a priori assumptions about the major differences between the strata or the determinants of these differences. It treats them rather as topics for empirical research. Unlike the other approaches in which class is defined in terms of easily researchable indices, the subcultural conception is harder to employ, however, for the characteristics and determinants of each class subculture must be carefully delineated.

The voluminous literature of class studies in America and elsewhere and the considerable similarity of the classes all over the industrialized world have made it possible to begin a delineation of the principal class subcultures. While I shall not attempt this task here, I do want to suggest what seem to me to be some of the major "focal concerns"[3] of four of the subcultures: working class, lower class, middle class, and professional upper-middle class. These brief outlines are based on observations made in the West End and elsewhere, and on the research literature. For the most part, they describe the subcultures in America and in one period of the life cycle: that of the family which is rearing children.

Perhaps the most important—or at least the most visible—difference between the classes is one of family structure. The working-class subculture is distinguished by the dominant role of the family circle. Its way of life is based on social relationships amidst relatives. The working class views the world from the family circle, and considers everything outside it as either a means to its maintenance or to its destruction. But while the outside world is to be used for the benefit of this circle, it is faced with detachment and even hostility in most other respects. Whenever feasible, then, work is sought within establishments connected to the family circle. When this is not possible—and it rarely

---

[3] I borrow this term from Walter Miller, who uses it as a substitute for the anthropological concept of value in his study of lower-class culture. See "Lower Class Culture as a Generating Milieu of Gang Delinquency," p. 261. I use it to refer to behavior as much as to attitude, and to phenomena of social structure as well as culture.

is—work is primarily a means of obtaining income to maintain life amidst a considerable degree of poverty, and, thereafter, a means of maximizing the pleasures of life within the family circle. The work itself may be skilled or unskilled; it can take place in the factory or in the office—the type of collar is not important. What does matter is that identification with work, work success, and job advancement—while not absolutely rejected—are of secondary priority to the life that goes on within the family circle. The purpose of education is to learn techniques necessary to obtain the most lucrative type of work. Thus the central theme of American, and all Western, education—that the student is an individual who should use his schooling to detach himself from ascribed relationships like the family circle in order to maximize his personal development and achievement in work, play, and other spheres of life—is ignored or openly rejected.

The specific characteristics of the family circle may differ widely —from the collateral peer group form of the West Enders, to the hierarchical type of the Irish, or to the classic three-generation extended family. Friends may also be included in the circle, as in the West Enders' peer group society. What matters most—and distinguishes this subculture from others—is that there be a family circle which is wider than the nuclear family, and that all of the opportunities, temptations, and pressures of the larger society be evaluated in terms of how they affect the ongoing way of life that has been built around this circle.

The *lower-class subculture* is distinguished by the female-based family and the marginal male. Although a family circle may also exist, it includes only female relatives. The male, whether husband or lover, is physically present only part of the time, and is recognized neither as a stable nor dominant member of the household. He is a sexual partner, and he is asked to provide economic support. But he participates only minimally in the exchange of affection and emotional support, and has little to do with the rearing of children. Should he serve as a model for the male children, he does so largely in a negative sense. That is, the women use him as an example of what a man should not be.

The female-based family must be distinguished, however, from one in which the woman is dominant, for example, the English working-class family. Although this family may indeed revolve around the "Mum," she does not reject the husband. Not only is he a member of the family, but he is also a participant—and a positive model—in child-rearing.

In the lower class, the segregation of the sexes—only partial in the working class—is complete. The woman tries to develop a stable routine in the midst of poverty and deprivation; the action-seeking man upsets it. In order to have any male relationships, however, the woman must participate to some extent in his episodic life style. On rare occasions, she may even pursue it herself. Even then, however, she will try to encourage her children to seek a routine way of life. Thus the woman is much closer to working-class culture, at least in her aspirations, although she is not often successful in achieving them.

For lower-class men, life is almost totally unpredictable. If they have sought stability at all, it has slipped from their grasp so quickly, often, and consistently that they no longer pursue it. From childhood on, their only real gratifications come from action-seeking, but even these are few and short-lived. Relationships with women are of brief duration, and some men remain single all their lives. Work, like all other relationships with the outside world, is transitory. Indeed, there can be no identification with work at all. Usually, the lower-class individual gravitates from one job to another, with little hope or interest of keeping a job for any length of time. His hostility to the outside world therefore is quite intense, and its attempts to interfere with the episodic quality of his life are fought. Education is rejected by the male, for all of its aims are diametrically opposed to action-seeking.

The *middle-class subculture* is built around the nuclear family and its desire to make its way in the larger society. Although the family circle may exist, it plays only a secondary role in middle-class life. Contact with close relatives is maintained, but even they participate in a subordinate role. Individuals derive most of their social and emotional gratifications from the nuclear family itself. One of the most important of these is child-rearing. Consequently, the middle-class family is much more child-centered than the working-class one and spends more of its spare time together. Outside social life takes place with friends who share similar interests. The nuclear family depends on its friends—as well as on some caretaking institutions—for help and support. Relatives may also help, especially in emergencies.

The middle class does not make the distinction between the family and the outside world. In fact, it does not even see an outside world, but only a larger society, which it believes to support its aims, and in which the family participates. The nuclear family makes its way in the larger society mainly through the career of its breadwinner. Thus work is not merely a job that maximizes income, but a series of related jobs or job advances which provide the breadwinner with higher income, greater responsibility, and, if possible, greater job satisfaction. In turn his career enhances the way of life of the rest of the family, through increases in status and in the standard of living.

Education is viewed, and used, as an important method for achieving these goals. The purpose of education is to provide the skills needed for the man's career and for the woman's role as a mother. In and out of school, it is also used to develop the skills necessary to the maintenance and increase of status, the proper use of leisure time, and the occasional participation in community activities. Thus, much of the central theme of education is accepted. But the idea that education is an end in itself, and should be used to maximize individual development of the person, receives only lip service.

The subculture I have described here is a basic middle-class one; a more detailed analysis would distinguish between what is currently called the middle-middle class and the lower-middle class. The upper-middle-class subculture is also a variant of the basic middle-class culture. There are at least two such subcultures, the managerial and the professional. Since I shall be concerned with the latter, it is of primary interest here.

The *professional upper-middle-class culture* is also organized around the nuclear family, but places greater emphasis on the independent functioning of its individual members. Whereas the middle-class family is a companionship unit in which individuals exist most intensely in their relationships with each other, the upper-middle-class family is a companionship unit in which individuals seeking to maximize their own development as persons come together on the basis of common interests. For this subculture, life is, to a considerable extent, a striving for individual development and self-expression, and these strivings pervade many of its relationships with the larger society.

Therefore, work is not simply a means for achieving the well-being of the nuclear family, but also an opportunity for individual achievement and social service. Although the career, income, status, and job responsibility are important, job satisfaction is even more important, although it is not always found. Indeed, professional work satisfaction is a focal concern not only for the breadwinner, but often for the woman as well. If she is not interested in a profession, she develops an alternative but equally intense interest in motherhood, or in community activity. Child-rearing, moreover, gives the woman an opportunity not only to maximize her own individual achievements as a mother, but to develop in her children the same striving for self-development. As a result, the professional upper-middle-class family is not child-centered, but adult-directed. As education is the primary tool for a life of individual achievement, the professional upper-middle-class person not only goes to school longer than anyone else in society, but he also accepts its central theme more fully than do the rest of the middle class.

This concern with individual achievement and education further enables and encourages the members of this subculture to be deliberate

and self-conscious about their choices. They are a little more understanding of the actions of others than the members of less educated
strata. Their ability to participate in the larger society, plus their high
social and economic status, also gives them somewhat greater control
over their fate than other people, and make the environment more predictable. This in turn facilitates the practice of self-consciousness, empathy, and abstraction or generalization.

The possession of these skills distinguishes the upper-middle class
from the rest of the middle class, and even more so from the working
and lower class. For the latter not only lives in a less predictable environment, but they are also detached from the outside world, which
increases their feeling that it, and, indeed, all of life, is unpredictable.
In turn this feeling encourages a pervasive fatalism that pre-empts the
optimism or pessimism of which the other classes are capable. The
fatalism of the working and lower classes, as well as their lack of education and interest in personal development and object goals, minimizes
introspection, self-consciousness, and empathy for the behavior of others.

Class: Opportunity and Response

The subcultures which I have described are *responses* that people make
to the *opportunities* and the *deprivations* that they encounter. More
specifically, each subculture is an organized set of related responses
that has developed out of people's efforts to cope with the opportunities,
incentives, and rewards, as well as the deprivations, prohibitions, and
pressures which the natural environment and society—that complex of co-
existing and competing subcultures—offer to them. The responses which
make up a subculture are compounded out of what people have retained
of parental, that is, traditional responses, the skill and attitudes they
have learned as children, and the innovations they have developed for
themselves in their own encounters with opportunity and deprivation.

These responses cannot develop in a vacuum. Over the long
range, they can be seen as functions of the resources which a society
has available, and of the opportunities which it can offer. In each of the
subcultures life is thus geared to the availability of specific qualitative
types and quantities of income, education, and occupational opportunities. Although I have used occupational labels to distinguish between
the major subcultures,[4] a man's job does not necessarily determine in

---

[4] It is relevant to note that the words I have used to label the class subcultures are somewhat misleading. For example, I describe the middle class not as
a group in the middle of the economic and power structure, but as a subculture
focally concerned with the nuclear family. Likewise, the working class obviously
works no more or less than any other group. Only the lower-class label fits well,
since this subculture is in so many ways a response to the deprivations to which it
is exposed.

which of these he shall be placed. In the long run, however, the existence of a specific subculture is closely related to the availability of occupational opportunities. For example, the functioning of the family circle and the routine-seeking way of life in the working class depend on the availability of stable employment for the man. The lower-class female-based family is a response to, or a method of coping with, the lack of stable male employment. The goals of middle- and upper-middle-class culture depend on the availability of sufficient income to finance the education that is necessary for a career, and on the availability of job opportunities that will allow middle-class individuals to find the type of job satisfaction for which they are striving.

When these opportunity factors are lacking, the cultural responses made by people are frustrated. Should opportunities be deficient over a long enough period, downward mobility results. Should they disappear entirely, the subculture will be apt to disintegrate eventually. For example, working-class culture can function for a time in a period of unemployment, but if no substitute sources of stability are made available, people initially resort to protest. Eventually, the family circle begins to break up under the strain, and its members adopt many if not all of the responses identified with the lower-class subculture.

Similar reactions take place in the other subcultures, although the ways in which they are expressed may differ. If job opportunities are lacking so as to frustrate the career desires of the middle class, or the professional desires of the upper-middle class, one reaction is to transfer aspirations elsewhere, for example, into non-work pursuits. Since upper-middle-class people are able and willing to act in the larger society, they may also develop social and political protest movements in order to create these opportunities, or to change society. Bourgeois socialist movements in America, taking their lead from the Marxist aim to "humanize" work so that it will provide quasi-professional job satisfaction to all people, are examples of such a reaction. Although downward mobility in the working class results in the adoption of lower-class responses, middle-class downward mobility does not bring about a working-class response. People may depend more on relatives as adversity strikes, but other differences between middle- and working-class subcultures remain in effect.

Downward mobility is also possible in the lower-class subculture. Since this culture is initially a response to instability, further instability can result only in family disintegration, total despair, and an increase in already high rates of mental illness, antisocial and self-destructive behavior, or group violence.

Conversely, when opportunity factors are increasingly available, people respond by more fully implementing their subcultural aspirations, and by improving their styles of life accordingly. For example, working-class people responded to the post-World War II prosperity by selecting from the available opportunities those elements useful for increasing the comfort and convenience of their way of life. They did not strive for middle-class styles. Nor did they reshape the family, adopt careers, or surrender their detachment from the outside world.

Periods of increased opportunity also encourage marginal members of each subculture to move into others to which they are aspiring. For example, lower-class women with working-class goals have been able to send their boys to school with the hope that they will be able to move into working-class culture. Whereas some of them have been able to make the move as adults, others have found that they could not summon the emotional and other skills necessary to succeed in school or job. In many cases, opportunities simply were not as freely available as expected, and sudden illness or other setbacks propelled them back into the lower-class culture.

Upward mobility that involves movement into another class subculture is relatively rare because of the considerable changes which people must make in their own lives, often against great odds. Thus the majority are content to improve the style of life within their own subcultures. They may, however, encourage their children to make the move in the next generation.

Although opportunities can increase or decrease rapidly and drastically over time, the subcultures I have described are relatively slow in changing their basic structure and content. In many ways contemporary working-class culture is a continuation of European peasant cultures, and some features of the middle- and upper-middle-class subcultures can be traced back to the post-Renaissance and to the beginnings of the urban-industrial revolution. Improvements and changes in the level of living take place all the time, as modern ideas, habits, and artifacts replace traditional ones. But the focal concerns of each subculture change more slowly.

Changes in the distribution and quality of opportunity factors do, of course, have significant effects. They influence the extent to which subcultural aspirations can be realized, and they help to determine the position of each subculture within the over-all class hierarchy. This in turn affects the political influence that each of them can exert on many matters in the national society, including the distribution of opportunities itself.

Moreover, new opportunities and the need for new skills can increase the number of people found in any one subculture, just as the demise of opportunities can reduce it. For example, whereas the reduction of temporary, unskilled labor is likely to shrink the lower-class sub-culture, the increased need for professionals has led to the enlargement of the middle and upper-middle class. In short, new opportunities bring higher incentives, which in turn encourage people to move into other subcultures, although a generation or two may pass before they adopt all of the primary focal concerns of their new way of life. At any one point in time, then, many people could be said to be living between subcultures. Radical changes in the society can even bring entirely new subcultures into being, although this has happened only infrequently in the course of history.

Selected Bibliography

1. Richard A. Cloward and Lloyd E. Ohlin. *Delinquency and Opportunities.* Glencoe, Illinois: The Free Press of Glencoe, 1960.

2. Elizabeth Herzog. "Some Assumptions About the Poor," *Social Service Review,* 37 (December, 1963).

3. Herbert Hyman. "The Value Systems of Different Classes. A Social Psychological Contribution to the Analysis of Stratification," *Class, Status, and Power,* edited by R. Bendix and S. M. Lipsett. Glencoe. Ill. The Free Press, 1953, pp. 426-442.

4. Oscar Lewis. *Five Families.* Basic Books, 1959.

5. ———. *La Vida.* Random House, 1966.

6. Seymour M. Lipset. "Democracy and Working Class Authoritarianism," *American Sociological Review,* 24 (August, 1959).

7. S. M. Miller. "The American Lower Class: A Typological Approach," *Social Research,* 31 (Spring, 1964).

8. S. M. Miller and Frank Riessman. "The Working Class Subculture: A New View," *Social Problems,* 9 (Summer, 1961).

9. Hyman Rodman. "On Understanding Lower Class Behavior," *Social and Economic Studies,* 9 (December, 1959).

10. Hyman Rodman. "The Lower-Class Value Stretch," *Social Forces,* December 1963.

11. Leonard Schneiderman. "The Culture of Poverty: A Study of the Value Orientation Preferences of the Chronically Impoverished," Unpublished Doctoral Dissertation, University of Minnesota School of Social Work, 1963.

12. ———. "Value Orientation Preferences of Chronic Relief Applicants," *Social Work,* 9 (July, 1964).

Chapter 6

The Life of the Poor

Poverty not only has many faces, connections, and ramifications, but also different loci—and, therefore, it shows variations in behavioral symptoms, and calls for different diagnoses and prognoses. Poverty is endemic in the center city slum, and it is no accident that there occurs the classic convergence of poverty with other ills. Poverty in the city is obviously not confined to the slum, but the fact that it is embedded there with other ills makes it more difficult to treat than if it were in a non-slum setting. Nor do all slum dwellers present examples of poverty or require or want intervention or help beyond ordinary expectations. Although it may be related to time or duration, there is a difference between the pandemic poverty of Appalachia and the epidemic poverty of a Detroit hit a few years ago by automation or slackening car demand. For example, it is important to distinguish between the family or person relatively recently hit by an incident of unemployment or local epidemic of poverty and the long time Negro resident of the slums who has known nothing but endemic poverty and who refuses to be mouse trapped into any belief that significant change is forthcoming or possible by talk, exhortation, or misguided efforts to teach him middle-class values that may already be known and appreciated. Middle-class values, highly advertised as they are, indeed may be well-known. But that does not make them realizable. For many, particularly for the young poor, the distance between knowing and being able to achieve them is the rub.

—Quoted from "The Contemporary Urban Poverty Syndrome." Speech delivered by Hylan Lewis to Howard Medical School students, April 28, 1964.

OUR UNDERSTANDING OF LOWER-CLASS BEHAVIOR is hampered by a series of stereotypes and misconceptions about the poor. The mass media dramatize the sensational in lower class life—violence, brutalization and deviance—and this is often the only benchmark for viewing the behavior and attitudes of the poor. We must add to this the fact that the more affluent groups of the community rarely engage in close personal contact with the poor and consequently there are few challenges to the images of the poor that are presented in the mass media. If contact is made, it is apt to be in situations that reinforce these stereotypes—the panhandler on the street or the domestic in the home. The geographical confinement of the poor to the slum and the contact limitations afforded by the opportunity structure make the poor invisible to other groups in the community and it is this invisibility that sustains these misconceptions and stereotypes of lower-class life.

These stereotypes and misconceptions are of three kinds. First, lower-class life is seen as unorganized or disorganized. The middle-class individual may deplore the fact that the poor let their children run wild; or that the poor do not organize their finances well; or that the poor are promiscuous; or that people who would live in such deteriorated, disorganized surroundings must themselves lack organization or predictability. What is usually the case is that organization does exist in the slum but that it is organization of a kind that is not intelligible to the middle class observer. In his classic study of street corner society, William Foote Whyte showed that what appeared to be a disorganized slum was actually a highly organized community but that organization was on a different basis than what the middle class observer has come to expect from his own experiences. The failure to see organization in the slum does not stem from the fact that it does not exist but rather that such *kinds* of organization have no prototypes in middle class surroundings. Leadership exists but all too often it is the leadership that is unfamiliar or repugnant to middle class values (e.g. the leader of a rent strike). Few people are able to appreciate the tensions and anxieties of a poverty situation and fewer still appreciate the life styles that develop in these surroundings.

A second misconception is to attribute the behavior pattern to some imperfection in the individual rather than to the stresses that are generated by a particular poverty situation. In a society where emphasis is placed on the individual's ability to master his environment, little thought is given to the structuring of behavior by situational stress or to the existence of a particular opportunity structure. The individual behaves as he does because he is "lazy, dirty, or ignorant" or because he is "ambitious, polished, and intelligent." Only a little more than a century ago, little thought was given to the structuring of behavior by situational stresses or the existence of a particular opportunity structure. The profound contribution made by such researchers as Allison Davis is that the motivation of the underprivileged worker was to be found in terms of the opportunity and reward structure of the community. But old explanations die hard. Even in the 1960's, the solutions suggested to combat unemployment stress the retraining and rehabilitation of the individual rather than the changing or regulation of the job opportunity structure.

Finally, there is a misconception regarding the goals set by the poor as well as the means that they use in the attainment of these goals. Again, this reflects the fact that middle class people are not familiar with lower class living conditions. Goals tend to be fitted to the realities of situations. Where economic resources are unpredictable, greater emphasis is placed on subsistence rather than achievement. The latter is only possible where the former has been assured. Just as affluence sets the goals for the middle class child, so poverty becomes a limiting factor in setting the goals for the lower class child. The means are also a reflection of reality. The middle class child is surrounded by a world in which education pays off and where the successful serve as models. In lower class life where there is a general lack of successful work models, the child is apt to see the futility of an education in a second-rate educational system. Goal setting and the availability of means are circumscribed by the stresses and unpredictability brought about by a scarcity of economic resources.

But the most common misconception in understanding lower class life is to look for a single theme. Poverty is characterized by actual and sensed powerlessness as well as social isolation from the cues and rewards of the larger community. These are the end results of the lack and unpredictability of economic resources. Lower class life must be seen within this framework as a composite of many situations, many themes, and many experiences. In this chapter Warren Haggstrom begins by describing the power and the psychology of the poor. Jeremy Larner discusses some of the self-perceptions of a particular group of lower-class school children against the context of the 1964 New York City school boycott. The problems and potentials for organizing the poor in community action are reviewed by George Brazer. Some problems of Negro urban life are described in Gordon Parks's poignant study of a Harlem family. Charles Lebeaux reviews the results of his study on the household budgets of fatherless families. Mary Wright concludes by describing a typical day in the life of a welfare recipient and his anxieties and frustrations with bureaucracy.

The Power of the Poor*

Warren C. Haggstrom

Syracuse University

[Reprinted from Mental Health of the Poor, edited by Frank Riessman, Jerome Cohen, and Arthur Pearl (New York, 1964) by permission of the Free Press of Glencoe, A Division of the Macmillan Company. Copyright © 1964.]

ON THE AVERAGE, the poor in the United States have bad reputations. They are regarded as responsible for much physical aggression and destruction of property; their support is alleged to be a heavy burden on the rest of the community; and they are said not even to try very hard to meet community standards of behavior or to be self-supporting. Poverty, it is said, is little enough punishment for people so inferior and so lacking in virtue.

Roughly speaking, these common opinions about the poor have some accuracy. Socially notorious varieties of deviancy and dependency do flourish in areas of poverty to a greater extent than in the remainder of our society. The middle classes, of course, have their own faults, which are sometimes perceptively observed and described by the poor. The relatively prosperous tend to use their verbal facility to conceal aspects of social reality from themselves and tend to use word-magic to make themselves comfortable about being in their generally undeserved positions of affluence, positions in which they manage to obtain the most pay and security for doing easy and interesting kinds of work.

Since the United States is a middle class society, those who emphasize the bad reputations of the poor are regarded as hard-headed realists, while those who stress the phoniness of the middle classes are considered rather extreme and overly suspicious. When a social worker reports that the lower classes tend in the direction of schizophrenia and character disorders, he is viewed as having made a sober report of the existing state of affairs. Or when a social scientist discovers that the poor are unsocialized, childlike, occupy an early category in *his* category system of degrees of socialization, his discovery is treated as an important basis for further scientific work. But suppose that a leader of the poor announces that social workers tend to be "phonies" and "half-queer" as well, or suggests in his own language that social scientists are

---

* Revised version of a paper prepared for presentation at the 71st Annual Convention of the American Psychological Association in Philadelphia, Pennsylvania, August 29–September 4, 1963.

usually fuzzy-minded and socially irrelevant. This invidious description is not seen as a suitable hypothesis for investigation and research; it is rather said (without benefit of evidence) to be a symptom of the ignorance or of the personal or political needs of the person making the statement.

We cannot, of course, simply shed the presuppositions which attach to our social positions, and those of us who see the poor from above are likely not to have viewed them from the most flattering perspective. But let us, in the following discussion, attempt to be critical and scientific by orienting ourselves to reasons and evidence rather than to common sense conceptual refinements of our current prejudices. We will first analyze a popular contemporary account of the psychology of poverty, and then advance a different orientation as a more precise explanation for available data.

Psychological Characteristics of the Poor

Social scientists have arrived at a rough consensus about the modal personality in neighborhoods of poverty:

(1) The poor tend to have a keen sense of the personal and the concrete; their interest typically is restricted to the self, the family, and the neighborhood. There is a particular stress on the intimate, the sensory, the detailed, the personal. Not struggling to escape their circumstances, the poor often regard their ordinary lives as being of much intrinsic interest. This is related to their primary concern with the problem of survival rather than with the problem of moving up in society, and to the value which they attach to skills needed in coping with deprivation and uncertainty as distinguished from skills required to make progress. It has frequently been reported that persons in areas of poverty appear to be apathetic, to have little motivation, to be unable to cooperate with each other in the solution of problems which they regard as important, and to lack occupational and verbal skills and leadership traits; and are characterized by parochialism, nostalgic romanticism, and prescientific conceptions of the natural and social orders. Instead of having love for one another as fellow human beings, they achieve positive mutual attitudes through seeing themselves as all in the same boat together.

(2) Caught in the present, the poor do not plan very much. They meet their troubles and take their pleasures on a moment-to-moment basis; their schemes are short-term. Their time perspective is foreshortened by their belief that it is futile to think of the future. Thus, when the poor use conventional words to refer to the future, those words tend to be empty of real meaning. They have little sense of the past and they

go forward, but not forward to any preconceived place. Their pleasures and rewards are sought in the present; they find it difficult to delay gratification, to postpone satisfaction.

(3) There is much egoism, envy, and hostility toward those who prosper. There is a feeling of being exploited. There are many negative attitudes and few positive ones. The unity of the poor comes about through suspicion of and resentment toward outsiders, through opposition to common enemies and hostility to powerful groups. Disillusion about the possibility of advancement stems from a victim complex in relation to the powerful. There is a sense of inability to affect what will happen, a lack of conviction that it is within their power to affect their circumstances. The outside world cannot be trusted; it must be defended against. Outsiders and the outside are seen as risky, likely to injure you when you least expect it. Pessimism and fatalism about being able to affect one's own situation stems from a feeling of being victimized by superordinate, capricious, and malevolent natural and social forces. Their lives appear to them to be fixed by the immutable forces of fate, luck, and chance. While well-to-do people tend to attribute causality to inner forces, the poor tend to make external attributes of causality, seeing themselves as subject to external and arbitrary forces and pressures.[1]

The Social Problem of Poverty and Its Natural Solution

The poor, in short, are commonly seen as apathetic, childlike, not very competent, and hostile-dependent. Other research, emphasized in the past few years, has pointed out the extent to which the poor tend to occupy specific social categories (minority racial and ethnic groups, the elderly, ADC families, and the like), as well as the continuing large proportion of the population who have low incomes even in such an affluent society as the United States. It has been natural to get concerned about a large proportion of the population, the members of which have

---

[1] This summary social scientists' image of the psychological characteristics of the poor was prepared on the basis of a survey of articles and books relating to poverty published by social scientists during the past fifteen years. Any particular author would be likely to differ on one or more points and would probably want to add others not recorded here. For example, in *The Children of Sanchez* (New York: Random House, 1961), Oscar Lewis includes "a strong present time orientation with relatively little ability to defer gratification and plan for the future, a sense of resignation and fatalism based upon the realities of their difficult life situation, a belief in male superiority which reaches its crystallization in *machisme* or the cult of masculinity, a corresponding martyr complex among women, and finally, a high tolerance for psychological pathology of all sorts." (Pages xxvi–xxvii) Lewis, of course, restricted his account to urban Mexican poor.

behavior patterns and psychological characteristics that tend to place them in opposition to or dependence on the remainder of the community.

Poverty has therefore again become a publicly recognized social problem in the United States. The general perception of a social problem leads to a search for its solution. Since a lack of money is the most universal characteristic of poverty, and since a general increase of income for some social groups would automatically abolish poverty, it seems clear to many persons that certain known steps are suitable to end poverty in the United States. Their view is that public policies should be developed and implemented that emphasize provision of jobs, increased access to education that leads to jobs, and higher minimum wage levels and welfare payments. Scientists, according to this view, can contribute by learning how to measure poverty with greater accuracy and by studying its adverse psychological and other consequences, and they should seek to understand how these consequences might be controlled.

In this natural line of reasoning it is assumed rather than demonstrated that the major problem of the poor is poverty, a lack of money. But this assumption is essential to the associated recommendations for scientific work and social policy. It may be well, therefore, to inquire in a more searching fashion whether the problems of the poor primarily result from a lack of money.

There are a number of phenomena which one could hardly anticipate on the basis of such an assumption:

(1) A given level of real income has various consequences depending upon the circumstances in which a person receives the income.

Among the poor, there are many subgroups, the members of which do not display the presumed psychological consequences of poverty. These include most of that portion of the leadership of the poor which is itself poor, those low income families with high educational aspirations for their children, low income members of religious groups such as the Hutterites, university student families with little income, and the like. In the past, of course, members of the lower middle class have survived on real incomes below those received today by comparable public welfare families—and without losing their capacity to struggle in the pursuit of distant ends. Many from the intelligentsia today in such countries as India and Japan have incomes that, in the United States, would place them with the poor. They may differ from educated Americans in personality characteristics, but they do not have the alleged psychology of poverty either.

(2) Increases in income often do not lead to a diminution of the expected psychological consequences of poverty.

For example, the rise in real per capita public welfare expenditures in the United States has not had a demonstrated effect on the psychological functioning of welfare recipients.

(3) Differences in income between otherwise comparable groups of poor do not appear to be accompanied by differences in psychological functioning.

For example, states vary greatly in the size of their payments to comparable welfare recipient families. Comparable families appear to resemble one another in psychological orientation regardless of relatively major differences in their incomes.

(4) When income remains constant, but persons in a neighborhood of poverty become involved in successful social action on important issues, in their own behalf, their psychological orientation does extend over a greater period of time, their feeling of helplessness does lessen, their skills and activities do gradually change.

For example, no one could have predicted on the basis of articles in the relevant scholarly journals that lowly Negroes from areas of poverty would, with some help, begin to organize with such effect that they would carry timid and ultra-conventional members of the Negro middle classes along with them into a militant struggle for freedom. It has also been reported that many "lower class" Negroes who have become part of the Muslim movement have had their lives transformed in the direction of greater order and achievement.

During this past summer I gathered some data concerning The Woodlawn Organization (two), a primarily "lower class," predominantly Negro organization which was initiated about two years ago in Chicago with the assistance of Saul Alinsky and the Industrial Areas Foundation. The poor constitute the bulk of active members, and are an important segment of the leadership of this community organization, which has already demonstrated its effectiveness and power. For example, two has delivered a majority of the votes from a Negro area to elect a white alderman who takes a strong civil rights position; the unsuccessful opponent was a Negro from the regular political organization. It has been able to secure its own conditions for implementation of an urban renewal development proposed by the University of Chicago for part of the Woodlawn area. two has carried out rent strikes and has taken other successful actions against owners of dilapidated slum buildings; it has organized picketing of stores that sell merchandise to people who cannot afford the high interest on installments; it has organized successful city hall demonstrations of more than a thousand persons. Over this period of widespread involvement, the poor appear to have gradually acquired skills of organization, longer range planning, and other qualities contrary to those which reputedly characterize areas of poverty. I observed a similar process occurring in "lower class" white neighborhoods in Northwest Chicago, where the Northwest Community Organization, another Alinsky associated enterprise, has been in existence for less than two years.

(5) When members of some groups lose or give up their wealth, they do not thereby acquire the psychology of poverty.

One has only to consider the vows of poverty taken by members of some religious orders to illustrate this assertion.

Since the psychology of poverty obtains only under specific and describable circumstances, one cannot therefore use poverty as an explanation for these psychological characteristics which often are associated with poverty.

We might briefly mention other problems involved in the ready identification of poverty as the major problem of the poor. First, it is invalid reasoning to proceed without evidence from the fact that the poor have distinctive failings to the assumption that poverty is important in the etiology of these failings. It is incorrect simply to take the defining characteristics of a social category to which a group of people belong (the category "poverty" in this case) and use it without further evidence to account for the peculiar afflictions of that group of people. Second, even if *all* poor today were to exhibit the psychology of poverty, this may be merely an accidental connection, and the fact of having little money could remain only distantly related, for example, to feelings of being dominated by irrational external forces. One should not confuse an observed regularity with an inevitable regularity, a conventional law with a natural law. Third, when a scientist observes that a group of persons, the poor, have adopted their own patterns of behavior and system of beliefs, this does not mean that the behavior and belief patterns are cultural or subcultural or that these patterns represent durable characteristics of the people involved over a wide variety of social situations. The patterns and beliefs may be situational, not internalized, and may shift readily as the situation changes. Just when social scientists appear to be getting the poor firmly in mind, the poor are transformed. Thus, the "psychology of the poor" may be quite different from the psychology of a neurosis the basis of which *is* internalized.

It is therefore likely that the natural solution to the problem of poverty is naïve: it merely assumes the determinants of the psychology of poverty.[2]

---

[2] The personality characteristics of the poor may themselves be different from those reported. Much of the scientific literature is based on reports of verbal

The Self-Help Doctrine and Its Consequences for Dependent Persons

In rapidly industrializing societies in which there are many opportunities for individual advancement there typically arises some form of the doctrine of self-help. The common core of self-help views can be stated as follows: A person is good to the extent to which he has assumed responsibility for and accomplished the realization of his potentialities for maximum use of his native capacities in a long, sustained, and arduous effort to reach a distant legitimate goal. With enough effort any normal person can attain such goals; no special ability is needed.

In the older Western industrial nations a growing appreciation of the limitations of opportunity has provided increasing support for modification of the traditional doctrine, with the qualification that ability as well as effort is necessary to success, and that some persons have been born with more ability than others. Also, since the nineteenth century, the common legitimate goal has changed from entrepreneurship of a prosperous independent business to a high position in a large work organization, and the struggle begins in the institutions of learning before the transfer to a work setting.

According to the doctrine of self-help, *anyone*, given enough time and enough effort, could achieve success. Thus, to be poor could have either of two meanings. On the one hand, poverty was regarded as the original accompaniment of the highest development of character, the struggling poor who were later to become successful were most worthy of respect. On the other hand, poverty indefinitely prolonged might mean a character defect, a lack of will power. Poverty, therefore, was ambiguous; from it alone one could reach no conclusion about virtue. However, an economy with limited opportunities for success plus the belief in equal opportunity for success according to merit made inevitable an assault on the self-esteem of the permanently unsuccessful.

Officially defined dependency was not usually regarded as ambiguous. The person on welfare has left the struggle altogether and has sat back to allow others to furnish his sustenance. It is true that some persons, the crippled, the very young, the seriously ill, and so forth,

---

or other behavioral responses of the poor in the presence of researchers, usually middle class persons of much higher status and greater power than those being studied. It is not easy for a powerful person accurately to understand one who is weak since the behavior of the latter in the research situation may depend very much on the behavior of the former. The massive failure of intelligent and educated Southern whites to withstand Negroes with whom they had maintained years of presumably close relationship should provide reason for researchers to use caution in their claims based on a few hours' contact with persons much different from their usual associates.

clearly could not have avoided dependency. But as for the rest, the presumption of their ability to work and succeed if they only tried hard enough led to the inevitable conclusion that those who have left off trying are bad. The intensity with which this conclusion was known was also related to the fact that dependent persons were seen to be living at the expense of the rest of the community. Not only did the scoundrels manage to exist without honest labor, but they actually made of the rest of the community a duped partner to their idleness. Inexcused dependency became a social symbol communicating defective character, toward which there was a feeling of superiority tinged with contempt. Even in the best of circumstances professional helpers were automatically considered morally as well as materially superior to those helped, and thus the helping relationship became a concrete carrier of the general meaning of dependency: the unworthiness of the dependent.

In affecting the psychology of dependency, the self-help doctrine has also, of course, affected the *behavior* of persons who are in need. One way to evade the unpleasantness of being dependent is to avoid getting help at all in a dependent situation. Families in trouble, as was discovered in various studies, often hide away when they need help the most. The stigma attached to receiving assistance prevents the use even of available resources.

Official dependency in modern society is a residual category of persons unable to enter into the normal types of income-producing relationships. Such persons are unable to relate to the normal avenues for gaining support, and the presence and location of such avenues is therefore the major immediate condition or cause of dependency in modern society. Inability to relate to normal avenues of support symbolizes failure, and perception by a dependent person of his own dependency is sufficient to produce shame and guilt and their complications. Official dependency is fundamentally the perception of the use of relative social power within a superordinate-subordinate relationship; the doctrine of self-help in a contractual economy made financial dependency the focal point for this definition in modern society. The official assumption is that all working adults are equal in that they have entered into work contracts on an equal basis, contracts which they could have chosen to enter or not to enter.

The financially self-responsible person is assumed to be responsible also in other areas of his life. For this reason dependency can concern any area of superordinate-subordinate relationship, and there is always some stigma associated with any dependency relationship, even though there is often pleasure in divesting oneself of the burden of self-responsibility. Even the relationship of citizen to expert can be distasteful since it makes the citizen intellectually dependent on the expert.

The sharpest psychological impact of dependency has occurred where it is officially defined and therefore clearly perceived and sanctioned by the community. However, most dependency is not so explicitly defined; most of the poor are not "on welfare." Even so, the poor are generally perceived, however unclearly, as having failed, and this perception has hardened the community against them. In the latter case, the doctrine of self-help has intensified the feelings of hopelessness among the poor.

The extent of self-support is only one measure of the extent of dependency, a measure stressed only in connection with the doctrine of self-help. More generally, dependency is the placement of one's destiny in other hands. It is therefore especially characteristic of the areas of poverty, but also characterizes many other aspects of society, including the low echelons of large organizations, organization men at any echelon, and so forth. In a general sense dependency is also destructive, but more subtly so. If extent of self-realization is a measure of personality development, then dependency, which erodes self-realization with the loss of self-responsibility, is a measure of personality inadequacy. If the human personality develops as a decision process through self-responsible choices, then the taking away of self-responsible choices through assuming the subordinate position in a dependency relationship necessarily destroys personality.

The Social Situation of the Poor

Most of the poor are heavily dependent on outside forces. In many places, a poor person is much more likely to be subject to police interrogation and search, or to public identification as the object of police activity, than is a member of a middle class family. Urban renewal programs periodically disrupt the neighborhoods of poverty, scattering the families in several directions in accordance with standards which the poor do not understand or support. Schools function impervious to the concerns of the low income families whose children attend, or else schools may seek themselves to "lead" in the areas of poverty in which they are located, that is, they seek to impose school standards and definitions on the neighborhoods. Settlement houses run recreation programs that meet their own traditional criteria, but neighborhood youth often do not understand these criteria, often cannot engage in accustomed and legal modes of behavior and still participate in settlement house activities, often, involuntarily and without understanding, have to disperse friendship groups in order to participate in a recreation program.

Many families, having bought more than they can afford, especially through high-interest installment financing, have no way to know whether or when their furniture will be repossessed or their check garnisheed. Medical and psychiatric care are inadequate, inadequately understood, and uncertainly available, especially to the poor who do not have connections through welfare. The securing of general relief or categorical assistance is a humiliating experience at best for people imbued with self-help ideas, but the deliberate rudeness intended to discourage as many applicants as possible, the complex agency rules which are not so much bases for action as after-the-fact rationales to provide support for decisions already made, and the subjective and unpredictable decisions of social workers representing agencies to the poor, all combine to place the economic foundation of many families at the mercy of completely incomprehensible forces.

The poor who seek employment must find it in a dwindling supply of jobs available to unskilled and semiskilled persons (including domestics), often seasonal or temporary work. In addition, the landlords of the poor are frequently discourteous, seldom inclined to make adequate repairs on their buildings, and likely to blame the tenants for the condition of the ancient and crumbling structures for which high rents are charged.

In other words, the poor, by virtue of their situation, tend to be more dependent than other groups on a larger number of powerful persons and organizations, which are often very unclear about the bases for their actions and unpredictable in their decisions, and which further render the poor helpless by condescending or hostile attitudes, explicit verbal communications which state or imply the inferiority of the poor, and callousness or actual harassment. If we divide the powerful persons affecting the poor into two groups, the benevolent in intention on the one hand, and the callous or punitive on the other, we will find that the majority of both types of power figure treat the poor as inferior and reach down to relate to them.[3]

The situation of poverty, then, is the situation of enforced dependency, giving the poor very little scope for *action*, in the sense of behavior under their own control which is central to their needs and values. This scope for action is supposed to be furnished by society to any person in either of two ways. First, confidence, hope, motivation, and skills for action may be provided through childhood socialization

---

[3] It should be remembered that not all sections of the poor are so much at the mercy of outside forces. The stably employed working class poor are less dependent on mysterious, unpredictable, arbitrary, and capricious forces. There are degrees and kinds of poverty, and the differences among them will be set forth elsewhere to supplement the general description contained in this paper.

and continue as a relatively permanent aspect of the personality. Second, social positions are provided which make it easy for their occupants to act, which make it possible for decisions of their occupants to be implemented in their futures. Middle class socialization and middle class social positions customarily both provide bases for effective action; lower class socialization and lower class social positions usually both fail to make it possible for the poor to act.

Thus, the dependency of the poor is not primarily a neurotic need to occupy dependency positions in social relationships, but rather it results from a deprivation of those minimal social resources, at every period of their lives, which the poor need and therefore must seek. The poor are not victims of the social system in the sense that "organization men" are victims. They are rather, as Michael Harrington has emphasized, the *other* America, outsiders to the major society. In consequence, members of the majority society are usually outsiders to the poor.

The initial dependency and its consequences are reinforced by the hardening of a consensus in the majority community about the nature of the poor, stabilization of the patterns of behavior in areas of poverty, and partial internalization of ideas and patterns of behavior in the children who grow up in both communities. Thus, the positions of poor persons in relationship to superordinate forces are expressions of two communities, a superior and powerful community and an inferior and weaker community; two communities with institutionalized ways of living which prop up the superordinate position of the one in relation to the other.

People isolate and segregate those they fear and pity. The stronger of the two communities has traditionally acted to alleviate the results perceived to be undesirable without changing the relationship of the two communities or ending the division into two communities. Since persons designing and implementing such programs did not consider the consequences of the division for their aims, they were able to maintain an intention to bring the poor into their society. The recommendations have been for improved law enforcement; public welfare; public housing; social settlements; higher horizons educational programs; social work with "hard core" families; urban renewal, clean-up, paint-up, and fix-up programs; block and neighborhood organizations; and the like. All these plans and programs have usually shared two characteristics: (1) they are initiated and supported from outside the neighborhoods of poverty and imposed on the poor; and (2) they fail to make any lasting positive impact on neighborhoods of poverty. That is, although a few persons and families become affluent and leave the neighborhoods, the majority remain poor and continue in an atmosphere of apathy, disorganization, and hostility, toward the programs designed to rescue them. These programs, presupposing the inferiority of the people in the area, perpetuate and exacerbate the inequality. Definitions of the poor are carried by the institutionalized helping hands. Insofar as these agencies have any *social* impact, the definitions embedded in them become self-fulfilling. But, although the powerful external social agencies —powerful in relation to the poor—are not very effective in carrying out their official tasks in areas of poverty, they do enable the stronger community to believe that something is being done about the social problem of poverty, reducing guilt and shame to such an extent that there remains little motivation to develop some effective means to bring the poor into the larger society.

On the basis of this sketch of the dynamics of the situation of the poor, the following classification can be made of the sources of the "psychology of poverty."

(a) In any modern industrial society the overall amount of power of the society tends constantly to increase, although the rate of increase may vary. Although everyone in the society may secure ownership of additional *material* goods as a result of technological progress, the additional *power* tends to be secured only by those persons and social systems with preexistent power. The poor boy with strong internalized drives and skills for success and the large corporation with effective control over technological advances in its field both illustrate the tendency for socially created power to attract to itself additional power. But the poor most often have neither the power created through childhood socialization nor that to be secured through attachment to a strong social system in which they have influence. In some countries, the population is predominantly poor, and this populace may have some power through the political process. But, in the United States the poor are an unorganized or ineffectively organized minority, unable even to exert influence in the political sphere. Thus, increments in power tend to attach to those with power, and the balance of power in a country such as the United States tends naturally to tilt against the poor.

(b) The fact of being powerless, but with needs that must be met, leads the poor to be dependent on the organizations, persons, and institutions which can meet these needs. The situation of dependency and powerlessness through internal personality characteristics as well as through social position leads to apathy, hopelessness, conviction of the inability to act successfully, failure to develop skills, and so on.

(c) As a consequence of the self-help doctrine, this "psychology of poverty" arouses the anger of the affluent toward the poor. Thus, the affluent can avoid the necessity to alter the social situation of the poor by assuming that the poor are bad and deserve their situation. This additional meaning of poverty makes rigid the dependency aspects of the social situation of the poor, and, to some extent, the poor accept the prevalent view of themselves. However, since the poor are not together in an unambiguously clear social category, they, at the same time, may reject being placed in such a category subject to the assumption of their dependency and inferiority. For example, persons eligible to live in public housing are not affected only by the convenience, space, and other physical characteristics of their living quarters. A large proportion seem to prefer dilapidated private housing operated by an indifferent landlord to better maintained, less crowded, less expensive quarters in a public housing project in which the management is concerned with tenant needs. The meaning of living in such a project may offset the superiority of the physical living arrangements.

(d) Over time the dependency relationship of the poor becomes institutionalized and habits, traditions, and organizations arise in both the affluent community and in the neighborhoods of poverty, maintaining the relationship between them. The poor react in part to the institutionalization itself. For example, "lower class" delinquency does not only stem from the fact that the poor have few and drab job opportunities. There is also the perception that the conforming poor tend to remain indefinitely in low social positions as well as the angry rejection by the adolescent poor of attempts, through law enforcement and social agencies, to control and manipulate them without altering their situation.

Consequences of this social process for the poor have been indicated at several points in the preceding discussion; we will only briefly recapitulate some of them here.

First, people tend either to retreat from or to attack forces controlling their lives which they cannot affect and which are not inescapable. For this reason the poor typically stand aloof from settlement houses, get minimally involved with social workers, drop out of school. Only forces too omnipresent to be escaped may ensure normative affiliation through identification with aggressors. It is easy to see the poor as paranoid since they are so often hostile to and suspicious of powerful objects which they may perceive in a distorted fashion. However, paranoia presumably requires origins in early childhood, while the hostility and suspicion of the poor naturally arise from their social position and their necessarily over-simplified and naturally personified perceptions of it.

Second, with less of their selves bound up in their self-conceptions than is the case with other groups, the poor do not entirely accept these definitions of themselves, but protect themselves by various psychological strategies from fully accepting the implications of their situation. The impact of the definitions then is primarily indirect; the definitions have consequences by creating the situation of the poor through the meaning of poverty to those who possess power. The situation gives rise to the typical absence of that hope which is associated with action and which give salience to intentions and attitudes. Thus, the poor frequently verbalize middle-class values without practicing them. Their verbalizations are useful in protecting their self-conceptions and in dealing with the affluent rather than in any pronounced relationship to non-verbal behavior. This does not imply deliberate falsification; a poor person may have the necessary sincerity, intention, and skill to embark on a course of action but there is so much unconscious uncertainty about achieving psychological returns through success that the action may never be seriously attempted. As has been discovered in social surveys, the poor may not only pay lip service to middle class notions, but may, for similar reasons, say to any powerful person what they believe he wants to hear. That is, much of the behavior of the poor does not relate primarily to their own basic values, beliefs and perceptions held by others about the poor. The poor are normally involved in partly involuntary self-diminution; their behavior may therefore be remarkably transformed when, as has happened through social action, they begin to acquire a sense of power, of ability to realize *their* aspirations. Thus, the so-called differential values of the poor, which are ill-defined at best, are more nearly comprehensible as the psychological consequences of a long continued situation of perceived powerlessness in contemporary industrial society. They become a subculture to the extent that the traditions, orientations, and habits of dependency become internalized.

Third, the situation of the poor, the inability of the poor to act in their own behalf, creates a less complex personality structure for them than is the case with affluent persons with more linguistic skills. This does not necessarily mean that the poor have less effective personalities, or are unsocialized in comparison, since the personalities of more highly educated persons are often partly constituted by social elaborated fantasies which conceal reality and rationalize avoidance of problem solving.

Fourth, awareness of their common fate typically leads the poor to engage in mutual aid activities, activities which, in spite of involving only very minor skills, are precursors to the joint social action which develops naturally as the poor acquire organizational skills and confidence in using them.

Fifth, because of the social situation of the poor and the fact that the majority society has relatively little normative basis for social control in areas of poverty, these areas are often characterized by high rates of publicly discernible types of deviance: juvenile delinquency, school dropouts, alcoholism, illegitimacy, mother-centered families, and the like.

Finally, there are differential consequences of institutionalized, uncompensated powerlessness for the poor who have various social positions within areas of poverty. For example, because of the greater expectation for men to be powerful and to be sources of power, the consequences of powerlessness for "lower class" men is usually greater than that for women.

All of this suggests that the problems of the poor are not so much of poverty as of a particularly difficult variety of situational dependency, a helplessness to affect many important social factors in their lives, the functioning or purpose of which they do not understand, and which are essentially unpredictable to them.

Not Enough Money Versus Situational Dependency

With increased money the poor could at least be better able to cope with such forces, could be less dependent on some. What, then, is the relationship between the poverty of the poor and their situational dependency?

Money is a generalized source of power over people through a right to control over goods and services. As such, money is one of many kinds of power. Poverty, therefore, is one of many kinds of powerlessness, of being subject to one's social situation instead of being able to affect it through action, that is, through behavior which flows from decisions and plans. Since there are several varieties of generalized power, an absence of money is often replaceable *insofar as the psychological reactions to powerlessness are concerned.* An American Indian who lives in poverty may have considerable influence through authority relationships traditional in his culture. Members of religious orders who have taken vows of poverty remain able to exercise influence through their order and through relationships of interdependence with colleagues. The college student with a very low income has influence through the expectations of his future social position. When the poor engage in successful social action they gain power, even when their incomes remain unchanged.

In other words, when social scientists have reported on the psychological consequences of poverty it seems reasonable to believe that they have described the psychological consequences of powerlessness. And many persons without money have, or get, other varieties of power, or else identify with powerful persons or groups and therefore fail to exhibit these consequences. Even the poor do not react entirely on the basis of the social definition of them. There are counter institutions and traditions (churches, unions, and clubs) which deflect the impact of the majority definition. Primary groups (family and peer) also mediate and modify the community definitions they transmit. The behavior of the poor may not, therefore, reflect their self-conceptions; we should not suppose that the poor feel as would middle class persons in their situations, or as their behavior suggests they feel. This very resistance of the poor makes it possible to attempt the otherwise herculean task of trying to get the major society to alter its relationship to poverty by helping the poor themselves to build a backfire, to become strong and effective enough to challenge the invidious definitions that have been made of them.

Human personality is a process of decisions and actions on the basis of decisions. One becomes fully human only through acting in important areas of one's life. All social arrangements which take responsibility out of the hands of the poor, which make decisions and action more difficult or operative over a more restricted area, feed the psychology of powerlessness which is so widely (and correctly) regarded as undesirable. For example, it is often noted that the poor lack a time perspective. But only through action (important decisions and behavior on their basis) does one acquire a history and, with the history, a practical concern with the future.

What consequences does the social situation of the poor have for programs to help the poor? We will next consider some general answers to this question.

Redefining the Social Situation of the Poor

We can reject two possible alternatives.

First, the solution most frequently suggested is to help the poor secure more money without otherwise changing present power relationships. This appears to implement the idea of equality while avoiding any necessary threat to established centers of power. But, since the consequences are related to *powerlessness*, not to the absolute supply of money available to the poor, and since *the amount of power purchasable with a given supply of money decreases as a society acquires a larger supply of goods and services,* the solution of raising the incomes of the poor is likely, unless accompanied by other measures, to be ineffective in an affluent society. Where the poor live in serious deprivation of goods and services, an increase in the supply of those goods and services would be an important source of power, that is, of access to resources which satisfy crucial needs. However, when the poor do not live in actual deprivation, increases in money make relatively little impact on the dependency relationships in which they are entangled. The opportunity to participate in *interdependent* relationships, as a *member* of the majority society, requires an increase in *power.*

Second, the *self-help* doctrine is normally related to conventional criteria of success, and persons who have not met these conventional criteria therefore are threatened with feelings of guilt and shame. One theoretically possible solution would seem to involve redefinition of success, allowing social support to lives which are now viewed as failures. This, however, presupposes an ability to meet some alternative criteria of success through action, a possible solution for philosophers, poets, or beatniks, but not now generally possible for the poor. It may, however, be that the meaning of the self-help doctrine could be adequately extended to reward the social action of the poor who can act successfully through their own organizations.

Along these lines the criteria for an effective solution are reasonably clear. In order to reduce poverty-related psychological and social problems in the United States, the major community will have to change its relationship to neighborhoods of poverty in such fashion that families in the neighborhoods have a greater stake in the broader society and can more successfully participate in the decision-making process of the surrounding community.

It is frequently said that we must provide opportunities for the poor. To render more than lip service to this objective demands more power and more skill and more knowledge than we now possess for the bureaucratic provision of such opportunities. For example, there are a finite number of jobs available, fewer than the number of people looking for work. There are severe limits to the extent to which the adult poor can be trained for existing openings. A large proportion of the poor have jobs which do not remove them from the ranks of the powerless. Any great shift in opportunities made available to the poor within the structure of the majority community will threaten more powerful groups with vested interests in those limited opportunities, and the proponents of creating opportunities for the poor cannot themselves affect the political or economic process enough to implement their good intentions.

It is important to develop opportunities in sensitive relation to the perception by the poor of their own needs. When this is not done, the poor are not likely to be able to use efficiently the opportunities created for them. And, most central of all, rather than to provide opportunities for the "lower class," the poor must as a group be helped to secure opportunities for themselves. Only then will motivation be released that is now locked in the silent and usually successful battle of the neighborhoods of poverty to maintain themselves in an alien social world. This motivation which will enable them to enter the majority society and make it as nurturant of them as it is at present of the more prosperous population.

The involvement of the poor in successful and significant social action provides both immediate and compelling psychological returns and also the possibility of initiative to help the bureaucratic organizations related to the poor to fulfill their officially stated purposes. The institutions of the major community can be forced to establish relationships of interdependence, not of dependence, with the poor; professionals can help by accepting professional roles as employees of the organizations of the poor.

In our society inner worth as expressed in action, striving, the struggle is held eventually to result in attainment of aspirations. If one is not successful, one is viewed as worthwhile so long, and only so long, as one struggles. The poor tend to be regarded as failures and not struggling, and hence as worthless. This perception of worthlessness is incorporated in the conception which others have of the poor and also, to some extent, in the conceptions which the poor have of themselves. One way in which the poor can remedy the psychological consequences of their powerlessness and of the image of the poor as worthless is for them to undertake social action that redefines them as potentially worthwhile and individually more powerful. To be effective, such social action should have the following characteristics:

1. the poor see themselves as the source of the action;
2. the action affects in major ways the preconceptions, values, or interests of institutions and persons defining the poor;
3. the action demands much in effort and skill or in other ways becomes salient to major areas of the personalities of the poor;
4. the action ends in success; and
5. the successful self-originated important action increases the force and number of symbolic or nonsymbolic communications of the potential worth or individual power of individuals who are poor.

The result of social action of this kind is a concurrent change in the view which the poor have of themselves and in the view of the poor by the outside world. There is a softening of the destructive social reality and immediate psychological returns to the poor, although not without hostile reactions from advantaged persons and organizations with known or hidden vested interests in maintenance of the areas of poverty.[4]

The only initial additional resources which a community should provide to neighborhoods of poverty should be on a temporary basis: organizers who will enable the neighborhoods quickly to create powerful, independent, democratic organizations of the poor. These organizations will themselves then seek from the rest of the community resources necessary to the neighborhoods for the solution of the problems they perceive. Agencies for the provision of training and education and opportunities can be developed under the control of the neighborhoods of

---

[4] The Syracuse University School of Social Work has developed a field placement in which graduate students are now receiving training in initiating social action projects by the poor to resolve problems of broad concern in neighborhoods of poverty. Experience indicates that social work students can learn to help the poor jointly to engage in efforts which meet these criteria. Social action efforts by the poor in areas of poverty have occurred in several places. For example, several

poverty, thereby ensuring that the poor are in interdependent rather than dependent positions in relation to the agencies. This would meet the professed objectives of most communities since it would effectively motivate the poor to maximum use of opportunities, since the requirements of professional practice will ensure the quality of services rendered, and since the communities state their intention not to allow their help to become an instrument of domination.

The comment that "we know the needs of the poor" is accurate in a very general sense. But there is a great distance between this observation and a knowledge of how, in practice, those needs can be met. If a community is not merely giving lip service to meeting them, if a community wants to be effective as well as to have good intentions, then the way of meeting needs must be appropriate to the personal and social characteristics of those being helped. In this case, effectiveness requires that the only *unilateral* additional help be given at the outset and in the form of temporary assistance in the creation of democratic and powerful organizations of the poor. Through such organizations, the poor will then negotiate with outsiders for resources and opportunities without having to submit to concurrent control from outside. The outcome will be maximal motivation to take advantage of resources and opportunities which are sensitively tailored to their needs.

Summary

There are two alternative ways to understand the psychological characteristics of the poor. These characteristics can be naïvely understood

---

years ago, Hope and Dan Morrow moved with their family into a block in East Harlem, New York City. With their help, the families in the block organized themselves formally and informally for a number of important purposes ranging from keeping streets clean to reducing juvenile delinquency. On a larger scale, some of the social action organizations originated by Saul Alinsky of the Industrial Areas Foundation have involved large numbers of people in neighborhood improvement through a conflict process around crucial neighborhood issues. IAF organizations have enabled areas to decrease or end exploitation by some absentee landlords and unethical businesses. They have also ended police brutality and secured police protection, street cleaning, and other services which low income neighborhoods had not previously received at a level equivalent to that of the remainder of the community. Several of the IAF organizations are engaging in "self-help" nonfederally assisted urban renewal. It remains true, however, that most social action programs in low income areas do not meet the above criteria. Such programs frequently attempt to mobilize neighborhoods of poverty without jeopardizing any existing power arrangement, even temporarily, and thus pursue two contradictory objectives simultaneously. They may, in any case, perform such useful functions as providing symbolic satisfaction for the conscience of the majority community and jobs for some estimable persons.

as resulting from poverty. But there are a number of reasons why it is more precise to view them as the psychology of the *powerlessness* of the poor.

These alternative points of view have also different consequences for social policy. If the problem were only one of a lack of money, it could be solved through provision of more and better paying jobs for the poor, increased minimum wage levels, higher levels of welfare payments, and so on. There would be, in that case, no real need for the poor to undertake any social action on their own behalf. This view is consistent with the idea that the poor are unable to participate in and initiate the solution of their own problems.

However, since it is more likely that the problem is one of powerlessness, joint initiative by the poor on their own behalf should precede and accompany responses from the remainder of society. In practice this initiative is likely to be most effectively exercised by powerful conflict organizations based in neighborhoods of poverty.[5]

The Disadvantaged Child and the Learning Process

Martin Deutsch

Columbia University

[Reprinted from Education in Depressed Areas, *A. Harry Passow, Editor. Copyright © 1963 by Teachers College, Columbia University. Reprinted by permission of the Bureau of Publications, Teachers College, Columbia University. All rights reserved.]*

THIS PAPER WILL DISCUSS the interaction of social and developmental factors and their impact on the intellectual growth and school performance of the child. It will make particular reference to the large number of urban children who come from marginal social circumstances. While

---

[5] Because of the nature of this paper there has been no attempt in it to marshal the data relevant to the various assertions made in the discussion of the psychology of areas of poverty as the psychology of powerlessness. This paper has not been designed as a contribution to science in the sense in which science is understood to be a body of verified statements. In the area under consideration there is no such body of statements now available. Contributions to science remain possible, but must be put forward as relatively tentative formulations in the early stages of a process which will move to the collection of additional data relevant to specific points. It is my hope that the above formulation can serve such a purpose.

much of the discussion will be speculative, where appropriate it will draw on data from the field, and will suggest particular relationships and avenues for future investigation or demonstration.

Among children who come from lower-class socially impoverished circumstances, there is a high proportion of school failure, school drop-outs, reading and learning disabilities, as well as life adjustment problems. This means not only that these children grow up poorly equipped academically, but also that the effectiveness of the school as a major institution for socialization is diminished. The effect of this process is underlined by the fact that this same segment of the population contributes disproportionately to the delinquency and other social deviancy statistics.

The thesis here is that the lower-class child enters the school situation so poorly prepared to produce what the school demands that initial failures are almost inevitable, and the school experience becomes negatively rather than positively reinforced. Thus the child's experience in school does nothing to counteract the invidious influences to which he is exposed in his slum, and sometimes segregated, neighborhood.

We know that children from underprivileged environments tend to come to school with a qualitatively different preparation for the demands of both the learning process and the behavioral requirements of the classroom. There are various differences in the kinds of socializing experiences these children have had, as contrasted with the middle-class child. The culture of their environment is a different one from the culture that has molded the school and its educational techniques and theory.

We know that it is difficult for all peoples to span cultural discontinuities, and yet we make little if any effort to prepare administrative personnel or teachers and guidance staff to assist the child in this transition from one cultural context to another. This transition must have serious psychological consequences for the child, and probably plays a major role in influencing his later perceptions of other social institutions as he is introduced to them.

It must be pointed out that the relationship between social background and school performance is not a simple one. Rather, evidence which is accumulating points more and more to the influence of background variables on the patterns of perceptual, language, and cognitive development of the child and the subsequent diffusion of the effects of such patterns into all areas of the child's academic and psychological performance. To understand these effects requires delineating the underlying skills in which these children are not sufficiently proficient. A related problem is that of defining what aspects of the background are most influential in producing what kinds of deficits in skills.

Environmental Factors

Let us begin with the most macroscopic background factors. While it is likely that slum life might have delimited areas that allow for positive growth and that the middle-class community has attributes which might retard healthy development, generally the combination of circumstances in middle-class life is considerably more likely to furnish opportunities for normal growth of the child. At the same time, slum conditions are more likely to have deleterious effects on physical and mental development. This is not to say that middle-class life furnishes a really adequate milieu for the maximum development of individual potential: it doesn't. The fact that we often speak as though it does is a function of viewing the middle-class environment in comparison to the slum. Middle-class people who work and teach across social-class lines often are unable to be aware of the negative aspects of the middle-class background because of its apparent superiority over the less advantageous background provided by lower-class life. We really have no external criterion for evaluating the characteristics of a milieu in terms of how well it is designed to foster development; as a result we might actually be measuring one area of social failure with the yardstick of social catastrophe.

It is true that many leading personalities in twentieth-century American life have come from the slums, and this is a fact often pointed out by nativistic pragmatists in an effort to prove that if the individual "has it in him" he can overcome—and even be challenged by—his humble surroundings. This argument, though fundamentally fallacious, might have had more to recommend it in the past. At the turn of the century we were a massively vertical mobile society—that is, with the exception of certain large minority groups such as the Negroes, the Indians, and the Mexican-Americans who were rarely allowed on the social elevator. In the mid-twentieth century it is now increasingly possible for all groups to get on, but social and economic conditions have changed, and the same elevator more frequently moves in two directions or stands still altogether. When it does move, it goes more slowly, and, most discouragingly, it also provides an observation window on what, at least superficially, appears to be a most affluent society. Television, movies, and other media continually expose the individual from the slum to the explicit assumption that the products of a consumer society are available to all—or, rather, as he sees it, to all but him. In effect, this means that the child from the disadvantaged environment is an outsider and an observer—through his own eyes and those of his parents or neighbors—of the mainstream of American life. At the same time, when the child enters school he is exposing himself directly to the values and anticipations of a participant in that mainstream—his teacher. It is not sufficiently recognized that there is quite a gap between the training of a teacher and the needs, limitations, and unique strengths of the child from a marginal situation. This gap is, of course, maximized when the child belongs to a minority group that until quite recently was not only excluded from the mainstream, but was not even allowed to bathe in the tributaries.

What are some of the special characteristics of these children, and why do they apparently need exceptional social and educational planning? So often, administrators and teachers say, they are children who are "curious," "cute," "affectionate," "warm," and independently dependent in the kindergarten and the first grade, but who so often become "alienated," "withdrawn," "angry," "passive," "apathetic," or just "trouble-makers" by the fifth and sixth grade. In our research at the Institute for Developmental Studies, it is in the first grade that we usually see the smallest differences between socio-economic or racial groups in intellectual, language, and some conceptual measures, and in the later grades that we find the greatest differences in favor of the more socially privileged groups. From both teachers' observations and the finding of this increasing gap, it appears that there is a failure on some level of society and, more specifically, the educational system. Was the school scientifically prepared to receive these children in the first place? And, in addition, were the children perhaps introduced to the individual demands of the larger culture at too late an age—that is, in first grade?

Before discussing these psychological products of social deprivation, it is appropriate to look more closely at the special circumstances of Negro slum residents. In the core city of most of our large metropolitan areas, 40 to 70 percent of the elementary school population is likely to be Negro. In my observations, through workshops in many of these cities, I have often been surprised to find how little real comprehension of the particular problems of these youngsters exists as part of the consciousness of the Negro or white middle-class teachers. While in middle-class schools there is great sensitivity to emotional climates and pressures and tensions that might be operating on the child in either the home or the school, in lower-class schools the problems of social adaptation are so massive that sensitivity tends to become blunted.

In the lower-class Negro group there still exist the sequelae of the conditions of slavery. While a hundred years have passed, this is a short time in the life of a people. And the extension of tendrils of the effects of slavery into modern life has been effectively discouraged only in the last few decades, when there have been some real attempts to integrate the Negro fully into American life. It is often difficult for teachers and the personnel of other community agencies to understand the

Negro lower-class child—particularly the child who has come, or whose parents have come, from the rural South. There is a whole set of implicit and explicit value systems which determine our educational philosophies, and the institutional expectation is that all children participate in these systems. And yet for these expectations to be met, the child must experience some continuity of socio-cultural participation in and sharing of these value systems before he comes to school. This is often just not the case for the child who comes from an encapsulated community, particularly when the walls have been built by the dominant social and cultural forces that have also determined the value systems relating to learning.

A recent article in *Fortune* magazine asked why the Negro failed to take full advantage of opportunities open to him in American life. At least part of the answer is that the Negro has not been fully integrated into American life, and that even knowledge about particular occupations and their requirements is not available outside the cultural mainstream. Implications of this for the aspirations and motivations of children will be discussed later.

Another source of misunderstanding on the part of school and social agency people is the difficulty of putting in historical perspective the casual conditions responsible for the high percentage of broken homes in the Negro community. Implications of this for the child's emotional stability are very frequently recognized, but the effects on the child's motivation, self-concept, and achievement orientation are not often understood.

The Negro family was first broken deliberately by the slave traders and the plantation owners for their own purposes. As was pointed out earlier, the hundred years since slavery is not a very long time for a total social metamorphosis even under fostering conditions—and during that period the Negro community has been for the most part economically marginal and isolated from the contacts which would have accelerated change. The thirteen depressions and recessions we have had since Emancipation have been devastating to this community. These marginal economic and encapsulated social circumstances have been particularly harsh on the Negro male. The chronic instability has greatly influenced the Negro man's concept of himself and his general motivation to succeed in competitive areas of society where the rewards are greatest. All these circumstances have contributed to the instability of the Negro family, and particularly to the fact that it is most often broken by the absence of the father. As a result, the lower-class Negro child entering school often has had no experience with a "successful" male model or thereby with a psychological framework in which effort can result in at least the possibility of achievement. Yet the value system of the school and of the learning process is predicated on the assumption that effort will result in achievement.

To a large extent, much of this is true not only for the Negro child but for all children who come from impoverished and marginal social and economic conditions. These living conditions are characterized by great overcrowding in substandard housing, often lacking adequate sanitary and other facilities. While we don't know the actual importance, for example, of moments of privacy, we do know that the opportunity frequently does not exist. In addition, there are likely to be large numbers of siblings and half-siblings, again with there being little opportunity for individuation. At the same time, the child tends to be restricted to his immediate environment, with conducted explorations of the "outside" world being infrequent and sometimes non-existent. In the slums, and to an unfortunately large extent in many other areas of our largest cities, there is little opportunity to observe natural beauty, clean landscapes or other pleasant and aesthetically pleasing surroundings.

In the child's home, there is a scarcity of objects of all types, but especially of books, toys, puzzles, pencils, and scribbling paper. It is not that the mere presence of such materials would necessarily result in their productive use, but it would increase the child's familiarity with the tools he'll be confronted with in school. Actually, for the most effective utilization of these tools, guidance and explanations are necessary from the earliest time of exposure. Such guidance requires not only the presence of aware and educated adults, but also time—a rare commodity in these marginal circumstances. Though many parents will share in the larger value system of having high aspirations for their children, they are unaware of the operational steps required for the preparation of the child to use optimally the learning opportunities in the school. Individual potential is one of the most unmarketable properties if the child acquires no means for its development, or if no means exist for measuring it objectively. It is here that we must understand the consequences of all these aspects of the slum matrix for the psychological and cognitive development of the child.

Psychological Factors

A child from any circumstance who has been deprived of a substantial portion of the variety of stimuli which he is maturationally capable of responding to is likely to be deficient in the equipment required for learning.

Support for this is found in Hunt who, in discussing Piaget's developmental theories, points out that, according to Piaget, ". . . the rate of development is in substantial part, but certainly not wholly, a function of environmental circumstances. Change in circumstances is required to force the accommodative modifications of schemata that constitute development. Thus, the greater the variety of situations to which the child must accommodate his behavioral structures, the more differentiated and mobile they become. Thus, the more new things a child has seen and the more he has heard, the more things he is interested in seeing and hearing. Moreover, the more variation in reality with which he has coped, the greater is his capacity for coping."

This emphasis on the importance of variety in the environment implies the detrimental effects of lack of variety. This in turn leads to a concept of "stimulus deprivation." But it is important that it be correctly understood. By this is not necessarily meant any restriction of the quantity of stimulation, but, rather, a restriction to a segment of the spectrum of stimulation potentially available. In addition to the restriction in variety, from what is known of slum environment, it might be postulated that the segments made available to these children tend to have poorer and less systematic ordering of stimulation sequences, and would thereby be less useful to the growth and activation of cognitive potential.

This deprivation has effects on both the formal and the contentual aspects of cognition. By "formal" is meant the operations—the behavior —by which stimuli are perceived, encouraged, and responded to. By "contentual" is meant the actual content of the child's knowledge and comprehension. "Formal equipment" would include perceptual discrimination skills, the ability to sustain attention, and the ability to use adults as sources of information and for satisfying curiosity. Also included would be the establishment of expectations of reward from accumulation of knowledge, from task completion, and from adult reinforcement, and the ability to delay gratification. Examples of "contentual equipment" would be the language-symbolic system, environmental information, general and environmental orientation, and concepts of comparability and relativity appropriate to the child's age level. The growth of a differentiated additudinal set toward learning is probably a resultant of the interaction between formal and contextual levels.

Hypothesizing that stimulus deprivation will result in deficiencies in either of these equipments, let us examine the particular stimuli which are available and those which are absent from the environment of the child who comes from the conditions discussed above. This reasoning suggests also certain hypotheses regarding the role of environment in the evolving of the formal and contextual systems.

As was pointed out in the previous section, the disadvantaged environment as well as certain aspects of the middle-class circumstance offers the child, over-all, a restricted range of experience. While one does see great individual variability in these children, social conditions reduce the range of this variation; with less variety in input, it would be reasonable to assume a concomitant restriction in the variety of output. This is an important respect in which social poverty may have a leveling effect on the achievement of individual skills and abilities. Concomitantly, in the current problem of extensive under-achievement in suburban lower-middle-class areas, the over-routinization of activity with the consequent reduction in variety may well be the major factor.

In individual terms, a child is probably farther away from his maturational ceiling as a result of this experiential poverty. This might well be a crucial factor in the poorer performance of the lower socio-economic children on standardized tests of intelligence. On such tests, the child is compared with others of his own age. But if his point of development in relation to the maturational ceiling for his age group is influenced by his experience, then the child with restricted experience may actually be developed to a proportionately lower level of his own actual ceiling. If a certain quantum of fostering experience is necessary to activate the achievment of particular maturational levels, then perhaps the child who is deficient in this experience will take longer to achieve these levels, even though his potential may be the same as the more advantaged child. It might be that in order to achieve a realistic appraisal of the ability levels of children, an "experience" age rather than the chronological age should be used to arrive at norms.

This suggests a limitation on the frequent studies comparing Negro and white children. Even when it is possible to control for the formal attributes of social class membership, the uniqueness of the Negro child's experience would make comparability impossible when limited to these class factors. Perhaps too, if such an interaction exists between experiential and biological determinants of development, it would account for the failure of the culture-free tests, as they too are standardized on an age basis without allowing for the experimental interaction (as distinguished from specific experimental *influence*).

Let us now consider some of the specifics in the child's environment, and their effects on the development of the formal, contextual, and attitudinal systems.

Visually, the urban slum and its overcrowded apartments offer the child a minimal range of stimuli. There are usually few if any pictures on the wall, and the objects in the household, be they toys, furniture, or utensils, tend to be sparse, repetitious, and lacking in form and color variations. The sparsity of objects and lack of diversity of home artifacts which are available and meaningful to the child, in addition to the unavailability of individualized training, gives the child few opportunities to manipulate and organize the visual properties of his environment and thus perceptually to organize and discriminate the nuances of that environment. These would include figure-ground relationships and the spatial organization of the visual field. The sparsity of manipulable objects probably also hampers the development of these functions in the tactile area. For example, while these children have broomsticks and usually a ball, possibly a doll or a discarded kitchen pot to play with, they don't have the different shapes and colors and sizes to manipulate which the middle-class child has in the form of blocks which are bought just for him, or even in the variety of sizes and shapes of cooking utensils which might be available to him as playthings.

It is true, as has been pointed out frequently, that the pioneer child didn't have many playthings either. But he had a more active responsibility toward the environment and a great variety of growing plants and other natural resources as well as a stable family that assumed a primary role for the education and training of the child. In addition, the intellectually normal or superior frontier child could and usually did grow up to be a farmer. Today's child will grow up into a world of automation requiring highly differentiated skills if he and society are to use his intellect.

The effect of sparsity of manipulable objects on visual perception is, of course, quite speculative, as few data now exist. However, it is an important area, as among skills necessary for reading are form discrimination and visual spatial organization. Children from depressed areas, because of inadequate training and stimulation, may not have developed the requisite skills by the time they enter first grade, and the assumption that they do possess these skills may thus add to the frustration these children experience on entering school.

The lower-class home is not a verbally oriented environment. The implications of this for language development will be considered below in the discussion of the contentual systems. Here let us consider its implication for the development of auditory discrimination skills. While the environment is a noisy one, the noise is not, for the most part, meaningful in relation to the child, and for him most of it is background. In the crowded apartments with all the daily living stresses, a minimum of non-instructional conversation is directed toward the child. In actuality, the situation is ideal for the child to learn inattention. Furthermore, he does not get practice in auditory discrimination or feedback from adults correcting his enunciation, pronunciation, and grammar. In studies at the Institute for Developmental Studies at New York Medical College, as yet unreported in the literature, we have found significant differences in auditory discrimination between lower-class and middle-class children in the first grade. These differences seem to diminish markedly as the children get older, though the effects of their early existence on other functioning remain to be investigated. Here again, we are dealing with a skill very important to reading. Our data indicate too that poor readers within social-class groups have significantly more difficulty in auditory discrimination than do good readers. Further, this difference between good and poor readers is greater for the lower-class group.

If the child learns to be inattentive in the pre-school environment, as has been postulated, this further diminishes incoming stimulation. Further, if this trained inattention comes about as a result of his being insufficiently called upon to respond to particular stimuli, then his general level of responsiveness will also be diminished. The nature of the total environment and the child-adult interaction is such that reinforcement is too infrequent, and, as a result, the quantity of response is diminished. The implications of this for the structured learning situation in the school are quite obvious.

Related to attentivity is memory. Here also we would postulate the dependence of the child, particularly in the pre-school period, on interaction with the parent. It is adults who link the past and the present by calling to mind prior shared experiences. The combination of the constriction in the use of language and in shared activity results, for the lower-class child, in much less stimulation of the early memory function. Although I don't know of any data supporting this thesis, from my observations it would seem that there is a tendency for these children to be proportionately more present-oriented and less aware of past-present sequences than the middle-class child. This is consistent with anthropological research and thinking. While this could be a function of the poorer time orientation of these children or of their difficulty in verbal expression, both of which will be discussed, it could also relate to a greater difficulty in seeing themselves in the past or in a different context. Another area which points up the home-school discontinuity is that of time. Anthropologists have pointed out that from culture to culture time concepts differ and that time as life's governor is a relatively modern phenomenon and one which finds most of its slaves in the lower-middle, middle-middle, and upper-middle classes. It might not even be an important factor in learning, but it is an essential feature in the measurement of children's performance by testing and in the adjustment of children to the organizational demands of the school. The middle-class teacher organizes the day by allowing a certain amount of time for each activity. Psychologists have long noticed that American Indian children, mountain children, and children from other non-industrial groups have great difficulty organizing their response tempo to meet time limitations. In the Orientation Scale developed at the Institute, we have found that lower-class children in the first grade had significantly greater difficulty than did middle-class children in handling items related to time judgments.

Another area in which the lower-class child lacks pre-school orientation is the well-inculcated expectation of reward for performance, especially for successful task completion. The lack of such expectation, of course, reduces motivation for beginning a task and, therefore, also makes less likely the self-reinforcement of activity through the gaining of feelings of competence. In these impoverished, broken homes there is very little of the type of interaction seen so commonly in middle-class homes, in which the parent sets a task for the child, observes its performance, and in some way rewards its completion. Neither, for most tasks, is there the disapproval which the middle-class child incurs when he does not perform properly or when he leaves something unfinished. Again, much of the organization of the classroom is based on the assumption that children anticipate rewards for performance and that they will respond in these terms to tasks which are set for them. This is not to imply that the young lower-class child is not given assignments in his home, nor that he is never given approval or punishment. Rather, the assignments tend to be motoric in character, have a short-time span, and are more likely to relate to very concrete objects or services for people. The tasks given to pre-school children in the middle-class are more likely to involve language and conceptual processes, and are thereby more attuned to the later school setting.

Related to the whole issue of the adult-child dynamic in establishing a basis for the later learning process is the ability of the child to use the adult as a source for information, correction and the reality testing involved in problem solving and the absorption of new knowledge. When free adult time is greatly limited, homes vastly overcrowded, economic stress chronic, and the general educational level very low—and, in addition, when adults in our media culture are aware of the inadequacy of their education—questions from children are not encouraged, as the adults might be embarrassed by their own limitations and anyway are too preoccupied with the business of just living and surviving. In the child's formulation of concepts of the world, the ability to formulate questions is an essential step in data gathering. If questions are not encouraged or if they are not responded to, this is a function which does not mature.

At the Institute, in our observations of children at the kindergarten level and in our discussions with parents, we find that many lower-class children have difficulty here. It follows that this problem, if it is not compensated for by special school efforts, becomes more serious later in the learning process, as more complex subject matter is introduced. It is here that questioning is not only desirable but essential, for if the child is not prepared to demand clarification he again falls farther behind, the process of alienation from school is facilitated, and his inattentiveness becomes further reinforced as he just does not understand what is being presented.

It is generally agreed that the language-symbolic process plays an important role at all levels of learning. It is included here under the "contextual" rubric because language development evolves through the correct labeling of the environment, and through the use of appropriate words for the relating and combining and recombining of the concrete and abstract components in describing, interpreting, and communicating perceptions, experiences, and ideational matter. One can postulate on considerable evidence that language is one of the areas which is most sensitive to the impact of the multiplicity of problems associated with the stimulus deprivation found in the marginal circumstances of lower-class life. There are various dimensions of language, and for each of these it is possible to evaluate the influence of the verbal environment of the home and its immediate neighborhood.

In order for a child to handle multiple attributes of words and to associate words with their proper referents, a great deal of exposure to language is presupposed. Such exposure involves training, experimenting with identifying objects and having corrective feedback, listening to a variety of verbal material, and just observing adult language usage. Exposure of children to this type of experience is one of the great strengths of the middle-class home, and concomitantly represents a weakness in the lower-class home. In a middle-class home also, the availability of a great range of objects to be labeled and verbally related to each other strengthens the over-all language fluency of the child and gives him a basis for both understanding the teacher and for being able to communicate with her on various levels. An implicit hypothesis in a recent Institute survey of verbal skills is that verbal fluency is strongly related to reading skills and to other highly organized integrative and conceptual verbal activity.

The acquisition of language facility and fluency and experience with the multiple attributes of words is particularly important in view of the estimate that only 60 to 80 percent of any sustained communication is usually heard. Knowledge of context and of the syntactical regularities of a language make correct completion and comprehension of the speech sequence possible. This completion occurs as a result of the correct anticipation of the sequence of language and thought. The child who has not achieved these anticipatory language skills is greatly handicapped in school. Thus for the child who already is deficient in auditory discrimination and in ability to sustain attention, it becomes increasingly important that he have the very skills he lacks most.

The problem in developing preventive and early remedial programs for these children is in determining the emphasis on the various areas that need remediation. For example, would it be more effective to place the greatest emphasis on the training of auditory discrimination, or on attentional mechanisms, or on anticipatory receptive language functions in order to achieve the primary goal of enabling the child to understand his teacher? In programming special remedial procedures, we do not know how much variation we will find from child to child, or if social-class experiences create a sufficiently homogeneous pattern of deficit so that the fact of any intervention and systematic training may be more important than its sequences. If this is so, the intervention would probably be most valid in the language area, because the large group of lower-class children with the kinds of deficits mentioned are probably maturationally ready for more complex language functioning than they have achieved. Language knowledge, once acquired, can be self-reinforcing in just communicating with peers or talking to oneself.

In observations of lower-class homes, it appears that speech sequences seem to be temporally very limited and poorly structured syntactically. It is thus not surprising to find that a major focus of deficit in the children's language development is syntactical organization and subject continuity. In preliminary analysis of expressive and receptive language data on samples of middle- and lower-class children at the first- and fifth-grade levels, there are indications that the lower-class child has more expressive language ability than is generally recognized or than emerges in the classroom. The main differences between the social classes seem to lie in the level of syntactical organization. If, as is indicated in this research, with proper stimulation a surprisingly high level of expressive language functioning is available to the same children who show syntactical deficits, then we might conclude that the language variables we are dealing with here are by-products of social experience rather than indices of basic ability or intellectual level. This again suggests another possibly vital area to be included in an enrichment or a remedial program: training in the use of word sequences to relate and unify cognitions.

Also on the basis of preliminary analysis of data, it appears that retarded readers have the most difficulty with the organization of expressive language.

In another type of social-class-related language analysis, Bernstein (1960), an English sociologist, has pointed out that the lower-class tends to use informal language and mainly to convey concrete needs and immediate consequences, while the middle-class usage tends to be more formal and to emphasize the relating of concepts. This difference between these two milieus, then, might explain the finding in some of our recent research that the middle-class fifth-grade child has an advantage over the lower-class fifth grader in tasks where precise and somewhat abstract language is required for solution. Further, Bernstein's reasoning would again emphasize the communication gap which exists between the middle-class teacher and the lower-class child.

Though it might belong more in the formal than in the contextual area, one can postulate that the absence of well-structured routine and activity in the home is reflected in the difficulty that the lower-class child has in structuring language. The implication of this for curriculum in the kindergarten and nursery school would be that these children should be offered a great deal of verbalized routine and regulation so that expectation can be built up in the child and then met.

According to Piaget's theories, later problem-solving and logical abilities are built on the earlier and orderly progression through a series of developmental stages involving the active interaction between the child and his environment. This is considered a maturational process, though highly related to experience and practice. Language development does not occupy a super-ordinate position. However, Whorf, Vygotsky, and some contemporary theorists have made language the essential ingredient in concept formation, problem-solving, and in the relating to an interpretation of the environment. Current data at the Institute tend to indicate that class differences in perceptual abilities and in general environmental orientation decrease with chronological age, whereas language differences tend to increase. These might tentatively be interpreted to mean that perceptual development occurs first and that language growth and its importance in problem solving comes later. If later data and further analysis support this interpretation, then the implication would be that the lower-class child comes to school with major deficits in the perceptual rather than the language area. Perhaps the poverty of his experience has slowed his rate of maturation. Then by requiring, without the antecedent verbal preparation, a relatively high level of language skill, the school may contribute to an increase in the child's deficit in this area, relative to middle-class children. Meanwhile, his increased experience and normal maturational processes stimulate perceptual development, and that deficit is overcome. But the child is left with a language handicap. The remedy for such a situation would be emphasis on perceptual training for these children in the early school, or, better, pre-school, years, combined with a more gradual introduction of language training and requirements.

This theory and interpretation are somewhat, but by no means wholly, in conflict with the previous discussion of language. In an area where there is as yet much uncertainty, it is important to consider as many alternatives as possible, in order not to restrict experimentation.

In any event, whether or not we consider language skills as primary mediators in concept formation and problem solving, the lower-class child seems to be at a disadvantage at the point of entry into the formal learning process.

The other contentual factors that so often result in a poorly prepared child being brought to the school situation are closely interrelated with language. Briefly, they revolve around the child's understanding and knowledge of the physical, geographic, and geometric characteristics of the world around him, as well as information about his self-identity and some of the more macroscopic items of general information. It could be reasonably expected, for example, that a kindergarten or first-grade child who is not mentally defective would know both his first and last names, his address or the city he lives in, would have a rudimentary concept of number relationships, and would know something about the differences between near and far, high and low, and similar relational concepts. Much of what happens in school is predicated on the prior availability of this basic information. We know that educational procedures frequently proceed without establishing the actual existence of such a baseline. Again, in the lower-class child it cannot be taken for granted that the home experience has supplied this information or that it has tested the child for this knowledge. In facilitating the learning process in these children, the school must expect frequently to do a portion of the job traditionally assigned to the home, and curriculum must be reorganized to provide for establishing a good base. This type of basic information is essential so that the child can relate the input of new information to some stable core.

From all of the foregoing, it is obvious that the lower-class child when he enters school has as many problems in understanding what it is all about and why he is there as school personnel have in relating traditional curriculum and learning procedures to this child. Some reorientation is really necessary, as discussion of these problems almost always focuses on the problems the school has, rather than on the enormous confusion, hesitations, and frustrations the child experiences and does not have the language to articulate when he meets an essentially rigid set of academic expectations. Again, from all the foregoing, the child, from the time he enters school and is exposed to assumptions about him derived from experience with the middle-class child, has few success experiences and much failure and generalized frustration, and thus begins the alienating process.

The frustration inherent in not understanding, not succeeding, and not being stimulated in the school—although being regulated by it, creates a basis for the further development of negative self-images and low evaluations of individual competencies. This would be especially true for the Negro child who, as we know from doll-play and other studies, starts reflecting the social bias in his own self-image at a very early age. No matter how the parents might aspire to a higher achievement level for their child, their lack of knowledge as to the operational implementation, combined with the child's early failure experiences in school, can so effectively attenuate confidence in his ability ever to handle competently challenge in the academic area, that the child loses all motivation.

It is important to state that not all the negative factors and deficits discussed here are present in every or even in any one child. Rather, there is a patterning of socially determined school-achievement-related disabilities which tends initially to set artificially low ceilings for these children: initially artificial, because as age increases it becomes more and more difficult for these children to develop compensatory mechanisms, to respond to special programs, or to make the psychological readjustments required to overcome the cumulative effects of their early deficits.

It is also important to state that there are strengths and positive features associated with lower-class life. Unfortunately, they generally tend not to be, at least immediately, congruent with the demands of the school. For example, lack of close supervision or protection fosters the growth of independence in lower-class children. However, this independence—and probably confidence—in regard to the handling of younger siblings, the crossing of streets, self-care, and creating of their own amusements, does not necessarily meaningfully transfer to the unfamiliar world of books, language, and abstract thought.

School Conditions

Educational factors have of course been interlaced throughout this discussion, but there are some special features that need separate delineation.

The lower-class child probably enters school with a nebulous and essentially neutral attitude. His home rarely, if ever, negatively predisposes him toward the school situation, though it might not offer positive motivation and correct interpretation of the school experience. It is in the school situation that the highly charged negative attitudes toward learning evolve, and the responsibility for such large groups of normal children showing great scholastic retardation, the high drop-out rate, and to some extent the delinquency problem, must rest with the failure of the school to promote the proper acculturation of these children. Though some of the responsibility may be shared by the larger society, the school, as the institution of that society, offers the only mechanism by which the job can be done.

It is unfair to imply that the school has all the appropriate methods at its disposal and has somehow chosen not to apply them. On the contrary, what is called for is flexible experimentation in the development of new methods, the clear delineation of the problem, and the training and retraining of administrative and teaching personnel in the educational philosophy and the learning procedures that this problem requires.

In addition, the school should assume responsibility for a systematic plan for the education of the child in the areas that have been delineated here by the time the child reaches kindergarten or first grade. This does not mean that the school will abrogate the family's role with regard to the child, but rather that the school will insure both the intellectual and the attitudinal receptivity of each child to its requirements. Part of a hypothesis now being tested in a new pre-school program is based on the assumption that early intervention by well-structured programs will significantly reduce the attenuating influence of the socially marginal environment.

What might be necessary to establish the required base to assure the eventual full participation of these children in the opportunity structure offered by the educational system is an ungraded sequence from age 3 or 4 through 8, with a low teacher-pupil ratio. Perhaps, also, the school system should make full use of anthropologists, sociologists, and social psychologists for description and interpretation of the cultural discontinuities which face the individual child when he enters school. In addition, the previously discussed patterning of deficits and strengths should be evaluated for each child and placed in a format which the teacher can use as a guide. In the early years this would enable diagnostic reviews of the intellectual functioning of each child, so that learning procedures, to whatever extent possible, could be appropriate to a particular child's needs. New evaluation techniques must be developed for this purpose, as the standardized procedures generally cannot produce accurate evaluation of the functioning level or achievement potential of these children.

Possibly most important would be the greater utilization by educators in both curriculum development and teacher training of the new and enormous knowledge, techniques, and researches in the social and behavioral sciences. Similarly, social and behavioral scientists have in the school a wonderful laboratory to study the interpenetration and interaction of fundamental social, cognitive, psychological, and developmental processes. Close and continuing collaboration, thus, should be mutually productive and satisfying, and is strongly indicated.

References

1. Bernstein, B., "Language and Social Class," *Brit. J. Psychol.*, 11:271–76, September 1960.
2. Hunt, J. McV. *Intelligence and Experience.* New York: Ronald Press, 1961.

The New York School Crisis
Jeremy Larner

[Excerpted from the article, "The New York School Crisis," by Jeremy Larner with permission, from Dissent, *Spring 1964.]*

The Circumstances

UFT OFFICIAL: *Why is it we can get young people to volunteer for the Peace Corps to teach in Ghana, yet we can't get them to teach in public schools in Harlem? Answer: Because in Ghana, there's hope.*

LET ME START WITH SOME STATISTICS. There are 132 elementary schools and 31 junior high schools in New York City whose students are almost entirely (over 90% in the elementary schools; over 85% in the junior highs) Negro and Puerto Rican. In the past six years, while Negro and Puerto Rican enrollment has gone up 53%, white enrollment has fallen 8%, and the number of predominantly Negro and Puerto Rican schools has doubled. Of New York's one million schoolchildren, roughly 40% are Negro and Puerto Rican, 60% "other." Efforts of the Board of Education in the past six years to eliminate blatant gerrymandering and allow some voluntary transfers have reduced by a third the number of schools where Negroes and Puerto Ricans are less than 10% of enrollment. But the problem gets more difficult all the time, as is indicated by the fact that 52%—an outright majority—of the city's 1st graders are Negro or Puerto Rican.

The increase in segregated schools is due to three factors. First, rural minority groups are moving into the city and middle-class urban whites are heading for the suburbs. Second, discrimination, economic pressures, and lack of effective planning confine the newcomers to ghettoes. Third, cautious whites send their children to private or parochial schools rather than "risk" a neighborhood school where minorities predominate. Over 450,000 New York children attend private or parochial schools, a figure that would represent a staggering percentage even for an exclusive suburb.

Thus New York City suffers from an educational problem which it has come to describe as *de facto* segregation. The Board of Education says the facts are essentially beyond its control; the civil rights groups say they are the facts of a racist society, and must in all justice be eliminated by whatever means possible.

Segregation in ghetto schools is more than racial; there is segregation by economic class as well. Wherever Negro parents reach the middle class, at least some of them send their kids to private schools. Lower-class Negro kids find themselves isolated in schools which are understaffed, underequipped, overcrowded, demoralized, and conspicuously lacking in the mixture of cultural backgrounds which can make life in New York such an educational experience. Many of them are children of parents who are in effect first-generation immigrants from southern and rural areas; for of New York's 1,100,000 Negroes, 340,000 have arrived in the last ten years, 630,000 in the last twenty years. Most of the 600,000 Puerto Ricans have come in the past decade, while the white population has dwindled by 500,000.

Teaching middle-class children the ins and outs of a culture made for them is obviously easier than struggling with ghetto children, most of whom are members of a racial group which has never been allowed to recover from the effects of slavery. Some minority schools have annual teacher turnover rates of over 60%. Some teachers flatly refuse to take assignments in such schools; others drop out as the school year proceeds. Not only is one out of every two teachers a substitute, but some classes may stay without a regularly assigned teacher all year, defeating one temporary substitute after another. One can see that the atmosphere in minority schools is hardly conducive to learning. It is estimated that 85% of the 8th-grade students in Harlem are "functional illiterates," which means that their reading is not above 5th-grade level —in many cases it is much below.

Though some authorities, e.g. Kenneth Clark, disagree, it is hard to believe that the social conditions under which most New York Negroes live are not responsible for some of the difficulty. According to

the Harlem Youth survey, whose figures many observers regard as conservative, only one-half of Harlem children under 18 are living with
both parents, more than one-quarter of Harlem youth receives welfare
assistance, and the rate of narcotics addiction in the area is ten times
that for the rest of the city.

By the time they reach junior high school, ghetto children are
well aware of their social situation, and it does not exactly give them a
feeling of unlimited possibilities. Let me quote from two batches of
essays which were gathered at different Harlem elementary schools from
a 6th-grade class of "slow" readers (S) and a 6th-grade class of "fast"
readers (F). I think the language shows as much about the children—
their educational retardation and yet their straightforwardness and
toughness—as about the conditions they describe.

> *6th-grade boy* (F): This story is about a boy namely me, who lives in
> a apartment in and around the slum area. I feel that other people
> should be interested in what I have to say and just like me, *try* to do
> something about it, either by literal or diatribe means. This book is
> only to be read by men and women boys and girls who feel deeply
> serious about segrigation and feel that this is no joke.

> *6th-grade girl* (S): I am not satifeyed with the dope addictes around
> our block. They take dope in our hallway every night. Another is they
> break in stores and bars. I am desatifed with the lady that live under
> us. she set fire to Doris's door. Some dope backs live under us. The
> lady under us robbed Teddy's aunt for $17.00's. One night a dope
> addict went cazey in our hally way. They are so many bums in our
> block. Please help to get and keep them out.

> *6th-grade girl* (S): I don't like people going around youing bad
> Lanugwsh around litter Kide a bearking in Store and fighting and
> youing dop. And Killing people. And drunk in hallwall. They should
> stop drink They are teacher the Kide how to Steel I see it alot of tim
> but I dont pay it no mind I am surrounded by them.

> *6th-grade boy* (S): Im not happy about the people who dink. wiskey
> and go to sleep And I not happy about the peole who come in my hall-
> way and go up stairs and take a neals and. stick there themselve in the
> arm. I am not happy about the people who buy wine and wiskey and
> broke the bottle in the hallway

> *6th-grade girl* (S): the be out there in the hall taking dope and I be
> freighten.

> *6th-grade boy* (S): I deslike the peple being hit by cars, the car
> crashes, peple fighting, the peple jumping of roofes, stelling paper
> from the stores, peple picking pocketes, the peple with out thir cubs on
> dogs and stop peple from taking dop in this naborhood.

6th-grade girl (F): (True) *What a Block!* (true)
My block is the most terrible block I've ever seen. There are at lease 25 or 30 narcartic people in my block. The cops come around there and tries to act bad but I bet inside of them they are as scared as can be. They even had in the papers that this block is the worst block, not in Manhattan but in New York City. In the summer they don't do nothing except shooting, stabing, and fighting. They hang all over the stoops and when you say excuse me to them they hear you but they just don't feel like moving. Some times they make me so mad that I feel like slaping them and stuffing bag of garbage down their throats.

The fact that these kids have been encouraged to describe their surroundings is the first sign of hope that they will be able to change them. The school should represent that possibility; it should be a fortress of security in which the children are respected, accepted and developed. Otherwise they are surrounded, as the little girl says; drug addiction, for example, will begin to appear in their ranks while they are still in junior high school—and addiction is only the most dramatic form of withdrawal and defeat.

Looking around him, the young Negro boy will find few "father figures" to imitate; for the men of his world have not been accorded the honorable work men need to earn self-respect. Bitter, confused, withdrawn, violent against one another, lower-class Negro men do not usually last long with their women. The families are matriarchal, the children remaining with their mothers while a successions of "uncles" come and go. There is small hope of that masculine self-respect which is the traditional basis of family pride. The little boy is regarded as inferior to the little girl, and has less chance of survival—by which I mean simply less chance of getting through life without cracking up, without sliding into some form of self-obliteration.

Dismal to tell, the schools in many ways duplicate the situation of the homes. The classroom confronts the child with the same old arrangement: a woman with too many kids. Far too few of the elementary schoolteachers are men, let alone Negro men. The size of classes, usually around 30 pupils per class, makes individual attention—and thus the development of positive identity and incentive—as unlikely at school as it is at home.

When lower-class Negro children enter elementary school, they are already "behind" in several important respects. In crowded tenement apartments children are in the way from the moment they are born. While the adults of the matriachal clan unit work or wander, children are brought up by older children, who have reasons of their own to feel impatient or harassed. According to the teacher whose "fast" 6th-grade pupils I quoted above,

. . . middle-class Negro kids need integration. But what the lower-class kids need right now is that somehow we conquer the chaos they live in. They have no stability whatever—no family, no home, no one to talk with them. They live in a world without space or time. I mean that literally. Even by the time these kids reach the 6th grade, most of them can't tell time. You can't talk to them about the future—say, about jobs—because they won't know what you're talking about. And when you refer to concepts of space, why you can't talk about "somewhere else," tell how far away another city is, how long a river is, or simple facts of geography. Though they're fantastically sophisticated, more sophisticated than maybe they ought to be, about how adults behave, their mental orientation is almost utterly without abstract concepts. Look: they don't even know who pays the welfare! They don't even know what checks are!

Of course this particular teacher will get his kids talking and thinking about time and space and jobs and where the money comes from. But there aren't enough like him, and one year of a good teacher can dispel the chaos for very few. The class he has taken such pains with finds itself a year later without an assigned teacher, and the boy who last year wrote a brilliant autobiography is in danger this year of flunking at junior high, breaking down, and spending his high school years in and out of institutions.

Why don't teachers make more progress with these children? Because they are woefully short of books and materials, especially good readers based on the facts of urban life. Because they have to spend so much time on discipline.[1] Because they get poor support from their principals and from the rest of the top-heavy school bureaucracy. But the truth is that most of New York's teachers are too middle-class, too insensitive or too fragile to teach ghetto children successfully. Not that they are worse than teachers in other places, they are simply less suited to their jobs. Not all of them are bothered by their failure; some stay in slum schools because apparently it gives them a sense of security to blame the kids for what they fail to teach them. Others, with the best will in the world, are baffled by children who literally speak a different language. One young white teacher, extremely hard-working and perhaps more honest than most, told me after a grueling day,

I hate these kids. They're impossible. How did they get this way? I never thought I'd become so authoritarian.

---

[1] Discipline as opposed to socialization. The 6th-grade teacher quoted above reports that with a "slow" class he begins with checkers, and that it takes weeks to get the children to play together without turning over the board and having at each other. Then he brings out the readers.

Most of the teachers are conscientious: that's one of the hallmarks of the professional person. But the manner in which teachers are trained and chosen—which I will discuss below—is practically guaranteed to eliminate those possessing the imagination and flexibility to get through to slum children.

As for the curriculum, it is hopelessly inappropriate. The readers still current in practically every school are those insipid productions featuring Sally, Dick and Jane, the golden-haired cardboard tots from Sterilityville. One could go on by describing a series of tests and achievement-levels, but tests and levels are irrelevant to children who mostly do not pass or reach them. Let me quote Martin Mayer (from his book, *The Schools*) on what our young tenement-dwellers are supposed to be learning by the time they get to high school:

> In New York . . . the major Theme Center for tenth-grade "Language Arts" is "Learning to Live with the Family." . . . The curriculum guide suggests "round-table, panel, and forum discussions" on "questions relating to allowances, dating, working after school, selecting and entertaining friends, choosing a career, minding younger brothers and sisters, helping with household chores, contributing earnings to the family, decorating one's own room, choosing family vacation places, using the family car."

But what difference does high school make? The battle is lost long before then. Perhaps it's already lost by the time 1st graders move to the 2nd grade, when only 10% of them are on reading level.

Yet, when all is said and done, are not these conditions surmountable by individual effort? Is it not possible for the majority of these youngsters to pull themselves up by their own bootstraps, as so many of their 2nd-generation American teachers say that they or their parents did? Or is this problem unique somehow, does it have to do with the unprecedented oppression and separation of a group that has never in the history of this country been free? Is it really true, as the 1954 Supreme Court decision contends, that "Segregation of white and colored children in public schools has a detrimental effect upon the colored children. . . . A sense of inferiority affects the motivation of the child to learn"?

In the opinion of this observer, no one could sit for long in Harlem classes without seeing overwhelming evidence of the demoralizing effects of segregation. These children are treated as inferior, just as their parents and grandparents and great-grandparents were—and there is no sense of any possibility that such treatment is ending! In the classroom of a 1st-grade teacher who was a militant supporter of the boycott, I was surprised to find cut-out pictures of white children used almost exclusively as bulletin board illustrations. Later I found the purified faces of Sally, Dick and Jane beaming out at me in ghetto classrooms of teachers Negro or white, liberal or not: as if to say, these are what good children are like.

> *5th-grade Lower East Side boy* (F): I have a problem that I am colored. I would like to be handsom but I cant because other people have strait blond hair and they are handsom.

In a 2nd-grade Harlem classroom the teacher, a lively, intelligent Negro woman, has her kids acting out a nursery tale. In front of the class stands a shy, finger-sucking little girl, her hair in pigtails, absolutely adorable and black. From her neck hangs a large square of cardboard, on which an adult has painted the head of a white girl with abundantly flowing golden hair. Caption: "GOLDILOCKS."

In another 2nd-grade classroom, where well cared-for Negro children are industriously and quietly working under the direction of a Negro teacher, I glance up and see a row of self-portraits above the front blackboard. I count: of 23 portraits, 1 red, 1 green, only 2 brown, and 19 white as the paper they're drawn on.

The sense of inferiority runs deeper than skin-deep. I remember a junior-high-school social-studies teacher trying to discuss the school boycott with his 9th-grade "slow" pupils. Most of them are long since lost; they look as though they have drawn curtains across the inside of their eyeballs. It develops that they do not know the words "boycott" or "civil rights," and to them "discrimination" is something that happens down South. And oh the tortured embarrassment with which they answer questions! From beneath the embarrassment there slinks a kind of arrogance, thriving it seems on the mere fact that the teacher is trying to teach them—as if to say, imagine this fool, asking *me* a question! Whereupon they laugh. They have to. And we are all relieved.

Whether they know the word "discrimination" or not, these kids know they are not worth much to the world they live in. Some of them, all too many, are not worth much to themselves, and lash out in self-hating violence at the nearest target, usually someone who reminds them of themselves. Already the white people of America are beginning to dread the day when these children, as some day they surely must, will recognize their real enemies. As they are at last beginning to . . .

> *West Harlem 6th-grade boy* (F): Teacher! In the caveman days, if there were Negro cavemen, did the white cavemen use them as slaves? . . .

The Aftereffects

What effects did the 1964 New York City school boycott have? In terms of Negro self-respect, undoubtedly positive. In terms of its own objectives, too, it was successful, forcing a more definite integration plan than the Board of Ed would ever have volunteered.[2] But in other areas the effects were moot.

The Schools

Anyone who knows anything about the New York schools cannot help but be uneasy about the gap between the strategy of the boycott and the situation it attacks. The issue is by no means so simple as Galamison often made it out to be:

> We feel that if we desegregate the public schools, these other problems—like overcrowding, low curriculum, etc.—will go away. Like when you have an infection, and you take a shot of penicillin.

One problem that will not go away is that of money. In the 1964–65 state budget. New York City, which has 34% of the state's school-children, is slated to receive only 25% of total state aid to schools. Due in part to the machinations of a rurally-dominated state legislature, the City and its residents pay 49.7% of all state taxes and get back only 37.3% in benefits. The rationale for low school aid is that New York has an abundance of taxable property with which to finance its schools; the catch is that the City also has stupendous upkeep expenses.

To be specific, the value of taxable property per pupil in New York City is $31,878, far above the state average of $26,600; and it is this ratio on which state aid is based. But whereas City taxes amount to $54.27 per $1000 of property valuation, the City spends $39.39 of that money for municipal purposes and only $14.88 for schools—which compares poorly with what is spent by surrounding districts. Even though the City tax rate is high, moreover, funds collected are minimized by the gross undervaluation of property holdings. Real estate in New York's five boroughs is currently valued at the bargain total of $35 billion; theoretically Manhattan is worth only $13.5 billion—but don't try to buy it if that's all you can raise. Furthermore, much of the non-school bite on New York's property taxes goes to pay for problems that only large cities have—such as the costs of tearing up streets and assigning extra police to direct traffic when property owners decide to pull down or put up new buildings for their private profit. And since current property taxes don't entirely cover the costs of municipal overburden, the City shifts the load to the public in regressive taxes such as the 4% city sales tax.

Financial shortages drastically affect the operation of the schools. According to a study of the New York schools sponsored jointly by the

---

[2] In September, 1964, however, the Board, under pressure from the well-financed P.A.T., ignored its "plan" and put into effect only two pairings.

PEA and the UFT, "30% of the daily instructional staff is made up of substitutes and other persons on similar temporary or emergency status." The schools are short by 27,500 permanent staff members, including 12,500 "professionals" who would be required to bring the City up to the *average only* of the school districts among which it once enjoyed leadership. That leadership position was held in the early 1940's, before suburban flight began in earnest, when the City spent more per child than its suburbs did. Now it spends $200 per child less, which amounts to about $200,000 per school and a total of $200 million per year simply to bring the system up to par in staff, materials, textbooks and upkeep.[3] The $200 million does not include extra funds urgently needed for new construction.

At present, there is not enough room, time, or personnel to take care of all the children. A major classroom problem is that one or two children can disrupt an entire class and dissipate most of the teacher's energy; and as one might expect, difficult children are more prevalent in slum schools. According to one assistant principal,

> It's the 2–3% who are unteachable and uncontrollable—the ones with very deep emotional disturbances—who take so much time and trouble in the lower neighborhood schools. There's no place to put them. We can't even assign them to a "600" [special problems] school without their parents' permission. The "600" schools have no more room anyway. Sooner or later these kids are caught committing a serious crime: you send them to a judge and he sends them right back to school.

There are also curriculum problems which integration will not necessarily solve. One of the most controversial is the practice of grouping the children according to reading level, and later, IQ test, so that fast, "achieving" children are in a homogeneous group entirely separate from the classrooms of the slow, "non-achieving" youngsters. One of the effects of such grouping is that in schools where a small population of whites remains, it is in effect segregated vertically in the advanced classrooms. So transporting kids from their neighborhoods will not by itself guarantee them an integrated classroom experience; in fact, since most Negro children lag in classroom skills, it might not do them much good to be thrown in with white children of their own grade level—at least not without drastic changes in the present set-up. Most experts now agree, however, that homogeneous grouping leads to stereotyping of

---

[3] New York City school supplies and equipment are ordered from a purchasing manual through a central department which buys from designated contractors *at list price only*—which is often two or three times the every-day retail price at New York's discount houses.

individuals and is not desirable on the grade school level. To quote Martin Mayer, "in New York, Wrightstone's study of comparative performance showed no significant advantage for bright kids grouped with their fellows over bright kids scattered through the school at random." But experts also agree that heterogeneous groupings cannot effectively be taught unless class size is reduced to no more than 15 children, a procedure which would require twice as many classrooms and teachers. For the present, boycotters might take some satisfaction in a provision of the February integration plan, wherein the Board agreed to eliminate IQ tests.

Also beyond the reach of the boycott is the teacher herself, who is often unaware of her middle-class attitudes and the damage they do her ability to teach. I remember one young teacher with an all-Negro "slow" 1st grade, extremely conscientious and worried that she is not more successful, yet unaware that her tone of voice is superior and humorless. At any given moment, only about five of her children are paying attention, and at least three-quarters of the words she utters are devoted to discipline. Let me give some flavor of her monologue:

> . . . well, why did you raise your hand if you had a pencil? I asked for only those who didn't have pencils to raise hands! That's not funny, Wilma! That's not funny! Boys and girls, we're not getting our work done and if we don't settle down we won't be able to have recess today. NOW I WON'T HAVE ANY MORE TALKING IN THIS ROOM! I'll start over again . . . we draw two lines across and that's the big A. Now I see that Freddy didn't hear me, Becky didn't hear me, Nicholas didn't hear me, Roger didn't hear me. And you're not looking! You can't learn to make the big A unless you're looking! Now can you make a big A? Let's see if you can. Raise hands if you need help. You don't have paper? Deborah, where is your paper? All right, I'll give you more . . .

After twenty minutes, a majority of the children are making big A's. As the teacher starts on the little a, I do what most of the kids want desperately to join me in: escape.

To give you an idea of these kids six years later, here is the teacher of a 7th-grade English class.

> Now take a sheet of lined paper and write at the top "English notes." I want all of you to copy down right this second the facts I'm going to give you. Norman, would you be so kind as to put your hand down. Now your assignment is going to deal with this, so get these facts accurately. Hurry up, I haven't got too much time.

Unfortunately, teaching attracts types who enjoy relations where they have undisputed superiority. Thus the effort to "understand the disadvantaged child" turns out in practice to be the science of patronizing the slum-child without feeling guilty about it. For the disadvantaged child, of course, is really not that at all, no matter what it helps one to know about his background: he is a person, and as such something splendid in his own right even before a teacher gets to him.

In every ghetto school I visited, teachers recommended a book called *The Culturally Deprived Child* by Frank Riessman. Reading this book, they told me, had helped them to understand the nature of the children they had to deal with. Sure enough, I found Riessman's book preaching "a sympathetic, noncondescending, understanding of the culture of the underprivileged." But neither Riessman nor the average teacher realizes how un-noncondescending sympathy delivered from the top can be:

> Moreover, self-expression and self-actualization, other aims of education, particularly modern education, are equally alien to the more pragmatic, traditional, underprivileged person.

No! You just can't talk that way about a child entering elementary school. Kids from "underprivileged" homes want to express themselves and realize themselves just as much as anyone else. Maybe the most important thing for them is to have a teacher who will *expect* something from them, let them know there is some authority who cares. The best teacher I met in Harlem had taken a class of bright 6th graders who up to that time were demoralized and undisciplined. Fortunately he did not assume they weren't interested in self-expression. He assumed that they had something to express, the fruits of their own experience, which is in so many ways deeper and more demanding than that of middle-class children. It was a long haul, after eleven years of neglect, but eventually he got them writing and writing well. He read them French translations and they wrote him parables and fables; it seems Negro children are natural-born fable-writers, for—as we have seen— they are not likely to pull their punches when it comes to the moral. He read them Greek myths and stories, and they wrote him back their own myths, classic transformations, and one boy even wrote an illustrated history of the Trojan War. (One of the transformations begins, "I was transformed from a poor little infant into a nice boy, and as I grew I was transformed into a magnificent extraordinary deceiving nuisance to the world.") Most of the children wrote novels, and one 11-year-old boy, without having read a single modern novel, began a remarkable autobiography with the sentence, "I am dreaming and crying in my sleep."

This was an ordinary 6th-grade Harlem class; there were some high IQ's, but it was not an "SP" (specially gifted) class and had attracted no special attention to itself. The teacher disciplined them, yes, kept them in order, but did it not to triumph but to show them he cared. He respected them, which is something you can't learn from books. He visited their homes, which is absolutely unheard-of. He worked patiently with each child, and got them to work with each other.

Now it is a year later, the kids are dispersed into a notoriously depressing junior high, and most of them have lost what they gained. Some are flunking; their former teacher bitterly wonders how the life in them can survive. But for that one year they produced a body of work uniquely theirs.

The Grouping of Groupings

If conditions within the classroom are bad enough, to look beyond them is to find oneself in a jungle of stumbling and makeshift, where stentorian voices boom from the tops of trees, and clusters of officious missionaries rush about distributing memoranda on the cannibal problem.

First of all, there is the school bureaucracy. According to Martin Mayer, "New York City employs more people in educational administration than all of France." I believe I have alluded to the public relations men on the Board of Ed staff, but I have perhaps failed to mention the endless associations, commissions, sub-commissions, advisory committees, deputy directors, associate supervisors, district superintendents, coordinators, directors, foundations and independent consultants who must be involved in every policy decision. The trouble with such a set-up is that the basic concern on every level points up, toward impressing the higher-ups, rather than down, toward serving the classroom teacher. Would it be heresy to suggest equal salary for every school position? With the present system, the classroom teacher can be in a panic for materials she ordered three years ago, while the assistant superintendent is sincerely assuring the area superintendent that everything is all right in his sub-sector. In such a bureaucracy, the people who move toward the top are the yes-men, the round pegs, whom the public pays to rise away from the children.[4] They have a priority on operating funds, too; if they could not get their paperwork properly submitted and filed, the system would collapse. In fact, despite the teacher shortage, there are a number of employees listed on the Board of Ed budget as classroom teachers who never report to their assigned schools; they are clerks and typists working in the central offices. Ironically, the policy directives they type, like great portions of our public

---

[4] Gross's 1965 school budget included approximately $5 million to increase salaries for "Commissioners" who make curriculum revision recommendations.

school funds, may never filter down to the classroom; but they do reach the publicity department, from which they are carefully distributed to the newspapers, which in turn describe to us a school system that doesn't really quite exist. Nevertheless, its paper achievements will be proudly recounted by the functionary flown to a conference of "educators" at public expense. Life in the big city goes on somehow, though where it goes no one knows.

The gap between theory and practice is nowhere more striking than among the school principals. Many of them know little of what goes on in their own schools and make no effort to learn. The job of the principal is to spend his time in educational conferences, or addressing committees, or preparing reports for higher-ups who never come to check. At the Harlem school where the 6th-grade "slow" letters I have quoted were written, the principal assured me,

> I don't notice any demoralization on this level. The children are happy, well-behaved and eager to learn.[5]

Small wonder that one of the best teachers at this school could not get enthusiastic about the boycott:

> What if the boycotters are successful and get the Board to come up with a plan? Who has to implement it but these same shits!

Then there is the problem of the teachers themselves and their organization, the UFT. It would be unkind to expect too much of an organization so urgently needed and besieged with such difficulties as is the UFT. But it must be said that an excessive concern of teachers black and white is their own respectability. The most pressing practical issues are submerged in the desire to preserve their "professional image." For instance, a teacher's license in New York City cannot be obtained unless the applicant has passed the expensive and utterly idiotic education courses offered at teachers' colleges. I never talked to a single good teacher who claimed to have learned anything of value in these courses. Furthermore, they discourage many of the specially talented people gathered in New York City from seeking employment as public school teachers. Bright, educated people who want to try their hands at teaching children can't, not in New York, not even if they have PhD's, unless they are willing to go back to school for their "education credits."[6] Yet

---

[5] This principal did not bother to use up several thousand dollars of his allotted budget for equipment and supplies. The kids at this school are short on books and have no musical instruments whatever.

[6] Education courses are not the only obstacles in the paths of potentially valuable teachers. Teachers from the South or from Puerto Rico with advanced academic degrees may find themselves disqualified on the interview section of the teachers' license exam for "speaking English with an accent."

the union, although ambitious to work out a joint recruiting program with the Board aimed at attracting Negro teachers from the South, shows little interest in this question. The current teachers' pay scale is based on these pointless credits, and to upset it would invalidate years of useless course-taking.

Finally, there is the conglomeration of civil rights groups, divided and sub-divided within itself, spreading out towards too many separate targets with only the most general slogans to hold itself together. The structure of the rights organizations is chaotic beyond description. Let me say simply that the end effect is too often the mirror image of the bureaucracy they are arrayed against. And the boycott offered no program for the Negro children to realize their own particular talents, no social-action program with which to unite the Negro community in self-respect. Was not the boycott in some sense one more appeal to the great white father to do right by his poor black children?

No Ending

Have I captured the confusion? Here is New York City with a mass of black people, most of whom have never been allowed to partake of our civilization. Now they must be allowed that dubious privilege; for there is no other place for them. In previous eras of American life, there was some room for a variegated lower class, which took care of the dirty work and was not permitted entrance into the cultural mainstream. Little by little most groups surfaced into the middle class, leaving behind among unlucky remnants of themselves a permanent body of American Negroes, who, handicapped by years of slavery and oppression, remained what a Negro teacher describes to me as "a colonial people encapsulated *within* the colonial country." But now automation is chopping away at the colony; we see the natives in the street, shaking their fists. We must open the door and let them in.

The big question is, will they come in having truly changed and purified and reformed our social structure, as some say they must? Will we have to chip away at our stone walls to let them in, as the Trojans did for the Greek horse? Or will the Negro scrape through bloody, bitter and confused, ready to perpetuate the authoritarian ethic he has so far, to his unique credit, managed to evade?

The answer to this question depends in part on our schools. But all school systems are—and have always been—failures. Even Leo Tolstoy, with all his genius, his wealth, his command, and with not a single bureaucrat to hamper him, could not educate his peasants into free men. His failure, our failure . . . the failure is always the same: the failure to educate each man—not for a prestigious "function" or "role"—but to fulfill his own capacities for living, for being alive, for finding and making his own kind of beauty, for respecting the diversity of life without, in his frustration, turning to violence, self-suppression, and the worship of authority.

So what the boycotters are demanding, ultimately (and more power to them!) is a change in the nature of the lives we lead.

> *6th-grade Harlem girl* (S): I wish that the hold city can chage. and that the governor make new laws. that there to be no dirt on streets and no gobech top off and wish that my name can chage and I wish that whether can trun to summer.
>
> *6th-grade Harlem boy* (F): *Fable*
> Once upon a time there was two men who were always fighting so one day a wise man came along and said fighting will never get you anywhere they didn't pay him no attention and they got in quarrels over and over again. So one day they went to church and the preacher said you should not fight and they got mad and knock the preacher out Can't find no ending.

Organizing the Unaffiliated in a Low-Income Area

George Brager

Mobilization for Youth

[Excerpted from the article, "Organizing the Unaffiliated in a Low-Income Area," from Social Work, Vol. 8, No. 2 (April 1963) pp. 34–40, with permission of the National Association of Social Workers, and the author.]

COMMUNITY ORGANIZATION EFFORTS generally have one of three broad objectives. In the first instance a substantive area of community change —a needed reform—is emphasized, as, for example, attention to housing needs and inequities. Another goal is the co-ordinated and orderly development of services, as evidenced in the planning of a welfare council. The third focuses upon citizenship involvement, regardless of the issues that engage citizen attention, in order to heighten community integration. These three goals are not necessarily mutually exclusive, although it may reasonably be argued that this is more true than is generally realized. In any event, programs that do not develop objectives in some order of priority risk diffuse and ineffective performance, as well as the impossibility of focused evaluation. There is, of course, some advantage in this nondefinition. One of the three arrows may hit *some* mark, and, in any case, one need not face up to his failures if he has not specified his goals.

An encompassing delinquency prevention effort may rightly concern itself with all three objectives, although perhaps to some degree different programs need to be devised to achieve different objectives. In order to sharpen this discussion, however, focus will be placed only upon issues relating to citizenship participation.

In a study of two lower-income neighborhoods of similar socio-economic levels it was found that in the more integrated neighborhood (in which people knew their neighbors, perceived common interests, shared common viewpoints, and felt a part of the community) delinquency rates were markedly lower.[1] Participation by adults in decision-making about matters that affect their interests increases their sense of identification with the community and the larger social order. People who identify with their neighborhood and share common values are more likely to try to control juvenile misbehavior. A well-integrated community can provide learning experiences for adults that enable them to serve as more adequate models and interpreters of community life for the young. In short, participation in community-oriented organizations is highly desirable in delinquency reduction efforts.

A program must, however, involve significant numbers of representative lower-class persons.[2] Such an organization ought to enable what has been called the "effective community" of working-class youth— that is, the individuals, families, and groups with whom these youth interact and identify—to exert more positive influence on them.[3] The learning that accrues from the collective process can result in better opportunities or more effective models for potential delinquents only when large numbers of working-class adults are members of community organizations.

However, such membership is not very common among the lower class. A considerable number of studies indicate that formal group membership is closely related to income, status, and education; the lower

---

[1] Eleanor Maccoby et al., "Community Integration and the Social Control of Delinquency," Journal of Social Issues, Vol. 14, No. 3 (1958), pp. 38–51.

[2] The word "representative" is used here in the sense of "typical of their group, i.e., class" rather than in the political sense of "functioning or acting in behalf of others." Elsewhere in the literature it has been restricted to the latter use. See Chauncey A. Alexander and Charles McCann, "The Concept of Representativeness in Community Organization," Social Work, Vol. 1, No. 1 (January 1956), pp. 48–52.

[3] Derek V. Roemer, "Focus in Programming for Delinquency Reduction" (Bethesda, Md.: National Institutes of Mental Health, 1961). (Mimeographed.)

one's income status and educational level, the less likely one is to participate in formal community groups.[4]

Furthermore, in every slum neighborhood there are adults who, in attitudes, strivings, verbal skills, and possession of know-how, are oriented toward the middle class. Although their children are less likely to experience strains toward deviance, these are precisely the parents who tend to join formal community organizations and to have faith and competence in the collective solution of social problems. In most organizations, therefore, persons who are in a minority among slum dwellers (*i.e.*, the upwardly mobile) unfortunately represent the majority of those working-class members who participate. Because lower-class persons tend to eschew formal organizations, organizers who set out to reach the effective community of the delinquent frequently settle for those slum dwellers who are easiest to enlist.

Although reports of failure only rarely find their way into the literature, the modesty of claims regarding the organization of the deprived population itself indicates a general lack of success. For example, in East Harlem in 1948 a five-block area was chosen for organization. Five trained social workers were assigned to organize these blocks and a program of social action was embarked upon, devoted to housing, recreational, and social needs of the neighborhood. Unfortunately, the East Harlem Neighborhood Center for Block Organization was able to attract only a limited number of participants during a three-year period. Subsequent research indicated that those who did participate were upwardly aspiring. Further, they were isolated from the rest of the community and therefore nonrepresentative.

Barriers to Community Integration

Characteristics of community life. Why are representative lower-income adults less likely to become closely involved in community affairs? The source of the barriers to their effective participation rests with all three elements of the interaction: the characteristics of community life, the nature of lower-income adults, and the structure of the community organization effort.

One such community characteristic is residential mobility. Local communities have been inundated by new migrants, many of them unfamiliar with the demands and opportunities of urban life. Although public housing mitigates some of the problematic aspects of slum life, the recruitment of single-family units from widely dispersed parts of

---

[4] Morris Axelrod, "Urban Structure and Social Participation," *American Sociological Review*, Vol. 21, No. 1 (February 1956), pp. 13–18.

the metropolitan area collects in one place thousands of deprived families, strangers to one another and to local community resources. Physical redevelopment programs and the consequent exodus of old residents have in many instances shattered existing institutions, so that they are unable to help in assimilation of the newcomers into the urban system. For example, the diminishing vitality of some local political machines, with their attentive political leaders, eliminates an important interpretive link to the new world.

Intergroup tensions are also a barrier to community integration, as are the bewildering operations of massive bureaucratic systems. The size, impersonality, concentrated power, and inflexibility of these large organizations makes them seem to local residents hardly amenable to their influence.

The community characteristic that may act as the major deterrent to involvement of lower-income people in community affairs, however, is the opposition of already entrenched organizations. New groups in a community—especially new minority groups—are often confronted with hostility from established groups whose positions of power are threatened by the possibility of forceful action by the newcomers. There is evidence, for example, that some political machines will avoid registering minority group members, even under the impetus of national campaigns. This is so even though the minority group member is assumed to support the machine's national candidates. It is recognized that the new group will inevitably challenge the dominance of incumbent leadership.

This resistance of political parties, governmental agencies, and private organizations is never directly specified. Ordinarily it takes the form of statements such as "the minority groups are not really interested," they are "not ready," "they'll take positions we don't agree with," or they will be "controlled by the left-wing agitators." Whatever its form, the opposition of established community groups is a formidable obstacle to indigenous community participation.

Lower-income life. The circumstances of lower-income life and the nature of lower-income persons constitute another set of obstacles. The realities of lower-class life, *i.e.*, the necessary preoccupation with the day-to-day problems of survival, hardly encourage attention to broad community matters. Furthermore, lower-class persons lack the verbal or literary requisites for organizational skills; neither do they tend to be comfortable with the formal methods of doing business in organizations. Their self-defeating attitudes also interfere with community integration. Lower-income groups tend to view life more pessimistically, with less hope of deliverance, and, as a consequence, they tend to retreat from struggle. A Gallup poll conducted in 1959 indicated that a higher percentage of respondents in the under-$3,000 income group expected World War III and a new depression than respondents in any other grouping. As one observer noted, "Seeing his chances for improvement as slim produces in the slum-dweller a psychology of listlessness, of passivity, and acceptance, which . . . reduces his chances still further."[5] Such defeatism, resulting in lack of participation, produces a loss of interest in changing their conditions.

Structure of community organization. The community organization itself, while purportedly seeking the involvement of lower-income persons, offers certain obstacles, whether inevitable or otherwise. Most community activities, for example, are staffed by middle-class personnel. To the extent that lower-class people feel that they are being dominated, they are likely to withdraw from collective activities. The predominance of the middle class in community organizations has a number of sources. When community problems become so severe that people are motivated to act, it is generally the middle-class element (or at least those who are oriented toward the middle class) that reacts first. Although lower-class persons may affiliate with the organization, its predominantly middle-class style soon becomes a subtle source of intimidation. Its leaders are likely to be businessmen, professionals, social welfare personnel, ministers, and other members of the middle class. The formality of the organization meetings, with predetermined agendas, concern with rules of procedure, and the like, tends to make the lower-class participant, unfamiliar with these matters, feel insecure and inferior.

Furthermore, organizers who insist on maintaining control of the activities and policies of the organization, subtly or otherwise, inevitably encourage the participation of lower-class persons whose values and skills are congenial with those of the middle-class organizer. Those whose values and skills differ, however, will gradually sense that such differences matter and that the organization exists to serve middle-class ends. They may, therefore, disassociate themselves.

It may be that, because of the disparity between lower- and middle-class "life styles," significant numbers of both groups cannot even be expected to participate together within the same organization. For example, a study conducted by the Girl Scouts, focused upon recruiting volunteers from working-class communities, was forced to conclude that the agency could offer no program suitable to both middle-

---

[5] Michael Harrington, "Slums, Old and New," *Commentary,* Vol. 30, No. 2 (August 1960), p. 121.

and lower-class groups. As noted by the authors, lower-income adults are less interested in "the joys of fully integrated personality in a democratic society" than in the need to better their standard of living. They do not even object to their children being handled authoritatively if it serves such end.[6]

The tendency of social workers to emphasize the amelioration of conflict and the reduction of tension, while often appropriate and helpful, may, in effect, also discourage lower-income participation. With issues flattened rather than sharpened, differences minimized rather than faced, there may be little to arouse the interest of a group that already lacks the predisposition to participate. Matters sufficiently vital to engage slum residents are almost inevitably fraught with controversy or are challenging to some powerful community interest. If they are avoided by a community organization, it may be expected that the organization will be avoided in turn.

The sponsorship of the community organization effort will also affect the character of participation. The primary interests of a sponsoring group will tend to determine membership selection, organizational form, objectives, and activities. Organizational maintenance requirements of the sponsor will inevitably limit the independence of an action-oriented affiliate. Further, its responsibility to a board of directors with widely variant views and connections to numerous community interest groups will limit a sponsor's freedom to encourage a free-wheeling community action program. When the sponsoring group is an already established community organization, it is likely to contain significant representation from groups that, as noted earlier, actively oppose the effective participation of lower-income and minority group people.

The formidable array of obstacles thus cited does not permit us to be sanguine about the success potential of any program oriented toward community action by representative lower-income adults. We may conclude, as a matter of fact, that the limitations to independence inherent in sponsorship by private or public social service organizations are hardly surmountable. Or we may discover that those obstacles least accessible to the social worker's means of intervention are most centrally required for program success. However discouraging, a specification of barriers is, nevertheless, a requirement of intelligent program planning. . . .

---

[6] Catherine V. Richards and Norman A. Polansky, "Reaching Working-class Youth Leaders," *Social Work*, Vol. 4, No. 4 (October, 1959), p. 38.

The Cycle of Despair: A Harlem Family

Gordon Parks

Free-lance writer

[Reprinted with permission from Life, *March 8, 1968.]*

THE COMING OF WINTER this year was a bad time for Norman Fontenelle Sr. When I first saw him, he had just been laid off his part-time job as a railway section hand. There was almost no money left, or food. None of his kids had winter coats, and if it turned much colder, they wouldn't be able to go to school. "It's awful," he said, squinting through eyes that are always bloodshot. "The black man gets the walking papers first. And he's the last to be called back. The white man does all the hirin' and firin'. Not much to do about it. I don't have a education so I can't get anything better. That's why I hang onto this job. But after working 11 years for a company, you'd think they'd take you on steady.

"I've got 10 mouths to feed here and there ain't enough in that icebox to even fill the baby's stomach. What can I do?" Norman Sr. is a quiet, short, powerfully built man but defeat is hanging off him. He came to Harlem 15 years ago, with big plans, from St. Lucia in the British West Indies. "It's a pretty place," he said wistfully. "I'd like to take my whole family there—away from this miserable damn place."

Four flights up in an old brick building on Eighth Avenue the Fontenelles hang on as best they can. There's Norman Sr., 38, and Bessie, 39, his wife; Phillip, 15; Roseanna, 14; Norman Jr., 13; Riel, 12; Lette, 9; Kenneth, 8; Ellen, 5, and Richard, 3. And a bad-tempered dog named Toe-boy and a cat, who are there really to keep the roaches and the rats in check. Many Harlem families keep pets for the same reason. Norman Sr. stays bitter about his plight. "The rent's $70 a month and the whole building's crawling with roaches and rats. The plaster is falling down. It ain't fit for dogs. But what can you do? My wife's always trying to get into one of those projects, but they won't let us in until I get a steady job. So we're always finding ourselves right where we started—nowhere." The Fontenelles once also had goldfish. One morning when I got there, little Richard was pointing at the bowl on the mantel. The heat had gone off the night before and three fish were floating on the surface, dead from the cold. "Fishies dead, fishies dead," he kept mumbling.

Bessie Fontenelle appears to be a strong woman, especially in the early part of the day, when she looks younger than 39. As the day wears on, she seems to age with it. By nightfall she has crumpled into herself. "All this needing and wanting is about to drive me crazy," she said to me one evening. "Now I've got double trouble. My husband is a good man but every time they fire him or lay him off, he takes it out on me and the kids. He gets his little bottle and starts nipping. By the time he nips to the bottom, he's mad with the whole world. Then the kids and I get it, especially Norman Jr. Those two don't get along at all. That boy keeps telling him he'll kill him if he keeps beating up on me. I wouldn't be surprised someday if he'll just up and do it."

Bessie tries to give warmth to this home, but it remains a prison of endless filth, cluttered with rags and broken furniture. Her touch shows in the shapeless, soiled curtains; the dime-store paintings on the walls; the shredded scatter rugs covering the cracked linoleum; the wax flowers and outdated magazines. It is a losing battle.

I have yet to see all the Fontenelles sitting down and eating together. One of the kids will cry his hunger and Bessie will scrounge up a sandwich of some kind. Norman Jr. seems to exist on tiny 7-cent sweet-potato pies from the grocery store. Little Richard was eating a raw potato one day. Sometimes four of the younger kids hungrily share one apple. But even if there was enough food for regular meals, the kitchen table is too small to accommodate all 10 of them at once.

Lette came into the room crying. Norman Jr. had thumped her on the head. Bessie dropped her head into her hands: "Oh, God, if it ain't one thing, it's another." Little Richard joined in the crying. His swollen lips were cracked and bleeding. "Oh, God, oh, God," Bessie said. She put on some ointment. Then, weary and distraught, she lay down and began to moan. Kenneth came in from the kitchen and sat down beside her. "You all right, Momma?" he asked. "You all right?"

Norman was holding a big roll of masking tape. "Look, Momma, what I got." He stripped a long piece off and cut it up with a paring knife. Then he began covering a hole in the wall by his bed.

"Is that to keep out the rats?" I asked.

"Naw," he said. "They eat right through this stuff. This is to keep out that cold wind."

I caught up with Mrs. Fontenelle and four of her kids at the antipoverty office. She was looking for help and wanted anyway to make some complaints about the rats and the roaches and the garbage and the broken windows and the heat going off. "The landlord looks and promises, but nothing happens. But just let us miss that $70 rent one month and he's threatening to put us in the street." Bob Haggins, the board director, sat in his overcoat and listened to her. The poverty office had also been without heat for the last three days. He asked her where she came from. "North Carolina," Bessie said. "I heard all about the big factories that were going up in the cities. I didn't know it would be like this."

"You have to keep faith," Haggins told her and said he would try to get Norman Sr. into some kind of job training that would pay him $2 an hour.

Norman Jr. and Kenneth lay on their sheetless bunks, fully clothed and under blankets, fighting the cold and their homework. Roseanna had given in momentarily to a comic book. Lette had been excused from studying. Her glasses were broken. Welfare had promised her a new pair but that had been two weeks before. Now she was having dizzy spells when she tried to read. It is Bessie who insists on homework. "Seems the most important thing now is to try to get them some kind of education," she said to me. "That's why I make them keep working. If just one of these kids can make it in some way, I'll be thankful." The way the kids keep their books so neatly stacked in all the rubble is amazing. In the quieter moments, the older ones help the others with their lessons. At such times the house seems to be filled with love.

Roseanna sat with her head buried in her hands, barefoot, with a black raincoat buttoned against the cold. She wouldn't talk to me. I walked past her into the kitchen. "Want to know what's the matter with Rosie?" Kenneth whispered. "Momma whipped her for staying out all night last night." I asked Rosie about it. "Us kids don't have any place to go. That particular night we were at a girl friend's house, dancing and having fun. It got so late we were all afraid to go home, so we just hung on until morning." Later, three of Rosie's friends—two boys and a girl—came by. They sat in the semidarkness of Rosie's room on a bundle of rags and the unmade bed, their coats on, hardly saying anything to one another, sharing a single cigarette. It was as though they had come not to visit but to escape the weather and share each other's misery.

Bessie Fontenelle reached over and straightened a picture of Christ that hangs over the baby's crib. I asked her if they were a religious family. Just as she was about to answer, Ellen screamed. Toe-boy had nipped her toe. Bessie sent the dog scurrying with a well-aimed kick. "Well, I guess we are—at least we used to be. We

just don't go to church any more. I have to be truthful. It's hard
keeping faith in something when everything's going so bad for you. I
teach the kids their prayers, and that's the best I can do."

It was snowing when I left and the flakes were swirling down
through an open skylight and piling up in a hallway by their door. On
the street below I came up on Norman Jr. peering through the
window of a fish-and-chips joint. "Want some chips?" he asked hopefully. I told him I'd love some. So we went in and filled our stomachs
with greasy fried potatoes and fish. He is a strange mixture. In his talk
there is a defiance for whites—the white policeman, the white butch-
er, the white grocery clerk. His eyes have the hard glint of older black
men in Harlem. At 13 he is already primed for some kind of action. He
is aggressive, determined and powerfully built for his age. But his
hostility is balanced by an overwhelming tenderness at times. He will
suddenly lift Little Richard off the floor and smother him with kisses.
At times he stands beside his mother, affectionately fingering her
earrings. "You're pretty, Momma, real pretty," he'll say without
smiling.

On another day, Rosie lured me into the fish-and-chips place.
Through the steamy window, Lette spotted us eating and came in to
join us. I asked Lette what she would like and she pointed to the
greasy potatoes. "No fish or chicken?" I asked. Her eyes lit up. "Chick-
en? That's too much money, ain't it?" I told her to order chicken.

Each day Bessie seems to sink into deeper despair. She com-
plains constantly about the filth and the falling plaster. "I could clean
this place every hour and it would still look the same. There's no
place to put anything. I stay tired all the time. Over at the hospital
they say it's my nerves. They want to open my throat and operate for
some reason. Sometimes I feel like jumping out the window. But
there's the kids to look after."

Two children of the family do not live at home. "My oldest
girl, Diana, is graduating from nursing school up in Massachusetts this
year," Bessie said. "She'll make it." Harry, 20, is confined as a narcotics
addict at Brentwood, 25 miles east of Harlem, in New York's Pilgrim
State Hospital. "He got on dope when 15," Bessie said. "I did everything I could—even took him to the police. But once he was hung up,
there was nothing to do. To protect the other kids I finally had to
throw him out of the house when he was about 18." Brentwood is
$4.50 in railway fare, too much; so none of the family has visited Harry
in the six months he's been there. On a Sunday morning I drove

Norman Sr. and Bessie up to see him. The first moments of the meeting were awkward.

"How's all the kids?" Harry asked.

"They're all fine and send you their love," said Bessie.

"They treating you all right?" asked Norman Sr.

"Everything's okay. I should be out in another seven months."

"You're fat."

"Think so? They got any heat in the house for you this year?"

"Oh yes," Bessie cut in. "Everything's just going fine at home." I swallowed the lie heavily. Then Bessie got to what was really on her mind. "I hope you come out good and clean, Harry. You've had enough trouble already."

"Oh, I'll be straight. Everything'll be straight, Mom."

"I hope to God you never touch the stuff again."

His answer stunned all three of us. "Well, I don't know—I can't say for sure I'll never go back on it. You see, I wasn't on heroin, just on cocaine—which isn't so bad."

Suddenly Harry saw how much his words had hurt Bessie. He choked out a sob and covered his face.

There was no heat in the apartment. There hadn't been any the night before. The 10 of them had slept huddled together on mattresses in the kitchen with the oven going all night. Bessie and the children were still there when I arrived in the morning. They were eating warmed-over fish for breakfast. Fish—just on the edge of spoiling—is a staple for them. It is cheaper than anything else. That night they were planning Thanksgiving dinner, their most luxurious meal in months: sausage and eggs.

"How's it going?" I asked one morning.

"Not good at all," said Norman Sr.

"Any hope for going back to work?"

"I was out for the shape-up every day this week." He rubbed his head. "Any other man would have been gone long time ago. A lot of these guys up here do. But I can't leave. All I want to be is a man," he said finally.

I found Norman Jr. standing around on the street corner, warming himself over a garbage-can fire. The smell of snow was in the air. The boy wore tennis shoes and a light windbreaker, the heaviest coat he owned. I asked him what he was doing out so late in the cold.

"Poppa put me out," he said, rubbing his hands together over the flame.

"For what?"

"For nothing. He's mad about not having any work, I guess."

I asked him if I could do anything.

"Naw," he answered. "Momma will fix things up. I'll be all right."

Upstairs, I could hear an argument through the door before I knocked. It stopped when I went in, but there was tension in the chilly apartment. Norman Sr. was slumped in a dark corner. I sat around for nearly half an hour in the uncomfortable stillness. Bessie went with me to the door. She was really down in the dumps. "Things are a little rough here tonight," she said softly. "One of his friends gave him a bottle."

Next afternoon when I arrived, Bessie was lying on her bed, groaning in misery. Little Richard had crawled beneath her arm. Her neck was scratched and swollen. She managed a painful half-smile. "He gave me a going-over last night. My ribs feel like they're broken." She began to cry. "I just can't take it no more. It's too much for anybody to bear." I asked where Norman Sr. was. In the hospital, she said. "When he got through kicking me, I got up and poured some sugar and honey into a boiling pan of water and let him have it in the face." Why the sugar and honey? "To make it stick and burn for a while."

Norman Jr. and I went over to the hospital. It was almost impossible to recognize the father. The honey and sugar still coated his neck and face, and his right hand was horribly burned. He sat up on the side of the bed and daubed at his eyes. "I don't know why your mother did it, boy," he said. "I just don't know why." Then he lay back down and lapsed into painful sleep.

Just another one of the thousands of violences that explode in a ghetto every week, I thought as we left. In the heat of summer they pile up and spill into the street. And buildings burn and people are killed and windows are smashed. And the Normans, big and small, dash in to loot what they don't have at home.

Snow was falling again. He headed back toward the cold apartment, and I wondered why they waited for summer.

Life on A.D.C.: Budgets of Despair

Charles Lebeaux

Wayne State University School of Social Work

[Reprinted with permission from New University Thought, *Winter 1963.]*

> *Editors' comment: One of the solutions to the state of poverty has been social welfare, but this article indicates the situation of those who are dependent on the help given within the present social ethic. Charles Lebeaux, who teaches in the School of Social Work of Wayne State University, undertook this study together with other faculty, social workers, and students—an indication of healthy concern within a much-derided profession.*

IN SEPTEMBER 1962 a grave crisis occurred in 6,000 needy families with children in Detroit. These families were recipients of Aid to Families with Dependent Children (AFDC), the aid program commonly known as ADC (Aid to Dependent Children) until its title was changed in 1962. In the early 1940's the Detroit welfare departments began supplementing AFDC grants out of general relief funds, because the Michigan state grant in AFDC was in many cases too small for the family to live on, and because it was often *less* than the same family would receive from general relief.[1] But due to Detroit's financial straits, about four years ago the city began cutting the amount of the supplement. In September 1962 the supplement was cut entirely. This last cut affected 6,000 of the city's 13,000 AFDC families—many more had been affected by earlier cuts. These many thousands of families are thus living below the minimum standards of health and decency, even as defined by this welfare program itself.

---

[1] AFDC is one of five categorical public assistance programs set up in the Social Security Act, in which the federal government shares costs with the states. These programs (AFDC, Old Age Assistance, Aid to the Blind, Aid to the Disabled, and Medical Aid to the Aged) are separate financially, and for the most part administratively, from general relief, which is run by the states and localities with no federal involvement. Detroit is in Wayne County where there are three relief offices: the Wayne County Bureau of Social Aid, which administers the categorical aid programs (including AFDC) for the entire county; the Detroit Department of Public Welfare, which handles general relief in Detroit; and the Wayne County Department of Social Welfare, which handles general relief in the rest of the county.

Few people in Michigan know about the plight of these families and even fewer seem to care. The AFDC mothers themselves, many without the clothes or carfare to go out of their homes, have almost no power to influence public policy or opinions. Although in the fall of 1962 members of the Detroit Chapter of the National Association of Social Workers (NASW) organized and supported efforts of some Negro organizations (primarily the Trade Union Leadership Council and the Federation of AFDC Mothers, a group of the mothers themselves), none of their appeals to rescind the cut, either to the mayor or the welfare department, were successful. When these efforts failed, the following survey of the families affected by the cut was made, in order to arouse the moribund consciences of the city and state.[2]

The People on AFDC

There are now about 7½ million people in the United States getting public assistance under all programs, special and general. Around four million of these are in AFDC families. There are about 33,000 AFDC families in Michigan; about 13,000 of these families with some 40,000 children, live in Detroit. AFDC is the most controversial of the public assistance programs, not only because of its size and persistent growth, but because of the social characteristics of the recipients. When the program started in the late 1930's, death of the father was the common cause for being in need of aid. Today, more than 60 percent of AFDC cases are due to estrangement of parents—divorce, separation, desertion, or unmarried motherhood. The American public regards these as bad or unworthy reasons to be in need, and is less inclined to give help.

Over 40 percent of AFDC families are Negro (compared to about 10 percent of the general population). In northern industrial cities, the caseload is largely Negro (about 81 percent in Detroit), and in cities

---

[2] After we were unable to obtain a list of the 6,000 from city, county or state agencies, which made a full random sample impossible, the NASW decided that it had to proceed on its own, and quickly. A list of some hundred odd names was supplied by the Federation of AFDC Mothers, and a questionnaire was devised by faculty and students of the Wayne State University School of Social Work. Twenty-five members of NASW and twenty-five social work students volunteered to do the home interviewing, which was accomplished in April 1963. Ninety-three usable interviews were held, and are the basis of this report.

Because we could not obtain the list of 6,000 supplement cut cases, we could not pick a statistically correct sample; but when a population is quite homogeneous with respect to the characteristic under investigation, just a few cases may represent all. So with the poverty aspect of our AFDC families. In fact, my guess is that our group is better off than the typical AFDC family, because women who participate in the Federation of AFDC Mothers also probably will be better managers than the average woman receiving AFDC.

like Detroit, the proportion of illegitimate children is unusually high (although less than one-quarter of all illegitimate children in the country receive AFDC assistance).

The federal law says that to qualify under AFDC a child must be in "need," but the states define that status and determine the actual amount of money that each child and his family receive. The Michigan AFDC law says that they shall receive enough to permit them to live with "health and decency," at a level below which something suffers— health, church and school attendance, or self-respect. However, most states, including Michigan, interpret a health and decency standard to mean "minimum subsistence."

Dollar costs of a minimum subsistence budget are determined by home economists and other experts in the Federal Department of Agriculture, the State Department of Social Welfare, and home economics departments in universities by adding together minimum amounts for food, shelter, utilities, clothing, household supplies, and personal incidentals. For example, on the scale prepared by the Family Budget Council of the Detroit Visiting Nurses Association, $266.21 per month was the minimum income required in January 1960, by a family consisting of a mother age thirty-five, a boy age fourteen, and two girls, nine and four, with rent assumed to be $55 per month. For the identical family, paying identical rent, the Michigan State Department of Social Welfare in January 1961, has $223.05 as the monthly amount required to meet basic needs.

In practice, the welfare worker on the case adds up the amount needed to meet basic needs of the family according to state standards, subtracts any income there may be, and the unmet need should be the amount of the AFDC check. But in most cases in Detroit that is *not what the family gets*. The state sets ceilings on what each family can get, no matter what the budget figures show they need, according to the 1963 formula shown in Table 1.

TABLE 1

Theoretical and Actual Grants

Family Size	Budget Requirements[1]	Maximum Grant
Mother and 1 child	$151	$120
Mother and 2 children	191	140
Mother and 3 children	228	160
Mother and 4 children	263	180
Mother and 5 children	300	200
Mother and 6 children	334	220
Mother and 7 children	368	240 (absolute) maximum)

[1] Includes food and incidentals allowance of $34 per person, $67 rent, and heat and utilities according to a standardized allowance based on family size.

How Are They Living?

Without important error, we can think of these families as living on the schedule of state ceiling grants. No income other than the relief grant was reported for seventy-nine families. This means that for 85 percent of the group, income is fixed by the state ceilings—$120 for a mother and one child, $140 for a mother and two children, and so on. Whenever income plus the ceiling grant exceeds the state subsistence standard for the family, the grant is reduced accordingly.

Court-ordered or voluntary support payments by the absent fathers of families on relief is the weakest of financial reeds. In many cases they are not actually forthcoming, and families dependent on them are chronically on the verge of utter destitution. Children over seventeen are excluded from the state-federal AFDC program, and since September 1962 are also eliminated from city welfare support. There are at least six families among our ninety-three with an unemployed child over seventeen living in the home with no provision for his support.

Out of the ceiling grant rent and utilities must get paid, usually first. Table 2 shows the combined cost of rent and utilities to these families in the month of March 1963.

TABLE 2

Combined Cost of Rent and Utilities—March 1963

Dollars	Public Housing	Private Housing	Type of Housing Not Ascertained
40-59	44	3	1
60-79	6	10	1
80-99	2	18	2
100-above	0	5	0
Total	52	36	4

Fifty-two of the families live in city public housing projects, thirty-seven in private housing. Living in public housing projects is cheaper—the median rent and utility cost is $56, compared with $86 in private housing, but few public housing units are large enough for the biggest families, who naturally pay more for bigger private quarters.

What do these reasonable rent and utility costs mean to an AFDC family? Consider a mother with two children. Say that rent and utilities are $70 per month. Out of their $140 grant that leaves $70. But the state welfare department says that three people need $102 a month for food and incidentals. It is clear that for these families "something suffers."

One mother, three days after receipt of her check (and twelve days before the next one would come), had 56c left. She had bought food and coal and paid the rent, but held off on the gas and electricity bills because there was no money to pay them. The gas and electricity may be cut off, she says, as they have been twice in the last two years. And what of school supplies, clothing, or carfare?

Sixteen mothers reported they were behind in rent. Half of these owed $50 or less, but one woman was $140 behind because her grant had stopped while the agency checked out a report that "a man was living with her." The lost income was never made up. Twenty-five families were behind in utilities; you need a roof overhead, at least in the winter, but you can exist without heat and light.

A surprising proportion of the mothers considered themselves not badly housed. In the words of the women:

> (Private housing): *"It's good because the rent is fair and it's near school, relatives and shopping. But the house is too small and the neighborhood is unfriendly."* (High-rise public housing project): *"It's cold in winter, causing excess use of electricity. It's too far from the children outside, too small, and the elevators are a problem. But it is burglar and fire proof, and there's a good incinerator."* (Also high-rise): *"It's too crowded, noisy, and too high,"* (woman has hypertension). *"But it's warm, fire proof, and the Neighborhood Service Organization has good programs for the kids."*

How Do AFDC Families Eat?

To get some detail on the quality of economic life on AFDC, we asked the mothers how much food they had on hand (meat, dairy products, and fresh or canned fruit). The information obtained was voluminous and interesting, but difficult to summarize and liable to misinterpretation. Just before check day, food stocks will naturally be low, and just after, there may be two weeks' supply of food newly purchased. Averages here would make no sense.

However, the trend of the information gathered indicated that hardly any mother had as much as a half-gallon of milk on hand, and very little meat. Often the meat listed was an inexpensive cut like neck bones, or a canned variety. There was a nearly universal report, "No fruit," "No fruit." And something we didn't inquire into was frequently volunteered: "No vegetables either." And in home economics courses in the schools they teach children about balanced diets!

Asked "Is your family adequately fed?" forty of the mothers answered "yes," six answered "sometimes," and forty-seven answered "no." "Never enough near the time the check is due. Hungry at other times too." "Before transfer to AFDC (from Detroit welfare) we ate well, but now food is inadequate." So the mothers respond who feel their families are inadequately fed. One mother had a doctor-prescribed high-protein diet (and TB too) that she has been unable to follow for two months.

Those that consider their families adequately fed have often given up something else. They say that they are getting behind in the rent, are without adequate clothing, and in one case without a phone, which was necessary because of a brain damaged child with frequent convulsions. Those who feel they are adequately fed usually go without fruit, and eat little meat and vegetables.

Food Stamps in the AFDC Program

For many years now the federal government has been disposing of some of the surplus foods accumulated under the farm subsidy program, by giving it to local relief agencies across the country who distribute it to poor people. In 1962 the food stamp program, which had been used before World War II, was started in a number of localities including Detroit to test whether it was a better way of distributing surplus foods. As a result, in Detroit surplus commodities are not now given directly to families, but food stamps are distributed by the City Department of Public Welfare to all low income people who wish to participate. The participant takes his cash to a stamp office and buys stamps which are worth more than the cash paid—for example, you may get $14 worth of stamps for $10. The amount one may purchase depends mostly on the size of the family, but most AFDC families qualify for less than a 50 percent bonus, e.g., for $30 cash, $43 in food stamps.

All AFDC families in Detroit are eligible to buy food stamps. Forty-seven out of our ninety-three families reported buying food stamps; forty-six did not. Most mothers who get the stamps say they are a great help. Those who do not get the stamps gave the following reasons (in order of frequency): not enough cash, restricts purchase selection, timing is off, and can't get to the stamp office.

Twenty-four families found the stamps restricted purchase selection. For example, the stamps don't buy soap, cleaning supplies, or toilet paper. They don't buy coffee or cocoa. These restrictions occur because the program, financed by the U.S. Department of Agriculture with farm subsidy funds, is designed to get rid of surplus food stores, not to help feed poor people. The resulting rules and procedures guard the interests of the farmers, who don't grow coffee or toilet paper, instead of the interests of the stamp users. Even a very careful home manager is penalized by the program's procedures; however, she still gains in dollars by using the stamps.

Not enough cash. This is the most important reason; and it causes all kinds of difficulties even for the families that buy food stamps. What happens is this: A family of mother and three children when receiving its semi-monthly AFDC check of $80 is certified to buy $30 worth of food stamps. But the rent of $55 is due and must be paid first; there is not enough left to get the food stamps. Suppose they pay only half the rent now (which many do); but some utility bills are due and a child must have a pair of shoes—again, not enough cash to buy the food stamps. They are not permitted to buy less than the amount they are certified for by the welfare department (this would be against the Department of Agriculture regulations). And they must buy regularly. Every time a family fails to buy the stamps at the appointed time, it is automatically decertified and must go through the application procedure again. If the family is very irregular in buying stamps, it becomes ineligible for the program for a while—a Department of Agriculture penalty to force regular participation. Thus those who most need the added food-buying power of the stamps are least able to get them.

Some find the "timing is off"—that the fixed time for buying stamps comes several days after (or before) the check comes. Meanwhile you have to eat, and there is then insufficient cash to buy stamps when the time comes. This problem is much less severe now than it was when the program was started because local relief officials, after fighting a long battle with Washington, have been able to get the check and stamp buying dates into approximate coincidence.

There are some cases where the mother wanted, and was able, to buy the stamps but couldn't get her relief worker to come out to certify her. Although occasionally workers are indifferent, the basic reason is that the Bureau of Social Aid is so understaffed that planned contacts with AFDC families have been made only once in every six to twelve month period. This period has been reduced under the 1962 welfare amendments. Yet when no worker comes around, the family doesn't get food stamps.

What Do the Children Wear?

As a further measure of the level of living on AFDC, information was obtained on the total wardrobe of the oldest school child in each family. As with the food data, the information obtained was voluminous and enlightening, but difficult to summarize and liable to misinterpretation. However, some startling facts emerged regarding what is one of the most critical problems in AFDC life, clothing for school children.

Only about half of the clothing is purchased, a good deal of it was bought before the supplement cut of September 1962, and a good deal of this purchased clothing is used. For the other half of their clothing the children depend on gifts, from relatives and neighbors, and from school teachers. About eight out of ten boys have but one pair of shoes; about half the girls have only one pair of shoes, and half have two pairs. About half the children have no rubbers or boots of any kind, and about three-fourths have no raincoats of any description. There is obviously no room in a state ceiling grant for clothing.

What Else Do They Spend Money On?

Although the grants hardly allow for it, the mothers are forced from time to time to spend money on things other than rent, utilities, and food. For the month prior to the interview they reported the following other expenditures—which, of course, are estimates from memory.

Sixty-nine had some expense for transportation, ranging in amount from under a dollar to $45 for a trip South to resettle a burned-out mother. Thirty spent one or two dollars, nineteen more spent three or four dollars. One woman said it cost $20 in carfare to make trips to the clinic for an asthmatic son. Twenty-four families apparently rode not at all.

A good deal of medical expense is reflected in the transportation figure, since the free clinic is their only medical provision. Many find Receiving Hospital care unsatisfactory because of long waits and responsibility for young children; thus we find thirty-one who had expenses for doctors, dentists, or medicines during the month. In twenty-four of these cases the amounts expended were less than $7, but one woman reported $48.68 for doctor and $4.25 for medicine, while another "pays what she can" on a $300 bill for braces for her son's teeth.

Eight families reported insurance premium payments of from $3 to $15 in the preceding month, and undoubtedly many more neglected to report such expenditures. Only ten families reported any expenditure for recreation, although all were specifically asked about this. Nine reported church expenses, from $1 to $6; nine had school expenses, from $1 to $10; eleven paid telephone bills; one paid $7.50 for house screens; one $2 for a horn mouthpiece for a child; one $3.09 for brooms and a mop; several had bought newspapers; one girl lost $10 from the sale of Girl Scout cookies and the mother had to make it good.

Life in Our "Affluent Society"

The significance of these other expenditures is twofold. First, that they should exist at all, since there is usually no allowance at all for them in the grim budgets of these families; and second, even more important, that they should be so few and so small considering that we live in a money economy. What does it mean that families should spend nothing at all for transportation for a whole month in a city like Detroit? That most should spend nothing at all for recreation in families averaging

over three children apiece? That with hundreds of school kids represented, only nine families reported expenses for school supplies?

As a refined measure of the economic situation of these families,
they were asked the combined value of cash and food stamps on hand,
and how many days until the next check came. AFDC checks are now
issued twice monthly, rather than once as formerly, to help families
spread their income over the entire month, although this interferes with
rent payment and purchase of food stamps. The essence of the financial
situation of these people is contained in the fact that thirty-one families
had between nothing and $4 on hand to last from three to fourteen days.
Asked if they ever ran out of money, they all answered yes.

When asked what they did about running out of money, two-
thirds said they borrowed, either from relatives and friends or store-
keepers, and one-third said they just "stayed run out." "Stay run out"
is the theme of their lives—and for those who borrow too, because the
loan must be paid back, and each month they sink a little deeper. Besides borrowing and staying run out, some found other ways to cope
with the continuing crisis: One "lets the bills go." (Where does this
end?) One cashes in bottles and borrows food. One cried in shame:
"The lady downstairs gives us food." One said, "If the children get sick,
I call the police to take them to Receiving Hospital."

One has been "borrowing" secretly from the funds of a Ladies'
Club of which she is treasurer. The club is her one meaningful adult
social contact. There is soon to be an election for new club officers and
she will be exposed. Her children ask: "Mama, why are you always so
sad?" Half crazy with worry, she feels sick; at Receiving Hospital they
have referred her to the psychiatrist.

One was in despair because a retarded son who delights in his
monthly visit home from the County Training School was coming tomorrow, and there was little food and no money or food stamps in the
house. One said bitterly: "A woman could always get $10 if she had to.
I prefer not to resort to this."

Consider our affluent society: in an economy generating wealth
sufficient to supply every family of four with nearly $10,000 per year
income, we reduce a family to cashing in pop bottles to get food, we
push a woman to thoughts of prostitution to feed her children, we force
an honest woman into theft and then provide her with $25 an hour
psychiatric treatment.

Impact of the Supplementation Cut

As noted above, only about two-thirds of the ninety-three families received a supplement cut in September 1962. The families that had been
cut were asked: Where did it hurt? What did you stop buying?

"No more clothes, fruit, milk. Clothes hurt most because mostly for school boy. Borrowed clothes to go to church." "Got behind in utilities—over $100." "Had to cut out food stamps. Hurt because came at time when children needed school supplies and clothing." "Shoes. Children have hard to fit feet so can't buy cheap shoes. Special treats cut out. We used to go as a family for small treats on holidays, but no more." "School clothing. They are ashamed of their ragged clothing. No spending money in school. This makes my children want to quit." "Boy dropped out of Boy Scouts. No shows, no getting away from the house."

No clothing, no school supplies, no gym shoes, no church, no Boy Scouts, no movies, no little treats, no ice cream cones—nothing like this if you want to keep the roof overhead. But after a while you lose interest even in that, and you quit school, quit church, quit Boy Scouts, begin to steal, or perhaps take money from a boy friend. Every single family which has its supplement cut was seriously hurt by the income reduction—all gave stories like those above.

When the 6,000 AFDC cases were cut off supplemental relief in September 1962, it was expected at the welfare department that many would come to the department asking for reinstatement of supplementation. But few showed up. It was then suggested by some public assistance officials, "Maybe they are not so bad off as we thought. Maybe they don't really need it." As we have seen they are wrong.

But how many went, what happened, and why didn't the rest go? Actually thirty-one of the sixty-five mothers who had received a budget cut *did* go to the city welfare to ask for help. None got it. Why didn't the other thirty-four mothers go? Perhaps they were wiser in anticipating refusal; they decided to save the time, the carfare, and the effort. Of course, in refusing aid the intake workers are simply carrying out departmental policy. So often in the position of having to deny aid to people who in their heart they know need help, the workers tend to develop what one former worker calls "the culture of intake"—methods of denying aid without fully examining the circumstances of the family.

Social Poverty

These people are not starving or out on the street. But in our world lack of buying power, even when it is not so absolute as to lead to starvation or death, leads to a very real social starvation and social death.

Well-off people easily forget that almost all social relationships depend on the ability to spend some money. To go to school costs money —for books, notebooks, pencils, gym shoes, and ice cream with the other kids. Without these the child begins to be an outcast. To go to church costs money—for Sunday clothes, carfare to get there, and a little offering. Without these, one cannot go. To belong to the Boy Scouts costs money—for uniforms, occasional dues, shared costs of a picnic. Without these, no Scouts.

Poverty settles like an impenetrable prison cell over the lives of the very poor, shutting them off from every social contact, killing the spirit, and isolating them from the community of human life.

The Dusty Outskirts of Hope

Mary Wright

Council of the Southern Mountains

[Reprinted from Mountain Life and Work, *Spring 1964, by permission of the Council of the Southern Mountains, Inc.]*

I KNOW A MAN, I'll call him Buddy Banks. He lives in a ravine in a little one-room pole-and-cardboard house he built himself, with his wife, their six children, and baby granddaughter. Mr. Banks, 45 years old, is a sober man, a kindly man, and a passive man. He can read and write a little, has worked in the coal mines and on farms, but over the years he's been pretty badly battered up and today is "none too stout." Last fall, when he could no longer pay the rent where he was staying, his mother-in-law gave him a small piece of ground, and he hastened to put up this little shack in the woods before the snow came. If, as you ride by, you happened to glance down and see where he lives, and see his children playing among the stones, you would say, "White trash." You would say, "Welfare bums."

When the newspaper announced the new ADC program for unemployed fathers, I thought of Buddy Banks. There is not much farm work to be done in the wintertime, and Mr. Banks has been without a job since summer. Here in their ravine they can dig their coal from a hole in the hill, and dip their water from the creek, and each month he scratches together $2 for his food stamps by doing odd jobs for his neighbors, who are very nearly as poor as he is. Other than this there is nothing coming in. I thought, maybe here is some help for Buddy Banks.

Mr. Banks does not get a newspaper, nor does he have a radio, and so he had not heard about the new program. He said, yes, he would be interested. I offered to take him to town right then, but he said no, he would have to clean up first, he couldn't go to town looking like this. So I agreed to come back Friday.

On Friday he told me he'd heard today was the last day for sign-ing up. We were lucky, eh? It wasn't true, but it's what he had heard and I wondered, suppose he'd been told last Tuesday was the last day for signing up, and I hadn't been there to say, well, let's go find out anyway.

Buddy Banks was all fixed up and looked nice as he stepped out of his cabin. His jacket was clean, and he had big rubber boots on and a cap on his head. I felt proud walking along with him, and he walked proud. (Later, in town, I noticed how the hair curled over his collar, and the gray look about him, and the stoop of his shoulders. If you saw him you'd have said, "Country boy, come to get his check.")

When we reached the Welfare Office it was full of people, a crowd of slouchy, shuffly men, standing around and looking vaguely in dif-ferent directions. I followed Buddy Banks and his brother-in-law, who had asked to come with us, into the lobby, and they too stood in the middle of the floor. Just stood. It was not the momentary hesitation that comes before decision. It was the paralysis of strangeness, of lost-ness, of not knowing what to do. A girl was sitting at a table, and after a number of minutes of nothing, I quietly suggested they ask her. No, they told me, that was the food stamp girl. But there was no other. So finally, when I suggested, well, ask her anyway, they nodded their heads, moved over, and asked her. I wondered how long they might have gone on standing there, if I'd kept my mouth shut. I wondered how long the others all around us had been standing there. I had an idea that if I hadn't been right in the way, Buddy Banks just might have turned around and gone out the door when he saw the crowd, the lines, and that smartly-dressed food stamp girl bending over her desk.

Yes, he was told, and after waiting a few minutes, he was shown behind the rail to a chair beside a desk, and a man with a necktie and a big typewriter began to talk with him. They talked a long long time, while the brother-in-law and I waited in the lobby. (They had asked the brother-in-law if he had brought the birth certificates. No, he hadn't, and so they said there wasn't anything they could do, to come back next Tuesday. He said nothing, stared at them a moment, then walked away. He stood around waiting for us all day long and never asked them an-other question. He said he would tend to it some other time. Fortu-nately, they got Mr. Banks sitting down before they inquired about the birth certificates.)

I knew what they were talking about: I have talked long times with Mr. Banks myself, and they were going over it again, and again, and I could imagine Mr. Banks nodding his head to the question he didn't quite understand, because he wanted to make a good impression, and it would be a little while before the worker realized that he hadn't understood, and so they would go back and try again, and then Mr. Banks would explain as best he could, but he would leave something out, and then the worker wouldn't understand, so that, in all, their heads were bent together for almost an hour and a half. It seemed a long time to take to discover Buddy Bank's need—a visit to his home would have revealed it in a very few minutes, but of course twelve miles out and twelve miles back takes time too, and there are all those eligibility rules to be checked out, lest somebody slip them a lie and the editorials start hollering "Fraud! Fraud!" Actually, I was impressed that the worker would give him that much time. It takes time to be sympathetic, to listen, to hear—to understand a human condition.

At last he came out, and with an apologetic grin he said he must return on Tuesday, he must go home and get the birth certificates. Then they would let him apply. (How will you come back, Mr. Banks? Where will you get the $3 for taxi fare by next Tuesday? Perhaps you could scrape it up by Monday week, but suppose you come on Monday week and your worker isn't here? Then perhaps you won't come back at all . . .)

While Mr. Banks was busy talking, I was chatting with one of the other workers. Because I am a social worker too, I can come and go through the little iron gate, and they smile at me and say, "Well, *hello* there!" We talked about all the work she has to do, and one of the things she told me was how, often, to save time, they send people down to the Health Department to get their own birth records. Then they can come back and apply the same day. I wondered why Mr. Bank's worker never suggested this. Maybe he never thought of it. (Maybe he doesn't live twelve miles out with no car, and the nearest bus eight miles from home. And no bus fare at that.) Or perhaps he *did* mention it, and Mr. Banks never heard him, because his head was already filled up with the words that went before: "I'm sorry, there's nothing we can do until you bring us the birth certificates," and he was trying to think in which box, under which bed, had the children been into them . . . ?

So I tried to suggest to him that we go now to the Health Department, but he didn't hear me either. He said, and he persisted, I'm going to the Court House, I'll be right back, will you wait for me? I tried to stop him: let's plan something, what we're going to do next, it's almost lunchtime and things will close up—until suddenly I realized that after the time and the tension of the morning, this was no doubt a call of nature that could not wait for reasonable planning, nor could a proud man come out and ask if there might not be a more accessible solution. And so, as he headed quickly away for the one sure place he knew, I stood mute and waited while he walked the three blocks there and the three blocks back. I wonder if that's something anybody ever thinks about when they're interviewing clients.

Mr. Banks and I had talked earlier about the Manpower Redevelopment Vocational Training Programs, and he had seemed interested. "I'd sure rather work and look after my family than mess with all this stuff, but what can I do? I have no education." I told him about the courses and he said, yes, I'd like that. And so we planned to look into this too, while we were in town. But by now Mr. Banks was ready to go home. "I hate all this standing around. I'd work two days rather than stand around like this." It wasn't really the standing around he minded. It was the circumstances of the standing around. It took some persuading to get him back into the building, only to be told—at 11:30 —to come back at ten to one. (Suppose his ride, I thought, had been with somebody busier than I. Suppose they couldn't wait till ten to one and kept badgering him, "Come on, Buddy, hurry up, will you? We ain't got all day!")

I tried to suggest some lunch while we waited, but they didn't want lunch. "We had breakfast late; I'm not hungry, really." So instead, I took him around to the Health Department and the Circuit Court and the County Court, and we verified everything, although he needed some help to figure which years the children were born in.

At ten to one he was again outside the Welfare Office, and he drew me aside and said that he'd been thinking: maybe he should go home and talk this whole thing over a little more. He felt that before jumping into something, he should know better what it was all about. This startled me, for I wondered what that hour and a half had been for, if now, after everything, he felt he must return to his cronies up the creek to find out what it all meant. So we stood aside, and I interpreted the program as best I could, whom it was for and what it required, and what it would do for him and his family, while he stood, nodding his head and staring at the sidewalk. Finally, cautiously, almost grimly, he once again pushed his way into that crowded, smoke-filled lobby.

"Those who are to report at one o'clock, stand in this line. Others in that line." Mr. Banks stood in the one o'clock line. At 1:15 he reached the counter. I don't know what he asked, but I saw the man behind the desk point over toward the other side of the building, the Public Assistance side, where Mr. Banks had already spent all morning. Mr. Banks nodded his head and turned away as he was told to do. At that point I butted in. "Assistance for the unemployed is over there," the man said and pointed again. So I mentioned training. "He wants training? Why didn't he say so? He's in the wrong line." I don't know what Mr. Banks had said, but what *does* a person say when he's anxious, and tired and confused, and a crowd of others, equally anxious, are pushing from behind and the man at the counter says, "Yes?" I butted in and Mr. Banks went to stand in the right line, but I wondered what the man behind us did, who didn't have anybody to butt in for him.

While Mr. Banks was waiting, to save time, I took the birth certificates to his worker on the other side. I walked right in, because I was a social worker and could do that, and he talked to me right away and said, "Yes, yes, this is good. This will save time. No, he won't have to come back on Tuesday. Yes, he can apply today. Just have him come back over here when he is through over there. Very good."

At 1:30 Buddy Banks reached the counter again, was given a card and told to go sit on a chair until his name was called. I had business at 2:00 and returned at 3:00, and there he was, sitting on the same chair. But I learned as I sat beside him that things had been happening. He had talked with the training counsellor, returned to his welfare worker, and was sent back to the unemployment counsellor, after which he was to return once more to his welfare worker. I asked what he had learned about the training. "There's nothing right now, maybe later." Auto mechanics? Bench work? Need too much education. There may be something about washing cars, changing oil, things like that. Later on. Did you sign up for anything? No. Did they say they'd let you know? No. How will you know? I don't know.

At last his ADC (Unemployed) application was signed, his cards were registered, his name was in the file. Come back in two weeks and we'll see if you're eligible. (How will you get back, Buddy? I'll find a way.)

It was four o'clock. "Well, that's over." And he said, "I suppose a fellow's got to go through all that, but I'd sure rather be a-working than a-fooling around with all that mess." We went out to the car, and I took him home. "I sure do thank you, though," he said.

While I'd been waiting there in the lobby, I saw another man come up to the counter. He was small and middle-aged, with a wedding band on his finger, and his face was creased with lines of care. I saw him speak quietly to the man across the desk. I don't know what he said or what the problem was, but they talked a moment and the official told him, "Well, if you're disabled for work, then there's no use asking about training," and he put up his hands and turned away to the papers on his desk. The man waited there a moment, then slowly turned around and stood in the middle of the floor. He lifted his head to stare up at the wall, the blank wall, and his blue eyes were held wide open to keep the tears from coming. I couldn't help watching him, and when suddenly he looked at me, his eyes straight into mine, I couldn't help asking him—across the wide distance of the crowd that for just an instant vanished into the intimacy of human communion—I asked, "Trouble?" Almost as if he were reaching out his hands, he answered me and said, "I just got the news from Washington and come to sign up, and . . ." but then, embarrassed to be talking to a stranger, he mumbled something else I couldn't understand, turned his back to me, stood another long moment in the middle of the crowd, and then walked out the door.

Disabled or not disabled. Employed or not employed. In need or not in need. Yes or no. Black or white. Answer the question. Stand in line.

It is not the program's fault. You have to have questionnaires, and questionnaires require a yes or no. There is no space for a maybe, but . . .

Nor is it the people-who-work-there's fault, for who can see—or take time to see—the whole constellation of people and pressures, needs and perplexities, desires and dreads that walk into an office in the person of one shuffling, bedraggled man—especially when there are a hundred other bedraggled men waiting behind him? You ask the questions and await the answers. What else can you do?

Then perhaps it is the fault of the man himself, the man who asks —or doesn't quite know how to ask—for help. Indeed, he's called a lazy cheat if he does, and an unmotivated ignorant fool if he doesn't. It must be his own fault.

Or maybe it's nobody's fault. It's just the way things are . . .

Selected Bibliography

1. Edwin W. Bakke. *The Unemployed Worker*. New Haven: Yale University Press, 1940.

2. M. Elaine Burgess and Daniel O. Price. *An American Dependency Challenge*. Chicago: American Public Welfare Association, 1963.

3. David J. Caplovitz. *The Poor Pay More: Consumer Practices of Low Income Families*. New York: Free Press of Glencoe, 1963.

4. Allison Davis. "Motivation of the Underprivileged Worker," *Industry and Society*, William F. Whyte, ed. New York: McGraw Hill, 1946.

5. Lenore A. Epstein. "Some Effects of Low Income on Children and Their Families," *Social Security Bulletin*, Vol. 24, February, 1961.

6. Louis A. Ferman. "The Irregular Economy: Informal Work Patterns in Urban Ghettos," Unpublished paper, Institute of Labor and Industrial Relations, The University of Michigan—Wayne State University, January 1966.

7. Herbert J. Gans. *The Urban Villagers*. Glencoe, Illinois: The Free Press, 1963.

8. Elizabeth Herzog. *Children of Working Mothers* (U.S. Children's Bureau Publication 383), Washington, Government Printing Office, 1960.

9. Joseph S. Himes. "Some Work Related Cultural Deprivations of Lower-Class Negro Youths," *Journal of Marriage and the Family*, November, 1964.

10. Frederick S. Jaffe. "Family Planning and Poverty," *Journal of Marriage and the Family*, November 1964.

11. Genevieve Knaupfer. "Portrait of the Underdog," *Public Opinion Quarterly*, II (Spring, 1947).

12. Mollie Orshansky, "Children of the Poor," *Social Security Bulletin*, Vol. 26, July, 1963.

13. Lee Rainwater and Karol Kane Weinstein. *And the Poor Get Children*. Chicago: Quadrangle Books, 1960.

14. David Riesman, et al. *The Lonely Crowd*. New York: Doubleday and Company, 1953.

15. Frank Riessman. *The Culturally Deprived Child*. New York: Harper and Row, 1962.

16. Nicholas von Hoffman. "Reorganization in the Casbah," *Social Progress*, April, 1962.

17. William F. Whyte. "The Social Organization of the Slum," *American Sociological Review*, 8 (1944).

Chapter 7

Policies and Programs

To meet the problems effectively will require the concerted efforts of all segments of our national life—all levels of government working with labor and management and private community groups and organizations. With such coordinated, positive action, we are confident that, in overall terms, the total cost will be low when measured by the positive economic gains which will be generated throughout the total economy and also when measured by the resultant strengthening of the forces which produce an alert, productive, and democratic society.

—From Joint Economic Committee, 84th Congress, Second Session, Senate Report 1311.

PREVIOUS CHAPTERS HAVE ATTEMPTED to delineate the general prevalence of poverty, its specific incidence on certain groups and its causal roots and sustaining conditions in the American political economy. We then looked more closely at the value patterns, life styles and family situation of the poor, highlighting conditions of education, social and economic participation.

We can draw several generalizations from this varied material:

(1) Poverty does not exist at the periphery of an otherwise healthy social and economic order, but is the result of deficiencies in the way in which the society allocates resources, judges worth and rewards achievement.

(2) Poverty is not of a piece. While there are certain common roots, the problems of old people are different from those of youth or those of obsolete workers in depressed areas or those of mothers with dependent children. Remedies must be specific as well as general.

(3) Poverty will not gradually disappear with the advance of American prosperity. Trends in manpower needs coupled with high concentration of children among the poor, suggest a growing new generation of poor, without an expanding job market to offer opportunity for economic advancement.

(4) Poverty is not simply a matter of deficient income. It involves a reinforcing pattern of restricted opportunities, deficient community services, abnormal social pressures and predators, and defensive adaptations. Increased income alone is not sufficient to overcome brutalization, social isolation and narrow aspiration.

(5) Poverty is not something that just happens. There are groups in the society that make a profit from the poor. There are other groups whose profit or power would be threatened if the poor were to become secure economically and active as social and political participants.

The range of policies and programs included in this chapter was selected with a view to their relative agreement or disagreement with these general points of orientation. Seven criteria or dimensions might aid in assessing these proposals.

(1) Does the proposal assume no difficulty in eliminating poverty from our wealthy society (consensus model of social change), or does it assume conflicts, in attempts to eliminate poverty, between current values and the uncompromisable interest of some social groups (conflict model of social change)?

(2) Does the proposal see poverty in primarily income-economic terms or in social, quality-of-life terms? The income definition implies a need to rebuild the basis of economic self-sufficiency, whereas the wider, quality-of-life definition implies a need to reshape the entire opportunity structure of the poor; this involves value judgments as to which opportunities and experiences are relatively more important for the good life.

(3) Does the proposal focus on symptoms or causes? Treatment of cause requires an analysis of why poverty exists and how anticipated social changes of the next decades will affect poverty. Following this analysis, programs are designed to correct the root conditions—in the individual and in the society—that generate poverty. Treatment of symptoms seeks primarily to alleviate individual hardship, to dissipate "social dynamite" and to aid individuals in breaking the hold of poverty. It is thus akin to a clinical program of individual treatment and sponsored mobility in contrast to a social program of environmental reform and general uplift.

(4) Is it directed to aid the next generation of poor or the present poor? Some programs concentrate on the problems of youth or even pre-school children, while essentially writing off the present adult poor as beyond help except for symptomatic relief. Other programs seek generally to improve economic opportunities, seeing that this will aid both children and their parents; still other programs are more specific in designing both causal and symptomatic remedies for distinct age,

occupational and geographical groups. The issues are often how best to allocate scarce anti-poverty resources and how to minimize the social conflict which anti-poverty aid might foster.

(5) Does the proposal operate within the present framework of the affluent society or does it see anti-poverty action as a vehicle for broader social change? Some proposals affirm the status quo of welfare capitalism and limited democracy as a close approximation to the good society and assume that the poor should be aided toward full participation within this structure. Other proposals premise major failures in the status quo and see anti-poverty action as coordinated with such goals as the creation of participatory democracy, broadening the definition of productive work, deepening the quality of culture, or reducing manipulative pressures for mass consumption.

(6) Is the proposal paternalistic or democratic? Some programs plan out the needs to be met and opportunities to be offered in advance and then operate through a high level coordination of community services, welfare agencies and business leaders to most efficiently implement the plan. In these, the poor are largely passive recipients of aid or special opportunities. Other proposals would sacrifice a degree of efficiency and predictability in exchange for the democratic participation of the poor in the planning, staffing and administration of programs. The one sees the problems as primarily an organizational job of reallocating certain resources and opportunities, best handled by those with organizational experience and with direct control of the needed resources. The other view places greater trust in the poor and is concerned with the human goal of giving individuals some control over the conditions of their life, both to break patterns of passivity and dependence and to release their creative energies to the benefit of the whole community.

(7) Does the proposal identify the forces of resistance and develop a strategy for implementation? Some programs develop theoretical solutions while ignoring the political realities of social change. Others gear their vision to the limits of the immediately possible. Any serious proposal must analyze the interacting forces that would be potential antagonists to the program and those that would be the potential allies.

Each of these dimensions sets up a polarity, which roughly approximates minimal and maximal positions for dealing with poverty. The minimal position seeks to reduce hardship, mitigate poverty generated social problems and minimize disruptive social conflict. The maximal position seeks a wide range of social change where not only the life of the poor, but the whole society is transformed in terms of spiritual opportunities and economic realities of the next decade. It is on the conflict between these positions that the debate over poverty will focus in the coming years.

The Triple Revolution: An Appraisal of the Major U.S. Crises and Proposals for Action

The Ad Hoc Committee on the Triple Revolution

THIS STATEMENT IS WRITTEN in the recognition that mankind is at a historic conjuncture which demands a fundamental reexamination of existing values and institutions. At this time, three separate and mutually reinforcing revolutions are taking place:

THE CYBERNATION REVOLUTION: A new era of production has begun. Its principles of organization are as different from those of the industrial era as those of the industrial era were different from the agricultural. The cybernation revolution has been brought about by the combination of the computer and the automated self-regulating machine. This results in a system of almost unlimited productive capacity which requires progressively less human labor. Cybernation is already reorganizing the economic and social system to meet its own needs.

THE WEAPONRY REVOLUTION: New forms of weaponry have been developed which cannot win wars but which can obliterate civilization. We are recognizing only now that the great weapons have eliminated war as a method for resolving international conflicts. The ever-present threat of total destruction is tempered by the knowledge of the final futility of war. The need of a "warless world" is generally recognized, though achieving it will be a long and frustrating process.

THE HUMAN RIGHTS REVOLUTION: A universal demand for full human rights is now clearly evident. It continues to be demonstrated in the civil rights movement within the United States. But this is only the local manifestation of a world-wide movement toward the establishment of social and political regimes in which every individual will feel valued and none will feel rejected on account of his race.

We are particularly concerned in this statement with the first of these revolutionary phenomena. This is not because we underestimate the significance of the other two. On the contrary, we affirm that it is the simultaneous occurrence and interaction of all three developments which make evident the necessity for radical alterations in attitude and policy. The adoption of just policies for coping with cybernation and for extending rights to all Americans is indispensable to the creation of an atmosphere in the United States in which the supreme issue, peace, can be reasonably debated and resolved.

Interaction of the Three Revolutions

The Negro claims, as a matter of simple justice, his full share in America's economic and social life. He sees adequate employment opportunities as a chief means of attaining this goal: the March on Washington (August, 1963) demanded freedom *and* jobs. The Negro's claim to a job is not being met. Negroes are the hardest-hit of the many groups being exiled from the economy by cybernation. Negro unemployment rates cannot be expected to drop substantially. Promises of jobs are a cruel and dangerous hoax on hundreds of thousands of Negroes and whites alike who are especially vulnerable to cybernation because of age or inadequate education.

The demand of the civil rights movement cannot be fulfilled within the present context of society. The Negro is trying to enter a social community and a tradition of work-and-income which are in the process of vanishing even for the hitherto privileged white worker. Jobs are disappearing under the impact of highly efficient, progressively less costly machines.

The United States operates on the thesis, set out in the Employment Act of 1946, that every person will be able to obtain a job if he wishes to do so and that this job will provide him with resources adequate to live and maintain a family decently. Thus job-holding is the general mechanism through which economic resources are distributed. Those without work have access only to a minimal income, hardly sufficient to provide the necessities of life, and enabling those receiving it to function as only "minimum consumers." As a result the goods and services which are needed by these crippled consumers, and which they would buy if they could, are not produced. This in turn deprives other workers of jobs, thus reducing their incomes and consumption.

Present excessive levels of unemployment would be multiplied several times if military and space expenditures did not continue to absorb 10% of the Gross National Product (i.e. the total goods and services produced). Some 6–8 million people are employed as a direct result of purchases for space and military activities. At least an equal number hold their jobs as an indirect result of military or space expenditures. In recent years, the military and space budgets have absorbed a rising proportion of national production and formed a strong support for the economy.

However, these expenditures are coming in for more and more criticism, at least partially in recognition of the fact that nuclear weapons have eliminated war as an acceptable method for resolving international conflicts. Early in 1964, President Johnson ordered a curtailment of certain military expenditures. Defense Secretary McNamara is closing shipyards, airfields, and army bases, and Congress is pressing the National Space Administration to economize. The future of these strong props to the economy is not as clear today as it was even a year ago.

The Nature of the Cybernation Revolution

Cybernation is manifesting the characteristics of a revolution in production. These include the development of radically different techniques and the subsequent appearance of novel principles of the organization of production; a basic reordering of man's relationship to his environment; and a dramatic increase in total available and potential energy.

The major difference between the agricultural, industrial and cybernation revolutions is the speed at which they developed. The agricultural revolution began several thousand years ago in the Middle East. Centuries passed in the shift from a subsistence base of hunting and food-gathering to settled agriculture.

In contrast, it has been less than 200 years since the emergence of the industrial revolution, and direct and accurate knowledge of the new productive techniques has reached most of mankind. This swift dissemination of information is generally held to be the main factor leading to widespread industrialization.

While the major aspects of the cybernation revolution are for the moment restricted to the United States, its effects are observable almost at once throughout the industrial world and large parts of the non-industrial world. Observation is rapidly followed by analysis and criticism. The problems posed by the cybernation revolution are part of a new era in the history of all mankind but they are first being faced by the people of the United States. The way Americans cope with cybernation will influence the course of this phenomenon everywhere. This country is the stage on which the Machines-and-Man drama will first be played for the world to witness.

The fundamental problem posed by the cybernation revolution in the United States is that it invalidates the general mechanism so far employed to undergird people's rights as consumers. Up to this time economic resources have been distributed on the basis of contributions to production, with machines and men competing for employment on somewhat equal terms. In the developing cybernated system, potentially unlimited output can be achieved by systems of machines which will require little cooperation from human beings. As machines take over production from men, they absorb an increasing proportion of resources while the men who are displaced become dependent on minimal and unrelated government measures—unemployment insurance, social security, welfare payments. These measures are less and less able to disguise a historic paradox: that a growing proportion of the population is subsisting on minimal incomes, often below the poverty line, at a time when sufficient productive potential is available to supply the needs of everyone in the United States.

The existence of this paradox is denied or ignored by conventional economic analysis. The general economic approach argues that potential demand, which if filled would raise the number of jobs and provide incomes to those holding them, is under-estimated. Most contemporary economic analysis states that all of the available labor force and industrial capacity is required to meet the needs of consumers and industry and to provide adequate public services: schools, parks, roads, homes, decent cities, and clean water and air. It is further argued that demand could be increased, by a variety of standard techniques, to any desired extent by providing money and machines to improve the conditions of the billions of impoverished people elsewhere in the world, who need food and shelter, clothes and machinery and everything else the industrial nations take for granted.

There is no question that cybernation does increase the potential for the provision of funds to neglected public sectors. Nor is there any question that cybernation would make possible the abolition of poverty at home and abroad. But the industrial system does not possess any adequate mechanisms to permit these potentials to become realities. The industrial system was designed to produce an ever-increasing quantity of goods as efficiently as possible, and it was assumed that the distribution of the power to purchase these goods would occur almost automatically. The continuance of the income-through-jobs link as the only major mechanism for distributing effective demand—for granting the right to consume—now acts as the main brake on the almost unlimited capacity of a cybernated productive system.

Recent administrations have proposed measures aimed at achieving a better distribution of resources, and at reducing unemployment and underemployment. A few of these proposals have been enacted.

More often they have failed to secure Congressional support. In every case, many members of Congress have criticized the proposed measures as departing from traditional principles for the allocation of resources and the encouragement of production. Abetted by budget-balancing economists and interest groups, they have argued for the maintenance of an economic machine based on ideas of scarcity to deal with the facts of abundance produced by cybernation. This time-consuming criticism has slowed the workings of Congress and has thrown out of focus for that body the inter-related effects of the triple revolution.

An adequate distribution of the potential abundance of goods and services will be achieved only when it is understood that the major economic problem is not how to increase production but how to distribute the abundance that is the great potential of cybernation. There is an urgent need for a fundamental change in the mechanisms employed to insure consumer rights.

The Cybernation Revolution—Facts and Figures

No responsible observer would attempt to describe the exact pace or the full sweep of a phenomenon that is developing with the speed of cybernation. Some aspects of this revolution, however, are already clear:

the rate of productivity increase has risen with the onset of cybernation;

an industrial economic system postulated on scarcity has been unable to distribute the abundant goods and services produced by a cybernated system or potential in it;

surplus capacity and unemployment have thus co-existed at excessive levels over the last six years;

the underlying cause of excessive unemployment is the fact that the capability of machines is rising more rapidly than the capacity of many human beings to keep pace;

a permanent impoverished and jobless class is established in the midst of potential abundance.

Evidence for these statements follows:

1. The increased efficiency of machine systems is shown in the more rapid increase in productivity per man-hour since 1960, a year that marks the first visible upsurge of the cybernation revolution. In 1961, 1962, and 1963, productivity per man-hour rose at an average pace above 3.5%—a rate well above both the historical average and the post-war rate.

Companies are finding cybernation more and more attractive. Even at the present early stage of cybernation, costs have already been lowered to a point where the price of a durable machine may be as little as one-third of the current annual wage-cost of the worker it replaces. A more rapid rise in the rate of productivity increase per man-hour can be expected from now on.

2. In recent years it has proved impossible to increase demand fast enough to bring about the full use of either men or plant capacities. The task of developing sufficient additional demand promises to become more difficult each year. A thirty billion dollar annual increase in Gross National Product is now required to prevent unemployment rates from rising. An additional forty to sixty billion dollar increase would be required to bring unemployment rates down to an acceptable level.

3. The official rate of unemployment has remained at or above 5.5 percent during the Sixties. The unemployment rate for teenagers has been rising steadily and now stands around 15 percent. The unemployment rate for Negro teenagers stands about 30 percent. The unemployment rate for teenagers in minority ghettoes sometimes exceeds 50 percent. Unemployment rates for Negroes are regularly more than twice those for whites, whatever their occupation, educational level, age or sex. The unemployment position for other racial minorities is similarly unfavorable. Unemployment rates in depressed areas often exceed 50 percent.

These official figures seriously underestimate the true extent of unemployment. The statistics take no notice of under-employment or feather-bedding. Besides the 5.5 percent of the labor force who are officially designated as unemployed, nearly 4 percent of the labor force sought full-time work in 1962 but could find only part-time jobs. In addition, methods of calculating unemployment rates—a person is counted as unemployed only if he has actively sought a job recently—ignore the fact that many men and women who would like to find jobs have not looked for them because they know there are no employment opportunities. Underestimates for this reason are pervasive among groups whose unemployment rates are high—the young, the old, and racial minorities. Many people in the depressed agricultural, mining and industrial areas, who by official definition hold jobs but who are actually grossly underemployed, would move if there were prospects of finding work elsewhere. It is reasonable to estimate that over 8 million people are not working who would like to have jobs today as compared with the 4 million shown in the official statistics.

Even more serious is the fact that the number of people who have voluntarily removed themselves from the labor force is not constant but increases continuously. These people have decided to stop looking for employment and seem to have accepted the fact that they will never hold jobs again. This decision is largely irreversible, in economic and also in social and psychological terms. The older worker calls himself "retired"; he cannot accept work without affecting his social security status. The worker in his prime years is forced onto relief: in most states the requirements for becoming a relief recipient bring about such fundamental alterations in an individual's situation that a reversal of the process is always difficult and often totally infeasible. Teenagers, especially "drop-outs" and Negroes, are coming to realize that there is no place for them in the labor force but at the same time they are given no realistic alternative. These people and their dependents make up a large part of the "poverty" sector of the American population.

Statistical evidence of these trends appears in the decline in the proportion of people claiming to be in the labor force—the so-called labor force participation rate. The recent apparent stabilization of the unemployment rate around 5.5% is therefore misleading: it is a reflection of the discouragement and defeat of people who cannot find employment and have withdrawn from the market rather than a measure of the economy's success in creating jobs for those who want to work.

4. An efficiently functioning industrial system is assumed to provide the great majority of new jobs through the expansion of the private enterprise sector. But well over half of the new jobs created during the period 1957–1962 were in the public sector—predominantly in teaching. Job creation in the private sector has now almost entirely ceased except in services; of the 4,300,000 jobs created in this period, only about 200,-000 were provided by private industry through its own efforts. Many authorities anticipate that the application of cybernation to certain service industries, which is only just beginning, will be particularly effective. If this is the case, no significant job creation will take place in the private sector in coming years.

5. Cybernation raises the level of skills of the machine. Secretary of Labor Wirtz has recently stated that the machines being produced today have, on the average, skills equivalent to a high school diploma. If a human being is to compete with such machines, therefore, he must at least possess a high school diploma. The Department of Labor estimates, however, that on the basis of present trends as many as 30% of all students will be high school drop-outs in this decade.

6. A permanently depressed class is developing in the United States. Some 38,000,000 Americans, almost one-fifth of the nation, still live in poverty. The percentage of total income received by the poorest 20% of the population was 4.9% in 1944 and 4.7% in 1963.

Secretary Wirtz recently summarized these trends. "The confluence of surging population and driving technology is splitting the American labor force into tens of millions of 'have's' and millions of 'have-nots.'

In our economy of 69 million jobs, those with wanted skills enjoy opportunity and earning power. But the others face a new and stark problem—exclusion on a permanent basis, both as producers and consumers, from economic life. This division of people threatens to create a human slag heap. We cannot tolerate the development of a separate nation of the poor, the unskilled, the jobless, living within another nation of the well-off, the trained and the employed."

Need for a New Consensus

The stubbornness and novelty of the situation that is conveyed by these statistics is now generally accepted. Ironically, it continues to be assumed that it is possible to devise measures which will reduce unemployment to a minimum and thus preserve the overall viability of the present productive system. Some authorities have gone so far as to suggest that the pace of technological change should be slowed down "so as to allow the industrial productive system time to adapt."

We believe, on the contrary, that the industrial productive system is no longer viable. We assert that the only way to turn technological change to the benefit of the individual and the service of the general welfare is to accept the process and to utilize it rationally and humanely. The new science of political economy will be built on the encouragement and planned expansion of cybernation. The issues raised by cybernation are particularly amenable to intelligent policy-making: cybernation itself provides the resources and tools that are needed to ensure minimum hardship during the transition process.

But major changes must be made in our attitudes and institutions in the foreseeable future. Today Americans are being swept along by three simultaneous revolutions while assuming they have them under control. In the absence of real understanding of any of these phenomena, especially of technology, we may be allowing an efficient and dehumanized community to emerge by default. Gaining control of our future requires the conscious formation of the society we wish to have. Cybernation at last forces us to answer the historic questions: What is man's role when he is not dependent upon his own activities for the material basis of his life? What should be the basis for distributing individual access to national resources? Are there other proper claims on goods and services besides a job?

Because of cybernation, society needs no longer to impose repetitive and meaningless (because unnecessary) toil upon the individual. Society can now set the citizen free to make his own choice of occupation and vocation from a wide range of activities not now fostered by our value system and our accepted modes of "work." But in the absence of such a new consensus about cybernation, the nation cannot begin to take advantage of all that it promises for human betterment.

Proposal for Action

As a first step to a new consensus it is essential to recognize that the traditional link between jobs and incomes is being broken. The economy of abundance can sustain all citizens in comfort and economic security whether or not they engage in what is commonly reckoned as work. Wealth produced by machines rather than by men is still wealth. We urge, therefore, that society, through its appropriate legal and governmental institutions, undertake an unqualified commitment to provide every individual and every family with an adequate income as a matter of right. This undertaking we consider to be essential to the emerging economic, social and political order in this country. We regard it as the only policy by which the quarter of the nation now dispossessed and soon-to-be dispossessed by lack of employment can be brought within the abundant society. The unqualified right to an income would take the place of the patchwork of welfare measures—from unemployment insurance to relief—designed to ensure that no citizen or resident of the United States actually starves.

We do not pretend to visualize all of the consequences of this change in our values. It is clear, however, that the distribution of abundance in a cybernated society must be based on criteria strikingly different from those of an economic system based on scarcity. In retrospect, the establishment of the right to an income will prove to have been only the first step in the reconstruction of the value system of our society brought on by the triple revolution.

The present system encourages activities which can lead to private profit and neglects those activities which can enhance the wealth and the quality of life of our society. Consequently national policy has hitherto been aimed far more at the welfare of the productive process than at the welfare of people. The era of cybernation can reverse this emphasis. With public policy and research concentrated on people rather than processes we believe that many creative activities and interests commonly thought of as non-economic will absorb the time and the commitment of many of those no longer needed to produce goods and services. Society as a whole must encourage new modes of constructive, rewarding and ennobling activity. Principal among these are activities such as teaching and learning that relate people to people rather than people to things. Education has never been primarily conducted for profit in our society; it represents the first and most obvious activity inviting the expansion of the public sector to meet the needs of this period of transition.

We are not able to predict the long-run patterns of human activity and commitment in a nation when fewer and fewer people are involved in production of goods and services, nor are we able to forecast the overall patterns of income distribution that will replace those of the past full employment system. However, these are not speculative and fanciful matters to be contemplated at leisure for a society that may come into existence in three or four generations. The outlines of the future press sharply into the present. The problems of joblessness, inadequate incomes, and frustrated lives confront us now; the American Negro, in his rebellion, asserts the demands—and the rights—of all the disadvantaged. The Negro's is the most insistent voice today, but behind him stand the millions of impoverished who are beginning to understand that cybernation, properly understood and used, is the road out of want and toward a decent life.

The Transition*

We recognize that the drastic alterations in circumstances and in our way of life ushered in by cybernation and the economy of abundance will not be completed overnight. Left to the ordinary forces of the market such change, however, will involve physical and psychological misery and perhaps political chaos. Such misery is already clearly evident among the unemployed, among relief clients into the third generation and more and more among the young and the old for whom society appears to hold no promise of dignified or even stable lives. We must develop programs for this transition designed to give hope to the dispossessed and those cast out by the economic system, and to provide a basis for the rallying of people to bring about those changes in political and social institutions which are essential to the age of technology.

The program here suggested is not intended to be inclusive but rather to indicate its necessary scope. We propose:

---

* This view of the transitional period is not shared by all the signers. Robert Theobald and James Boggs hold that the two major principles of the transitional period will be (1) that machines rather than men will take up new conventional work openings and (2) that the activity of men will be directed to new forms of "work" and "leisure." Therefore, in their opinion the specific proposals outlined in this section are more suitable for meeting the problems of the scarcity-economic system than for advancing through the period of transition into the period of abundance.

1. A massive program to build up our educational system, designed especially with the needs of the chronically undereducated in mind. We estimate that tens of thousands of employment opportunities in such areas as teaching and research and development, particularly for younger people, may be thus created. Federal programs looking to the training of an additional 100,000 teachers annually are needed.

2. Massive public works. The need is to develop and put into effect programs of public works to construct dams, reservoirs, ports, water and air pollution facilities, community recreation facilities. We estimate that for each $1 billion per year spent on public works, 150,000 to 200,000 jobs would be created. $2 billion or more a year should be spent in this way, preferably as matching funds aimed at the relief of economically distressed or dislocated areas.

3. A massive program of low-cost housing, to be built both publicly and privately, and aimed at a rate of 700,000–1,000,000 units a year.

4. Development and financing of rapid transit systems, urban and interurban; and other programs to cope with the spreading problems of the great metropolitan centers.

5. A public power system built on the abundance of coal in distressed areas, designed for low-cost power to heavy industrial and residential sections.

6. Rehabilitation of obsolete military bases for community or educational use.

7. A major revision of our tax structure aimed at redistributing income as well as apportioning the costs of the transition period equitably. To this end an expansion of the use of excess profits tax would be important. Subsidies and tax credit plans are required to ease the human suffering involved in the transition of many industries from manpower to machine-power.

8. The trade unions can play an important and significant role in this period in a number of ways:

a. Use of collective bargaining to negotiate not only for people at work but also for those thrown out of work by technological change.

b. Bargaining for perquisites such as housing, recreational facilities, and similar programs as they have negotiated health and welfare programs.

c. Obtaining a voice in the investment of the unions' huge pension and welfare funds, and insisting on investment policies which have as their major criteria the social use and function of the enterprise in which the investment is made.

d. Organization of the unemployed so that these voiceless people may once more be given a voice in their own economic destinies, and strengthening of the campaigns to organize white-collar and professional workers.

9. The use of the licensing power of government to regulate the speed and direction of cybernation to minimize hardship; and the use of minimum wage power as well as taxing powers to provide the incentives for moving as rapidly as possible toward the goals indicated by this paper.

These suggestions are in no way intended to be complete or definitively formulated. They contemplate expenditures of several billions more each year than are now being spent for socially rewarding enterprises, and a larger role for the government in the economy than it has now or has been given except in times of crisis. In our opinion, this is a time of crisis, the crisis of a triple revolution. Public philosophy for the transition must rest on the conviction that our economic, social and political institutions exist for the use of man and that man does not exist to maintain a particular economic system. This philosophy centers on an understanding that governments are instituted among men for the purpose of making possible life, liberty and the pursuit of happiness and that government should be a creative and positive instrument toward these ends.

Change Must Be Managed

The historic discovery of the post-World War II years is that the economic destiny of the nation can be managed. Since the debate over the Employment Act of 1946 it has been increasingly understood that the Federal Government bears primary responsibility for the economic and social well-being of the country. The essence of management is planning. The democratic requirement is planning by public bodies for the general welfare. Planning by private bodies such as corporations for their own welfare does not automatically result in additions to the general welfare, as the impact of cybernation on jobs has already made clear.

The hardships imposed by sudden changes in technology have been acknowledged by Congress in proposals for dealing with the long and short-run "dislocations," in legislation for depressed and "impacted" areas, retraining of workers replaced by machines, and the like. The measures so far proposed had not been "transitional" in conception. Perhaps for this reason they have had little effect on the situations they were designed to alleviate. But the primary weakness of this legislation is not ineffectiveness but incoherence. In no way can these disconnected measures be seen as a plan for remedying deep ailments, but only, so to speak, as the superficial treatment of surface wounds.

Planning agencies should constitute the network through which pass the stated needs of the people at every level of society, gradually building into a national inventory of human requirements, arrived at by democratic debate of elected representatives.

The primary tasks of the appropriate planning institutions should be:

―――― to collect the data necessary to appraise the effects, social and economic, of cybernation at different rates of innovation;

―――― to recommend ways, by public and private initiative, of encouraging and stimulating cybernation;

―――― to work toward optimal allocations of human and natural resources in meeting the requirements of society;

―――― to develop ways to smooth the transition from a society in which the norm is full employment within an economic system based on scarcity, to one in which the norm will be either nonemployment, in the traditional sense of productive work, or employment on the great variety of socially valuable but "nonproductive" tasks made possible by an economy of abundance; to bring about the conditions in which men and women no longer needed to produce goods and services may find their way to a variety of self-fulfilling and socially useful occupations.

―――― to work out alternatives to defense and related spending that will commend themselves to citizens, entrepreneurs and workers as a more reasonable use of common resources.

―――― to integrate domestic and international planning. The technological revolution has related virtually every major domestic problem to a world problem. The vast inequities between the industrialized and the underdeveloped countries cannot long be sustained.

The aim throughout will be the conscious and rational direction of economic life by planning institutions under democratic control.

In this changed framework the new planning institutions will operate at every level of government—local, regional and federal—and will be organized to elicit democratic participation in all their proceedings. These bodies will be the means for giving direction and content to the growing demand for improvement in all departments of public life. The planning institutions will show the way to turn the growing protest against ugly cities, polluted air and water, an inadequate educational system, disappearing recreational and material resources, low levels of medical care, and the haphazard economic development into an integrated effort to raise the level of general welfare.

We are encouraged by the record of the planning institutions both of the Common Market and of several European nations and believe that this country can benefit from studying their weaknesses and strengths.

A principal result of planning will be to step up investment in the public sector. Greater investment in this area is advocated because it is overdue, because the needs in this sector comprise a substantial part of the content of the general welfare, and because they can be readily afforded by an abundant society. Given the knowledge that we are now in a period of transition it would be deceptive, in our opinion, to present such activities as likely to produce full employment. The efficiencies of cybernation should be as much sought in the public as in the private sector, and a chief focus of planning would be one means of bringing this about. A central assumption of planning institutions would be the central assumption of this statement, that the nation is moving into a society in which production of goods and services is not the only or perhaps the chief means of distributing income.

The Democratization of Change

The revolution in weaponry gives some dim promise that mankind may finally eliminate institutionalized force as the method of settling international conflict and find for it political and moral equivalents leading to a better world. The Negro revolution signals the ultimate admission of this group to the American community on equal social, political, and economic terms. The cybernation revolution proffers an existence qualitatively richer in democratic as well as material values. A social order in which men make the decisions that shape their lives becomes more possible now than ever before; the unshackling of men from the bonds of unfulfilling labor frees them to become citizens, to make themselves and to make their own history.

But these enhanced promises by no means constitute a guarantee. Illuminating and making more possible the "democratic vistas" is one thing; reaching them is quite another, for a vision of democratic life is made real not by technological change but by men consciously moving toward that ideal and creating institutions that will realize and nourish the vision in living form.

Democracy, as we use the term, means a community of men and women who are able to understand, express, and determine their lives as dignified human beings. Democracy can only be rooted in a political and economic order in which wealth is distributed by and for people, and used for the widest social benefit. With the emergence of the era of abundance we have the economic base for a true democracy of participation, in which men no longer need to feel themselves prisoners of social forces or of decisions beyond their control or comprehension.

Programs in Aid of the Poor*

Sar A. Levitan
The George Washington University

[From Poverty and Human Resources Abstracts, *Vol. I, No. 1, Jan.-Feb., 1966. With permission.]*

> *"A decent provision for the poor is the true test of civilization."*
> *Samuel Johnson*

Who Are the Poor?

POVERTY IS A generic term for many types of deprivation. Its roots penetrate deeply and affect many elements of society. Yet to measure even the material dimensions of poverty is an elusive task, for there exists no one universally accepted definition of economic poverty. This is hardly surprising, in view of the large number of factors which determine the amount of money income necessary to provide for the basic needs of any individual or family. Programs supported by government, such as free education, subsidized food, or medical care, reduce the amount of money required to support a family. Differentials in the cost of living between urban and rural areas and among regions raise the income requirements of some people and lower them for others. And, finally, the concept of basic (or minimum) needs does not remain constant as our society becomes more affluent generally. It is no wonder, then, that experts differ as to the amount of cash income necessary for a family to reach a minimum acceptable level of economic welfare.

*This paper is part of a W. E. Upjohn Institute for Employment Research study, *The Great Society's Poor Law: A New Approach to Poverty,* devoted to an evaluation of the Economic Opportunity Act and financed by a grant from The Ford Foundation.

The American Welfare System

Over the past thirty years, the United States has developed an intricate, though far from comprehensive, welfare system. The underlying assumption of this system is that special programs are needed to take care of the diverse needs of the poor. It has been suggested that in practice these programs are more a series of makeshift measures than tailormade programs, and that millions of needy receive little or no aid. And the assistance offered in most cases is inadequate to raise the beneficiaries above the poverty level.

The welfare system consists of three types of programs:

1. Programs which offer cash assistance mainly to those outside the labor force. These programs include Old Age, Survivors, and Disability Insurance; public assistance programs under the Social Security Act; pensions for needy veterans; and general assistance for needy persons not covered by the Social Security Act and financed exclusively by states and localities.
2. Programs to aid those in the work force. These programs include training to equip the poor with skills that are saleable in the labor market, aid to depressed areas, unemployment insurance, minimum wage protection, job creation, and work relief.
3. Programs that provide services and goods to the poor on the basis of need regardless of labor force status. Included in this group of programs are child care, subsidized housing, medical services and drugs, and several forms of food distribution.

The distinction between programs aimed for the working poor and for those outside the labor force is useful and in accordance with the prevailing values of our society. This distinction is reflected in existing programs and is likely to be a controlling factor in developing further programs in aid of the poor.

It is assumed that special tailormade programs are needed to bolster the level of living of the working poor. This might be accomplished best by providing them with services and goods which are not likely to diminish the incentive to work, and by equipping them for more productive jobs whenever feasible. For those outside the labor force, burdened with impediments which preclude gainful employment, society's help to the poor must consist of providing a combination of services and income; in some cases, however, as conditions of individuals and family responsibilities change, training may also be appropriate.

The inherent difficulties of dividing the poor according to their labor force status are obvious. Official definitions of labor force are of only limited help. Many of the poor move in and out of the labor force, depending upon overall economic conditions and personal circumstances. It is also difficult to determine a priori those individuals who should be provided basic income through work (wages), and those who should be provided support through public assistance. For example, should a female head of a family with minor dependents and no regular income be required to work for support, or should the state assume the obligation of making direct contributions for her family's sustenance? Experts disagree as to whether society would be better served by providing work for the mother (assuming jobs are available), or by providing income which would permit the mother to devote full time to rearing her children. Some who favor the latter approach suggest that a redefinition of remunerative work may be necessary in order to include, for example, child rearing.

Observers would also disagree concerning the usefulness of providing the poor with income maintenance in addition to services and goods. Some would argue that the most appropriate way of assisting the poor is to supply them with cash, under the assumption that the family unit itself is the best judge in allocating the minimum available resources. Others maintain that the government can provide the services more efficiently by utilizing economies of large-scale enterprise, and that in any event existing institutions are often inadequate to supply the needs of the poor. It has been argued, for example, that adequate housing facilities for the poor will not be provided without direct government action, particularly where racial discrimination is involved. A final argument against income maintenance is that persons of low educational and economic attainment are only too frequently poor managers of even the limited resources available to them.

The inclusion of some of the specific programs within each of the three categories is also subject to controversy. For example, the inclusion of Old Age, Survivors, and Disability Insurance as part of the welfare system may be questioned since the eligibility test for OASDI is not based on personal need. OASDI is paid to the rich and poor alike, and about half the funds distributed under this program go to those who are above the poverty threshold. . . .

Alternative Income Support Programs

Public assistance is currently the prime vehicle for transmitting aid to the poor. The shortcomings of this program have already been reviewed. The income support provided is inadequate to meet basic needs of recipients, and even this support tends to discourage initiative because benefits are based on a stringent means test. Except for minor exemptions, earnings by relief recipients are normally deducted from benefits they receive, thus creating an incentive for the beneficiaries to withdraw from the labor force. Moreover, the majority of needy persons do not receive any assistance, and nearly four of every five persons do not receive public assistance. The federal government shares the cost of public assistance to selected groups—aged, blind, permanently disabled, and families with dependent children. States and local governments provide some assistance to needy persons outside these categories. But in many areas the destitute depend on private charity or have no support at all.

An additional problem of public assistance programs is that they have limited applicability to the working poor. Related programs intended to aid workers in the labor force, employed as well as unemployed, tend to bypass most of the poor, yet minimum wage legislation has raised the level of income of many working poor. The result of these inadequacies, as noted earlier, is that two million family heads (in 1963) having full-time, year-round jobs received earnings insufficient to raise them above the poverty threshold.

Family Allowances

While the acceptance of the principle of equal pay for equal work is desirable as a means of eliminating discrimination based on color or sex, it ignores the needs of families with children and tends to deprive children of large families of basic needs. The underlying justification for family allowances is that the well-being of children should be the concern of society as a whole. Family allowances also recognize that the wage system alone is an inadequate basis for distribution of income.

Providing minimum family needs under the wage system is an age-old problem which has occupied policymakers since the early days of the industrial revolution. It was tried first on a modest basis in England 170 years ago and has spread widely during recent decades. It is now practiced, under one form or another, by most industrial countries. Family allowances are given in all European countries and in about a third of the nations outside Europe. In several countries, these allowances account for a significant share of the total income received by families whose heads are low-wage earners and by families without breadwinners.

The family allowance programs for minimum needs in France and Canada illustrate two diverse types of systems. In France it is estimated that for a family of five, including three children, family allowances amount to about a quarter of total average wages paid in manufacturing; for a family with five children the family allowances would add about two-thirds to the average wages earned in manufacturing. Family allowances in France are financed by employers and amount to 13.5 percent of total payrolls. In Canada, by contrast, family allowances are paid by the government from the general revenue. The monthly allowance amounts to $6 (Canadian) for each child under 10 years of age and $8 for each child between the age of 10 and 16. Thus, the Canadian family allowances supply a small proportion of total family income.

Our wage system is not adapted to take account of the diverse needs of workers: except for some adjustments in income taxes, for example, the take-home pay from two identical jobs is the same for a bachelor as for the head of a family with dependents. Despite the wide acceptance of the family allowance principle in other countries, the idea has never received active consideration in the United States— though it has been advanced on numerous occasions.[1] An exception has been made under AFDC for most needy children. Expenditures under this program account for 0.3 percent of national income. A number of countries spend 10 times this percentage or more of their national income for family allowances. France, for example, allocates about 5.0 percent of national income to family allowances. And the trend in these countries has been to raise the proportion of national income devoted to family allowances.

Negative Income Tax

With the current commitment to wage war on poverty, various proposals have been advanced to supply additional income for the poor. The ultimate goal of these proposals is to raise the income of the poor and to eliminate poverty. The Social Security Administration has estimated that the addition of $11.5 billion would permit the 34.6 million persons designated as poor in 1963 to escape poverty.

The most widely discussed proposal is utilization of the income tax machinery as a vehicle to supply income to the poor. The law, providing now only for the collection of taxes, might be extended to include grants based on family or individual needs. Professor Robert J. Lampman of Wisconsin University has prepared the most careful and detailed cost estimates of different types of negative income tax proposals. The cost estimates presented in this section are based on Lampman's calculations.[2]

In its simplest form, a negative income tax would allow non-taxable individuals or families to claim the unused portion of their current exemptions. Such a plan would tend to spread the benefits thinly among most of the poor, but would still cost about $2 billion. If it were limited to families with children, the cost would be reduced by about one-half. A family of four with zero income would be entitled to a "rebate" of $420. An "average" AFDC family—a mother with three children—would receive somewhat more than $200 in addition to the nearly $1,500 of AFDC benefits, assuming that the states will continue current levels of assistance.

At the other extreme, negative income tax proposals would overhaul the present tax system to pay the poor enough income to close the poverty income gap which, as stated, amounted to $11.5 billion in 1963. Poverty would thus be eliminated. However, such an income maintenance level would rob any pecuniary incentives for millions of people to work since the guaranteed income would be equal to or in excess of their earned wages. A workable plan would therefore permit low-wage earners to keep at least a portion of their earned income in order to provide them an incentive to continue working. This would, of course, increase the cost of the income maintenance program by a larger amount than the $11.5 billion poverty income gap. Lampman estimates the cost of such a program would be double the present poverty income gap, or about $23 billion. This appears to be a conservative estimate.

A compromise between the above two plans would guarantee income to cover 50 percent of the poverty income gap. Thus a family of four would receive a guaranteed annual income of $1,565, based on the Social Security Administration estimates of basic needs. The cost of such a plan would be $8 billion. But this amount includes about $3 billion which is now currently paid to public assistance recipients. The net cost would therefore be about $5 billion. If the plan were limited to families with children, the cost would amount to $4.8 billion less the $1.3 billion now paid to public assistance recipients. As in the previous proposal, this scheme would also have to provide for continued incentive to work and allow low-income earners to keep all or part of their earnings. The cost would therefore be raised appreciably above the estimated $5 billion.

The three variations of negative income tax schemes suggest the cost magnitude of any negative income tax plan. The costs of the three proposals listed above range from an annual cost of $2 billion per year to $23 billion or higher. Different variations of these plans would involve a cost anywhere between these two extremes. Huge as these sums might appear, an addition of $5 to $23 billion to the income of the poor—ignoring the first scheme which would distribute the limited funds broadly—might be an attainable goal, given our society's present commitment to combat poverty. However, providing the poor with added income is only one aspect of combating poverty. The poor also need better schools, housing, training, and diverse services to improve their ability to compete for jobs in the labor market. Any adequate public welfare system, whose goal is to reduce poverty, must therefore aim at a judicious distribution of resources, both for raising the income level of the poor and for providing them with needed services.

Competing Goals

The goal of eliminating poverty is only one of many aspirations of our society which involve substantial financial resources. Alfred C. Neal, President of the Committee for Economic Development, suggested that the efficient pursuit of our national goals is "the Number One economic challenge" for the immediate and foreseeable future:

> Our Number One problem is not growth as such. Nor is it domestic poverty or the economic development of the emerging countries. It is not even the suffocating problems of the metropolitan cities—air and water pollution, traffic jams, urban sprawl, dropouts, crime and delinquency, important as each of these may be. Nor is our principal economic problem supremacy in space, or even better education.[3]

The National Planning Association has recently attempted to calculate the cost of realizing the major goals of our society. Along with the 15 major goals—including education, health, urban development, social welfare, and defense—outlined by President Eisenhower's Commission on National Goals,[4] the National Planning Association added space exploration as a 16th major program which has developed during the 1960's. Assuming an annual growth in GNP of 4 percent, the NPA estimated that the cost of achieving the major goals of society by 1975 would exceed the projected GNP for that year by $150 billion, or 15 percent. Leonard A. Lecht, director of the NPA study, concluded:

> We could well afford the cost of any single goal at levels reflecting current aspirations, and we could probably afford the cost for any group of goals over the next decade. We could rebuild our cities, or abolish poverty, or replace all the obsolete plant and equipment in private industry, or we could begin to develop the hardware to get us to Mars and back before the year 2000. We could make some progress on all the goals, perhaps substantial progress on many, but we cannot accomplish all our aspirations at the same time.[5]

It is not likely that society will decide in the foreseeable future to allocate the resources needed to win total victory over poverty, nor would excessive reliance upon transfer payments appear to constitute sound public policy. While allocation of additional income for the poor is an essential element in the war on poverty, simply raising income to fill even their minimum requirements would result in economic dislocations by eroding incentives to work. It may also be preferable in many cases to stress income in kind rather than in cash. This might apply to alcoholics and others afflicted with diverse maladjustments.

It is apparent that the waging of a successful war on poverty is a complex and costly undertaking. Even the 89th Congress, which is generally acknowledged as being the most welfare-conscious Congress in more than a generation, has not shown any inclination to commit the necessary resources to eliminate poverty in the immediate years ahead. As shown earlier, it has been particularly parsimonious in allocating additional income to the poor. Only about 2 percent ($150 million) of the multibillion-dollar 1965 amendments to the Social Security Act were allocated to raising federal contributions to public assistance. Nor has the Administration, which is committed to a total war on poverty, urged Congress to adopt programs which would raise the income level of the poor in the immediate years ahead. Whatever may be the merits of the varied income maintenance programs discussed above, there does not appear to be any wide consensus supporting their adoption. Although such a plan might receive serious consideration at some indeterminate future, to improve the lot of the poor in the short run we must realistically turn to more modest programs.

Short-Run Priorities

> If to do were as easy as to know what were good to do, chapels had been churches, and poor men's cottages princes' palaces.
>
> William Shakespeare

> The needy shall not always be forgotten; the expectation of the poor shall not perish forever.
>
> Psalms 1:18

The programs in aid of the poor reviewed in this summary carry an annual price tag of about $13 to $15 billion. The exact cost of these programs cannot be determined since many of the programs in aid of the poor are closely interwoven with general government activity; but rough estimates can be made about the portion which is allocated to the poor on the basis of need. Other programs not discussed in this summary—aid to Indians, workmen's compensation, farm aid measures and business loans as they pertain to the poor, and other programs—would add another billion to the total cost. Private philanthropic efforts on behalf of the poor raise the total funds allocated in aid of the poor by about another billion dollars. The total cost of programs is of little operational significance, since there exist no adequate criteria to suggest what percentage of GNP, or even of governmental expenditures, should be allocated to the poor. The $11.5 billion poverty gap, noted earlier, is a poor measure, at best, since it ignores the cost of additional services and goods that should be made available to the poor.

The above rough estimate of resources allocated to the poor on the basis of need does, however, help to lend perspective to the recently much-heralded commitment for a war on poverty embodied in the Economic Opportunity Act of 1964. Assuming that all the funds appropriated under this legislation actually reach the poor—a questionable assumption—the Economic Opportunity Act increased the antipoverty funds by about 5 percent during its first year of activity; this amount was doubled during the second year.

It would be misleading, however, to measure the war on poverty solely in terms of direct expenditures. Minimum wage legislation, to which no price tag can be attached, may be a more significant tool in the war on poverty than the expenditures of billions under other programs, but its negative effect in causing disemployment cannot be measured. Some programs that may bring the greatest returns in the war on poverty may require little or practically no financial resources. Chief among these programs is an educational campaign to reduce, and possibly obliterate, discrimination practiced against minorities, particularly Negroes. The Voting Rights Act of 1965 may turn out to be a more important tool to secure equal rights for Negroes and thus to combat discrimination and poverty than other legislation involving huge expenditures. Michael S. March, one of the Administration's early architects of the current poverty program, stated:

> Poverty has a formidable ally in our own ignorance of what we must do to root out poverty. When one stands "eyeball to eyeball" with poverty, preparing for mortal struggle, he will admit, if he is candid, that he does not know exactly what is best to do or how to do it.
>
> There is a surprising dearth of hard knowledge about the root causes and dynamics of poverty . . . Our prescriptions for the cure of poverty are unsure and lacking in consensus.[6]

Yet the significant gaps in our understanding of the causes of poverty and the best means for eradicating its roots are no valid reason, as March argues, for inaction. We need not await returns from all the precincts to continue a vigorous campaign to reduce poverty. Lacking comprehensive knowledge for eliminating the roots of poverty, we can focus on specific programs which would aid selected groups among the poor. This suggested emphasis upon helping specific groups is not intended to supplant the generalized societal goal of eliminating all poverty. A free and affluent society should aim at nothing less. But we should realize this is an ultimate goal and only one of numerous and pressing demands upon society's attentions and resources. For the time being, more modest and specialized strategems should be selected with a view to achieving the ultimate objective. Grand designs for the good society have been avoided, not only because there is little evidence that society is ready to allocate adequate resources to a speedy reduction of poverty and because of the many pressing and competing goals faced by society, but also because the road leading to the millenium of a poorless society is not fully charted.

Even assuming that consensus can be reached on the amount of additional resources that need to be allocated for the war on poverty, it is not at all clear how these resources should be distributed. What share of any additional dollar should be allocated to raising the cash income of the poor as compared with improving the quality and quantity of services in kind? The poor are not a homogenous mass. Additional income will provide for the basic needs of some; many others require services that will enable them to enter the mainstream of our society. Until these special services and income in kind are adequate, it is premature to hope to achieve a rational guaranteed level of acceptable minimum income—whether this is to be achieved through negative income tax or other similar schemes.

Major steps have been taken during the past year in the difficult and long journey whose goal is a poorless society. Whether all the programs will advance the journey is not yet known. The new anti-poverty and related programs have strained the limited technical resources in the areas of social services and training. However, new programs and techniques developed by the Office of Economic Opportunity may provide for more efficient utilization of existing resources. For example, Head Start utilized unused school resources during the summer of 1965. Similarly, various projects stressing participation by the poor may expand services with hitherto unutilized resources.

Judicious allocation of resources would suggest, however, the need of appraising the newly sponsored programs before additional funds are made available to OEO. The expected expansion in demand

of medical care provided for in the 1965 legislation will more than ex-
haust available medical facilities and services. Any major attempt further to expand medical services to the poor during the next few years
would, therefore, mean the redistribution of existing resources rather
than an expansion of aggregate services.

A realistic program aimed at reducing poverty should therefore establish priorities and determine appropriate resources to be
allocated. Leaving aside rhetoric about the elimination of poverty, it
is assumed here that if society continues to increase resources allocated
for alleviating poverty, say, at the cumulative rate of about 6 to 7 percent per year—about half again as much as the anticipated growth of
GNP—this would increase the anti-poverty kitty by about $4 billion
per year by the end of this decade. Given this modest, though far
from negligible, short-term goal, the immediate question is which
existing or new programs should claim priority for the additional
resources.

Looking to the future, the most promising means of reducing
poverty is to help the poor control the size of their families. This can be
achieved at negligible cost to the public. Primary emphasis should be
placed on helping the impoverished to plan parenthood and thus
reduce the number of unwanted children. Measured in terms of additional expenditures, the largest amount of expanded assistance would
go in aid of poor children, and to help create jobs for their parents.

It makes little sense to wage war on poverty without providing
an adequate diet and other basic needs for millions of children who
are being reared with an insufficient income. To repeat the social
worker's slogan: "Services do not fill an empty stomach." Most observers would, however, agree that it would be preferable to provide
income to impoverished families through the creation of jobs rather
than through providing cash assistance. This would suggest the desirability of creating publicly subsidized jobs for parents of poor children,
even though the creation of such employment may involve greater
direct public outlays than mere cash assistance. Finally, in the area
of providing goods to the poor, housing should claim top priority, not
only because attainment of adequate shelter is outside the reach of
most poor families, but because outlays for subsidized housing would
also help absorb general economic slack.

Planned Parenthood

> The problem, everyone talks of it, is that of birth control. . .
> It is an extremely grave problem. It touches on the main-
> springs of human life.
>
> Pope Paul VI

The first priority in the war on poverty should be given to dissemination of education about methods of birth control; and consistent with the religious beliefs, assistance should be made available to those who cannot afford private medical aid to plan parenthood. No major religious group in the United States is opposed to regulation of family size, though differences do exist on the methods that may be used to achieve this goal and on the appropriate role of the state in this area. But without entering into the theological aspects of the birth control controversy, the views of Richard Cardinal Cushing are pertinent for the purposes of this discussion. He recognized the necessity for the state to follow, on occasion, a path which may differ from the views of a religious group, when he stated:

> Catholics do not need the support of civil law to be faithful to their religious convictions, and they do not seek to impose by law their moral views on other members of society.[7]

However, the official Catholic position on birth control remains unchanged. In October 1965, Pope Paul VI addressed the United Nations urging the representatives of the nations:

> You must strive to multiply bread so that it suffices for the tables of mankind, and not rather favor an artificial control of birth, which would be irrational, in order to diminish the number of guests at the banquet of life.[8]

Broad support exists for dissemination of birth control information. In reply to a recent Gallup Poll question: "Do you favor or oppose the distribution of birth control information?" no less than 80 percent of Protestants, 60 percent of Catholics, and 84 percent of other religious groups answered in the affirmative.

With regard to the role of birth control in combating poverty, former President Eisenhower expressed the prevailing general attitude about federal support of birth control when he wrote:

> I realize that in important segments of our people and of other nations this question is regarded as a moral one and therefore scarcely a fit subject for Federal legislation. With their feelings I can and do sympathize. But I cannot help believe that the prevention of human degradation and starvation is likewise a moral—as well as a material—obligation resting upon every enlightened government. If we now ignore the plight of those unborn generations which, because of our unreadiness to take corrective action in controlling population growth, will be denied any expectations beyond abject poverty and suffering, then history will rightly condemn us.[9]

One of the most tragic aspects of poverty is that many of the children born to poor families are unwanted. The National Academy of Sciences concluded that the poor have more children than affluent families because the poor "do not have the information or the resources to plan their families effectively according to their own desires.[10] The same study found that 17 percent of white couples and 31 percent of nonwhite couples had unwanted children in 1960. But among couples with the least education, and thus likely to be also poor, the comparative percentages were 32 percent for white couples and 43 percent for nonwhite couples.

Medical science has developed effective birth control methods that are within the means of poor families. Given the widespread desire on the part of poor parents to regulate the size of their families, birth control could be used as an effective tool to reduce future poverty. It is important that information about these methods and the necessary devices be made available to the general public without further delay because children born during the "baby boom" years are marrying and procreating. In 1960 there were 4.7 million women aged 18 to 21. Five years later their number increased to 6 million, and by 1968 it is expected that this figure will increase by another million.

With minor exceptions, federal agencies have thus far avoided the funding of birth control programs. Even the Office of Economic Opportunity has shunned this controversial area. Only about 1 percent of the first 1,000 OEO-backed community action programs carried specific budgets for birth control programs.

It may be expected that the federal government will offer more positive support of birth control in the future. Katherine B. Oettinger, Chief, Children's Bureau, Department of Health, Education, and Welfare, declared recently that birth control services should be available to all as a matter of "right:"

> . . . For it is the families of the poor who too long have suffered spiritual dejection and demoralization after bearing successive babies without hope of these children being able to achieve their full potential or breaking the cycle of poverty.[11]

Potentially more effective support of birth control programs came from President Johnson when he stated on June 25, 1965: "Let us act on the fact that less than $5 invested in population control is worth $100 invested in economic growth." The President did not specify the basis on which he made his estimates, but ample evidence exists to indicate the savings that accrue to the public as a result of family-planning services. For example, a birth control program initiated in Mecklenburg County, North Carolina, in 1960 was estimated to have saved $250,000 in AFDC benefits within three years.[12] Expenses involved in operating the program amounted to one-twentieth of the savings. Many other examples could be cited. The arithmetic is simple. Even considering the low cost of AFDC support, averaging just about a dollar a day, the few dollars expended per case on birth control save the government the support of an AFDC child for years to come, not to mention that it also reduces poverty.

Aiding Impoverished Children

> The child was diseased at birth, stricken with hereditary ill that only the most vital men are able to shake off. I mean poverty—the most deadly and prevalent of all diseases.
>
> Eugene O'Neill

If the current battle cry, "break the chains of poverty," is not to become a hollow slogan, society must allocate additional resources to prevent the rearing of children in abject poverty and deprivation. The child from an impoverished home is likely to become a school dropout, an unemployable person, and a perpetual relief recipient when he grows into adulthood. Therefore, the next priority for any increased allocation of funds should go to helping poor children.

Though in need of radical overhauling, the AFDC program provides a suitable vehicle for this purpose. The nearly one million families, with about three million children, who are currently recipients of AFDC are among the neediest and most impoverished families in the United States; therefore, they deserve the most immediate attention. The average income paid by the government to AFDC recipients is about $1.00 a day. Since the minimum cost of food for a balanced diet is 70 cents per person per day and accounts for only a third of the basic needs, it is quite apparent that AFDC children exist on an inadequate diet, even if total food costs of young children are somewhat lower than the 70-cent average.

Before AFDC can be adopted as the main instrument for a decent relief system and as a tool for rehabilitation, the program will have to be overhauled. Not only will the level of allowances paid to recipients have to be increased, but the method of distribution will also have to be changed. The Veterans Administration pension system, described earlier, should be adopted as a model, since the VA experience has shown that the government can offer assistance to needy persons without subjecting them to harassment or degradation. And, unlike the AFDC program, the Veterans Administration does not discourage initiative of recipients.

In most states, earnings received by members of AFDC families are deducted from the total allowances the family is entitled to receive, allowing only minimal exemptions. The Economic Opportunity Act provides that the first $85 and half of additional monthly income earned under the provisions of the Act (except work experience) are not to be counted as income for purposes of determining basic needs under public assistance programs. The 1965 amendments to the Social Security Act are less generous and permit states to disregard for purposes of benefit payments the monthly earnings of dependent children, not exceeding $50 per child or $150 per family. But the choice is left to each state; and if past experience is any indication of future action, most states are not likely to permit this exemption. In all but a few states the allowable exemption exceeds the total payments made by the state per child. AFDC as now operative in most states is not aimed at rehabilitating recipients or encouraging initiative and promoting self-respect. The resources of the system are concentrated on providing a substandard income, thereby leaving most recipients in abject poverty.

An effective AFDC program which does more than pay lip service to the rehabilitation of clients must also raise payments made to recipients. Even assuming that $600 per individual is the minimum income needed—and for a family of four this is 23 percent below the Social Security poverty threshold level of income—it would be necessary to increase current benefits paid to AFDC recipients by about two-thirds in order to reach this income level. This suggested figure takes account of free food distribution available to many AFDC recipients. Such a boost in the level of payments would also increase the number of eligible recipients. The few states which meet or approach the level of benefits suggested above would not have to raise their AFDC outlays.

To meet the proposed standards, AFDC expenditures would have to be raised by about a billion dollars. And expansion of coverage would possibly double the cost, though an effective birth control program would tend to reduce the number of children in impoverished households and decrease future costs. The 1965 Social Security amendments raise the maximum amount of federal contributions to AFDC recipients by only $15 a year, and state action to match these benefits is required before the increased federal grants can be paid to recipients. The miniscule increase in payments made possible by the 1965 federal action indicates the resistance that exists in Congress and elsewhere to higher AFDC payments. State and local resistance may be even more difficult to overcome. The federal share of contributions to AFDC will therefore have to be increased appreciably if an effective program is to materialize.

It makes little sense to spend $6,000 a year, and possibly more, to rehabilitate a Job Corps trainee while at the same time depriving children in impoverished homes of basic needs and thus assuring a supply of future Job Corps candidates. This is not to disparage the potential accomplishments of the Job Corps or other programs initiated under the Economic Opportunity Act, but it does suggest the serious gaps that now exist in the anti-poverty program.

Job Creation and Work Relief

> Anticipate charity by preventing poverty; assist the reduced fellowman . . . so that he may earn an honest livelihood, and not be forced to the dreadful alternative of holding out his hand for charity. This is the highest step and the summit of charity's golden ladder.
>
> Moses Ben Maimon

Creation of jobs for which the poorly educated and unskilled would qualify is the third on our list of priorities. After almost complete neglect of work relief programs during the past two decades, the Economic Opportunity Act provided for job creation under its work-experience and youth employment programs. The continued high level of unemployment among the unskilled, particularly among Negroes, indicates the need for generating government-supported jobs for those who cannot qualify for gainful employment in private industry. This does not mean that the government should create make-work jobs.

Despite the gloomy forebodings of the prophets of cybernation, much of society's needed work is not being done; and the need for this work is going to increase rather than disappear. Many of these jobs can be performed by relatively unskilled and unemployed workers. And the work can be found in rural areas and urban centers. Stream clearance, reforestation, and park maintenance are some of the simple traditional work relief jobs. Many new ones can be added, for example: school aides, health aides, simple maintenance jobs in public buildings, and renovation of slum areas. Medicare, when it becomes effective, will not only expand the demand for services of physicians and technicians, but also require the addition of many unskilled workers in hospitals and nursing homes.

The need for creating jobs for unskilled workers may become more pressing in the years ahead. Proposed congressional action boosting the statutory minimum wage by 75 percent within a period of nine years, if it materializes in 1966, is likely to cause additional disemployment of unskilled workers. If no new jobs are created for these workers, relief will be the only method of providing income maintenance.

A major barrier to the creation of new public jobs for the unemployed is the determination of appropriate wage rates. Unions normally oppose the allocation of work, even when unskilled jobs are involved, at rates which undermine existing prevailing standards. Creation of these jobs is bound to be costly. A million dollars will buy no more than about 300 jobs, including some part-time jobs, paying modest wages and including cost of overhead and equipment. A program which will create 300,000 jobs, not an overambitious goal, is thus going to cost about one billion dollars annually.

Housing

> They turn the needy out of way; the poor of the earth hide themselves together . . . and embrace the rock for want of a shelter.
>
> Job 24:4-8

Housing for impoverished families is given high priority because it is evident that adequate shelter cannot be provided by private enterprise at a profit, considering the rent that they can pay. It thus meets the generally accepted maxim of Lincoln that "the legitimate object of government is to do for the people what needs to be done, but which they cannot by individual effort, do at all, or do so well, for themselves." The alternative to government subsidization of housing for the poor is slums and dilapidated housing which, in turn, breed poverty. Adequate housing is therefore a major instrument in "breaking the chains of poverty."

A continuing vigorous program of public subsidized housing would also act as an overall economic stimulation which would help decrease employment and expand job opportunities. Such a program is therefore a multipurpose tool in fighting poverty.

The great shortage of adequate housing available to the poor cannot be surmounted in the short run. It would require, even under the most conservative estimates, an investment in excess of $30 billion to eliminate substandard housing. The principle of housing subsidies has already been accepted, as witnessed by congressional action in 1965. The question now is how rapidly the program is to be implemented. A constraining factor should be the extent to which underutilized resources, both human and physical, are available for the purpose of building housing. This is not to suggest that construction of housing for the poor is inherently of low priority compared with the supply of other consumer goods. Most consumer goods are produced in the free market and are not subject to government regulation. A vigorous implementation of public housing during a period of shortages would intensity inflationary pressures, particularly in the field of housing construction where boosts in wage costs have tended to exceed increases in productivity. Since construction of subsidized housing is subject to government control, the degree of priority assigned to this program is diminished if it is to be undertaken at the risk of intensifying inflationary pressures.

Under the conditions that prevailed in the country between 1958 and 1964, expansion of housing for the poor could have been vigorous and rapid. With developing labor shortages and increased commitments to expand defense activities, subsidized housing expansion must be more moderate and selective. However, the level of unemployment and the amount of unutilized plant resources still remain high in many areas where additional construction activity could absorb some of the existing economic slack.

Since the supply of adequate housing for the poor will remain necessarily far short of need, priority in allocating the limited supply should be given to the working poor. This judgment is not based necessarily on the assumption that the working poor are more deserving. It is advanced because pragmatic considerations favor the working poor for the allocation of subsidized housing. Public housing has been criticized on the basis that it subsidizes the indolent, but this argument could be minimized if the bulk of subsidized housing were allocated to the working poor. Even opponents of the welfare state find it difficult to argue against helping the "deserving" poor.

Is Business As Usual Feasible?

> If there be among you a poor man . . . thou shalt not harden thine heart, nor shut thine hand from thy poor brother . . . and shall surely lend him sufficient for his need, in that which he wanteth.
>
> Deuteronomy 15:7-8

The cumulative addition of a billion dollars a year in aid of the poor during the next four years would alleviate poverty for only some of the poor. Large segments of the poor would hardly benefit by the programs outlined above. Included in these groups are more than five million persons aged 65 and over and most of the four million families headed by gainfully employed, unemployed, or underemployed workers. The aged group has been aided by the passage of Medicare and the boost in Social Security benefits, but much more will have to be done to raise the income of the aged poor above the poverty threshold. To improve the lot of the poor in the work force, reliance is placed on the achievement of full employment, job creation, and protective wage legislation. Though the achievement of full employment is a *sine qua non* in the war on poverty, it is not discussed in this paper because this goal is essential to the achievement of many of society's aspirations. Sustained full employment will not only absorb many of the unemployed poor in the work force, but will also raise their level of income.

It would take the absorption of more than three million poor into the work force to achieve the same proportion of gainfully employed among the poor as among the nonpoor. Given the educational, demographic, and other impediments of the poor, such conditions cannot be achieved even with full employment. It is questionable whether sustained full employment can be maintained in the next few years—assuming that it will be achieved before the end of this decade.

In brief, the anticipated allocation of an additional one billion dollars a year in aid of the poor assumes that society will stop short of assigning top priority to the war on poverty and that the goal of accelerating the reduction of poverty will remain one of several societal aspirations, competing for available limited resources. It represents only a modest effort in combating poverty and will result in little redistribution of income. It is not at all clear that such a situation will remain tenable in the years ahead in face of the widespread Negro unrest and the commitment of the Great Society to eliminate poverty. Half of the Negro population lives in poverty, compared with one of every seven whites. It is likely that the civil rights movement is going to stress even more the attainment of broader economic opportunities for the Negro population. And recent incidents indicate that some sectors of the Negro population are not inclined to rely exclusively upon orderly procedures to achieve a greater measure of economic and political equality. Society may find it therefore necessary to allocate far greater resources in aid of the poor than was anticipated in this paper.

References

1. Paul H. Douglas, in *Wages and the Family* (Chicago: University of Chicago Press, 1925), advocated a family allowance system financed by employers. The late Senator Richard L. Neuburger of Oregon, a more recent advocate, proposed a Senate study of the feasibility of

family allowances. His resolution (S.Res. 109, 84th Cong., 2nd sess.) was cosponsored by seven other Senators, including Paul H. Douglas, Hubert H. Humphrey, and John F. Kennedy; but never received a hearing.

2. "Approaches to the Reduction of Poverty," *Papers and Proceedings of The Seventy-seventh Annual Meeting of the American Economic Association*, May 1965, pp. 521-529; "Income Distribution and Poverty," in Margaret S. Gordon, ed., *Poverty in America* (San Francisco: Chandler Publishing Co., 1965), pp. 102-114; and others which are now in press.

3. "Toward the Efficient Pursuit of Happiness," address before the National Association of Business Economists, Chicago, Illinois, October 1, 1965 (scheduled for publication in *Business Economics*, Fall 1965).

4. President's Commission on National Goals, *Goals for Americans* (Englewood Cliffs, New Jersey: Prentice-Hall, 1960).

5. National Planning Association, *The Dollar Cost of Our National Goals* (Washington: The Association, 1965), p. 6.

6. "Poverty: How Much Will the War Cost?" *The Social Service Review*, June 1965, pp. 154-155.

7. U. S. Congress, Senate, Committee on Government Operations, Subcommittee on Foreign Aid Expenditures, Hearings, June 22, 1965, 89th Cong., 1st sess., on S. *1676 and Related Bills* (Washington: U.S. Government Printing Office).

8. "Consensus Grows on Birth Control," *Business Week*, October 9, 1965, p. 36.

9. Hearings on S. *1676 and Related Bills, op. cit.*

10. National Academy of Sciences, *The Growth of U.S. Population* (Washington: The Academy, 1965), p. 10.

11. Katherine B. Oettinger, "This Most Profound Challenge," *Congressional Record* (daily edition), September 24, 1965, p. 24201.

12. Jack Shepherd, "Birth Control and the Poor: A Solution," *Look*, April 7, 1964, p. 67.

Perspectives on Recent Welfare Legislation, Fore and Aft

Samuel Mencher

University of Pittsburgh Graduate School of Social Work

[Reprinted with permission of the National Association of Social Workers from Social Work, *Vol. 8, No. 5, (July 1963), pp. 59–64.]*

THIS IS A PERIOD of stock-taking for the field of public welfare. It is a time to re-examine the direction of welfare policy. The New Frontier symbolizes a new era for welfare, as it does for other areas of public policy. To what extent has there been a genuine reassessment of welfare programs? To what extent do the public welfare policies of the Kennedy administration only represent a cashing-in of old debts incurred during former eras of welfare innovation? Are the amendments of 1962 only catching up with the accounts left over from the New Deal of the 1930's, or are they projecting welfare policy for the decades ahead?

The history of public welfare, except in time of crucial emergencies such as in the thirties has more often been patchwork stitched onto outworn garments than a thoroughgoing policy of reform relevant to current needs and future requirements. There seems to be a compulsion among public welfare reformers and administrators to concentrate on the major inequities of previous decades rather than to plan policies for the future. This is not to deny the pressing need for such changes, but these may hardly be considered the symptoms of the "forward look" in welfare policy. Frequently, when these reforms do occur they may even be ill-suited to present conditions. For example, the great crusade against child labor has now been reflected in an abnormal number of school dropouts and the expansion of programs extending opportunities to youth. Early retirement of the aged, considered progressive in the thirties, has now exacerbated the psychological and physical difficulties of increasing longevity.

Underlying Philosophy

What has been the total contribution of the 1962 Public Welfare Amendments to the American welfare scene? A great part of these measures and their underlying philosophy are reforms of the original social security legislation or of more recent changes in the original act.

1. *Increased federal participation in present welfare programs—*increased grants to assistance programs of the states, for child welfare, and for the administration of public assistance.

2. *Efforts to make present programs more effective*—encouragement, albeit gentle, of combining the categorical or specific assistance programs—aid to the blind, aged, disabled; exemptions of small amounts of income from means test, particularly in old age assistance and AFDC; enlargement of responsibility for families with dependent children.

These are positive and praiseworthy, although hardly major, shifts in program. Yet, however much one might believe such changes inevitable, they were not undertaken previously and their contribution should not be minimized.

They are balanced, however, by other changes, and while in the long run these other measures may not be significant, they are important as indicators of an underlying philosophy among the present welfare leadership. There has been a retreat along the lines of work relief and controlled payments to assistance recipients. These are old sores of public assistance, and it was to be hoped that they would not be reopened. They must, of course, be handled gingerly, but no matter what the euphemisms employed they cannot but recall to us the earlier days of repressive poor relief policy. And there is no reason why they should not. One of the unpleasant facts of public welfare history is that it has a tendency to repeat itself, and very little of it bears repeating. Why work relief in a society less attuned to its success should be a valid policy today when it was found wanting from the seventeenth century onward is an interesting question. It is and has always been a sterile policy, and no new rationales have been found to explain away its 300-year failure.

It must be recognized frankly that controls placed upon economically dependent groups are discriminatory practices. While the sophisticated, the trained, the expert always find facile rationalizations for intervention, the intervention of the well-meaning specialist deprives the patient, the client, the citizen of his freedom as does any other kind of intervention. From an objective point of view the "Big Brother" of Orwell's *1984* is no more pleasant in the guise of a social practitioner than in the armband of an agent of political thought control. Almost a half-century ago Austin Chamberlain, the well-known British politician, made clear that although the Webbs' prescription for reform might be socially therapeutic it was psychologically unpalatable.[1]

Similarly we must be constantly on guard that merely because some citizens are dependent for economic support on the community's treasury, they must perforce accept the community's prescription for

---

[1] Beatrice Webb, *Our Partnership* (London: Longmans, Green & Co., 1948), p. 450.

their way of life. It would be better to be part of a society that gives the same freedom to its dependent members, whatever the consequences, than rely on the good will of a society willing to intervene in the lives of those of its members whose economic and social failures make them amenable to social control. The principle of assistance should be that the recipient of public aid will be subjected to no greater controls than other citizens. Why should the assistance recipient be deprived of discretion about the use of his income by administrative fiat and for more stringent reasons than apply to the great body of his neighbors? Why are Americans so generous and sensitive in their foreign aid program and so picayune and miserly in helping their less fortunate fellow citizens?

Unpleasant as they are, these measures might be considered political hostages for really significant advances on the welfare scene. However, one must look sharply to recognize important constructive and compensatory action. There is a general emphasis on prevention and rehabilitation, but specific or concrete examples are few. The references to day care and the provision of welfare services to persons not actually on relief, but who have been or might be, are heartening. However, the combination of the administration of child welfare with financial aid to dependent children and the broad emphasis on services and control as an integral part of assistance-giving overshadow these beginning attempts at making public welfare a rational and humane system. A recent study of child welfare services in the United States and England concluded that "administrative submergence of child welfare services under the massive weight of public assistance is a severe deterrent to program development of child welfare services." This conclusion was bolstered not only by American data but by the advances made in England's child care services since their divorce from "departments otherwise fully occupied with markedly different programs and philosophies."[2]

Even the laudatory attention given to the training of professional personnel in the 1962 amendments must be viewed in the light of the larger policy issues involved. As a professional group, social workers have prized self-criticism and placed even more emphasis than other groups on the upgrading of their profession. There has, however, been a tendency to identify with any program that provides for professional training or the expansion of professional personnel. Yet it is incumbent upon us neither to be so self-concerned nor so blind objectively as to

---

[2] Gladys M. Kammerer, *British and American Child Welfare Services* (Detroit: Wayne State University Press, 1962), pp. 414–417.

judge the value of programs only from the vantage of our own professional interest or involvement. We are quick to criticize the AMA and other professional groups who maintain that what is good for them is good for the national welfare. In a most arresting essay, Richard M. Titmuss, a leading British welfare authority and educator, points out that health and welfare bureaucracies may threaten the general welfare as much as bureaucracies devoted to other less humanitarian ends.[3] Any professional group whose practice or program is determined by the attention given it or the respect paid it should seriously reconsider its devotion to the ethic of disinterested service.

Major Issues

The major issues in regard to contemporary public welfare revolve around the provision of economic security and of other welfare services essential for the psychological, social, and physical health of this country's citizenry. The question is strategically different from those pointed up by the 1962 American welfare amendments.

Underlying the structure of the present program and its reforms are problems that concerned the charity organization movement and the English Fabian reformers in the latter quarter of the nineteenth century and culminated in the Majority Report of the Royal Commission on the Poor Laws of 1905–1909. The report of this famous commission, influenced by Charity Organization Society thinking, espoused a philosophy of welfare not far different from that current in this country. However, the sea of circumstances and popular opinion had already swept past the Majority's barrier to fundamental poor law reform. British society clearly pressed toward both a sound system of economic assistance and a system of universal social and health services that culminated in the great acts immediately following World War II.

American welfare policy, nevertheless, seems to regress to the level of the early 1900's. True, contemporary American programs are, on the whole, more liberal than those conceived by the COS in 1900. There is certainly less emphasis on institutional care and greater support of community care, but these differences are hardly sufficient to represent a half-century of major social and economic change. The major issues of welfare policy since the great industrial and urban expansion have been related to (1) the function of the welfare system, (2) the attitudes and beliefs as to the causes of the need for societal help or support and particularly the extent to which social or extra-individual

---

[3] *Essays on "The Welfare State"* (New Haven: Yale University Press, 1959), p. 202.

factors may be held accountable and responsible for economic dependency, and (3) the development of an effective organization of socioeconomic supports.

The basic welfare program of the United States, including its current amendments, has been guided by principles whose formulation both in the United States and Great Britain goes back *not* to the English Poor Law of 1601 (as is frequently stated) but to the poor law reforms of the first third of the nineteenth century. The original English act was a progressive measure solidifying the formulation of public responsibility. The reforms of the 1820's and 1830's in the United States and England were formulated at the height of *laissez-faire* influence and aimed to revoke the original commitment to social responsibility as well as the liberalization of earlier welfare practices. The present United States welfare program is in keeping with the philosophy of 1830 as revitalized by the Majority Report of the Royal Commission of 1905–1909 and the charity organization movement in the United States and England. In the contemporary American program the function of public welfare is viewed almost exclusively in relation to economic dependency, economic dependency is interpreted as much as possible from an individual or personal context rather than a social and environmental context, welfare services are elaborated almost entirely with regard to the groups receiving economic aid, and economic assistance programs are kept separate from other important economic measures.

This is an outmoded and anachronistic view of the welfare function. In addition, whatever the philosophy, the history of public welfare has demonstrated the sterility and the failure of such an approach. Philosophical rigidity has caused welfare leadership for some 150 years to focus on the technical aspects of problems rather than on the basic functional relationship to society of the welfare system. For 150 years the same philosophy, except for brief periods such as the early years of the Roosevelt administration, has dominated American policy. Tacking with the times, changes in the specifics of techniques or institutions have taken place, all in the hope that these measures would corroborate a basic *laissez-faire* philosophy. Indoor relief gave way to outdoor relief, local control to state and federal participation. Social insurance programs were introduced. At times, of course, society reverts to more primitive practices, e.g., work relief or protective payments and payments in kind. But the goal has always been the reduction and eventual dissolution of public support for the economically deprived rather than the establishment of a sound system of economic security.

There has been a continuous belief that it is somewhat immoral for a society to have, let alone recognize the existence of, an economically dependent population. While the presence of an economically dependent population is a problem not to be overlooked and hopefully to be remedied, the onus of its existence does not fall upon the public assistance mechanism. Nor can public assistance solve the great and complex social and economic maladjustments resulting, for example, in this country's continuing 6 percent unemployment rate during the past several years. Automation, mobility, depressed communities, changing family mores, the growing aged population, and the lack of opportunity for youth are not caused by, nor can they be cured by, an economic assistance program—no matter how well buttressed by psychosocial know-how!

The value of Galbraith's *Affluent Society* was that it stimulated a reassessment of the distribution of wealth in America. A variety of recent statistical analyses has shown that there are still large pockets of impoverished citizens, varying between 25 and 40 percent of the total population according to the criteria used. This is a social, not individual, phenomenon, as are the great number of the unemployed dependent on unemployment insurance and public assistance. In addition, there are several million persons on public assistance who are not employable according to contemporary principles and practices affecting employment—children, aged, blind, and disabled.

Dependency and poverty are part of the economic realities of America; it is not a question of a group of psychosocial misfits. Even Community Research Associates, who justify their existence by their ability to turn assistance recipients into self-supporting citizens, have found only a minor proportion of assistance clients to be employable. Thus there is a clear-cut problem of economic need responsive to the continuing and fluctuating conditions of the market economy of our society. It would seem overly euphoric, if not fatuous, to have this problem dominate the total pattern of welfare services when it only concerns a minority of the population. Economic problems will be solved more rationally if they are linked to the vast and complex network of programs related to the economic stability of the nation. There will be further consideration of this later.

Distinct from the problem of economic need are the many psychological and social problems indigenous to our society. Whatever the economic condition, whatever the occasion of their occurrence there is a broad and general need for programs aimed at the promotion of maximum psychosocial health. The prevalence of such problems is widespread, not limited to one economic group or to any particular element of the population. The children, the aged, the handicapped are society's concern wherever they are found. Their treatment is as necessary for the growth of a healthy society and for the fulfillment of our traditional humanitarian values as is maintenance of a sound economic structure. Many have been critical of the Marxist emphasis on the primacy of economic and material factors, yet our concentration on the centrality of economic dependence in welfare suggests that we are, in effect, victims of an overly simplified philosophy of economic determinism.

Separate the Economic from the Social

At this juncture, then, it is appropriate to accept responsibility and determine rational programs for two distinct functions whose prior symbiosis should not prevent future farsighted planning. There is as little or as much logic in combining the economic with the social in welfare agencies as maintaining that surgical wards should be in barber shops because they started out that way and frequently people are served by both. It is significant that Gordon Hamilton and Eveline Burns, approaching the issue from different vantage points, reached similar conclusions—the advisability of separating the income maintenance and service functions.[4]

Our society can afford to invest in the social and psychological welfare of its citizenry without maintaining a double bookkeeping account against which their economic return must be weighed. To a large degree this was the rationale of earlier relief programs and whatever their effectiveness they had the logic of a society of scarcity. Such efforts were not successful, but sometimes had momentary and spectacular results that still entice emphasis on, and investment in, programs aimed solely at rehabilitation of the economically dependent. The history of public welfare from the time of the famous houses of industry in late seventeenth-century Restoration England is replete with experiments and crusades to make the poor self-supporting. However, as Daniel Defoe, the author of *Robinson Crusoe*, pointed out in the early eighteenth century, if the means of economic support had been available to the poor, few would have been on relief.[5] The problem of economic assistance is linked to the economic organization of society, not to the welfare system.

American society must break away from this unholy alliance of welfare and economic security. Perhaps, as the British did, we must

---

[4] *See* Gordon Hamilton, "Editor's Page," *Social Work*, Vol. 7, No. 1 (January 1962); and Eveline M. Burns, "What's Wrong with Public Welfare?" *Social Service Review*, Vol. 36, No. 2 (June 1962).

[5] Dorothy Marshall, *The English Poor in the Eighteenth Century* (London: George Routledge & Sons, 1926), p. 50.

establish a national system of economic security unrelated to, and un-encumbered by, functions of social and psychological prevention and rehabilitation. We may even go further by unifying and rationalizing the total mechanism for economic security through creating a federation of the various agencies dealing with the problems of economic security for our citizens. Such a system might incorporate assistance programs, insurance programs for the aged and unemployed, and the various economic planning efforts related to retraining, job-finding, job-placement, and employment-creation, such as public works. These agencies could develop an approach to their problems fully as oriented to human values as are present programs. Hopefully, by working directly and effectively toward the practical solution of economic dependency and poverty, they will not require the compensating mechanism of the personalized treatment so heavily emphasized at present. Rather than needing social work to make palatable the bitter medicine of economic deprivation, they will provide dignified and realistic solutions to economic problems.

On the other side of the ledger, let us be free to develop a broad panorama of social services geared to the psychosocial development of our total citizenry. Serving the problems of marital discord, personal confusion, delinquency, and others should not be limited to the economically dependent. Many of these problems, in fact, affect economic potential and should be treated before they too greatly handicap the individual's contribution to his own and society's well-being. Those who see public assistance as a significant contribution to psychosocial health may be interested in the findings of the recently published study of the Survey Research Center of The University of Michigan. This research concluded that less than one-quarter of those families defined as "poor" had received any public assistance.[6] The public assistance system thus cannot even be considered a reliable mechanism for case-finding among those suffering from poverty alone.

A full-scale program to aid children and parents, adolescents and the aged, that will neither be impeded by their tie to the public assistance mechanism nor psychologically weakened by the traditional stigma of economic dependency would be a major advance. Perhaps we might ask ourselves why we are among the few western countries without a family allowance system and at the same time find aid to dependent children our most controversial program. Are we really concerned with

---

[6] James N. Morgan et al., *Income and Welfare in the United States* (New York: McGraw-Hill Book Co., 1962), pp. 216–217.

child and family welfare, or do we enjoy the inquisitorial satisfactions of puritan morality?

Are these criticisms of current welfare policy faint quibblings? Are they the resonant chords of a never-to-be-stilled compulsive and unnatural perfectionism? The author thinks not. Today the core of internal democratic policy is social welfare, which is the economic and social counterpart of the political democracy achieved almost two centuries ago in this country. It is the fruition of the political in the social and economic fields that will decide the future of this nation and much of this world. Failure in exporting political democracy without its social and economic equivalents has been illustrated in Latin America and in a great number of so-called underdeveloped regions. It is this country that is still undecided about its commitment to social and economic democracy. How far are we willing to go in guaranteeing equality of opportunity in health, education, and welfare?

The issue at this time is not the *size* of case loads in public assistance, but whether *we shall have* case loads in public assistance. The issue is whether we shall have a sound health program for all our citizenry, not whether a minority of the most and least fortunate shall enjoy the privileges of modern scientific medicine. The issue is whether education will be recognized as the social heritage of a civilized people, not solely as the vocational necessity of a cold war.

Program for the Social Orphans: The Next Step in Social Security

Alvin L. Schorr

U. S. Department of Health, Education, and Welfare

[From New York Times Magazine, *March 13, 1966*. © *1966 by The New York Times Company. Reprinted by permission.*]

THIS GENERATION's orthodoxy was last generation's revolution.

Those who are old enough may remember how visionary Social Security seemed until President Roosevelt signed it into law over 30 years ago. "It would be a wonderful world," said a carpenter at the time, "if we could simply be secure and know that in our old age, particularly, we would not have to depend on anybody." Now Social

Security has come to seem familiar and, with health insurance, even complete. But viewed in terms of 1965 instead of 1935, Social Security is far from complete. In a nation called the most child-centered in the world, the striking omission is children.

Prof. Eveline Burns of Columbia University's School of Social Work made the point to Congress 10 years ago. "Of all persons affected by our income-security and welfare programs," she said, "children are the least favored."

The children for whom we provide no protection similar to Social Security have been called the socially orphaned. They are the children of divorce, separation or of no marriage at all, who live with only one parent or with neither. Between seven and eight million children in the United States—say, one out of nine—are socially orphaned. Most of them live with their mothers; perhaps a third live with grandparents or other relatives; about half a million live in institutions or alone.

In 1960, about 10 million children lived in houses that lacked a proper toilet, bath, or hot water. About 4 million lived in houses that census enumerators called "dangerous." If we may judge by surveys of Aid to Families with Dependent Children—the public-assistance program originally designed to help broken families—socially orphaned children live in the poorest of these dwellings. The state of Florida found their families were paying "excessively high rents for unspeakably inadequate slum homes." In Maine, most families did not have central heating, not to speak of other necessities. Even clothing may be a problem. Winter after winter in the nation's capital, some newspaper carries the pathetic story of children who alternate days at school because they share a pair of shoes or who truant on "shower" days because they do not have underclothing.

Before considering what is done and might be done for socially orphaned children, we should understand why they are poor. Many "intact" families are able to escape poverty because, although the husband earns little, the wife provides a second income. A divorced woman, however, is forced to manage on a single income. In this situation, a mother may decide to work. But she then has to arrange for her younger children's care. Even if these arrangements do not cost her too much, her children's demands on her energy and attention make her an erratic or weary employe. Besides, women's wages are generally lower than men's and, on the average, women are less well trained for work. If a mother manages to work 40 hours a week at the minimum wage ($1.25 an hour), she will keep herself and two children just above the poverty line (reckoned at $3,000 a year for a family of four). Any illness, any upset with her children, any dip in the prosperity of her employer (she will be the first to be laid off) will drop her into poverty. If she has more than two children, she both needs more income and has more difficulty in working.

What of the father who has left and his income? A Maryland carpenter has provided an unwilling illustration of the limitations of divorced fathers. The carpenter divorced his wife in Boston and subsequently remarried and moved to Maryland. Authorities in Boston corresponded with him for four years, asking him to support his school-age son. Finally, he was extradited to Massachusetts, tried for nonsupport and sentenced to a year in prison. His second wife and their four children promptly became eligible for welfare payments—to the chagrin of authorities in Maryland. The carpenter's imprisonment may serve as a warning to errant fathers, but obviously matters were not improved for the child in Boston or the four in Maryland.

Three-fourths of all divorced persons remarry within five years. So, too, fathers of illegitimate children often separate from their families and without great delay enter into new family relationships. Divorce or separation are, therefore, likely to mean that two families look to one man for support. A man needs at the very least an income to $6,000 a year just to keep two small families out of poverty, but $6,000 is more than the average father's income. At the same time divorce and separation are more prevalent among those who earn less than average. Besides, fathers who might split their income equally are few; second wives who would be amenable to such a division are fewer, and no court would enforce it.

The earning problem of a lone mother or the limited support provided by a father with two families may be the chief problem for some socially orphaned children, but for many the situation is a great deal more complicated. Family breakdown and poverty quite enclose their lives. A poor youth, for example, is likely to marry younger, diminishing his chance of completing education or job training. Children come sooner, adding to financial and marital strain. A family quickly finds itself in the situation Mirra Komarovsky describes in "Blue Collar Marriage": "A 33-year-old man, a bottler in a beer company, struggles to support his wife and three children on $3,000-a-year pay. He does not like his job, but he also feels that he cannot risk giving up a secure job." Though comparatively young, the family is trapped.

The man's alternative is to become what researcher Hylan Lewis has called a "marriage dropout." It becomes clear that the father can never earn enough, and things are not so sweet at home anyway. At the third or fourth pregnancy, he deserts. Or his wife, conscious of his failure and her own misery, precipitates a divorce.

(Lewis has pointed out that, although middle class women may not be happy in their marriages, they can at least settle for being kept comfortably. A poor woman does not have this to settle for.) When each member of the couple remarries, they take trouble along—children already requiring support, and, sometimes, the idea that escape is an ultimate solution for any further trouble.

When we turn to the question of what is being done to aid children in poor families, we think immediately of the poverty program. However, the Economic Opportunity Act was not designed to provide support but to provide the equipment necessary for holding jobs. In the war on poverty, programs have emphasized education, training and work, and the conditions, such as good health, that are necessary to them. Financial help is available for children and youths if their parents are in Work Experience programs or if they themselves are in the Job Corps or Neighborhood Youth Corps, but children so aided represent a very small part of those who need help.

The major national program that provides financial support to socially orphaned children is called Aid to Families with Dependent Children. Under A.F.D.C., Federal funds supplemented by state contributions are dispensed by local welfare departments according to a "means test." With such a test, which varies from community to community, an investigator measures family income and needs in order to determine the amount of the payment. More than three million children are being aided under this program, two-thirds of them socially orphaned and the others actually orphaned or with fathers disabled or unemployed. It is difficult to conceive how we might do less than this, yet, as one Federal official puts it, "the trouble with the means test is that it is so mean." Families in the A.F.D.C. program receive an average of about $1 a day per person; thus virtually all the children remain poor even while they are being helped.

At the same time there are millions of socially orphaned children who are not helped by A.F.D.C. because, although their families have only a niggardly income, it is above the prescribed minimum, or because they run afoul of other regulations. For example, families may not be eligible under a state's regulations because it appears that a man has been living in the house. (Despite Federal encouragement, most states have not yet chosen to include families with an unemployed father in their A.F.D.C. programs.) Again, families may not be eligible because the local welfare department thinks that the mother or children ought to work. Families may not be eligible because the mother refuses to sue the father for support. (She may be glad he is gone and reluctant to have him brought back—for all the good it will do her, or she may be afraid of him.)

Indeed, families may be ineligible simply because it is assumed that the father is supporting them, whether he is actually doing so or not. And families may not be eligible because they do not have legal residence in a state. In short, although A.F.D.C. was originally enacted by Congress for the benefit of socially orphaned children, the majority of them are not entitled to help under local regulations.

Although the restrictions applied to A.F.D.C. vary from state to state, to a large extent they represent the same underlying problems. The number of socially orphaned who need help is increasing. The states with the largest proportion of poor people most lack the money to operate the program. Although A.F.D.C. is heavily subsidized by the Federal Government, poor states have difficulty in raising their share of the money. Regulations and paperwork have multiplied to the point where no one will defend them.

At least since World War II, legislative and public attitudes to the program have been plainly unfriendly. Negroes make up a substantial percentage (40 per cent) of the beneficiary families, as they do of the poor in general; this contributes to unfriendliness in many places. Public unfriendliness is widely transmuted into private chivying of those who receive assistance. From these families up through all the layers of professionals and officials who are concerned, no one regards A.F.D.C. with satisfaction. The U.S. Commissioner of Welfare, Dr. Ellen Winston, has criticized payment levels as "inadequate . . . to break the cycle of poverty and dependency." The National Association of Social Workers has declared its "stand for the abolition of the means test in the archaic form in which it is applied."

The problem of seven or eight million socially orphaned children calls for a Federal, non-relief solution, for it is a problem of national consequence. The cities and states lack the funds necessary to solve it. For example, if poor children were to be assured the extremely modest level of living that is provided in the Old Age Assistance program—the companion to A.F.D.C.—the additional cost would approach $5-billion.

In any event, food and shelter for these children cannot long be left subject to local prejudices. As protection against all the other contingencies that interfere with family income—disability, unemployment, retirement, death of a husband or father—the Government has provided Social Security or unemployment compensation. There is no reason why we should leave this last serious risk—loss of the father for social reasons—solely to an embattled program of public relief. Obviously all poor children deserve our concern and attention. We spotlight the socially orphaned because they represent a recognizable, nationally significant category whose income is subject to risk. The risk shows no signs of diminishing; if anything, it is growing.

Nothing inherent in the situation of children makes it impossible to devise a nonrelief program for them. We are the only developed country in the Western world without such a program. Most countries make provision for children's allowances—monthly payments for each child to the father or mother, regardless of income. A family with four children receives $25 to $30 a month in neighboring Canada and about $100 a month in France. (The precise amount varies with the age of the children.) New Zealand and Australia have a program designed specifically for socially orphaned children, who receive social security payments, just as do children whose fathers have died. Denmark ties a payment for children to the income-tax return. Those who owe tax receive a credit against it. Those who do not owe tax, who are naturally poorer, receive a payment from the government.

It is difficult to compare these countries to the United States. None is as wealthy as we, and their programs were established for differing reasons. France was hoping to increase its birth rate. Canada was seeking to avoid a depression after World War II and to deliver on the promise of a better world. However, we may take two kinds of reassurance from the experience of Western countries.

First, there is no evidence that their programs lead to an increase in the birth rate. Sweden has a lower birth rate now than it had when it began a program of children's allowances. The most remarkable fact about postwar birth rates in France and in Canada is that they closely resemble trends in the United States. Second, a number of countries feared that children might not benefit from the money that was paid out in their behalf. Some, therefore, specified that the mother should receive the payment even when there was a father in the household. The problem has turned out to be illusory. A microscopic proportion of families divert the money to personal or frivolous uses, but this is also true of families that receive income from work or widow's pensions.

At least three types of programs are available that provide a Federal, non-relief solution to the problems of socially orphaned children. Two of them are suitable to the problems of all poor children; all have been tried out somewhere in the Western world. We can call them the negative income tax, fatherless-child insurance, and children's allowances.

(1) Under a negative income tax, as in Denmark, families with income so low that they fail to benefit from income-tax exemptions would receive a payment from the government. (To some extent, the plan would correct an inequity in the present tax law. That is, rich people—because they pay a higher tax rate—benefit through deductions

for their children; poor people, paying no tax, do not benefit at all from any allowable deductions for children.) The plan seems simple and it could easily cover all needy children or all needy people. However, the sums of money saved because of the income tax deduction for children are small—around $100 a year for each child. A program that was limited to such sums would, like A.F.D.C., leave most children who benefit from it still poor. This is a damaging drawback.

Schemes can readily be devised that would be administered in connection with the income tax but deal with somewhat larger sums of money. For example, Prof. James Tobin, the Yale University economist, has proposed a payment of $400 per person to families with no other income. Payments to families who have other income would be diminished by a third of their other income. In effect, parents with three children would be assured a minimum income of $2,000 a year and at least some assistance up to an income of $6,000. Experts have so far seemed cool to this proposal, partly no doubt because it is expensive. More troublesome, although a man or woman would always stand to gain from working, the threat of stark privation would be eliminated for those who did not work—no matter what their reason. It is not clear that Americans are ready to take this step.

(2) Fatherless-child insurance was first proposed in the Beveridge Report, which charted Great Britain's course in social security after World War II. Mothers divorced in circumstances for which they were not responsible were to be treated like widows under Social Security. Under such a provision, in the United States, a mother would receive benefits for her children until they were 18 (or older, if in college). The mother would receive a small benefit for herself until the children grew up, unless she remarried or earned a moderate income.

One advantage of such a program is that families would receive meaningful amounts of money. Establishing that mothers were not responsible for the divorce, as Lord Beveridge proposed, would require a judge's opinion in each case. No doubt, this accounts for the omission from the Beveridge Report of parents who were merely separated. Yet children whose parents are separated constitute a substantial proportion of the socially orphaned; a program that ignored them would be seriously limited.

(3) Professor Burns at Columbia and others have put forward proposals for a children's allowance. Lord Beveridge supported this idea, too. (He read an early book on the subject in order to review it and was forthwith a convert.) A Government payment would be made to every father (or mother) for each child. It would be possible to pay more for the first child than the third or fourth, or vice versa. It would be possible to limit the allowance to preschool children or,

on the other hand, to children in school. The payment would not be related to income. Undoubtedly, however, the institution of children's allowances would be coupled with the reduction or elimination of the income-tax deduction for children. As a consequence, higher-income-families would suffer a tax loss in exchange for the payment.

A program of children's allowances has much to recommend it. It is the simplest of all programs. The allowance would be welcomed even by families of little means who were destined to have adequate incomes later on, for it would come in the years when they needed it most. A program of family allowances has one major drawback: making a payment for every American child is very expensive.

Clearly, each program has advantages and disadvantages. The choice is not automatic and requires thoughtful debate. The cost might fall anywhere between $3- and $10-billion a year, depending on the program selected and how it is drawn up. A program that costs less than $3-billion is not likely to be worth the bother. At an average of even $20 a month, 15 million poor children in the United States would require an allotment well over $3-billion. It is probably not necessary, in this Year of the Economist, to observe that this minimum sum of $3-billion is less than one-tenth of the amount that national production *increases* in a single year.

Funds for a negative-income-tax program or children's allowance would come from the Federal income tax. On the occasion of the last general tax reduction, President Johnson observed that the next tax reduction would be for poor people. Tax reduction may now seem some time off, but we should not forget the President's promise in whatever tax changes are to be made. A negative income tax would, obviously, represent a tax change for poor people. A program of family allowances carefully formulated to benefit poor families would not be far afield.

Fatherless-child insurance, as it represents an expansion of the Social Security system, would naturally be financed from the Social Security tax paid by employers and employees. But the burden of the Social Security tax falls rather more heavily on low-income families than does the income tax. Now, however, with health insurance, the precedent of a Government payment to support Social Security has been established, and it should be possible, following this precedent, to finance fatherless-child insurance by a Government payment to the Social Security fund.

Whatever the mechanism, the nation must somehow bear the cost if socially orphaned children are to be assured adequate support. Against the cost, we balance the fact that many parents can do little more to feed and clothe their children than they are already doing. Mothers will buy children what they need but they cannot do so without money. The nurture of children is at stake. For want of nurture, all their future may be lost.

The late Frances Perkins has reported that the first reaction of Franklin D. Roosevelt to the idea of unemployment compensation was: "Oh, we don't want the dole; not the dole." In 1935, the principle that a worker should be taxed so he could retire at 65 seemed quite possibly unconstitutional, even to proponents of Social Security.

These are the revolutions of a generation that is now growing old. Now, partly because we have solved other problems and partly because the problem of socially orphaned children looms larger every year, we confront an intrinsic irony in Social Security: it is far worse for children that their father should be separated from them than that he should die. We may be facing a national debate on the next stage in Social Security. Only in 10 or 15 years will the course that we take seem to have been inevitable.

The Negative Income Tax

Christopher Green
North Carolina State College

[From Christopher Green, Negative Taxes and the Poverty Problem, *published by The Brookings Institution, 1967.*]

PROPOSALS FOR NEGATIVE TAXES have been attracting increasing interest and support in universities, research organizations, and government circles. Because of variations among the plans—differences not only in content and cost, but also in purpose—it seems important that the crucial issues relating to negative taxes be singled out and investigated.

Objectives of Negative Income Taxation

Because the purpose of negative income taxation is to help fill the poverty income gap, the implication is that any negative tax plan is a welfare proposal with the main attention paid to raising the income of the poor. In general, negative income taxation is viewed primarily as a device to meet the needs of the poor rather than as a means of improving upon the distribution of income. The point has been made that, since World War II, Americans have not been agitated about the distribution of income but they have recently become concerned with the problem of poverty. Thus the focus of negative income taxation should be to get more income into the hands of the lowest fifth in the income distribution, not to redistribute generally from the upper fifths to the lower ones. (In fact, negative income taxation would tend to flatten the Lorenz curve by raising low incomes relative to high incomes.)

Strong exception has been taken to the view that negative income taxation should be set up and sold simply as an antipoverty weapon. There are good grounds for reducing inequality in the distribution of income. A negative tax plan could help the poor, but should be designed also to include those who are not poor. Admitting that measures which systematically redistribute income have not been popular, it might still be a mistake to single out the poor for special treatment. In fact, some wealthy persons might receive allowances, even under a plan aimed solely at the poor, because of important deficiencies in defining poverty on the basis of annual income. Moreover, a plan confined to the poor might not overcome the feeling of stigma presently associated with "relief."

While income is not an altogether satisfactory measure of poverty, it is the best available. The averaging of income would solve problems created by using annual income as the definition of poverty. It is commonly accepted that the negative income tax should be so structured as to reduce the possibility of stigma associated with a plan designed to help only the poor.

A few feel that an objective of negative income taxation should be eventually to replace many or all of the existing public programs. Even they qualify their position by saying that while replacement of existing programs would be desirable, it perhaps would not be possible. There has been general agreement that most present public transfer and service programs—notably social insurance and social services now associated with the war on poverty—would and should be maintained. However, some hope that a negative income tax would simplify and streamline the U.S. system for income maintenance. Many contend that the income maintenance function of public assistance programs should be reduced, and perhaps eventually eliminated. However, some of the social services associated with public assistance would continue to be necessary.

The adoption of negative income taxation might achieve greater vertical equity in the tax system. Negative tax rates would allow the poor to share in tax cuts and would partially offset the growth of regressive taxes.

Attractive Features of Negative Income Taxation

Proponents of a negative income tax argue that it is attractive on several grounds: (1) It is universal rather than categorical, applying to all low-income units. (2) The rate at which benefits are reduced as income rises can be held well below 100 percent, thereby reducing adverse effects on incentives to work. (3) Considerably less stigma would be involved than with the present public assistance programs. (4) The rules of the income tax would be substituted for the discretion of welfare workers. There is no general agreement that each of these features is desirable or that an operative negative income tax would, in fact, include each of these features.

Universal Coverage

The negative income tax may be understood as a universalization of income maintenance for which U.S. society is ready. The nation needs a program which sticks to a single simple definition of poverty so that the program can reach the large number of persons who are missed by more closely defined programs. At any given time, many poor persons receive neither public assistance nor social insurance benefits. The poor are generally employed people with low wages or with relatively large families against that low wage, and that is the category that is not now being reached even minimally with transfers.

Some do not agree that the categorical approach to income maintenance should be dropped. By separating the poor into categories it would be easier to deal with the problem of incentives. For example, 100 percent of the poverty income gap of the aged could be filled without creating an important work incentive problem. Another view is that instead of "rocking the boat," public assistance categories might be broadened or increased. Those who find universalization of income maintenance attractive also note that there is some reason for the categories. The categories essentially represent persons who are not in the labor force and who, therefore, rest more heavily upon the social conscience than do persons who could be attached to the labor force. Prevailing ethical standards seem to suggest income maintenance at higher levels for the aged, disabled, and families with dependent children than for persons who can work but choose not to do so.

High Marginal Tax Rate

There is wide agreement that an attractive feature of a negative tax proposal is that, unlike many other forms of assistance, it would allow beneficiaries to increase their disposable income by earning more —that is, an implicit marginal tax rate of 100 percent would be avoided. A tax rate of less than 100 percent is not an inherently unique feature of a negative income tax plan, nor is a 100 percent rate a feature inherent in public assistance and social insurance programs.

Stigma Effect

A negative income tax administered in a manner similar to the present individual income tax could reduce, perhaps eliminate, the stigma presently associated with being on relief. The concern over stigma might be one reason why many families eligible for public assistance are not receiving it. Public assistance may be demoralizing a good part of the poor population, But the negative income tax, if it were confined to the poor, might not avoid the stigma problem. Also, in a few years the present image of public assistance could apply to a negative income tax.

Rules versus Discretion

It might be useful to think of the negative income tax in terms of emphasizing the use of rules, whereas discretion plays a much more important role in public assistance. But this is not an inherent distinction—there is no lack of rules in public assistance. Nevertheless, a high degree of objectivity is identified with the administration of the income tax law. There is a strong feeling, however, that discretion is needed. Some people have above-average needs which will not be met by a program which makes payments attuned to average need. Many variables, assessed by the social worker, go into determining a given public assistance payment, thus making public assistance particularly useful in meeting special needs. In this respect, public assistance might win more support if it were added to the top of a program that provides some sort of income floor.

An important aspect of a negative income tax is that it would transfer power to make decisions on welfare operations from the states and localities to the federal government. But taxpayers may object to unsupervised transfers to the poor.

Basic Problems in Negative Income Taxation

Having discussed the objectives and attractive features of a negative income tax, there remain three more thorny problems in negative taxation: (1) the trade-offs involved in choosing the income guarantee, the negative tax rate (or rates), and the breakeven level of income; (2) the definition of income and the tax unit; and (3) the administration of a negative tax plan.

Trade-offs

A negative tax plan—in fact, any plan that would provide an income floor—involves some inescapable arithmetic. Any two of the three basic variables (the guarantee, tax rate, and breakeven level of income) determine the third in an uncomfortable manner. For example, the arithmetic indicates that the objective of a high guaranteed minimum income combined with a tax rate that keeps disincentives to work low is not compatible with the objective of confining allowances to the poor. Conversely, a low breakeven level of income and a reasonably low negative tax rate is not compatible with a high guaranteed minimum. Something has to give. Since a schedule of rates averaging much above 50 percent probably would not be acceptable, either the guarantee would be too low or the breakeven level of income would be too high. There is no general agreement, however, as to which objective—a high guarantee or a low breakeven level of income—is more expendable.

At very low levels of income the marginal tax rate might, without a great deal of harm, be allowed to go well above 50 percent. Income lost by dulling the incentives of working members of families whose income is below, say, $1,000 would not amount to much. However, those who hold this view feel that it is very important to keep marginal rates at or below 50 percent as income approaches the poverty line. Thus, if the tax schedule is to include more than one rate it should take on a regressive form: high marginal rates on the first several hundred dollars, declining to considerably lower rates as before-allowance income reaches more substantial levels.

Rates much in excess of 50 percent might not be enforceable. The Internal Revenue Service might collect more revenue with a 60 percent rate than with an 80 percent rate. Possibly this would suggest a per capita tax credit plan, with a single tax rate for all income levels—a rate in the neighborhood of 25 or 30 percent. However, this would mean paying net allowances to many families which are not poor. One has to decide if this price is too high. Some feel that low rates would push the breakeven levels of income to politically unacceptable levels. Congress has been opposed to granting a zero tax, in the form of higher personal exemptions, to present taxpayers. The minimum standard deduction (which is effectively an increase in personal exemptions) was passed by Congress in the belief that it would not cost much money. If Congress has been unwilling to increase the number of low-income units who are exempt from income taxation, it is unrealistic to believe that Congress would now grant a negative tax to these presently taxable low-income units.

However, there is some support for the idea of paying allowances to families whose income is above the present level of their exemptions and deductions. In the context of using transfer payments for eliminating poverty it would seem reasonable to provide a floor at or near the poverty line and still provide for work incentives. This means, even with a 50 percent negative tax rate, breakeven levels of income well above poverty lines, and probably close to the median income.

A somewhat different view has been proposed by those who suggest that the function of the negative tax plan might be limited to supplementing low incomes. The function of guaranteeing a high minimum income would be dispensed with, and it should be made clear to the public that the allowances would not do much for families with little or no income. Under such a plan, both tax rates and breakeven levels of income could be kept at acceptably low levels.

It is apppropriate to ask—especially in view of the hard facts of the inevitable trade-off—how significant the incentive problem really is. It is striking that most people worry about incentives for other people and never for themselves. However, there is the example of a group of disabled public assistance recipients who stopped work when they no longer could keep what they earned and began to face an effective 100 percent tax rate. Perhaps this experience cannot be generalized. It is estimated that in money terms the net cost of a plan that simply brings incomes up to poverty line levels might have been, in 1964, as high as $24 billion (when increases in negative tax allowances due to substitution of the allowances for other transfer income received by the poor are excluded). Approximately $12 billion of this cost is accounted for by the 1964 poverty gap. The maximum real cost in terms of output lost is the remaining $12 billion—a very rough guess —representing elimination of all the earnings of the poor, plus a small amount of earnings of some families with incomes close to, but above, the poverty lines.

It is probably politically and ethically intolerable to do nothing for a family earning $3,001 while giving $3,000 to another family whose members are unwilling to do any work. From the standpoint of incentives it is important to avoid a sharp discontinuity between negative and positive rates.

Definitions of Income and Tax Unit

With regard to the question of how income and the tax unit should be defined for purposes of the negative income tax, both efficiency (confining payments to poor families) and equity (similar treatment of equally poor families) demand a broad definition of money income and a tax unit resembling the consumer unit which pools its income for major items of expense. The present income tax unit and definition of income do not meet these specifications. Thus, if a negative income tax were not tied to reform of the existing individual income tax system, two different definitions of income and the tax unit would be needed in a system with both positive and negative rates. An additional question is whether dual definitions or concepts would create important administrative problems.

Those who stress the definition of income agree that a broad definition is necessary. However, payments made under the public assistance programs should be excluded from the income concept used in calculating negative tax allowances. Imputed rent might be included unless it is quantitatively insignificant. There is also the question whether special treatment could be given to earned income. An earned income credit might reduce the incentive problems created by high marginal negative income tax rates.

Congress might not adopt a system under which income maintenance payments would depend on the same rules as those applied to the present positive tax system. Though this is a double standard, it may be politically necessary. However, two definitions of income probably would not create important administrative problems. In fact, two different definitions of income might allow tax filers to transfer income to their children in order to benefit from the negative income tax. However, this eventuality could be met by carefully defining the tax unit for negative income tax purposes.

A definition of the basic tax unit as spouses, children under 19 years of age, and students under 22, has drawn some criticism for being rather arbitrary. Also, a definition of a family tax unit might create incentives to split the family; because of this, a per capita tax credit might be more appropriate.

Administration

There is sharp division over whether the Treasury Department and its Internal Revenue Service could or should administer negative tax allowances. There is also division over whether negative income taxation requires stricter enforcement and guidance than does present positive income taxation.

Several lines of thought have developed on the question of who should be responsible for administration of a negative income tax plan. Technical problems and the need for discretionary powers to prevent any wealthy persons from receiving allowances could prevent the

Treasury from administering negative and positive taxation as a single system. The Treasury might not be able to administer a welfare system and a tax system at the same time. Also, even if the Treasury administered the plan it might still be identified as a welfare program with a means test. A contrasting view is taken by those who suggest that it would be necessary for the Treasury to administer negative taxation in order that the public would not view the plan as just another form of welfare. Proponents of this view feel that an important asset of negative income taxation is its relation to the tax system. Since almost all families have some dealings with the Internal Revenue Service, any stigma attached to receipt of allowances might be reduced. Still others believe that tying the negative tax to the tax structure is not important so long as the administering authority is a federal agency, and not the state and locally controlled welfare apparatus.

ENFORCEMENT. There is some concern that the satisfactory level of self-assessment and enforcement now attained in the positive income tax system might not be attainable under a negative tax system using existing approaches to enforcement. It is difficult to visualize the Treasury transferring large amounts of money without making "validations and certifications" of the income claims of potential allowance recipients. Some believe there would have to be adjustment for regional differences in the cost of living. In addition, there would be difficulties in getting allowances to the families who were eligible for them. At present, numerous potential public assistance recipients receive no assistance because they do not know about the public assistance program. It would be important to see that the allowances are usefully spent—at least where children are concerned.

It is more than rhetorical to ask whether it is a greater crime to cheat the government out of a dollar by not paying tax or by collecting a dollar that is not deserved. It is better to argue for symmetry and less worry about enforcement. Most reject the idea of a special welfare-type apparatus for administering a negative income tax. Aside from safeguards against fraud, the negative income tax can be administered through a set of rules applying universally, both in demographic and geographic terms.

LENGTH OF ACCOUNTING PERIOD. There has been concern over how to collect overpayments of negative income tax allowances. Payments would have to be current, instead of at the end of the year. This could mean overpayments because of a miscalculation of the recipient's yearly earnings. Overpayments might be repaid directly or similar amounts withheld from payments in the following year. However, these solutions could create a real hardship for families with few resources.

The accounting period for determining eligibility for allowances and the level of payments would have to be very short—much shorter than a year—unless a system can be found that is sensitive to weekly or monthly changes in annual rates of earnings.

Relation to Existing Social Welfare Programs

There is a prevailing view that a negative tax would supplement, rather than substitute for, present public transfer and service programs. To some, this is not a matter of despair. They believe that a negative tax would usefully complement the present income transfer and income-in-kind programs as well as the war on poverty programs. Others somewhat unhappily indicate that a politically feasible negative income tax would not provide payments high enough to relieve the need for some public assistance and the continuation of public housing, medical, counseling, and legal aid programs. It has been suggested that there is a qualitative, as well as a quantitative, difference between a small negative income tax plan and a "sufficient" program. The latter would alleviate, to a great extent, the need for many of the existing programs.

The before-transfer poor receive about half of total public transfer payments, and the after-transfer poor receive about a quarter of the total. In addition, available evidence indicates that, for the most part, the payments-in-kind programs—for example, medical, educational, and counseling—do not channel their funds only to the poor. A negative income tax could be thought of as an income-conditioned family allowance which would, by fitting into a whole battery of programs, mainly benefit those elements of the poor population, especially the working poor, who receive the least benefit from the present transfer programs. It is important that the negative income tax be visualized against a background of progress in the fields of services and payments-in-kind.

Social Insurance and Public Assistance

Those who address themselves to the subject state that negative income tax allowances should supplement old-age, survivors and disability insurance (OASDI) and unemployment compensation. That is, OASDI and unemployment compensation should be included in the definition of income, and negative income taxes would fill—partially or wholly—whatever gap was left after an individual's or family's social insurance benefits had been accounted for. In contrast, public assistance would be excluded from the definition of income and would be treated as a supplement to negative income tax payments. Some proponents visualize a negative income tax of modest size in the near future supplemented as necessary by public assistance, but eventually growing to a level at which the need for public assistance would be eliminated in all but the most unusual cases. While public assistance is gradually being eliminated, OASDI could be developing to the point at which it would assure a poverty-free income to the aged.

War on Poverty

It is argued that under no circumstances should a negative income tax plan be considered a substitute for the so-called opportunity programs—the education and training programs which are such basic parts of the current war on poverty. However, while programs of the Office of Economic Opportunity are for the long run, the poor have not accepted this premise. The poor would like to get money directly from Washington, and now. Thus a negative income tax could be regarded as an additional front in the war on poverty. There is another belief that transfer programs and opportunity programs are cooperative approaches to the same problem, and that what is most attractive about the negative tax type of transfer is that it does support incentives to work.

Minimum Wage Legislation

There is spirited discussion of the question whether a negative income tax would allow a reduction in the minimum wage or an elimination of minimum wage legislation. The view is expressed that a negative income tax could provide all low-paid workers with a minimum income without jeopardizing the employment opportunities of any of them. Minimum wages, on the other hand, effectively apply only to workers actually employed and can—potentially, at least—create unemployment. Some observers are distressed by the implication that minimum wages should be reduced or eliminated. They say a negative income tax would not eliminate the need for a floor under wages. There is also the view that the minimum wage issue is entirely unrelated to the negative income tax issue.

A negative income tax might compete for financing with other social welfare programs. If it came to a question of financing a negative income tax or raising social security benefits many groups, probably including organized labor, would prefer to have larger social security payments than the negative tax.

Alternatives to Negative Income Taxation

Since most agree that the main object of negative income taxation is to close the poverty income gap, it seems important to judge other income maintenance proposals on the basis of how well they would close that gap. Public assistance gains the most attention in this respect, despite criticisms leveled at it. The attention paid to public assistance as an alternative to negative income taxation can be explained by the fact that public assistance, of all existing transfer payment programs, is most directly concerned with poor people—even though it deals only with special categories of poor people. The social insurances and family allowances are perhaps given less attention because, for reasons explained below, they are not efficient means of closing the poverty income gap.

Public Assistance

At least three lines of thought are evident with regard to the reform of public assistance. One view is that there is nothing in the public assistance statute that makes adequate care of the poor impossible other than the distribution of power among national, state, and local governments. In the late 1940's there were proposals to make public assistance a comprehensive noncategorical program with federal standards. Although the proposals did not receive much political attention then, real efforts in the same direction today might achieve the same results that a negative income tax is supposed to achieve. In addition, public assistance is more flexible than a negative tax because it can quickly meet special needs and it can account for regional differences in the cost of living.

Some proponents of this new line of thought advocate broadening the categories, adding new ones, or both. The rate at which benefits are reduced as income increases could be lowered. In this regard there were amendments in 1962 to the public assistance section of the Social Security Act which were designed to provide public assistance recipients with greater work incentives. In 1965, there was a further increase in the amount of monthly earned income which may be exempted in determining public assistance payments. The real problem is that very few states have taken advantage of these amendments to the federal statute. The view that public assistance can be reformed can be summed up by stating that if one is trying to hit a target population with a fair degree of efficiency and keep resource outlays low and the benefits high, there is nothing inherent in the present welfare system preventing the attainment of these goals.

A contrasting view is that public assistance is currently inadequate, that in practice it will not be reformed, and that even a broadening of coverage and a lowering of the penalty rate (marginal tax rate) on earnings would not relieve recipients of the stigma presently associated with being on relief. Even some supporters of reform of public assistance admitted reform might no longer be politically feasible. One student of the problem who has been close to the public assistance programs believes that refinements could be made in public assistance, but he suspects that the present public assistance programs will never provide adequate coverage and adequate payments. He notes that public assistance is basically unpopular, and carries a stigma in the United States. In addition, it is wasteful because welfare workers spend a very high percentage of their time on investigations. He thinks that a net decrease in cost could be achieved by eliminating investigations. Furthermore, he believes it would be helpful to separate the services and the income maintenance functions, and to recognize that many persons will need some form of monetary assistance no matter what levels of services they receive. One objective of a negative income tax is to get away from the tradition in public assistance of close supervision of the manner in which the money is spent. Although a 100 percent penalty on increases in income is not inherent in public assistance, a negative income tax is a more likely route to getting rid of the 100 percent rate than would be a beefed-up public assistance program. Eliminating the 100 percent rate might necessitate a reconsideration of the basic ideas about how public assistance ought to work.

A third view—more implicit than explicit in discussions of public assistance—is that the necessary reforms of public assistance would make it identical in form to a negative income tax. If public assistance were made universal, conditioned only on the basis of a family's income and size, the penalty rate substantially reduced, national minimum standards of assistance payments introduced, and residence requirements eliminated, then public assistance would differ from a negative income tax only with respect to who administers the program. However, this route gives less assurance than does a negative income tax that the stigma now associated with receipt of assistance payments will be reduced or eliminated.

Social Insurance

The present social insurance system, with its wage-related system of benefits, has important limitations as a general approach to reducing and eventually eliminating the poverty gap. It helps, at present, only a fraction of the after-transfer poor—and these are mainly the aged poor. It keeps out of poverty a somewhat larger number of aged persons who would be poor were it not for their benefits. However, it is not designed to deal with the problem of inadequate earnings of persons who are still employed. Since social insurance replaces earned income for persons at all income levels (although in larger proportion at lower earnings levels) an increase in benefits to bring the aged or unemployed poor out of poverty necessitates an increase also in benefits to the aged and unemployed who are not poor. Hence, it is an inefficient approach if the aim is to direct redistribution of income to the poor. That is illustrated by the fact that it would cost an additional $10 billion to $11 billion to bring about a half of the aged poor out of poverty by way of the OASDI route. Only about a third of this sum would be received by those who had been, or who remained, poor.

Family Allowances

There is relatively little discussion of family allowances, even though this approach to income maintenance is quite popular in most other Western nations. Family allowances paid to all families with children is an expensive way in which to aid poor children, since most of the benefits would be received by children who are members of nonpoor families. Presumably, this problem could be surmounted by having income-conditioned family allowances. Such an approach, however, would not differ from a negative income tax plan which confined its allowances to families with children.

Specific Transfer-by-Taxation Plans

Four specific transfer-by-taxation plans may be used as a basis for estimating costs, benefits, and financing. The four types of plans discussed are defined briefly as follows:

1. A negative rates taxation plan would use poverty lines as breakeven levels of income and a single 50 percent negative tax rate applied against the poverty income gap. In 1964, a plan of this type would have cost the federal government $6.3 billion.

2. A set-aside plan also would use poverty lines as breakeven levels of income, but it would exempt from tax all income below 50 percent of the poverty line income. Thereafter the negative tax rate would be 50 percent. It is estimated this plan, in 1964, would have cost $4.7 billion.

3. A social dividend plan would guarantee income equal to the poverty line and would tax income below this breakeven level of income at a 50 percent rate. The gross cost, in 1964, of this plan would be $155 billion with a redistribution, or net cost, of $31 billion, which could be financed by a 15 percent tax rate on income above the breakeven income levels.

4. A tax credit plan would have two basic features: a proportional income tax with no exemptions, and a flat-sum credit per capita. For purposes of comparison with the plans outlined above, this plan suggests a $400 tax credit per capita. In order to finance the tax credit

plan plus other expenditures normally financed by the federal personal income tax, it would be necessary to levy a 25 percent income tax rate against an income base which would no longer be reduced by personal exemptions and which would be broadened still further through tax reform in the area of personal deductions and tax exempt income. This plan is similar to the social dividend plan described above, but its guaranteed minimum income is only about half as great. Also, the tax credit plan adopts a single flat-rate income tax schedule rather than distinguishing between the social dividend tax schedule and the existing positive tax schedule. The breakeven levels of income of both of these plans, however, are similar. For example, the breakeven level of income for a family of four is $6,000 ($3,000 divided by .50) under the social dividend plan above and $6,400 ($400 times 4 divided by .25) under this tax credit plan. It is estimated that, in 1964, the gross cost of the tax credit plan would have been $76 billion ($400 times a population of approximately 190 million), with a redistribution, or net cost, of about $16 billion.

There is concern that the proposals for the negative rates plans do not include an indication as to how they would grow over time. Some of those who have studied the problem are willing to begin with a small program—one which filled only half of the poverty gap—but they wanted it to grow so that it would provide an income floor at or near poverty line levels of income. Thus they suggest still another plan. This one would begin as a negative rates plan (such as the first plan summarized above) and would grow to proportions similar to the social dividend plan described above. There is a feeling that the first two plans—the negative rates and set-aside plans—are pragmatically sound from a political point of view compared with the social dividend and tax credit plans. But their attractiveness is reduced by the need for continuing to provide substantial amounts of supplementary public assistance payments. Concern has also been expressed that Congress would not give a plan which started on a relatively moderate basis a chance to expand. It is hard to get Congress to change the tax laws. One might also ask whether the $5 billion to $6 billion set-aside and negative rates plans would be big enough to prevent real disappointment with respect to their effectiveness as a means for improving income maintenance.

A variant on the negative rates plan might increase incentives to work. The variant would provide allowances equal to some fraction of the poverty gap plus some fraction of the change in a family's earnings. It has been noted, however, that this would create a "notch" problem by making allowance payments to a family whose income had risen above the poverty line—though this would happen for only one year. Also, is there need for further reduction of the allowance when a family's earnings fall?

Of those who say they favor a particular plan, a large number choose the negative rates plan with a 50 percent rate. This plan is favored because its target is the poor; it fills 50 percent of the poverty income gap in the most efficient manner; and because it holds out the greatest likelihood politically of getting a "foot in the door." However, the negative rates plan gains support from some persons only on condition that it would grow beyond its initial modest proportions. But it might be a mistake to undersell a plan which began by providing $5 billion to $6 billion to the poor. In this connection, the cost figures given for both the negative rates plan and the set-aside plan include estimates that overstated the initial reduction in public assistance expenditures. It might also be better for the breakeven levels of income to be the value of personal exemptions and minimum standard deductions rather than the calculated poverty lines. A few supporters of the negative rates plan favor separating it from the tax system and treating it as an income-conditioned family allowance.

Support for the tax credit proposal comes from those who think an objective of negative income taxation is to reduce inequality in the distribution of income. Further support comes from those who like the way in which a tax credit fits into the existing personal income tax system and the way it avoids distinguishing between the poor and nonpoor. The Tobin plan very nicely integrates the negative and positive tax schedules; there are similarities between the Tobin and tax credit plans. Some interest in the tax credit plan is indicated by those who want a plan tied to the tax structure. However, there is concern that the negative rates and set-aside plans have little relation to the positive income tax system, and therefore might well be administered apart from it.

In Conclusion

Full-bodied discussion of negative income tax indicates that a negative income tax is neither a simple, nor a wholly satisfactory, device for improving the current income maintenance system. It also indicates that the alternatives to negative taxation have very serious limitations. Despite this lack of consensus either for or against negative income taxation, it is significant that few people are willing to stand behind any other single income maintenance program as the primary means of better meeting the income needs of the poor. There has been widespread agreement that some form of income-conditioned grant which would not be restricted to special categories of the poor is desirable.

Poverty and New Careers for Nonprofessionals

Arthur Pearl

University of Oregon

Frank Riessman

New York University

[Chapter 1 in New Careers for the Poor, *Arthur Pearl and Frank Riessman, New York: The Free Press, 1965. Reprinted with permission of The Macmillan Company from* New Careers for the Poor, *by Arthur Pearl and Frank Riessman. Copyright © The Free Press, a Division of The Macmillan Company 1965.]*

FOR TOO MANY YEARS widespread and pervasive poverty has existed in this country and the public has been either unaware or unconcerned about the problem. Today there is awareness and concern, frenzied activity and legislation, demonstration programs, and volunteers in the field—all functioning with but one stated ambition—to help the poor. The concern is laudable although the activity might not be.

There should be no confusion on one point. *Poverty will not be easy to eradicate.* Poverty is not a superficial blemish on an otherwise healthy structure. It is not a passing phase of a society in flux. The causes of poverty are deep-seated. Short term stop-gap measures will not bring about a permanent solution to the problem. The need to reorganize and revitalize many of the structures and institutions central to society is the alternative to relegating large numbers of citizens to a spectator class—a permanent, stable "nonworking" class, whose children and grandchildren will also be unable to perform meaningful functions in our society. The prospect of many millions of Americans in such a nonproductive situation is not a science-fiction terror. The danger is real and upon us.

This presentation will include a description of the problem, an analysis of its causes and effects, an evaluation of suggested remedies, and a proposal for redress of the condition.

The complex of goals of the new career proposal includes the following:

1. A sufficient number of jobs for all persons without work.

2. The jobs to be so defined and distributed that placements exist for the unskilled and uneducated.

3. The jobs to be permanent and provide opportunity for life-long careers.

4. An opporunity for the motivated and talented poor to advance from low-skill entry jobs to any station available to the more favored members of society.

5. The work to contribute to the well-being of society.

To devise a program which will provide, in sufficient numbers, socially useful, compensated positions and which will also furnish equal chances for upward mobility, is no small task. If the poor and the currently unemployable are going to be brought into productive society there must be some determination of the capabilities of this group. What can the poor do? How can useful functions be developed that will meet the limitations of the population? What must be done to educate the uneducated in the labor force? What must be done to prevent future uneducated generations from developing? What responsibilities for providing the necessary jobs should be delegated to private industry? And, what is the public sector's responsibility? These are the basic questions confronting us.

It must be abundantly clear that in the solution of poverty every aspect of American life will undergo change. Organizational structures and institutions which have come to be accepted as basic and immutable must be transformed. Education in particular must be reappraised and adjustments must be made at every level. However, as will be stressed here, the modifications which take place must be keyed to the needs of the society. No good can come from a panic which demands change only for change's sake.

The methods of securing and changing employment in this country must also be overhauled. There is too much slippage between the referral office and the job. Too much of the job-securing mechanism concern is in satisfying the short-term needs of the employer. There is no articulated process for the job-seeker to obtain security. Too much of the risk in job preparation is absorbed by those least able to absorb risk—the poor. Civil service merit systems based primarily on an ability to perform written examinations may need to be updated to allow all persons, regardless of background, a more equal chance to obtain career placements.

The roles played by highly-skilled technicians and professionals need to be reviewed. Many functions currently performed exclusively by professionals must be delegated to persons with limited education, experience, and skill. Society insists that training take place prior to job placement. Such a system made sense (although it reinforced inequality) when only a small percentage of the population was engaged in highly skilled occupations, while most of the work force required little formal training. This condition no longer exists. Most of the needs of society can be satisfied only by the highly-skilled and the well-trained. In an era of rapid technological development even the skills of the professional rapidly become obsolete. Training cannot be considered a prerequisite for employment. While this is often understood for some functions it is not yet appreciated as a general proposition. There can be no end to poverty unless it is fully appreciated that, for the most part, training for the poor must take place *after* employment is secured. This may not be necessary in the future, when all of the population, rich and poor alike, are well-educated. But today, and certainly for the next decade, at least, many millions of persons will be seeking employment who have not had adequate education. This group, not only because of its plight, but also because it contains the parents of future generations, is the norm-setter. The poor job-seeker of the 1960's will develop and model the value systems, loyalties, and aspirations of those who are to benefit from new approaches to education. They must be permitted to play a useful, meaningful role in today's world. There can be no sacrifice of a population of today under the mantle of concern for tomorrow. Inability to deal with the poor of today will be transmitted to the poor of tomorrow.

Ours has been, and still is, a vigorous society. Growth has been rapid, and in the exciting, untrammeled course of that growth, much of the institutional structure has grown up unplanned. This lack of planning is often given accolades equal to those awarded the accomplishments. But the course of growth has necessitated interdependence and reliance upon government-sponsored activity. There is no denying the importance of the public sector, nor is there a path back from it. Education, welfare, recreation, and corrections are public responsibilities. A consequence of unimpeded and unplanned growth is lack of continuity and linkage between institutions, organizations, and agencies. This deficiency in connection is most strongly felt by the poor since they lack resources of their own. There is often no passageway for the poor from education to employment, from institutional commitment to living in free society, from economic calamity back to a sound economic footing. With limited resources, skill, and flexibility, the poor have little chance to recover from serious injury or prolonged illness. If there is to be a path from poverty, not only must there be change within structures, but there also must be integration between structures.

Changes of the nature outlined above can only come about when there is public consensus for their necessity. Therefore, many entrenched belief systems must be reconsidered and many myths exposed, with more adequate concepts offered in exchange.

One such fabrication places full responsibility on the poor. The details may vary, but there is a common theme; the poor are poor because of innate inferiority, a lack of desire—or the romantic variation—because they want to live the good, simple life. All of these are status-quo positions, implying that there is no cause for alarm and that the situation truly requires no change.

A variation of the theme is that the poor become poorer because they react violently, impulsively, and senselessly against middle-class values; or, conversely, the poor remain poor because the middle class can only maintain relative superiority by denying the poor equal access to opportunities.

This paper will espouse an emphatic rejection of the desirability or inevitability of wholesale poverty. It is our thesis that no segment of our society stands to gain over the long run from the existence of a nonproductive class.

The poverty issue presents the United States with a totally new crisis, one that defies previously used solutions. It is a chronic crisis which does not lend itself to any partisan political position and would only worsen if atavistic procedures were employed as remedial measures. The crisis, on one hand involves the permanent poor, and on the other, involves an inability to provide, in sufficient numbers, persons to fill the most needed technological and professional roles. In oversimplified terms, there exist simultaneously large numbers of people without jobs and a great many jobs without people.

It is difficult to estimate accurately the number of jobs currently unfilled. There is a tendency for all operations to "make-do" with what is available. Administrators are often given credit for a "sound fiscal" operation when savings accrue from unfilled budgeted positions. However, there can be no doubt that were there thousands more fully accredited teachers, social workers, librarians, engineers, nurses, and doctors, the economy would absorb them.

The jobs which are needed are primarily in the public sector or are sustained by public financing. One reason that it is difficult to estimate job vacancies precisely is that definition of need is arbitrary. The public, through elected representatives, makes this determination. There are no established efficiency standards or guidelines to be applied to operations which are designed to provide helping services. Nor can there be any.

The value of an educated child, for example, cannot be reduced to a simple accounting of income obtained from tax investments. Adequate health, education, welfare, and recreation are available only to citizens of an affluent society. All societies need as much of these services as can be afforded.

The central thesis of this paper is that in an affluent automated society the number of persons needed to perform such tasks equals the number of persons for whom there are no other jobs.[1]

The persons without jobs are not difficult to identify. They are the unskilled, the uneducated. In disproportionate numbers they are young; they are Negro. They are likely to remain poor and so are their children. There is almost nothing that they can do about it. Lack of control over destiny is a unique feature of today's poverty. The poor of the past, because of differences in structure and organization of society, had a much better chance to change status than do the poor of today. (The Negro poor of the past—the slave—was an exception. He was denied opportunity to improve himself and the consequences of enforced poverty have an important bearing on the existing scene.)

The distinguishing feature of the modern economic scene is that unskilled labor is ceasing to be a necessary component of functioning society. Traditionally, the poor have possessed one marketable commodity—unskilled labor. By means of their labor the poor could gain a toehold on the economic ladder, and many of the children of these poor could advance to higher stations through education or entrepreneurial enterprise. Technological advancement was on the side of the poor (in the long run, at least). Technological advance stimulated the economy and provided work opportunity. The history of the United States can almost be charted by immigration of impoverished people linked to specific technological changes.

Railroading was but one technological development of the 19th century, which, on a mass scale provided entrance to viable society for the poor immigrant. Many members of the establishment proudly refer to antecedents who, as poor immigrants, worked the mines, laid the track, or manned the foundries and mills. It was this profound influence of technological advance on the economy that encouraged immigration. If there had been nothing for the unskilled immigrant to do, the "dream" of America, the open society would not have been sustained. The promise of America continued because it was based on a hard core of truth.

The automotive industry further stimulated the economy and provided continued opportunity for the unskilled laborer. Technological advances in the 20's and 30's led to the assembly line which was specifically designed for the unskilled laborer. Complexity and variability of job performance was reduced to an absolute minimum. The

---

[1]Impoverished nations with relatively few persons in helping services are not without need for these services. They are simply unable to afford them.

essential feature of the assembly line was the reduction of job complexity to allow for interchangeability of workers regardless of skill. In a variety of settings increased affluence was accomplished at the expense of the skilled craftsman. Technological advance in shoemaking resulted in modern assembly line production, new jobs for the unskilled, and the elimination of the highly-skilled craftsman. Job evolution, however, has come full circle. The unskilled workers' functions, to a large extent created by the machine, are now being replaced by the machine.

Automation must be recognized for what it is, a permanent fixture in American life which will enable private industry to produce efficiently, increase the gross national product, *and*—eliminate jobs. John I. Snyder, President and Chairman of U.S. Industries, Inc., estimates that two million jobs are eradicated each year by automation.[2]

A magnificent year for the general economy was 1963. There was a healthy increase in gross national product; a new high was set for median income. In this same year, however, rising unemployment widened an even greater economic gap between the poor and nonpoor, and the Negro and non-Negro. Between 1957 and 1962, 500,000 fewer workers produced significantly more goods and one million jobs were eliminated in agriculture, although farm surpluses continued to accumulate.[3]

The future augers for more of the same; the unskilled worker is to be replaced by automated devices and the labor force augmented by the trained technicians. It is projected that approximately the same number of persons will be employed as laborers in 1975 as were employed in 1960—a period in which it is expected that 20 million more workers will enter the labor market. There will be in excess of a million and a half fewer workers in agricultural pursuits in 1975 than there were in 1960. These workers and their families will steadily flow to urban centers where they will lack resources, skills, and education—possessing only the qualities necessary to become part of the permanent poor.

To expect the private sector to absorb these additional workers while being confronted with decreasing need of currently employed, meagerly skilled workers is unrealistic. Industry can engage in extensive job analyses and by redefinition create a considerable number

---

[2]Snyder, John I., The Myths of Automation, *American Child,* 1964, Vol. 46, No. 1.

[3]United States Labor Department, *Manpower Report of the President and a Report on Manpower, Requirements, Resources, Utilization and Training,* U.S. Government Printing Office, Washington, D.C., 1963.

of jobs which do not require extensive training or experience and industry should be encouraged along these lines by government subsidy.
However, the greatest potential for new careers is in the public sector.

To offset the relative loss of employment in the private sector,
there has been rapid growth in the public domain:

> Total government civilian employment rose from 5.5 million
> in 1947 to 9.2 million in 1962. . . . The addition of 3.7 million public
> employees accounted for one-third of the total increase in nonagricul-
> tural employment in the post war years.[4]

The bulk of the growth has been in education and health. In
these areas the number of persons presently employed exceed by over
60 per cent the number employed 10 years ago.[5]

A Glance into the Future

The areas of health, education, and other services intended to help or
uplift persons offer the greatest promise for employment opportunities
in the future. Through extrapolation of populations, it is projected
that between the years 1960 and 1975 there will be a 65 per cent
increase in professional, technical, or kindred worker occupations.[6]
During this interval the elementary school population will increase by
15 per cent. There will be in excess of 50 per cent more youth of
secondary school age, and at least a 70 per cent increase in youth
of college-attending age.[7]

The increase in numbers of persons of school age cannot by
itself be used as the sole gauge for estimating teacher need. Not only
will students increase in number, but there will be a tendency for students to stay in school longer. Even without campaigns and public concern, the drop-out rate in this country has been declining steadily.
Many more youth complete high-school now than was the case thirty
years ago. A constantly increasing proportion of high school graduates
go on to college. A higher percentage of those who enter college
achieve graduation, and a higher percentage of those who complete
college go on to attain higher degrees.

Between 1960 and 1970, 7.5 million youth will terminate an educational process without attaining a high school education, only if no
remedial steps are instituted in this decade.[8] If youth could be attracted

---

[4]*Ibid.*, p. 16.
[5]*Ibid.*, p. 16.
[6]*Ibid.*, page 100.
[7]Source: U.S. Department of Commerce, Bureau of the Census.
[8]Schrieber, Daniel (ed.); *The School Dropout,* National Education Association, Washington, D.C., 1964, page 2.

to education, and, most importantly, if education could be realistically perceived by youth to have value, many more students would be retained in high school than is currently estimated. The increased enrollment resulting from more effective programming would further increase demand for teaching personnel. Most projections of demand for teachers not only rely on a substantial loss of youth before high school graduation, but also assume that the teacher-pupil ratio will remain fairly constant.

> The estimated pupil-teacher ratio for elementary, secondary, public and private schools combined for 1960 was 24.7 to 1. This rate is projected to decline to 24.3 to 1 by the middle of the decade and then remain stationary.[9]

Neither the assumed drop-out rate nor the assumed class size can be accepted without challenge. While no recommendation is made here that persons should be hired as teachers because our society can find nothing else for them to do, it is strongly urged that many more persons could play productive roles in the educational systems of the country than are currently being utilized. It is lamentable that research findings which give a factual base for the determination of optimal (or even tolerable) loads are almost totally lacking. To accurately appraise the maximum educational return for tax dollar investment it would be necessary to experimentally manipulate and compare outcomes in a variety of situations and contexts. Assessment would have to be made for teachers with differing skills and attributes, for youth of different ages, and for youth from diverse social backgrounds in schools and classrooms with different intellectual and emotional climates. There would have to be evaluation of the impact that the kind and level of course content had upon optimal classroom population, and also the influence of different techniques used to present material. In the absence of definite findings, any assumption that pupil-teacher ratio is relatively fixed is unnecessary and unwise.

The proposal to substantially increase the numbers of persons with teaching responsibilities carries with it a call for rigorous evaluation. If such an investment should not result in significantly improved educational outcomes for any substantial segment of the population, and if careful study of the process of utilization of "new careers" in teaching does not reveal faulty execution, then deployment of available manpower in such channels should be discontinued in favor of investments where "pay-off" could be demonstrated.

Central to this presentation is a very simple thesis—for the present and the foreseeable future our society can and should afford many

---

[9]Manpower Report of the President, op. cit., page 126.

improvements and additions to the services offered its citizens. As long as there are people without work and work which, most agree, should be done, then the role of a rational society is to provide the machinery and the procedures which make possible a connection between worker resource and manpower requirements. Improving education is one generally recognized need. The symptoms are clear. High incidence of school failure, premature school leaving, inability to generalize obtained education to work or life experience, are all obvious indices that what we possess is not the best of all education worlds. As will be elaborated later, advocating the addition of indigenous low-income people to the education system has both experimental and theoretical justification. Such a proposal is intended to produce a better educational system as well as affording employment to millions of persons.

Education is not the only area where expansion of work opportunities can be anticipated. In the next decade it is expected that more managers, officials, proprietors, clerks, sales persons, craftsmen, foremen, and service workers will be needed. Only for the unskilled laborer in the city or on the farm are the prospects poor for increased employment opportunity.[10] Those developing job opportunities which do not require substantial change in job definition are treated but lightly in this book. There have been procedures established which allow for the entrance of the disadvantaged into these available job openings. The point being emphasized, however, is that the available opportunities are too limited. There are not enough jobs being developed to accommodate the numbers who need work. There is no assurance that the work is permanent, and there is often no path to a better station from the entry job.

Another area where potential for employment is great is in the broad field of health services. Almost every aspect of health service could be enlarged and improved. One segment of the population whose health needs are likely to require special attention are the elderly.

Between 1960 and 1975 the population over the age of sixty-five will increase by almost one-third. There will not only be more persons of retirement age, but they will live longer, and they will be less reluctant to call for health services. The number of persons needed, in a variety of roles, to attend to the problems of the aging, even under current definition, are already beyond the call of available resources. With increased demands for service, the solution can come only from increasing the numbers of persons involved in health work. Therefore, in this field, as in education, there is perceived to be a major opportunity for career development.

---

[10]*Ibid.*, page 100.

The New Career Concept

The new career concept has as a point of departure the creation of jobs normally allotted to highly-trained professionals or technicians, but which could be performed by the unskilled, inexperienced, and relatively untrained worker; or, the development of activities not currently performed by anyone, but for which there is a readily acknowledged need and which can also be satisfactorily accomplished by the unskilled worker.

There is a common need for careful scrutiny of the job function for the purpose of defining duties which are structured at the level of the jobless.

Providing jobs which the poor can perform is only a first step along the path to a new career. The job must be made permanent and must be incorporated into the matrix of the industry or agency. If the position, for example, is in government, there must be legitimation of the activity by civil service certification and incorporation of the function into the agency table of organization. In the private sector, created positions must, by similar procedures, become securely fused into the organic operation.

Persons filling entry positions must have latitude for limited advancement without being required to undergo extensive additional training. This type of opportunity is generally available to governmental and private agency personnel assigned to clerical or non-professional services. Advancement within the "same line" provides an inducement to "life career" for the least capable and gifted. For the many who aspire to more, and are capable of it, such a narrow range of possible achievement would hardly suffice.

The chance for truly substantial advancement in job station is crucial to the new career concept. If significant rise to higher stations is to be a genuine possibility for the entering unskilled worker, then jobs which will require knowledge, experience and skill, and present more challenge than the entry positions, must be created. These jobs would have to be intermediate between the unskilled beginning duty and the terminal professional status. To be eligible for an intermediate position a worker would be required to perform notably at the less advanced position and participate in a training program offered partially on the job and partially in a sequence of college courses (or receive training which could be allowed college credit).

Establishing a continuum ranging from nonskilled entry positions, extending through intermediate sub-professional functions, and terminating in full professional status, changes the nature of the upward mobility in our society. No longer would professional status be attained *only* by first completing between five and eight years of college. The requiring of this training *prior* to entrance into a field of endeavor effectively eliminates almost all of the poor from eligibility. A sequence beginning with the unskilled aide and proceeding through an assistant (two years of college equivalence plus experience); an associate (four years of college equivalence plus experience); and terminating in an accreditation as professional is manageable and opens areas to which the poor can now hardly hope to aspire.

If such a program were accepted in the field of medicine, it would be possible for a person to enter the field as a hospital aide (menial worker, only); graduate to a medical assistant (engage in slightly more responsible work); move upward to a medical associate (engage in a more demanding relationship with patients under direct supervision of doctor); continue up a sequence of increasing challenge and responsibility until ultimately the status of medical doctor was reached.

The unique quality of the new career proposal might be best emphasized by consideration of the present inability of a registered nurse to obtain credit for training and skill toward becoming a medical doctor. It is proposed that ultimately such a course would be available. The nurse-to-doctor sequence, while probably more fraught with difficulty than most, would indicate the nature of resistance to be encountered and overcome before the new career concept can become a reality.

Probably only a small percentage of the persons who would enter a new career sequence as nonskilled aides would emerge as full-fledged professionals. Each advance based on merit would constitute a screening process which only the most sensitive, motivated, and capable would ford, but while all might not achieve the highest rung, the *opportunity* for attainment of a higher station would be available to all.

It is not recommended that there be only this arduous and circuitous route to professional status. The traditional path to the M.D., the Ph.D., the education or social work degree would be always an available alternative. However, there would be advantages to the aspiring professional in the development of a sequence of "landings" designed for subprofessionals. At the present time, if a student fails to attain full professional status there is no defined role for him. A person might invest almost a decade in education, only to be informed that he is not to be allowed to become a professional. There is no designated function for the "almost" doctor, lawyer, teacher, social worker, or psychologist. If a sequence of positions had been established, the person unable to attain full status might be eligible for an intermediate position.

Defining the Entry Jobs

For *full* implementation of the new career concept there must be large-scale study of the activities performed by professionals in the fields mentioned above (and others) to delineate specific duties and functions which the unskilled can perform. Such studies must define precisely the relative challenge, complexity, and time expended on each function. The number of jobs required at each level and the number of levels necessary for a complete sequence can be *initially* estimated from the results obtained from such a study. Continued study would be needed for revision of job needs and duties arising from changing situations and technological development.

Inauguration of the new career concept should not, however, await the conclusions of an extensive job study. There is need for immediate test of the concept by demonstration and experimentation in a diversity of settings, with a broad range of persons, and in the performance of a variety of tasks.

There is sufficient experience for initial experimentation. An educated reckoning of job activities which the unskilled can perform can be continually refined after experimentation. Research, while needed, cannot be an excuse for inactivity. It is only through activity that data can be obtained for use in evaluation and further development.

On the other hand, the exigencies of the moment cannot justify unthinking exuberance. *Any* activity is not necessarily good activity. The plight of the poor is tragic and action is needed, but the action which is needed is long-term commitment to an ultimate solution, not a transient concern with superficialities.

The Trouble with Crash Programs Is That Often They Do Just That

Poverty seems so ridiculously out of place in an affluent society, and so readily susceptible to remediation that enthusiasm and concern alone appear sufficient to produce change. The answer to poverty may seem to be found in a single word—"money." This is too sanguine a view. If care is not taken, money designed to aid the poor can be channeled in many useless directions. In the haste to meet the emergency, jobs which might, with careful preparation, be tailored for the poor could be filled by those in less dire need—e.g., middle class housewives, students, or retired persons—or they might become second jobs for persons already employed.[11] A strategy which might satisfy both

---

[11]There is no attempt being made in this article to arrange for employment of the poor at the expense of more affluent groups. The point being stressed is that persons with means and education have job opportunities available to them; this simply is not the case for the uneducated poor.

short-term concern for the jobless and long range interest in ultimate solutions might combine both types of programs. Investment in short run or symptom solution programs would be reduced as long range programs, attacking the significant causes of poverty gain a foundation of knowledge and experience.

Will the Best New Careerist Please Stand Up

Selecting persons to enter new career sequences presents a formidable problem. The sequences are projected in areas of considerable sensitivity and persons will be requested to play significant roles in education, in the socialization of children, and in the care and treatment of the sick. These are not positions which can be filled in a cavalier fashion. However, it should be clearly appreciated that if traditional measures are used to screen prospective workers, those who most need employment will in all probability be excluded.

If applicants are to be denied opportunity for employment in new career sequences on the basis of measured intelligence or aptitude, or delinquency record, or lack of school attainment, then the current jobless will, in disproportionately large numbers, remain jobless. There is a compelling reason to reject screening procedures which are based on test scores or prior records. These indices may reflect only the effect of an impoverished existence and would therefore not predict capabilities in a new context. Alien and defeated, the poor have had little incentive to excel in conventional academic activity.

One of the objectives of experimental demonstration with new career programs should be determination of attributes of persons best suited to perform new roles. In the absence of criteria which have been subjected to rigorous validation, the fewer the prejudgments of potential ability the better.

Selecting new career candidates without discrimination is not as reckless a procedure as it might appear at first blush. All candidates would be subjected to short-term intensive training which would constitute a preliminary screen. To be eligible for placement, trainees would have to demonstrate an ability to perform the job and give some evidence of motivation and personal stability.

The new career assignment itself provides the greatest protection against abuse. In his initial assignment the new careerist is in a position of minimal sensitivity and responsibility. He is closely supervised by highly-trained professionals. He can attain more responsibility only by demonstrating capability. He is to be judged not on past record or tenuously related tests, but on actual performance.

Despite precautions and protections, there will be some risk in permitting persons with dubious backgrounds to perform in new career positions but it must also be recognized that there is risk in denying such persons an opportunity to participate in the program. The most obvious consequence will be that the program will fail to come to grips with one of the prime reasons for its existence. The result would be perpetuation of dynastic dependence—a vicious phenomenon of welfare recipient begetting welfare recipient.

Denial of opportunity to play a meaningful role in society may not only result in passive noncontribution, but could also trigger off violent reactions among the alienated and rejected. One likely course of action of any group denied access to status, dignity, and self-esteem by activity within the system would be the development of codes and behaviors affording status and leadership and an acceptable self-image. The recent violent outbursts by groups of slum youth in many cities in the country, resulting in wanton destruction of property and injury to persons, seem to have come about precisely because of the frustration of enforced exclusion from functioning society.[12]

Not all the risks would, however, take the form of affronts to society. Harm might come from failure to realize the specific talents of those persons who are excluded from jobs without trial. It may be precisely those persons who have exhibited leadership capacity in delinquent gangs who possess attributes to make unique contributions in new career roles.

A profound change must be made to occur in programs designed for slum youth. Schools must be revitalized, rehabilitation programs tailored to the needs of the community, health services altered —all of which will require enthusiastic workers, workers who can inspire the residents, and can offer trust and support, thus serving as ego models. It may well be that the very person who today is most troublesome to society can tomorrow become its most valuable contributor.

---

[12]Although varying in specific details and emphasis, many social scientists explain organized juvenile delinquency as the result of denial of equal access to the benefits of society. See, for example:

Richard A. Cloward and Lloyd E. Ohlin, *Opportunity and Delinquency: A Theory of Delinquent Gangs*, Glencoe, Ill., The Free Press, 1960.

Albert K. Cohen, *Delinquent Boys: The Culture of the Gang*, Glencoe, Ill., The Free Press, 1955.

Louis Yablonsky, *The Violent Gang*, New York, The Macmillan Co., 1962.

From Protest to Politics:
the Future of the Civil Rights Movement
Bayard Rustin

A. Philip Randolph Institute

[Reprinted from Commentary, *February 1965, copyright © 1965 by the American Jewish Committee.]*

There are 50 million poor in this country. And the Negro poor will never rise up until there is no more poverty. I hate to say this to young Negro people, but it is blindness to say anything else. We are sending them down a blind alley to pretend that by some hook or crook we can deal with slums on our own and with a few isolated whites. Or that somehow we can really deal with the housing problem, or that we can deal with the school problem or with jobs. Now there must be a great revolution in this country which is prepared to turn things upside down on these fundamental questions.

The war on poverty is a contribution of the Negro struggle to the American revolution. . . . We have to see that we have an American revolution and not simply a civil rights movement in isolation. . . . Let some of the white students who are so happy to go to Mississippi . . . put on old clothes and go into the ghettoes of Detroit and Chicago and take on the really tough task of finding the leadership among the white poor and educating them and getting them marching in the streets. . . . For the civil rights movement, life now depends on whether other segments of the society can adopt a political platform, program, and broad movement to deal with the poor of this country, black and white.

—From a speech to the Michigan Regional Conference of the Congress of Racial Equality, May 1, 1964.

I

THE DECADE spanned by the 1954 Supreme Court decision on school desegregation and the Civil Rights Act of 1964 will undoubtedly be recorded as the period in which the legal foundations of racism in America were destroyed. To be sure, pockets of resistance remain; but it would be hard to quarrel with the assertion that the elaborate legal structure of segregation and discrimination, particularly in relation to public accommodations, has virtually collapsed. On the other hand, without making light of the human sacrifices involved in the direct-action tactics (sit-ins, freedom rides, and the rest) that were so instrumental to this achievement, we must recognize that in desegregating public accommodations, we affected institutions which are relatively peripheral both to the American socio-economic order and to the fundamental conditions of life of the Negro people. In a highly industrialized, 20th-century civilization, we hit Jim Crow precisely where it was most anachronistic, dispensable, and vulnerable—in hotels, lunch counters, terminals, libraries, swimming pools, and the like. For in these forms, Jim Crow does impede the flow of commerce in the broadest sense: it is a nuisance in a society on the move (and on the make). Not surprisingly, therefore, it was the most mobility-conscious and relatively liberated groups in the Negro community—lower-middle-class college students—who launched the attack that brought down this imposing but hollow structure.

The term "classical" appears especially apt for this phase of the civil rights movement. But in the few years that have passed since the first flush of sit-ins, several developments have taken place that have complicated matters enormously. One is the shifting focus of the movement in the South, symbolized by Birmingham; another is the spread of the revolution to the North; and the third, common to the other two, is the expansion of the movement's base in the Negro community. To attempt to disentangle these three strands is to do violence to reality. David Danzig's perceptive article, "The Meaning of Negro Strategy," correctly saw in the Birmingham events the victory of the concept of collective struggle over individual achievement as the road to Negro freedom. And Birmingham remains the unmatched symbol of grass-roots protest involving all strata of the black community. It was also in this most industrialized of Southern cities that the single-issue demands of the movement's classical stage gave way to the "package deal." No longer were Negroes satisfied with integrating lunch counters. They now sought advances in employment, housing, school integration, police protection, and so forth.

Thus, the movement in the South began to attack areas of discrimination which were not so remote from the Northern experience as
were Jim Crow lunch counters. At the same time, the interrelationship
of these apparently distinct areas became increasingly evident. What
is the value of winning access to public accommodations for those who
lack money to use them? The minute the movement faced this question,
it was compelled to expand its vision beyond race relations to economic
relations, including the role of education in modern society. And what
also became clear is that all these interrelated problems, by their very
nature, are not soluble by private, voluntary efforts but require government action—or politics. Already Southern demonstrators had recognized that the most effective way to strike at the police brutality they
suffered from was by getting rid of the local sheriff—and that meant
political action, which in turn meant, and still means, political action
within the Democratic party where the only meaningful primary contests in the South are fought.

And so, in Mississippi, thanks largely to the leadership of Bob
Moses, a turn toward political action has been taken. More than voter
registration is involved here. A conscious bid for *political power* is being
made, and in the course of that effort a tactical shift is being effected:
direct-action techniques are being subordinated to a strategy calling for
the building of community institutions or power bases. Clearly, the implications of this shift reach far beyond Mississippi. What began as a
protest movement is being challenged to translate itself into a political
movement. Is this the right course? And if it is, can the transformation
be accomplished?

II

The very decade which has witnessed the decline of legal Jim Crow
has also seen the rise of *de facto* segregation in our most fundamental
socio-economic institutions. More Negroes are unemployed today than
in 1954, and the unemployment gap between the races is wider. The
median income of Negroes has dropped from 57 percent to 54 percent of
that of whites. A higher percentage of Negro workers is now concentrated in jobs vulnerable to automation than was the case ten years ago.
More Negroes attend *de facto* segregated schools today than when the
Supreme Court handed down its famous decision; while school integration proceeds at a snail's pace in the South, the number of Northern
schools with an excessive proportion of minority youth proliferates. And
behind this is the continuing growth of racial slums, spreading over our
central cities and trapping Negro youth in a milieu which, whatever its
legal definition, sows an unimaginable demoralization. Again, legal

niceties aside, a resident of a racial ghetto lives in segregated housing, and more Negroes fall into this category than ever before.

These are the facts of life which generate frustration in the Negro community and challenge the civil rights movement. At issue, after all, is not *civil rights*, strictly speaking, but social and economic conditions. Last summer's riots were not race riots; they were outbursts of class aggression in a society where class and color definitions are converging disastrously. How can the (perhaps misnamed) civil rights movement deal with this problem?

Before trying to answer, let me first insist that the task of the movement is vastly complicated by the failure of many whites of good will to understand the nature of our problem. There is a widespread assumption that the removal of artificial racial barriers should result in the automatic integration of the Negro into all aspects of American life. This myth is fostered by facile analogies with the experience of various ethnic immigrant groups, particularly the Jews. But the analogies with the Jews do not hold for three simple but profound reasons. First, Jews have a long history as a literate people, a resource which has afforded them opportunities to advance in the academic and professional worlds, to achieve intellectual status even in the midst of economic hardship, and to evolve sustaining value systems in the context of ghetto life. Negroes, for the greater part of their presence in this country, were forbidden by law to read or write. Second, Jews have a long history of family stability, the importance of which in terms of aspiration and self-image is obvious. The Negro family structure was totally destroyed by slavery and with it the possibility of cultural transmission (the right of Negroes to marry and rear children is barely a century old). Third, Jews are white and have the *option* of relinquishing their cultural-religious identity, intermarrying, passing, etc. Negroes, or at least the overwhelming majority of them, do not have this option. There is also a fourth, vulgar reason. If the Jewish and Negro communities are not comparable in terms of education, family structure, and color, it is also true that their respective economic roles bear little resemblance.

This matter of economic role brings us to the greater problem— the fact that we are moving into an era in which the natural functioning of the market does not by itself ensure every man with will and ambition a place in the productive process. The immigrant who came to this country during the late 19th and early 20th centuries entered a society which was expanding territorially and/or economically. It was then possible to start at the bottom, as an unskilled or semi-skilled worker, and move up the ladder, acquiring new skills along the way. Especially was this true when industrial unionism was burgeoning, giving new dignity and higher wages to organized workers. Today the situation has changed. We are not expanding territorially, the western frontier is settled, labor organizing has leveled off, our rate of economic growth has been stagnant for a decade. And we are in the midst of a technological revolution which is altering the fundamental structure of the labor force, destroying unskilled and semi-skilled jobs—jobs in which Negroes are disproportionately concentrated.

Whatever the pace of this technological revolution may be, the *direction* is clear: the lower rungs of the economic ladder are being lopped off. This means that an individual will no longer be able to start at the bottom and work his way up; he will have to start in the middle or on top, and hold on tight. It will not even be enough to have certain specific skills, for many skilled jobs are also vulnerable to automation. A broad educational background, permitting vocational adaptability and flexibility, seems more imperative than ever. We live in a society where, as Secretary of Labor Willard Wirtz puts it, machines have the equivalent of a high school diploma. Yet the average educational attainment of American Negroes is 8.2 years.

Negroes, of course, are not the only people being affected by these developments. It is reported that there are now 50 percent fewer unskilled and semi-skilled jobs than there are high school dropouts. Almost one-third of the 26 million young people entering the labor market in the 1960's will be dropouts. But the percentage of Negro dropouts nationally is 57 percent, and in New York City, among Negroes 25 years of age or over, it is 68 percent. They are without a future.

To what extent can the kind of self-help campaign recently prescribed by Eric Hoffer in the *New York Times Magazine* cope with such a situation? I would advise those who think that self-help is the answer to familiarize themselves with the long history of such efforts in the Negro community, and to consider why so many foundered on the shoals of ghetto life. It goes without saying that any effort to combat demoralization and apathy is desirable, but we must understand that demoralization in the Negro community is largely a common-sense response to an objective reality. Negro youths have no need of statistics to perceive, fairly accurately, what their odds are in American society. Indeed, from the point of view of motivation, some of the healthiest Negro youngsters I know are juvenile delinquents: vigorously pursuing the American Dream of material acquisition and status, yet finding the conventional means of attaining it blocked off, they do not yield to defeatism but resort to illegal (and often ingenious) methods. They are not alien to American culture. They are, in Gunnar Myrdal's phrase, "exaggerated Americans." To want a Cadillac is not un-American; to push a cart in the garment center is. If Negroes are to be persuaded that the conventional path (school, work, etc.) is superior, we had better provide evidence which is now sorely lacking. It is a double cruelty to harangue Negro youth about education and training when we do not know what jobs will be available for them. When a Negro youth can reasonably foresee a future free of slums, when the prospect of gainful employment is realistic, we will see motivation and self-help in abundant enough quantities.

Meanwhile, there is an ironic similarity between the self-help advocated by many liberals and the doctrines of the Black Muslims. Professional sociologists, psychiatrists, and social workers have expressed amazement at the Muslims' success in transforming prostitutes and dope addicts into respectable citizens. But every prostitute the Muslims convert to a model of Calvinist virtue is replaced by the ghetto with two more. Dedicated as they are to maintenance of the ghetto, the Muslims are powerless to affect substantial moral reform. So too with every other group or program which is not aimed at the destruction of slums, their causes and effects. Self-help efforts, directly or indirectly, must be geared to mobilizing people into power units capable of effecting social change. That is, their goal must be genuine self-help, not merely self-improvement. Obviously, where self-improvement activities succeed in imparting to their participants a feeling of some control over their environment, those involved may find their appetites for change whetted; they may move into the political arena.

III

Let me sum up what I have thus far been trying to say: the civil rights movement is evolving from a protest movement into a full-fledged *social movement*—an evolution calling its very name into question. It is now concerned not merely with removing the barriers to full *opportunity* but with achieving the fact of *equality*. From sit-ins and freedom rides we have gone into rent strikes, boycotts, community organization, and political action. As a consequence of this natural evolution, the Negro today finds himself stymied by obstacles of far greater magnitude than the legal barriers he was attacking before: automation, urban decay, *de facto* school segregation. These are problems which, while conditioned by Jim Crow, do not vanish upon its demise. They are more deeply rooted in our socio-economic order; they are the result of the total society's failure to meet not only the Negro's needs, but human needs generally.

These propositions have won increasing recognition and acceptance, but with a curious twist. They have formed the common premise of two apparently contradictory lines of thought which simultaneously nourish and antagonize each other. On the one hand, there is the reasoning of the New York *Times* moderate who says that the problems are so enormous and complicated that Negro militancy is a futile irritation, and that the need is for "intelligent moderation." Thus, during the first New York school boycott, the *Times* editorialized that Negro demands, while abstractly just, would necessitate massive reforms, the funds for which could not realistically be anticipated; therefore the just demands were also foolish demands and would only antagonize white people. Moderates of this stripe are often correct in perceiving the difficulty or impossibility of racial progress in the context of present social and economic policies. But they accept the context as fixed. They ignore (or perhaps see all too well) the potentialities inherent in linking Negro demands to broader pressures for radical revision of existing policies. They apparently see nothing strange in the fact that in the last twenty-five years we have spent nearly a trillion dollars fighting or preparing for wars, yet throw up our hands before the need for overhauling our schools, clearing the slums, and really abolishing poverty. My quarrel with these moderates is that they do not even envision radical changes; their admonitions of moderation are, for all practical purposes, admonitions to the Negro to adjust to the status quo, and are therefore immoral.

The more effectively the moderates argue their case, the more they convince Negroes that American society will not or cannot be reorganized for full racial equality. Michael Harrington has said that a successful war on poverty might well require the expenditure of $100 billion. Where, the Negro wonders, are the forces now in motion to compel such a commitment? If the voices of the moderates were raised in an insistence upon a reallocation of national resources at levels that could not be confused with tokenism (that is, if the moderates stopped being moderates), Negroes would have greater grounds for hope. Meanwhile, the Negro movement cannot escape a sense of isolation.

It is precisely this sense of isolation that gives rise to the second line of thought I want to examine—the tendency within the civil rights movement which, despite its militancy, pursues what I call a "no-win" policy. Sharing with many moderates a recognition of the magnitude of the obstacles to freedom, spokesmen for this tendency survey the American scene and find no forces prepared to move toward radical solutions. From this they conclude that the only viable strategy is shock; above all, the hypocrisy of white liberals must be exposed. These spokesmen are often described as the radicals of the movement, but they are really its moralists. They seek to change white hearts—by traumatizing them. Frequently abetted by white self-flagellants, they may gleefully applaud (though not really agreeing with) Malcolm X because, while they admit he has no program, they think he can frighten white people into doing the right thing. To believe this, of course, you must be convinced, even if unconsciously, that at the core of the white man's heart lies a buried affection for Negroes—a proposition one may be permitted to doubt. But in any case, hearts are not relevant to the issue; neither racial affinities nor racial hostilities are rooted there. It is institutions—social, political, and economic institutions—which are the ultimate molders of collective sentiments. Let these institutions be reconstructed *today*, and let the ineluctable gradualism of history govern the formation of a new psychology.

My quarrel with the "no-win" tendency in the civil rights movement (and the reason I have so designated it) parallels my quarrel with the moderates outside the movement. As the latter lack the vision or will for fundamental change, the former lack a realistic strategy for achieving it. For such a strategy they substitute militancy. But militancy is a matter of posture and volume and not of effect.

I believe that the Negro's struggle for equality in America is essentially revolutionary. While most Negroes—in their hearts—unquestionably seek only to enjoy the fruits of American society as it now exists, their quest cannot *objectively* be satisfied within the framework of existing political and economic relations. The young Negro who would demonstrate his way into the labor market may be motivated by a thoroughly bourgeois ambition and thoroughly "capitalist" considerations, but he will end up having to favor a great expansion of the public sector of the economy. At any rate, that is the position the movement will be forced to take as it looks at the number of jobs being generated by the private economy, and if it is to remain true to the masses of Negroes.

The revolutionary character of the Negro's struggle is manifest in the fact that this struggle may have done more to democratize life for whites than for Negroes. Clearly, it was the sit-in movement of young Southern Negroes which, as it galvanized white students, banished the ugliest features of McCarthyism from the American campus and resurrected political debate. It was not until Negroes assaulted *de facto* school segregation in the urban centers that the issue of quality education for *all* children stirred into motion. Finally, it seems reasonably clear that the civil rights movement, directly and through the resurgence of social conscience it kindled, did more to initiate the war on poverty than any other single force.

It will be—it has been—argued that these by-products of the Negro struggle are not revolutionary. But the term revolutionary, as I am using it, does not connote violence; it refers to the qualitative trans-formation of fundamental institutions, more or less rapidly, to the point where the social and economic structure which they comprised can no longer be said to be the same. The Negro struggle has hardly run its course; and it will not stop moving until it has been utterly defeated or won substantial equality. But I fail to see how the movement can be victorious in the absence of radical programs for full employment, aboli-tion of slums, the reconstruction of our educational system, new defini-tions of work and leisure. Adding up the cost of such programs, we can only conclude that we are talking about a refashioning of our political economy. It has been estimated, for example, that the price of replacing New York City's slums with public housing would be $17 billion. Again, a multi-billion dollar federal public-works program, dwarfing the cur-rently proposed $2 billion program, is required to reabsorb unskilled and semi-skilled workers into the labor market—and this must be done if Negro workers in these categories are to be employed. "Preferential treatment" cannot help them.

I am not trying here to delineate a total program, only to sug-gest the scope of economic reforms which are most immediately related to the plight of the Negro community. One could speculate on their political implications—whether, for example, they do not indicate the obsolescence of state government and the superiority of regional struc-tures as viable units of planning. Such speculations aside, it is clear that Negro needs cannot be satisfied unless we go beyond what has so far been placed on the agenda. How are these radical objectives to be achieved? The answer is simple, deceptively so: *through political power.*

There is a strong moralistic strain in the civil rights movement which would remind us that power corrupts, forgetting that the absence of power also corrupts. But this is not the view I want to debate here, for it is waning. Our problem is posed by those who accept the need for political power but do not understand the nature of the object and there-fore lack sound strategies for achieving it; they tend to confuse political institutions with lunch counters.

A handful of Negroes, acting alone, could integrate a lunch counter by strategically locating their bodies so as *directly* to interrupt the operation of the proprietor's will; their numbers were relatively unimportant. In politics, however, such a confrontation is difficult be-cause the interests involved are merely *represented*. In the execution of a political decision a direct confrontation may ensue (as when federal marshals escorted James Meredith into the University of Mississippi—to turn from an example of non-violent coercion to one of force backed up with the threat of violence). But in arriving at a political decision, numbers and organizations are crucial, especially for the economically disenfranchised. (Needless to say, I am assuming that the forms of political democracy exist in America, however imperfectly, that they are valued, and that elitist or putschist conceptions of exercising power are beyond the pale of discussion for the civil rights movement.)

Neither that movement nor the country's twenty million black people can win political power alone. We need allies. The future of the Negro struggle depends on whether the contradictions of this society can be resolved by a coalition of progressive forces which becomes the *effective* political majority in the United States. I speak of the coalition which staged the March on Washington, passed the Civil Rights Act, and laid the basis for the Johnson landslide—Negroes, trade unionists, liberals, and religious groups.

There are those who argue that a coalition strategy would force the Negro to surrender his political independence to white liberals, that he would be neutralized, deprived of his cutting edge, absorbed into the Establishment. Some who take this position urged last year that votes be withheld from the Johnson-Humphrey ticket as a demonstration of the Negro's political power. Curiously enough, these people who sought to demonstrate power through the non-exercise of it, also point to the Negro "swing vote" in crucial urban areas as the source of the Negro's independent political power. But here they are closer to being right: the urban Negro vote will grow in importance in the coming years. If there is anything positive in the spread of the ghetto, it is the potential political power base thus created, and to realize this potential is one of the most challenging and urgent tasks before the civil rights movement. If the movement can wrest leadership of the ghetto vote from the machines, it will have acquired an organized constituency such as other major groups in our society now have.

But we must also remember that the effectiveness of a swing vote depends solely on "other" votes. It derives its power from them. In that sense, it can never be "independent," but must opt for one candidate or the other, even if by default. Thus coalitions are inescapable, however tentative they may be. And this is the case in all but those few situations in which Negroes running on an independent ticket might conceivably win. "Independence," in other words, is not a value in itself. The issue is which coalition to join and how to make it responsive to your program. Necessarily there will be compromise. But the difference between expediency and morality in politics is the difference between selling out a principle and making smaller concessions to win larger ones. The leader who shrinks from this task reveals not his purity but his lack of political sense.

The task of molding a political movement out of the March on Washington coalition is not simple, but no alternatives have been advanced. We need to choose our allies on the basis of common political objectives. It has become fashionable in some no-win Negro circles to decry the white liberal as the main enemy (his hypocrisy is what sustains racism); by virtue of this reverse recitation of the reactionary's litany (liberalism leads to socialism, which leads to Communism) the Negro is left in majestic isolation, except for a tiny band of fervent white initiates. But the objective fact is that *Eastland and Goldwater* are the main enemies—they and the opponents of civil rights, of the war on poverty, of medicare, of social security, of federal aid to education, of unions, and so forth. The labor movement, despite its obvious faults, has been the largest single organized force in this country pushing for progressive social legislation. And where the Negro-labor-liberal axis is weak, as in the farm belt, it was the religious groups that were most influential in rallying support for the Civil Rights Bill.

The durability of the coalition was interestingly tested during the election. I do not believe that the Johnson landslide proved the "white backlash" to be a myth. It proved, rather, that economic interests are more fundamental than prejudice: the backlashers decided that loss of social security was, after all, too high a price to pay for a slap at the Negro. This lesson was a valuable first step in re-educating such people, and it must be kept alive, for the civil rights movement will be advanced only to the degree that social and economic welfare gets to be inextricably entangled with civil rights.

The 1964 elections marked a turning point in American politics. The Democratic landslide was not merely the result of a negative reaction to Goldwaterism; it was also the expression of a majority liberal consensus. The near unanimity with which Negro voters joined in that expression was, I am convinced, a vindication of the July 25th statement by Negro leaders calling for a strategic turn toward political action and a temporary curtailment of mass demonstrations. Despite the controversy surrounding the statement, the instinctive response it met with in the community is suggested by the fact that demonstrations were down 75 percent as compared with the same period in 1963. But should so high a percentage of Negro voters have gone to Johnson, or should they have held back to narrow his margin of victory and thus give greater visibility to our swing vote? How has our loyalty changed things? Certainly the Negro vote had higher visibility in 1960, when a switch of only 7 percent from the Republican column of 1956 elected President Kennedy. But the slimness of Kennedy's victory—of his "mandate"—dictated a go-slow approach on civil rights, at least until the Birmingham upheaval.

Although Johnson's popular majority was so large that he could have won without such overwhelming Negro support, that support was important from several angles. Beyond adding to Johnson's total national margin, it was specifically responsible for his victories in Virginia, Florida, Tennessee, and Arkansas. Goldwater took only those states where fewer than 45 percent of eligible Negroes were registered. That Johnson would have won those states had Negro voting rights been enforced is a lesson not likely to be lost on a man who would have been happy with a unanimous electoral college. In any case, the 1.6 million Southern Negroes who voted have had a shattering impact on the Southern political party structure, as illustrated in the changed composition of the Southern congressional delegation. The "backlash" gave the Republicans five House seats in Alabama, one in Georgia, and one in Mississippi. But on the Democratic side, seven segregationists were defeated while all nine Southerners who voted for the Civil Rights Act were re-elected. It may be premature to predict a Southern Democratic party of Negroes and white moderates and a Republican Party of refugee racists and economic conservatives, but there certainly is a strong tendency toward such a realignment; and an additional 3.6 million Negroes of voting age in the eleven Southern states are still to be heard from. Even the *tendency* toward disintegration of the Democratic party's racist wing defines a new context for Presidential and liberal strategy in the congressional battles ahead. Thus the Negro vote (North as well as South), while not *decisive* in the Presidential race, was enormously effective. It was a dramatic element of a historic mandate which contains vast possibilities and dangers that will fundamentally affect the future course of the civil rights movement.

The liberal congressional sweep raises hope for an assault on the seniority system, Rule Twenty-two, and other citadels of Dixiecrat-Republican power. The overwhelming of this conservative coalition should also mean progress on much bottlenecked legislation of profound interest to the movement (e.g., bills by Senators Clark and Nelson on planning, manpower, and employment). Moreover, the irrelevance of the South to Johnson's victory gives the President more freedom to act than his predecessor had and more leverage to the movement to pressure for executive action in Mississippi and other racist strongholds.

None of this *guarantees* vigorous executive or legislative action, for the other side of the Johnson landslide is that it has a Gaullist quality. Goldwater's capture of the Republican party forced into the Democratic camp many disparate elements which do not belong there, Big Business being the major example. Johnson who wants to be President "of all people," may try to keep his new coalition together by sticking close to the political center. But if he decides to do this, it is unlikely that even his political genius will be able to hold together a coalition so inherently unstable and rife with contradictions. It must come apart. Should it do so while Johnson is pursuing a centrist course, then the mandate will have been wastefully dissipated. However, if the mandate is seized upon to set fundamental changes in motion, then the basis can be laid for a new mandate, a new coalition including hitherto inert and dispossessed strata of the population.

Here is where the cutting edge of the civil rights movement can be applied. We must see to it that the reorganization of the "consensus party" proceeds along lines which will make it an effective vehicle for social reconstruction, a role it cannot play so long as it furnishes Southern racism with its national political power. (One of Barry Goldwater's few attractive ideas was that the Dixiecrats belong with him in the same party.) And nowhere has the civil rights movement's political cutting edge been more magnificently demonstrated than at Atlantic City, where the Mississippi Freedom Democratic Party not only secured recognition as a bona fide component of the national party, but in the process routed the representatives of the most rabid racists—the white Mississippi and Alabama delegations. While I still believe that the FDP made a tactical error in spurning the compromise, there is no question that they launched a political revolution whose logic is the displacement of Dixiecrat power. They launched that revolution within a major political institution and as part of a coalitional effort.

The role of the civil rights movement in the reorganization of American political life is programmatic as well as strategic. We are challenged now to broaden our social vision, to develop functional programs with concrete objectives. We need to propose alternatives to technological unemployment, urban decay, and the rest. We need to be calling for public works and training, for national economic planning, for federal aid to education, for attractive public housing—all this on a sufficiently massive scale to make a difference. We need to protest the notion that our integration into American life, so long delayed, must now proceed in an atmosphere of competitive scarcity instead of in the security of abundance which technology makes possible. We cannot claim to have answers to all the complex problems of modern society. That is too much to ask of a movement still battling barbarism in Mississippi. But we can agitate the right questions by probing at the contradictions which still stand in the way of the "Great Society." The questions having been asked, motion must begin in the larger society, for there is a limit to what Negroes can do alone.

A Freedom Budget for All Americans

A. Philip Randolph Institute

[*From* A "Freedom Budget" For All Americans, *by permission of the A. Philip Randolph Institute.*]

Introduction

The "Freedom Budget" contends that this nation has the resources to abolish poverty, for the first time in human history, and to do so within a decade. Indeed, the very process of abolishing poverty will add enormously to our resources, raising the living standard of Americans at all income levels. By serving our unmet social needs—in slum clearance and housing, education and training, health, agriculture, natural resources and regional development, social insurance and welfare programs—we can achieve and sustain a full employment economy (itself the greatest single force against poverty) and a higher rate of economic growth, while simultaneously tearing down the environment of poverty. All of these problems interact, whether viewed as causes or results, and they are in truth both.

Only such a massive and sustained program—which sees poverty in terms of the national economy, and not only in terms of the personal characteristics of the poor—can bring success. Goals must be set, along with timetables for achieving them. We must plan the allocation of our resources in accord with our priorities as a nation and people.

I. The "Freedom Budget" in Brief

Basic objectives

The seven basic objectives of the "Freedom Budget" are these:

(1) *To restore full employment as rapidly as possible,* and to maintain it thereafter, for all able and willing to work, and for all whom adequate training and education would make able and willing.

(2) *To assure adequate incomes for those employed.*

(3) *To guarantee a minimum adequacy level of income to all those who cannot or should not be gainfully employed.*

(4) *To wipe out the slum ghettos, and provide a decent home for every American family, within a decade.*

(5) *To provide, for all Americans, modern medical care and educational opportunity up to the limits of their abilities and ambitions, at costs within their means.*

(6) *To overcome other manifestations of neglect in the public sector, by purifying our airs and waters, and bringing our transportation systems and natural resource development into line with the needs of a growing population and an expanding economy.*

(7) *To unite sustained full employment with sustained full production and high economic growth.*

The key role of our Federal Government

The "Freedom Budget" is a call to action. But the response to this call must take the form of national programs and policies, with the Federal Government exercising that leadership role which is consistent with our history, our institutions, and our needs. The six prime elements in this Federal responsibility are now set forth.

(1) *Beginning with 1967, the President's Economic Reports should embody the equivalent of a "Freedom Budget."* These Reports should quantify ten-year goals for full employment and full production, for the practical liquidation of U.S. poverty of 1975, for wiping out the slum ghettos, and indeed for each of the seven basic objectives set forth in the "Freedom Budget."

(2) *The bedrock civilized responsibility rests with our Federal Government to guarantee sustained full employment.*

(3) *The Federal Government should exert the full weight of its authority toward immediate enactment of a Federal minimum wage of $2.00 an hour, with coverage extended to the uppermost constitutional limits of Federal power.*

(4) *A new farm program, with accent upon incomes rather than prices, should focus upon parity of income for farmers and liquidation of farm poverty by 1975.*

(5) *To lift out of poverty and also above deprivation those who cannot or should not be employed, there should be a Federally-initiated and supported guaranteed annual income, to supplement rather than to supplant a sustained full-employment policy at decent pay.*

(6) *Fiscal and monetary policies should be readjusted to place far more weight upon distributive justice.*

The "economic growth dividend"

We cannot enjoy what we do not produce. The "Freedom Budget" recognizes that all of the goals which it sets must be supported by the output of the U.S. economy. This output should grow greatly from year to year, under policies designed to assure sustained maximum employment, production, and purchasing power in accord with the objectives of the Employment Act of 1946.

The "Freedom Budget" does not contemplate that this "economic growth dividend" be achieved by revolutionary nor even drastic changes in the division of responsibility between private enterprise and government under our free institutions. To illustrate, in 1965, 63.7 percent of our total national production was in the form of private consumer outlays, 16.5 percent in the form of private investment, and 19.8 percent in the form of public outlays at all levels for goods and services. Under the "higher" goals in the "Freedom Budget," these relationships in 1975 would be 63.5 percent, 16.9 percent, and 19.6 percent.

But while the "Freedom Budget" will not be regarded as socialistic, it is indeed socially-minded. It insists that we must make deliberate efforts to assure that, through combined private and public efforts, a large enough proportion of this "economic growth dividend" shall be directed toward the great priorities of our national needs: liquidation of private poverty, restoration of our cities, abolition of the slum ghettos, improvement of rural life, and removal of the glaring deficiencies in facilities and services in "the public sector" of our economy. The "Freedom Budget" thus has moral as well as materialistic purposes.

Responsibilities of the Federal Budget

The following table reveals the "Freedom Budget" proposals for the Federal Budget (measured in 1964 dollars).

These proposals for the Federal Budget will seem excessive only to those who do not appreciate the growing productive powers of the U.S. economy, under conditions of sustained full employment and full production.

Looked at even more broadly, the whole program set forth in the "Freedom Budget" would not subtract from the income of anyone. It would facilitate progress for practically all, but with accent upon the dictates of the social conscience that those at the bottom of the heap should make relatively the most progress.

	1967 (Actual)		1970		1975	
	Total Bil. $	$ Per Capita	Total Bil. $	$ Per Capita	Total Bil. $	$ Per Capita
All Federal Outlays	104.1	521.79	135.0	645.93	155.0	685.84
National Defense, Space Technology, All International	64.6	323.77	77.5	370.82	87.5	387.17
All Domestic Programs	39.5	198.04	57.5	275.12	67.5	298.67
Economic Opportunity Program	1.5	7.39	3.0	14.36	4.0	17.70
Housing and Community Development	0.1	0.57	3.4	16.03	3.8	16.81
Agriculture and Natural Resources	5.9	29.75	10.5	50.24	12.0	53.10
Education	2.6	13.10	7.0	33.49	9.5	42.04
Health Services and Research	3.3	16.74	4.8	22.97	7.0	30.97
Public Assistance; Labor, Manpower, and Other Welfare Services	4.4	21.92	6.6	31.58	7.5	33.18

II. The Role of The American Negro In The "Freedom Budget"

The "Freedom Budget" will benefit all

In one sense the American Negro, relative to his numbers, has an unusually large stake in a "Freedom Budget." When unemployment is excessive, the rate tends to be more than twice as high among Negroes as others. Viewing U.S. multiple-person families in 1964, 37.3 percent of the nonwhites lived in poverty with annual incomes under $3,000, contrasted with only 15.4 percent of the whites. About 14 percent of the nonwhite families had incomes between $1,000 and $2,000, contrasted with 5.4 percent of the whites. And 7.7 percent of the nonwhite families had incomes below $1,000, contrasted with only 2.7 percent of the whites. Among unattached individuals, 52.3 percent of the nonwhites lived in poverty with annual incomes under $1,500, contrasted with 40.5 percent of the whites; and 35.8 percent of the nonwhites were below $1,000, contrasted with 24.4 percent of the whites.

Thus, the only reason why the Negro will benefit relatively more than others from the liquidation of excess unemployment and poverty is not because he is a Negro, but rather because he is at the bottom of the heap.

Aside from this dismal phenomenon, which is a liability rather than an asset to the Negro, others will benefit far more in absolute numbers through achievement of the goals of the "Freedom Budget." There are far more unemployed among whites than among non-whites. In 1964, 6.6 million white families and 4.2 million white unattached individuals lived in poverty, contrasted with 1.8 million nonwhite families and 0.9 million nonwhite unattached individuals.

The "Freedom Budget" in relation to civil rights

There is an absolute analogy between the crusade for civil rights and liberties and the crusade which the "Freedom Budget" represents. This is because the "Freedom Budget" would achieve the freedom from economic want and oppression which is the necessary complement to freedom from political and civil oppression. And just as the progress thus far made on the front of civil rights and liberties has immeasurably strengthened the entire American political democracy, so will the "Freedom Budget" strengthen immeasurably our entire economic and social fabric.

The Negro's greatest role on both of these fronts is not as a beneficiary, but rather as a galvanizing force. Out of his unique suffering, he has gone a long way toward awakening the American conscience with respect to civil rights and liberties. The debt which the whole nation owes him will be increased many times, as he helps to win the battle against unemployment and poverty and deprivation.

Poverty Programs and Policy Priorities

Martin Rein, *Bryn Mawr College School of Social Work*

S. M. Miller, *Ford Foundation*

THE WAR ON POVERTY is financially boxed in—on the one side, by the military priorities for the war in Vietnam, and on the other, by conservative domestic politics and assaults. In this state of siege, its progress is limited. But even if the conflict in Vietnam—and in Congress —were to end tomorrow, the anti-poverty program would still face major battles and possible defeat. For success in any program depends on strategy as well as resources. Given vastly greater funds and lowered political opposition, basic questions would still have to be answered: Which projects should the government support? How well are they planned? What can they realistically accomplish? What goals come first?

It is not the purpose of this article to recommend specific programs, whether old or new, which should be continued or started. Rather, we are concerned with helping to construct a workable framework for making such decisions—a framework needed under any circumstances of war or peace.

To set up priorities, we must consider what is wanted (values), what could be effective (rationality), and what is politically and organizationally *feasible*. We must not only know what benefits we seek, and why, but what we are willing to pay, or give up, to achieve them. Goals very often conflict; to promote one may not only mean neglecting others, but even working against them. Values must not be buried under technical considerations—the "whys" lost sight of because of the "hows." The kind of nation and life we think worthwhile—our view of the good society—must help determine the programs we choose.

There are no final or absolute answers here. Rather, let us explore what choices are available, how people choose, and how they should go about choosing.

Most programs for reducing poverty to date, whether in the planning or implementation stage, fall under six major headings: amenities, investing in human capital, transfers, rehabilitation, participation, economic measures.

Amenities. These are concerned with supplying services that strengthen and enrich the quality of life, that directly modify the environment of the poor. They serve as increments to personal and family welfare, whether as household help, child care facilities, or information centers. They extend the quality of living; if the poor have them, they are less poor in the sense of being without services. Alfred Kahn calls them "social utilities" and considers them as necessary as such public utilities as water and roads. They should not be considered remedies for a disease, but a normal and accepted service.

Investing in Human Capital. Investment of wealth is a means of creating more wealth. Investments in "human capital" (an in-term among economist) concentrate resources on making the poor more self-sufficient and productive: schooling, job training, health care, and various techniques of fitting them into the job market. Theodore W. Schultz believes that "changes in the investment in human capital" are the basic and most effective means for "reducing the inequality . . . of personal income," rather than such devices as progressive taxes.

But what is a good investment? The purposes of "investments in human capital" are not as clear-cut as the parallel with investment in physical capital implies. What purposes, for instance, are educational programs in the war on poverty designed to accomplish? There is considerable confusion about this. In the nineteenth century, the emphasis in the charity schools was on inculcating character—good work habits and such traits as industry, promptness, and reliability—rather than in teaching the specific skills and abilities necessary to rise in the world. The Job Corps and Neighborhood Youth Programs frequently seem intent on following this nineteenth-century model. The rhetoric of these programs implies that the goal is increasing lifetime earnings rather than conformity. On the other hand, "good character" seems to be a prerequisite for higher salaries.

Transfers. Transfers provide cash to the poor (and to other groups in society). Devices include the proposed negative income tax, fatherlessness insurance, children's allowances, guaranteed income, and various cash subsidies. They are a means of redistributing income outside the market place. Cash transfers to the poor could be provided in a way that promotes self-respect and perpetuates the myth that they, like the farmer or subsidized industry, are actually helping the country by accepting the money. Transfers emphasize a way to build up and assure total income, instead of the 1930's emphasis on replacing income lost because of illness, unemployment, accident, or old age.

But American public policy has been biased against the use of transfer payments to reduce poverty. We seem continually haunted by that legacy of Victorianism that a guaranteed income (for the poor) must increase shiftlessness, immorality, and illegitimacy. Subsidy payments to farmers or industry rouse few doubts about the danger to the moral fiber of their recipients. Public assistance programs seem less concerned with whether the poor get enough as the harm it might do them if they did. The prevailing orthodoxy (see Title V of the Economic Opportunity Act and the 1962 amendments to the Social Security Act) is committed to change sources of income rather than to increase it, to "get people off the dole"—Title V by work training and the amendments by social services.

Rehabilitation. This approach concentrates on changing people, usually by psychological means, to restore social functioning. It ranges from guidance and counseling, through casework, to psychotherapy and psychoanalysis. Rehabilitation hopes to overcome poverty by overcoming personal and family disorganization and deviancy. Those

adequate livelihood. Whether or not children remain in the same social and occupational classes as their parents, therefore, can be used as a measure of the reduction of poverty and the rigidity of the social order.

Poverty and Social Control. For many, improved income and services cannot be enough—for they are concerned with the social problems associated with poverty: alcoholism, delinquency, illiteracy, illegitimacy, mental illness. In the rhetoric of professionals, rehabilitation contributes to "self-actualization," but in fact it is more often used for social control—getting the poor to behave according to accepted standards. This view frequently merges into a broader concern with social harmony and equilibrium. If reducing poverty among Negroes did not eliminate race riots, the programs would be considered failures.

Poverty and Social Inclusion. In this view, people are poor when they cannot participate in the major institutions of our society, particularly the institutions that affect their lives—that is, when they have little or nothing to say about schools, employment, law enforcement, or even welfare and other social services. "The meaning of poverty," writes Peter Marris, "is humiliation: lack of power, of dignity, of self respect. . . . It is a mark of inferiority, and so more damaging than want itself."

Some experts justify reducing poverty for economic reasons—the poor will spend their increased incomes for necessities and comforts and improve the economy; if the money went instead to the middle class, more would simply go into savings. Therefore, as the poor prosper, all will prosper. Humanitarian and economic goals coalesce.

But what if they should come to conflict? Then, to follow this concept to its logical conclusion, economic considerations must be given priority. We must prevent inflation even at the cost of preserving, or increasing, poverty; economic growth is more important than redistribution. At these points, the concern with the economy sharply displaces the interest in helping the poor or reducing poverty.

Policy Models

These different concepts lead us to at least three basic models of how to view the overall purposes of social policy:

Allocative Justice. Policy is guided by a commitment to the more equitable distribution of benefits—who gets what, where, why and how. This model emphasizes equal opportunity for investment in career jobs and education and for the redistribution of amenities, income, and resources necessary for well being.

Policy as Handmaiden. This strategy seeks to promote programs that reduce poverty, but these are subordinate to other goals, such as economic growth, social stability, or physical renewal of cities. Thus, transfer payments to the poor could be primarily supported because they stimulate the economy. Or services and amenities to the poor could be aimed at reducing social unrest, providing a silent strategy for riot control. Or the major purpose of rehabilitation of the poor in slums could be to make them good tenants and to facilitate the relocation of those displaced by urban renewal programs aimed at increasing the real estate values of downtown areas. These programs are designed to win the joint support of what might otherwise be competing groups. But in case of conflict the secondary role of poverty policy becomes evident.

Policy as Therapy. Many people, including a disproportionate number of the poor, do not behave according to our prevailing, accepted, and predominantly middle class standards. Poverty programs may exact conformity. Rehabilitation programs illustrate this approach.

This analysis leads to four fundamental policy questions. What are the purposes of the programs? How effective are they in achieving them? How feasible are they politically (what are the chances of getting them adopted and implemented)? How do we choose between competing desirable programs or goals?

Purposes of Poverty Programs

The question of purpose involves much more than technical classifications. It includes value judgments about goals. For instance, do we consider adequate housing and health programs for the poor *amenities* (to make the quality of their lives more comfortable) or *investments* (good housing to prevent poverty, and good health to reduce unemployment and improve learning in school)?

It is a political question as well: Will legislators vote funds for an anti-poverty program unless we contend it will reduce poverty and crime or welfare costs? But a technical and rational question also is involved: What is the evidence that better housing and medical care will prevent poverty? Can we document the charge that the poor are really the most victimized by these insufficiencies?

Alvin Schorr has made an impressive and persuasive attempt to bring together evidence on the relationship between housing and poverty. He concludes:

The following effects may spring from poor housing: a perception of one's self that leads to pessimism and passivity, stress to which the individual cannot adapt, poor health, and a state of dissatisfaction; pleasure in company but not in solitude, cynicism about people and organizations, a high degree of sexual stimulation without legitimate outlet, and difficulty in household management and child rearing; and relationships that tend to spread out in the neighborhood rather than deeply into the family.

He believes that malnutrition, poor health, and inadequate housing reinforce each other in causing, and intensifying, poverty. As he sees it, it is not the "life styles" of the poor that disable them so much as the lack of means to live properly. What they need is not psychological or sociological analysis but health, housing, adequate incomes.

Others disagree. Their studies indicate to them that improved housing has little effect on such things as deviant behavior or physical illness. Nathan Glazer, for instance, challenges Schorr's assumption:

> The chief problems of our slums are social—unemployment, poor education, broken famiiles, crime. . . . Nor can they be solved by physical means, whether by urban renewal projects or . . . housing directly for the poor.

In fact, Glazer believes that social relationships have more effect on housing than vice versa; that broken families can nullify the effects of even the best housing. The facts Glazer quotes are impressive: Two-thirds of the poorest urban families (under $2,000 a year) do not live in substandard housing; further, most of substandard housing is not occupied by the poorest.

What about the traditional relationship between morbidity and poverty? Charles Kadushin concludes: "A review of the evidence . . . leads to the conclusion that . . . there is very little association between getting a disease and social class, although the lower class still feel sicker." That is, Kadushin says, the poor complain more about illness and stay away from work longer for it, but are not necessarily more ill.

Others challenge Kadushin's interpretation. Further, these data do not provide an argument against the development of health and housing programs for poor people. If health and housing seem unrelated, this may be because of difficult problems of measurement. Are the poor who live in standard housing overcrowded? Do they pay too high a portion of their income for this housing? They may be largely older people living in their own homes, while the families with many children live in substandard apartments. Inadequate statistics can distort the total picture.

Let us consider health in the same light. Even if morbidity rates among the poor are low, infant mortality is high, life is shorter, hospitalization longer, and disability has more severe consequences.

The fact is that we have so little good policy-oriented research that we cannot make any firm conclusion about the relationships between poverty and housing and health care. Consequently, we cannot be sure that better housing and health would help raise the poor from poverty.

But housing and health can be justified on other grounds than reducing poverty. Equality, as noted, is one. Inequalities and loss of dignity might be the crucial aspects of poor housing. According to Schorr: "It makes little difference whether bad housing is a result or a cause of poverty, it is an integral part of being poor." And the psychology of poverty is reinforced by seeing, all about, how the other half lives. By this definition, then, people without adequate housing or access to medical care are poor; adequate amenities reduce poverty. It is not that housing is instrumental to improved education or income; it is a goal in itself.

Program Effectiveness

The second policy issue is effectiveness. What good is a program that does not accomplish its purpose? But, in the first place, what is a program's purpose? Anyone who tries to get a straightforward statement of goals from a social agency usually finds that they react as though their very reason for being were under challenge.

But if the agencies will not provide clear answers, what of social science itself? For instance, do present rehabilitation programs actually reduce deviancy? When the score is finally totaled, the answer turns out to be, mostly, no. Social science research generally winds up exploding myths rather than giving solutions. William Kvaraceus, who recently reviewed the literature on delinquency, has reached the gloomy conclusion that nothing works very well. Other studies support him. Social work techniques may make youths and groups more democratic, more willing to join in approved sports and dancing, but they have little effect on law-breaking. Walter Miller has concluded that delinquency depends largely on age and sex—young men commit most crimes—and therapy will not change these conditions.

Will rehabilitation and counseling help broken or ineffective families or reduce economic dependency? A number of studies—including the most recent analysis of a vocational high school by Henry Meyer—and his associates—indicate that intensive casework makes little difference in reducing social problems.

However, ineffectiveness alone is not always enough reason to abandon a strategy. A program can be effective in unplanned ways. Even if rehabilitation does not reduce pathology and poverty much, its ethical, moral, and humanitarian value should not be discounted.

Another practical political factor impedes effectiveness: We frequently adopt programs not because of demonstrated validity, but because they are feasible—we can get them adopted and financially supported. "It is always easier to put up a clinic than tear down a slum," Barbara Wootton argues. "We prefer today to analyze the infected individual rather than the infection from the environment." Rehabilitation as a means of reducing dependency has become a national policy. Also, for political reasons we have reversed the usual procedure by starting programs and *then* testing the concepts in demonstration projects. In such situations the pressure to find exactly the answers we are already committed to is hard to resist. Thus, what is politically possible makes a rational analysis difficult.

What of the argument that the poor should, as a policy, be encouraged to achieve power through collective action and pressure? Alvin Schorr has summarized the arguments against such grassroots involvement:

> Efforts to promote self-organization fail more often than they succeed. . . . First, poor people have learned cynicism from bitter experience. They do not widely and readily respond to efforts to organize them. Second, when they do seek serious ends for themselves, they threaten established institutions or interest groups. At that point they are likely to learn once more that they are comparatively powerless. Third, the professionals who try to help them have, with rare exceptions, one foot in the "establishment." The ethical and practical problems that arise in their marginal situation are not solved simply by an effort of will.

Political Feasibility

The foregoing leads us to the third policy issue—the feasibility of programs that invest in human resource development. If we say that investment in education or training will result in jobs, can we deliver? Is there a coherent relationship between the learning and the job?

More education or training usually pays off in more and better employment. But how much education—and expense—before the payoff starts? College graduates are better off than others, and the income differences between them and the non-college population are expanding. But the differences in job opportunities and wages between high school graduates and dropouts are not great, especially for non-whites. They seem, in fact, to be declining. For males age 35 to 44 in 1939, dropouts earned 80 percent as much as high school graduates; in 1961, 87 percent. As more people get more education, the tipping point for education may come later and later. Investing in human resources may have a limited gain if would-be dropouts do not go to college.

How much education, how good, and how relevant to the job market are all important questions in job training. And on one or more of these counts most of our training programs have fallen down. A study of "successful" ex-convicts shows that only 17 percent were working at the trades they had learned in prison. Of 1,700 young people who applied to Mobilization for Youth for training, only "roughly one in four eventually achieved competitive employment as a direct result . . . ," according to Richard A. Cloward. And these were mostly for marginal jobs, paying marginal salaries. As Herbert E. Klarman says: ". . . in the past the market economy has apparently not absorbed appreciable numbers of rehabilitated persons."

The relationship between occupational training and unemployment is very low. First, whatever its faults, we have done a much better job of rehabilitating people than of preparing society to receive them; and training means little if it does not lead to jobs. The connection between jobs and training is frequently very loose. Second, our training programs are often simply not good or relevant enough. Cloward reveals that the youths who did graduate from the MFY program could not read better than when they started, and had failed to get skills that could qualify them for the higher pay jobs. Training just to improve character or work habits—the intent of many if not most training programs for low-income youth—is a poor investment.

Moreover, employers tend not to take this training seriously, or consider it a legitimate "credential" of employability. One of the great virtues of a diploma, or even an honorable military discharge, is that an employer will recognize it as a "credential" of employability and character.

Why train if that training is inadequate, discounted, or if no jobs are available? Real improvement can only come about with changes in our educational, referral, and economic institutions—which are untouched by the training programs. In short, unless relevant institutions themselves are changed, even highly promising programs will be frustrating rather than improving prospects. Training can be an effort to evade the issue of job availability.

Few people will argue that better training and more jobs for the poor are not desirable goals. But the stubborn facts are that most training is not good enough, and that the jobs which follow training are too often marginal or scarce. Education, to yield large payoffs, will need large investments. Are we willing to face these difficulties?

Competing Goals

What happens when goals conflict, whether the conflict is real or apparent, recognized or ignored?

As Isaiah Berlin has astutely observed, there is a "natural tendency of all but a few thinkers to believe that all the things they hold good must be intimately connected or at least compatible with one another." In social policy, as in other fields, this is a delusion; goals often conflict, and we must decide on priorities. Here are four major areas of real or assumed value conflict:

Prices and Poverty. Paul Samuelson and Robert Solow have concluded that a 5.5 percent level of unemployment is necessary to keep prices stable; anything less must result in inflation. "It may be doubted . . . that we can achieve both a satisfactory level of employment and price stability without major improvements in our antiinflationary weapons." Similarly, the British Labor government has recently discovered, with some distress, that if it strengthens its international economic position, it may have to let unemployment rise and renege on its promise to raise pensions.

In short, we may have to choose between social welfare programs and rising prices. As James Tobin says:

> We are paying much too high a social price for avoiding creeping inflation and for protecting our gold supply and "the dollar." . . . The interests of the unemployed, the poor and the Negroes are underrepresented in the consensus which supports and confines current policy.

Income Plans and Incentives. Raising incomes through payments can conflict with trying to get the poor into the labor market. Is providing an incentive to work more important than assuring adequacy of income? As Evelyn Burns puts it:

> Workers whose normal incomes are very low and whose economic horizons are very limited may, if social security income is adequate for their modest wants, prefer benefit status to securing an income from employment, particularly if their normal type of employment is arduous or unpleasant, or if they are unmarried with no family responsibilities.

Rights and Misuse. Support programs contain various tests of eligibility, and provisions to punish violators. These are supposed to prevent cheating and make sure that welfare does not interfere with the free labor market and private economic incentives. These goals, however, conflict with those of economic costs and social rights. Obviously, the greater the gap between benefits and wages, the less effectively welfare can serve to increase demands in time of recession, and generally stabilize the economy; and the more rigid the rules and administrative control over welfare payments, the less chance of reducing feelings of powerlessness among the poor, and of establishing social benefits as legal *rights*.

Order and Conflict. The goals of keeping public order and protecting the well-to-do and of safeguarding the social and constitutional rights of the poor often conflict. We have not only a law about the poor, which seeks to deal with their condition, but a law *of* the poor, based on police powers. As Jacobus Ten Broek has declared, it is "designed to safeguard health, safety, morals, and well-being of the fortunate rather than directly to improve the lot of the unfortunate." The goal is the protection of society against the poor rather than safeguarding the poor from an indifferent or callous society. When we encourage the poor to be militant and independent, to secure and exercise the legal rights to assistance and protection, we tend to sharpen this conflict. If they are to try to shape policy, they may become involved in boycotts, pickets, strikes, and other dramatic forms of protest—in other words, in threatening the "well-being of the fortunate." In such areas as school desegregation, the interests of the fortunate will be directly pitted against those of the unfortunate. These are natural conflicts in a pluralistic society.

Thus, the single, seemingly simple aim of reducing poverty hides the many and often contradictory goals deriving from different conceptions of what poverty is. They call for many different kinds of strategy, which cannot hope to satisfy everybody.

Cost-Benefit Analysis

How do we establish rules to allocate limited resources to promote goals that are in partial conflict? Can we develop more effective methods of making decisions that specifically recognize contrasting objectives and give policymakers a clearer choice of the costs and benefits of various combinations?

Cost-benefit analysis has become more popular as older decision-making methods have proven inadequate for fighting poverty. The economic market had long been the traditional way of making decisions —automatic, impersonal. More recently, politicians and their administrators have made many important decisions—reflecting the play of political and value preferences. But though it moderated some of the dangers of market decisions, political determination has brought new strains of its own—arbitrariness, and the obscuring of national needs because of political traditions and expediency. Cost-benefit analysis seeks to professionalize decision-making. It offers a rational, as opposed to a market or political (value) basis for making decisions. Means are in agreement with goals.

It makes important contributions. But it does not provide a mechanism for superseding questions of value and preference. When used that way, it has important defects. Our criticism of cost-benefit analysis is six-fold: it suffers from technical limitations; it can lead to a quantitative mentality; the issue of operational feasibility is largely ignored; it has no ready-made response to the basic question of what costs and which benefits; goals are difficult to delineate; and it does not deal with the issue of competing goals. The large-scale danger in cost-benefit analysis is that values surreptitiously and inevitably creep in. The covert handling of values limits democratic discussions. Nor does it, we believe, strengthen in the long-run an effective policy of poverty or inequality-reduction.

It implies knowledge and confidence about social data that are ill placed. One does not have to agree with the doubts that we have raised in this paper about the efficacy of housing or the connection between health and poverty to doubt that one can have much confidence in measurements of costs and benefits. Hunches are frequently more important than scientific determination. Obviously social science will develop and some uncertainties will diminish. But we cannot be confident that all our evaluations are based upon scientific proof and that in the future we will always have a firm scientific basis for choices to be faced.

Another technical problem is the question of the "interest rate." In order to calculate cost and benefits which are received or expended over a number of years, it is necessary to use some way to calculate future benefits in terms of their present value. Since present gains are valued more than future, the latter should be reduced by an appropriate discount. The level of the discount can markedly affect total benefits. For example, cost-benefit analysis of much vocational education would have different results if a higher discount rate were employed than in some present calculations. The appropriate level of the discount is not undebatable.

The result of looking at benefits over a long number of years is, therefore, inevitably an emphasis on youth. The longer individuals can benefit from a program, the greater the return. It pays them to concentrate on youth rather than on the aged. But are there not other reasons for concentrating on older workers?

Cost-benefit analysis tends to emphasize those variables that can be reduced to figures. For example, the inability in urban renewal to assign a monetary value to the aesthetic pleasure of greenery may be a serious difficulty. There is danger of sliding into the position that the only goals with merit and legitimacy are those that are quantifiable and convertible into money. Quantitative reasoning may lead to stressing productivity (return per unit of expenditure) over total results. Productivity can be high while total returns may be less than in some other kind of activity which has a high relative cost per unit of expenditure. For instance, it may be more "productive" to work with the highly educated, "cream" unemployed because it is easier to get them jobs than it is for the hard-core, long-term unemployed individuals. But which activity comes closer to solving the problems of unemployment?

Quantitative reasoning also tends to underestimate the importance of feasibility. Here we do not refer to the political issues, but to the effective implementation of a program. It may be that a particular program is highly productive with a likelihood of a return far outweighing its cost. But this program may be extremely difficult to mount because of manpower or administrative obstacles. Another program may have a much poorer prospect in terms of productivity and costs, but be much easier to implement.

In making these points, we do not argue that the defects cannot be remedied, rather that current practice tends to ignore them. But now we move into issues which are more basic to the long-term difficulties of cost-benefit analysis.

What is a cost and what is a benefit is not so obvious as it seems. To a large extent cost-benefit analysis narrows the definition of both cost and benefit. To what extent are second and third order effects of any action included in the analysis? This is largely a political and value question more than a technical one.

What is the goal? Our foregoing analysis has stressed competing goals. Which should have priority is not only a question of rational calculations but of political issues and value preferences. Cost-benefit analysis provides some important kinds of information, but it does not resolve the issues of values, direction, purposes, or priorities. Is the goal to bring the poor up to a certain income level? Or is it a larger one of reducing inequalities within society?

Which is preferable cannot be determined by cost-benefit analysis alone. Cost-benefit analysis at best is only a tool. It may be useful, but it also can be misleading when assumed to have greater clarifying power than it actually has.

We must not be lulled into thinking that cost-benefit analysis can rescue us from choice. Three solutions—cost-benefit analysis, the marketplace, the political process—are probably necessary, but none is sufficient alone, or even together. Policy is not all about technical rules for implementing value-neutral hardware. No simple choices are on hand. The crucial issues remain: How do we define a good society? How do we implement it?

These questions must be confronted. Technology must serve

a purpose. There are several ways to reveal the techniques of policy-making as the politics that they are. One good way may be to create a pluralistic system of advisory planning where many interest groups have their own experts to develop and support their own policies. Herbert Gans suggests that this may have already developed in city planning, where a progressive wing concentrates on social planning and a conservative wing defends "traditional physical planning and . . . middle class values."

Value judgments have to be made—but who, specifically, shall make them? However it is done—overtly or covertly, consciously or unconsciously, democratically or dictatorially—it occurs. The planner is not a value-free technician serving a value-free bureaucracy. The assumption that politics is without content—only efficient or inefficient —is unacceptable. As Paul Davidoff says: "Appropriate policy in a democracy is determined through a political debate. The right course of action is always a matter of choice, never a fact." The search for "rationality" cannot avoid the issues of objectives and ideologies.

There should be many analyses, based on competing outlooks as well as assumptions. In a pluralistic, competitive society the people should weigh competing values, vigorously promoted, before they can make just decisions. But ultimately, after all technical analyses are made, the selection of goals and timing must depend on judgment; and judgment must depend on those brute preferences we call values.

Selected Bibliography

1. Edgar S. and Jean C. Cahn. "The War on Poverty: A Civilian Perspective," *Yale Law Journal,* 73 (July, 1964).

2. Joel Cogen and Kathryn Feidelson. "Rental Assistance for Large Families," *Pratt Planning Papers.* Brooklyn: Pratt Institute, June, 1964.

3. Rennie Davis. "The War on Poverty: Notes on Insurgent Response," Economic Research and Action Project, Ann Arbor, Mich., 1965.

4. Economic Opportunity Act of 1964. Hearings before Select Committee on Poverty of the Committee on Labor and Public Welfare, United States Senate, June, 1964.

5. Economic Opportunity Act of 1964. Report of the Committee on Labor and Public Welfare together with minority and individual views, Report Number 1218, July, 1964.

6. Milton Friedman. *Capitalism and Freedom*. Chicago: University of Chicago Press, 1962.

7. Herbert Gans. "Some Proposals for Government Policy in An Automating Society," *The Correspondent*, 30 (January–February, 1964).

8. Eli Ginzberg. *The Pluralistic Economy*. New York: McGraw Hill, Inc., 1965.

9. Christopher Green and Robert J. Lampman. "Schemes for Transferring Income to the Poor." *Industrial Relations*, 6, No. 2 (February 1967).

10. Hubert H. Humphrey. *War on Poverty*. New York: McGraw Hill, 1964.

11. David Komatsu. "Mr. Johnson's Little War on Poverty," *New Politics*, Spring, 1964.

12. Sar A. Levitan. *Programs in Aid of the Poor*. Washington, D.C.: Upjohn Institute for Employment Research, December 1965.

13. ———. *The Design of Anti-Poverty Strategy*. Ann Arbor: Institute of Labor and Industrial Relations, The University of Michigan, 1967.

14. Peter Marris and Martin Rein, *Dilemmas of Social Reform: Poverty and Community Action in the United States*. New York: Atherton Press, 1967.

15. Martin Oppenheimer. *Disarmament and the War on Poverty*. American Friends Service Committee, 1964.

16. Mobilization for Youth, Inc. *A Proposal for the Prevention and Control of Delinquency by Expanding Opportunities*. New York: Mobilization for Youth Inc., 1961.

17. Martin Rein and S. M. Miller. "Poverty Policy and Purpose: The Axes of Choice," *Poverty and Human Resources Abstracts*. Vol. I, No. 2 (March-April 1966), pp. 9-22.

18. Ben Seligman, Ed., *Poverty as a Public Issue*. New York: Free Press of Glencoe, A Division of the Macmillan Company, 1965.

19. ———. *Permanent Poverty*. Chicago: Quadrangle Books, 1968.

20. Alvin Schorr. "Poverty and Money," *New Society*, August 17, 1967.

21. Robert Theobald. *Free Men and Free Markets*. New York: Potter, C. N., 1963.

22. U. S. Office of Economic Opportunity. *Catalog of Federal Assistance Programs: A Description of the Federal Government's Domestic Programs*. Washington, D.C.: Government Printing Office, 1967.

23. Adam Walinsky. "Keeping the Poor in Their Place," *New Republic*, July 4, 1964.

Selected Agencies and Organizations

American Friends Service Committee,
Inc.
160 North Fifteenth Street
Philadelphia, Pennsylvania 19102

American Jewish Committee
165 East 56th Street
New York, New York

American Management Association
135 West 50th Street
New York, New York 10020

American Psychological Association
1200 Seventeenth Street, N.W.
Washington, D.C. 20036

American Public Welfare Association
1313 East 60 Street
Chicago, Illinois

Association on American Indian Affairs
475 Riverside Drive
New York 27, New York

Center for Labor Education
and Research (CLEAR)
Economics Department
University of Colorado
Boulder, Colorado 80304

Center for the Study of Democratic
Institutions
Box 4068
Santa Barbara, California 93103

Center for Studies in Vocational and
Technical Education
Social Science Building
1180 Observatory Drive
The University of Wisconsin
Madison, Wisconsin 53706

Center for Urban Education
33 West 42 Street
New York, New York 10036

Citizens' Crusade Against Poverty
132 Third Street S.E.
Washington, D.C. 20003

Commission on Automation and
Technological Progress
900 North Michigan Avenue
Chicago, Illinois 60611

Committee for Economic Development
1001 Connecticut Avenue, N.W.
Washington, D.C.

Committee for Miners
1165 Broadway
New York, New York 10001

Committee on Pockets of Poverty
1020 Connecticut Avenue N.W.
Washington, D.C. 20036

Conference of Economic Progress
1001 Connecticut Avenue, N.W.
Washington, D.C. 20036

Congress of Racial Equality
38 Park Row
New York, New York

Department of Housing and
Urban Development
1626 K, N.W.
Washington, D.C.

Economic Research and Action Project
1100 West Ainslie
Chicago, Illinois

Gray Areas Project
Ford Foundation
477 Madison Avenue
New York, New York 10022

Human Resources Administration
250 Broadway, 28th Floor
New York, New York

Industrial Areas Foundation
8 South Michigan Avenue
Chicago 3, Illinois

Industrial Union Department
A.F.L.–C.I.O.
815 16th Street, N.W.
Washington, D.C. 20006

Institute for Policy Studies
1900 Florida Avenue, N.W.
Washington, D.C. 20090

Institute for Poverty Research
University of Wisconsin
Madison, Wisconsin 53706

Institute for the Study of Human
  Problems
584 Mayfield
Stanford University
Stanford, California

Jewish Labor Committee
25 East 78th Street
New York, New York

Joint Center for Urban Studies
Harvard University
Cambridge, Massachusetts

Kentucky Child Welfare Research
  Foundation, Inc.
P. O. Box 713
Frankfort, Kentucky 40601

Labor Policy Association
1815 H Street, N.W.
Washington, D.C.

League for Industrial Democracy
112 East 19th Street
New York, New York 10003

National Advisory Committee on
  Farm Labor
112 East 19th Street
New York, New York 10003

National Association for the
  Advancement of Colored People
20 West 40th Street
New York, New York

National Committee for Children
  and Youth
1145 19th Street, N.W.
Washington, D.C.

National Committee for Full
  Employment
Box 232, Village Station
New York, New York 10014

National Committee on Employment
  of Youth
145 East 32nd Street
New York, New York

National Consumers League
1029 Vermont Avenue, N.W.
Washington, D.C.

National Planning Association
1606 New Hampshire Avenue, N.W.
Washington, D.C.

National Sharecroppers Fund
National Urban League
112 East 19th Street
New York, New York 10003

14 East 48th Street
New York, New York

Research Department
A.F.L.–C.I.O.
815 16th Street, N.W.
Washington, D.C. 20006

Southern Regional Council
5 Forsythe, N.W.
Atlanta, Georgia

Student Non-violent Coordinating
  Committee
360 Nelson Street, N.W.
Atlanta, Georgia

United States Office of Economic
  Opportunity
1156 15th Street, N.W.
Washington, D.C.

The W. E. Upjohn Institute for
  Employment Research
709 South Westnedge Avenue
Kalamazoo, Michigan

Contributors

FAY BENNETT is the executive secretary of the National Sharecroppers Fund.

BARRY BLUESTONE is in the Department of Economics of The University of Michigan.

GEORGE BRAGER is with the United States Department of Labor.

DAVID CAPLOVITZ is on the faculty of Columbia University and a staff member of the Bureau of Applied Research.

RAYMOND F. CLAPP is with the United States Department of Health, Education and Welfare.

RICHARD CLOWARD is on the faculty of the Columbia University School of Social Work.

MARTIN DEUTSCH is on the staff of the New York Medical College.

RICHARD M. ELMAN is a free-lance writer.

HERBERT J. GANS is on the faculty of the Teachers College, Columbia University.

CHRISTOPHER GREEN is on the faculty of the North Carolina State College of Agriculture and Engineering.

WARREN C. HAGGSTROM is with the School of Social Work, University of California, Los Angeles.

MICHAEL HARRINGTON is chairman of the board of the League for Industrial Democracy.

HERBERT HILL is National Labor Director of the NAACP, and on the faculty of the New School for Social Research.

TOM KAHN is the executive secretary of the League for Industrial Democracy.

CHARLES C. KILLINGSWORTH is on the faculty of the School of Industrial and Labor Relations, Michigan State University.

JEREMY LARNER is a free-lance writer.

CHARLES LEBEAUX is with the School of Social Work, Wayne State University.

HYLAN LEWIS is on the faculty of Brooklyn College and Associate Director of the Metropolitan Applied Research Center.

OSCAR LEWIS is on the faculty of the University of Illinois.

SAR A. LEVITAN is with the George Washington University.

DWIGHT MACDONALD is a staff writer for the *New Yorker* and a free lance writer.

SAMUEL MENCHER is on the faculty of the University of Pittsburgh.

HERMAN P. MILLER is with the Bureau of the Census.

S. M. MILLER is with the Ford Foundation.

WALTER B. MILLER is on the faculty of the Boston University School of Social Work.

OSCAR ORNATI is on the graduate faculty of the New School for Social Research.

MOLLIE ORSHANSKY is with the Social Security Administration of the Department of Health, Education and Welfare.

GORDON PARKS is a free-lance writer.

ARTHUR PEARL is on the faculty of the University of Oregon.

FRANCES FOX PIVEN is on the faculty of the Columbia University School of Social Work.

MARTIN REIN is with the Department of Social Work and Social Research at Bryn Mawr College.

FRANK REISSMAN is on the faculty of New York University.

BAYARD RUSTIN is the director of the A. Philip Randolph Institute.

ARTHUR A. SEAGULL is on the faculty of Michigan State University.

PATRICIA C. SEXTON is on the faculty of New York University.

HAROLD L. SHEPPARD is with the W. E. Upjohn Institute for Employment Research.

ALVIN L. SCHORR is with the United States Department of Health, Education and Welfare and in the Research Division of the Social Security Administration.

MARY WRIGHT is a staff member of the Presbyterian Child Welfare Agency in Buckhorn, Kentucky.

Index